Cisco® Security Bible

Cisco® Security Bible

Rajesh Kumar Sharma, NIIT

WILEY

Wiley Publishing, Inc.

Cisco® Security Bible

Published by

Wiley Publishing, Inc.

111 River Street

Hoboken, NJ 07030

www.wiley.com

Copyright ©2000 by Wiley Publishing, Inc., Indianapolis, Indiana

Published simultaneously in Canada

Library of Congress Catalog Card Number: 2001093436

ISBN: 0-7645-4878-6

1B/SQ/QS/QS/IN

About the Authors

Rajesh Kumar Sharma holds a Bachelor of Engineering in computer technology. He is also a Certified NetWare Engineer and Cisco Certified Network Administrator (CCNA). Rajesh has worked on a variety of networking projects; his work involves network consulting, management, and administration.

Rashim Mogha is a Microsoft Certified Solution Developer (MCSD). She has worked for two years at NIIT Ltd. Her first year was spent in the Career Education Group (CEG), where she taught NIIT students, handled computer installation and maintenance, and managed resources. For the past year, she has been working on varied technical assignments in the Knowledge Solutions Business (KSB) division of NIIT—including design, development, testing, and implementation of instructor-led training courses. Her primary responsibilities include training development executives, project management, instructional review, technical review, and ensuring ISO compliance. She loves writing.

Credits

Acquisitions Editors
Melody Lane
Katie Feltman

Project Editor
Amanda Munz Peterson

Technical Editor
Jeff Keller

Copy Editors
Barry Childs-Helton
Kala Schrager

Editorial Manager
Ami Frank Sullivan

Senior Vice President, Technical Publishing
Richard Swadley

Vice President and Publisher
Joseph B. Wikert

Project Coordinator
Regina Synder

Graphics and Production Specialists
Kelly Hardesty
Gabriele McCann
Erin Zeltner

Quality Control Technicians
Laura Albert
David Faust
John Greenough
Andy Hollandbeck
Angel Perez

Cover Illustrator
Kate Shaw

Proofreading and Indexing
TECHBOOKS Production Services

Cover Design
Murder By Design

This book is for my family. Thank you, Mom and Daddy, for patiently waiting for me, never complaining, and for putting up with the late nights and weekends when I was working on this book. Mom, thanks for giving me your love and encouragement when I needed it the most. Shweta and Shilpa, I couldn't do without your support. Last but not least, this book is for all network professionals who constantly try to secure networks.

— Rashim

Preface

The last couple of decades have seen a significant change in the business scenario. As the concept of globalization gained popularity, many organizations penetrated remote geographical markets. Along with this new global presence (not to mention the emergence of e-commerce) came a new and urgent question: How can an organization transmit information quickly, reliably, and cost-effectively? Use of the Internet added another criterion — security. Dedicated private networks emerged as one way to provide the all-important protection and data integrity that online business requires.

Most up-to-date organizations use dedicated private networks to facilitate faster transmission of information. Without proper safeguards, however, these networks are prone to security threats (for example, hackers taking control of the file server and gaining access to confidential data) that can result in considerable losses.

In the past few years, incidents involving security breaches have increased at an alarming rate. Granted, network monitoring techniques have improved — and better intrusion-detection systems are available, so more network attacks are being identified and reported — but these measures are no panacea for the problem. In fact, not even a reliable and accurate tally of such incidents is available; only one in ten are actually reported.

Why have these attacks increased in number? One reason is that the capabilities of personal computers have evolved. Scattered "road warrior" laptops and work-at-home office environments now bristle with features such as mobile computing, VPN connectivity, and telecommunications; one byproduct of this progress is that computer hackers have readier access to networks through security loopholes — and are often harder to track down.

Computer professionals also point to the new technologies' ease of use as a factor that tends to boost the number of security attacks. Many newer technologies are easy to use and require minimal technical expertise; thus more people are tempted to try their hands at attacking the security of networks. According to many security analysts, *employees working for the company* carry out (or aid in) 90 percent of computer attacks. These disgruntled employees have access to the network and can inflict maximum damage to company property (such as computer equipment) and to data.

Network administrators, security consultants, and independent security services must now shoulder the responsibility of protecting the world's networks against security threats — but these professionals also face a daunting challenge: Network technology is still (and always) evolving. As it becomes more complex and even easier to use, networks become even more susceptible to security threats. Network administrators must select an effective—but practical—"right mix" of technologies to achieve coherent and consistent security policies. They must then tailor those policies to large and small networks—while still allowing regular upgrades to network equipment.

Ironically, the open standards and architecture that made the original Internet a viable means of institutional communication pose real—and chronic—security problems. Implementing security mechanisms for all networks uniformly has become difficult; no standard security-solution package can be implemented across all networks. Even so, network security has become a sort of growth industry, with new solutions coming online constantly. Current preventive measures against network-security attacks include firewalls, perimeter routers, and encryption tools—and they, too, evolve as they must.

Cisco Systems, in its attempt to make the online world safer and more secure for business networks, has recently launched a sweeping security initiative. Cisco has introduced new products and services, upgraded versions of existing products, set up certification programs for security technicians and third-party products, and established a Web database of best practices. Two Cisco products illustrate the initiative's priorities:

✦ **Cisco IOS Firewall** is a security-specific option for Cisco IOS software. It enhances the security features of Cisco IOS software by adding application-based filtering, dynamic (and user-specific) authentication and authorization, tools for detecting and preventing common network attacks, filters that can exclude Java applets, and other advanced features.

✦ **Cisco PIX Firewall** is an integrated hardware/software product that offers excellent security performance on an enterprise-wide scale. PIX Firewall provides maximum security without affecting network performance. It is available in various models to meet the requirements of different networks.

Cisco Systems also provides tools for maintaining and managing network security after it's set up. These tools include CiscoWorks 2000 ACL Manager, Cisco Secure Policy Manager, Cisco ACS, Cisco PIX Firewall Manager, and VPN/Security Management Solution.

This book seeks to provide networking professionals with the knowledge and skills needed to install, configure, operate, manage, and verify Cisco network-security products and Cisco IOS security features.

Icons Used in This Book

Each icon used in this book signifies a special meaning. Here's what each icon means:

Note   Notes elaborate on technical points, providing supplemental information that is often vital (although usually it isn't obvious).

Tips provide special information or advice. They offer handy networking techniques, useful approaches, and effective shortcuts.

Caution icons warn you of a potential problem, risk, or error.

This icon directs you to related information elsewhere in the book.

How This Book Is Organized

The basic aim of this book is to equip the networking professionals with the knowledge required to install, configure, operate, and manage Cisco network security products. The book starts with the basics of network security, which provides the reader an insight to the details of network security. After the reader is thoroughly familiar with the concept of network security, the book moves on to cover the Cisco tools and techniques that can be used to protect the network.

The book is divided into seven parts.

Part 1: Understanding Network Security

Part One is an overview network security threats, the motivations behind them, a range of ways to protect against them, and the need to raise users' awareness of security. It presents the need to formulate and evaluate a security policy, describes security measures at the Transport, Network, and Data Link layers of the OSI model, and summarizes appropriate Cisco hardware and software products.

Part 2: Securing Networks

This part discusses the methods of securing the network infrastructure. It discusses campus security problems and solutions. It then discusses how to secure a network by using Access Control Lists. Standard, extended, dynamic, and reflexive access lists are discussed in detail. This part of the book also discusses perimeter routers, details the architecture and configuring procedure required for Network Address Translation, and reviews Cisco's encryption technology.

Part 3: Security Using Firewalls

Part Three discusses the role of firewalls in securing a network. It provides an overview of Cisco IOS Firewall (including the product's major components), and describes the appropriate ways to deploy and configure Cisco PIX Firewall.

Part 4: Understanding and Implementing AAA

This is part of the book discusses authentication, authorization, and accounting methods. It also describes how to configure your network access server for Authentication, Authorization, and Accounting (AAA) security.

Part 5: Virtual Private Networks

Part Five summarizes the role of virtual private networks and describes how to implement and configure basic VPN technologies securely—including IPSec and Cisco Secure VPN clients.

Part 6: Cisco Technologies and Security Products

This part of the book discusses Cisco IOS IPSec and how to configure it. A brief review of some Cisco security products follows, including CiscoWorks 2000 ACL, Cisco PIX Firewall Manager, VPN/Security Management Solution, and Cisco Secure Policy Manager.

Part 7: A Networking Primer

This part of the book summarizes basic networking concepts as a crash course for the new administrator and a review for the veteran. Included are the types of networks, networking models and topologies, and network cabling and devices. Next, it presents the layers of OSI model of networking, along with the protocols associated with each layer.

Appendixes

Use this section to test and hone your knowledge of Cisco security. It provides assessment questions that test your knowledge of topics covered in the book and a set of lab exercises.

Glossary

For quick reference, this section provides brief definitions of the terms used in the book.

Acknowledgments

I would like to take the opportunity to thank everyone involved in creating this book. At NIIT: Project Manager Ms. Anita Sastry, the graphics team, and the technical editors. At Hungry Minds, Inc., Acquisitions Editors Melody Lane and Katie Feltman, Project Editor Amanda Munz Peterson, Technical Editor Jeff Keller, and Copy Editors Barry Childs-Helton and Kala Schrager for their support and encouragement. I also take this opportunity to thank all who have directly or indirectly contributed in writing this book.

—Rajesh

I would like to acknowledge the contributions of all who were involved in creating this book, at NIIT and Hungry Minds. My special thanks go to the Project Manager at NIIT, Ms. Anita Sastry, the Editor of the book at NIIT, Ms. Anisha Chauhan, the Technical Reviewers at NIIT, Ashish Kr Chugh and Vikas Khatri, and the Graphics Designer at NIIT, Sunil Kumar Pathak. Without their valuable contribution, this book wouldn't be possible. A very special thanks to Kartik Bhatnagar, Meeta Gupta, and Ashok Appu for their timely help. Thank you, all my dear friends, for giving me the support of solid friendship when I needed it the most. Thanks, Kurien, for always patiently answering my queries.

Also, my special thanks go to the Acquisitions Editors, Melody Lane and Katie Feltman and Project Editor Amanda Munz Peterson for giving me an opportunity to write this book. Very special thanks to Technical Editor Jeff Keller and Copy Editor Barry Childs-Helton for their valuable input and constant support.

—Rashim

Contents at a Glance

Contents

Chapter 11: Configuring the Network Access Server for AAA Security 361

Part V: Virtual Private Networks 377

Chapter 12: Fundamentals of Virtual Private Networks 379

Understanding Network Security

T his part shows you how to identify threats to network security — and examines the reasons for network intrusions. Such identification is the first step toward selecting the best way to protect the security of your site; this part also takes the next step — helping you determine specific security requirements for the components of your network that correspond to different layers of the OSI model. This part also touches on the hardware and software Cisco provides for IP security, and describes methods of detecting network intrusions.

Identifying Threats to Network Security

Networks have become indispensable for conducting
business worldwide. With the increase in use of the
Internet (and other networked information infrastructure),
network intrusions by unauthorized users have increased
in frequency and severity. Thus, networking professionals
have had to develop and maintain a detailed awareness of
the vulnerabilities within their networks — and assess them
periodically.

This chapter explores possible reasons for potential security
threats — from inside and outside the network perimeter,
explains the need to implement network security, and examines the most common security threats (including the
reasons and tools that drive them). In addition, the chapter
summarizes the major categories of network security threats
(and methods to counter them). It covers the process of
evaluating a network-security policy within the enterprise
network, and outlines the key components of a network-
security policy.

Motivations Behind Security Threats

The Internet has changed the way business is conducted—including the ways people communicate, interact, and purchase items. Today, every business model is so centered on the options available over the Internet that business gurus worldwide accept its strategic role and importance in delivering better "Quality of Service" (QoS).

Even before the widespread acceptance of the Internet, the enterprise networks were susceptible to security threats, such as a hacker taking control of the file server and gaining access to confidential data. As use of the Internet has become commonplace, the networking model and the motivations of hackers have changed. Although the primary reason to break into private networks remains consistent (access to secure data) the hacker community is also excited with the sheer challenge of defeating so-called state-of-the-art security technologies.

What are they after?

These days, the main motivating factors that drive network intrusions are more diverse:

✦ **To gain access to the secure and confidential data of a corporation or government agency—and make unauthorized use of it.** A hacker may be acting out of commercial rivalry or hostile (even warlike) intent.

✦ **To check for security bugs in newly released software.** In such cases, the software vendor has usually hired authorized consultants to test the product before its commercial release—and report any security bugs that must be fixed.

✦ **To access money being transferred electronically.** Often the hacker seeks to capture data-transmission packets and decipher the codes used while money is transferred between bank accounts (or when credit cards are used for electronic transactions over the Internet). E-commerce sites promise secure electronic payment and fund transfer—and back up the promise with certificate servers and 128-bit encryption—but the sheer amount of money involved is inevitably a lure for hackers.

✦ **To crawl into a network out of curiosity.** Such curiosity can often lead to accessing server data or modifying online content—intentionally or inadvertently. A community of hackers develops shareware or freeware applications whose purpose is network intrusion; users of such programs decide whether to use them as a legitimate test or as a hack. Over time, the Web and mailing servers have become easy targets because of open standards and the ease with which they can be connected.

✦ **To execute malicious scripts or install applications on a network server for destructive purposes.** Many hackers develop applications and executables that can damage the data on your server.

What can they do to my network?

The Internet is not the only source of danger to private networks. Organizations that have no interconnectivity to the Internet should not assume their networks are secure. Any network is susceptible to security threats. Hackers working within an organization can take control of the file server and gain access to confidential data. The following types of impact can result from such intrusion:

✦ **Unauthorized access to network resources:** Deploying networks enables organizations to make resources, such as printers, applications, and data, available to multiple users. However, not all users must use all network devices. If proper permissions are not set, unauthorized users can gain access to network resources and misuse them.

✦ **Manipulation of data:** Organizations deploy networks to make resources (such as printers, applications, and data) available to multiple users. However, not all users need the same level of access rights. For example, a sales representative would not require rights to modify the personal details of employee records in an organization. If proper access rights are *not* defined for the users, unauthorized users can gain access to sensitive data and use it for malicious purposes.

✦ **Interference with network functions:** Organizations deploy networks to transmit information accurately and efficiently within their structures. Hackers can disrupt this accuracy and efficiency by changing the configurations of network devices (such as hubs), interfering with the basic functionality of the network.

✦ **Spoofing of data packets:** Data packets that travel over the network can be intercepted and altered (even counterfeited) by hackers who pose as legitimate users. Such users can send malicious or incorrect data to unsuspecting legitimate users on the network, interfering with workflow.

Need for Network Security

An organization's network is prone to a variety of security threats, which can be divided into various categories:

✦ **Disruption of network services:** Most organizations provide their employees with access to the Internet and e-mail service, which inevitably entail the risk of external attacks that can disrupt network services. Virus infections, buffer overflows, and other denial-of-service attacks are the most common methods used by hackers to keep the network from doing its job.

✦ **Exploitation of sensitive data:** Data that flows over the network is a valuable resource that hackers seek to access and control for their own political or economic ends. Hackers use methods such as IP spoofing to gain access to this data, after which they can distort, falsify, reroute, or otherwise misuse it.

✦ **Destruction of network resources:** Some network attacks can destroy resources by making records inaccessible or wiping out data (for example, by formatting hard drives).

✦ **Interception of restricted information:** Hackers or intruders can gain control of the network by discovering the usernames and passwords of authorized users, thereby gaining access to network resources.

✦ **"Social engineering" attacks:** Hackers, intruders, or competitors can gain access to network resources by compromising and manipulating employees of the organization.

As organizations expand their networks, network security technologies are increasingly vital in preventing intrusion and eliminating network security vulnerabilities. Security consultants and service providers can provide easy and reliable access to advanced security technologies and expertise — but remember: Networks were created to prevent data isolation. Security and privacy are (by their nature) at odds with sharing and distribution. "Perfect" security would mean nobody gets to use the data — in which case, why generate it at all? Any practical and effective plan for network security must always balance two goals:

✦ Provide appropriate access to authorized users.

✦ Safeguard the network and its data from unauthorized users.

The Internet was intended as a backup communication system for vital information in the event of a global disaster. Designed to facilitate easy communication between computers, it is according to open standards and architecture — which poses problems for the administrator who seeks to implement security mechanisms for all networks uniformly. No one security solution offers a standard package that can be implemented across all networks. Network engineers and system administrators are *always* faced with the challenge of selecting a best-possible mix of technology that achieves coherent and homogenous security for both large and small networks (while still allowing network upgrades) and then creating a comprehensible policy to describe it.

Cisco has developed and supported security technologies and products that can support networks of any size and technology mix. Developed under the Cisco's SAFE architecture (a security blueprint for e-business networks), these solutions are designed to counter Internet-based security threats to enterprise networks.

Security Vulnerabilities

The typical modern organization uses distributed client/server network architecture: Computers configured as servers and clients communicate through networks — both internal and external (most often the Internet) — to sustain a visible business presence with customers, partners, and suppliers. Although computer networks continue to revolutionize the way business is done, the risks they introduce can be fatal for an organization if left unmanaged.

Networks are growing in size and technology every day, becoming more complex—which has led to the use of various *internetwork* technologies (combinations of network and computing devices). Internetworks have security imperfections of their own; security loopholes can result from misconfiguration or improper management.

Network security is vulnerable in three primary areas:

✦ **Technology:** As more technical innovations and technologies are integrated to provide Internet access, security threats rise because each networking technology has its own inherent security problems.

✦ **Implementation:** Designing and deploying a network for an enterprise environment can render a company vulnerable to security threats if the components are not configured and managed properly.

✦ **Policy framework:** Securing the network by implementing security policies (however sound they may be) can lead to security threats unless the policy is reviewed frequently.

The following sections cover these vulnerabilities in detail.

Technology

An enterprise network comprises multiple hosts and network servers interconnected through network devices. Although the makers of these components design and test them to provide security, each product has inherent security vulnerabilities. Figure 1-1 illustrates this principle.

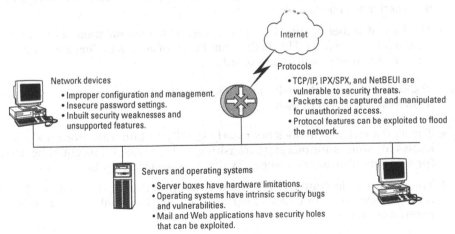

Figure 1-1: Vulnerabilities of network components

Intranets are prone to security breaches that exploit the particular vulnerabilities of servers, operating systems, protocols, and network devices.

Servers and operating system

Each server has its own unique security issues, rooted in the inherent limitations of its hardware and software (which are usually documented on the makers' Web sites).

Note A network is not possible without a server running a proper network operating system. The server itself is a hardware box, equipped with server-class (high-capacity/heavy-duty) hardware and running a compatible operating system.

Operating systems have their own security issues, problems, and bugs that cause security threats. Security issues in operating systems are addressed by releasing fixes and patches. The Web, e-mail, and database applications, supported by each of these operating systems, are also prone to security threats.

Protocol

To enable communication over the network, a network protocol is necessary. By negotiating the connections among devices, network protocols (such as TCP/IP, IPX/SPX, NetBEUI, and AppleTalk) allow smooth implementation and integration of networks. Each protocol has its own documented security issues. The following section discusses security issues associated with TCP/IP, which is used primarily for Internet communications.

TCP/IP is the most widely used internetwork protocol designed as an open standard to enable communication. Major factors that make TCP/IP prone to a security attacks are as follows:

✦ The contents of the packet headers of TCP, UDP, and IP can be viewed and modified using hacking tools.

✦ The lack of authentication in IP packets leads to manipulation of the information in its source field. This is the foundation of all IP spoofing and, consequently, the major issue in IP security.

Note *IP spoofing* is an attack in which an attacker pretends to be sending data from an IP address other than its own.

✦ The TCP specification does not clearly specify certain transitions and thus allows for some spurious state transitions. These transitions could be used for a variety of attacks — especially denial-of-service attacks.

✦ The Network File System (NFS) does not support user authentication. It uses random UDP ports for establishing sessions, making it vulnerable to unsecured user access.

✦ Unix is a refined and open operating system in which the source code is available and reviewable. It has TCP/IP applications embedded into it to provide various services. Unix also has some unsecured legacy applications, such as `telnet`, `rlogin`, FTP, and SMTP.

Tip   For more information about TCP/IP, consult the *TCP/IP Bible,* published by Hungry Minds, Inc.

Network devices

All networks use interconnectivity devices to connect to the Internet and increase the scalability of the network. Typically, these devices are routers, switches, and remote access devices. All these devices have some sort of security issues, which are addressed by the vendor. Each vendor documents these issues and then releases patches and fixes to counter the problems. Even then, numerous issues crop up — such as authentication, unsecured password handshaking, firewall placement, packet manipulation, and routing protocols — all of which can harbor security loopholes.

Each vendor tries to update its network devices by notifying users of any bugs or security holes it finds and providing patches and fixes. Cisco also keeps its security product line updated through Internet Security Advisories, and documents each possible reported security bug (along with its fix) on the Cisco support site, `www.cisco.com`.

Implementation

The most common security breaches result from improper implementation or configuration of the network components. Internetwork devices usually require some configuration to safeguard the network. These configurations are device- and vendor-specific; take special care when you configure a mix of technologies.

The most common configuration error is to allow unlimited access at the router (or at the proxy configured for the external network or Internet access), as shown in Figure 1-2. The router shown is configured with an extended IP access list that permits all IP traffic to pass — this is a big mistake. The router doesn't keep track of any incoming or outgoing traffic, which allows an intruder to penetrate the network easily. The router also has the console login enabled with an easy-to-guess password, which leaves the gateway essentially open to any hacker who wants to access your internetwork devices and exploit the vulnerabilities of various network components.

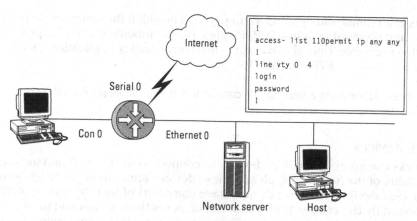

```
!
access- list 110permit ip any any
!
line vty 0  4
login
password
!
```

Figure 1-2: Improper configuration resulting in security threat

To get a head start on identifying and fixing security holes in your implementation, scrutinize your network for the following common vulnerabilities:

✦ **Misconfigured network equipment.** Almost all network equipment has features for managing traffic and access. Misconfiguring these features can cause security problems. Most devices come with default settings that enable easy implementation — but unless you change them, they also enable security holes, especially the settings that govern access and traffic control. Check the default settings of every network device — and don't be surprised if you find some default settings you must reconfigure for proper security.

✦ **Unsecured user accounts.** Network devices usually interoperate through proper handshaking mechanisms. These mechanisms typically require usernames or passwords — which are often carried over the network unsecured. Be sure to configure your handshaking mechanisms so security credentials are never exposed to general view. Also make sure that the usernames and addresses of system accounts are not generally visible — and the passwords that protect them are not easy to guess — as you configure your network servers.

✦ **Improper configuration of network services.** To implement a functional enterprise network, normally you must provide network users with various services such as access to the Web and e-mail; remember that each of these services requires proper configuration on both the server and client sides. A common security threat in Web access, for example, is when clients enable cookies and Java applets in their Web browsers. Such a setting inadvertently gives hackers direct access to your network resources. The security of e-mail servers is also a concern — it's often the target of malicious e-mail messages that carry viruses or other attachments that disrupt your e-mail service.

Such implementation errors are serious issues because they invite security threats. Fortunately, you can identify and address these errors relatively easily. They can be rectified whenever they are diagnosed or intrusion is detected — but early diagnosis is the best option — and though calling in an independent security consultant may take additional time, the informed second opinion may well pay off in terms of enhanced security. Vendors that provide security products often devise their own mechanisms to detect intrusion, which can change your basic implementation scenario; they may also request configuration changes — and such advice usually goes well beyond the basic checklist included here. Most implementation and configuration vulnerabilities are discussed in white papers on security.

 Note   You can refer to the white papers on network security at Cisco's site, www.cisco.com.

Policy framework vulnerabilities

A well-thought-out security policy should define your organization's expectations of computer and network usage — as well as some standard procedures to follow that can help prevent (or at least minimize the impact of) security incidents. A strong policy document is the foundation of network security; it outlines the assets worth protecting, the operations that threaten those assets, and the appropriate responses.

To create a security policy, you must first assess the risk to the network and build a team to respond to these security risks. The security policy document should also make provision for any changes in the network security needs and include a schedule for periodic monitoring of the network to check for security violations.

When the policy document is in place, implementing better security requires several ongoing commitments:

✦ To keep up to speed on your network's current needs, schedule a regular analysis of network usage according to industry-standard security parameters.

✦ To complement and support your routine analysis, have several team members cross-verify their assessments of network conditions.

✦ To counter the lack of awareness that makes a security policy hard to enforce, make sure you have adequate procedures in place for revising the policy document, distributing it to employees, and briefing your managers and teams.

Regular monitoring and auditing, backed by proper documentation, can help counter the worst effects of an attack — and validate a properly implemented security policy.

Categories of Security Threats

Studies reveal that each case of network intrusion has its own degree of severity and complexity of method. The methods chosen depend on the exploitable vulnerabilities of particular networks. These intrusions can be performed either by someone who is within the network or by someone over the Internet.

Who are the intruders?

Security threats run the gamut from crude (brute-force guessing of passwords) to sophisticated (penetrating the network to gain unauthorized access to corporate assets). The severity of the intrusion can range from a simple file hack to a disruption that crashes the whole network infrastructure.

Internal threats

Network attacks or intrusions are not exclusively external; in-house users can carry out hacks with equal (sometimes worse) impact. Internal users have an advantage as potential attackers: They work for the target organization and already have some level of network access. They understand their organization's business structure and its network architecture. Some employees even gather information about network operation, management, and security implementation — and then use this information to penetrate the network. In fact, most security breaches that result in financial and operational loss occur as a result of unauthorized access by internal users.

Most users within an organization are not aware of the benefits of network security. They can make mistakes — sometimes intentionally, for the sake of immediate convenience — such as using easy-to-guess passwords or leaving their desktops unlocked. These practices can leave security holes big enough to appeal to any hacker; an easy target is likelier to be attacked.

Note   *Social engineering* is a hacker's method of gaining access by influencing or manipulating people inside the company so they provide (often unwittingly) the information needed to break into the network security system. Posing as a company official or network technician on the phone is a common example of social engineering.

The only way to counter such security threats is to educate users and make them understand the importance of network security. Employees should be warned about the dangers of allowing other users to use their accounts. It is also important that employees are warned against using predictable passwords or writing the passwords on their workstations. A good idea is to advise the employees to change their passwords at frequent intervals.

Tip   Most network administrators use policies to force the users to change the passwords at a regular interval

Most viruses enter an organization's network through e-mail attachments; employees should be warned against opening the e-mail attachments coming from unknown people. In fact, employees should be advised to scan the attachments for viruses before opening. To prevent intrusions from internal users, the recruitment division should take precautions while recruiting employees. The organization should gather information about an employee's background and references before hiring a person.

External threats

Most network intrusions today are from outside the network. External network intrusions are usually serious and not as easy to trace. Since these attacks can be launched by practically anyone outside the network (amateur as well as professional hackers), it is difficult to trace the origin and the purpose of these attacks. Data communication links — often unsecured and easily tapped — are prime targets for external threats. Most susceptible and vulnerable to such attacks are networks, which are connected to the Internet and host online applications. The attacker can penetrate the network to gain information and then destroy the contents to erase his/her identity.

There are multiple solutions to prevent networks from external threats. These can range from configuring access control lists to implementing firewalls with intrusion detection devices. If you implement virtual private networks (VPNs) — which encrypt any data sent over unsecured communication links — you can close that particular entryway to intruders.

Note   Most organizations outsource some (or all) routine functions of their information system; common examples include backing up data, storing the backups, and providing communication links. However, few organizations bother to find out how secure their data is in the care of the outsourcing company. Normally such companies provide services to many organizations; make sure each organization's data is stored separately and securely.

Classifications of security threats

There are several methods used to exploit vulnerabilities of a network and penetrate the network security. Three major categories of security threats are

- ✦ Unauthorized access
- ✦ Denial of service (DoS)
- ✦ Data diddling (unauthorized changing of data)

Hackers first investigate and collect system information about the target network. Then they disrupt the network to withhold services from valid and authenticated network users — while they gain unauthorized access for themselves and can then manipulate network data. Cisco provides security products like PIX Firewall, intrusion-detection devices, access control servers, and Cisco Secure Scanner (in conjunction with Cisco IOS security configurations) to counter network intrusions.

 For more about Cisco security products, see Chapters 3, 9, 10, and 15.

Investigation

Almost every hacker first investigates and monitors the system and possible loopholes in the network before intruding into it. Monitoring the network traffic constantly with specially developed applications can provide the required network information. Information compiled from this investigation can be used to gain unauthorized access to the enterprise network. The following sections describe the tools and techniques used in the process of investigation.

Locating the device

The first step for any intrusion is to identify and locate the target host or network device. A valid IP address range or specific IP address is the best source of information to identify the target. Intrusion becomes easy if the attacker knows the target IP address. But, if there is no logical information of the target, then the hackers use query-based commands to locate the target host. The following methods are used to *identify* the target host:

✦ **Network utilities:** These are basic TCP/IP network commands like ping, trace, whois, finger, telnet, rusers, rpcinfo, nslookup, and other commands or custom utilities. Utilities, such as crawlers and Trojans, help in gathering information about the target.

✦ **Port scanning:** The first stage of penetrating into a network or auditing a remote host is to prepare a list of available open application ports. These ports are used by applications to establish sessions between communicating peers using TCP or UDP protocols. The type of application is specified using port numbers in each data transmission sequence when one application communicates with another application on another host over the Internet. These ports are specific to applications and are assigned by Internet Corporation for Assigned Names and Numbers (ICANN).

Port scanning is one of the techniques most widely used to discover and map services by listening to traffic on a specific port. Programs called *port-scan utilities* can verify all possible ranges of TCP and UDP ports on a remote host to determine what network services are available. Port-scanning techniques allow an attacker to locate open/closed ports on a remote host. The scan method used in a given environment depends entirely on the type of network topology, IDS, and logging features enabled at the remote end. A common tool for port scanning is System Administrators Tool for Analyzing Networks (SATAN).

✦ **ICMP sweeps:** Messages that use the Internet Control Message Protocol (ICMP) can detect whether the target host is alive or reachable on an organization's intranet. ICMP checks are usually performed individually on a single host. ICMP sweep scans a range of configured IP addresses or all possible IP addresses. Accordingly, this (relatively slow) process is only practical to use on midsize networks.

Note   Using the same method to query multiple hosts is known as an ICMP or `ping` *sweep*.

Network snooping

Network snooping gives the hacker better control over the collected information. A sniffer is placed on a host on the network. It captures all the data packets traversing on the connected network. Observing the network traffic and capturing the relevant packets (using filters) for analysis is an effective way to gather the necessary information. This process of snooping is also called *sniffing*. Network intruders use this method to prepare a pattern for the data traversing the medium and use this pattern for gaining unauthorized access or personal security IDs used for money transactions. Network sniffers are hard to detect; they use minimal system resources and their activity is not logged.

Tip   In legitimate use, network sniffers are efficient tools for monitoring network traffic. Network administrators need the information sniffers provide — but this tool can also pose a threat to network security if a hacker uses it to size up network traffic for an attack and gather information that travels over the network.

Unauthorized access

After gathering the relevant information about the remote host and available options to reach it, the intruder tries to gain access over the networked servers and clients and the networking devices. The primary motive of the intruder is to take administrative control of the target server.

An intruder can gain unauthorized access from many possible entry points. How far the penetration goes into the internetwork depends on whether the intruder has obtained a system-level username/password combination. If the hacker is internal to the network, authentication credentials can be obtained by influencing the system administrator, by eavesdropping; external hackers often use packet sniffers to capture the username and password. When an intruder (whether internal or external) has that vital information, access to the network is easy.

Cracking the password

Possession of the correct username or password gives an intruder rights to manipulate data — usually in the form of administrative or privileged access to network components. Stealing the right combination of username and password is supposed to be tough, but various password-cracking programs are available to ease the task. A *password cracker* is a program designed to decrypt passwords or disable password protection. Some of these programs look into security database files in your network operating system to extract the information; others use several algorithms to make and try possible combinations.

Enforcing strict password policies can block such attempts. A strong policy should require users to include unusual alphanumeric characters (including both alphabets as well as numbers, for example `John#1266abc`) — and define a short life for the password (ranging from 10 to 15 days). In addition to the users' habits, the network itself can use some direct attention: for example, some third-party utilities (such as Securpass and RSA SecurID) that help in password management.

Intrusion from remote access

Enterprise users require remote access to the company's information systems. The facility of remote access can provide e-mail, ftp, and extranet access to traveling employees or to sales people to confirm business orders. By its nature, remote access to computer systems adds vulnerabilities by increasing the number of access points. Most applications providing remote access do not have built-in security. Also, most methods used for remote access do not have secure authentication mechanisms. The three major modes of remote access are

✦ **Service-specific.** This type of remote access is limited to remote operation of one service, usually e-mail or HTTP/FTP.

Often software programs (such as Microsoft Outlook, Lotus Notes, and cc:Mail) support mobile connections without making provision for general network services. Applications that do support such services (for example, `SMTP`, `POP`, `MIME`, and `sendmail`) have inherent security vulnerabilities that leave them open to exploitation by intruders.

Attacks on Web servers make up the most common type of network intrusion. Intruders exploit the bugs and security holes on the Web server and the operating system to take control of the Web server and gain access to the Web content. The intruder can then manipulate the data.

File transfer — another operation performed by remote users — is another service often targeted by hackers. As useful as network protocols such as FTP or TFTP are for file transfer, they are prone to intrusions. TFTP is an unsecured protocol because it requires no authentication; FTP can be misused for transferring spurious content if a hacker is using anonymous access.

✦ **Remote control:** An offsite user operates a personal computer situated at another location. The other computer can be a special purpose system or the user's desktop computer. This is usually allowed on networks for remote administration. The remote computer is used strictly as a keyboard and a display. Remote control restricts the remote users to use the software programs resident on the other computer.

Some multiuser remote-control products also provide enhanced auditing and logging, but they are vulnerable because they require only username and password for initiating a session.

✦ **Remote node operation:** A remote computer connects to a remote-access server and accesses applications stored on it. The remote computer provides application software as well as local storage space to the users. Remote node operation provides all network services to remote users, unless access control software is used. This form of remote access can be accomplished using dial-in connections, Telnet sessions, or using software products that support remote access. Although remote node operation is becoming the most popular form of remote access, it introduces the highest level of vulnerability to corporate systems.

In any of the cases mentioned above, once the intruder gains access to operating systems and applications running at both ends can be exploited. To keep a check on this intrusion, the remote access devices and software programs should be regularly monitored. Vendors customarily use a part of their Web sites to list bugs discovered in their software and patches to apply to their software to counteract the bugs.

Cisco has devised multiple solutions to block intrusions. The most widely accepted are Cisco PIX Firewalls and Cisco Secure control servers. You can, for example, implement and configure Cisco PIX Firewalls at your network perimeter to control access according to your security policies — or interoperate such a firewall with the IOS features built into Cisco routers and Cisco Secure Access Control Server (which use encrypted authentication for even greater security).

For more about Cisco routers and Cisco Secure Access Control Server, see Chapters 4, 10, and 15.

Denial-of-service attacks

Denial-of-service (DoS) attacks leave the target computers inaccessible to the authorized users of the network. Usually, hackers flood the servers and communication links with useless data, temporarily halting data access and eventually crashing the computers.

DoS attacks are easy to launch and are becoming common because they don't require advanced technical skills — or even any access to the target server. In addition, DoS attacks are easy to keep anonymous; although several methods exist for initiating them, no one countermeasure can always determine the identity of the attacker.

Denial-of-service attacks are different from other network attacks because they target network services and try to make them unavailable to authorized users. Other network attacks attempt to gain access to data on the network.

Hackers who use DoS attacks exploit inherent vulnerabilities — especially those of the IP protocol and of communication technologies. In fact, any IP packet being sent across the network can be used to execute a DoS attack; such attacks can come from any point on the network. Figure 1-3 illustrates some of the possible origin points for DoS attacks.

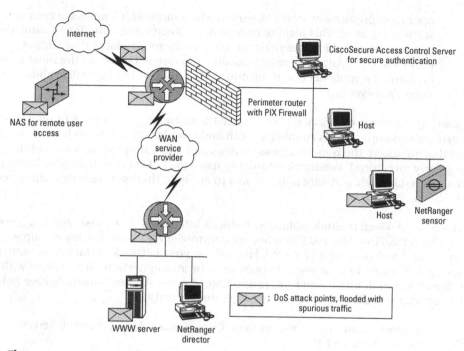

Figure 1-3: Common DoS-vulnerable points on a network

DoS attacks can take different forms, target a variety of network services, and have one or more of the following goals:

✦ Unauthorized use of resources

✦ Physical destruction or modification of network devices

✦ Destruction or modification of network-configuration information

The following sections describe the most commonly employed tools and mechanisms for DoS attacks.

Ping of death

In this mechanism of DoS attack, the network is flooded with large-sized ICMP packets targeted to a specific host. The target host receives the ping command in fragments and starts reassembling the packet — but the packet is large; when fully reassembled, it's too big for the buffer. The resulting overflow causes unpredictable results such as reboots, hangs, or even a system crash. Such oversize ICMP packets can be sent from computers running Microsoft Windows 95 and Windows NT by typing this command:

```
ping -l 65527 -s 1 {destinationIP}
```

where

✦ -1 65527 sets the buffer size to 65527

✦ -s 1 specifies the timestamp for hop counts

On a Unix platform, source codes such as simping.c and pingdd.c can be used to create ping floods.

A solution to counter the ping attack is to block only fragmented pings rather than blocking all regular pings. This will allow regular 64-byte pings through almost all systems and block the fragmented pings, which are bigger than the MTU size of your link.

SYN floods

The basic purpose of a DoS attack called a *SYN flood* is to use up all new network TCP connections at a site and thus prevent legal users from connecting. A TCP connection uses a three-way handshake mechanism to start a session. The steps involved in establishing a TCP connection are as follows:

1. The first host sends the first data packet to the second host. This data packet is referred to as *SY*nchronize sequence *N*umber (SYN) and contains the ID of the host.

2. The second host acknowledges the receipt of the data and sends the second data packet to the first host. This second data packet is referred to as the ACK.

3. The second host also sends its SYN along with ACK for the first host.

4. The first host on receiving the data from the second host sends back the third data packet or ACK.

The complete process involves a transfer of only three data packets (thus the term *three-way handshake*). If a fake ID is sent in the SYN packet, the receiving system would never get a connection acknowledgment. Eventually, the connection times out; the incoming channel on the receiver becomes available for another request. SYN floods send so many requests that all incoming connections are tied up waiting for acknowledgments. If a fake ID is sent in the SYN packets, acknowledgments never come; the server waits for them, unavailable to legal users. TCP interception tools are the only way to counter this problem; Cisco provides such tools in IOS software and Cisco PIX Firewall.

Mail bombing and spam mailing

In an *e-mail bomb* attack, the hacker repeatedly sends identical copies of e-mail messages to an address. Hackers use scripts to create such fake mails, which keep replicating at the server end. This causes the target mail server to process all incoming mails. The target server might not be capable of handling this due to low bandwidth, low disk space, or other processing constraints. This puts the mailing server in a looping process and eventually leads to a server crash.

Spam mailing is a method that sends e-mails with fake reply addresses. When the receiving users try to send a reply to these e-mail messages, the reply e-mail bounces back because of an unrecognizable e-mail address. If this happened for only one e-mail, the effect would be negligible — but if a reply is sent to spam mails that get replicated many times, the process soon monopolizes resources and brings down the mail server.

Smurf DoS

Smurf DoS is one of the latest network-level attacks: A hacker sends a large number of IP `echo` requests to the IP broadcast address of the network, all using the spoofed address of the victim so that all computers on the network respond to these requests by sending the `echo` reply message. This leads to network traffic congestion. The situation can be even worse in a multiaccess broadcast system; hundreds of computers would reply to each `echo` request.

Note   This attack is named after a DoS tool called Smurf that performs the actual attack.

Broadcast storm

A *broadcast storm* is a popular DoS attack method that introduces a large number of packets into a network, addressed to a destination that doesn't exist. Each host tries to forward the packets to the fake destination address; the packets bounce around the network for a long time until they halt the regular network processes. Network tools (such as `ping`, `finger`, and `sendmail`) can be misused for generating broadcast storms.

Organizations should consider the extent to which they can afford any disruption and take steps to lessen unacceptable risks. The variety of DoS attacks has resulted in a range of countermeasures:

✦ Creating and maintaining regular backup schedules.

✦ Creating and maintaining appropriate password policies.

✦ Implementing route filters to filter large or fragmented ICMP traffic.

✦ Configuring filters for IP-spoofed packets.

✦ Installing patches and fixes for TCP SYN attacks.

✦ Disabling unused or unneeded services on the network. If the operating system supports multiple partitions or volumes, then partition the file system to separate application-specific files from regular data.

✦ Establishing system performance baselines and monitoring daily activity for any deviations.

✦ Routinely examining the physical security environment with respect to current needs.

✦ Using tools such as Tripwire to detect changes in configuration information or other files. Implementing an Intrusion Detection System would also help detect the problem.

You can address the problems of DoS attacks with the implementation of PIX Firewall and Cisco Secure Intrusion-Detection System. There are many built-in features within the Cisco IOS that can be used to secure the perimeter router from DoS attacks. You can also use Context-Based Access Control (CBAC) for detecting and countering DoS attacks.

Data diddling

Data diddling involves capturing, modifying, and corrupting the data on the trusted host. The intruder can also replay the data sent over the wire and reroute the network traffic. This is possible due to inherent flaws in the protocol and operating system. Web site attacks are the most common data-diddling attacks, in which the intruder modifies the contents of the Web pages. Some common data-diddling methods are described in the following sections.

IP spoofing

A spoofing attack involves hiding the source address. IP spoofing is when an attacker masquerades his computer as a host on the target's network. The IP spoofing attack is unique as it can only be implemented against a certain class of computers running TCP/IP. A network intruder uses this method to imitate the identity of host or application used to establish a session with peer target. The intruder uses a spoofed valid address to penetrate into the network. This can be done either to avoid the IP filters on the perimeter router or firewalls.

Spoofing provides IP address authentication, which uses the IP address as an index. The target computer authenticates a session with other computers by examining the IP address of the requesting computer. There are different forms of IP authentication, and most of them are prone to attacks. For spoofing to be successful, an attacker has to forge the source address and needs to maintain a TCP sequence number with the target. The second task is the most complicated one because when a target sets the initial sequence number, the attacker must send the correct response. An attacker who correctly guesses the sequence number, can synchronize with the target and establish a valid session. Some common services vulnerable to IP spoofing are as follows:

✦ Remote Procedure Call (RPC) services

✦ Any service that uses IP address authentication

✦ The X Window system

✦ Unix-based R services, such as `rlogin` and `rsh`

IP spoofing attacks are on the rise, and it is hard to detect such attacks. The following security measures can be used to prevent IP spoofing.

✦ Avoid using source address authentication. Implement cryptographic authentication system-wide. If external connections from trusted hosts are allowed, enable encryption sessions at the router.

✦ Configure your network to reject packets from the Internet that claim to originate from a local address. This can be easily configured on the perimeter router.

Cisco recommends implementing Cisco Secure Intrusion Detection System (IDS) and packet filtering to detect and prevent IP spoofing attacks.

Session hijacking

When a hacker takes over a TCP session between two computers it is called TCP session hijacking. Because most authentications occur at the start of a TCP session, it allows the hacker to gain access to any computer. The hacker captures the TCP/IP session packets and manipulates necessary fields in the header.

A popular method of hijacking a session is by using source-routed IP packets. The hacker participates in a conversation between two other devices by encouraging the IP packets to pass through his computer. If source routing is turned off, the hacker can use "blind" hijacking and guess the responses of the two computers. Thus, the hacker can send a command but can never see the response.

The refined version of this hijacking is termed as session replay in which the intruder replays a counterfeit and manipulated data stream to gain unauthorized advantage. This data stream is captured from the network that does not implement authentication. Using proper secure and encrypted authentication methods, this problem can be avoided to some extent. You can prevent session replay attacks by

✦ Using packet filters and controlling access to the network.

✦ Using encryption technologies for security credential transaction and maintaining security over data.

✦ Configuring security on Web browsers so cookies and applets cannot be executed on the computers.

Cisco Secure Access Control Server should be implemented to support TACACS+, RADIUS, or SSL authentication. Cisco PIX Firewall is ideal on the network perimeter to filter packets and apply policy-based filtering.

Rerouting

A router is the easiest target for any hacker because it is the gateway to a network. A hacker can gain unauthorized access to the routing device and manipulate the routing information or host configuration. This results in routing misconfigurations within the intranet — resulting in loss of data packets. The hacker masquerades the router identity in a manner such that the local users are unable to locate the route to the external network.

There are various methods to counter such attacks. Rerouting can be prevented by limiting access to the routing device itself, filtering source-routed packets, disabling source routing on hosts, and using Cisco IOS authentication features. The CiscoSecure IDS can be configured to detect these activities on the device and take action against it.

Formulating and Evaluating a Security Policy

A *network-security policy* defines an organization's vision of using computer and network infrastructure for providing better service and productivity. It also outlines the procedures to counter and respond to the security threats. A network-security policy streamlines the risk factors and possible threats associated with any corporate asset. You should have the company's network policy in hand before you start planning the security of the network.

In practice, network-security policy is a delicate balance that weighs possible threats against the value of personal productivity and efficiency. As a network administrator, you should also realistically assess the benefits to be gained from implementing the policy. Without a proper network security policy, a functional and operational security framework cannot be established.

A functioning security policy is not only a set of rules governing all users' access to corporate assets, it's also a general agreement to accept and abide by those rules. The ideal security policy is a framework that safeguards corporate resources, enforces security regulations, and still allows secure and transparent user access (as illustrated in Figure 1-4). A real-world security policy must always keep those three goals in a dynamic balance.

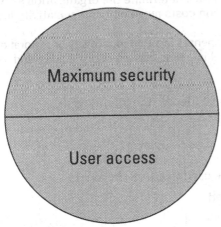

Figure 1-4: Network security policy: The ideal

Naturally, consistency is an essential ingredient, and formulating a policy document is an essential step toward standardizing security activities. Such formulation should be a collaborative effort of IT managers, administrative officers, front-line managers, and executives. The actual policy document must be approved and issued by the organization's senior management after they evaluate the cost-benefit ratio.

As you strive for balance between maximum security and transparent user access, a good rule of thumb is to impose as few restrictions as possible from the users' point of view.

Considering the risks posed by an unsecured network, implementing security measures such as encryption does not unduly restrict access or adversely affect productivity. Inadequate security planning can result in failure to resist attack, which can massively reduce productivity and performance. Network-security policy should match the economic health and realistic budget of the company to relative ease of implementation and use. To determine an appropriate starting point, perform a risk analysis before you formulate your security policy — identify any assets prone to security threats and assess the level of protection each asset requires. The following section discusses risk analysis in detail.

Risk analysis

Sensitivity to specific risks varies from one organization to another. Risk analysis helps you identify the assets and security measures that your security policy must address — one at a time. Each asset has its own particular sensitivity to risk; each risk has its own degree of likelihood, taken into consideration during risk analysis. The consequence of a security breach is a major factor that affects an organization's level of sensitivity. All security breaches, however insignificant they might seem, lead to restoration costs — which in turn determine the organization's level of sensitivity. Bottom line: Higher restoration costs mean a higher sensitivity level.

Tip

Restoration costs are not confined to expenses incurred in recovery or restoration. They also include the costs of personnel idle time, missed opportunities, and lost customer trust.

In the process of risk analysis, you first must identify the following:

✦ Assets that must be protected

✦ People who can attack the assets

✦ Tools (and their sources) that can be used to attack the assets

✦ Immediate cost if the asset is attacked

✦ Time needed to recover the attacked asset

The following sections discuss these points in detail.

Assets that must be protected

The assets of an organization can be broadly classified into two categories.

✦ **Tangible assets:** Refer to the assets that have physical form. Tangible assets include computers, printers, network hubs, cables, network devices, and computer peripherals. Often the process of risk analysis ignores tangible assets.

However, as one of the basic aims of risk analysis is to help in the formulation of security policy, it is important that the security risks for all assets are taken into consideration.

✦ **Intangible assets:** Refer to the assets that do not have a physical form. Intangible assets include time and goodwill. Consider intangible assets while performing risk analysis. Since many organizations survive on goodwill, it becomes important to consider the impact of a security breach on the goodwill of an organization. While performing risk analysis, also take into account the worth of time spent in restoring the required functionality of devices or the network.

Tip   You must consider both tangible and intangible resources in the process of risk analysis.

A variety of classifications can be applied to an organization's hardware and software to help you decide the appropriate level of security to apply. Some categories you can use to classify your hardware and software are as follows:

✦ **Strategic systems:** This category includes hardware and software that conform to the organization's computing standards.

✦ **Tactical systems:** This category includes hardware and software that no longer meet the criteria for strategic systems are still functional in the organization's current computing environment. These systems must be upgraded to (or replaced with) strategic systems.

✦ **Legacy systems:** This category includes hardware and software that do not conform to the strategic standards of the organization. Usually, database applications and e-mail systems fall into this category, hence it becomes important to support these systems.

✦ **Unsupported systems:** This category includes hardware and software that can no longer be supported by the organization.

In today's fast-changing computing world, systems quickly move from strategic to tactical and then to unsupported category. Consider phasing out of unsupported systems in favor of strategic systems that offer greater security and conform to strategic computing standards.

People who can attack the assets

An organization's network is prone to security attacks from a variety of people. A network administrator should identify the people who can attack the network assets and their motivation. The most common potential attackers to network security are

✦ Internal users or employees of the organization

✦ Hackers

✦ Competitors

Note   Most security policies make the mistake of addressing threats from external intrusions but neglecting those from internal users. During risk analysis, consider possible security threats from internal users and the employees of your organization.

Sources that can be used to attack network assets

Potential attackers can gain access to an organization's assets from one or more of the following sources:

✦ Remote offices

✦ The Internet

✦ Local-area networks

✦ Modem pools

Immediate cost

Immediate cost refers to an attack's impact in terms of the costs imposed when an asset is compromised or dysfunctional. Consider an example: If a problem in network connectivity prevents your employees from accessing data on the server, the result is reduced work output and decreased productivity — proportional to network downtime — and this loss in productivity is the immediate cost.

One of the most important resources of an organization is the business and operational information that it produces or processes. Thus, most network attacks are targeted at organizational data — and if they succeed in compromising it, the result is significant financial and operational loss. Hence, an effective risk analysis categorizes your organization's data according to its sensitivity to loss, manipulation, or destruction. You can start such a classification by applying four categories to your data:

✦ **Sensitive data:** This category is vital to the reputation and mission of most organizations; special precautions are needed to deflect security attacks. Be sure to protect this data from unauthorized modification, access, or deletion.

✦ **Confidential data:** Data meant strictly for use within the organization. Disclosure of confidential data can have adverse impact on the organization, its clients, and business partners.

✦ **Private data:** Information meant for use of specific departments within the organization (such as personal records of employees) falls into this category. It is important that private data is *not* accessible to all the employees of the organization.

✦ **Public data:** Public data refers to data that doesn't fall in any of the earlier-mentioned categories. It is assumed that disclosure of public data would not have any significant adverse effect on the organization.

You should document all your findings during risk analysis. The information that you gather after risk analysis serves to formulate the network security policy.

Note Although in most organizations it is the network administrators who perform risk analysis, ideally a team of individuals that comprises business managers and network administrators should be involved in risk analysis.

Components of a network-security policy

Before formulating a security policy, it is mandatory to study the requirements of a security policy. A network-security policy depends on various factors of an enterprise — such as network size, topology, internetwork devices, and usage — that make such policies considerably subjective. Every factor should be considered. Thus network-security policy can be different for different organizations. Certain issues, relevant and important in designing the security policy, are discussed in the following sections.

Physical security

An enterprise network can span floors, buildings, and even wide geographical locations. Implementation of such a network involves many components and devices. A network security policy must address the physical security of the actual components and devices in the network.

Brass-tacks security issues — such as maintaining the confidentiality and integrity of data over the communication cable — cannot be effectively considered before a proper framework to provide security for physical components and devices is in place.

Network security

In addition to its role as a vital enterprise system, a network has resources and data repositories shared within the user accounts. These resources are valuable to an organization and must be protected. Your network security policy should address how the organization's data repositories stored on the network have to be protected. It also includes the implementation and configuration of security components for access controls, firewalls, network auditing, remote access, directory services, Internet services, and file-system directory structures.

Access control

Access control is the mechanism used to ensure that only legitimate and authorized users have access to resources and services. Your security policy should define a guideline for access-control mechanisms that streamlines legitimate user access within — or outside — the network, while allowing legitimate remote access and blocking possible intrusions from the Internet. Your policy should not be overly complex; it should be easy to implement.

Software security

Although software security is often a misinterpreted topic, software security policy should define how the commercial and non-commercial software packages would be installed, implemented, and used on the network. The policy should also address software copyright and OEM support issues, as well as how to purchase, upgrade, or procure licenses for the software. Be sure to include security guidelines for downloading new software, upgrades, or patches from the Internet.

Auditing and review

Your security policy must be reviewed and audited regularly to keep it relevant to current conditions, address any need to update security measures, and ensure that all components and users are complying with the standards. Monitoring resources and components for inconsistencies is a natural outgrowth of this practice. If an organization does not review or make regular audit checks, it has no basis for a documented action plan — and no ready response in case of a security breach. Auditing helps in identifying new security holes that might have developed during the time.

Note   Although audits and reviews play a significant role in ensuring the security of a network, fewer than 50 percent of organizations periodically audit and review their network security policies.

Security awareness

Implementing a network security policy demands that each user on the network understand its importance. Users with little or no idea of security are a threat to network security. Users who do not understand the importance and proper use of security measures can unintentionally disclose security credentials causing threat to the network security. Every network user should be confronted with the same clear statement that underscores the importance of usernames and passwords — and of keeping them secure.

Incident response and disaster contingency plan

Your security policy should include procedures to follow in case of disaster. Such a *disaster contingency plan* works out how an organization would recover from a natural disaster, in the event of hardware failure, or attacks from hackers. The security of corporate data is most important for a network. Apart from regular access policies and user permissions, planning backup and restoration of data in case of disaster is essential. The backup plan should indicate the frequency and scheme of backup, where to store backup media (onsite or offsite), and how to recover data in case of a failure.

Your disaster contingency plan should also include information about the people who should draft the plans and respond to natural disasters or attacks on the network. These people would have the responsibility of raising awareness among the users regarding the importance of backup — and training them.

Preparing the security policy

What makes a good security policy? You can move toward an effective one by considering the following aspects of creating it:

✦ **Accessibility:** An organization's security policy affects all its employees. Hence, it is important that all employees have access to the policy. A good idea is to include the security policy in the employee handbook or the intranet Web site (if your organization has one).

✦ **Outlining the goals:** Any change in the existing setup of an organization is bound to meet resistance from the employees. The same holds true when you try to introduce the security policy. It is important that goals and objectives of a security policy are outlined. Employees must know why security policy is important to the organization.

✦ **Clarity:** Because security policy affects all employees of the organization, it should be clear, easily understandable, and precise to avoid any misinterpretation. The language of the security policy document should be accurate and unambiguous; the role of the organization should be well defined.

✦ **Defining roles and responsibilities:** Security policy should clearly define the roles and responsibilities of the employees in maintaining the network security. The policy should also define people who are responsible for enforcing the security policy, taking backups, and conducting audits.

✦ **Defining the consequences:** Employees should know the impact of noncompliance to the security policy. Hence, the security policy should include the consequences that an employee would face if he/she does not comply with a particular issue in the policy.

Before implementing a security policy within the network, it is necessary to study and create analytical reports on the following issues:

✦ **Usage policy statements:** A usage policy statement is necessary to define a user's role and responsibilities within the security framework. It should provide the users with an understanding of the security policy and define their security responsibilities. It should also contain guidelines for improving security practices. This security policy should be able to address the issues of user account administration, enforcement of policies, and the review of user privileges. It should explicitly mention rules regarding access to corporate data and user passwords.

✦ **Risk analysis:** Before devising the network policy, it is necessary to do a risk analysis to identify the risks to resources, devices, and data on the network. The primary objective of risk analysis is to identify security threat points within the network. After identifying the security threat points, you must apply an appropriate level of security according to risk levels.

✦ **Security and support team:** A security support team comprising IT managers and members from senior management who are aware of the security policy and its technical implementation should be constituted. Key responsibilities of this support team would be to develop policies, encourage policy usage, and respond to any security attack. The security team should periodically review the security policy. Also, the security team should review the security policy if there is a change in:

- Network design
- Firewall configuration
- SNMP configuration
- User or management requirements
- Access-control lists (ACLs)

The security policy of an organization should provide answers to the following questions:

- ✦ Who should have rights to access the organization's network? If required, how would clients, partners, and vendors be provided access to the organization's network?
- ✦ Who can connect to external networks, such as those of clients and partners?
- ✦ Who can access the Internet from the organization's network?
- ✦ How would the employees of the organization access the Internet?
- ✦ When should a person's (employee or external user) account be deleted?
- ✦ How secure must computers be before they are placed in a network with unprotected access to the Internet?
- ✦ Can (and should) users download random executables from the Internet?
- ✦ How would the data traveling over the organization's network be protected?
- ✦ How would the confidential information about employees be protected? Are there any laws regarding the handling of this type of information?
- ✦ What kinds of passwords should employees use, and how often should they change passwords?
- ✦ What safety measures must be taken against viruses on personal computers?
- ✦ How would the computers of remote and mobile users be secured? How would they get secure access to the organization's network?

Tip   Know what goes into your network-security policy. You should also know what should *not* go into it. For example, if employees display obscene pictures on their computers, it isn't an issue that needs to be addressed in network-security policy. It is an issue that needs to be addressed by the human resource department. Also, the problem of employees playing computer games or surfing the Internet during office hours needs to be addressed by management in some way other than the network-security policy.

A security policy template

This section lays out a template for a security policy; you can use it as the basis for your organization's policy document.

<Company name> Network-Security Policy

1. Purpose

This section should make clear the purpose of creating the security policy, highlighting the policy's goal: To prevent the organization's network from security breaches rather than restricting user access.

2. Audience

This section should list the audience for whom the security policy is intended. For example, it should list who is expected to comply with the security policy. It should also mention who would implement and support the policy.

3. Scope

In this section, the scope of the security policy is defined. Specify any relevant national or international rules and laws.

4. Responsibility

This section should clearly define the people who would be responsible for drafting, maintaining, and enforcing the security policy. It should also define the responsibilities of the system administrator with respect to network security.

5. Implementation

This section should describe how the security policy would be implemented in the organization. It should also define the network devices used in implementing the policy.

6. Maintenance plan

This section should define when audits would be done, if the audits would be random, and who would be the auditor. It should also define the time period after which the security policy must be revised or updated.

7. Training plan

This section should describe how the employees would be educated about the security policy. Emphasize educating the employees to prevent them from being socially engineered by would-be intruders.

8. Usage policy

This section should clearly define what consequences an employee would have to face if he/she fails to comply with the security policy.

9. Authentication methods

This section defines the authentication methods that would be used for user authentication and identification. This section should include the password management plan, if any.

10. Encryption policy

This section should define whether encryption would be used to secure data transmission.

11. Internet access

This section should define methods to be used for gaining access to the Internet. It should also list who can access the Internet; include a list of specific sites that you don't expect the employees of the organization to access. Also specify whether the employees may download executables from the Internet and run them on their personal computers.

12. Campus access

This section defines the different access levels that would be assigned to the employees in the network.

13. Remote access

This section defines the measures or safety precautions that would be taken to secure remote access to the organization's network.

14. Branch office access

This section defines the level of access that would be given to the branch offices.

15. Extranet access

This section defines the level of access that would be given to the offices of business partners, customers, and vendors.

16. Disaster and accident handling

This section should define how the organization plans to handle security threats posed by natural disasters and accidents.

17. Backup hardware

This section should list the backup equipment that needs to be kept in the inventory to ensure immediate replacement in case of hardware failure.

18. Backup procedure

This section defines the time interval at which data backup would be made. It should also define the medium on which the backup would be made, and identify the person who would be responsible for making the backup.

19. Physical security

This section should define how the physical security of data, as well as network devices, would be ensured. For example, you should specify a separate server room (and limit access to it) to prevent unauthorized physical access to the server.

20. Intrusion detection

This section defines the mechanisms that would be used to detect network intrusions.

Cross-Reference   For details on intrusion detection, refer to Chapter 3.

The security policy template given in this section includes the basics — each organization must enhance and edit it to meet specific needs. As a network administrator, you must decide what to add or delete from the basic template, fine-tuning your policy template to meet the security needs of your network.

Monitoring network security

An effective network-security policy should have provisions for auditing and monitoring the secured network. It should specify techniques and procedures to identify and respond to any inconsistency within the network. The basic aim of security monitoring is to detect changes in the network and determine whether these changes can lead to security violation. The regular monitoring and auditing of network resources and components can be performed using a variety of tools and methods. Some common methods used for monitoring the network components are described in the following sections.

Note   Where network security is concerned, creating a security policy is not the end of the job — in fact, it's the beginning. After you formulate your policy, make sure it's implemented effectively.

Log files

Every networking device and software has inherent capabilities of creating logs of events that occur. These logs can be configured to capture specific events concerned with security. Log files can be analyzed to list all users currently logged on; the results can be compared with previous logs. Some advanced logging features even log the incidents of resource access and violations of security. These log files can be saved and stored for reference and pattern analysis. The `syslog` utility in Unix and Event Viewer utility in Windows NT maintain an event log of all configured activities.

Tip   Most network administrators prefer to set SNMP thresholds or DMI events to warn them in case of an emergency.

Enterprise-management systems

The growing size of networks and use of heterogeneous technologies have made the management of enterprise networks even more difficult. There are vendors like HP, IBM, and Cisco who have enterprise-management system suites. These packages provide real-time monitoring of the network and give detailed information about the health of the network and its operating status. Apart from monitoring all network devices and the servers on the network, these packages are also capable of detecting events (such as unauthorized access, unusual traffic, changes to the firewall, access granted to the firewall on the network) that might pose a security threat.

The monitored computer runs agent software that generates and sends security alerts when it detects a problem or erratic traffic pattern. Management systems respond to these alerts by taking appropriate actions. These actions can be an operator notification, event log, system shutdown, and automatic attempts for a system repair. The management stations also log all these events, which can be later used for analysis.

Network intrusion-detection systems

Security monitoring can be accomplished with the implementation of an intrusion-detection system (IDS). Network-based intrusion-detection systems monitor all layers of the network communication in real time. Because these systems operate by analyzing network traffic, the monitors often protect only local segments. There are four common deployment strategies for intrusion-detection devices:

✦ Implement it on every critical segment within the intranet. This would protect the network against any security breaches from within the organization.

✦ Implement it in the network's DMZ (demilitarized zone) to protect devices, such as firewalls within the area.

✦ Deploy it inside the intranet firewall to monitor a firewall and ensure that there are no tunnels being established through the firewall to infringe on the network system.

✦ Implement the IDS on the hosts having critical data. The IDS implementation on each host provides protection by having intrusion-detection agents that monitor unusual administrative activities or configuration changes.

Intrusion-detection systems can be either host-based or network-based.

✦ *Host-based IDS* are implemented on a specific host to monitor and secure network servers. Host-based IDS are also implemented on secure hosts having important corporate data. The agents are installed on each corporate asset; the information they provide is compared to a defined set of rules to determine if a security breach has occurred.

✦ *Network-based IDS* monitor the activity on a specified network segment. They are different host-based agents because network-based systems are dedicated platforms. Network-based IDSs have two major components:

   • A sensor that analyzes network traffic in the background

   • A management system configured to send an alert after receiving information from the sensor

Cisco Secure IDS supports only network-based systems. A typical implementation of network-based IDS is shown in Figure 1-5.

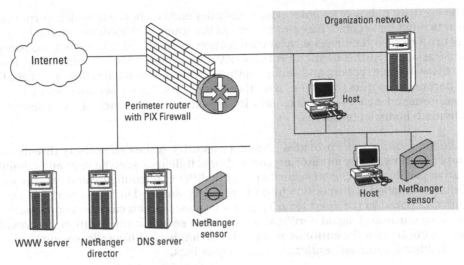

Figure 1-5: A network-based IDS

Intrusion-detection technology is a complementary tool that must be used with traditional security products. It works with firewalls, encryption and authentication technologies, and access-control lists.

Apart from implementing IDS, it is necessary to regularly audit the network-security system to generate reports on the security state. Cisco Secure Scanner is a tool that enables you to measure security, manage risks, and eliminate security vulnerabilities enabling secure network environments. Cisco Secure Scanner offers unique auditing features, such as network mapping, security vulnerability assessment, risk management analysis, decision support, and security policies validation through an easy-to-use interface.

A monitoring policy should be created for each network entity identified in risk analysis. How often you monitor should depend on two factors:

✦ How important the device is to the network

✦ How susceptible the device is to attack

A good policy could be that low-risk devices be monitored on a weekly basis, the medium-risk devices on a daily basis, and high-risk devices hourly.

Your security policy should also address issues such as how to notify the security team of security violations. Network monitoring software should trigger a notification to the operations center when it detects a security violation. The operations center should in turn notify the security team using various wireless paging and notifying mechanisms.

The security policy of an enterprise largely depends on how and which corporate assets must be secured. An *open security policy* framework assumes minimum security risks and outlines easy authentication methods using cleartext passwords and Password-Authentication Protocol (PAP) for remote-access handshaking. It has no firewalls, encryption, and secure authentication methods. It relies on access lists at perimeter routers to prevent unauthorized access. Such a security policy is compromised easily — and is usually implemented due to a lack of awareness or adequate financial resources.

A *closed security policy* provides maximum security against all security threats with emphasis on security monitoring and auditing. It defines specific user and adminis-trative privileges. A closed security policy is difficult to configure and manage and requires detailed introspection into the risk assessment. The investment can be high compared to the open security policy framework. You can use a combination of smart cards and digital certificates to provide secure authentication. To provide access control for the entire network, you can implement firewalls, encryption mechanisms, route authentication, and access lists.

System integrators can devise a security policy that provides a balance between open and closed policies. The security policy of an organization can be open or closed. A security policy midway between open and closed is a *restrictive security policy*. As a rule, the cost of security implementation increases as a policy become more restrictive.

Case Study

AllSolv, Inc., an IT solution provider, is based in Boston and has branch offices in New York, Connecticut, and Washington, D.C. All remote users access the network resources through a single point. They must provide only their usernames and passwords to gain access.

The network structure of AllSolv is illustrated in Figure 1-6.

However, due to the expansion of its business and increasing security threats, AllSolv, Inc. has decided to implement a security policy for its network. This policy will form the basis for securing the network of AllSolv, Inc. and at the same time educate the users on how to make the best use of the organization's network resources.

The following section gives a detailed account of the security policy, which AllSolv, Inc. plans to implement. The different sections included in the security-policy document are as follows:

1. Definition of scope and authority

2. Policy for computer usage

3. Policy for authenticating and identifying users

4. Policy for remote access

5. Policy for accessing the Internet

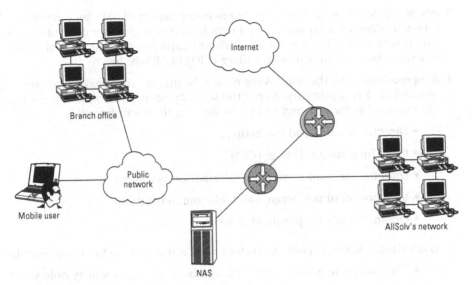

Figure 1-6: AllSolv's network

Definition of scope and authority

This policy document defines the scope as well as the various entities involved with the management, implementation, and design of the security policy. Every employee of AllSolv, Inc. needs to be well acquainted with the security policy so he/she can better understand the need for a secure network and help ensure data integrity.

The shareholders of the company have vested upon the board of directors and the executives of the organization the right to formulate and implement the security policy as per the national and international rules and regulations. The following sections are included in this document:

1. **Audience.** According to AllSolv's security policy, it is meant for the following audience:

   • Users (internal as well as remote) of the AllSolv, Inc. network resources

   • Support engineers who provide support services (in addition to implementing the policy)

   • Auditors and lawyers of the organization who help uphold the name and reputation of the organization

- Executives of the organization who are responsible for data integrity and must control the cost of network security

- Managers of the organization who are responsible for data security and the cost implications of the policy

2. **Scope.** AllSolv's security policy covers every aspect of data security from internal users, Internet access, and remote access to disaster control measures. The policy states that the responsibility of implementing the security policy lies with the Chief Information Officer (CIO) of AllSolv, Inc.

3. **Responsibility.** All the employees of AllSolv, Inc. are responsible for ensuring network and data integrity. As per the security policy, the following employees are involved in formulating and implementing the security policy:

- Director of sales and marketing

- Chief Information Officer (CIO)

- Director and senior manager information systems (IS)

- Vice president networking and telecommunications

- Organization's corporate attorney

In addition, the system administrators must adhere to the following guidelines:

- The username and password should be as per the security policy.

- The user accounts should be deactivated after the termination of the employee.

- The accounts should be assigned to individuals only and not to groups.

- To check for system configuration and data integrity, network security management tools should be run regularly.

- The system log files should be reviewed every day. In case the system administrator finds a serious security breach, it should immediately be reported to the security officer. In case of minor incidents of security breach, such as failed login attempts, the system administrator should send a fortnightly report to the security officer.

4. **Implementation:** It is the responsibility of the vice president of networking and telecommunications to design the network. This network design should include the network topology, hardware, and software requirements used to implement the security policy. Also, the vice president needs to verify that the network design is in compliance with security policy.

5. **Maintenance plan:** Regular audits should be conducted by the IS division to check whether the guidelines given in the policy are being adhered to. Also, results of the audits must be properly documented.

6. **Training plan:** Every employee should be trained and made aware of AllSolv's security policy. There should be a security policy awareness session at the time of induction of the employee. Also, every employee should read and sign the computer-usage policy every year.

Policy for computer usage

This policy document defines the dos and don'ts with respect to the use of hardware and software and the access (internal as well as external) to AllSolv's network resources.

1. **Use of network resources:** Unless authorized by the system administrator, no employee can access or copy system configuration files, such as router configuration or password files. Also, no employee other than the system administrator can have root or EXEC access to the network equipment. Employees who maintain network connections between AllSolv's network and other networks must ensure that users accessing these network connections do not pose a threat to AllSolv's network resources.

2. **Conforming to policy requirements:** User access rights can be changed at any time and are at the sole discretion of AllSolv Inc. Moreover, the employees must follow these rights and any changes made to them. Failure to conform to the policy rules can result in a disciplinary action from AllSolv.

Policy for authenticating and identifying users

This document gives various guidelines for managing user authentication.

1. **Password authentication:** To use passwords as a means of user authentication, the following guidelines can be followed:

   • The password should be changed every two months.

   • Every account an employee has should have its own unique password.

   • A password should have a minimum length of seven characters, with at least one special character.

   • Passwords should not be disclosed to anyone.

2. **Guideline for authentication:** For authentication, AllSolv will use a remote security database with Terminal Access Controller Access Control System (TACACS) + protocol.

Policy for remote access

This document defines the rules relating to remote access of the resources of AllSolv, Inc. Users accessing network resources remotely must be well aware of the remote access policy rules. These rules are as follows:

✦ Remote-access connection must be authenticated.

✦ All the computers used to access the network of AllSolv must be protected by passwords. In addition, these computers must be configured in such a way that any unauthorized remote user attempting to gain access to the network resources cannot execute an application to establish a connection with the network of AllSolv.

✦ It is the responsibility of the IS department to specify all details pertaining to computer type and the tools or utilities it uses to protect confidential data.

Policy for mobile users

Mobile employees who must access the campus network of AllSolv should be allowed to gain access only through the network access servers (NAS). Employees should only use those software which the IS department has specified.

Mobile users should use only dial-up connections to access AllSolv's network resources. Only the employees of AllSolv, Inc. can use dial-up connections, and no outsider can access the resources of AllSolv, Inc. through a dial-up connection. Access via dial-up connection should support one-time password authentication.

Policy for branch-office access

Access to network resources by branch offices should be first approved by the IS department. Only after the approval has been granted by the IS department can the branch offices gain access to AllSolv's network.

Policy for home-based remote access

Use CHAP authentication to authenticate employees working from home-based offices.

Policy for encryption

All remote access processes should be encrypted. Use only those algorithms specified by the IS department.

Policy for accessing the Internet

This document specifies the rules and guidelines for accessing the Internet. The following sections are covered under the security policy.

Policy for firewall

There should be a firewall system to prevent unauthorized users from accessing the campus network from the Internet. This firewall system should consist of a bastion host and a perimeter router.

Policy for public services

For HTTP, e-mail, and FTP, users accessing AllSolv's network should pass through the bastion host.

Policy for acceptable use

Employees of AllSolv can access the Internet only for official purposes and not for personal use.

Summary

This chapter described various security threats to a network and the motivations behind them. You also learned about various tools and techniques used to invade and attack networks — including protocol analyzers, port scanners, and customized executables. After introducing various categories of security threats, the chapter outlined the necessity of a practical and coherent security policy, outlined risk assessment, and discussed the need to identify and safeguard corporate assets with appropriate security mechanisms.

✦   ✦   ✦

Internet Protocol Network Security

When organizations connect their networks to the outside world, security risks increase by leaps and bounds. A truly effective understanding of those risks must go beyond the basics — into the details of specific threats to each layer of the OSI networking model. Such an understanding helps equip an organization to prevent security threats — and the process of updating security policy and security devices is ongoing thereafter.

This chapter provides an overview of security mechanisms (including technologies that ensure network integrity), identifies security issues specific to each layer of the OSI networking model, and points out ways to address those issues. Protocols, technologies, and mechanisms that work at the individual layers have their own vulnerabilities to security threats. Therefore this chapter reviews these weaknesses and describes major Cisco security-related products that protect network infrastructure and Internet Protocol (IP) security.

Protecting a Site

With organizations striving to reach their markets more efficiently, network designers turn to the Internet as a cost-effective way to transport their data. This potential advantage comes at a price: Connecting Internet technologies to corporate networks unleashes vulnerabilities and increasingly complex security threats — both internal and external. Securing your network depends on staying informed and up to date about the evolving threats that target your operating systems and software.

Connecting a private network to the Internet means connecting to tens of thousands of unknown networks and their users. Such connections open doors to many useful applications and provide great opportunities for sharing information with network users. Some of those users may be potential customers — and some are almost certainly potential intruders of two general types:

✦ **Hackers:** These unauthorized users often see themselves as mere pranksters. Usually they are trying to frighten their targets and impress each other by gaining access to private networks, looking at confidential data, and leaving their mark. Apart from stealing a look at corporate data, however, hackers' hijinks often paralyze the organization's network setup, requiring expensive fixes.

✦ **Crackers:** These intruders are even more dangerous to your network than hackers; the difference between a hacker and a cracker can be as costly as it is crucial. A cracker's goal is actually hostile: Gain access to your network and do damage — for example, crashing the network, reformatting hard drives on servers or workstations, reformatting the IOS on network devices, exposing your company's vital information to the world via the World Wide Web (WWW), or a combination of attacks.

If a network has valuable resources to share — and needs instant access to data mines — then isolating that network from all risk is almost impossible. The situation is further complicated when a network is exposed to the Internet; such exposure provides hackers with several ready routes toward penetrating security and accessing sensitive information. To anticipate and deal with security issues, an organization must draft and implement a security policy.

 For details on creating and implementing a security policy, refer to Chapter 1.

Protecting sensitive data

Data can exist in two ways on a network — as a file on storage media (such as hard disks) or in transit in the form of packets. In both forms, the data is prone to attacks from hackers — *especially when it's in transit*. Therefore your organization must take steps to ensure the security of sensitive information *before* sending it out.

You have a better chance of securing your information effectively if you have a good working understanding of the methods hackers use when they attack network security. To help you give your security framework a firm foundation, upcoming sections describe some common ways of attacking a network.

IP spoofing

IP spoofing exploits the vulnerabilities of TCP/IP and the network. In this type of attack, the hacker either uses one of the IP addresses on the network or a trusted external IP address to access the network. Hence, the hacker poses to be a trusted computer of the network. Often this type of attack inserts malicious data or commands into the data stream traveling over the network — but doing so requires two-way unauthorized communication. To get it, a hacker has to change all the routing tables so they point to the spoofed IP address. The idea is to prevent a response from an application if the hacker tries to get your system to send a sensitive file via e-mail.

Network packet sniffing

Data travels over the network in the form of packets. A *packet sniffer* is software that captures all data packets traveling on the network. To do so, a packet sniffer makes use of the *promiscuous mode* built into network adapter cards. In this mode, the adapter card captures not only the packets meant for it, but also all *other* packets sent across a network — even if their destinations have addresses that don't match the network card. Promiscuous mode is not hard to activate under protocols such as TCP/IP — the most widely accepted network protocol for transferring packets. Although TCP/IP specifies how the packets are identified and labeled — and enables a computer to determine whether a packet is intended for it by looking at specific fields — it falls short as a security-friendly protocol. The trouble is that most network applications that use TCP/IP distribute network packets unencrypted — as *cleartext*.

Because network packets are not encrypted, they can be processed and understood by a packet sniffer, which can give a hacker a look at the information by querying the network database. The sniffer can also determine the username and password that provide access to the network database.

Distribution of confidential data

Although a perfectly secure network is unlikely in the real world, an effective network-security policy demands appropriate control over the distribution of confidential data. The policy must give an organization the tools for deciding — carefully — which people should have access to confidential data. Unless access rights are appropriately granted, users within the organization might exploit network services (such as e-mail and FTP) to access sensitive data and pass it to rival organizations for lucrative offers. Security policy should define proper and adequate permissions for all internal users.

Password attacks

The basic aim of a password attack is to identify usernames and passwords. These attacks can use methods such as IP spoofing, Trojan horse applications, packet sniffing, and brute force. Brute-force attacks use an application that runs across the network and attempts to log on to a shared resource, trying a large range of alphanumeric combinations quickly in an attempt to determine the password. After gaining access to a resource, a hacker can exploit internal users' privileges and manipulate data repositories.

Man-in-the-middle attacks

Man-in-the-middle attacks are carried out to gain access to confidential data. In this type of attack, the hacker uses transport protocols and packet sniffers to capture network packets as they traverse the network. Consider an example where in-house users A and B are exchanging messages in the form of network packets. Hacker C gains access to one of the nodes on the network through which the packets travel. Now C has access to the messages exchanged between A and B; C can read and alter the messages — even pose as A and reply to B's messages (or vice versa). Man-in-the-middle attacks can hack an ongoing session, alter the transmitted data, or introduce spurious information into the network.

Application-layer attacks

The Application layer is the uppermost layer of the OSI model of TCP/IP. Attacks on the Application layer use weaknesses in applications such as Web browsers to launch attacks on the network. These attacks use various methods — such as exploiting the inherent vulnerabilities of the FTP server — but one of the most common methods is to use a Trojan horse program to capture the login information of an authorized user. Then the Trojan horse e-mails the login information to the hacker, who can obtain access to the network by using the stolen user credentials. The typical goal of an Application-layer attack is to capture or alter the data on the network — or install a sniffer to analyze network traffic for further attacks.

The most recent method of launching an Application-layer attack is to use special Java applets and ActiveX controls built to act like Trojan horses. Hackers transmit these on the network, with the intention that other computers on the network download the programs (often by using a Web browser). Once downloaded, the applets and controls perform malicious operations such as overwriting or deleting files or executing harmful commands.

Classifying networks by trustworthiness

For a network administrator, thinking in terms of security must become second nature. One useful way to develop that habit is to classify networks according to how trustworthy they are — or are not. The three standard categories for doing so are *trusted*, *untrusted*, and *unknown*.

Trusted networks

In practical terms, *trusted* networks can only exist inside the security perimeter of your network. A trusted network comprises computers, storage boxes, and application servers configured and run according to the organization's security policy. The network administrator monitors these assets; the organization controls the trusted network's security measures. The network administrator has a duty to protect trusted networks against attack.

To secure a trusted network, you should set up a firewall and explicitly identify the type(s) of networks that must connect to the firewall server. As a rule, after the initial configuration, trusted networks include the firewall server and all networks *behind* the firewall. The only exceptions to this rule are the organization's virtual private networks (VPNs). Although VPNs transmit data across an untrusted network infrastructure (such as the Internet), any network packets that traverse a VPN originate from within the internal perimeter — that is, from within a trusted network. To operate a VPN safely, however, be sure to deploy security measures that help the firewall server authenticate the origin of any data packet and verify data integrity.

Untrusted networks

An *untrusted* network is also subject to a practical definition. Any network that is outside the security perimeter of your organization (and not under its administrative control) is untrusted. These networks are private shared networks from which the internal network of your organization must be protected. When a firewall is configured, the untrusted network from which it can accept requests must be explicitly identified.

Rule of thumb: If a particular network is not subject to the security policies of your organization, treat it as untrusted.

Unknown networks

Networks that are neither trusted nor untrusted are referred to as *unknown* networks. Because your firewall cannot be explicitly configured to identify these networks as trusted or untrusted, the firewall must treat them as "strangers."

If all trusted networks are located inside the firewall, an equally simple rule applies to unknown networks: They are located outside the firewall.

Creating a security perimeter

To create and maintain a secure boundary between your network and the unsecured outside world, your network-security policy should seek to accomplish three goals:

✦ Define the correct and appropriate use of network resources.

✦ Define the measures and steps the organization takes to secure network devices.

✦ Control network traffic and usage.

When you deploy a network-security policy, you should consider the boundaries within the network. These strategic boundaries are called *perimeter networks*. Setting them up entails two tasks:

✦ **Identifying the security perimeter.** Your organization needs a complete inventory of all potential contact points between internal and external networks. Then you can set up specialized *perimeter routers* to keep internal networks separate from external networks.

✦ **Selective adaptation of security-design principles.** A perimeter router has a distinct mission that requires a firewall: It monitors network traffic and enforces restrictions specified in the security policy.

The following section details the process of setting up your perimeter security.

Perimeter networks

Before setting up your perimeter networks, you must decide what networks to protect — and select appropriate security measures to protect them. Then you can divide your organization's network into multiple perimeter networks, categorized by their security requirements, their topologies, and their positions relative to each other. Three basic categories are useful here — outermost, internal, and innermost perimeters — as illustrated in Figure 2-1.

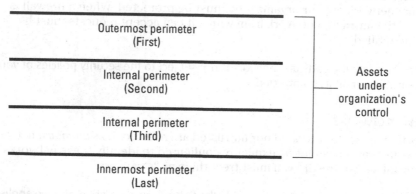

Figure 2-1: Three types of perimeter networks

The *outermost* perimeter network separates an internal network from an external network (say, an ISP or the Internet itself) — usually by means of a perimeter router. You can also implement *internal* perimeter networks by using other security mechanisms such as intranet firewalls and filtering routers configured to handle internal traffic. Figure 2-2 shows a network-security design based on two perimeter networks — one outermost and one internal — defined by the placement of internal routers, external routers, and the firewall server.

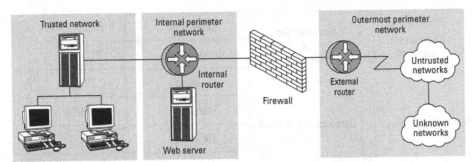

Figure 2-2: An example of a two-perimeter network-security design

Although the implementation of a firewall between an external and an internal router does not significantly secure the network from the attacks on either side, it does increase the performance of the firewall. This is because of a significant reduction in the traffic that the firewall server has to evaluate. As discussed earlier, the outermost perimeter network is where the external network connects with the internal network, making it the most insecure area in a network infrastructure. Therefore you should *never* place (or implement) devices that contain sensitive information in the outermost perimeter network.

Securing the site

Securing the network is essential not only to keep data from unauthorized users, but also to keep the business running smoothly. Organizations that use the Internet to conduct online business assume a certain risk when they connect their Web and application servers to the Internet: A successful hack can make these servers unusable.

You can deploy a multitude of security solutions to make Internet usage safer for your organization, but your overall strategy is likely to favor one of two general approaches:

✦ **Application-coupled security:** This approach imposes its security measures on individual applications or builds those measures into the OSI Transport layer.

✦ **Network-coupled security:** This approach builds its security measures into the Network layer — either in the operating system or in a higher layer of the system architecture.

Figure 2-3 associates these two security models with their specific OSI layers.

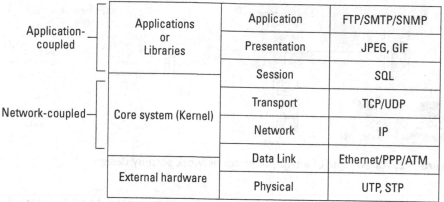

Figure 2-3: Application- and network-coupled security models, with their corresponding OSI layers

Application-coupled security

Application-coupled security ensures security requirements for private and reliable communication between applications. Its effective implementation requires the following three features in an application:

✦ It should be security-aware.

✦ It should be capable of handling errors and special conditions.

✦ It should provide proofs of authenticity, such as certificates.

Some advantages of implementing application-coupled security are as follows:

✦ It offers higher efficiency and reliability. The application determines the security requirements and constraints for each type of network traffic it encounters; the lower layer need not re-evaluate security requirements type by type. To determine the security requirements, the application should be specifically designed to be security-aware. However, in dynamic and configurable approaches, this can be achieved by specifying the applications relevant for security requirements.

✦ It reduces the network administrator's worries about security at the lower layers. The Application layer itself handles security, which improves data-transfer speed on intermediate devices.

Network-coupled security

As a feature built into the Network layer, network-coupled security does not depend on reliable transport mechanisms for its effectiveness. It can also be placed on intermediate systems.

Network-coupled security offers two major advantages:

✦ Security mechanisms and interfaces are common to all applications on a machine. No additional operation is required by individual applications after the cryptographic elements have been tested for correctness and security.

✦ Intermediate devices, such as routers and firewalls, can also handle security aspects for the traversing data. This enables the intermediate devices to handle virtual networks and soft link encryption with intelligence.

Both security models have benefits; plan a security policy that can use both. The security model must be able to prevent most attacks from affecting valuable network resources. Attacks can originate by penetrating into the first line of defense or from inside the network. These attacks must be accurately detected and quickly contained to minimize their effect on the rest of the network. However, the network should not only be secure but also continue to provide critical services that users expect.

The security framework should stay as close as possible to the functional requirements of present enterprise networks. Security implementation decisions can vary, depending on the network services offered. Security design objectives should include the following:

✦ Security measures and attack mitigation based on the policy

✦ Security implementation throughout the infrastructure and not just on specialized security devices

✦ Secure management and reporting

✦ Authentication and authorization of users and administrators who must use critical network resources

✦ Detection of intrusion into any network containing critical resources and subnets

✦ Support for emerging networked applications

Network Integrity

Even after securing the network, you cannot be sure of the complete integrity of the network. Any security breach in the integrity of a network can open multiple avenues for continued attacks. Therefore your security policy should also include methods that ensure consistent data integrity for the network. The most common methods used to compromise network integrity are

✦ Network packet sniffers

✦ IP spoofing

✦ Password attacks

✦ Denial-of-service attacks

✦ Application-layer attacks

Network integrity is the goal when you protect your network from three specific threats:

✦ Destruction or corruption of information by e-mail-borne viruses

✦ Loss of network service through spam and spoof attacks

✦ Congestion resulting from system misuse

To ensure and maintain a productive network environment, the network integrity should verify the identity of computers and users, ensure proper operation of the services that the network provides, and provide optimal network performance.

Widespread acceptance of TCP/IP along with the ease of integration has overshadowed the necessity to secure network assets. The TCP protocol itself checks the integrity of data transmitted, but with a weak checksum algorithm. Numerous tools ensure data integrity; the most commonly used are the MD5 algorithm and Pretty Good Privacy (PGP) cryptography

MD5

Message Digest 5 (also known as MD5) is a tool that guarantees the integrity of network data and ensures that the data has not been altered in transit. It is a one-way hash algorithm that produces a 128-bit *message digest* when applied to the data. This message digest is irreversible; one cannot simply apply a reverse process to the digest to obtain the original data.

The MD5 algorithm is also used for digital-signature applications under a public-key cryptosystem such as RSA. Whenever a file is downloaded or uploaded, one of the first things to be done is to make an MD5 hash of the file. Then the message digest from the MD5 hash algorithm is compared with a known message digest stored at the remote site. The integrity of the file is ensured only if the message digests match.

 Note   The MD5 Message-Digest Algorithm is described in RFC 1321.

Pretty Good Privacy

Encryption is widely accepted as an ideal method of ensuring network data integrity. Two types exist:

✦ **Symmetric cryptosystems** encrypt and decrypt data with the same key.

✦ **Asymmetric (public-key) cryptosystems** encrypt data with one key and decrypt the data with another key.

Symmetric cryptosystems require secure transport of the secret key from the sender to the recipient. Trusted couriers may serve this purpose, but the security of the electronic key itself cannot be guaranteed on the Internet. Therefore, the efficient and reliable solution is a public-key cryptosystem such as RSA, which is used in a popular security tool called Pretty Good Privacy (PGP).

PGP is a public-key encryption program that has become a *de facto* standard for encrypting e-mail on the Internet. Before encrypting the plaintext, PGP first compresses it. For encrypting the data, PGP creates a one-time secret *session key*, which is randomly generated. This session key then serves to encrypt the plaintext. When the encrypted data reaches the recipient end, it must be decrypted. To do so, the session key also must be sent to the recipient in an encrypted form. The public key of the recipient serves to encrypt the session key. This encrypted session key is transmitted along with the encrypted data to the recipient. The recipient must recover the session key (by using the private key) before the encrypted data can be recovered (decrypted); the session key decrypts the data.

In the process just described, the public key plays a crucial role in the entire transmission. Public keys are freely available, which questions the authenticity of the key itself. This problem has been solved by the use of *digital certificates,* which establish whether a public key truly belongs to the owner. A digital certificate has the same significance as a physical certificate. Use of digital certificates counters attempts to substitute one person's key for another. A digital certificate requires some authority to validate that a public key and the name of the key's owner can travel together. With PGP certificates, anyone can play the role of a validator, as compared to X.509 certificates that essentially require a Certificate Authority to act as a validator.

Note The X.509 standard defines what information can go into a certificate and the format for writing that information.

Understanding Transport-Layer Security

TCP/IP is the network protocol used over the Internet for providing connectivity and services. TCP/IP itself does not provide any security. Security is more often dependent on the application. The Transport layer of the OSI model provides reliable end-to-end transparent data communication through a network. The Transport-layer security protocol provides confidentiality and integrity services to data transmitted between computers.

Note Security at the Transport layer is independent of network technology.

The Transport layer uses application port numbers to identify an active session between two communicating hosts. Port numbers are assigned to individual applications in a communication meant to establish unique sockets.

TCP/IP uses two modes of connection at the Transport layer: connection-oriented and connectionless.

✦ **Connection-oriented mode:** TCP uses this mode; data transfer happens after a connection is established between the two computers.

✦ **Connectionless mode:** UDP uses this mode; data transfer happens without establishing a connection between two computers.

Depending on the configurations of the upper OSI layers, the application can use TCP or UDP ports. The traditional method to provide security at the Transport layer is by blocking unused port numbers. Blocking the unused ports on a host prevents a hacker from establishing a connection with that host by using the exposed ports. You can block unused ports by using firewalls at the edge of the network and configuring a policy to block susceptible ports on specific hosts.

> **Tip**   Extended access lists on Cisco routers can also block specific application ports.

The idea of providing security services at the Transport layer is not new; two protocols were proposed (years ago) to meet this need: NSA/NIST SP4 and ISO TLSP. By now, however, these protocols are obsolete as anything more than steppingstones to the development of more advanced Transport-layer security protocols. Several other such protocols have been proposed more recently for use on the Internet:

✦ Secure Shell (SSH)

✦ Secure Sockets Layer (SSL)

✦ Private Communications Technology (PCT)

✦ Transport-Layer Security (TLS)

Secure Shell protocol

Secure Shell (SSH) is a protocol and software package that was originally developed at the Helsinki University of Technology. SSH was designed to replace Berkeley r-tools like `rlogin`, `rsh`, `rcp`, and some other utilities. Secure Shell technology is considered as the de facto standard for securing remote access connections over IP networks. SSH secures connections over the Internet by encrypting passwords and other data. After being launched, SSH transparently provides strong authentication and secure communication over unsecured networks. SSH provides host and user authentication, data compression, and protection for data confidentiality and integrity.

The SSH protocol consists of three major components:

✦ The Transport-layer protocol (SSH-TRANS) provides secure authentication, confidentiality, and network integrity. It might provide encryption also. Transport is typically run over a TCP/IP connection, but can also be used on top of another reliable data stream.

✦ The user authentication protocol (SSH-USERAUTH) authenticates the client-side user to the server. It runs over the Transport-layer protocol.

✦ Connection protocol (SSH-CONN) multiplexes the encrypted tunnel into several logical channels. It runs over the user authentication protocol.

The SSH Transport layer is a secure, low-level Transport protocol. SSH allows users to login to a remote computer over the network, execute commands on it, and move files from one computer to another. The steps involved in an SSH connection are as follows:

1. The client sends a request to the server. When the request is intercepted, both the client and the server exchange an identification string, followed by a new line.

   The maximum length for an identification string (including the new line) is 255 characters.

2. If data compression was negotiated during the transmission, then the data is compressed.

   If data compression was not agreed upon, key exchange begins. During the key exchange, an encryption algorithm and a key are negotiated. Both the client and the server agree upon a common algorithm.

3. The client sends its authentication message.

   After the client is authenticated, the service request is issued.

SSH provides strong encryption, cryptographic host authentication, and integrity protection. However, SSH is not designed to protect against flaws inherent in the operating system, such as poorly developed IP stack and insecure storage of passwords.

Secure Sockets layer protocol

The TCP/IP protocol handles the transport and routing of data over the Internet. Commonly used protocols, such as HyperText Transport Protocol (HTTP), Lightweight Directory Access Protocol (LDAP), or Internet Messaging Access Protocol (IMAP), use TCP/IP for communication purposes. The SSL protocol (refer to Figure 2-4) runs between Transport-layer protocols and high-level protocols, such as HTTP or IMAP, for providing security to data. It uses TCP/IP on behalf of high-level protocols to establish secure connections. The SSL protocol does this by enabling SSL-enabled devices, such as servers and clients, to authenticate themselves and allows them to establish an encrypted connection.

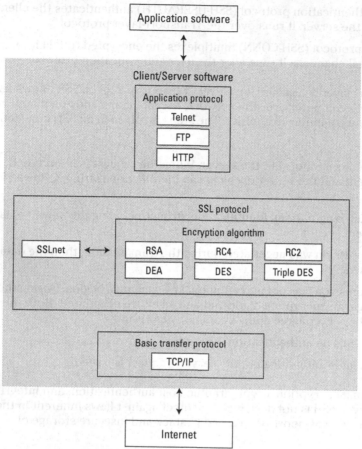

Figure 2-4: Relationship of SSL to other protocols

SSL supports a variety of cryptographic algorithms, including the following:

✦ **DES:** Data-encryption Standard (DES) is a cryptographic algorithm approved by the National Bureau of Standards and Technology (NIST) and published in Federal Information Processing Standards (FIPS) 46. DES is mainly for government and public use.

✦ **DSA:** Directory Service Agents (DSA) is a part of digital authentication standard used in X.500.

✦ **KEA:** Key Exchange Algorithm (KEA) is a variation of Diffie-Hellman key exchange.

✦ **MD5:** Message Digest Algorithm (MD5), released by RSA Laboratories, is for digitally signed messages.

✦ **RC2:** Rivest's Cipher (RC2) is a 64-bit block cipher algorithm that uses variable-sized keys.

✦ **RC4:** RC4 is an advanced version of RC2. It is a variable key-size cipher algorithm.

✦ **RSA:** RSA is a public-key algorithm, developed by Rivest, Shamir, and Adleman. RSA is for both authentication as well as encryption.

✦ **3DES:** Triple DES (3DES) is a cryptographic algorithm that encrypts data three times.

Cross-Reference   For more about cryptographic algorithms, see Chapter 7.

The SSL protocol serves to provide privacy and reliability between two communicating applications. The SSL protocol includes two subprotocols: the *SSL record protocol* and the *SSL handshake protocol*.

SSL record protocol

The SSL record protocol defines the format used to transmit data. It uses session keys to encrypt the data in transit. SSL record protocol divides the data into blocks, which undergo the following stages:

✦ **Fragmentation:** In this stage, the data is fragmented into records in plaintext format. The size of each record should be 16,384 bytes or less. Messages with the same content type can be combined into a single record; alternately, one single message can be broken down into multiple records.

✦ **Compression:** In this stage, the data to be transmitted is compressed by using a compression algorithm. The compression algorithm should ensure that during compression no data is lost. After compression, the data is encrypted and transmitted. At the receiver's end, a decompression algorithm decompresses the data.

✦ **Record payload protection:** After the data is compressed, integrity check value is computed. This check value is known as the *Message Authentication Code* (MAC). The compressed data and MAC value is then encrypted and transmitted. At the receiving end, the data is decrypted and then decompressed. The MAC value is also recomputed to verify data integrity.

After the authentication process is complete, an SSL session can be established by using cryptographic algorithms.

SSL handshake protocol

The SSL handshake protocol uses the SSL record protocol to establish an SSL connection between the two SSL-enabled devices by exchanging a series of messages. This exchange of messages performs different functions which include authenticating the server to the client, (optionally) authenticating the client to the server, selecting the commonly supported cryptographic algorithms or ciphers, generating shared secrets by using public-key encryption techniques, and establishing an encrypted SSL connection. The SSL handshake protocol determines the cryptographic algorithms used by the client and server to authenticate each other, to establish session keys, and to transmit certificates.

An SSL session starts with an exchange of messages between the client and server. During this exchange of messages (called the *SSL handshake*), the server authenticates itself to the client by using a public key. The steps involved in an SSL session are as follows:

1. The client sends its SSL version number, cipher settings, and other information to the server. The server uses this information to communicate with the client that uses SSL.

2. The server sends its SSL version number, certificate, cipher settings, and other information to the client. The client uses this information to communicate with the server. If the client must be authenticated for accessing a resource, the server sends a request for the client certificate.

3. Based on the information sent by the server, the client authenticates the server and an SSL session is established.

4. The client creates a pre-master secret for the current session. The client then encrypts the pre-master secret (using the public key of the server) and sends the encrypted pre-master key to the server. If the server has requested client authentication, the client also sends its certificate and signed data.

5. The server authenticates the client based on the certificate and the signed data sent by the client.

   If the client is authenticated, the server decrypts the data sent by the client by using its private key. The server uses the decrypted data to generate a master secret. The client also uses the same data to generate the master secret.

6. The client and the server use the master secret to create *session keys*. These session keys are symmetric and are used to encrypt and decrypt the data transmitted during the SSL session.

7. The client informs the server that all future messages, which it will be sent during the SSL session to the server, will be encrypted using the session key. It also sends an encrypted message to the server to indicate that the client-side handshake is over.

8. The server also informs the client that all future messages from the server will be encrypted by using the session keys. It also sends an encrypted message to the client to indicate that the server-side handshake is over. After the SSL handshake is over, the client and server use the session keys to encrypt and decrypt the information that they send to each other. SSL protocol has the following features:

   • **Server authentication:** SSL-enabled client software uses public-key cryptography to verify the server's certificate. Using it, the client can verify that a trusted Certificate Authority (CA) issues the server's certificate.

- **Client authentication:** SSL-enabled server software allows the server to verify the identity of the client. The SSL-enabled server software uses public-key cryptography to verify the validity of the client's certificate — and that it was issued by a Certificate Authority (CA) that the server recognizes as trusted.

- **Encrypted connection:** All information transferred between the client and server is encrypted. This provides a high level of confidentiality to the data in transit.

The SSL protocol provides connection security that has three basic properties:

✦ The connection is private. After the algorithm is decided, encryption is used after an initial handshake to define a secret key. Symmetric cryptography is for data encryption. Examples of symmetric cryptography are DES and RC4.

✦ Asymmetric (public-key) cryptography such as RSA and DSS can be used to authenticate the peer's identity.

✦ The connection is reliable. Message transport includes a message integrity check by using secure hash functions, such as SHA and MD5.

Private Communications Technology protocol

Microsoft adapted the SSL protocol in another protocol called Private Communication Technology (PCT). Internet Information Server is built upon PCT, which is a superset of the SSL protocol. The PCT protocol is designed to provide privacy between two communicating applications in client/server architecture. It can also authenticate the server and the client.

The PCT protocol is independent of the application protocol. Any application protocol, such as HTTP, FTP, and Telnet, can work along with the PCT protocol transparently. The PCT protocol initiates with a handshake phase that negotiates an encryption algorithm and session key — and authenticates a server to the client based on certified asymmetric public keys. After the transmission of application protocol data begins, all the data is encrypted (using the session key negotiated during the handshake). In addition to encryption and authentication, the PCT protocol verifies the integrity of messages by using a hash function-based message authentication code (MAC).

The Transport-layer Security protocol

The Transport-layer Security (TLS) protocol is actually an improved version of the SSL 3.0 protocol specification. Although the two protocols are only minimally different, they are not interoperable with each other. The TLS protocol provides critical security features to help protect the privacy and integrity of the network. These security features are as follows:

✦ Authentication based on RSA and Diffie-Hellman/DSS with X.509v3 certificates

✦ Encryption based on DES, Triple DES, RC4, and IDEA

✦ Message integrity based on SHA1 and MD5

✦ Framework that enables new cryptographic algorithms (such as Kerberos) to be easily incorporated into the specification

TLS ensures privacy and data integrity between two applications communicating with each other. TLS is a combination of two protocols, the TLS record protocol and the TLS handshake protocol. The following sections discuss these protocols.

TLS record protocol

TLS record protocol is layered over a transport protocol, such as TCP. The TLS record protocol has the following features:

✦ It ensures a secure, reliable, and private connection between communicating applications.

✦ It uses symmetric cryptography for encrypting data. For each new connection, unique keys are generated.

These unique keys are based on a session key negotiated by another protocol, such as TLS handshake protocol.

The TLS record protocol serves to encapsulate a variety of higher-level protocols, such as TLS handshake protocol.

TLS handshake protocol

TLS handshake protocol allows the client and the server to authenticate each other. It also allows them to negotiate an encryption algorithm and cryptographic keys before the Application layer starts the transmission of data. TLS handshake protocol has the following features:

✦ It provides connection security. The identity of the peers is authenticated by using asymmetric cryptography. However, this authentication can be made optional.

✦ It ensures secure and reliable negotiation of the session key.

TLS uses RSA public-key cryptography mechanism for authentication, where each application has an associated public key and private key. Data encrypted using the public key can be decrypted only after applying the private key. The reverse process is also supported when data encrypted with the private key can be decrypted only with the public key. The TLS protocol permits a special handshake process where a previously established session can be resumed. This prevents the complicated public key computations. The TLS handshake also facilitates the negotiation of ciphers to be used in a connection.

When a client authenticates a server, the public key of the server can be used to encode confidential data to be sent by the client. For decoding this data, the user has to use the corresponding private key, which is only available with the actual server application. As a result, it is only the server application that can decode this data. After authentication is complete, the TLS client application sends an encoded data value to the server. This unique session-encoded value is a key to a symmetric cryptographic algorithm.

To maintain the integrity of network data, the authentication and privacy features of TLS ensure that applications can exchange confidential data that cannot be eavesdropped. However, these features do not prevent encrypted messages transmitted between applications from being modified.

Understanding Network-Layer Security

Security provided at the Network layer has a number of advantages over security provided on the layers of the protocol stack. Network semantics are usually hidden from applications, which automatically and transparently benefit from whatever network-layer services are provided by their environment. The Network layer offers flexibility not available at any higher layer. Network-layer security can be configured in various ways, for example

✦ End-to-end to protect traffic between two communicating hosts

✦ Route-to-route to safeguard traffic passing over a particular set of links

✦ Edge-to-edge to protect traffic between trusted networks when it travels over an untrusted network

✦ Any configuration that identifies network nodes as appropriate security endpoints

If the Network layer provides secrecy by encrypting all the data carried by IP datagrams, any packet stream at the Network layer can be assumed to be secure. This would require that whenever a host wishes to send a datagram, it should encrypt the data field of the datagram before exposing it to the network. As already discussed, the encryption can be done with symmetric-key encryption, public-key encryption, or with the session keys negotiated by using public-key encryption. The data field can be a TCP segment, a UDP segment, or an ICMP message. If such a Network-layer service is made available, then all data sent by hosts (including e-mail, Web pages, and control or management messages) is secured.

Apart from providing data integrity, the Network layer provides source authentication. Whenever a destination host receives an IP datagram with a particular IP source address, it might authenticate the source by ensuring that the IP datagram was indeed generated by the host with that IP source address. Such a network service prevents hackers from spoofing IP addresses.

Network-layer protocols, such as IPSec, have been standardized and implemented by commercial vendors. However, the current standards for Network-layer security do not address the management of policies governing the handling of packets in a transaction. The security protocol itself protects packets from external tampering and eavesdropping. However, it does not enforce a policy so the hosts are authorized to exchange specified traffic. Such policies can be complex in configuration scenarios that use Network-layer security to build firewalls and virtual private networks.

The easiest way to accomplish security at the Network layer is to base firewalls in that layer and configure them for packet-level filtering. Although all firewalls support policy-based, packet-level filtering, some products can also be configured to filter traffic according to attributes associated with layers above the Network layer. Two security mechanisms at the Network layer itself are IPSec and IPv6. The next two sections offer a brief overview of the IPSec protocol and the inherent security of IPv6.

IPSec protocol

IPSec is the standard suite of protocols devised for providing Network-layer confidentiality and authentication of Internet traffic. IPSec is based on *datagram encapsulation*: Encrypted Network-layer packets are placed inside other (unencrypted) packets as payload. Intermediate nodes that process packet headers for routing never have to deal with the encrypted payload. Outgoing packets are encapsulated, encrypted, and authenticated just before sending. Incoming packets are verified, decrypted, and de-encapsulated immediately upon receipt. The IPSec protocol suite that does all these tasks has two principal protocols within it:

✦ **Authentication Header (AH):** The AH protocol provides source authentication and verifies data integrity.

✦ **Encapsulation Security Payload (ESP):** The ESP protocol provides data integrity and ensures secrecy.

In effect, IPSec transforms the traditionally connectionless Network layer of the Internet into a layer of temporary logical connections. When a source host transmits secure datagrams, it uses either the AH protocol or the ESP protocol. Both AH and ESP protocols require a *handshake* between source and destination hosts — the formation of a logical connection at the Network layer — before sending secured datagrams. This logical channel is called the *Security Agreement* (SA). An SA has three identifiers, each of which must be a unique value:

✦ A security protocol (AH or ESP) identifier

✦ The source IP address for the simplex connection

✦ A 32-bit connection identifier called the *Security Parameter Index* (SPI)

Note Information can flow in only one direction (from source host to destination host) along an SA. If both hosts send secure datagrams to each other, they must establish two SAs.

Identifying and verifying with the AH protocol

The AH protocol identifies the source host and verifies data integrity. When a source host sends secured datagrams to a destination host (after the two hosts establish the required SA), each secured datagram must include the *AH header*, inserted between the original IP datagram data and the IP header, as shown in Figure 2-5.

Protocol number 51

| IP header | AH header | TCP/UDP segment |

Figure 2-5: Position of an AH header in an IP datagram

The AH header adds the original data field (encapsulated as a standard IP datagram). A value of 51 for the `protocol` field in the IP header indicates that the datagram includes an AH header. After identifying the AH header, the destination host uses the AH protocol to processes the datagrams. Intermediate routers ignore the encrypted payload, routing the datagrams after verifying the destination IP address.

After receiving an IP datagram and verifying that it has an AH header, the destination host authenticates and verifies the integrity of the data in the packet. At this point, IPSec authentication uses a scheme called Hash Message Authentication Code (HMAC) — in which the destination host uses a secret key shared between two hosts (instead of public-key methods) to unlock an encrypted digest of the message.

Protecting and authenticating with the ESP protocol

The ESP protocol serves two purposes: Ensure the secrecy of encrypted data encapsulated at the Network layer and authenticate the source host. The source host sends secured datagrams to the destination host after establishing SA. Encapsulating the encrypted data consists of padding the original IP datagram's data with header and trailer fields. Once encapsulated, the data is inserted into the data field of a different IP datagram, as shown in Figure 2-6.

An ESP header consists of a 32-bit field for both SPI and the sequence number. To indicate that the IP datagram includes an ESP header and trailer, the `protocol` field is assigned a value of 50. After identifying the appropriate value in the protocol field, the destination host uses the ESP protocol to process the datagram.

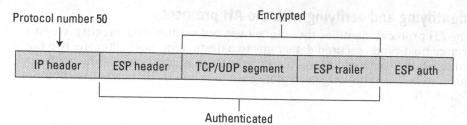

Figure 2-6: ESP fields in the IP datagram

Successful deployment of IPSec has two main requirements:

✦ **A scalable and automated method of establishing SA:** The Internet Security Association and Key Management Protocol (ISKMP) defines procedures for establishing and tearing down SA.

✦ **A key-management scheme to keep the shared key secret:** The Internet Key Exchange (IKE) algorithm is the default IPSec protocol that serves this vital purpose.

For a detailed discussion of IPSec, see Chapter 13.

IPv6

Internet Protocol version 6 (IPv6) is the Next-Generation Internet Protocol, which was approved by the Internet Engineering Steering Group (IESF) in 1994 as a proposed standard.

IPv6 was intended to overcome the limitations of the then-existing (IPv4) standard. IPv4 used a 32-bit IP addressing scheme and had many Network-layer vulnerabilities that could be easily exploited by hackers.

Many IESF workgroups have their own designated IPv6 projects under way. Such projects include the basic IPv6 protocol specification itself, as well as schemes for address architecture, domain name servers (DNS), security, transition mechanisms, and an Internet Control Message Protocol (ICMP).

Though still in use today, IPv4 specifications have inherent security problems that make them unable to support the robust security features needed for Network-layer components. One prominent problem is a lack of interoperability due to proprietary security extensions. To overcome such limitations, IPv6 bases its data-security capabilities on flexible header extensions.

For example, the header extension that IPv6 uses for authentication ensures that a packet is actually coming from the host indicated in its source address — which helps to safeguard data, passwords, and network-control utilities against compromise by IP-spoofing techniques.

Tip   Although some enterprises block IP spoofing by implementing firewalls at the edges of their networks, these devices can introduce other problems such as performance bottlenecks, restrictive network policies, and limited connectivity to the Internet.

The authentication mechanism built into IPv6 provides the industry with a standard method for determining the authenticity of packets. Vendors can create more interoperable authentication services thanks to the consistency of authentication headers as defined in IPv6.

Note   IPv6 implementations are required to support the MD5 algorithm for authentication. In networks that use autoconfiguration services (such as DHCP), hackers can exploit the lack of Network-layer authentication in IPv4. IPv6 authentication blocks illicit autoconfiguration.

IPv4, by contrast, has no native data-encryption scheme. OSI layers higher than the Network layer must resort to various (and less interoperable) methods of encryption. IPv6 encryption headers provide fields to carry encryption keys and other handshaking information—features that make the payloads in IP packets easier to encrypt and decrypt appropriately. IPv6 security headers are also versatile enough to use directly between hosts or with a specialized security gateway.

This new version of IPv6 is nearly mature enough to make available to all network devices. Doing so would ensure greater reliability of data by using the intrinsic features of IPv6 as well as interoperable security standards.

Understanding Data Link Layer Security

The Data Link layer of the OSI model is where transmission of data takes place, using the physical medium and the addresses of devices on the network. In terms of security policy, this layer is where the administrator must define protocols for data packets and the manner in which they are transmitted. Although it handles communication at the level of network links, the Data Link layer does not depend on any particular transmission medium; its place in the OSI scheme is just above the Physical layer.

The Data Link layer ensures reliable transmission of data across a physical network link. Specifications at this layer define network and protocol characteristics, including network topology, error-notification procedures, physical addressing, flow-control mechanisms, and the sequencing of frames. This layer encapsulates packets from the Network layer into corresponding frames. If a transmission error occurs, error notification warns the upper-layer protocols; sequencing of data frames reorders any frames transmitted out of sequence. A flow-control mechanism moderates transmission of data to avoid flooding the receiving device with more traffic than it can handle at one time.

The Data Link layer has two sublayers:

✦ **Media Access Control (MAC):** The MAC sublayer of the Data Link layer inter-operates with the Physical layer to identify the host on the network by assigning appropriate physical addresses. To establish a communication session between any two hosts, translation of logical addresses at the Network layer to physical address at the Data Link layer is necessary. This translation of the address provides potential security loopholes.

✦ **Logical Link Control (LLC):** The LLC sublayer of Data Link layer uses the services of MAC to provide services to the Network layer. The LLC sublayer monitors data-flow control and handles errors.

The Data Link layer also has distinctive vulnerabilities; for example, it may not register when the connected state of the Physical layer has changed. The result may be a security lapse due to excessive reliance on the integrity and security of the network's switching systems. An insertion attack at Data Link layer might go undetected. A hacker who can spoof the legitimate calling identity might be able to avoid a link authentication.

Switches operating at Layer 2 are most vulnerable to attacks. The methods to access a switch from a console and Telnet can be compromised. This can be exploited to take administrative control of switch. Any SNMP-enabled switch, if not configured properly, can provide a wealth of information to a hacker — for example, the topology of a network and its configuration parameters.

Point-to-Point Protocol

Point-to-Point Protocol (PPP) is the most widely implemented Layer 2 encapsulation protocol for transporting IP traffic over point-to-point links. PPP has built-in features for assigning and managing IP addresses. It supports asynchronous and bit-oriented synchronous encapsulation; multiple network protocols to run link configuration, link-quality testing, error detection; and data-compression. PCP supports these functions by virtue of two components, *Link Control Protocol* (LCP) and *Network Control Protocols* (NCPs).

LCP performs all the functions related to link management, such as encapsulation format options. It also handles negotiating limits on sizes of packets, detecting a looped-back link, and common misconfiguration errors. Another important (but optional) feature of LCP is authentication during the call setup process.

Caution   The authentication feature of LCP can be exploited because security credentials travel over the cable used for communication — and eavesdropping is easy.

NCPs establish and configure Network layer protocols. They also control the operations of Network-layer protocols. Usually, each Network-layer protocol has its own NCP.

PPP supports Password Authentication Protocol (PAP), Challenge Handshake Authentication Protocol (CHAP), and MS-CHAP authentication protocols.

 Note   MS-CHAP is a proprietary protocol, supported only by Microsoft client/server architecture.

Password Authentication Protocol

Password Authentication Protocol (PAP) provides a simple method for a remote node to establish its identity using a two-way handshake. This is done only upon initial link establishment. The remote node is in control of the frequency and timing of the logon attempts. It is not a secure authentication protocol because passwords are sent in clear text and there is no protection from playback or trail-and-error attacks.

Such an authentication scheme does not guarantee security at all. After the PPP link establishment phase is complete, a username and a password pair is repeatedly sent by the remote node across the link until authentication is acknowledged or the connection is terminated.

Challenge Handshake Authentication Protocol

Challenge Handshake Authentication Protocol (CHAP) is a more secure method of authentication that periodically verifies the identity of the remote node by using a three-way handshake. This is done when the initial link is established and can be repeated any time after the link has been established.

After the PPP link-establishment phase is complete, the authenticating host sends a *challenge* message to the remote node, beginning authentication. The remote node, yet to be authenticated, must respond appropriately to the challenge or be refused. The correct response is a value calculated by using a one-way hash function (typically the message-digest algorithm MD5). The authenticating host also generates the value in a way similar to that used by the remote node. It then checks the response against its own calculation of the expected hash value. If the values match, authentication is complete. Otherwise the connection is terminated.

CHAP protects against playback attack through use of repeated challenges with a variable challenge value, which make every challenge value unique and unpredictable. Use of repeated challenges is intended to limit the time of exposure to any single attack. The host (or a third-party authentication server such as Terminal Access Controller Access Control System) is in control of the frequency and elapsed time of the challenges.

 Note   Apart from ensuring secure authentication at the Data Link layer, additional security schemes that use TACACS+, RADIUS, and Kerberos can be implemented.

Virtual LAN

Virtual LAN (VLAN) refers to a group of computers that behave as if they are physically connected to each other to form a network. You implement a virtual LAN by using software (rather than hardware) to break a single broadcast domain into several smaller broadcast domains, configuring them separately. Each of these groups is a VLAN. This approach solves the scalability problems of large flat networks. Virtual LANs offer easier moves and changes in network design; LAN switches segment the networks into logically defined virtual workgroups. This logical segmentation (called *VLAN communication*) is a fundamental change in how LANs are designed, administered, and managed, making security easier to implement and network broadcast easier to manage across the enterprise.

This solution reduces the scope of attack and minimizes vulnerabilities at the Data Link layer. In the case of the Cisco Catalyst, VLANs are created at Layer 2 of the OSI network model by assigning each port for appropriate VLAN. To enable interVLAN communication, a Layer 3 device (router) is required. Figure 2-7 shows a typical VLAN setup.

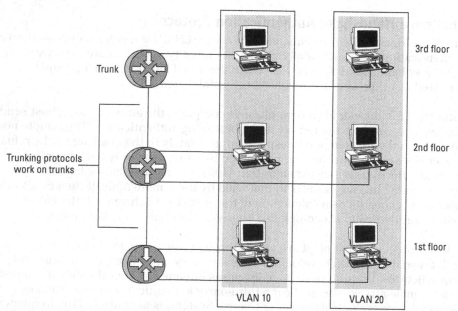

Figure 2-7: A typical VLAN setup

VLANs might be extended beyond a single switch. Trunk links are used between the switches for carrying the traffic of multiple VLANs between them. Because the trunk lines carry traffic of multiple VLANs, it is necessary to identify VLAN information across the trunk lines. Do so by wrapping the Ethernet frame in a trunking protocol. Cisco has created a proprietary trunking protocol called ISL, but the

802.1q standard is also supported. It is suggested that VLAN should be not used as a direct security measure. You can ensure security on VLANs by implementing the following precautions:

✦ Disable trunk settings explicitly, rather than using the auto mode on ports which are not being used as trunks. This denies a host from receiving all the traffic being carried on the trunk. It is advisable to disable all the ports not in use. This would restrict any hacker from plugging into any vacant port and misusing it.

✦ Assign a VLAN ID to a trunk port not in use elsewhere on the switch. This prevents packets tagged with the same VLAN as the trunk port from reaching another VLAN without crossing a Layer 3 device. VLAN ID 1 is reserved for the management and troubleshooting of VLAN across the network.

Note VLANs should not be used as the sole method of securing access between two subnets. The VLAN tagging protocols were not designed with security in mind. While implementing VLANs in security deployments, pay close attention to the configurations and guidelines just mentioned.

Organizations implement VLANs for one or more of the following reasons:

✦ Enhanced security

✦ Easier management

✦ Performance optimization

✦ Flexible segmentation

Security

In a network there are computers that store critical and sensitive data and computers that access this data. Computers that store critical data are attacked more often by hackers than any other computers on the network. Organizations usually implement VLANs to separate computers storing sensitive data from other computers in the network. These VLANs create a virtual boundary that can only be crossed through routers. You can appropriately configure the routers that act as the entry point to VLANs and prevent sensitive data from hackers.

Management

VLANs are implemented by using software rather than hardware devices. Hence, it is easier to manage relocation of a computer, which is a part of a VLAN. Also, it is easier to add nodes in a VLAN than adding nodes to a LAN.

Note Moving nodes in a LAN or adding nodes to a LAN involves physically reorganizing wires and is at times cumbersome. However, VLANs are implemented using software, moving or adding nodes can be easily handled from the management console.

Performance optimization

One major reason why organizations use VLANs is to increase the network performance. Network administrators can plan VLANs in a way that the number of router hops in a network reduces. Because there would be less router hops in the network, the apparent bandwidth would increase, leading to better network performance.

Flexible segmentation

VLANs allow grouping of the computers that must communicate more often, regardless of their physical location. This not only reduces the extraneous traffic, as the computers that communicate frequently are in the same VLAN, but also offers internal security benefits. Most organizations prefer to place different departments on different VLANs because of security reasons. The idea behind placing different departments in different VLANs is that the users in one department should have restricted access to the data of other departments. This reduces the security threats from internal users.

Virtual private networks

A virtual private network (VPN) is an extension of an organization's private network across a public network such as the Internet by creating a secure private connection (*tunnel*) over the public infrastructure. A VPN tunnel encapsulates data within IP packets that transport information; it does not otherwise conform to Internet-addressing standards — which means that remote users become *virtual nodes* on the network into which they have tunneled (that of your organization) and do not interact with the public network through which the tunnel passes.

 For more about VPNs, see Chapter 12.

The data to be transferred can be the frames or packets of another protocol. Instead of sending the original frame produced by the originating node, the tunneling protocol encapsulates the frame in an additional header. The additional header provides routing information so the encapsulated data can travel over the intermediate internetwork.

Tunneling technology can be based on one of two tunneling protocols:

✦ **Layer 2 tunneling protocols** correspond to the OSI Data Link layer.

✦ **Layer 3 tunneling protocols** correspond to the OSI Network layer and use packets.

Layer 2 tunneling protocols

VPNs use Layer 2 tunneling protocols to ensure the reliability and integrity of data that travels across the public infrastructure. These protocols provide compression, encryption, and encapsulation to protect the actual payload. The three different Layer 2 tunneling protocols in current use are as follows:

✦ **Point-to-Point Tunneling Protocol (PPTP)** is an extension of the basic PPP protocol used for communications. PPTP uses the existing PPP connection between two hosts. It then encapsulates the data traffic inside IP packets. Because PPP itself does not support multipoint connections, the PPTP connection must be point-to-point. PPTP only supports TCP/IP.

For more about PPTP, see Chapter 13.

✦ **Layer 2 Forwarding (L2F)** is a tunneling technology proposed by Cisco that enables secure private network access through public infrastructure. L2F is a transmission protocol that allows dial-up access servers to frame dial-up traffic in PPP and transmits it over WAN links to an L2F server. The L2F server then unwraps the packets and injects them into the network. L2F does not depend on the IP protocol only. It can work with other network native protocols, such as ATM and FDDI. L2F uses PPP for authentication and supports TACACS and RADIUS technologies.

For more information on L2F, refer to Chapter 13.

✦ **Layer 2 Tunneling Protocol (L2TP)** is a fast-emerging technique for providing secure access to remote users. It is derived from L2F by Cisco and PPTP by Microsoft. L2TP can be used on a variety of connections. You can use an IP Internetwork, Frame Relay Private Virtual Circuits (PVCs), X.25 VCs, and ATM VCs. L2TP supports multiple tunnel connections from the same Virtual Private Dial-up Network (VPDN) client.

For more information on L2TP, refer to Chapter 13.

Layer 3 tunneling protocols

Layer 3 tunneling protocols correspond to the Network layer of the OSI model. Layer 3 protocols such as IP over IP and IPSec Tunnel Mode use packets as their unit of exchange. These protocols encapsulate IP packets in an additional IP header before sending them across an IP internetwork.

For more information on IPSec, refer to Chapter 13.

Cisco Hardware and Software for IP Security

Cisco offers several security products. Different products are suitable for different requirements of customers. Dedicated security products, such as PIX Firewall, are a combination of software and hardware dedicated to providing security, while others, such as Cisco IOS Firewall, enhance the capabilities of the Cisco IOS Software on the router.

Key security products from Cisco are as follows:

✦ Cisco Secure PIX Firewall

✦ Cisco IOS Firewall

✦ Cisco Secure Scanner

✦ Cisco Secure Policy Manager

✦ Cisco Secure Intrusion-Detection System

✦ Cisco Secure Access Control Server (ACS)

✦ Cisco IOS software

✦ Cisco Security Assessment Posture

These products are reviewed in the following sections.

Cisco Secure PIX Firewall

Cisco Secure PIX Firewall (PIX) acts as a gatekeeper of the network, which prevents intruders from entering the network. The PIX Firewall enables the internal network to connect the Internet and other external networks securely and safely.

Cisco Secure PIX Firewall is a stateful firewall (combination of hardware and software) that completely hides the internal network from the external world. PIX Firewall is available in several models, such as Cisco Secure PIX 506, Cisco Secure PIX 515, Cisco Secure PIX 520, Cisco Secure PIX 525, and Cisco Secure PIX 535. As the model numbers increase the capacity of PIX Firewall also increases. The capacity can be in terms of the number of concurrent connections supported by the PIX Firewall. Port density also varies with each model. Each new model comes equipped with a stronger processor and higher RAM up to 512MB and even 1GB, respectively. Higher models also support Gigabit Ethernet ports and Token-Ring interfaces.

Key features of Cisco Secure PIX Firewall are as follows:

✦ It gives excellent performance along with security. It can support up to 250,000 connections.

✦ The operating system of the firewall is a real-time embedded operating system.

✦ It is located between the corporate network and Internet access routers.

✦ It provides Ethernet, Fast Ethernet, Token-Ring, or FDDI LAN interfaces.

✦ Adaptive Security Algorithm (ASA) provides stateful security and allows connections to external networks to be made only from within the networks.

✦ Uses the highly efficient cut-through proxy server for authentication and authorization.

✦ It can be integrated with the HP OpenView product.

✦ It provides a GUI for configuration and management.

✦ It also provides an alert and an alarm notification service.

✦ It also supports VPN with the Private Link encryption card.

Cisco IOS Firewall

Cisco IOS Firewall is a security-specific option for Cisco IOS software and available for a wide range of router platforms. It enhances Cisco IOS software's security capability by integrating the robust firewall features and intrusion detection capabilities into the IOS software. Cisco IOS Firewall adds stateful, application-based filtering, dynamic user-specific authentication and authorization, detection and prevention of common network attacks, Java applets filtering, and a host of other features to the Cisco IOS Firewall.

Key features of Cisco IOS Firewall are as follows:

✦ Context-based access lists. These enhanced access lists allow only certain packets to enter the internal network; such packets must come only from valid sessions initiated by hosts on the internal network. This feature detects and prevents the denial-of-service attacks and network intrusions.

✦ Intrusion detection includes real-time monitoring of the network traffic. This feature detects any unauthorized user sending traffic into the network, and any misuse of the network-by network users. Denial-of-service attacks by checking Transport-layer headers for any suspicious information and also by keeping track of how many sessions are half-open to hosts.

✦ IOS Firewall prevents internal users from inadvertently downloading malicious Java applets.

✦ Real-time alerts and audit trails log alert messages for attacks on the network (or any misuse of network resources). It also logs the details of the transactions occurring over the network along with the timestamp and other details for each event.

✦ IPSec encryption secures data being transported over untrusted networks such as the Internet.

✦ Supports Cisco IOS software encryption, tunneling, and QoS features to provide support to secure VPNs. It also supports advanced bandwidth management and service-level validation.

Cisco Secure Scanner

Cisco Secure Scanner is an enterprise-class security software tool. It is a network vulnerability scanner and network mapping system. Cisco Secure Scanner also enables an organization to diagnose and repair security problems in its network by informing the network administrator about the possible vulnerabilities.

Cisco Secure Scanner provides an efficient network system identification and data management. It enhances the end-to-end network security and can be installed on Windows NT and Unix systems.

Key features of Cisco Secure Scanner are as follows:

✦ It provides a license that suits the needs of individual customers.

✦ It provides a user-friendly GUI that allows the user to configure a network scan. This does not require pre-existing knowledge of the network or security vulnerabilities.

✦ It is a complete scanning tool that analyzes and identifies specific network devices and systems. This can identify Web servers, firewalls, routers, switches, and workstations.

✦ It can analyze the data in depth and report the information in a flexible manner. This includes graphical representation of reports and wizards to generate reports.

✦ It allows users to configure scheduling, specialized profiles, and flexible scanning rules for standardized and proprietary systems.

✦ It provides unique matrix browser and display technology that allows the users to view the data as required.

✦ It provides a database consisting of security problems and options to fix them that help the user in time of need.

Cisco Secure Policy Manager

Cisco Secure Policy Manager (CSPM) is a powerful security policy management system. It can be used for enhancing the security provided by Cisco firewalls, virtual private network (VPN) gateways and intrusion detection system (IDS). It enables administrators to define, distribute, enforce, and audit network-wide security policies from a central location. It simplifies the task of managing network security elements and can be used to manage perimeter access control, Network Address Translation (NAT), IDS, and IPSec-based VPNs.

Key features provided by Cisco Secure Policy Manager are as follows:

✦ It supports up to 500 Cisco PIX Firewalls and Cisco routers, thus providing huge scalability.

✦ It supports a distributed architecture. This is the reason it can support PIX Firewalls on the Internet, intranet, and extranet.

✦ It enables the remote configuration of PIX Firewalls.

✦ It can be installed as a stand-alone system, a client/server system, or a distributed system.

✦ It provides the facility of network address translation by using NAT. It allows the administrator to configure NAT policies for the PIC Firewall.

✦ It allows the administrator to configure high-level policy for the IPSec environment.

✦ It also provides auditing and reporting features. It helps in monitoring the network and its security.

✦ It supports Web browsers, such as Internet Explorer 4.01 or later.

Cisco Secure Intrusion-Detection System

Cisco Secure Intrusion-Detection System is a security tool that can monitor a large number of networks through centralized management; it can operate on both the Internet and the intranet. Cisco Secure Intrusion-Detection System detects, reports, and drops unauthorized activity on the network. It detects and responds to unauthorized activities as and when they take place.

Unauthorized activity could be an attempt to break through an existing firewall, router, and network security policies or the misuse of authorized services. It makes use of two components to detect and prevent unauthorized activity on the network. The two components are as follows:

✦ **Sensor:** It analyzes the content of each packet and determines whether the traffic is authorized or unauthorized. If the traffic is unauthorized — and is causing unauthorized activity on the network — the sensor forwards an alarm of the activity to the Director console and removes the offender from the network.

✦ **Director:** The Director displays events, monitors sensors, and analyzes data. It communicates with one or more sensor systems to collect data.

Key features of Cisco Secure Intrusion Detection System are as follows:

✦ Intrusion detection is real time. Therefore, no time is lost between detection and action taken. The offender is immediately disconnected from the network. Intrusion detection is transparent to the authorized traffic on the network.

✦ It can detect a wide range of attacks. It can also detect content and context-based attacks.

✦ It supports a range of interfaces, such as Ethernet, Token Ring, and FDDI.

✦ It provides sensors that send alarms. The alarms include information, such as source and destination IP addresses, source and destination ports, and attack description.

✦ It is scalable to large and distributed networks.

Cisco Secure Access Control Server

Cisco Secure Access Control Server (ACS) ensures the security of the network and tracks the activity of the users connected to the network. It uses Authentication, Authorization, and Accounting (AAA) to provide network security. For ensuring AAA, Cisco Secure ACS uses security protocols, such as Terminal Access Controller Access Control Server + (TACACS+) or Remote Access Dial-In User Service (RADIUS). ACS can enable the management of user access for all Cisco devices, including Cisco IOS routers, VPNs, firewalls, and Voice over IP (VOIP).

You can centrally control user AAA. It provides a Web-based control and a graphical interface. You can also adopt a distributed approach where you can distribute those controls to hundreds of access points on the network.

Tip   Cisco Secure ACS is available for Windows NT and Unix operating systems. Cisco Secure ACS now supports the industry's leading relational database technologies, such as Sybase and Oracle.

Cisco Secure ACS supports an unlimited number of Cisco NASs. It can support any third-party device that supports TACACS+ or RADIUS protocols. It also supports Token cards and servers.

Cisco IOS software

Cisco IOS software consists of a number of built-in security features, which include access-control lists. Access-control lists permit or deny packets traveling through the router based on the criteria specified by the administrator. Cisco IOS software can be used to control traffic of various protocols, such as TCP/IP, SPX/IPX, AppleTalk, and DECnet.

Tip   Reflexive and dynamic access lists further enhance the security of a network by keeping track of the session information.

Cisco IOS software supports various security features, including

✦ VPN capabilities on VPN-enabled routers, which provide security to the traffic traveling through tunnels

✦ Data encryption for sending data securely over the network

✦ PAP and CHAP authentication over its serial ports

✦ Security protocols such as TACACS+, RADIUS, and AAA

Using a Cisco Security Posture Assessment

Cisco has also developed a Security Posture Assessment (SPA). Cisco SPA helps the organizations and service providers to determine the vulnerabilities in their networks. When the organizations and service providers know about these security gaps in their network, they can take appropriate security measures to fill the security gaps. It also helps the organizations to assess their networks and identify the areas of improvement. Thus, SPA offers a comprehensive analysis on the security vulnerabilities that exist in a network.

When a SPA is conducted for a service provider, the security experts examine external connectivity to assess the following factors:

✦ Effectiveness of the current security measures

✦ Extent of existing security vulnerabilities

✦ How well security devices on the network detect and respond to attacks

A typical posture assessment includes four major phases:

✦ Mapping the network topology and analyzing it as a potential target of security attacks

✦ Analysis of vulnerabilities that exist for each network service

✦ Reviewing security design to determine loopholes

✦ Reporting on findings and offering recommendations to management

After the organizations get a report on the vulnerabilities in their network and the suggested changes, they can use the services provided by Cisco to implement the recommendations.

Summary

This chapter explained the need for protecting a site. It also described the need for network integrity and the network integrity tools — MD5 tool and PGP cryptography. The chapter covered the security aspects at the Transport, Network, and Data Link layers of the OSI model:

✦ SSH protocol, SSL protocol, PCT protocol, and TLS protocol provide security at the Transport layer.

✦ The common protocols providing security at the Network layer are IPSec and IPv6. IPSec uses two component protocols, AH protocol and ESP protocol, to provide Network-layer security. IPv6 has built-in security features.

✦ At the Data Link layer, the data can be securely transmitted using VLANs and PPP authentication. The PPP authentication protocols are PAP and CHAP.

The chapter briefly described security products offered by Cisco, such as Cisco Secure PIX Firewall, Cisco IOS Firewall, Cisco Secure Scanner, Cisco Secure Policy Manager, and Cisco Secure ACS. You also learned that Cisco IOS software also has built-in security features. The chapter also discussed Cisco Secure Posture Assessment (SPA), which helps the organizations and service providers determine the vulnerabilities in their networks.

✦   ✦   ✦

Detecting Intrusions

As networked computing has become an indispensable corporate tool, network security has become a primary concern for any modern organization. To ensure network security, organizations must secure their networks from external as well as internal intruders. The aim of network intruders is to gain access to the network, disrupt network traffic, and manipulate data or information on the targeted computers; it is important that the network security mechanisms are designed in a way that they prevent unauthorized access to the network resources. You can secure networks by using the Cisco *intrusion-detection system* (IDS) — a set of features designed to detect intrusion attempts and respond by sending alerts.

Caution

Despite the availability of network-security products on the market, security breaches are not entirely preventable. Intrusion-detection systems can, however, help you detect attacks on network — and limit their effect.

This chapter explains the concept and technology of intrusion detection — and looks into the reasons why networks face attacks and intrusions. The chapter also covers the weaknesses in the TCP/IP protocol suite and lists the various Cisco Internet Operating System (IOS) intrusion-detection systems. Before you delve into IDS, you may want to review the fundamentals of intrusion detection presented in the next section.

Understanding Intrusion Detection

In security terms, an *intruder* is anyone — whether individually or as a group — who attempts to gain unauthorized access to a network. Once in, an intruder can manipulate data, misuse network resources, and/or disrupt network services. Therefore Cisco offers its own version of an *intrusion-detection system* (IDS) — a set of features designed to detect intrusions into the network.

A typical IDS can run on all the local computers or monitor the network from a central computer. When it spots an intrusion, the IDS responds according to predefined instructions (for example, by sending an alert).

IDS products can be either network-based or host-based; each type has its advantages, as the upcoming sections of this chapter explain.

Network-based IDS

Network-based IDS searches a specified section of the network for intruders. It draws its data from network packets and uses a network adapter (running in promiscuous mode) to monitor traffic flowing over the network. To identify an attack, a network-based IDS uses four criteria:

✦ **Frequency or threshold crossing:** When a normal activity occurs several times in an unusually short period, it can exceed a preset threshold and make the IDS send an alert. For example, if a logon attempt fails once, it could easily be an everyday user mistake. If the same password failure occurs repeatedly and crosses the threshold, the system identifies the event as a possible attack.

✦ **Bytecode, expression, or pattern matching:** To verify whether an attack has occurred, the IDS matches bytecodes, expressions, or patterns of activity to entries in its database. This is the most common method of detecting attacks.

✦ **Correlation of lesser events:** The IDS checks for a specific sequence of events.

✦ **Statistical anomaly detection:** The IDS monitors an activity for a predefined period of time (to establish a normal behavioral model) and then checks for the occurrence of abnormal activities.

Figure 3-1 shows a typical network-based IDS.

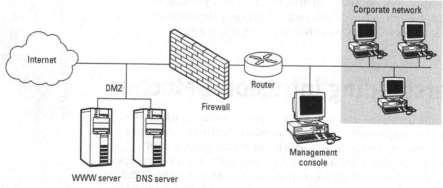

Figure 3-1: Network-based IDS

Detecting an intrusion

Network IDS consists of two components — a *detection agent* that constantly scans the network and a *managing agent* that responds to a detected intrusion. The detection agent constantly checks the network activity and compares it with a set of rules that defines acceptable network traffic. When the detection agent finds any deviation, an alert is sent to the managing agent. The managing agent is configured to carry out a set of actions when the detection agent alerts it. These actions can include logging the address of the computer and stopping the computer from accessing the network.

A detection agent uses either *profile-based detection* or *signature-based detection* to detect the presence of an intruder in a network.

Profile-based detection

In profile-based detection, the system maintains a list of profiles for each user. Each profile lists the activities performed by its user on the network — including the network resources, files, and folders that the user accesses and the time for which the user was logged in. Any change in the behavior pattern specified in the profile is considered an intrusion. Although detailed, this method of intrusion detection has two major disadvantages — high cost and unreliability. Users might not remain in the same organizational position (or at the same physical location) long enough for the system to achieve effective monitoring. For example, they might get transferred or go on leave and access their computers remotely — which the IDS would consider an attempted intrusion. Such a situation leads to frequent false alarms, wastes resources, and increases cost because a powerful managing agent must keep track of the ever-changing profiles.

Signature-based detection

In signature-based detection, the vendor provides a list of *attack signatures* — patterns of online activity (or sets of such patterns) that together constitute an attack. The managing agents check the network activity against this list of attack signatures; if an intruder is detected, the agent takes appropriate action — either recording the address of the computer in a log or sending an alert to the managing agent.

To detect a possible intrusion, an IDS scrutinizes the data packets transmitted in a TCP connection and checks them against the signatures of identified network attackers. Although most vendors have given users the right to customize the list of signatures according to their own security requirements, most vendors also periodically provide updated signature lists.

Tip   Users can create customized, *string-based* signatures to detect common attacks. For example, users can create a signature to identify e-mail attachments that contain the `.vbs` file extension — which can help identify the viruses that contain the `.vbs` file extension (as did the notorious I Love You virus).

Organizations can also create customized signatures that identify and keep track of e-mail containing certain keywords (such as `confidential`).

Although versatile, signature-based detection is not always reliable; the agent could interpret normal actions of the computer as malicious activities of intruders. For example, a security administrator might use `ping` to identify vulnerable TCP ports — which the agent might identify as an intrusion. Signature-based detection may work for documented attacks, but what about the types of attacks (such as Trojan horses or encrypted viruses) that still have not been documented? Such attacks are invisible to signature-based IDS. Newer and better intrusion-detection systems overcome this limitation by examining the data flow between the devices using IP. Any change between normal network communication and unusual transactions quickly becomes apparent to the IDS.

Types of network-based IDS

Two general types of network-based IDS are currently in use:

✦ Static or built-in signature IDS

✦ Stateful dynamic signature inspection

Static or built-in signature IDS

This type of IDS has a built-in database engine that analyzes attack signatures as a method of detecting attacks. Static or built-in signature IDS cannot, however, detect new attacks for which signatures do not yet exist in the database. Also, as the list of attack signatures lengthens, the performance of this IDS decreases; a longer list takes longer to process.

Stateful dynamic signature IDS

This type of IDS is based on Stateful Dynamic Signature Inspection (SDSI) technology. SDSI uses a virtual processor that executes attack signatures as a set of instructions. This virtual processor is dedicated to intrusion detection and is independent of the attack signatures; it keeps track of the current states of all application sessions on the network.

Features of a network-based IDS

Network-based IDS provides various features not offered by host-based IDS. The following features make network-based IDS a preferred approach:

✦ The system is deployed at strategic access points, where network traffic destined to a number of network devices is monitored; network-based IDS does not require installation of software on all network devices — which not only reduces the cost of ownership but also reduces managing responsibilities.

✦ The system checks the headers of all data packets in transit for attacks; network-based IDS provides protection against attacks, such as denial-of-service attacks, which can be identified only by checking packet headers.

✦ The system checks the content of each data packet for the specific commands or syntax used to launch specific attacks.

✦ The system uses data packets themselves to detect network attacks — hence the data that this IDS captures includes the method of attack. Hackers have a much tougher time trying to remove the evidence of the attack.

✦ The system detects attacks as soon as they occur, providing faster notification of attacks.

✦ The system provides information about failed network attacks — which helps network administrators keep track of all attacks (successful or unsuccessful) and gauge the effectiveness of security measures and policies.

✦ The system is independent, functioning apart from the operating system of the host computer.

Drawbacks of network-based IDS

Network-based IDS monitors data packets transmitted over the network. Sensitive data is usually encrypted before being sent; decrypting these packets before analyzing them is usually not practical. Thus network-based IDS can't monitor the content of encrypted packets — which is a significant drawback, especially if the attack comes in the form of an encrypted virus.

Note In most encrypted data packets transmitted over a network, the header is not encrypted. Network-based IDS can (at least) scan the header information in such data packets.

IDSs worked well on conventional networks, but with the improvement in technology, networks have migrated to high-speed networks. However, IDSs do not perform well with high-speed transmission. Unable to match these speeds, they fail to scan data packets properly.

As a solution, vendors have created detection systems designed to monitor entire networks; these run at speeds measured in gigabits (rather than megabits) per second. Because such systems are compatible with existing technology, organizations need not spend large sums to upgrade their networks before they can implement these new security measures. An added benefit is that network administrators can use their existing IDS consoles to monitor enterprise routers, subnets, and networks at this higher speed.

Caution Although obtaining all your IDS capabilities from a single vendor can mean easier protection and management across all types of processors, a single-vendor solution is often easier for hackers to penetrate and collapse — sometimes they need find no more than a single weakness to bring down the entire network.

Host-based IDS

In a host-based system (as shown in Figure 3-2), detection agents are installed on all computers, reporting intrusions to a managing agent installed on a central computer. The detection agent then searches for intruders, using resources (such as disk space and memory) available on the computer on which it is installed. Of course, when the agent uses resources on the destination computers, the performance of the destination computer inevitably degrades somewhat. Host-based IDS is best suited to small networks with a limited number of computers to monitor — or a network with servers that must be consistently monitored.

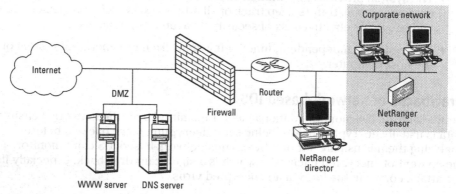

Figure 3-2: Host-based IDS

Host-based IDS is a powerful tool for analyzing previous security breaches and determining methods for preventing their recurrence. In the Windows environment, a host-based IDS monitors the event, system, and security logs for this purpose; in a Unix environment, it monitors `syslog`. If any entry in these log files changes, the IDS compares the new entry with existing attack signatures. If the entry matches an attack signature, the IDS sends appropriate alerts.

Note   Until a few years back, host-based IDS was a common way to review audit logs for security breaches and intrusions. Today, host-based IDS still uses audit logs — but they are much more automated.

Types of host-based IDS

Host-based IDS solutions are of two broad categories (as detailed in the upcoming sections):

✦ **OS-specific IDS** is tailored to the capabilities and functions of specific operating systems.

✦ **Application-specific IDS** is tailored to the security needs of particular applications.

OS-specific IDS

An OS-specific IDS monitors the OS *audit trails*, lists of activities that result when a user session is established with the server. This type of IDS uses the *behavioral model of normal use* — a model defines the usual pattern of activity that a user

follows after login. The IDS collects information from OS log files and audit trails —
for example, time of session, number and types of files created, and the number and
types of files accessed on the network. During the monitoring process, abnormal
sessions, such as unsuccessful login attempts, are identified. Algorithms then
compare these sessions against the behavioral model for normal use. All suspicious
sessions are classified and reported.

Application-specific IDS

This type of host-based IDS monitors intrusions or attacks attempted against a specific application server. The primary use of an application-specific IDS is to protect
servers that store critical data. Such an IDS monitors the activities of particular applications and selects details to create a set of rules. This set of rules establishes normal
usage and helps identify abnormal activities. To detect intrusion, the IDS periodically
checks the occurrence of selected rules for any departure from normal usage.

How a host-based IDS works

Because operating systems (including those of hosts) log all events in which user
accounts are added, modified, and deleted, a host-based IDS can detect such
changes in an active user account. All host-based intrusion-detection systems,
whether OS-specific or application-specific, share the following ways of working:

- ✦ Use of event logs to verify whether a security attack is successful.

- ✦ Monitoring user activities and file-access operations.

- ✦ Monitoring any changes made to file permissions, including attempts to install
  executable files.

- ✦ Monitoring changes to critical system and executable files; it can detect any
  attempts made to manipulate system files or install Trojan horses.

- ✦ Provides almost a real-time response. Whenever there is a new log file entry, a
  host-based IDS receives an interrupt from the operating system. The new
  entry can then be analyzed immediately; hence, the time between the attack
  and response is significantly reduced.

- ✦ Implemented on the existing network infrastructure, such as file servers,
  Web servers, and other computers in the network and does not require any
  additional hardware; host-based IDS is cost-effective to implement.

Drawbacks of a host-based IDS

A host-based IDS has the following disadvantages:

- ✦ It is dependent on the type of computers. Most host-based IDS can monitor
  only specific types of computers. For example, a host-based IDS designed to
  protect a Web server will not be effective for a Web server that runs multiple
  services, such as DNS and POP3.

- ✦ It runs as a background process and does not provide protection against
  attacks on protocol stacks.

Host-based IDS versus network-based IDS

Host-based and network-based IDS each have their inherent features and drawbacks. The following list compares the two systems.

✦ Host-based IDS can monitor and detect the attempts of attacks made on system files and executables more effectively.

✦ Host-based IDS can detect attacks not attempted through the network. Network-based IDS can only detect the attacks attempted through the network.

✦ Host-based IDS provides better protection to the networks that use switches.

✦ Network-based IDS does not provide protection against attacks in an encrypted environment. However, host-based IDS is effective in encrypted environment — when the data reaches the host-based system, it has already been decrypted and can be easily monitored.

✦ Host-based IDS is less expensive than network-based IDS.

✦ Host-based IDS is dependent on the operating system; different host-based IDSs must be deployed for different systems. However, network-based IDS is independent of the operating system.

✦ In network-based IDS, it is more difficult for hackers to remove the evidence of attacks. In host-based IDS, removing evidence is relatively easy; audit logs can be manipulated without much difficulty.

✦ Network-based IDS can detect attempted attacks that were rejected. However, host-based IDS is unable to do so as the information never reaches the host. This information about rejected attempts of attacks is important in evaluating and updating the security policy.

Since both host-based and network-based IDS have some inherent drawbacks, most advanced intrusion detection systems use both host-based and network-based approaches. In intrusion detection systems that use both these approaches, network-based sensors monitor the network traffic and host-based sensors monitor the host. However, both sensors report to a single console and provide integrated reporting.

Caution   Analyze your network-security requirements *before* you purchase an IDS. If your network needs both host-based and network-based IDS, purchase an integrated solution.

Reasons for Network Attacks and Intrusions

The extent of threat to network security that an organization faces depends on the nature of an organization's business. In the past few years, network-security threats have increased considerably — partly because access to networks has diversified to include mobile computing, VPNs, and telecommunication. Hackers now have more ways to gain easy access through security loopholes. Also, with the improvement of network monitoring techniques and the availability of better IDSs in the market, more network attacks are being identified and reported. Besides the increase in number of attacks, hackers have changed their attack strategies and goals. Often, for example, the hackers' intent has shifted from merely disrupting the network to corrupting it over time.

According to many security analysts, employees carry out (or aid) more than half the computer attacks. Disgruntled employees who have access to the network can inflict maximum damage on network resources. One way they do so is by purposefully creating areas in the network that are open to attacks by hackers.

Aside from spiteful or vengeful attacks, another (more commercial) reason to attack a network can be industrial sabotage. One organization might hack into a competitor's network to disrupt its functions or steal sensitive (or confidential) data.

To counter network intrusions, organizations form *intruder-protection teams* — in effect, industrial counterintelligence teams who set up special servers to act as bait for hackers. These servers work like virtual cul-de-sacs: An intruder is allowed to enter the network up to a predefined point — and then is not allowed to exit. The IP address of the intruder's machine and other information is recorded to protect the network from future attacks from the same source.

Security threats also exist for other reasons — some of which are less aggressively hostile, as described in the following sections.

Improperly configured technologies

Incorrect configuration of network equipment can hamper network security — often, in fact, default settings must be considered incorrect from a security standpoint. Fortunately, when such problems are identified, they can be easily corrected without spending too much time or money. Changing the default settings on network components can help close security loopholes that hackers could otherwise exploit; informing the manufacturers or vendors of any security loopholes you find in their products is an important step toward correcting such loopholes.

In particular, your configurations should prevent the easy transfer of user names and passwords across the network. If hackers can gain access to this information, they can wreak havoc on your network — no less than if in-house users fail to change their passwords frequently enough (or use easy-to-guess passwords). Policy and configuration should operate together to bar hackers from easy access to your network; Figure 3-3 shows an improperly configured network.

Unsecured network services — especially those connected to the Internet — pose a grave danger to your network security. Java and JavaScript codes that run in Web pages can easily be reconfigured to cause damage to network components; unsecured TCP services can give hackers easy remote access to your network.

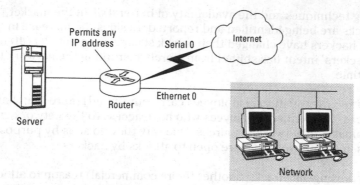

Figure 3-3: Improperly configured network

Ineffective network-security policies

Security policies (overt rules that you apply consistently to your security devices so they know which network traffic to permit or deny) can actually hurt your network if they're not well documented and consistently applied. Some drawbacks that immediately crop up in such a situation are as follows:

✦ Security cannot be implemented consistently across the network, making loopholes more likely.

✦ If employees are transferred within a short span of time, no single document provides requirements and guidance for changing the employees' permissions to maintain network security.

✦ A lack of proper monitoring and auditing gives hackers an opportunity to attack the network. IDS must take corrective actions the moment an intrusion is detected; to guide in the configuration and use of your IDS, the documentation of your security policy must provide all the needed information about intrusion detection and preventive actions.

✦ In the absence of a documented policy, a hacker may have an easier time changing your hardware settings or installing unauthorized software without the knowledge of the network administrator — and without triggering an alert or other security precaution.

✦ Failure to select (and prepare for) backup measures (or other actions) in case of network attack means a lack of proper implementation — and a lack of protection for your network.

Weaknesses in technology

A common source of security threats (often inadvertent) is unnoticed weakness in a key technology. Systems that typically display such weaknesses are the TCP/IP protocol suite, the operating system, and the network infrastructure. All operating systems — whether Windows-based, Unix- or Linux-based, IBM OS/2, or any other — have inherent imperfections that can become security problems. An effective network-security policy helps the organization find, analyze, and compensate for such weaknesses — and that means documentation. All this documentation is stored in the CERT archives.

Different components have different characteristic weaknesses. For example, some firewalls cannot protect a network from attacks that are not attempted through the network itself. Some of these problems — unreliable password protection, lack of authentication, unsecured routing protocols, and breaches in firewalls — can be remedied by applying service packs or an operating system upgrade. In an ideal world, all makers of network components should analyze the problems documented in the CERT archives and find solutions to them. A wise administrator checks to find out whether such is the case.

Weaknesses in TCP/IP Protocol Suite

The strength of TCP/IP as a communications tool — its open standards — can also become a security liability. TCP/IP applications that have known vulnerabilities to security threats are listed below.

✦ Network File System (NFS) tries to provide network access to all types of users — even hosts that are not authenticated. The file system doesn't follow user-authentication procedures; nor does it assign specific UDP ports for particular tasks. Bottom line: The network is left vulnerable.

✦ Since hackers can modify UDP, IP, and TCP packet headers easily, the contents of these packets can be easily modified and resent. This leads to a leakage of secured information.

   The `sendmail` daemon present in Unix allows direct access to the `root` account — which has, in effect, total power over the network. `sendmail` also allows unauthorized users to send e-mails in Unix. Hackers can put `sendmail` commands in bogus e-mail messages to access the `root` level — for example, a command to send the version number of the OS back to the hacker, which helps in the custom-tailoring of an attack on the network. Hackers can even use `sendmail` commands to determine the domain name of the host and redirect messages to unauthorized addresses.

✦ Although originally a useful online tool, Telnet is often misused by hackers. Typically, a hacker uses Telnet to start a transaction with an unsecured host — by providing no more than an unused port number and an IP address.

Security weaknesses that are specific to TCP/IP can be analyzed at four layers of the 7-layer OSI model (as shown in Figure 3-4).

Hackers can bring down the network by exploiting any of these weaknesses. You can refer to CERT to find out any new weaknesses in the TCP/IP suite.

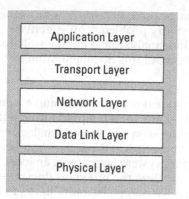

Figure 3-4: The layers of the OSI model where TCP/IP can be analyzed.

| Application Layer |
| Transport Layer |
| Network Layer |
| Data Link Layer |
| Physical Layer |

Physical and Data Link layers

At these layers, the main concern is to ensure full access control and maintain the information about the physical transmission medium. Data in the physical layer is in the form of bits; hence, you cannot implement any security measures at this layer.

Network layer

Maintaining security at the Network layer means ensuring security of data packets. The threats to packet security are various:

✦ **Network sniffers:** Hackers can use sniffer software to extract valuable information from a network. Similarly, hackers can use any computer on the network to read the data packets being transmitted over the network. Because the network-sniffing tools are also the network-troubleshooting tools, they are easily available and therefore widely used. Hackers also make use of these sniffer software to extract names and passwords of accounts. Hackers use sniffers to put the network interface of computers in multi-user mode and extract all information from any data packet that passes through the network.

✦ **Modifying messages:** Currently, it is difficult to ensure the integrity of the datagram being transmitted across a network. Hackers not only modify the contents of data packets, but also modify the header information to ensure that the recipient is unable to notice the difference.

✦ **Delay or denial in sending messages:** Hackers can disrupt and even deny transmission of data packets by modifying the routing rules. They can overload the network with junk data so that the network becomes slow and is unable to transmit the actual data packets. This happens only if the routers and other hosts discard data packets, which they cannot store. This is hazardous if you are using UDP packets, which are then lost and are irretrievable. However, if you are using TCP data packets, they can be retransmitted.

✦ **Masked IP addresses:** Hackers could use the same address as that of another computer on the network. In this way, the network services (such as NFS) can take this address as an authorized address and let it access the resources; these services look only for the appropriate network address and provide service to the first IP address matching their search criteria.

✦ **Address spoofing:** A spoofing attack targets certain weaknesses of the TCP/IP system, such as the trust relationship between two computers, the lack of variation in the TCP's Initial Sequence Number (ISN), and weak authentication methods used by some commands.

✦ **Attacks through routing:** Because no secure mechanism for authentication is used, many of the routing protocols receive false or fictitious update messages. The source routing option in IP allows hackers to provide the routing path of the packet from its source to its destination.

✦ **Tunneling:** You can encapsulate IP within TCP, which is called tunneling. Hackers use such tunnels to evade firewalls. The extent of damage done through tunneling depends on the amount and type of information passed through the tunnel.

✦ **Hacking into legitimate sessions:** If hackers get access to the root of the network system, any tool can be used to make changes to the root. After gaining access to the root, hackers can access any computer on the network.

✦ **Message replay:** In such attacks, the hacker records a message sent by a user to the host and then replays the recorded message to access the network. For example, to log in to a remote host, User A sends his password to the host machine. Hacker C captures the password sent by A (even if it is encrypted). Hacker C can then replay this captured password and log in to the host computer.

At the Network layer, the computers (rather than the users) are authenticated, using IP addresses. Accordingly, hackers can use such methods as address masquerading and address spoofing to gain access.

Transport layer

Data packets are transmitted over the network as either TCP or UDP data packets. Due to certain weaknesses that exist at the Transport layer, it is difficult to maintain the confidentiality, authenticity, and integrity of data packets. Some of these weaknesses are packet storm denial-of-service (DoS) attack (in the case of UDP) and the Session hijacking (in the case of TCP). In a UDP packet storm DoS attack, a single computer or the entire network is affected. When a single computer is attacked, it might not give the desired level of output; however, if multiple computers are attacked, the attack can bring down the entire network. When a session is established between two systems by using UDP, a lot of data packets are created. This large number of data packets can block the network and cause the DoS attack on the computer providing the service. Because no special user account is required to carry out such attack, anyone who has access to the network can attack the network.

Application layer

Even if a secured connection is established between two networks or computers, you cannot ensure the security of a remote connection or avoid attacks on the application level protocols, such as SMTP, FTP, or HTTP.

In addition to weaknesses in the layers of OSI model, some other weaknesses associated with TCP/IP are as follows.

Weakness in ICMP

The Internet Control Message Protocol (ICMP) serves to send and receive information about the status of the Internet connectivity by using the ping utility. The ping utility of ICMP sends an echo request to the host. It then waits for the host to send an echo reply message. Hackers often use the ping utility to launch network attacks and disrupt network services. To disrupt network services, a hacker sends a large number of request messages to the target computer. The target computer then keeps on sending replies to these requests. This leads to an increased traffic on the network, and as a result the legitimate users are denied network services.

Note   Network administrators find ping utility a useful tool for testing and troubleshooting network connectivity issues. However, it is equally popular among hackers, who use it to launch network attacks.

Hackers use ICMP messages, such as "time exceeded" or "destination unreachable" to launch DoS attacks. These messages indicate that data packets could not be successfully sent to the intended host. The "time exceeded" message is a result of routing loops or inability to reach a distant host. When a host receives any one of these messages, it ends the connection. A hacker can send forged ICMP messages to the hosts and thus break the connection between the two communicating hosts.

Weakness in RIP

Routing Information Protocol (RIP) serves to transmit routing information on the network to hosts. Normally, hosts using RIP assume that all information sent to them comes from a trusted host; they do not check the source of the information. An untrusted host or hacker can pose as a legitimate host, gain access to the network, and send incorrect routing information to divert information from the network to an unauthorized site.

After gaining access to the network, the hacker can participate in ongoing transactions in the network. For example, in a LAN, two hosts A and B are communicating with each other. At the same time, hacker C poses as A and eavesdrops in the ongoing communication between A and B. C can thus capture passwords and sensitive information. It can also send malicious information to the target host.

The weaknesses in the TCP/IP suite make it prone to security attacks — but what can be done to prevent these attacks? One immediate step you can take as an administrator is to alter the parameters that govern TCP/IP timing and queue size: You can increase the queue size to handle more requests and decrease the timeout to free the network resources for more connections.

Tip   To prevent RIP and ICMP attacks, you should turn off the RIP at routers and should not permit ICMP redirects.

Cisco Security Strategies

Cisco uses three methods to provide security: firewalls, the encryption and authentication of data packets, and access lists.

Firewalls

A firewall is a system that serves to implement access-control policy between networks. The most important point to remember about firewalls is their access-control policy. Unless you know the kind and level of access you want to allow or deny, a firewall would not be effective. A firewall's configuration is also an important factor that must be considered while deciding on the policy that has to be enforced; all hosts that connect to a firewall inherit any policy applied to it.

A firewall's primary function can differ from one network to the next. Some firewalls place a greater importance on blocking traffic; for others, permitting traffic is more important. Figure 3-5 illustrates a typical firewall and lists its functions.

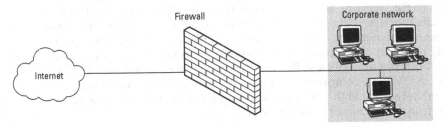

1. Keeps miscreants out
2. Internal users are able to connect to the Internet but not vice-versa
3. Single point of entry to the network

Figure 3-5: A typical firewall and its functions

One network can have various firewalls, each carrying out different activities. Some firewalls allow only e-mail traffic to pass, protecting the network against all types of attack except those that target e-mail. Other firewalls provide less stringent protection, and block only those network services known to create problems.

Most firewalls are configured to protect the network against hackers and other intruders — blocking outside traffic (especially unauthorized login attempts) from entering the local network. Often they allow users on the internal network to communicate with outside networks — such as the Internet — without restraint.

A firewall customarily serves as the exclusive point of entry for the network — which ensures that proper and efficient security can be implemented and the network traffic can be audited periodically. In situations where hackers dial in the network by using modems, it is difficult to locate the source of attack. Using firewalls makes it easy to locate the source since all traffic flows in through a single point of entry. All network traffic logged in and audited provides a summarized report to the administrator about the kind and amount of traffic passing through the network and the number of attempts made to break into the network.

Although the purpose of the Internet is to share information, there are people who use it to gain unauthorized access to an organization's network and carry out illegal activities. A firewall's primary purpose is to keep such miscreants out of the network while at the same time allowing authorized users to get their jobs done.

Network restrictions

You can use one of two general approaches to controlling the use of your network:

✦ **Allow specified network-access rights:** Any rights not specifically allowed to users are restricted.

✦ **Restrict specified network-access rights:** Any rights not specifically denied to users are allowed.

The most commonly assigned restriction limits the right to access network resources. Providing such access is often risky; if certain services are allowed access to the network, a hacker can use these services to disrupt the network. Firewalls function differently from intrusion detection; they control access to all devices on the network — which slows down throughput. On the other hand, an IDS simply monitors the network and constantly searches for intruders. The best way to use both the firewalls and IDS together is to place the IDS in a *demilitarized zone* (DMZ). A DMZ is a computer or a local-area network located between a corporate internal network and the Internet. It acts as a central hop for incoming and outgoing traffic from or to the corporate network.

Cross-Reference   For more information on DMZ, refer Chapter 6.

You can place your IDS outside or inside the firewall. In either case, the sensor tracks all the traffic entering and leaving the network. Figure 3-6 shows a firewall placed within a DMZ.

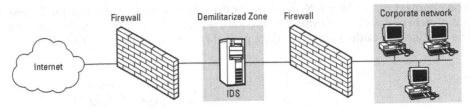

Figure 3-6: An IDS within a demilitarized zone

The second type of restriction, right not to access network resources, can also be considered dangerous if it is not properly implemented. For example, if an administrator allows access to remote hosts through a specific port but doesn't restrict the right to access the port to only authorized users, then hackers can use this port to gain entry to the network.

Firewall drawbacks

Although the firewall is an effective way to ensure security, there are a number of security threats against which the firewall cannot protect the network. First, a firewall cannot protect the network against attacks that do not go through it. For example, a hacker could steal data by copying it on a magnetic disk. For such attacks a firewall is ineffective. Second, employees can also reveal sensitive information over the telephone, such as through "social engineering" attacks. If an employee accidentally or intentionally discloses his or her password, a hacker could break into the network by bypassing the firewall. Third, firewalls can't protect the network against tunneling attacks that use application protocols, such as HTTP and SMTP, to access the network.

Firewalls are also not effective against viruses. Organizations concerned about viruses should implement virus control measures throughout the organization, such as installing anti-virus applications and applying anti-virus updates periodically. Instead of detecting viruses at firewalls, the organization must make sure that every computer has virus-scanning software installed that checks for viruses when the computer is rebooted or accessed. In recent years, a large number of firewall vendors are offering virus detection bundled along with the firewall software. Nevertheless, a robust firewall can never be a substitute for an anti-virus software that recognizes the type of virus and takes appropriate action.

Firewall classification

Firewalls can vary in operation depending on whether you install them at the Network layer or the Application layer of your network.

Network-layer firewall

This firewall scans the source and destination addresses and the ports of individual IP packets. It then accepts or rejects data packets according to this information.

The simplest example of a Network-layer firewall is a router (as shown in Figure 3-7) not concerned with the content of the data packets. It only looks at the source and the destination addresses of the data packets to transmit them further.

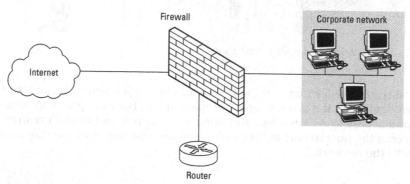

Figure 3-7: A Network-layer firewall

A Network-layer firewall can either act as a packet filter or as a circuit layer gateway. When a Network-layer firewall acts as a packet filter, it scans the IP packets and accepts or rejects them according to specific information (such as source and destination). Network-layer firewalls that act as circuit layer gateway not only scan the source and destination address in the IP packet but also scan for protocols. Thus, the Network-layer firewalls also check inbound requests for validity before allowing the IP packets inside the network.

Network-layer firewalls use an access list to verify whether the source and destination address of data packets is valid. As these firewalls do not scan the contents of data packets, they cannot detect the vulnerabilities in data. However, as Network-layer firewalls do not scan data of IP packets, the packets are processed faster; Network-layer firewalls are used in the scenarios where speed is important.

Note   Network-layer firewalls scan connections to servers, such as Web servers and e-mail servers, that have high traffic flow, and speed is a major concern.

Nowadays, Network-layer firewalls have advanced considerably and internally maintain information about the state of connections passing through them and the contents of some data streams. In addition, Network-layer firewalls are fast and transparent to users.

Network-layer firewalls are prone to security threats, such as buffer overruns and ICMP tunneling.

✦ **Buffer overruns:** This refers to a situation when the size of data in a buffer exceeds the allocated size. Hackers can use buffer overruns to exploit network resources. For example, if a buffer of length 600 bytes is created for a command, hackers can overload this buffer with an executable code of their own, and thus perform malicious activities. Because a Network-layer firewall does not scan the content of data packets, it is prone to buffer overrun attacks.

✦ **ICMP tunneling:** Hackers use ICMP tunnels to insert malicious data into legitimate ICMP packets, thereby inserting malicious data into the network or gaining access to network resources.

Application-layer firewalls

Application-layer firewalls treat the information flowing over the network as a stream of data and scan this stream of data to decide whether it should be allowed in the network. This decision to allow or disallow data is based on a set of predefined rules.

Because Application-layer firewalls scan the content of each data packet, they are more effective against security threats than Network-layer firewalls. However, this scanning can also retard system performance.

Application-layer firewalls are the hosts running proxy servers, which do not allow traffic to pass directly between networks, as shown in Figure 3-8. These Application-layer firewalls also carry out complex logging and auditing activities on the traffic that passes through them. As a result, it becomes easier to track the attempted security attacks.

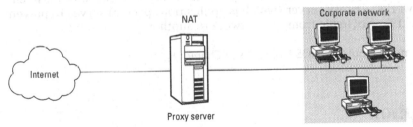

Figure 3-8: An Application-layer firewall

Application-layer firewalls can serve as network-address translators, passing data packets through an application that disguises the original address of the data packet and replaces it with another global IP address. In addition, Application-layer firewalls provide more in-depth audit reports and enforce more conventional security models than Network-layer firewalls.

Most modern firewalls can no longer be strictly classified as belonging to either the Application layer or the Network layer. They have become hybrids, seeking to address the security needs of both layers. Since they vary in the extent to which they serve either the Application or the Network layer, be sure to evaluate them accordingly before you implement.

Regardless of whether you implement them at the Application layer or the Network layer, firewalls have inherent drawbacks. Analyze your organization's security requirements carefully before purchasing a firewall solution.

Tip   Look for a Network-layer firewall if speed is the overriding concern. If security is your number-one concern, look for an Application-layer firewall.

Firewall technology

Firewalls can be built on a variety of technologies. The most frequently used technologies are as follows:

✦ **Static packet filtering:** Uses the information in the packet headers to scan and control the network traffic. When a filtering device that uses this technology receives data packets, it compares the information stored in the packet header against the access list (ACL). Depending on the result of comparison, it allows or rejects data packets. Static packet filtering uses information (such as source IP address, destination IP address, and service ports of destination and source) to regulate the traffic flow.

✦ **Dynamic packet filtering:** Besides using the information in the packet headers to scan and control network traffic (like static packet filtering), dynamic packet filtering also maintains a connection table. It uses this connection table to monitor the status of a session — which offers better control over traffic monitoring.

✦ **Proxy:** An application called proxy server is used as a mediator between two networks. A proxy server (which is application specific) serves to prevent a direct flow of traffic from one network to another.

Cross-Reference   For more about Cisco IOS Firewall, see Chapter 8.

Encryption

One of the most common methods of securing information and resources on a network is by using encryption and authentication. Despite their popularity, these methods have certain problems associated with them.

Most organizations are distrustful about communicating sensitive data over networks. There is a constant fear that this data might be viewed or altered during transfer or used by hackers to harm the organization. Data encryption serves to protect such sensitive data. Encryption involves encrypting data so that it can pass securely between the various points on a network. These points could be between two clients, between a client and a server, or between two routers on the network. Encryption of data provides the following three services:

✦ Maintaining the integrity of data

✦ Maintaining data privacy

✦ Ensuring the authenticity of the transaction

By using Cisco's Network-layer encryption technology, you can easily integrate the security features provided by encryption. The integration is invisible to end users, applications, intermediate routers, and the network devices. Encryption is best configured at the edge of the network where the confidential data enters or leaves the network. Another advantage of encryption is that decryption is not required until the data reaches the destination router. Data packets are encrypted once the header information is classified as User Datagram Protocol (UDP) or Transmission Control Protocol (TCP). By using the Cisco IOS Network-layer encryption, all intermediate routers and switches forward the data packets just like any other IP packets. Users can therefore send encrypted data transparently over the Internet.

Integrity should be maintained not only of the transmitted data, but also of the device used to transmit the data. You have to ensure that the device is secure and not a part of a hacker's attack. You also must ensure that the integrity of data is protected at both the ends of the network as well as during transit. For data authentication, Cisco uses technologies, such as Digital Signature Standard (DSS), the Diffie-Hellman (DH) public-key algorithm, and data-encryption Standard (DES). DSS is for peer router authentication. The DH algorithm and DES standard initiate and conduct encrypted communication sessions between participating peer routers.

Implementing encryption at different OSI layers

Network administrators can implement encryption at three layers of the Open Systems Interconnection (OSI) model:

✦ **At the Application layer:** Each application that generates sensitive data should support encryption — and should do so on every host that runs it. All hosts with which the application interacts must use the same encryption language.

✦ **At the Data Link layer:** Apply encryption on devices other than the router, but make sure the transferred data is decrypted before it enters the router. This process has to be repeated at every link where you need security. Because this method does not provide the IP addresses for routing, the processes of decryption and re-encryption must occur again and again — which can slow down the network traffic or even cause a security loophole.

✦ **At the Network layer:** Apply encryption anywhere in the network; to enhance overall network security, users must enable Quality of Service (QoS) at both ends. You can ensure privacy by encrypting data at the source before transmission — and only decrypting it at the destination. Only the source and destination computers have the encryption and decryption keys; a hacker who intercepts a data packet in transit can't get at the data without them.

Tip

Using digital signatures ensures authenticity of the source of the transaction. Because it is attached at the source, identifies the senders and contains the time the message was sent. The authenticity of the data packets can easily be verified at the destination.

You can either encrypt all the data together at the source or you can encrypt it at the session level. If you encrypt all the data at the source, it remains encrypted as it passes through the network. On the other hand, if data is only encrypted during transit from the Web page back to the database, it becomes vulnerable the moment it is decrypted at the database end. A hacker might gain access to the data at the database level and delete or modify the data or crash the server. Even a host-based ID might not detect this attack because the request to modify the data would seem to originate from an authenticated source.

Cross-Reference   For information on Cisco Encryption Technologies, refer to chapter 7.

Understanding cryptography

Cryptography is one of the main methods of encryption. By using cryptography, you can ensure the privacy of communication. Fundamentally, cryptography uses an algorithm for encrypting plain text and changing the text to a series of apparently random bits. This encrypted data can then be transmitted over the network or the Internet and decrypted on the destination, where it becomes meaningful data again.

Numerous algorithms encrypt data. DES is the most widely used algorithm and has been a standard for over 20 years. It is considered to be totally secure and practical. The National Security Agency (NSA) of the U.S. government first reviewed this algorithm in the early 1970s. After being reviewed by NSA, DES was used by the U.S. government to secure sensitive communication. It is still widely used in both hardware and software encryption. Because DES is global in nature, it can also be exported for allowing interoperation between corporate partners existing in different parts of the world.

Note   DES was the algorithm chosen for Cisco's Network-layer encryption as it was faster than its closest competitors.

The most secure factor in using cryptographic algorithm is that it is hard to decipher. The security of the cryptographic system relies on the level of difficulty a hacker faces to decipher the contents of the encrypted text. In most protocols, the security depends on ensuring the secrecy of the key used to encrypt data. In DES, the construction of the algorithm is such that it is almost impossible for anyone to decrypt the text without having the key. Therefore, the most critical factor in ensuring the success of cryptography is protecting the confidentiality of the encryption key. Because Cisco appreciates the importance of maintaining this secrecy, two of the three algorithms used in the Cisco IOS cryptographic system focus more on ensuring key distribution and secrecy rather than the encryption of data.

Two routers use the shared secret key to communicate with each other while using the DES encryption algorithm. The length of the key is an important factor to be kept in mind; a larger key is harder to guess than a smaller one. Although the secret key is the only way to decrypt data encrypted by using DES, given enough computing power and time, a hacker can find the algorithm of the key. If a hacker can crack even a single key, the hacker could easily decrypt every packet that was encrypted — simply by using the key. Therefore, frequently changing the session keys makes it more difficult for hackers to decrypt the data; any individual key loses importance as a target. The data is safe, even if the key to the encrypted data was discovered.

Cryptography advantages

Cryptography provides the security services, such as confidentiality, entity authentication, data integrity, digital signatures, and PKI base. These services are described here:

✦ **Confidentiality:** During the process of encrypting data, it is important that confidentiality of the interacting entities is maintained. You can do this by using cryptography wherein only authorized entities have the information about the encryption keys. For example, if a user on a remote network sends an encrypted mail to another user, you ensure by using cryptography that hackers do not alter the message while it is transmitted over the network.

✦ **Entity authentication:** Before data is transmitted across a network, the identity of the recipient must be verified to ensure that the data has been transmitted from a secure source. You also must ensure that the data has not been tampered with during transit. You can do this by using the entity authentication service in cryptography. Verify that only the authorized person possesses the secret key. However, even during the process of the data encryption the key is not disclosed.

✦ **Data integrity:** Cryptography also maintains the data about the original sender of the data packets. Thus, the sender authenticates the encrypted data, and it is proved that the information is not altered by any other entity.

✦ **Digital signatures:** Digital signatures prove that the sender of the document has legally bound the document. For example, digital signatures can prove that a person actually used his credit card in a transaction.

✦ **PKI base:** Public-Key Infrastructure (PKI) is a system to verify and authenticate users sending data across the network. You can authenticate users by using one of the three methods by which PKI is implemented. These methods are hash function, secret keys, and by using the public and private keys.

Authentication

Authentication is a vital component for ensuring the security of your network and is now an integral part of almost all operating systems. It is a procedure to verify the identity of users through the use of user IDs and passwords. A cryptographic algorithm serves to authenticate the user IDs and passwords. Although this method might seem secure, it is not completely foolproof. Hackers can still take advantage of weak password policies and security loopholes in the network. If hackers can break through your network security, they might install programs that give them full access to your network.

You can effectively use intruder-detection systems to prevent hackers from taking advantage of these weaknesses. You can configure the IDS to send out administrative alerts the moment an intruder is detected.

As an authentication tool, Kerberos has the advantages of encrypting passwords and using a single login (a Unix-based primary ID) to access all the resources on the network. Kerberos is used in DCE, and even in Windows 2000. Other techniques such as SSH encrypt passwords and use digital certificates for authentication. For example, SSH allows the use of public keys in place of encrypted passwords. Thus a single sign-on is enough to initiate login or other sessions.

You can also use authentication techniques such as smart cards and digital signatures to authenticate valid users. A smart card is similar to a credit card in size. It stores all information that is required by a user to get authenticated. A digital signature is a digital code that uniquely identifies the sender. Digital signatures are becoming an integral part of authentication processes.

Note   For information on smart cards, visit the Cisco Web site at `www.cisco.com`.

Cross-Reference   For more information on generating digital signatures, refer to Chapter 7.

Access lists

An access list (ACL) is a list of rights that informs a server of the level of access rights assigned to each user for a specific system object, such as a directory or an individual file. Each object has a security attribute assigned to it, which is recorded in the access list. The most common privileges include the permission to read the contents of a file or a directory, write to a file, and execute a file. Operating systems, such as Microsoft Windows NT/2000, Novell's NetWare, Digital's OpenVMS, and Unix-based systems, use access lists. The implementation of the list differs for each operating system.

You can use the ACL to indicate who has the access to a particular file or directory. The level of access can be limited to just read or write permissions, or can include both. The access can be assigned to an individual user or to a specific group of users. You can assign similar rights at the router level by setting either the packet's source IP address or the port it's using as a criterion for allowing or denying access. If the network administrator wishes to extend the right to make modifications to other users, the `acledit` command serves to edit ACL permissions. You must specify an editor before the `acledit` command when you use it for the first time.

You use access lists to filter network traffic by implementing them at router interfaces. The router scans each packet, deciding whether to forward or drop it according to the criteria specified in the access lists.

There are numerous good reasons to configure access lists. For example, by using access lists you can restrict the contents that pass through a router or regulate the network traffic. But the most vital reason to configure access lists is to secure the network. Access lists provide a fundamental level of security for accessing the network. If access lists are not configured on the router, malicious data packets can pass through the router and enter any part of the network.

Access lists should optimally be configured on the routers that form a part of the firewall. Placed between the internal and external networks, these routers serve as checkpoints for monitoring network traffic as it enters and exits the network. Access lists can also be configured on routers placed between two parts of the internal network to supervise traffic that enters or exits a particular part.

To derive the maximum-security benefits from access lists, you should install access lists on routers placed on the edges of a network — which provides a buffer between the internal network and the Internet or between a secured part of the network and the rest of the network. You must configure access lists for each network protocol on each of the routers. Both the incoming traffic or outgoing traffic or both should be filtered by the interface.

The main drawback of these access lists is that if they are not properly configured, they cease to be useful. For example, if you do not configure the router or firewall to keep track of the type of the data that enters or leaves the network, any violation to the rules would not be detected.

 Tip Although most protocols use their own sets of specific tasks and rules to filter network traffic, every one must define an access list and apply it to an interface.

Cisco IOS Intrusion-Detection System

Cisco provides a wide range of intrusion-detection devices, such as the NetRanger Sensor, the Cisco Internet Operating System (IOS) intrusion-detection system, and the access lists. A device called the NetRanger Director installed on a central machine manages the NetRanger Sensor and Cisco IOS intrusion-detection system. The director receives and processes alerts from all the intrusion-detection devices.

Computers on which a Cisco IDS is already deployed can also deploy the Cisco IOS software-based IDS signatures to make the existing IDSs more secure. For example, Cisco IOS software-based IDS signatures can be implemented on systems that do not support the NetRanger Sensor. You can implement these signatures along with the standard features supported by the Cisco IOS Firewall. A new mechanism for reporting exists in the Cisco IOS Firewall IDS that logs intrusions not only in the Cisco IOS syslog but also in Cisco Secure IDS Director.

Features of Cisco IOS intrusion-detection system

Cisco IOS intrusion-detection system has the following features:

✦ Acts as an authentication proxy

✦ Detects and prevents denial-of-service attacks

✦ Allows Dynamic port mapping

✦ Blocks Java applets

✦ Supports IPSec encryption, VPN, and QoS

✦ Allows configuring of real-time alerts, audit trails, and event logs

The following sections discuss the features and associated benefits of the Cisco IOS intrusion-detection system.

Authentication proxy

Cisco IOS Firewall is LAN-based, dynamic, and allows the administrator to create authentication and authorization sessions for each user. Earlier, the authentication of user ID was based on either a user's static IP address or a single security policy applied to entire group (or subnet). With Cisco IOS firewall software (which you can download from a TACACS+ or RADIUS authentication server), you can create policies for each user. Users can use HTTP to log in to the network or the Internet; their individual access profiles are automatically downloaded. These profiles are available as and when required, and they protect the network from a uniform policy being applied to a group of users. The router interface is secured at both ends of the network for implementing authentication and authorization services, which secures both incoming and outgoing information on the Internet, intranet, and the extranet. Figure 3-9 shows a typical Cisco IOS Firewall setup.

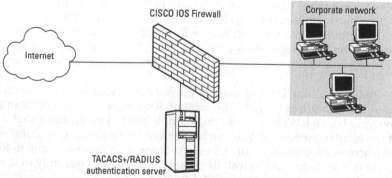

Figure 3-9: A Cisco IOS Firewall implementation

Detecting and preventing DoS attacks

You need to protect the network against different types of DoS attacks, such as packet injection, SYN flooding, and port scanning. You can do this by inspecting the sequence of packets in a TCP connection.

If the number of data packets being transmitted over the network is greater than a specified range, the router drops the rest of the data packets. Similarly, if the router notices that a large number of connections are being requested, an alert message is automatically sent and all unopened TCP connections are dropped so that the network stabilizes.

If an attack is detected, a trace is made either for the source or the destination address and the ports used. All the details of the transaction are recorded and audited.

Dynamic port mapping

CBAC-supported applications can run on nonstandard ports (if variable and per-application port mapping is used). In this way, network administrators can customize access control for certain applications and services — in cases where the need of the network requires such a change.

Blocking Java applets

Since Java applets now form an integral component of all Web pages, it has become necessary to protect the network from dangerous Java applets that threaten network security. You can configure the Java blocking feature of the Cisco IOS Firewall to filter out or completely deny entry to Java applets into the network.

 For details on how to configure the Cisco IOS Firewall to filter Java applets, refer to Chapter 8.

IPSec encryption, QoS, and VPN support

The Cisco IOS Firewall is used along with Cisco IPSec encryption technology to provide the virtual private network (VPN) functionality. VPNs have developed rapidly and provide safe transfer of data over the Internet, secure and economical connection between the remote branch offices and the main office, and on the extranet. VPNs also improve the reliability of quality of service (QoS).

The Network layer encryption prevents hackers from accessing or altering data as it is transmitted over the network. The Cisco Firewall provides secure VPNs by combining itself with features, such as Cisco IOS software encryption, tunneling, and QoS. The firewall uses Internet Protocol Security (IPSec) to encrypt data being transmitted over distributed networks. The Cisco IOS software also supports multiple tunneling protocol standards, such as Layer 2 forwarding (L2F), Generic Routing Encapsulation (GRE), and Layer 2 tunneling protocol (L2TP). QoS functions manage network congestion, prioritize the use of applications, and classify traffic.

You can install a Cisco IOS Firewall on Cisco VPN-enabled platforms to increase the scope of existing networks to VPNs. VPNs not only provide secure encrypted tunnels for transferring data, but also ensure that data is delivered safely and in time at destinations. They also provide a strong security layer between corporate portals and the Internet. Other advantages offered when the Cisco IOS Firewall is integrated together with a 7100 serial router are intrusion detection, bandwidth maintenance, service-level validation, and enhanced security.

Note   Authentication and authorization features of the Cisco VPN client software are also implemented by using Cisco IOS firewall authentication proxy feature.

Configuring alerts, event logging, and audit trails

The moment an intrusion is detected, an alert in the form of a syslog error message is sent to the central management console so that the network manager can immediately handle the threat. The audit feature uses the syslog to keep track of transactions, record timestamps, gather information about the source and the destination hosts, types of ports used, the time duration for which the session lasted, and the amount of data transferred during the session.

You can configure Cisco IOS Firewall alerts and audit trails, which allow more adaptable reporting and tracking of errors. You can configure the audit trail feature for Java blocking and modular tracking of specific CBAC-supported applications.

Cross-Reference   For details on configuring the audit trail of the Cisco IOS Firewall, refer to Chapter 8.

Managing firewalls

Firewalls can be efficiently and effectively managed from a central control by using the GUI-based management console, such as Cisco ConfigMaker 2.1. The management console also supports NAT and IPSec. The Cisco ConfigMaker 2.1 can be installed on Microsoft Windows 95, Windows 98, or Windows NT 4.0. As a wizard-based application, ConfigMaker is easy to install and configure. You can use it to configure networks of Cisco routers, hubs, switches, and various other network devices from a single computer.

Note   You can refer to www.cisco.com to get installation information on ConfigMaker.

Using Cisco IOS software with Cisco IOS Firewall

Both Cisco IOS software and Cisco IOS Firewall combine together to provide an effective security solution for the network. A secure solution consists of not only setting up and managing the firewall, but it must be an integrated component of the network itself. The Cisco IOS software allows managers to apply security policies as and when it grows. The Cisco IOS Firewall is interoperable with the Cisco IOS software. As a result, it supports Cisco IOS features, such as NAT and Cisco encryption technology and Cisco IOS IPSec. Hence, you can use Cisco IOS Firewall with other Cisco security solutions, such as VPN solutions to enhance security in your network.

Customers of Cisco IOS Firewall

The following people should set up a Cisco IOS Firewall:

✦ People who require a low-cost system of increasing the scope of their network. They must provide connections to branch offices and create intranets or extranets.

✦ People who need a single software program to take care of the organization's security, intrusion detection, VPN functionality, multiprotocol routing, user authentication, and authorization requirements.

✦ People who require additional security, such as with less-trusted partner networks.

✦ People who are service providers and want to set up a Cisco IOS Firewall as a firewall or router for providing services.

✦ People who have small or medium-sized businesses and need an economical router with firewall and intrusion-detection capabilities bundled with it.

✦ Organizations that need further security on their Internet connection.

✦ Organization requiring connections between remote branch offices and the corporate headquarters or the Internet.

✦ People who are currently using Cisco IOS but do not want another firewall platform.

✦ People who want to have firewall protection integrated with their network environment.

Cisco IOS IDS signature list

As discussed previously in this chapter, in signature-based detection the IDS compares the data packets transmitted over the network against a list of attack signatures. Here are some signatures on the Cisco IOS IDS signature list:

✦ 1000 IP options-Bad Options List

✦ 1001 IP options-Record Packet Route

✦ 1002 IP options - Timestamp

✦ 1003 IP options - Provide

✦ 1004 IP options - Loose Source Route

✦ 1005 IP options - SANET ID

✦ 2000 ICMP Echo Reply

✦ 2001 ICMP Host Unreachable

✦ 2002 ICMP Source Quench

✦ 2003 ICMP Redirect

✦ 2004 ICMP Echo Request

✦ 2005 ICMP Time Exceeded for Datagram

Cisco Secure Intrusion-Detection family

The Cisco Secure Intrusion-Detection family provides high-performance security solutions to a variety of environments — especially as a defense against denial-of-service (DoS) attacks, exploits, and misuse of network resources.

The benefits of Cisco Secure IDS family are as follows:

✦ Provides most platform options without compromising the benefits on an integrated system.

✦ Provides scalable sensing performance. Although Cisco Secure IDS 4230 supports performance up to 100 Mbps, IDS 4210 provides support up to 45 Mbps and is cost-effective.

✦ Does not impact network performance and is transparent to the end user.

✦ Offers comprehensive intrusion-detection capabilities against exploits, DoS attacks, and misuse.

✦ Provides an integrated solution. The IDS 4200 Sensors are packaged as plug-and-play solutions and IDS module is integrated within Catalyst 6000; both these solutions are fully integrated into the Cisco Security IDS management infrastructure for operational consistency.

✦ Offers a variety of management options, such as Windows-based Cisco Secure Policy Manager and Unix-based Cisco Secure IDS Director. It is also compatible with third-party management products, such as netForensics.

✦ Allows configuring to automatically terminate specific connections by changing ACLs on Cisco routers; Cisco Secure IDS supports proactive response facility.

Due to these aforementioned benefits, Cisco Secure IDS family has become a market-leading IDS product. It is now an accepted standard for organizations as well as service providers.

Cisco Secure Intrusion-Detection family consists of an IDS Catalyst 6000 security module and Cisco Secure IDS 4200 appliances. The following sections discuss these components.

IDS Catalyst 6000 security module

The IDS module allows network administrators to monitor the network traffic at the switches. It detects unauthorized activities on the network. IDS module allows network administrators to monitor the traffic flowing through the Catalyst 6000 family switches in the network. The IDS module can be deployed on Catalyst 6000 family chassis and has the following features:

◆ Provides real-time intrusion detection.

◆ Is cost-effective and has low cost of ownership.

◆ Does not impact switch performance. Instead it is a passive monitoring module that scans copies of data packets.

◆ Detects a wide range of security intrusions and attacks.

◆ Can be easily updated to include new signatures to detect intrusions, without affecting the switch.

◆ Can monitor network traffic on multiple VLANs simultaneously.

◆ Is simple to install, configure, and manage.

◆ Is interoperable with other Cisco Secure IDS devices and management consoles.

◆ Can monitor 100 Mbps of traffic and about 47,000 packets per second.

IDS Catalyst 6000 security module requires Catalyst Operating System Version 6.1 or higher and a policy feature card for VLAN ACL capture facility. The management platforms required by IDS Catalyst 6000 security module are Cisco Secure Policy Manager and Cisco Secure Intrusion Detection Director.

Cisco Secure IDS 4200 appliances

Cisco Secure IDS 4200 Sensor appliances have the following features:

◆ Easy to install

◆ Self-contained as they include both hardware and software and do not require electronic licensing

◆ Can be placed almost anywhere in the network, such as in front or behind the firewall or in internal network segments

◆ IDS 4210 supports performance of 45 Mbps; IDS 4230 supports performance of 100 Mbps

The system requirements for IDS-4210 Sensors are as follows:

◆ Celeron 566 MHz processor

◆ 256MB RAM

◆ Autosensing 10/100 BaseT Ethernet Network Interface Card

◆ Autosensing 10/100 BaseT Ethernet Command and control interface

The system requirements for IDS-4230 Sensors are as follows:

✦ Dual PIII 600 MHz processor

✦ 512MB RAM

✦ Autosensing 10/100 BaseT Ethernet Network Interface Card

✦ Autosensing 10/100 BaseT Ethernet Command and control interface

Summary

This chapter explained intrusion detection, discussed intrusion-detection systems (both network-based and host-based), analyzed some reasons behind network attacks and intrusions, and examined some network problems caused by a weak security policy. The chapter listed weaknesses in the TCP/IP protocol suite (both generally and in each layer) and outlined the Cisco security strategies — firewalls, encryption, authentication, and access lists. A discussion of intrusion-detection systems (in particular, a Cisco product that works at the level of the IOS) led into an examination of authentication proxy, detecting and preventing DoS attacks, using dynamic port mapping, and blocking Java applets. For more intense security needs, an outline of Cisco Secure IDS included common signatures found in the product's signature list.

✦   ✦   ✦

Securing
Networks

Part II describes campus security problems, approaches to securing the different parts of a network, and the best available methods for protecting networks from security threats. This part also examines the process of securing networks by using ACL and perimeter routers — and explains how to configure and implement current encryption technology.

Securing the Network Infrastructure

The lack of a proper security policy is often a factor in major security breaches — and their resulting damages. A coherent, consistent, well-documented security policy is an indispensable tool for maintaining the integrity of campus networks and reducing risks and losses associated with security threats.

The first realistic step toward establishing such a policy is to define the security goals of your enterprise network — and the most convenient approach is to use the *Open Systems Interconnection* (OSI) *Reference Model* (commonly called the *OSI model*) that the International Standards Organization created as an industry-standard definition of a network. Using it, you can address specific security concerns at the Physical layer, Data Link layer, Network layer, and Application layer.

Cross-Reference For more information on the OSI model, refer to Chapter 18.

The specific areas of an internal network that need maximum protection can vary from one company to the next. The proper degree of restriction to impose on user access to these areas is also unique to each company, as is the best way to filter network services. But the goal is (or should be) consistent: to prevent potential security breaches without unduly hampering productivity.

Any company that has Internet access must plan to implement proper security for the protocols by which most users commonly access the Net: SNMP and HTTP. You can use access lists and distribution lists to establish basic control over network traffic, permitting or denying specific host(s) across your network's routers and switches. If your organization has deployed these as a *campus*—a consistent information system that coordinates several local-area networks (LANs)—then you have some uniquely complex security issues to address.

This chapter provides an overview of the threats that target campus networks and offers methods of securing the campus environment by implementing physical security of network devices, securing administrative interfaces of network devices, managing secured router-to-router communications, and providing security to Ethernet switches.

Campus Security Problems

Cisco Systems provides products designed to ensure the security of campus networks. The most relevant features include capabilities for two key security measures:

✦ Controlling access to the administrative interfaces of network devices

✦ Securing the console port, virtual terminal lines, and auxiliary ports

> **Tip**
> Securing routers and switches secures the campus infrastructure; an unsecured router or switch is potentially a serious security hole. A wise administrator should investigate any possibility that the network is tapped at this level.

By default, Cisco products allow access to routers and switches through various means. As you formulate your network-security policy, consider all such access mechanisms and set security safeguards in place to counter potential attacks. Some security vulnerabilities that specifically threaten campus infrastructures are as follows:

✦ **Console and Telnet ports:** Allow users to log in to the network device to view and modify configuration files.

✦ **HTTP access to routers:** Can monitor and modify the configuration.

✦ **Router configuration files:** Can be modified by unauthorized access to the TFTP server on which they are stored.

✦ **SNMP information:** Can be captured to get network device configurations.

✦ **Routing updates:** Can be captured and modified by spoofing.

To secure the network infrastructure from all these potential threats, the following areas of the network need careful scrutiny and analysis for appropriate security measures:

✦ Physical devices

✦ Administrative interface

✦ Router-to-router communications

✦ Ethernet switches

Every security system has vulnerabilities. Be sure you understand your particular system's potential security holes and determine actions to reduce them. The entire network environment should have barriers at different points so intruders who access one part of the system can't automatically access the rest of the system. Avoid relying only on one type of technology (or one OSI layer) to solve all security problems; a more effective approach targets the special vulnerabilities of every layer.

Proper and timely auditing can help ensure the appropriate and consistent enforcement of your security policy. Check the audits periodically, with an eye toward modifying (as needed) not only your policy but also the implementation of your technology.

Securing the Administrative Interface

The *administrative interface* (also called the *management interface*) is, in effect, a storehouse of information about network devices such as Cisco routers and Ethernet switches. If an intruder can successfully access the administrative interface, it can become an illicit treasure trove; your device configurations are there for the taking. The intruder can also use Telnet and HTTP to access other network equipment. Ensuring proper security for administrative interface requires a checklist of security measures that include the following:

✦ Restricting and protecting console access

✦ Encrypting passwords

✦ Managing session timeouts

✦ Blocking all display of banner messages

✦ Managing Telnet access

✦ Controlling HTTP access

✦ Managing SNMP access

Protecting console access

Passwords should be assigned to every access point of every management interface — whether in-band (such as TFTP and VTY access) or out-of-band (such as console and auxiliary ports).

Note   A *console* is a terminal attached directly to the router through (logically enough) the console port. Its primary function on the network is to control the activities of servers.

In a classic example of default settings that an administrator must know about and change, *no passwords are assigned by default to the console.* As a basic and readily useful security measure, you should assign such passwords immediately. Then two more tasks complete the job:

✦ Configure console security so all users must be authenticated before they can log in.

✦ Ensure the physical security of the console port so intruders can't reset the password by password-recovery processes.

The console of a Cisco router has two modes of access:

✦ **User-level mode:** This is the default access mode. The user may execute certain commands but may not modify device configuration or use the debugging tool.

✦ **Privileged-level mode:** This mode is primarily for administrative use. At the privileged level, the user may issue commands to modify configurations or use the debugging tool.

To secure access to the router through the console port, you can set passwords for both these modes. Console passwords can range from 1 to 25 alphanumeric characters that can be either uppercase or lowercase.

User-mode passwords

To configure a console password in user mode, enter the following commands:

```
Router(config)#line console 0

Router(config-line)#login

Router(config-line)#password abc
```

In this configuration, the password abc is case-sensitive. When you log in to the router, it asks for verification before it allows user-mode access, using the following prompt:

```
User Access Verification

Password:
```

A user must enter the password abc (for example) to gain user-mode access to the router. The router response to a successful login looks like this:

```
Router>
```

User mode is signified by the hostname of the router followed by the > prompt. (The hostname is configured by the hostname global configuration command.) In user mode, you cannot change the configuration of the router.

Caution   For best results, never use cisco or other obvious words as passwords.

Privileged-mode passwords

You can access privileged mode from the user mode by typing the enable command at the router prompt. If privileged mode has no password already in place, then it's operating under the default setting—and you can gain access to it without using a password at all (convenient, yes, but appalling from a security standpoint). Set a password for privileged mode by using either the enable password command or the enable secret command.

Using the enable password command

The syntax for the enable password command is

```
Router(config)#enable password [level level] {password | [encryption-type]
encrypted-password}
```

where

+ level sets the privilege level for which the password applies.

+ password sets the password for users to enter the enable mode.

+ encryption-type is a proprietary Cisco algorithm you can select and use for encrypting the password. (The only value currently available for this parameter is 7.)

+ encrypted-password is the password itself, in encrypted form.

Tip   When you specify encryption type, the user must supply the encrypted password to get access.

Cisco enables 16 levels of user access (ranging from 0 to 15) to the administrative interface of a device. These levels range from 0 to 15. Level 1 is the default user EXEC privilege. Privilege level 15 provides full access to the device. Level 0 can be used to define a subset of the EXEC-level privilege. Levels 2 to 14 can be used to customize user-mode privilege levels. At other privilege levels, the commands to be used must be specified (by default, every user is given privilege level 15).

You can configure the privileged-mode console password by entering the following sequence of commands:

```
Router(config)# enable password xyz
```

In this case, the password is xyz. When you access privileged mode from user mode, the router asks for the enable password by displaying

```
Router>enable

Password:
```

After you enter the password as xyz, the following prompt appears.

```
Router#
```

Privileged mode is indicated by the hostname of the router followed by the # prompt. In this mode, you can enter all commands that govern viewing statistics; you can also configure the router by accessing various configuration modes. The enable password command stores the passwords in cleartext — you can view them easily by using the show running-configuration and show configuration commands. If necessary, you can use the enable secret command to encrypt the passwords so they cannot be viewed.

Using the enable secret command

The enable secret command automatically encrypts the password according to the MD5 hashing function. The syntax is

```
Router(config)#enable secret [level level] {password | [encryption-type]
encrypted-password}
```

where

   ✦ level can have any value from 0 to 15.

   ✦ password sets the password for users to enter the enable mode.

   ✦ encryption-type is the Cisco proprietary algorithm by which the password can be encrypted. The only available value for this parameter is 7.

   ✦ encrypted-password is the encryption password.

The enable secret command is available in Cisco IOS Software versions 10.0(9), 10.2(5), 10.3(2), and later versions.

Setting privilege modes

The Cisco IOS command set provides a range of privilege levels for users; you set them by using the privilege level command. (Either the enable password or enable secret command, when used in conjunction with the privilege command, can provide better access control when you specify different levels.) The syntax is

```
Router(config)#privilege mode {level level command | reset command}
```

where

   ✦ reset: serves to reset a designated command of the privilege level.

   ✦ mode: specifies various privilege command modes.

For example, to set a password for a level-4 user and give that user two specific rights — to execute the `ping` command and view the running configuration — enter the following sequence of commands:

```
Router>enable

Router#config terminal

Router(config)#enable password level 4 pwd

Router(config)#privilege exec level 4 ping

Router(config)#privilege exec level 4 show running-config

Router(config)#end
```

The valid modes for the privilege command are as follows:

- controller
- configuration
- hub
- exec
- interface
- ipx-router
- line
- map-class
- map-list
- route-map
- router

Encrypting passwords

By default, passwords are stored in cleartext form in the router's configuration except for the enable secret password. Passwords can easily be observed by viewing the executing or saved configuration. Two ways to secure passwords exist: using the enable secret password (which only secures the privileged-mode password) or by using the `service password-encryption` command.

The `service password-encryption` command stores all the passwords in an encrypted form so anyone viewing the router configuration would not be able to determine the configured passwords. Although encryption is helpful, it can be compromised and thus should not be the only password-security strategy. Syntax for the `service password-encryption` command is

```
Router(config)#service password-encryption
```

This command encrypts the cleartext `enable` password so it appears as a string of characters in the router-configuration files. The command also works for passwords that govern other functions and components such as VTY ports, consoles, usernames, and passwords.

To disable this feature, use the following command:

```
Router(config)#no service password-encryption
```

Passwords already encrypted using the `service password-encryption` command remain encrypted even after this feature is disabled.

Managing session timeouts

Setting the login and enable passwords may not provide enough security in some cases. The use of automatic logout mechanism ensures that if a terminal is left connected or unattended after a user has finished work, no one can use it and modify the configuration. A timeout for an unattended session provides additional security. You can change the login timeout by using the command `exec-timeout` *mm ss*, where *mm* is minutes and *ss* is seconds. The sequence of commands looks like this:

```
Router(config)#line console 0

Router(config-line)#exec-timeout 2 10

Router(config)#line  vty 0 4

Router(config-line)#exec-timeout 5 30
```

In this code, the session would timeout if the console were left unattended for 2 minutes and 10 seconds. The Telnet session would be disconnected if left unattended for 5 minutes and 30 seconds.

Using banner messages as greetings and indicators

You can use a banner message as a greeting for a user, an indicator of who is allowed to access the system, or as a warning against unauthorized entry.

Tip   If using a banner as a *keep out* sign seems redundant, consider: Hackers have been acquitted of unauthorized entry because a network administrator used a friendly message-of-the-day banner that was legally construed as a welcome into a system. Although such an interpretation may vary with the laws of a particular state or country, a good rule of thumb is to study the relevant laws before you set your message—and then *say exactly what you mean.*

The syntax of the command that configures the banner is

```
Router(config)#banner {exec | incoming | login | motd} delimiter message-text
delimiter
```

where

+ exec specifies that the banner message is displayed during an exec process, such as console and VTY.

+ incoming specifies that the banner message is displayed during connection to an asynchronous line.

+ login displays a banner message before the username and password during login.

+ motd specifies that the banner is the message of the day and is displayed at login.

+ delimiter specifies any delimiting character.

+ message-text specifies the message text to be displayed.

The banner message is defined as text between two delimiter characters. The delimiter can be any character — but it can't be used within the message text.

Controlling Telnet access

In addition to connecting through the console port, users may want to connect to the router remotely using the Telnet utility. Both the user mode and the privileged mode can be accessed on the router through Telnet. As with the console port, Telnet security is provided when users are prompted by the router to authenticate themselves by using passwords.

A Telnet port on a router is also called a *virtual terminal* because it emulates the function of a terminal. By default (on most Cisco routers), the Telnet port is dedicated to VTY communications, handling five virtual-terminal (VTY) lines that allow up to five users to access the device simultaneously.

On the router, ports that can handle VTY transactions are numbered from 0 through 4 — but an administrator has no way to determine which VTY line a particular user is actually using. Therefore, setting identical access restrictions on every VTY line ensures consistency of access.

To configure your VTY lines, follow these steps:

1. Using Telnet, access your router.

   You enter user mode by default.

2. Enter your privileged-mode password and press Enter.

You enter privileged mode. Here you can encrypt passwords and specify time-outs for Telnet sessions.

3. Set a timeout for your VTY lines.

For example, to give your VTY lines with a password def and a timeout of 2 minutes, enter the following commands:

```
Router#configure terminal

Router(config)#line vty 0 4

Router(config-line)#login

Router(config-line)#password def

Router(config-line)#exec-timeout 2 0

Router(config-line)#end
```

Now any login command given when the router is in line-configuration mode launches the password-checking feature. The sequence of commands shown in Step 3 modifies all five VTY lines (the second command specifies VTY lines 0 through 4). When a user Telnets to a router's IP address, the router does not provide immediate access but instead displays a prompt similar to the one shown in Figure 4-1.

```
% telnet router

Trying. . .

Connected to router.

Escape character is  ' ^ ] ' .

User Access Verification

Password:
```

Figure 4-1: Using Telnet to access a router

The user now has the user-mode access to the router and can enter the privileged mode by entering the enable command.

You can secure the access to VTY lines by using access-list and access-class commands. These commands allow access to virtual lines from specific hosts or a group of hosts. The access-class command applies the access list to the line. A standard access list can be defined to permit or deny specific IP addresses. The following sequence of commands shows an access list that permits incoming Telnet connections only if they come from the 172.16.1.0/24 subnet:

```
Router(config)#access-list 2 permit 172.16.1.0 0.0.0.255

Router(config)#line vty 0 4

Router(config-line)#access-class 2 in
```

The following configuration shows an access list applied to AUX and VTY lines.

```
Router(config)#access-list 1 deny 0.0.0.0 255.255.255.255

Router(config)#access-list 2 permit 192.168.1.2

Router(config)#line aux 0

Router(config-line)#access-class 1 in

Router(config-line)#line vty 0 4

Router(config-line)#access-class 2 in
```

The preceding commands would deny all inbound Telnet access to the auxiliary port. However, they would allow Telnet access to the router only if the packet comes from IP address 192.168.1.2 on VTY lines.

 Cross-Reference Access lists are covered in detail in Chapter 5.

Terminal Access Controller Access Control System (TACACS) provides a way to authenticate users on an individual basis before they can gain access to the router or the communication server. It is defined in RFC 1492. It controls the user access to the router in the user mode and privileged mode.

A TACACS server runs on a Unix workstation and is for Authentication, Authorization, and Accounting (AAA) services. When authentication via TACACS server is enabled, the router prompts the user for a user-name and a password. The router, after querying the TACACS server, allows the user to log in after supplying the correct username and password.

The tacacs-server host command designates the Unix host running the TACACS server to authenticate users. Multiple TACACS servers can also be specified for a single router.

Authentication failures would occur if none of the TACACS servers are available because of some configuration problem or failure. In such a situation, use the following command to give your users access:

```
tacacs-server last-resort [password | succeed]
```

The keyword succeed allows the user to log in to the router with no password. The keyword password serves to force the user to supply the standard login password.

The following configuration allows the user to log in without a password *only* when host 192.168.1.1 is designated as the TACACS server:

```
Router(config)#tacacs-server host 192.168.1.1
Router(config)#tacacs-server last-resort succeed
```

To force users to access the router through Telnet and authenticate themselves by using TACACS, enter the following configuration commands:

```
Router(config)#line VTY 0 4
Router(config-line)#login tacacs
```

The TACACS server can also provide support for the Token Card system. The Token Card system relies on a physical card to provide authentication. The TACACS server code can be modified to provide support for this system. You need not make any changes to the setup or configuration to support a Token Card system.

Managing HTTP access

The Cisco IOS software release 11.0(6) and later has the capabilities of a Web server for configuring network devices. Access to the Web interface can be restricted in the same way as VTY lines.

HTTP access should be secured properly after it is enabled. It is disabled by default. You can easily monitor a router — and modify its configuration — by using the Cisco Web-browser interface. The command used to enable the HTTP server is

```
Router(config)#ip http server
```

Password security for Web access is similar to console and VTY lines. Authentication information can come from various sources: an AAA server, the enable password, the local user database, or the TACACS server. The command that does the job looks like this:

```
Router(config)#ip http authentication {enable | aaa | local |
tacacs}
```

where

+ enable: serves to enable password authentication.

+ aaa: is the AAA server that authenticates the user.

+ local: is the local database where the username and password have been specified.

+ tacacs: is the TACACS server that provides authentication.

As with VTY lines, you can limit remote connections by specifying an access class that defines a standard access list. To enable connections from the 172.16.1.0/24 subnet, for example, use the following commands:

```
Router(config)#access-list 2 permit 172.16.1.0 0.0.0.255

Router(config)#ip http access-class 2
```

Controlling SNMP access

Simple Network Management Protocol (SNMP) is an Application layer protocol. It is a part of the TCP/IP protocol suite and facilitates the exchange of management information between SNMP agents and managers. It enables network administrators to manage network performance, find and solve network problems, and plan for network growth. The basic components of an SNMP-managed network are as follows:

✦ **Managed devices:** These contain the SNMP agent that collects and stores management information and makes this information available to Network Management Systems (NMSs) by using SNMP. For example, network devices such as routers, switches, and hubs could be managed devices if an SNMP agent is installed on them.

✦ **Agent:** This is network-management software that resides in a managed device and translates the local management information into an SNMP-compatible form.

✦ **Network-Management System (NMS):** This serves to communicate with agents in managed devices to get statistics and alerts. It is an SNMP management application.

Figure 4-2 shows the three components of an SNMP-managed network.

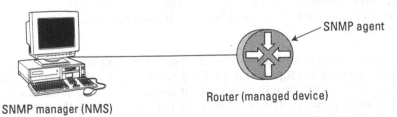

Figure 4-2: A network with a topology optimized for SNMP

 An intruder can use SNMP to learn — and change — device configurations *and internal network topology.* The intruder can easily access Management Information Bases (MIBs) by using the SNMP discovery tool or by capturing SNMP messages.

Basic SNMP commands include `read`, `write`, and `trap`, as well as commands that govern *traversal operations* (an NMS method of determining which variables a managed device supports and gathering that information into tables). The `read` command monitors managed devices such as routers, on which the SNMP agent is installed. The `write` command controls managed devices. The SNMP manager uses both these commands. Managed devices use the `trap` command to send asynchronous reports of events to the SNMP manager.

In addition to the `trap` command, the `inform` request can also be used as an SNMP notification of events. Traps are unreliable because the receiver does not send any acknowledgment on receiving a trap. However, inform requests are reliable because the SNMP manager sends an acknowledgment on receiving this request from an agent. If the agent does not receive the acknowledgment, it will resend the `inform` message.

SNMP Management Information Base (MIB) is a hierarchical collection of information. It consists of managed objects and is identified by object identifiers. An *object identifier* uniquely identifies a managed object in the MIB hierarchy.

The following versions of SNMP are supported by Cisco IOS release 12.0:

✦ **SNMP version 1 (SNMPv1):** It is described in RFC 1157 and operates over protocols, such as UDP, IP, CLNS, AppleTalk, and IPX. The network-management system issues a request, while the managed devices return responses.

✦ **SNMP version 2 (SNMPv2):** It is an evolution of SNMPv1. In addition to `Get`, `GetNext`, and `Set` operations used in SNMPv1, it has some enhanced protocol operations such as modified SNMPv2 `Trap`, `GetBulk`, and `Inform` operations.

SNMP has no authentication capabilities of its own, which leaves it vulnerable to security threats. Thus, an unauthorized entity can assume the identity of an authorized management entity and attempt to perform management operations. An unauthorized entity may attempt to alter a message generated by an authorized entity. This may result in unauthorized accounting management. When an unauthorized entity reorders, delays, or copies (and then replays) a message generated by an authorized entity, modifications in the sequence and timing of the message may occur.

SNMP uses the get-request and get-next-request messages to gather statistics and set-request messages to configure routers. Each message possesses a *community string*, a cleartext password sent in every packet between a management station and the SNMP agent (router). The community string authenticates the messages sent between the manager and agent.

The agent will respond only after receiving a message with the exact community string configured from the manager. SNMP has various access levels — including read-only (`ro`), which allows reading of MIBs, and read/write (`rw`), which allows both reading and writing to MIBs. You can configure more than one community string on your router by using the following command:

```
Router(config)#snmp-server community string [ro | rw] [access-list-number]
```

where

- *string* configures community string.
- ro allows only read access to MIBs.
- rw provides both read and write access to the SNMP agent.
- *access-list-number* specifies the list of IP addresses that may use the community string and gain access to the agent.

The SNMP agent on the router enables you to configure different community strings for nonprivileged and privileged access. Nonprivileged access allows users on a host to send SNMP get-request and SNMP get-next-request messages to the router. Privileged access allows users on a host to send router SNMP set-request messages.

To provide nonprivileged access to routers, use the ro option like this:

```
Router(config)#snmp-server community string ro
```

To provide privileged access to the routers, use the rw option like this:

```
Router(config)#snmp-server community string rw
```

To specify a list of specific IP addresses permitted to access an agent via the community string, use the following command:

```
Router(config)#access-list 10 permit 192.168.1.1

Router(config)#access-list 10 permit 192.168.1.2

Router(config)#snmp-server community private rw 10
```

This command grants privileged-mode access to the router to only two hosts — 192.168.1.1 and 192.168.1.2 — and the community string remains private. Granting nonprivileged access to a public community string requires the following sequence of commands:

```
Router(config)#access-list 10 permit 192.168.1.1

Router(config)#access-list 10 permit 192.168.1.2

Router(config)#snmp-server community public ro 10
```

Because SNMP community strings are sent on the network as cleartext (in ASCII format), always use the no snmp-server trap-authentication command. An intruder may capture SNMP packets to discover the SNMP community string; from there they can easily query your router — or even change your router configuration. The no snmp-server trap-authentication command prevents intruders from sending trap messages between SNMP managers and agents (as they would have to do to discover community strings).

The SNMP agent sends a `trap` message to an NMS when an event occurs. The event could be any defined condition. The router should send SNMP traps only to hosts identified or designated as NMS systems.

The following command allows the router to send trap messages only to NMS hosts:

```
Router(config)#snmp-server host host trap
```

The following command allows the router to send `inform` messages only to the NMS hosts:

```
Router(config)#snmp-server host host informs
```

Protecting the Physical Devices

A user can misuse any physical device in many ways, such as extract information out of a secured connection, break the connection, or introduce unnecessary traffic on the network. Almost all network devices have some mechanism to bypass the access password, and if a device is physically accessible, an intruder may be able to reconfigure the device. For example, a password breaking mechanism for almost all Cisco devices makes them prone to unauthorized access. A security policy is of little use without physical security for network devices. Physical security should, therefore, be the first and the primary step in securing a campus network. Your organization should have a physical security policy in place for every device on your network.

You can physically secure a network by developing a checklist from the following items and applying it to all your network devices:

✦ Formulating a security plan for each site that details how the device and links will be secured. To ensure physical security, implement regular security audits and careful monitoring.

✦ Making provisions for locking the room, proper ventilation, temperature and humidity controls, and backup power supply.

✦ Planning for adequate physical security, which can consist of door lock combinations and security alarms.

✦ Controlling authorized entry or access to rooms by using identification cards.

✦ Physically securing the rack in which the actual network device is placed.

✦ Setting up access passwords for the device and disabling ports such as an auxiliary port if they are not in use.

✦ Providing the security for the wiring closet. A lot of damage can be done in a short span of time by unauthorized access to a wiring closet.

Securing Router-to-Router Communications

Several router-to-router communications are susceptible to eavesdropping, resulting in problems such as invalid routing updates and unauthenticated data access. Such problems can have severe security implications. Router-to-router communications can be secured by

✦ Configuring file security

✦ Routing protocol authentication

✦ Controlling traffic using filters

Configuration-file security

Trivial File Transfer Protocol (TFTP) is the most commonly used protocol to upload and download configuration files stored in routers. These configuration files are stored on the TFTP server. Any unauthorized person, who can access the TFTP server, can modify these configuration files. The file transfer process during the TFTP operation is also susceptible to eavesdropping.

Since TFTP does not require any authentication password, it is not a secure protocol. Port-scanning software can detect the TFTP server; be sure to enable or disable TFTP software manually. Protecting — and limiting access to — TFTP servers is vital, especially when they contain router configuration files. Cisco IOS supports uploading and downloading of router configuration files through File Transfer Protocol (FTP) also. FTP is preferred over TFTP since it authenticates each user before connecting. If you are using a TFTP server to copy configuration files through SNMP, be sure to use the following command so it sends the copied files only to the servers specified in the access list:

```
snmp-server tftp-server-list number
```

Authenticating your routing protocols

Routers exchange routing information with the neighboring routers by using routing protocols. This functionality is prone to eavesdropping and spoofing. Essentially, the wrong routing updates can be introduced from unauthenticated sources, causing routing problems.

Cisco IOS software has features to prevent the spoofing of routing updates. One way to prevent spoofing of routing updates is by authenticating the routing updates to verify that the routing information has come from a valid and authorized source. This would prevent any unauthorized and unknown source from generating false routing updates. This is also called *neighbor authentication*.

During neighbor authentication, the receiving router authenticates the source router for each routing update message received. For this, an authenticating key or signature is configured and exchanged on both the source and destination router. Figure 4-3 explains the neighbor authentication process.

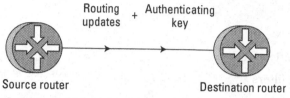

Figure 4-3: Neighbor router authentication

In Figure 4-3, the routers A and B are configured for the routing protocol authentication. Router A sends a routing update to B with an authentication key. Router B accepts the update after verifying the key with its configured value to ensure that the information is coming from a valid source and is not altered during the transmission.

Plaintext authentication and Message Digest 5 (MD5) are the two authentication methods supported by Cisco IOS release 12.0. The following sections discuss these authentication methods.

Plaintext authentication

In this method, an authenticating key is exchanged between neighboring routers (the key is configured on each of them). Some protocols allow multiple keys to be configured, where a unique key number identifies each key. For the protocols that use only one key, the key number is always 0.

The routing update sent from the source router contains the configured key and the key number. The receiving router verifies this key with its own configured key. The routing update is accepted if both the keys match. If the keys don't match, the update is rejected. Cisco IOS supports plaintext authentication for routing protocols such as IS-IS, OSPF, and RIP version 2.

However, plaintext authentication does have security vulnerabilities. Because the authenticating key is sent over the network, it can easily be captured with its packet during transmission — and there it is in plaintext for the hacker to read and use. A better option is to use MD5 authentication.

MD5 authentication

The MD5 authentication method does not send the key in plaintext over the network. Instead, it calculates its hash value by using the MD5 algorithm and sends the hash value (or message digest of the authentication key) over the network. Cisco IOS supports the MD5 authentication method for routing protocols, such as BGP, EIGRP, OSPF, and RIP version 2.

This authentication method is more secure than plaintext because the key is never sent on the wire minimizing the chances of eavesdropping during transmission (often done by discovering the key and modifying the routing updates).

Traffic control using filters

An access list is also called a *filter* because it controls router traffic by filtering (allowing or denying network access to) a specific group of IP addresses. It can be used to deny connections identified as security risks — and permit all other connections — or to permit only the connections considered acceptable and deny the rest. Access lists filter traffic according to the source address, source port number, destination address and destination port number, and specific protocols.

Routing updates filtering is done to control and prevent the exchange and propagation of routes. Cisco IOS software can filter the incoming and outgoing routing updates using distribute lists. Before processing a routing update, the router checks the routes within the update against the distribute list (if configured). If a distribute list is associated, the software checks the various statements in the list to find a match for the update. If a match occurs, the entry is processed while configuring. If no match for the entry occurs, the implicit denial at the end of the distribute list will cause the router to drop the received update message (or to send no update). If no filter is found associated with the routing protocol, the update is normally processed.

Route filtering can be done by defining a standard access list to permit or deny routes and by applying it to inbound or outbound routing updates. The command used to define a distribute list for outbound updates is

```
Router(config-router)# distribute-list {access-list-number | name} out [type
number | routing-process | autonomous-system-number]
```

The command used to define a distribute list for inbound updates is

```
Router(config-router)# distribute-list {access-list-number | name} in [type
number]
```

where

- ✦ *access-list-number | name* specifies a numbered or named standard access list to define the specific routes to be processed.

- ✦ in specifies the incoming routing updates.

- ✦ out specifies the outgoing routing updates.

- ✦ *type number* defines the outbound or inbound interfaces associated with the updates.

- ✦ *routing-process* specifies the routing process from which updates will be filtered. It can be either static or connected.

- ✦ *autonomous-system-number* specifies the autonomous system number.

Figure 4-4 shows an example of IP route filtering.

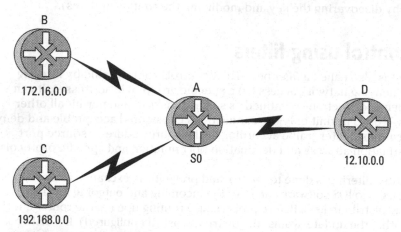

Figure 4-4: Network diagram showing IP route filtering (first example)

In Figure 4-4, a distribution list is applied at the serial 0 interface of router A. This distribution list only permits routing information for the network 192.168.0.0 from the router C through its serial 0 interface. Hence, it filters the network 172.16.0.0 from being revealed to the outer world. The configuration of router A is

```
Router(config)# access-list 1 permit 192.168.1.0 0.0.0.255

Router(config)# router eigrp 100

Router(config-router)# distribute-list 1 out serial0
```

Figure 4-5 shows another example of IP route filtering.

In Figure 4-5, a distribute list is applied at the serial 1 interface of the router D. This distribute list will only accept routing information for the network 192.168.1.0 from its serial 1 interface. Hence, it filters the network 172.16.0.0 from being accepted from the outer world. The configuration of the router D is

```
Router(config)# access-list 2 permit 192.168.1.0 0.0.0.255

Router(config)# router eigrp 100

Router(config-router)# distribute-list 2 in serial1
```

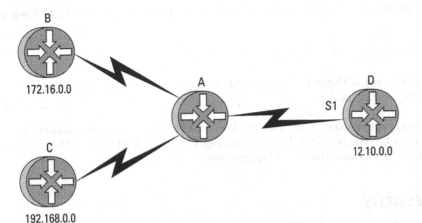

Figure 4-5: Network diagram showing IP route filtering (second example)

You can also control the routing of traffic by using the `passive-interface` command to prevent all routing updates from being sent through an interface. Although the interface can still receive updates, it can't send them. The command that does the job looks like this:

```
Router(config-route)# passive-interface type number
```

Securing Ethernet Switches

Security management on switches controls unauthorized access so sensitive information cannot be accessed without appropriate authorization. This may include

   ✦ Access control

   ✦ Port security

   ✦ Access security

Controlling access to Ethernet switches

To set the access password for the normal (`login`) mode, use the following command:

```
Switch(enable) set password
```

To set the privileged (enable) mode or administrator password, use the following command:

```
Switch(enable) set enablepass
```

After you enter any of these commands, the switch will prompt you to enter the password to be configured.

IP access lists can be used to control the limited Telnet access on the switch. To control access to switches with the set authentication and set authorization command, you can configure the AAA features.

Port security

Port security is a feature of Cisco Catalyst switches that enable the switch to block packets that enter a port if the source MAC address does not match the allowed MAC address configured on the port. This is known as the MAC address lockdown. Secured ports restrict the use of a port to a user-defined group of stations. The number of devices on a secured port can range from 1 to 132. By default, the switch allows all MAC addresses to access the network. A network administrator can configure a set of allowed devices or MAC addresses for additional security by using the port security feature.

There are two methods to configure port security on a switch: static and dynamic. In *static* configuration, you enable the port by manually entering the MAC addresses. This is the more secure method of configuration—but difficult to manage because you have to enter the MAC addresses manually. In the *dynamic* configuration, the first source MAC address learned on a particular port becomes secure and is the only allowed MAC address for that port. All other source MAC addresses are restricted. When a source address assigned to another secure port is received on a secured port or when the port tries to learn an address that exceeds its address table size limit, address violation occurs. The action can then be suspended, ignored, or disabled. After the port is suspended, it is re-enabled when a packet containing a valid address is received. If this action is ignored, the switch ignores the security violation and keeps the port enabled. When a port is disabled, the administrator must manually enable it. The address-violation global configuration command specifies an action for a port-address violation. The default action is to suspend.

You can configure port security on the set-based devices as follows:

```
Switch(enable) set port security mod/ports {enable | disable} [mac-addr]
```

If mac-addr is not supplied, it signifies a dynamic configuration. Supplying the optional mac-addr signifies static security configuration. To view the security settings, use the following command:

```
Switch(enable) show port security mod/ports
```

On Cisco IOS-based devices, only dynamic port security is available. The following commands configure port security and make it available for viewing:

```
Switch(config-if)#port secure [max-mac-count count]

Switch#show mac-address-table security
```

Access security

You can control access to a network switch by using any combination of authentication methods — for example, Local, RADIUS, TACACS+, and Kerberos authentication. The incoming Telnet and SNMP access can be restricted using IP permit lists.

> **Note** Outbound Telnet, TFTP, and other IP-based services are unaffected by the IP permit list.

The *IP permit list* is a security mechanism that provides network authentication and authorization. If TACACS is enabled on a network, it provides a first level of checking based on a source IP. Once enabled, the IP permit list authorizes Telnet access and SNMP services only for the IP addresses of the hosts configured on the permit list. SNMP traps and syslog messages notify unauthorized access attempts.

You can enable either the SNMP permit list or the Telnet permit list, or both lists. If you do not specify SNMP or Telnet, both the SNMP and Telnet permit lists are enabled. Up to 10 entries can be configured in a permit list. The commands that define and enable a permit list look like this:

```
Switch(enable) set ip permit ip-addr [mask]

Switch(enable) set ip permit enable
```

By default, the IP permit list feature is disabled; make sure it's disabled before you clear the permit entries or host addresses. Doing so keeps the switch you are configuring from dropping the connection if you clear your current IP address. The following commands disable and clear an IP permit list:

```
Switch(enable) set ip permit disable

Switch(enable) clear ip permit ip-addr

Switch(enable) clear ip permit ip-addr mask snmp

Switch(enable) clear ip permit ip-addr telnet

Switch(enable) clear ip permit all
```

The following command verifies an IP permit list:

```
Switch(enable) show ip permit
```

Case Study

The following case study depicts how to configure routers to protect an organization from internal threats.

Scenario

AllSolv, Inc. must configure campus routers to prevent its network from internal threats. Figure 4-6 shows the positioning of campus routers R1 and R2 in the network of AllSolv, Inc.

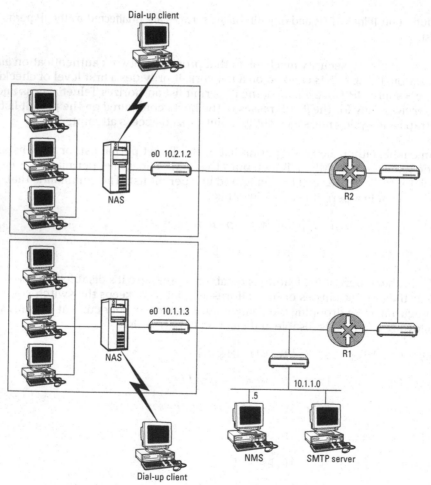

Figure 4-6: Router positioning in the network of AllSolv, Inc.

The network-security policy also highlights the following points:

✦ Appropriate session timeouts should be configured to exit the EXEC mode on idle sessions.

✦ Console and Telnet access should be secured.

✦ Control and secure router-to-router traffic.

Keeping these points in mind, the network administrator decides to configure routers R1 and R2.

Sample configuration

The following code is the sample configuration for router R1.

```
service password-encryption
no service udp-small-servers
no service tcp-small-servers
hostname R1
```

The `service password-encryption` **command encrypts the console and Telnet passwords:**

```
enable secret 5 $2$w2s6$3a4JHKnvBm5bQcb5TrXd1
enable password 7 16489230345012
line VTY 0 4
login
password 7 3rtyup2
ip host modem 2002 10.1.1.3

interface FastEthernet0
ip address 10.1.1.3 255.255.255.0
ip access-group 101 in
no mop enabled
```

The commands just given apply access list 101 to incoming traffic on the interface.

```
interface Serial0
physical-layer async
ip address 10.2.1.3 255.255.255.0
ip tcp header-compression passive
encapsulation ppp
bandwidth 40
async mode interactive
peer default ip address pool classpool
no fair-queue
no cdp enable
```

To secure router-to-router communications, the transmission of RIP routing updates should be permitted and routers should be configured to protect the identity of internal hosts to the dial-up clients.

The following commands are used to permit the transmission of RIP routing updates and to prevent the identity of internal hosts from being viewed by the dial-up clients.

```
router rip
network 10.0.0.0
distribute-list 21 out Ethernet0
distribute-list 22 out Serial2
distance 2

ip local pool classpool 10.1.2.2 10.1.2.15
ip classless
access-list 20 permit 10.1.1.5

access-list 22 deny 10.1.0.0 0.0.255.255
```

To allow only the network management server to read and write SNMP messages, use the following command:

```
access-list 25 permit 10.1.1.5
```

To discourage unauthorized users, you can create a banner message for your router that clearly spells out a *keep out* message. Use the following command:

```
banner motd ^C Unauthorized users not permitted ^C
```

To configure session timeouts to exit EXEC mode on idle sessions, use the following command:

```
exec-timeout 5 0
```

Summary

This chapter examined the various threats to a campus network. Although campus security problems — and their solutions — are specific to each institution's network, implementing security in four general areas can be useful in all cases: physical devices, the administrative interface, router-to-router communications, and Ethernet switches.

✦   ✦   ✦

Securing Networks Using ACL

Cisco IOS provides policy-based routing by using *access-control lists* (also known as *access lists*) to filter the packets that pass through a router. Access lists can be configured to handle all routed network protocols (for example, IP, IPX, and AppleTalk) and to filter the packets delivered under those protocols. Access lists can also keep certain traffic from entering (or exiting) a network. This chapter discusses IP access lists in particular.

Policy-Based Routing

Most organizations today deploy high-performance internetworks to meet their business requirements. Inevitably, however, such deployment leads to a considerable increase in security threats; the internetworks use public networks to transmit data, and the public always includes at least some potential attackers. Implementing customized security policies has thus become the price of doing e-business. Policy-based routing allows network administrators to implement security policies that require data packets to take specific routes. Hence, network administrators can use policy-based routing to implement routing and packet forwarding according to the security policy of the organization.

Policy-based routing is a flexible and efficient method for routing data packets. It allows implementation of routing policies to permit or deny packets according to the following criteria:

> ✦ **Address of an entire network:** Use this criterion when you want to permit or deny packets coming from a specific network.

✦ **Application:** Use this criterion when you want to permit or deny packets coming from a specific application.

✦ **Protocol:** Use this criterion when you want to allow or deny the use of a specific protocol.

✦ **Size of packets:** Use this criterion when you want to allow or deny packets according to their size.

Some primary benefits of policy-based routing are as follows:

✦ **Source-based selection of transit providers:** You can route packets originating from specific users through different Internet connections.

✦ **Ensuring quality of service (QoS) to network traffic:** You can not only assign different routes to specific data packets at the periphery of the network, but also control the network queue by prioritizing the data packets it contains.

✦ **Dynamic load sharing:** You can distribute network traffic to multiple paths according to your policy specifications.

✦ **Cost-effective use of network bandwidth:** You can distribute interactive traffic over low-bandwidth paths and batch traffic over high-bandwidth, switched paths.

Normally you apply policy-based routing only to incoming packets. When packets reach an interface that has policy-based routing in place, the interface filters packets by using *route maps* — sets of commands that control and modify routing information. Each entry in a route map contains `match` and `set` commands. The `match` command defines match criteria for the packet; the `set` command defines how the packet should be routed if the match criteria are met (the following sections of the chapter focus on the `match` and `set` commands). Thus the entries in a route map give a packet its route to the next hop.

The match command

A `match` command defines the criterion that must be met for the set command to be effective. Using the `match` command, you can specify match criteria based on source address, application, protocol type, precedence, and (if necessary) a packet size between specified minimum and maximum values.

The set command

A `set` command defines how to route or forward a packet if a match occurs. The `set` command defines this routing or forwarding according to criteria specified in the `match` command — and evaluates the criteria in the order shown in the following list:

✦ **Interfaces through which the packet can be routed:** If more than one interface is specified, the packet is routed through the first interface found working.

✦ **IP addresses of the adjacent hop:** Specifies the next address used to forward the data packet toward its destination.

✦ **Default interface:** Specifies a default interface that would be used to route the data packet if it has no specified interface for that purpose. If more than one default interface is specified, the packet is routed through the first one found working.

✦ **Default IP addresses of the adjacent hop:** Specifies the default IP address of the adjacent hop (toward the destination) that would be used to forward the data packet if the IP address of the adjacent hop is not explicitly specified.

✦ **IP TOS:** Serves to specify the type of service that must be set in the IP packets.

✦ **IP precedence:** Serves to set the precedence in the IP packets.

Note   One route map can contain more than one set of `match` and `set` combinations. In each combination, however, all matches must occur before the route map applies the `set` command.

Cisco IOS software supports the use of access lists to implement policy-based routing. The following sections discuss access lists in detail.

Overview of Access Lists

Although an *access list* is a simple tool—a list of statements that control access to resources (both to and from network segments)—it's also a powerful aid to security. It can filter unwanted packets (which helps control packet movement through the network) by placing specific limits on network traffic and restricting network use by certain users or devices. Access lists are a vital means of implementing an organization's security policies; in effect, they challenge and identify network traffic.

Even so, access lists can't do anything by themselves; the way you apply them defines their purpose. If you apply them to an interface, you can block undesired packets from entering or leaving the router—or permit only the desired packets to enter or leave the router. If you apply access lists to routing tables, they filter routes. All an access list really indicates to the router is whether a particular packet is of interest. A packet could attract such attention if its source has to be blocked, if its destination must not be allowed access, or if it is carrying specified information.

An access list has two main uses:

✦ Permit or deny network access to packets moving through the router

✦ Permit or deny Telnet (VTY) access to or from the router

Other uses are as follows:

✦ Define interesting traffic for dial-on-demand routing

Note "Interesting traffic" simply means any traffic you want to monitor.

✦ Route the filtering in routing updates

✦ Define traffic for priority and custom queuing

Although an access list may consist of several statements in a sequence, each statement must consist of two parts:

✦ **Test condition:** Defines the characteristics that a packet should have to match with the statement.

✦ **Action:** Defines the action to be taken on the packets that satisfy the test condition. Action can be one of two types:

   • **Permit:** Allows the packet to proceed

   • **Deny:** Blocks the packet

After an access list is created, it can be applied in one of two ways:

✦ **As an inbound access list:** It filters incoming traffic. When a data packet reaches the router, the router checks the source address of the data packet against the access list. If the access list permits the source address, the router processes the data packet. However, if the source address is not permitted by the access list, the router rejects the data packet and sends a host unreachable message.

✦ **As an outbound access list:** It filters outgoing traffic. In this case, after receiving and routing the data packet to the controlled interface, the router checks the source address of the packet against the access list. If the access list permits the source address, the router processes the data packet. However, if the source address is not permitted by the access list, the router rejects the data packet and sends a host unreachable message.

Access-list operations

The sequence of events that occur when a routable packet arrives at the interface of a router is as follows:

1. After receiving the packet at the interface, the router checks the inbound interface to see whether an inbound access list is applied there. If so, then the packet is tested against the statements of the inbound access list and Step 2 follows; if not, Step 3 follows.

2. If the result of the packet's test of the access list is deny, then the packet is dropped. If the result is permit, Step 3 follows.

3. The router identifies the destination address of the packet and scans the routing table for the destination network address. If there is no entry for the destination network address, the packet is dropped. If the router finds an entry (which can be a default route) for the destination network address, then the router finds the outbound interface for the entry and Step 4 follows.

4. The router checks whether the outbound interface has an outbound access list applied to it. If it does, the packet is tested against the statements in the access list for a match and Step 5 follows. If the outbound interface has no access list, Step 6 follows.

5. If the result of the test is deny, the router drops the packet. If the result is permit, then Step 6 follows.

6. The router sends the packet from the outbound interface.

This sequence of steps is illustrated in Figure 5-1.

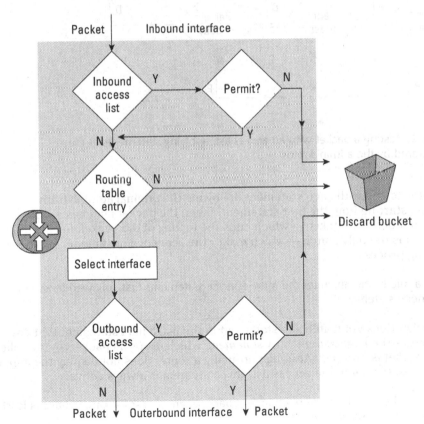

Figure 5-1: A diagram of access-list operations

If an access list contains several statements, they appear in the order in which the administrator entered them (as shown in Figure 5-2).

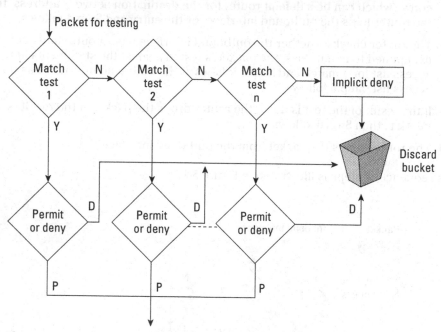

Figure 5-2: Testing a packet with an access list, applying statements in the order entered by the administrator

A packet is tested with each statement, following the original administrative sequence, starting from the first statement. When the packet matches a statement, the action it defines is taken — which ends the testing of the packet. In effect, the first match is the only match — which makes the sequence of statements crucial for the testing process.

Tip   As a rule of thumb, enter the more specific statements first, followed by the more general statements.

If the packet does not match any statement in the list, a final statement that covers all packets — the *implicit deny any statement*, which drops all packets — is applied and the packet is dropped. Although normally a router does not display the implicit deny any statement in the access list, this statement is always active.

Tip   To avoid inadvertent loss of important packets, any access list should have at least one permit statement.

Depending on a company's specific security policy, it can use one of two strategies to provide security:

✦ **Deny some and allow the rest:** If you want to deny access to some networks and grant it to the rest, then enter all your `deny` statements first. Then, enter a `permit all` statement to allow the rest of the networks access.

✦ **Permit some and deny the rest:** If you want to allow access to certain networks and deny it to the rest, then simply enter the `permit` statements. Any network not among those specifically permitted is automatically denied.

Note   For more information on access lists, refer to `www.cisco.com`.

Guidelines for implementing access lists

Some general principles can help you successfully implement access lists:

✦ **You can apply an access list to multiple interfaces.** Remember, however, that you can use *only one access list per protocol per interface per direction.* For example, if one access list handles TCP/IP outgoing packets sent from the outbound interface, a different list must handle TCP/IP incoming packets received at the inbound interface.

✦ **When you organize your access list, enter the more specific statements first, followed by the general statements.** For example, you can spell out the addresses you want to permit or deny, and then enter general rules that apply to all other addresses.

Note   When you add a statement, the router puts it at the end of the access list (but before the implicit `deny any` statement).

✦ **Every access list should have at least one `permit` statement.**

✦ **Create your access list before you apply it to an interface.** Applying an access list before you specifically create it permits all traffic on the interface.

✦ **An access list filters only the traffic going through the router.** It does not act on packets originating from the router.

Tip   Actually, an access list *can* filter some packets that originate from the router — in particular, its own routing updates and any Service Advertisement Protocol packets created in IPX. Applying access lists to VTY lines can also filter Telnet packets that originate from the router.VTY

Basic commands for configuring access lists

Configuring an access list requires two main steps:

✦ **Create and define the access list in global configuration mode.** You assign a number to the access list, define the permit or deny actions to be taken, and define the test conditions. You may define several statements in an access list.

✦ **Apply the access list to an interface or to a command line.** To do so, you use (respectively) either *interface configuration mode* or *line configuration mode.* You can apply the list as either inbound or outbound.

The command for creating and defining an access list is as follows:

```
Router(config)#access-list access-list-number {permit|deny} {test-condition}
```

where

✦ *access-list-number* is the number assigned to the access list (it also indicates the type of list).

✦ permit|deny is a keyword defining the action to be taken if a packet satisfies the test condition. The *test-condition* could be as simple as checking for a source address or as complex as checking specific protocols and socket numbers.

Caution

Plan carefully before you configure a numbered access list — because if you want to modify the list, you can only append statements. If you want to delete specific statements, you have to delete the entire access list — and then recreate it without the unwanted statement(s). This is not the case with named access lists, as discussed later in the chapter.

The command for applying the access list to an interface is as follows:

```
Router(config-if)#protocol access-group access-list-number
[in|out]
```

where

✦ *protocol* could be IP, IPX, AppleTalk, and so on, in or out terms define how the access list is applied. The in option specifies an inbound access list; the out option specifies an outbound access list.

✦ *access-list-number* identifies an access list uniquely. It also indicates the network protocol that the list filters. Each protocol suite has its own range of reserved numbers to identify the access list(s) that can filter its packets. Table 5-1 lists these ranges of reserved numbers.

Table 5-1
Reserved Number Ranges for Access Lists

Number Range	Type of List, Arranged by Protocol
1–99	Standard IP access lists
100–199	Extended IP access lists
200–299	Ethernet type code, as well as access lists that use source-route bridging protocols and transparent bridging protocols
300–399	DECnet and extended DECnet access lists
400–499	XNS access lists
500–599	Extended XNS access lists
600–699	AppleTalk access lists
700–799	Ethernet addresses, as well as access lists that use source-route bridging (vendor code) and transparent bridging (vendor code)
800–899	Standard IPX access lists
900–999	Extended IPX access lists
1000–1099	SAP Filter IPX access lists

To identify the software it must use to process the list correctly, the router uses the number given to the access list. (This chapter discusses only IP access lists.)

Although the access lists associated with most protocols are easy to identify by number, some protocols require that their access lists be identified by name. The following protocols impose this requirement:

✦ Apollo Domain

✦ ISO CLNS

✦ NetBIOS IPX

✦ Source-route bridging NetBIOS

Access-list operations are easier to gauge if you know the performance criteria that define an effective access list. As discussed earlier, ACLs are a sequence of permit and deny statements. When a data packet reaches a router, the router checks the rules in the access list until it gets the first match. This checking stops when the first match occurs. If no match is found, the deny end-rule is applied.

Tip   The entire sequence of checking involves processing—and affects the performance of your CPU. You can use various switching techniques to reduce the processing requirements of your access lists; even so, every access list inevitably imposes a per-packet performance cost.

TCP/IP Access Lists

Separate types of access lists filter the different network protocols. For example, two types of TCP/IP access lists filter IP (Internet Protocol) traffic:

✦ **Standard IP.** This type of access list filters according to source IP address and can do so for packets sent under any protocol in the entire TCP/IP suite. The reserved number range for standard IP lists is 1to 99.

✦ **Extended IP.** This type of access list can filter packets by source address, destination address, specific protocol, and the port numbers of both source and destination. The number range reserved for extended IP lists is 100 to 199.

Three more aspects of access lists require an introduction: IP addressing scheme, subnets, and subnet masking. The following sections discuss these in detail.

IP Address

The Internet address, or *IP address*, is the address assigned to a particular network and the hosts within that network. The IP address has two parts: the *network address* and the *host address*.

Format of an IP address

An IP address consists of 32 bits. These 32 bits are segmented into four octets of 8 bits each. The octets are converted to decimal numbers and separated by dots. This format of an IP address is known as *dotted decimal notation*. Each octet can have a value ranging from 0 to 255. Here is an example of an IP address in binary format:

```
10000000 00000010 00000111 00001001
```

The same address, converted to a dotted decimal notation, looks like this:

```
128.2.7.9
```

Classes of IP addresses

The Internet is a vast and complex environment that has equally vast potential for confusion; therefore the Internet Assigned Numbers Authority (IANA) formulated a hierarchy of IP addresses — Class A, Class B, Class C, Class D, and Class E — each of which has its own requirements and purposes. Using this structure, the Internet Network Information Center (InterNIC) assigns IP addresses to organizations. Any IP address must occupy one of the five classes designated by IANA.

Class D and Class E are reserved for multicasting and experimentation. The rest of the classes — Class A, B, and C — are assigned to public entities, schools, government, and organizations.

The class of an IP address determines which octets constitute its network address and host address. For Class A, the first octet represents the network address and the remaining three octets represent the host address. For Class B, the first two octets represent the network address and the remaining two octets represent the host address. For Class C, the first three octets represent the network address and the remaining one octet represents the host address. Upcoming sections take a closer look at the IANA address classes.

Class A addresses

The Class A addresses are usually reserved for governments worldwide. For Class A, the first octet represents the network address; the remaining three octets represent the host address. Class A addresses always begin with a zero when written in a binary format. For example, the first Class A address is

```
00000001.00000000.00000000.00000000
```

and the last Class A address is

```
01111110.0000000.00000000.00000000
```

In decimal format, these addresses contain numbers ranging from 1 to 126 in their first octet. In decimal format, the first Class A address is 1.0.0.0 and the last Class A address is 126.0.0.0.

Class A addresses use their first 7 bits for a network address and the remaining 24 bits for a host address. Thus the number of possible networks supported in a Class A address would be 2^7-2 or 126; the number of hosts supported would be $2^{24}-2$ or 16777214.

Although 127.0.0.0 should ideally be the last Class A address, it's actually assigned as a *loopback* address used to diagnose the network. (A familiar command that uses a loopback address is ping.).

Class B addresses

IANA assigns Class B addresses to medium- or large-scale organizations. For Class B, the first two octets represent the network address and the remaining two octets represent the host address. In a binary format, a Class B address begins with 10. Thus the first octet of a Class B address must have a minimum value of 128 and a maximum value of 191. A Class B address uses its first 14 bits as the network address and the remaining 16 bits as the host address.

Class C addresses

In binary format, a Class C address begins with 110. Thus the first octet of a Class C address has a minimum value of 192 and a maximum value of 223. For Class C, the first three octets represent the network address and the remaining one octet represents the host address. In Class C addresses, the first 21 bits are the network address; the remaining 8 bits are the host address.

Class D addresses

Class D addresses are reserved as multicast addresses. In binary format, Class D addresses begin with 1110. Therefore the first octet of a Class D address has a minimum value of 224 and a maximum value of 239.

Class E addresses

Class E addresses are reserved for experimentation purposes. In binary format, Class E addresses begin with 1111. Therefore the first octet of a Class E address starts with 240. As the last class of IP addresses in the IANA hierarchy, Class E addresses have no maximum value.

Note   In addition to being used for experimentation, Class E addresses are reserved for future use.

Subnetting

For better manageability, a network may be split into smaller networks, a process known as *subnetting*. The resulting smaller networks (called *subnets,* short for *subnetworks*) provide functional flexibility, more consistent network organization, and ease of optimizing network addresses — all of which helps control network traffic. Subnetting helps an organization attain a range of goals:

✦ **Reducing traffic over the network:** Subnets allow network administrators to significantly reduce network traffic. All subnets connect to each other via routers; thus subnetting leads to more routers on the network. Despite the greater complexity involved, this greater number of routers can boost efficiency and reduce traffic by blocking the *broadcasting* of messages (sending to all hosts on the network).

✦ **Meeting the needs of the organization's physical design:** Splitting the network according to the physical design of an organization can give each physical division the network resources it needs. For example, if an organization occupies seven floors of a building, then the network can be split into seven subnets.

✦ **Meeting the needs of a functional structure:** Splitting a network to match the functional structure of an organization — for example, one subnet per department — can help make data easier to access.

✦ **Meeting future needs:** As an organization grows, the network can reorganize accordingly into an appropriate number of subnets. For example, adding a department can routinely include creating a subnet for the new department.

Note   Subnetting a network is an internal process; it does not affect entities external to the organization, and subnets are not visible to external entities.

Of course, keeping the network consistently organized requires that the network's routers be able to differentiate between the address of a subnet and that of the host. Providing this distinction is a process called *subnet masking,* covered in the next section.

Subnet masking

Though an ordinary IP address consists of two parts (network address and host address), a subnetted network splits its IP addresses this way:

✦ Network address

✦ Subnet address

✦ Host address

Splitting the normal IP host address into subnet-and-host address requires a *subnet mask* — a 32-bit number used to differentiate the network address from the host address.

In subnetting, the IP address is divided into a network (or subnet) address and host address. Some sites use the term *local address* to mean *subnet address plus host address.* Regardless of the variations in terminology, a subnet mask differentiates between network address and host address by using the binary values of its bits:

✦ All bits set to 1 denote a network address.

✦ All bits set to 0 denote a host address.

Each class of IP address has a standard subnet mask:

✦ **Class A subnet mask:** InterNIC specifies the mask for the first octet of a Class A address: Setting all these digits to 1 denotes the network address; the subnet cannot use these bits. The standard Class A subnet mask looks like this:

• **In binary format:** 11111111 00000000 00000000 00000000

• **In decimal format:** 255.0.0.0

✦ **Class B subnet mask:** In Class B addresses, the first two octets are masked by InterNIC and are set to all 1s denoting the network address. The standard Class B subnet mask looks like this:

• **In binary format:** 11111111 11111111 00000000 00000000

• **In decimal format:** 255.255.0.0

✦ **Class C subnet mask:** In Class C addresses, the first three octets are masked by InterNIC and are set to all 1s. The standard Class C subnet mask looks like this:

• **In binary format:** 11111111 11111111 11111111 00000000

• **In decimal format:** 255.255.255.0

Basics of binary ANDing

The ANDing process uses the AND operator. In ANDing, comparing anything with 1 returns 1; comparing 0 with anything returns zero. (And that *is* the only "truth" you need to remember.) You can use a truth table to perform ANDing, as shown here.

Truth Table for AND

Binary Digit	Binary Digit	Result
0	0	0
0	1	0
1	0	0
1	1	1

One excellent use for the ANDing operation is in calculating the network address: ANDing the IP address (in binary form) with the subnet mask (in binary form) results in a network address, also in binary form.

TCP/IP hosts use the subnet mask to obtain the network address from the IP address. The operation that does so is called a *binary ANDing operation*.

What the computer does during a binary ANDing operation is compare bits. When both bits being compared are 1s, the result is a 1 — but for any other combination, the result is 0. Performing a binary ANDing that compares the IP address and the subnet mask results in a value for the network address. For example, consider the following IP address:

```
10000001 00111000 10111101 00101001
```

with the following subnet mask:

```
11111111 11111111 11110000 00000000
```

The binary ANDing operation results in the following network address:

```
10000001 00111000 10110000 00000000
```

Note The binary ANDing operation can also determine whether the addresses are on the same subnet or on different subnets. When a router receives a data packet, it performs the binary ANDing operation. Then it compares the network address of the received data packet with the sender's address. If the addresses match, then the data packet is sent to the local subnet; otherwise it is sent to the relevant gateway.

Subnet masking involves borrowing bits from the host ID. When the subnets are created, a certain number of bits are borrowed from the host ID. The number of bits borrowed determines the number of subnets and hosts available per subnet. For example, consider a Class B address 172.17.0.0. With the subnet mask 255.255.255.0 (the third octet being masked), 254 (2^8–2) subnets are available, with 254 hosts per subnet.

You can use Table 5-2 as a reference to help determine the number of subnets and hosts available for a Class B address — as well as the corresponding subnet masks.

Table 5-2
Reference for Determining the Number of Subnets and Hosts Available for a Class B Address

Bits	Subnet Masks	Subnets	Hosts per Subnet
2	255.255.192.0	2	16,382
3	255.255.224.0	6	8190
4	255.255.240.0	14	4094
5	255.255.248.0	30	2046
6	255.255.252.0	62	1022
7	255.255.254.0	126	510
8	255.255.255.0	254	254
9	255.255.255.128	510	126
10	255.255.255.192	1022	62
11	255.255.255.224	2046	30
12	255.255.255.240	4094	14
13	255.255.255.248	8190	6
14	255.255.255.252	16,382	2

For Class C addresses, the first three octets are masked; therefore only the last octet can be used. Table 5-3 shows the subnet masks for Class C addresses.

Table 5-3
Reference for Determining the Number of Subnets and Hosts Available for a Class C Address

Bits	Subnet Masks	Subnets	Hosts per Subnet
2	255.255.192.0	2	62
3	255.255.224.0	6	30
4	255.255.240.0	14	14
5	255.255.248.0	30	6
6	255.255.252.0	62	2

Wildcard mask

Security needs vary in complexity. Yours may (for example) require your router to filter packets by checking for specific hosts, a range of hosts, a subnet, range of subnets, a network, or a range of networks. Some mechanism is needed to tell the router which specific bits to check and which to ignore. The wildcard mask provides this mechanism.

A *wildcard mask* is a 32-bit notation divided into four octets, where each octet is represented in a decimal form. A bit can be either 1 or 0, and it indicates how the corresponding bit of the IP address should be treated:

✦ A wildcard mask bit 0 means *Check the corresponding bit of the IP address.*

✦ A wildcard mask bit 1 means *Ignore the corresponding bit of the IP address.*

Figure 5-3 shows how IP address bits are matched against the wildcard mask.

To check for a specific host, the administrator has to specify the host address in the access list and the corresponding wildcard mask, which is 0.0.0.0. This may be tedious. Cisco has given an abbreviation for this type of situation. You can use the keyword host along with the host address in place of host address and wildcard mask of 0.0.0.0. For a host 10.0.0.100, instead of entering 10.0.0.100 0.0.0.0, you can enter host 10.0.0.100.

A common condition is when you want to apply the same action regardless of the IP address. The IP address 0.0.0.0 indicates any IP address, and the wildcard mask 255.255.255.255 will ignore all bits. Therefore, no bits will be checked, and the action specified will be taken on all packets. Cisco allows the use of the keyword any in such situations. So, in place of entering 0.0.0.0 255.255.255.255, just type **any**.

Wildcard Masks

Bit position	128	64	32	16	8	4	2	1
Check all bits	0	0	0	0	0	0	0	0
Check first two bits	0	0	1	1	1	1	1	1
Ignore all bits	1	1	1	1	1	1	1	1

Wildcard Mask   0 . 0 . 255 . 255

IP address   A . B . C . D
      Check Ignore
      bits bits

Figure 5-3: Matching IP address bits with the wildcard mask

For example, suppose you want to test a range of subnets from 10.8.0.0/16 to 10.15.0.0/16 that would be permitted or denied. The task is to find a wildcard mask to match the specified subnets. Figure 5-4 shows the wildcard mask that would accomplish this.

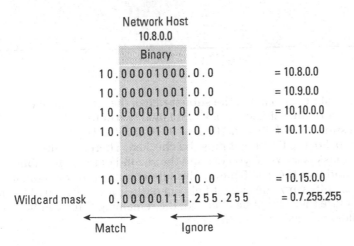

Address and Wildcard mask: 10.8.0.0   0.7.255.255

Figure 5-4: Determining the wildcard mask

Wildcard mask or inverted subnet mask?

Although a wildcard mask is often referred to as an inverted subnet mask, there is a significant difference between the two.

You can calculate inverted subnet masks by using the following formula:

```
Inverted subnet mask=local broadcast-subnet mask
```

For example, if the subnet mask is 255.255.172.0 and the local broadcast is 255.255.255.255, then the inverted subnet mask would be 0.0.83.255.

The following list shows wildcard masks and their corresponding subnet masks.

Wildcard Masks and Their Corresponding Subnet Masks

Wildcard Mask	Subnet Mask
255	0
252	3
248	7
240	15
224	31
192	63
128	127
0	255

Since all hosts of each subnet also fall in the subnet range, the host bits of the subnets are ignored. Therefore the wildcard mask has a final two octets of 255.255. To determine whether a subnet lies between 10.8.0.0/16 and 10.15.0.0/16, the first octet should be 10. So, the first octet must be checked. Therefore, the first octet of the wildcard mask is 0. When you expand the second octet of all subnets in a binary format, you find that the first 5 bits of the subnet range are common. In addition, if any of these bits vary, the subnet falls out of the range 10.8.0.0/16 to 10.15.0.0/16. Therefore these must be checked; the remaining three can be ignored. Thus the wildcard mask is 0.7.255.255.

Standard IP access lists

The two steps involved in configuring a standard IP access list are as follows:

1. Create and define the access list by using the command

```
Router(config)#access-list access-list-number {permit|deny}
source-addr [source-mask]
```

where

- *access-list-number* identifies the list. It is a number from the range 1 to 99.
- permit|deny specifies whether the matching packets should be blocked or allowed to proceed.
- *source-addr* identifies the source IP address.
- *source-mask* identifies the wildcard mask for the source IP address. The default wildcard mask is 0.0.0.0.

2. Apply the access list to an interface using the command

   Router(config-if)#ip access-group *access-list-number* [in|out]

   where

   - *access-list-number* identifies the access list to be applied.
   - in|out specifies whether the access list is applied as inbound or outbound. If neither is specified, the default is out.

Only one access list per protocol per interface per direction is allowed.

The following sections illustrate how to configure standard IP access lists.

Configuring standard IP access lists to block network traffic

Using the network shown in Figure 5-5, the task is to block all traffic from network 172.16.7.0/24 to 172.16.5.0/24.

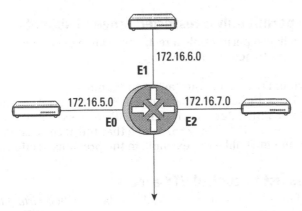

```
Router (config) #access-list 1 deny 172.16.7.0.0.0.0.255
Router (config) #access-list 1 permit 0.0.0.0.255.255.255.255
Router (config) #interface ethernet 0
Router (config-if) #ip access-group 1 out
```

Figure 5-5: Configuring an access list to block all traffic from network 172.16.7.0/24 to 172.16.5.0/24

The following list highlights the key parameters from the command sequence shown in Figure 5-5:

✦ 1 is the access list number indicating that it is a standard IP access list.

✦ deny indicates that the matching packets will be blocked.

✦ 172.16.7.0 is the source IP address.

✦ 0.0.0.255 is the wildcard mask for the source IP address, indicating that only the first three octets should be checked.

✦ 1 in the second statement indicates that it is the next statement of access list 1.

✦ permit in the second statement indicates that the matching packets should be permitted.

✦ 0.0.0.0 indicates the source IP address (in this case, any IP address).

✦ 255.255.255.255 indicates the wildcard mask for the source IP address. (In this case, the address is an instruction that signifies *Ignore all bits*.) You can get the same result by using the keyword any instead of the combination 0.0.0.0 255.255.255.255.

✦ ip access-group 1 out applies access list 1 to the interface Ethernet 0 as outbound.

Tip

If you apply access list 1 on interface Ethernet 2 as inbound, the router blocks all packets coming from network 172.16.7.0 — regardless of whether they are destined for 172.16.5.0 or for any other network. Therefore, the router will block network 172.16.7.0 for all networks. So, the router should be placed on Ethernet 0.

Configuring access list to permit only a restricted range of subnets

The task is to configure access list to permit only a restricted range of subnets (10.8.0.0/16 to 10.15.0.0/16) to access the Internet.

The network diagram is shown in Figure 5-6. Your task is to permit only subnets 10.8.0.0/16 to 10.15.0.0/16 — the same subnet range as in the example in the wildcard mask section — to access the Internet. The source IP address and the wildcard mask combination is 10.8.0.0 0.7.255.255. Notice that the access list does not have the permit all statement (unlike the example in the previous section).

Using a standard IP access list to control VTY access

A router has not only physical interfaces, but also virtual interfaces called *virtual terminal lines* (VTYs). By default, a router has five VTY lines, numbered from VTY 0 through 4. These VTY lines are used to telnet to the router. You can apply standard IP access lists to these VTY lines to secure them against unauthorized Telnet access.

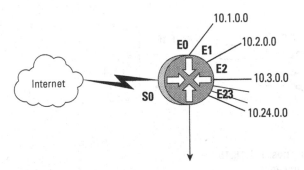

Router (config) #access-list 10 permit 10.8.0.0.0.7.255.255
(Implicit deny any statement - not visible)
Router (config) #interface serial 0
Router (config-if) #ip access-group 10 out

Figure 5-6: Configuring an access list so it permits only specific subnets to gain Internet access

To control VTY access, follow these steps:

1. Create and define a standard IP access list, using the command described earlier. This list consists of one entry: the IP address of the host, which is of interest to you.

> The host may be of special interest if it is either the source or the destination of the telnet session.

2. Apply the access list to the VTY lines using the following commands

   ```
   Router(config)#line VTY 0 4
   ```

   ```
   Router(config-line)#access-class access-list-number [in|out]
   ```

   where

   - *access-list-number* is the number of the standard access list created in Step 1.
   - The in option specifies that the access list will filter incoming sessions. The address specified in the access list will be treated as the source address.
   - The out option specifies that the access list must filter outgoing sessions initiated from the router. (The address specified in the access list is treated as the destination address.)

For example, consider the network diagram shown in Figure 5-7. You want to keep the router from initiating a telnet connection to host 172.16.16.1—thus you have to block the telnet connection initiated from router R1 for host 172.16.16.1.

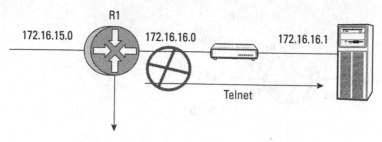

R1 (config) #access-list 10 deny host 172.16.16.1
R1 (config) #access-list 10 permit any
(Implicit deny any statement - not visible)
R1 (config) #line vty 0 4
R1 (config-line) #access-class 10 out

Figure 5-7: Network diagram for controlling VTY access

The Standard IP access list specifies the address 172.16.16.1. This access list is applied on all VTY lines for filtering outbound Telnet connections. Note that identical restrictions are applied on all VTY lines from 0 to 4 because you cannot control the VTY line to which a user will connect.

Extended IP access lists

Standard access lists provide broad security based on no more than the source IP address. In real life, you require more detailed security measures that conform to specific protocols, port numbers, and other factors. You can use extended IP access lists to attain this level of detailed implementation. *Extended IP access lists* check both source and destination IP addresses. In addition, they can filter packets according to specific protocols and optional TCP/UDP port numbers.

Well-known port numbers

For study or quick review, some well-known port numbers are given in Table 5-4.

Table 5-4 Well-known TCP/UDP Port Numbers	
Services	**Well-Known Port Numbers**
TCPMUX	1
NBP	2
ECHO	4
RJE	5

Services	Well-Known Port Numbers
ZIP	6
ECHO	7
USERS	11
DAYTIME	13
NETSTAT	15
QUOTE	17
MSP	18
CHARGEN	19
File Transfer Protocol (FTP) data	20
FTP Control	21
SSH	22
Telnet	23
Simple Mail Transfer Protocol (SMTP)	25
MSG-AUTH	31
DSP	33
TIME	37
RLP	39
GRAPHICS	41
NAMESERV	42
WHOIS	43
LOGIN	49
Domain Name System (DNS)	53
BOOTPS	67
BOOTPC	68
Trivial File Transfer Protocol (TFTP)	69
GOPHER	70
FINGER	79
WWW	80
HOSTNAME	101
X400	103
Remote telnet	107

Continued

Table 5-4 (continued)

Services	Well-Known Port Numbers
POP-2	109
POP-3	110
RPC	111
Network News Transfer Protocol	119
Network Time Protocol	123
NetBIOS Name Service	137
NetBIOS Datagram Service	138
NetBIOS Session Service	139
IMAP2	143
Simple Network Management Protocol (SNMP)	161
SNMP-TRAP service	162
CMIP-MAN	163
CMIP-AGENT	164
XNS-COURIER	165
Border Gateway Protocol	179
IRC	194
SMUX	199
AppleTalk-Routing Management Protocol	201
AppleTalk-Name Binding Protocol	202
Quick Mail Transfer Protocol	209
IPX	213
Unix List Server	372
Simple Network Paging Protocol	444
SSMTP	465
SAFT	487
EXEC	512
LOGIN	513
PRINTER	515
TALK	517
TEMPO	526

Services	Well-Known Port Numbers
CONFERENCE	531
NETWALL	533
WEBSTER	765
RSYNC	873
SOCKS	1080
Internet Cache Protocol	3130
MYSQL	3306
FAX	4557
BBS	7000
WWW Caching Service	8080
TPROXY	8081
ISNDNLOG	20011
Address Search Protocol	27374

Configuring an extended IP access list

To configure an extended IP access list, follow these steps:

1. Create and define the access list by using the following command:

```
Router(config)#access-list access list-number {permit|deny}
protocol source-addr source-mask [operator port] destination-
addr destination-mask [operator port] [established] [log]
```

where

- *access-list-number* identifies the list using a number from the range 100 to 199.

- permit|deny specifies the action to be performed on the packets that match the access list.

- *protocol* can be TCP, UDP, ICMP, GRE, or IGRP.

- *source-addr* and *source-mask* are the source IP address and the wildcard mask for source address.

- *destination-addr* and *destination-mask* are the destination IP address and the wildcard mask for the destination address.

- *operator* can be less than (lt), greater than (gt), equal to (et), or not equal to (neq).

- *port* specifies the protocol port number.

- established is a keyword to use for inbound TCP sessions only. It allows TCP traffic to proceed if the packet uses an established connection.

- log is a keyword that sends a login message to the console when a packet violates the access list.

Note   In TCP, an established connection has an ACK bit set.

2. Apply the access list to an interface using the following command, which is the same as that used in applying a standard IP access list to an interface:

```
Router(config-if)#ip access-group access-list-number [in|out]
```

The following example illustrates configuring an extended IP access list.

Consider the network diagram shown in Figure 5-8. You have to block all FTP traffic from network 172.16.7.0/24 to network 172.16.5.0/24. Therefore your task is to block all FTP packets with the source network 172.16.7.0/24 and the destination network 172.16.5.0/24.

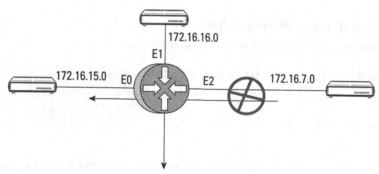

```
Router (config) #access-list 101 deny top 172.16.7.0.0.0.0.255 172.16.5.0
0.0.0.255 eq 21
Router (config) #access-list 101 deny top 172.16.7.0.0.0.0.255 172.16.5.0
0.0.0.255 eq 20
Router (config) #access-list 101 permit ip any any
Router (config) #interface ethernet 2
Router (config-if) #ip access-group 101 in
```

Figure 5-8: Configuring an extended access list to block all FTP traffic from network 172.16.7.0/24 to network 172.16.5.0/24

Tip   FTP uses two TCP ports, 20 and 21. Port 20 is for FTP data and 21 for FTP control. You must block both.

The following list highlights the key points of the commands used to configure this extended access list:

✦ 101 is the number assigned to this access list. The number range reserved for extended IP access lists is 100 to 199.

✦ deny implies that the matching packets should be blocked.

✦ tcp indicates TCP protocol in the protocol number of the IP packet header. If the transport layer protocol is TCP, protocol number 6 in the IP packet header indicates this.

✦ 172.16.7.0 0.0.0.255 indicates the source address and the wildcard mask for the source address. The router compares the first three octets of the source IP address.

✦ 172.16.5.0 0.0.0.255 indicates the destination address and the wildcard mask for the destination address. The router compares the first three octets of the destination IP address.

✦ eq 21 specifies that the router should check for port number 21 of the destination.

✦ eq 20 specifies that the router should check for port number 20 of the destination.

✦ access-list 101 permit ip any any is the permit any statement. The first any is for the source; the second any is for the destination.

✦ ip access-group 101 in applies access list 101 on Ethernet 2 as inbound.

Guidelines for placing access lists

An access list controls traffic by filtering and eliminating unwanted packets. Thus you can reduce unnecessary traffic by appropriately placing access lists.

Note   Traffic denied access to a destination host should not be allowed to use network resources along the route from the source to the destination. This would be an inefficient implementation of your access list. The more efficient way to drop unwanted traffic is near the source of the traffic itself (which may not always be possible).

Consider the network in Figure 5-9. If you want to block the traffic from the source network to the destination network, you should choose and apply access lists. Be sure, however, to block only the traffic to the intended destination network; avoid disrupting traffic to the rest of the networks.

If you want to block traffic in this manner by using a standard access list, you would configure it to deny packets only by source network address. If you apply this access list on the E0 interface of Router A as inbound, all traffic from the source network is blocked — regardless of the destination. Therefore place the standard access list near the destination, at an accurate distance from the destination so only the traffic to the intended destination is blocked.

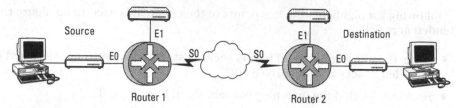

Figure 5-9: Configuring an access list to block traffic from the source network to the destination network

If you want to accomplish the same goal with an extended access list, configure it to check both source and destination address. If you apply this access list on interface E0 of Router A, you block only those packets from the source network that are destined for the destination network. As a result, you avoid blocking traffic for other networks. Place the extended access list in close proximity to the source.

Named IP access list

The *named IP access list* is a feature of Cisco IOS 11.2 and later versions. Instead of numbers, this type of access list is uniquely identified by its name.

Named access lists offer some distinctive advantages:

✦ You can name an access list to indicate the purpose of the access list.

✦ You can create a maximum of 99 standard IP access lists and 100 extended IP access lists. However, named access lists have no such restrictions.

✦ You can delete specific statements from named IP access lists. This is not possible with numbered access lists. In numbered access lists, you need to delete the entire access list and recreate the access list with the required statements.

You must consider the following before implementing named IP access lists:

✦ This type of access list is available only in Cisco IOS versions 11.2 and later.

✦ Names are case-sensitive.

✦ Names should be unique.

To configure a named IP access list, follow these steps:

1. Create the named IP access list by using the following command:

```
Router(config)#ip access-list {standard|extended} name
```

where

- standard|extended specifies the type of access list, whether standard or extended.

- *name* identifies the access list.

2. Define the statements in the access list created in Step 1.

After executing the command in Step 1, the router enters configuration mode for the named access list; there you define the statements. The command is as follows:

```
Router(config-{std|ext}-nacl)#{permit|deny} {test condition}
```

To remove a statement, prefix the command with no in the same configuration mode:

```
Router(config-{std|ext}-nacl)#no {permit|deny} {test condition}
```

Tip You can remove specific statements because of the separate configuration mode.

3. Apply the access list to an interface by using the following command:

```
Router(config-if)#ip access-group name [in|out]
```

Dynamic Access Lists (Lock-and-Key Security)

Dynamic access lists are IP access lists dynamically created and filter IP protocol traffic. Normally you configure them using IP dynamic extended access lists — although you can also use them in combination with other standard and static extended access lists.

Dynamic access lists enable designated users whose IP traffic is normally blocked at the router to gain temporary access through the router: When a user first telnets to the router and is authenticated by the lock-and-key procedure, the extended IP access list takes on a temporary configuration that allows equally temporary access to the designated host. You can use various methods to do the authentication, such as TACACS+ or RADIUS.

In effect, a lock-and-key dynamic access list is user-based. After the extended IP access list allows temporary access to an appropriate user, the interface is reconfigured to its original state — and blocks the same traffic as before.

A dynamic access list provides the following security advantages over static access lists:

✦ It uses the challenge mechanism for the authentication of the user.

✦ It reduces the chances of security breach by network hackers.

◆ In several situations, it reduces the required processing power of routers for access lists.

◆ It simplifies management in large networks.

◆ The permissions are user-based, which enhances security.

Dynamic access lists are useful in situations where you want remote users to gain access to a host on your network. These users may connect to the network through the Internet or other unsecured networks. The authentication process eliminates the possibility of any unauthorized user entering the network. You can also limit the access of the network to the user to a specific time.

Another common situation where dynamic access lists is useful is when you want only a particular subnet or a subset of hosts on the local network to gain access to a host on a remote network protected by a firewall. In this situation, you should enable access to the remote host only for the set of local users' hosts.

Lock-and-key operation

The steps in the lock-and-key access-list operation are as follows:

1. The user starts a `telnet` session to a firewall router configured with dynamic access lists.

2. The router prompts for the password and performs user authentication, which may use TACACS+, RADIUS, or any other method. The user has to pass the authentication before the router allows temporary access to the designated host or hosts.

3. After the user is authenticated, the router terminates the Telnet session and creates a temporary entry in the dynamic access list to allow the user's host to gain access to the designated host or hosts.

4. The user gains access to the host permitted by the access list and exchanges data traffic.

Note   It is recommended that while creating dynamic access lists, you should configure timeouts, which may be idle timeout or absolute timeout for the dynamic access list. If no timeout is configured, the only way to get rid of a temporary access-list entry is to have the administrator delete it manually.

5. The router deletes the temporary access-list entry either when the configured timeout is reached or when the administrator manually deletes the entry. After this, access to the designated host is blocked again.

Cisco IOS releases prior to release 11.1 are not compatible with the lock-and-key access-list enhancements. Therefore, access lists saved with IOS prior to release 11.1

will not be interpreted correctly by releases 11.1 and later. As a result, you need to save the access lists again to use them with IOS releases 11.1 and later.

Dynamic access lists can affect the performance of the router in the following situations:

✦ When lock-and-key is triggered, the dynamic access list forces an access-list rebuild on Silicon Switching Engine (SSE). This momentarily slows down the SSE switching path.

✦ Dynamic access lists require idle timeout facility. Therefore, they cannot be SSE-switched. These entries must be handled in the protocol fast-switching path.

✦ As temporary entries in the access lists are created on user authentication, the access lists grow in size. Large access lists can degrade the packet switching performance of the router.

Configuring dynamic access lists

The steps to configure a dynamic access list are as follows:

1. Create and define the dynamic access list, which serves as a template and placeholder for temporary access-list entries. The command is

```
Router(config)#access-list access-list-number [dynamic
dynamic-name [timeout minutes]] {deny|permit} protocol
source-addr source-mask destination addr destination-mask
[precedence precedence] [tos tos] [established] [log]
```

where

- access-list-number is the number assigned to the access list. This is a decimal number between 100 and 199 or between 2000 and 2699. 2000–2699 is the expanded range of extended IP access lists.

- dynamic dynamic-name identifies the access list as dynamic access list and assigns a name to it.

- timeout minutes specify the absolute time in minutes for which the temporary access-list entry can remain in the dynamic access list. The default is infinite.

- deny|permit specifies the action to be taken on matching packets.

- protocol specifies the IP protocol, which may be TCP, UDP, ICMP, or IGMP.

- source-addr source-mask specifies the source IP address and wildcard mask for the source address.

- *destination-addr destination-mask* specify the destination IP address and wildcard mask for the destination address.

- precedence *precedence* specifies the precedence level of the packets to be filtered. It may have a value from 0 to 7.

- tos *tos* specifies the type of service value to be checked in the IP header of the packets for filtering. It can have a value from 0 to 15.

- The established keyword is valid only for TCP. It specifies that the router should allow the packets that are part of an established connection to proceed.

- The log keyword sends the console an informational logging message about the packet that matches with the entry.

2. Apply the dynamic access list created in Step 1 to an interface by using the command

   ```
   Router(config-if)#ip access-group access-list-number
   ```

3. Configure user authentication on VTY lines by using the following commands:

   ```
   Router(config)#line VTY {number|range}

   Router(config-line)#login tacacs
   ```

   or

   ```
   Router(config)#username name password password
   ```

   or

   ```
   Router(config-line)#password password

   Router(config-line)#login local
   ```

   where

   - login tacacs selects the Terminal Access Controller Access Control System (TACACS)-style user ID and password-checking mechanism.

   - username *username* password *password* specifies username and password for authentication.

   - password *password* specifies a password in the line.

   - login local configures local password checking.

4. Configure the VTY lines to create temporary access-list entries by using the command

   ```
   Router(config-line)#autocommand access-enable [host] [timeout
   minutes]
   ```

where

- host specifies that the router should allow access only for the host from which the Telnet session originated. If not specified, the router allows all the hosts on the defined network to gain access. The dynamic access list contains the network mask to be used for enabling the new network.

- timeout *minutes* specifies the idle timeout for the temporary access-list entry. If the access-list entry is not used within this period, it is automatically deleted and the user has to be authenticated again. The default timeout value is infinite. This value should be equal to the idle timeout set for the WAN connection.

The access-enable command creates a temporary access-list entry in a dynamic access list. Using the autocommand command along with this command causes the access-enable command to automatically execute when a user telnets to the router.

Consider the following points while executing the autocommand command:

✦ Use the autocommand command on VTY lines if you want to use the local authentication command. However, if you want to use the TACACS+ server for authentication, execute the autocommand command on the TACACS+ server as a per-user autocommand.

✦ All VTY lines should have the same configuration and restrictions. Configure all VTY lines with the same autocommand command.

✦ You need to define at least one timeout value out of absolute timeout or idle timeout to enable the deletion of the access-list entry after some time. If you configure both the timeouts, the absolute timeout should be greater than the idle timeout.

If both timeouts are not configured, the administrator has to manually delete the temporary entries by using the following command:

```
Router>clear access-template [access-list-number] [dynamic-name] [source]
[destination]
```

where

✦ *access-list-number* specifies the number or name of the extended access list from which the entry is to be deleted.

✦ *dynamic-name* specifies the name of the dynamic access list from which the entry is to be deleted.

✦ *source* specifies the source IP address in a temporary access-list entry to be deleted.

✦ *destination* specifies the destination IP address in a temporary access-list entry to be deleted.

At times, the administrator is required to create a temporary entry manually. The following command does so:

```
Router>access-template [access-list-number] [dynamic-name] [source]
[destination] [timeout minutes]
```

where

✦ *access-list-number* specifies the number assigned to the access list.

✦ *dynamic-name* specifies the name of the dynamic access list.

✦ *source* specifies the source IP address in the dynamic access list. All other attributes are inherited from the original access-list entry.

✦ *destination* specifies the destination IP address in a dynamic access list. All other attributes are inherited from the original access-list entry.

✦ *timeout minutes* specifies a maximum time limit for each entry within this dynamic list. This is the absolute timeout value, in minutes.

Configuration tips for dynamic access lists

Keep the following points in mind while configuring dynamic access lists:

✦ The router refers to only the first dynamic access-list entry defined in a dynamic access list. Therefore, do not create more than one dynamic access list for any access list.

✦ All named dynamic access-list entries should be globally unique within the configuration. Assigning the same dynamic-name to more than one access lists instructs the router to use the existing list.

✦ Configure telnet as the protocol in the extended access list, so that the user should telnet to the router to be authenticated before gaining access through the router.

✦ The only value replaced in the temporary entry is the source or destination address, depending on whether the access list was in the input access list or output access list. All other attributes, such as port, are inherited from the main dynamic access list.

✦ Each addition to the dynamic list is placed at the beginning of the dynamic list. You cannot specify the order of the temporary access-list entries.

✦ Temporary access-list entries are not written to NVRAM.

Consider the network diagram shown in Figure 5-10. You need to configure lock-and-key with local authentication. Also, you need to configure a dynamic access list such that User1 of the subnet 10.0.0.0 is authenticated. The user should be able to access host 10.1.1.100 on subnet 10.1.1.0 whenever required. The router should delete the entry if, after five minutes, User1 has not used the available access to host 10.1.1.100.

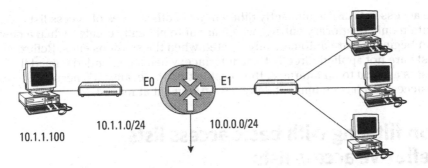

```
Router (config) # access-list 100 permit top any host 10.0.0.1 eq telnet
Router (config) # access-list 100 dynamic test permit ip any host 10.1.1.100
Router (config) # int el
Router (config-if) # ip address 10.0.0.1  255.255.255.0
Router (config-if) # ip access group 100 in
Router (config) # username user1 password userpwd
Router (config) # line vty 0  4
Router (config-line) # login local
Router (config-line) # autocommand access-enable host timeout 5
```

Figure 5-10: Configuring lock-and-key with local authentication

Figure 5-10 also shows the commands that can implement lock-and-key security with local authentication.

Reflexive Access List (IP Session Filtering)

If you allow the users on your network to access the Internet and you do not want any session to be initiated by anybody from the Internet, you need to ensure that packets received from the Internet are a part of a session initiated by an internal user. To accomplish this, you need the router to keep track of the side that initiated the session. Even if a packet coming from the Internet has the ACK bit set, it should be dropped unless it is a part of a session initiated from an internal network host.

Reflexive access lists allow IP packets to be filtered on the basis of upper-layer session information. You can use reflexive access lists to permit IP traffic for the sessions originating from within your network and to block IP traffic for the sessions originating from outside your network. Reflexive access lists can be defined with extended named IP access lists and not with numbered or named standard IP access lists. They provide a reasonable level of security against spoofing and certain denial-of-service attacks.

Reflexive access lists are significantly different from other types of access lists. They contain only temporary entries, which are automatically created when a new IP session begins and are automatically deleted when the sessions ends. Reflexive access lists are not applied directly to an interface; when an extended named IP access list is applied to an interface, they nest within it. Because it's nested, a reflexive access list has no implicit deny any statement at its end.

Session filtering with basic access lists and reflexive access lists

Session filtering in basic access lists occurs through the keyword established with the permit command. Using this keyword, the router checks the ACK or RST bit in the TCP header. If the ACK or RST bit is set, it is a part of an established session and is permitted to proceed by the router. However, this does not ensure that the session was initiated within the internal network. Thus, anybody from outside the network can send IP traffic with the ACK bit set and the router will allow such traffic. Moreover, this method is available only for TCP upper-layer protocols. For UDP and ICMP, you must define permissions separately.

Reflexive access lists match more filter criteria before permitting packets. Besides checking the ACK and RST bits, reflexive access lists also check the source and destination addresses. Moreover, they use temporary filters automatically created when the session is initiated from inside the internal network and removed after the session ends. This allows less time for hackers to operate.

Reflexive access lists operation

When a host from the internal network initiates an IP upper-layer session with outside network hosts, a reflexive access list is triggered. The reflexive access list creates a temporary entry, which permits traffic to enter the internal network only if it is a part of the session.

For example, if a host on your internal network initiates a UDP session with a host on the Internet, on receiving the first packet of the session from the internal host, it creates a temporary reflexive access list entry. This entry applies to the packets entering the internal network only. The temporary entry has the following characteristics:

✦ The temporary entry will test the packet arriving at the internal network, and the matching packets are permitted.

✦ The protocol permitted is the same protocol as the original outbound packet.

✦ The source address in the entry is the same as the destination address of the original outbound packet. The destination address is the same as the source address of the original outbound packet.

✦ The source port and destination port are the same as in the original outbound packet. The only difference is that the ports are swapped like the source and destination addresses. For other protocols that do not have port numbers, such as ICMP and IGMP, other criteria applicable to each are specified. In ICMP, type numbers are used.

✦ The entry expires and is deleted if the router detects no packet of the session for a configurable length of time, also called the time-out period. For protocols connection-oriented, such as TCP, the router deletes the entry on detecting the last packet of the session passing through the interface. For TCP sessions, the entry is removed either five seconds after two FIN bits are detected or immediately after matching the TCP packet with the *RST bit set*. An RST bit set represents an abrupt ending of a session.

Problems with FTP

Reflexive access lists do not work with those applications that use port number that change during a session. If an application uses different port numbers for return packets from the originating packets, the reflexive access lists do not allow them to enter the internal network.

For example, FTP uses two ports, port 21 for control functions and port 20 for data transfer. Consider a client located on the internal network and FTP server located on the Internet. The client opens a control session, using destination port 21 and a source port above 1023. The FTP server opens a data-transfer session with source port 20 and a destination port above 1023 (different from the source port that the client is using for the control session). Thus, for a reflexive access list, the data-transfer session is a *new* session initiated from outside the internal network.

The solution is to use passive FTP. In passive FTP, the server chooses its port for data transfer and informs the client. The client opens the data session to the FTP server, and then the FTP server transfers data. Thus the client initiates both the sessions.

Configuring reflexive access lists

The configuration of reflexive access lists depends on whether you want to apply the reflexive access list on the interface directly connected to your internal network, also called internal interface, or on the interface connected to the outside world, also called external interface.

Reflexive access list on internal and external interface

Putting a reflexive access list on an external interface prevents IP traffic from entering the router and the internal network unless the traffic is a part of a session initiated *from* the internal network. To configure a reflexive access list on an external interface, first define the reflexive access list for an external interface in an outbound IP extended named access list. Next, nest the reflexive access list within an inbound IP extended named access list. Finally, set the global timeout values.

The defined outbound reflexive access list evaluates traffic moving out of your network. If the defined reflexive access list is matched, temporary entries are created in the nested (inbound) reflexive access list. These temporary entries will then be applied to the traffic traveling into your network.

A reflexive access list on an internal interface blocks the external traffic to enter the internal network unless the traffic is a part of a session initiated from within your internal network. You will configure a reflexive access list on an internal interface if you are configuring a reflexive access list in a demilitarized zone topology. The external network can gain access to DNS servers, but they will not be allowed to initiate sessions to any host on the internal network. To configure a reflexive access list on the internal interface, first, define the reflexive access list in an inbound IP extended named access list. Next, nest the reflexive access list within an outbound IP extended named access list. Finally, set a global timeout value.

The defined reflexive access list evaluates the traffic traveling out of your internal network. If it finds a matching access list, it creates temporary entries to apply to the traffic traveling into the internal network.

Defining reflexive access list

You create an extended IP named access list by using the command

```
Router(config)#ip access-list extended name
```

where *name* specifies the name of the access list.

After entering this command, the router enters the named IP access list configuration mode. You define the reflexive access list in this mode by using the command

```
Router(config-ext-nacl)#permit protocol any any reflect reflex-
name [timeout seconds]
```

where

+ *protocol* could be IP, TCP, UDP, ICMP, GRE, or IGMP, or an integer in the range from 0 to 255 representing an IP number.

+ *reflex-name* specifies the name of the reflexive access list up to 64 characters long.

+ *timeout seconds* specifies the number of seconds to wait when no session traffic is detected before entries expire in this reflexive access list. The *seconds* can have value ranging from 0 to $2^{32}-1$. If not specified, the number of seconds defaults to the global timeout value.

Then, this access list may be applied (as inbound or outbound) to an interface by using the command

```
Router(config-if)#ip access-group name [in|out]
```

where *name* specifies the name of the named extended IP access list to be applied.

Tip   Apply the extended IP named access list as outbound to external interface and inbound to internal interface.

Nesting reflexive access list

After you define the reflexive access list, you must nest the reflexive access list within a separate extended IP named access list. After you nest the reflexive access list, the packets heading into your internal network can be evaluated against any reflexive access list temporary entries.

To nest and apply a reflexive access list, follow these steps:

1. Issue the following command

```
Router(config)#ip access-list extended name

Router(config-ext-nacl)#evaluate reflex-name
```

where

• evaluate *reflex-name* adds an entry pointing to the reflexive access list.

• *reflex-name* is a command that nests the reflexive access list inside an extended IP named access list.

The reflexive access list is now nested.

2. Apply the extended IP named access list to the interface in the following manner:

- Apply list as inbound if you are applying it to an external interface. Do so by using the following command:

  ```
  Router(config-if)#ip access-group name in
  ```

- Apply list as outbound if you are applying it to an internal interface. Do so by using the following command:

  ```
  Router(config-if)#ip access-group name out
  ```

The entire process of nesting a reflexive access list can be summarized in two general steps with explanations:

1. Define a reflexive access list in an extended named IP access list, which is applied on an interface.

   If the interface is internal, the access list is applied as inbound. If it is an external interface, the access list is applied as outbound. The purpose of this access list is to detect the packets that start a session from the hosts on the internal network to the hosts on the external network. As soon as it detects the first packet sent by an internal host to an external host to initiate a session, it creates a temporary entry in another extended IP named access list where you nest the reflexive access list.

2. Nest the reflexive access list in another extended IP named access list.

   This extended IP named access list can be applied on either external or internal interface in such a direction that it tests the packets coming from the external into the internal network. The temporary access list mentioned in Step 1 is created in this access list. This temporary entry checks whether the packets coming from the external network to the internal network are part of a session initiated by a host on the internal network. If these packets are not part of such a session, the packets are blocked.

Setting a global timeout value

The temporary entries in the reflexive access lists are removed after no packets in the session are detected for a certain period, called the timeout period. You can configure the timeout period for a reflexive access list while you are defining the reflexive access list. If you do not specify the timeout while defining the reflexive access list, the list will use the global timeout value.

The command to configure global timeout value is:

```
Router(config)#ip reflexive-list timeout seconds
```

where *seconds* specify the timeout in seconds. The default value is 300 seconds.

The following examples depict how to configure reflexive access lists.

Restricting access at the internal interface

Consider the network shown in Figure 5-11. The task is to configure the reflexive access list such that packets coming from an external network can enter network 10.0.0.0/24 (the internal network) only if they are a part of a session initiated by hosts on the internal network.

The router is connected to an internal network, the external network (Internet), and demilitarized zone (DMZ). The external hosts should not be able to initiate a session to the internal hosts, but they should be allowed to initiate a session that connects them to the hosts from the DMZ. For this reason, the reflexive access list is configured at the internal interface of the router.

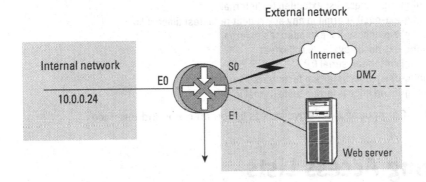

```
Router (config) # ip access-list extended testinternal
Router (config-ext-nacl) #permit ip any any reflect reflextest timeout 60
Router (config) #ip access-list extended testexternal
Router (config-ext-nacl) #evaluate reflextest
Router (config) #interface ethernet 0
Router (config-if) #ip access-group testinternal in
Router (config-if) #ip access-group testexternal out
```

Figure 5-11: Configuring a reflexive access list

Restricting access at the internal interface

Consider the network shown in Figure 5-12. The task is to configure a reflexive access list so packets coming from an external network may enter network 10.0.0.0/24 (the internal network) only if they are a part of a session initiated by hosts on the internal network.

This network is the same as in Figure 5-1 — except it does not have a DMZ. Because the router is connected to only the external and internal networks, the reflexive access list is configured on an outbound interface.

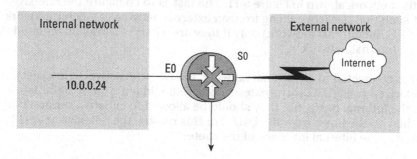

```
Router (config) # ip access-list extended testinternal
Router (config-ext-nacl) #permit ip any any reflect reflextest timeout 60
Router (config) #ip access-list extended testexternal
Router (config-ext-nacl) #evaluate reflextest
Router (config) #interface serial 0
Router (config-if) #ip access-group testinternal out
Router (config-if) #ip access-group testexternal in
```

Figure 5-12: Configuring a reflexive access list on an outbound interface

Monitoring Access Lists

You can monitor access lists according to protocol type. You can also monitor a specific access list by using its number or name, and you can view the access lists applied to an interface.

To view the access lists applied on an interface, use the command

```
Router#show ip interface intf-type intf-number
```

where

✦ *intf-type* specifies the type of interface, such as Ethernet, token ring, and serial.

✦ *intf-number* specifies the number of the interface.

Tip   You can't use the command

```
show interface intf-type intf-number
```

to display the access lists applied to the interface. Instead, use the following command:

```
show ip interface intf-type intf-number
```

Figure 5-13 shows the settings that apply access lists to an interface.

```
Router#show ip interface ethernet0
Ethernet0 is up, line protocol is up
Internetaddress is 172.16.6.1/24
Broadcast address is 255 255 255 255
Adress determined by setup command
MTU is 1500 bytes
Helper address is notset
Directed broad cast forwarding is disabled
Outgoing access list is not set
Inbound access list is 101
Proxy ARP is enabled
Security level is default
Splithorizon is enabled
ICM P redirects are always sent
ICM P unreachables are always sent
ICM P mask replies are never sent
IP fastswitching is enabled
IP fastswitching on the same interface is disabled
IP Feature Fastswitching turbo vector
<incomplete output>
```

Figure 5-13: Access lists applied to
an interface — correct settings

To view the statements in all access lists or a specified access list, use the following command

```
Router#show [ip] access-list [access-list-number|name]
```

where *access-list-number|name* specifies the number or name of the access list you want to view.

If you do not specify the access list number or name, the contents of all the access lists are displayed. If you do not specify IP in the command, the contents of all the access lists, whether they are IP, IPX, AppleTalk, or DECnet, are displayed.

Figure 5-14 shows the statements in the access list 101.

```
Router#show ip access-list 101
Extended IP access list101
 deny tcp host 172.16.5.1 host 172.16.6.1 eq telnet
 permit ip any any
```
Figure 5-14: Statements of an access list

Case Study

The following scenario depicts how to configure ACLs.

Scenario

According to the security policy of AllSolv, Inc. only the directors of the company should be able to access the confidential information on the server whose IP address is 10.0.2.100. The IP addresses of the computers used by directors are from 10.0.0.32 to 10.0.0.48. The network administrator has decided to configure an access list to accomplish this task. Figure 5-15 shows the network diagram of AllSolv, Inc.

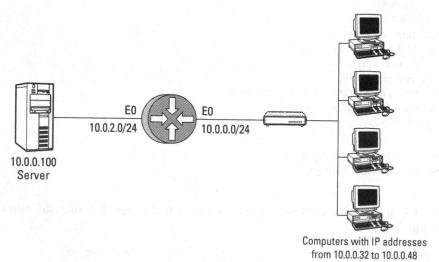

Figure 5-15: Network diagram of AllSolv, Inc.

Sample configuration

The IP address and wildcard mask to check the range of hosts from 10.0.0.32 to 10.0.0.48 are (respectively) 10.0.0.32 and 0.0.0.7. The two steps to configure the access list are as follows:

1. Create and define the access list:

   ```
   Router(config)#access-list 100 permit ip 10.0.0.32 0.0.0.7
   host 10.0.2.100
   ```

2. Apply the access list to the interface Ethernet E2:

   ```
   Router(config)#interface Ethernet 2
   Router(config-if)#ip access-group 100 out
   ```

Summary

Policy-based routing is a flexible and efficient method for routing data packets. This chapter explained how setting up policy-based routing helps reduce security threats in a network. To implement policy-based routing, you create and apply access lists, using guidelines discussed in this chapter. Access lists can be standard, extended, dynamic, and reflexive: The chapter explains each of these in detail and shows how to implement the various scenarios.

✦   ✦   ✦

Protecting Networks Using Cisco Perimeter Routers

CHAPTER 6

♦ ♦ ♦ ♦

In This Chapter

Fitting a perimeter router into your network-security strategy

Understanding and working with NAT

Implementing NAT operations

Configuring NAT

Verifying and troubleshooting NAT

Balancing the advantages and disadvantages of NAT

♦ ♦ ♦ ♦

Of prime importance in any network-security strategy is securing the *perimeter* — the logical and physical boundary where an internal network comes in contact with external networks such as the Internet. The perimeter is the entry point not only for data, but also for attacks on the network.

This chapter discusses the concept of the perimeter router, which is the first level in network security. After providing an overview on perimeter security, the chapter discusses the Network Address Translation (NAT) feature in Cisco routers. The chapter covers the basic concept of NAT, various types of NAT mappings, the configuration of NAT, and verifying and troubleshooting commands in NAT.

Perimeter Routers

Security is a major concern when you are using the Internet to connect to the outside world. Any such connection can mean exposure to the risk of intruders and hackers gaining entry. Therefore perimeter security — a process of segregating the internal network from the external network — is essential to the secure operation of your internal network.

To enable perimeter security by means of a perimeter router, you must first identify the inside and outside networks. The corporate network behind the firewall is the *internal* network; the network outside the firewall is the *external* network. The perimeter router acts as the first line of defense against any intrusion.

Define security parameters and policies before implementing the perimeter router. Various policies or considerations (such as determining the resources to be protected and the level of security required) must be kept in mind while implementing security on a network. Other factors that should be considered while implementing security are the size of the network and the budget allocated for network security.

Before securing your network and implementing perimeter security, analyze the sensitivity of the network and applications and know the type of incoming traffic. In addition, take into account all types of intrusions that could be harmful to your organization — which is particularly important for organizations that offer Web-hosting services, such as FTP or DNS.

Figure 6-1 illustrates perimeter security as implemented using edge routers and firewalls. The perimeter router connects to the Internet and the corporate internal network — which is located in the *demilitarized zone* (DMZ), a protected area that contains bastion hosts and other servers. The internal network connected to the edge router is considered a *semi-secure* (or *dirty*) DMZ. The firewall, placed between the external and internal networks, provides the second line of defense against external intrusion.

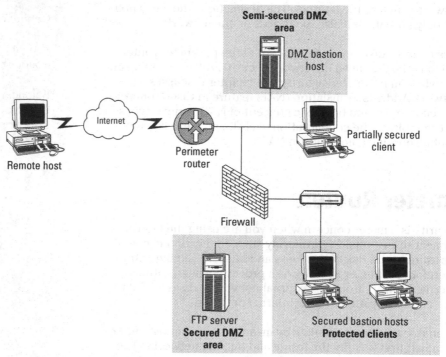

Figure 6-1: Perimeter security

DMZ area

A DMZ is a separate local-area network, distinct from the outer networks and the internal network of an organization. Located between a corporate internal network and the Internet, a DMZ is the network that is generally visible to the outside world, acting as a central hop for incoming and outgoing traffic. The outside world can establish connections only to the resources in the DMZ.

The standard way to create a DMZ is to implement perimeter security by using specially configured devices (such as routers and firewalls) at the perimeter of the network. The perimeter router creates a semi-secure network area (the dirty DMZ) where the organization places its public servers that offer services such as Web hosting and application services.

Bastion hosts

A *bastion host* resides in the secured DMZ area behind the firewall or another (second) level of security. Bastion hosts are typically secured servers that offer their organization a more secure way to use such Internet resources as FTP services, e-mail SMTP services, or DNS services. They also act as proxy servers through which the internal network can connect to the Internet, and as a common gateway to the Internet for internal users. Since internal users and external Internet users must both access the bastion hosts, they should also be highly secure.

As a proxy server, a bastion host provides TCP and UDP communications to the Internet. As a firewall server (in a dual-homed configuration), bastion host can have two network cards installed in the same machine — one for the internal network and one for the outside network.

The following sections discuss the steps involved in designing and building a bastion host.

Selecting a computer

Since a bastion host plays a critical role in a network, it is important that you choose the computer carefully. It should allow configurations that support all the functions a bastion host must perform.

Choosing a physical location

After you have chosen the computer to use as a bastion host — and decided its configuration — the next step is to decide where to locate it. Because a bastion host provides critical services to users — and any loss or damage to it would adversely affect those services — try to put it in a relatively impregnable place. An ideal location for your bastion host would be a locked room — with appropriate air conditioning and an uninterruptible power supply.

Selecting a location for bastion host in the network

Place your bastion host on a part of your network that does *not* carry confidential data. Ethernet interfaces can work in promiscuous mode and capture all packets; thus they can be used by intruders to launch security attacks — and compromise the bastion host. Hackers look for a portal through which they can get to sensitive resources. Your bastion host should not provide such an entryway, so a perimeter network is a better place to put it than an internal network that carries confidential data. An ideal approach would be to create an entire *separate network* for your bastion host.

Deciding on services that the bastion host must provide

You can configure a bastion host to provide a variety of services, using the following four categories as a guide:

✦ **Secure services:** This category includes all services that are secured, usually provided by means of packet filtering.

✦ **Services that are normally unsecured but can be secured:** You can provide these services in a safer manner by using a bastion host.

✦ **Services that are normally unsecured and cannot be secured:** Avoid even providing these services on your bastion host.

✦ **Services you don't need:** Disable all services that your organization does not need.

Disabling user accounts on the bastion host

Don't allow user accounts on your bastion host; disable them when you set it up. Active user accounts on a bastion host can curtail its performance — and hackers can easily exploit a user account to break in to the bastion host.

Building a bastion host

After you have decided on the configuration, physical location, and services for your bastion host, the next step is to build it. In this process of setup, configuration, testing, and connection — known as *hardening* — you configure the bastion host to resist security attacks. This process involves the following tasks.

1. Physically securing the computer that would act as bastion host.

2. Disabling all services that are not required.

3. Installing all required services.

4. Configuring the bastion host as per your requirements.

5. Establishing a security baseline by running security audit.

6. Adding the bastion host to the network.

Caution   Make sure you finish configuring the bastion host *before* you add it to the network. If the bastion host is vulnerable to the Internet while it's being configured, it could as easily become an inadvertent attack mechanism as a defense mechanism.

Typically, Cisco routers are used as perimeter routers, acting to keep secure networks apart from unsecured networks. In addition to securing the internal network, a Cisco router protects the firewall against direct intrusion.

Cisco IOS software has flexible security features that can adapt to any requirements and is more economical than a dedicated firewall. The Cisco perimeter router uses access lists to filter data packets according to established security policies.

Features of Cisco perimeter routers

Properly configured, Cisco routers can control access to their internal networks. The Cisco IOS has several built-in security features for securing the network perimeter:

✦ **Controlling TCP/IP services:** Perimeter routers are highly susceptible to attack; they are the first line of defense against intrusion. The Cisco IOS uses several powerful features to control the specific services offered by these routers. Once configured, these features provide extra protection against eavesdropping and DoS attacks.

Tip   One rule of thumb for configuring your perimeter routers is to enable only those services that a specified network requires. In addition, depending on the IOS version, many services are enabled or disabled by default; avoid assuming that the default is the appropriate setting for your network.

✦ **Packet filtering:** The perimeter router keeps track of incoming and outgoing traffic, using standard and extended access lists to filter packets as a protection against data manipulation through unauthorized access. Both inbound and outbound packet-filtering processes use protocols such as FTP, Telnet, SMTP, TFTP, and BootP — which helps to prevent IP-address spoofing attacks, remote-access attacks, and direct intrusion into the firewall.

✦ **Rate limiting:** The perimeter router provides the first line of defense against DoS attacks (such as continuous re-routing attacks) — which reduces the chances of eavesdropping and undesirable remote access. The perimeter router also limits the rate of ICMP and SYNC flood attacks.

✦ **Dynamic access lists:** The perimeter router provides lock-and-key security feature by using dynamic access lists — which provides an enhanced level of security over standard access lists by granting or denying access on a per-user basis (through the user-authentication process). You can also implement lock-and-key security in the firewall. Then, when a remote user tries to gain access to the corporate network, the system first authenticates the user and then allows access according to the parameters of a dynamic access list.

◆ **Address translation:** Network Address Translation (NAT) and Port Address Translation (PAT) give the network greater flexibility by using internal and external address translations. Address translation helps you work around the long-standing global problem of too few unique IP addresses.

◆ **TCP intercept:** This Cisco IOS feature protects the servers from attacks such as SYNC flooding and rerouting. TCP "interceptor" software filters incoming SYNC packets according to extended access lists (which validate each packet's client before connecting to the server). The software stays at the center of communication between client and server — maintaining connectivity throughout the session, limiting any would-be floods of traffic by restricting the size of threshold values. It maintains two sessions at a time — one with the client and another with the server — and binds the two sessions.

◆ **Router-to-router authentication:** Perimeter routers can also use protocol-specific authentication techniques. Using these techniques, perimeter routers provide stability to the network. Before exchanging updates with the peer routers, the routers can use MD5 or plaintext authentication to ensure that these updates are arriving from a trusted source of information — which helps prevent eavesdropping and reduces the vulnerability of routing updates.

Tasks performed by a perimeter router

You can configure a perimeter router to perform the following tasks:

◆ Managing TCP/IP services

◆ Preventing rerouting attacks

◆ Controlling user access

◆ Preventing DoS attacks

◆ Enabling Network-layer encryption

The following sections discuss these tasks.

Managing TCP/IP services

By default, a Cisco perimeter router has a variety of TCP/IP services turned on — and your network may not need all of them. To reduce the router's susceptibility to unauthorized access and eavesdropping, manually turn off the TCP/IP services that your network doesn't need. Table 6-1 lists the commands that switch off specific TCP/IP services in the global and interface configuration modes.

Table 6-1
Commands for Disabling Specific TCP/IP Services

Command	Service Affected	Configuration Mode to Use
no service tcp-small-servers	Turns off minor TCP services that are available for the Echo, Chargen, Daytime, and Discard ports.	Global
no service udp-small-servers	Turns off minor UDP services that are available for the Echo, Chargen, Daytime, and Discard ports.	Global
no service finger	Stops queries from remote users by preventing the use of finger protocol requests.	Global
no ip domain-lookup	Disables the IP DNS-based hostname-to-address translation.	Global
no ip source-route	Disables IP source routing.	Global
no ip bootp server	Disables the BOOTP service on the network.	Global
no ip tcp selective-ack	Disables TCP selective acknowledgment, which provides protection against DoS attacks.	Global
no mop enabled	Disables the Maintenance Operations Protocol (MOP).	Global
no cdp run	Disables the Cisco Discovery Protocol (CDP).	Global
no ip rcmd rcp-enable	Prevents remote users from using the rcp command to copy files to and from the router.	Global
no ip rsh-enable	Prevents remote users from using the rsh utility to execute commands on the router.	Global
no ip identd	Switches off support for TCP port identification.	Global
no ip redirects	Disables the sending of redirect messages.	Interface
no ip proxy-arp	Disables the proxy ARP on the network.	Interface

Continued

	Table 6-1 *(continued)*	
Command	**Service Affected**	**Configuration Mode to Use**
`no ip tcp path-mtu discovery`	Disables the path MTU discovery service for all new TCP connections from the router.	Interface
`no ip unreachable`	Stops a specified interface from generating `ICMP unreachable` messages.	Interface
`no ip route-cache`	Turns off autonomous switching caches for IP routing; can turn off fast-switching caches.	Interface
`no ip mroute-cache`	Default command for turning off IP multicast fast switching.	Interface
`no ip directed-broadcast`	Default command for switching off IP-directed broadcasts.	Interface
`no cdp enable`	Switches off CDP at a designated interface.	Interface

Preventing rerouting attacks

Static routes are unchanging routing instructions given to a perimeter router. A static route that tells the router to forward all data packets it receives to a specific hop in the network (whether to a specific router or other destination) is a *default route*. After a static route has been configured to send data packets destined for the Internet to the ISP's router, the ISP's router must forward the packets to their ultimate destination; the perimeter router need not reveal any details of the internal network to get its job done. To configure static routes, use the `ip route` command in global configuration mode.

Controlling user access

You can configure a perimeter router to control user access between networks — just set up standard and extended access lists on the router and configure them to scan incoming and outgoing traffic. While configuring inbound and outbound packet filtering, follow these guidelines:

✦ To prevent spoofing attacks, filter incoming packets by using RFC-reserved addresses as source addresses.

✦ To prevent remote-access attacks, you should filter incoming packets by `bootp`, TFTP, SNMP, and `traceroute` and allow incoming connections to access only your DMZ servers.

✦ To prevent IP spoofing attacks, you should allow initiation of TCP connections only from *inside* the network.

Consider the following guidelines when you configure outbound packet filtering:

✦ Allow only those packets that have source address from within the internal network or the source address of the bastion host to be transmitted to the Internet.

✦ Block all packets that have disallowed IP addresses, as documented in your organization's security policy.

Preventing DoS attacks

You can configure the perimeter router to prevent against DoS attacks. To prevent your network from DoS attacks, you can

✦ **Use the no** `ip directed-broadcast` **command on the interface.** Doing so prevents the perimeter router from amplifying the broadcast messages.

✦ **Apply rate limiting or policing to inbound, outbound, or both interfaces.** To apply rate limiting, use committed access rate (CAR), which is available with devices running IOS version 11.1cc or 12.0+.

✦ **Use access lists to filter incoming traffic by private and reserved address.**

✦ **Use access lists and the** `ip verify unicast reverse-path` **interface command to filter out packets from sources other than the DMZ or permitted addresses.**

✦ **Configure rate limiting for SYN packets.** You can also use TCP intercept to control SYN-flooding attacks.

Enabling Network-layer encryption

You can configure a perimeter router to use Network-layer encryption. Network-layer encryption encrypts the data packets that are transmitted from one application to another or from one subnet to another. However, Network-layer encryption encrypts only the payload and leaves the network headers unencrypted. Network-layer encryption can be used with CET and IPSec.

Cisco routers and Cisco IOS software

The Cisco IOS Software images deployed on Cisco routers also come with the Cisco IOS Firewall feature set. Of these features, the most significant is Context-Based Access Control (CBAC), which further enables security features such as blocking Java applets and establishing audit trails. The features of Cisco IOS Firewall feature set are discussed below.

✦ **CBAC:** This feature provides a secure, per-application access control for all data that travels across network perimeters. You can configure CBAC inspection rules to send alerts and audit trail messages.

✦ **Java blocking:** This feature of Cisco IOS Firewall feature set provides protection against known malicious Java applets

✦ **Real-time alerts:** Real-time alerts are used to log alerts when an intrusion or abnormal activity is detected.

✦ **Intrusion-detection system:** This feature detects the attempted intrusions on a network. The data packets that flow through the routers are scanned and checked for IDS signatures. If any intrusion attempt is detected, the event is logged in Cisco IOS syslog.

✦ **Audit trail:** This feature records connection information, such as source and the destination address, ports, and the number of bytes transmitted. It also records all unaccounted activities.

✦ **Authentication proxy:** This feature enables you to specify security policy for every user. It uses an HTTP session to authenticate and authorize a user to a security database.

✦ **ConfigMaker support:** ConfigMaker is a Windows 95/NT-based configuration tool that provides a wizard to speed the process of configuring your network and implementing your firewall.

✦ **DoS detection:** This Cisco IOS Firewall feature prevents DoS attacks by scanning the packet headers. The packets that do not meet the configured parameters are dropped. It also prevents the router resources against half-open TCP and UDP attacks.

NAT Overview

The Internet has grown enormously over the last few years, greatly stressing the infrastructure of the Internet and the protocols running on the Internet. Internet technology operates according to the Internet Protocol (IP). To communicate using IP, each device participating in the communication must have a unique IP address — not a problem, provided your organization limits its network activity to its own internal physical network and has no connection to the Internet. However, after the network of an organization connects to the Internet, each IP address has to be globally unique.

IPv4 — the fourth version of the Internet Transport Protocol (or Internet Protocol) — does not provide enough globally unique addresses to accommodate all the hosts on the Internet. The IP address is a 32-bit address, which places a theoretical limit on how many hosts the Internet can support — about 4 billion — and the practical limit is much lower (due to inefficient IP address allocation). This situation causes problems for organizations that need a finite number of IP addresses. Although it is not possible to assign valid, registered IP addresses to all hosts currently communicating over the Internet, organizations can use private IP addresses without prior permission from the regulatory bodies. However, if these addresses must connect to the Internet — a public network — they need public IP addresses.

One possible solution to this scarcity of valid IP addresses is a more flexible protocol — a new Internet protocol, known as IPv6 or *IP next generation*, would help overcome the limitations of IPv4. IPv6, not yet released, would require all existing applications and protocols to become compatible with it. A different solution is to use a proxy server, allowing the use of private addresses on your internal network while granting Internet access to internal hosts. The proxy would be assigned one or more registered IP addresses, using them while sending packets from the internal network to the Internet.

A more general solution is to *convert* private, internal addresses to official addresses when packets move out beyond the perimeter of the internal network. A technique known as Network Address Translation (NAT) — defined in RFC 1631 — allows the use of one or more registered IP addresses for a group of computers. Internal IP addresses are translated to one or more IP addresses while sending packets out of the internal network.

NAT operates at the boundary between the public Internet and the internal network of an organization. It works by rewriting the IP addresses and/or port numbers in a packet's IP header so the packet appears to be coming from (or going to) a public IP address that corresponds to the NAT device (instead of the actual source or destination). NAT makes use of the fact that only a few hosts in an organization connect to the Internet at any specified time. As a result, the IP addresses of only a few internal networks need be translated to globally unique IP addresses.

Cisco IOS NAT allows an organization with unregistered private addresses to connect to the Internet by translating the private addresses into globally registered IP addresses. Cisco IOS NAT also increases network privacy by hiding internal IP addresses from external networks.

The Internet faces two scalability challenges: the depletion of registered IP address space and the scaling of routing. NAT conserves the registered IP addresses on large networks and simplifies IP address management. It also translates IP addresses within private internal networks, giving packets unique IP addresses to be sent over public external networks. Incoming traffic is retranslated to the original address for delivery within the internal network. This whole process of conversion is not visible to the end user.

Working with NAT

NAT performs either a one-to-one or a many-to-one IP address translation. A private, inside IP address is mapped to a global, outside IP address — which implies that an inside IP address is replaced by the appropriate outside IP address (and vice versa). The inside network sends a packet by using the NAT perimeter router, which converts the internal private address or addresses to legal and registered IP addresses so that the packets can pass to the Internet.

NAT implementation

The NAT functionality is provided by Cisco IOS. It is available in Cisco IOS 11.2 and later versions. The Cisco NAT implementation uses some common terms:

✦ **Inside local IP address:** This is an IP address assigned to an inside network host. It can be allocated from the private address space or can be randomly picked. However, it must be unique within the internal network.

✦ **Inside global IP address:** This is a legal or public IP address assigned by the service provider that might represent one or more inside local IP addresses to the outer world. This address is allocated from the globally unique address space.

✦ **Outside global IP address:** This is an IP address assigned to an outside network host and is allocated from the globally routable address space.

✦ **Outside local IP address:** This is the IP address of an outside host as it appears to the inside network and is allocated from the routable address space or private address allocation. This address may or may not be a legal or public address.

Types of address translation

There are two types of address translations, static and dynamic. NAT solves the problem of scarce IP addresses by reassigning IP addresses. It contains a pool of available global addresses that are constantly reused. Internal network addresses are allocated according to the internal considerations of the network. Global addresses must remain unique to distinguish different hosts. When a packet is routed, NAT replaces the internal corporate address with a temporary global address. As soon as the application session is over, the global address is returned to the pool to be reassigned.

Static address translation allows access to an internal IP address from the Internet although the real IP address remains unknown to the outside world. The internal IP address always uses a specific outside IP address. Each internal IP address mapped by static NAT is converted to a different global IP address.

Dynamic address translation enables the administrator to define a pool of global addresses to be shared among local users when there are more users than the available global IP addresses. Each address mapped by dynamic NAT is allowed access to the Internet or the intranet. However, no request from outside is allowed access to the internal network. Each time an internal host wants to communicate with the Internet, the IP address of the host is mapped to an IP address from the pool of available IP addresses.

Single-address translation allows all users on the private network to have one global source. Each address mapped by a single NAT is allowed access to the Internet, but external hosts are not allowed the access to the network.

Static NAT

In static NAT translation, an internal host always uses a specific external IP address. As the name implies, static NAT defines a fixed address translation, from the inside (local) network to the outside (global) network, as shown in Figure 6-2.

As the communication infrastructure requirements of an organization grow, they must publish IP addresses for public servers, such as FTP and Web servers. Static mode supports this requirement and provides a one-to-one assignment between the published IP address and the internal IP address. Static mode would typically be implemented when administrators do not wish to expose the real IP addresses of the network servers.

In Figure 6-2, when the inside local IP addresses of the network 11.0.0.0 pass through the NAT perimeter router, they are translated to the inside global IP addresses to reach the remote host.

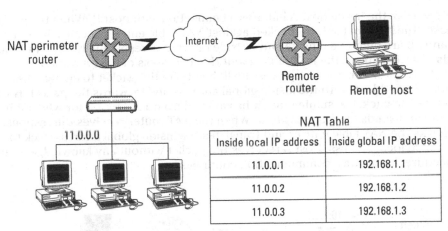

NAT Table

Inside local IP address	Inside global IP address
11.0.0.1	192.168.1.1
11.0.0.2	192.168.1.2
11.0.0.3	192.168.1.3

Figure 6-2: Static NAT table

Dynamic NAT

Dynamic NAT provides users access to the Internet while conserving registered IP addresses and hiding the actual IP addresses of network resources. Dynamic NAT translates from a pool of local IP addresses to either a pool of global IP addresses or a single global IP address. The user must define both pools of IP addresses. The pool of multiple internal IP addresses can have a single outside IP address — which conserves address space. Many internal IP addresses can be mapped to a single public IP address. The NAT-enabled router automatically assigns the address, either by multiplexing the ports or by changing the source port on the outbound packet. The NAT border router protects after the inside host has initiated a session. Once the mapping is done, all outside hosts can access the internal host.

NAT Operations

A user can implement either static or dynamic address translation on Cisco routers. These translations are stored in the *translation table* (also known simply as the *NAT table*). As the size of the translation table increases, the number of CPU cycles taken for looking up the table to translate the IP address also increases. Hence, with an increase in the size of the translation table, the CPU utilization increases. The different NAT implementation scenarios are discussed below.

Inside local address translation

In this type of implementation, the source IP address in the IP header of the packet is replaced with the inside or outside IP address — which implies that mapping is done between the inside local and global addresses — which results in a one-to-one mapping of the inside local and inside global IP addresses.

In Figure 6-3, the inside host A initiates a connection with host B. When the packet crosses the NAT router, it is checked against NAT table entries because interfaces e0 and s0 are defined as inside and outside interfaces, respectively. The NAT router finds a static entry in the NAT table about the IP address of host A, which is 192.168.1.10. The router replaces the IP header of the packet to change the inside local address with the inside global address and forwards the packet. Host B receives the packet, assuming that it has arrived from 10.1.1.10 for which it has a route and sends the response to it. When the NAT router receives the response, it checks the NAT table entries and translates the inside global address back to the inside local address. Host A receives the packet without any knowledge of the procedure. In this way, communication continues.

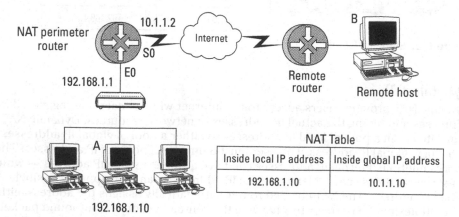

NAT Table	
Inside local IP address	Inside global IP address
192.168.1.10	10.1.1.10

Figure 6-3: Scenario for inside local address translation

Overloading inside global addresses

An overloading feature reduces the public IP addresses required by the network to a great extent. Unlike inside local address translation, it translates multiple private IP addresses to a single public IP address, conserving address space.

As stated earlier, these translations are stored in the NAT table. Since all the inside local addresses are translated to the same inside global address, it becomes important to have a mechanism by which the router can identify which packets belong to whom. You can do so by translating the TCP/UDP port numbers. The port numbers in the TCP/UDP header of the packets are replaced with the new port numbers. Even though different inside local IP addresses are mapped to the same inside global IP address, the sessions of the different internal hosts are identified by the TCP/UDP port numbers of the inside host. This process is known as *overloading* inside global addresses. The checksum for the IP packet is recalculated and checked for integrity. The TCP header checksum must also be recalculated since this checksum is calculated using the new inside or outside IP address, the new port, and the payload. To make the NAT transparent to the Application layers, the NAT process must also convert any application packet that contains a reference to the addressing scheme that is being translated to reference the new addressing scheme. Figure 6-4 explains the process.

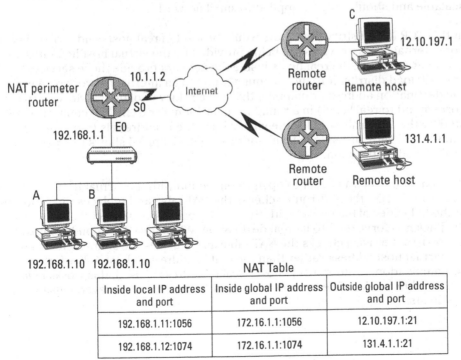

Inside local IP address and port	Inside global IP address and port	Outside global IP address and port
192.168.1.11:1056	172.16.1.1:1056	12.10.197.1:21
192.168.1.12:1074	172.16.1.1:1074	131.4.1.1:21

Figure 6-4: Scenario showing the overloading of inside global addresses

In Figure 6-4, when host A opens an FTP connection with remote host C, a random port number is generated. The NAT router checks for the mapping and translates its address to the inside global IP address. When overloading is enabled, any inside host can use the same inside global IP address for communication with another remote destination. The remote destinations respond to the NAT router with the same destination IP address, which is the inside global IP 172.16.1.1. The NAT router delivers the packet to the specific inside host address according to port address mappings.

This overloading feature of NAT that uses port numbers to identify different communications is also known as Port Address Translation (PAT). PAT uses port addresses to map inside (local) and outside (global) IP addresses. This arrangement allows you to map many-to-one IP addresses from inside (local) to outside (global) addresses.

TCP load distribution

The TCP load distribution feature is a very useful aspect of NAT implementation on Cisco routers. This feature is applied for the traffic received from the outside or external network to access a particular service hosted on the internal network. Using this feature, you can enable load distribution for the service located on the internal network at minimal cost. The limitation of this solution is that it is not scalable and should only be applied to small networks.

In this TCP load distribution, there would be a set of real hosts and a virtual host. For external users, services are being provided by the virtual host IP address. However, in reality, the real hosts inside the network provide those services. For TCP load distribution, the incoming traffic to an internal network receives the destination address or mapping through a rotary pool of IP addresses (which correspond to real hosts) in a round-robin fashion. For each TCP connection initiated by the external users for the virtual host, the IP address is translated and established with an inside local IP address pool. Figure 6-5 shows the mechanism of TCP load distribution.

When host C sends a packet to open a connection with the virtual host 192.168.1.127, the NAT router checks the NAT table and replaces the IP address in the IP header of the packet with that of the real host, 192.168.1.11. In this way, the packet is forwarded to its real destination. When host A responds to host C, the NAT router again checks the NAT table and replaces the source address with the virtual host address rather than the real IP address of host A. For further communication, another inside host's real IP address is used; this works in a round-robin fashion. The incoming load is distributed among several inside real hosts.

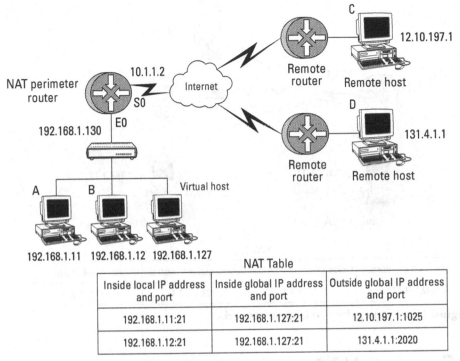

NAT Table

Inside local IP address and port	Inside global IP address and port	Outside global IP address and port
192.168.1.11:21	192.168.1.127:21	12.10.197.1:1025
192.168.1.12:21	192.168.1.127:21	131.4.1.1:2020

Figure 6-5: Scenario for TCP load distribution

Overlapping networks

Sometimes the internal IP addresses of one network overlap those of another network with which connectivity must be established (for example, when two companies merge). In such a case, address translation of both the source and destination addresses must be done. Figure 6-6 explains the NAT process in case of inside and outside network overlapping.

In Figure 6-6, the two companies are using the same network addresses. The inside hosts contact a DNS server to resolve the host name of the remote host to the IP address. The DNS server responds with the IP address of the remote host to the internal host, which has generated the query. A router configured to handle this overlapping address situation intercepts and examines the DNS replies — and replaces the destination address with the outside local IP address of the remote hosts. When host A wants to communicate with host B (having the same network address), first it must send a query to the DNS server for the IP address of host B. The NAT router checks the returned address and translates it into a separately configured pool of outside local addresses for an overlap of networks. The router forwards the packet to the actual host with a different source address (taken from a dynamic pool of addresses). In this example, communication between the overlapped networks takes place.

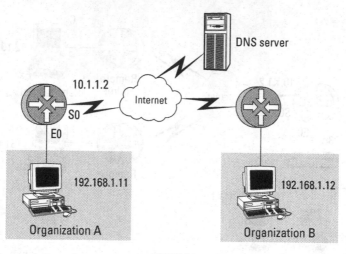

DNS server

10.1.1.2

Internet

S0

E0

192.168.1.11

Organization A

192.168.1.12

Organization B

NAT Table

Inside local IP address	Inside global IP address	Outside global IP address	Outside local IP address
192.168.1.11	172.16.1.1	192.168.1.12	172.16.2.1

Figure 6-6: Scenario for overlapping networks

Configuring NAT

Before configuring NAT, identify the interface that connects the internal network and the Internet. The inside part of this interface, connected to the internal network, is the *inside* interface; and the part connected to the Internet is the *outside* interface. After identifying the inside and outside interfaces, follow these steps to configure NAT:

1. Define the inside interface.
2. Define the outside interface.
3. Define the NAT mappings.

Before defining these parameters, be sure to enable IP routing on the router and ensure that its routing table contains all appropriate routes. To configure the NAT *inside interface* on the Cisco router, issue the following command in interface configuration mode:

```
Router(config-if)# ip nat inside
```

In the above command, `inside` is the interface that connects to the internal network.

To configure the NAT *outside interface* on the NAT perimeter router, issue the following command in interface configuration mode:

```
Router(config-if)# ip nat outside
```

Here outside is the interface that connects to the external or outside network. In this case, NAT translates the IP addresses of only those packets that move through an inside *and* an outside interface.

NAT offers various possible static and dynamic configurations on Cisco routers; the upcoming sections examine each major type.

Static NAT mapping

For static NAT configuration, the inside and outside interfaces are first defined with appropriate IP addresses configured on them. For each address that must be translated, there has to be an entry in the configuration file. You use the following command to configure a static mapping:

```
Router(config)# ip nat inside source static local-address global-address
```

where

   ✦ local-address is the local IP address assigned to an inside host and defines the address that must be translated.

   ✦ global-address is the global IP address of an inside host as it appears to the outside world and defines the outside address to which to translate.

   ✦ static specifies a single static translation.

In static translation, only packets from the inside interface destined to the outside interface are translated. A packet that is received on the inside interface but not destined for the outside interface is not translated. The following sample configuration illustrates static NAT mapping:

```
!
interface Ethernet0
    ip address 192.168.1.1 255.255.255.0
    ip nat inside
!
interface Serial0
    ip address 10.1.1.2 255.255.255.0
    ip nat outside
!
ip nat inside source static 192.168.1.10  10.1.1.10
!
```

This configuration defines Ethernet0 as the inside interface and Serial0 as the outside interface. A static mapping has been made to translate the IP address 192.168.1.10 to the IP address 10.1.1.10.

Dynamic NAT configuration

Before NAT can perform dynamic mappings, a pool of addresses must be defined. The inside hosts use IP addresses from this defined pool to gain access to the outside world. A NAT mapping is defined when an inside host begins a session with the outside host. First, at least one inside and one outside interface are defined using the `ip nat {inside|outside}` command. To configure the pool of outside addresses NAT is to use for dynamic mapping, issue the following command:

```
Router(config)# ip nat pool pool-name start-ip end-ip netmask netmask
```

where

- ✦ *pool-name* defines the name of the pool.
- ✦ *start-ip* defines the first outside IP address in the range of addresses in the address pool.
- ✦ *end-ip* defines the last outside IP address in the range of addresses in the address pool.
- ✦ *netmask* defines the network mask of the network to which the address pool belongs.

A standard access list defines the inside hosts that must be translated. The command used is as follows:

```
Router(config)# access-list access-list-number {permit|deny}
network-address wildcard-mask
```

where

- ✦ *access-list-number* defines a standard access-list number.
- ✦ *network-address* defines the inside network.
- ✦ *wildcard-mask* defines the wildcard mask.

The access list is mapped to the NAT address pool by using the following command:

```
Router(config)# ip nat inside source list access-list-number pool pool-name
```

where

- ✦ *access-list-number* defines the number of standard access lists.
- ✦ *pool-name* defines the NAT pool name.

NAT configuration translates only those packets from the inside interface that are destined for the outside interface. A packet received on the inside interface but not destined for the outside interface is not translated. An example of such configuration demonstrates dynamic NAT mapping:

```
!
interface Ethernet0
    ip address 192.168.1.1 255.255.255.0
    ip nat inside
!
interface Serial0
    ip address 10.1.1.2 255.255.255.0
    ip nat outside
!
access-list 1 permit 192.168.1.0 0.0.0.255
ip nat pool dynamic 172.16.1.1 172.16.1.254 netmask 255.255.255.0
ip nat inside source list 1 pool dynamic
!
```

In the preceding configuration, pool dynamic allows access to the outside hosts. The IP addresses used in this pool range from 172.16.1.1 through 172.16.1.254. The standard access list defines the range of inside host addresses that can be mapped to any of the addresses defined in the dynamic pool of outside addresses.

Configuring inside global address overloading

To configure global address overloading, you first must define the inside and outside interfaces — which is required to enable NAT. The standard access list defines the inside addresses to be translated to the inside global addresses, and a NAT pool defines the range for outside addresses. (This topic is discussed in the previous section.)

To define the dynamic address translation, use the following command:

```
Router(config)# ip nat inside source list access-list-number
pool pool-name overload
```

where

   ✦ access-list-number defines the standard access-list number.

   ✦ pool-name defines the dynamic pool name.

   ✦ overload enables the overloading of inside global addresses.

The following router configuration illustrates the implementation of global-address overloading:

```
!
interface Ethernet0
   ip address 192.168.1.1 255.255.255.0
   ip nat inside
!
interface Serial0
   ip address 10.1.1.2 255.255.255.0
   ip nat outside
!
access-list 1 permit 192.168.1.0 0.0.0.255
ip nat pool global-overload 172.16.1.1 172.16.1.2 netmask 255.255.255.0
ip nat inside source list 1 pool global-overload overload
!
```

In this configuration, the access list defines the range of inside addresses, which are mapped to the two global addresses 172.16.1.1 and 172.16.1.2 by using the keyword overload.

Configuring TCP load distribution

To configure TCP load distribution, you first must define the pool of real IP addresses. You can do so using the following command:

```
Router(config)# ip nat pool pool-name start-ip end-ip
netmask netmask type rotary
```

where

- ✦ *pool-name* defines the name of the pool.

- ✦ *start-ip* defines the first IP address in the range of addresses in the address pool.

- ✦ *end-ip* defines the last IP address in the range of addresses in the address pool.

- ✦ *netmask* defines the network mask of the network to which the address pool belongs.

- ✦ type rotary defines a rotary type pool.

A standard access list is used to define and permit the IP address of the virtual host. The command used is

```
Router(config)# access-list access-list-number permit IP-address
```

where

- ✦ *access-list-number* defines a standard access-list number.
- ✦ *IP-address* defines the IP address of the virtual host.

The following code associates the access list with the defined pool:

```
Router(config)# ip nat inside destination list access-list-number
pool pool-name
```

where

- ✦ *access-list-number* defines the standard access-list number.
- ✦ *pool-name* defines the dynamic pool name.
- ✦ destination is a keyword that enables the translations from outside to inside.

The following configuration demonstrates TCP load distribution:

```
!
interface Ethernet0
   ip address 192.168.1.130 255.255.255.0
   ip nat inside
!
interface Serial0
   ip address 10.1.1.2 255.255.255.0
   ip nat outside
!
access-list 1 permit 192.168.1.127
ip nat pool load-distribution 192.168.1.1 192.168.1.126 netmask 255.255.255.0
type rotary
ip nat inside destination list 1 pool load-distribution
!
```

In the preceding code, the incoming load is distributed among several hosts (ranging from 192.168.1.1 to 192.168.1.126) that provide the same service.

Configuring NAT to map overlapping addresses

Several tasks are needed to configure NAT so it maps overlapping addresses. First you define the inside and outside interfaces. Then you specify one pool of addresses for the inside network and another to define the outside network, using the following command:

```
Router(config)# ip nat pool pool-name start-ip end-ip netmask netmask
```

where

- ✦ *pool-name* defines the name of the pool.
- ✦ *start-ip* defines the first IP address in the range of addresses in the address pool.
- ✦ *end-ip* defines the last IP address in the range of addresses in the address pool.
- ✦ *netmask* defines the network mask of the network to which the address pool belongs.

To define a standard access list to block overlapping addresses, use the following command:

```
Router(config)# access-list access-list-number
permit network-address wildcard-mask
```

where

- ✦ *access-list-number* defines a standard access list number.
- ✦ *network-address* defines the overlapped network.
- ✦ *wildcard-mask* defines the wildcard mask of the overlapped network.

You associate this access list with both pools of addresses by using the following command:

```
Router(config)# ip nat {inside|outside} source list access-list-number
pool pool-name
```

where

- ✦ *access-list-number* defines the standard access-list number.
- ✦ *pool-name* defines the dynamic pool name.
- ✦ inside defines the mapping of the standard access list and the inside pool of addresses.
- ✦ outside defines the mapping of the standard access list and the outside pool of addresses.

The following router configuration shows how to map the inside and outside addresses of overlapping addresses:

```
!
interface Ethernet0
   ip address 192.168.1.130 255.255.255.0
   ip nat inside
!
interface Serial0
```

```
   ip address 10.1.1.2 255.255.255.0
   ip nat outside
!
access-list 1 permit 192.168.1.0 0.0.0.255
ip nat pool pool-in 192.168.1.1 192.168.1.254 netmask 255.255.255.0
ip nat pool pool-out 172.16.1.1 172.16.1.254 netmask 255.255.255.0
ip nat inside source list 1 pool pool-in
ip nat outside source list 1 pool pool-out
!
```

In the code just given, two pools are defined for inside and outside addresses. In addition, access-list 1 is mapped to the inside and outside pools. For overlapping networks, if the internal host needs access to a remote host in the overlapping address space, then the DNS server must be used to resolve the name.

Verifying and Troubleshooting NAT

To verify and troubleshoot NAT operations, you can use various show and debug commands. To verify NAT operations, you can use the following command:

```
Router# show ip nat statistics
```

This command displays the configured inside and outside interfaces, along with the total active translations. It also shows the static or dynamic mappings configured. The following output is displayed by this command:

```
Total active translations: 1 (0 static, 2 dynamic; 0 extended)
 Outside interfaces:
 Serial2
 Inside interfaces:
 Ethernet1
 Hits: 40  Misses: 2
 Expired translations: 0
 Dynamic mappings:
 -- Inside Source
 access-list 7 pool sample refcount 1
 pool test: netmask 255.255.255.0
 start 172.16.1.1 end 172.16.1.126
 type rotary, total addresses 2, allocated 1 (50%), misses 0
```

where

✦ Hits is the number of times the router has looked up the NAT table.

✦ Misses is the number of times the NAT router created a new entry because no entry was present.

✦ Expired translations is the number of expired translations due to restarting.

✦ `pool` is the name of the NAT pool.

✦ `type rotary` indicates that the TCP load distribution feature of NAT is being implemented.

The following command is another method to display the current status of NAT translations. It shows the NAT table and current mappings:

```
Router# show ip nat translation
```

The output of this command is as follows:

```
Pro    Inside global    Inside local    Outside local    Outside global
---    172.1.1.1        192.168.1.10    ---              ---
---    172.1.1.10       192.168.1.1     ---              ---
```

The following output shows a table of address translations. The host with the IP address 172.1.1.1 is being translated to IP 192.168.1.10 to use the public network.

```
Pro Inside global      Inside local      Outside local    Outside global
tcp 172.1.1.1:1540     192.168.1.10:1540 10.1.1.1:21      10.1.1.1:21
tcp 172.1.1.10:1980    192.168.1.1:1980  10.1.2.1:80      10.1.2.1:80
```

The above output is displayed when the NAT overload feature is being used. It displays the TCP or UDP port numbers associated with the communication.

For troubleshooting NAT, use the following `debug` command:

```
Router# debug ip nat
```

This command displays a line of output for each packet being translated in real time, as follows:

```
NAT: s=172.16.1.1->192.168.1.1, d=10.1.1.1 [20]
NAT: s=10.1.1.1, d=192.168.1.1->172.16.1.1 [30]
NAT*: s=172.16.1.10, d=192.168.2.1->10.1.2.1 [40]
NAT: s=10.1.2.1, d=192.168.2.1->172.16.1.10 [50]
NAT*: s=172.16.2.2, d=192.168.2.1->10.1.1.1 [60]
```

The asterisk mark (*) in the above output indicates that the NAT translation is using a fast path — which implies that the first packet will be process-switched and subsequent packets will follow the fast path if an entry is present in the cache.

To clear all NAT translation entries from the translation table, use the following command:

```
Router# clear ip nat translation *
```

This will clear all the entries in the NAT table as displayed by the `show ip nat translation` command. You can use this command if the entries in the table are incorrect, old, or in need of refreshing. After clearing the NAT table, you can check for new translation entries.

Advantages and Disadvantages of NAT

The primary objective of NAT is to conserve legally registered IP addresses. Its approach to this goal is to allow private intranets to access the Internet by using pools of legal addresses. The approach has its strengths and limitations.

Advantages of NAT

As a factor of network design, NAT offers great flexibility to the network administrators by the unlimited availability of addressing schemes. In addition, when organizations merge, NAT allows for a seamless network merger while maintaining the existing addressing schemes.

Another advantage is the reduction of overlapping in addressing schemes. If an addressing scheme is originally set up within an intranet and then the intranet is connected to the other remote networks without address translation, chances of address overlapping increases. Because routing protocols cannot provide reliable routing for ambiguous addressing, this is a serious problem. NAT avoids such overlaps by translating network addresses — and maintains full connectivity.

By hiding customers' internal networks behind one IP address, NAT helps protect against IP spoofing and `ping` attacks, providing an effective level of security. It also enhances security within the network by hiding the network's internal structure.

NAT increases the flexibility of an Internet connection. Multiple pools, backup pools, and load-sharing pools can be implemented to help ensure reliable Internet connections.

Disadvantages of NAT

Any advantage has a downside; one disadvantage of NAT is the loss of end-to-end IP traceability. Packets become much harder to trace as they undergo numerous changes over multiple NAT hops. However, this scenario leads to more secure links; hackers find those same packets just as difficult (if not impossible) to trace — which makes the original IP addresses for source or destination harder to obtain illegitimately.

Switching paths also introduces delays; translating each IP address within the packet headers takes time. Within the intranet, packet modification can put some performance limitations on the networking design.

Case Study

The following case study depicts how to configure NAT.

Scenario

Organization A and Organization B are merging, which has led to the merger of their networks (as shown in Figure 6-7). The organizations' Cisco perimeter routers are connected via a frame-relay WAN link. Both organizations are using the same internal network-addressing scheme, which is posing a problem in IP connectivity between the two organizations.

The network administrator of Organization A decides to implement the Network Address Translation feature of Cisco routers and configure address translation on Router A to overcome this problem and to establish the IP connectivity between Organizations A and B.

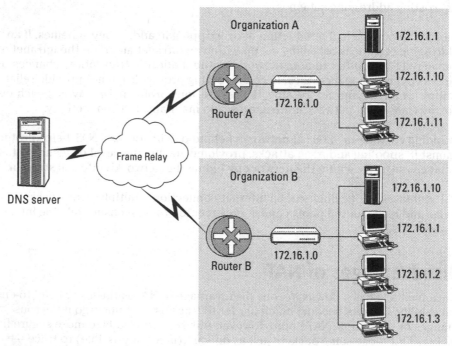

Figure 6-7: Network diagram of Organization A and Organization B

Sample configuration

The steps and code involved in configuring Router A are as follows:

1. Enter the global configuration mode of Router A; execute the following commands to create a global address pool and configure NAT for address translation from inside to outside:

```
ip nat pool pool-in 10.0.0.1 10.0.0.254
netmask 255.255.255.0
access-list 1 permit 172.16.1.0 0.0.0.255
ip nat inside source list 1 pool pool-in
interface Ethernet0
 ip address 172.16.1.1 255.255.255.0
 ip nat inside
```

2. Enter the global configuration mode of Router A; execute the following commands to create a global address pool and configure NAT for address translation from outside to inside:

```
ip nat pool pool-out 10.0.2.1 10.0.2.254
netmask 255.255.255.0
ip nat outside source list 1 pool pool-out
interface Serial0
    ip address 10.0.1.1 255.255.255.0
    ip nat outside
```

Summary

This chapter discussed the concept of perimeter security — and the use of Cisco products to set up a perimeter router. Topics covered included the selective disabling of TCP/IP services to enhance security, address translation, and NAT — how it works, how to configure it, how to troubleshoot it, and how to weigh its advantages and disadvantages against the needs of your network.

✦　✦　✦

Cisco's Encryption Technology

Data transmitted over a network can face a multitude of attacks from hackers and crackers. To protect your data against such attacks, you can encrypt it. *Encryption* is the process of converting plain text into indecipherable text by using an algorithm of complex code. For this purpose, Cisco uses *Cisco Encryption Technology* (CET) to ensure the security and confidentiality of data transmitted over the organization's network.

This chapter defines encryption, describes standard methods of encryption, and examines not only the contents of Cisco Encryption Technology but also how to configure it.

Cisco Encryption Technology Overview

When you connect an organization's network to some other remote network or to the Internet, you are virtually connecting the network to several unknown networks. Hackers can gain access to the data transmitted over these networks by using any of the numerous network hacking tools available to them. These tools pose a serious security risk — not only to the network but also to the data passing through it. Therefore you should be aware of the problems involved in transmitting data over an organization's network before you implement security measures such as encryption. The next section details some common security problems that virtually all networks face.

Common attacks against network security

Network attacks are attempts to disable or overwhelm the network security by taking advantage of its limitations. Some common problems in ensuring network security are as follows:

✦ **Network packet sniffers:** Hackers can use sniffer programs to gain control of data transferred over the network. A *sniffer* is an application or a device that serves to read, monitor, and capture data being transferred over the network. It also reads network packets.

✦ **Internet Protocol (IP) spoofing:** Hackers can modify the header of a packet. They can simulate a situation where the packet appears to originate from a trusted computer on the network. They do this by replacing the original IP address of the packet with another one from within the range of IP addresses used on the network. They can also use an authorized and trusted external IP address.

✦ **Network blocking:** By taking up the available network bandwidth with "junk" data transfers, hackers can block access to network services and prevent users from accessing data.

✦ **System-backdoor exploitation:** Hackers can use *system backdoors* — accounts created for administrators in case the original accounts become corrupted — to gain access to the network. Hackers can use these accounts to impersonate the network administrators and obtain administrative rights to access the entire network.

✦ **Unmonitored-service exploitation**: Hackers can misuse unmonitored services (such as remote-access services) to break into the network. For example, you might install RAS service to provide remote access to remote users. If this service is not secured, hackers can misuse it to access the network resources. Either remove or disable such services — or implement proper security measures to secure the data transmitted through these unmonitored services.

✦ **Brute-force password attack:** Hackers can attempt to gain entry to the network by trying different combinations of characters until they hit upon one or more passwords used on the network. You can prevent this type of attack by setting a lockout after a number of incorrect logins — although some hackers may use such a response as another way to tie up bandwidth, forcing the system to lock out again and again. The best countermeasure to this type of attack is to implement and enforce a strong password policy.

✦ **Retrieval of deleted data and misuse of default accounts:** Hackers can misuse deleted confidential files. They can use undelete utilities to retrieve the deleted files and misuse the data in them. Default accounts can also be misused to access confidential data.

✦ **Session takeover:** Developers leave buffer space in their code as a place for allocating variables in programs. A hacker can misuse this space by overwriting the code buffer, resulting in an overflow of code that stymies a session in progress. When this happens, the hacker can execute administrative functions at the security level of the application.

✦ **Application-layer attack:** Hackers can exploit weaknesses in network applications by altering the operating-system files and the contents of data files to interfere with network security. Hackers can also execute programs that return company information to them and block network addresses.

✦ **Man-in-the-middle attack:** When data packets pass between two computers, a hacker can get access to confidential data by impersonating the identity of either the sender or the receiver. When authenticated, the hacker can alter, delay, or destroy messages.

✦ **Social engineering:** Hackers can gain access to the passwords of authenticated users by impersonating help-desk staff or network administrators (which might also provide hackers with access to sensitive information).

Your data's best first line of defense as it travels over your organization's network is encryption.

Understanding encryption and decryption

You can use either hardware or software methods to encrypt data. For example, you encrypt only the data that passes from one Cisco router to another, as shown in Figure 7-1.

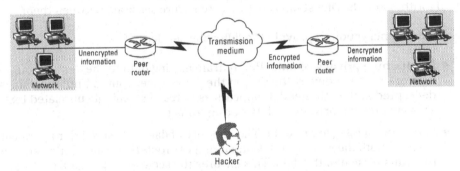

Figure 7-1: Encrypted data as it passes through the network

You can configure your Cisco routers to specify the essentials of encryption or decryption for your data packets. By default, only IP data packets are encrypted or decrypted; if you want to send packets prepared under a network protocol other than IP, you must encapsulate the packets in an IP packet before encryption. Cisco uses IP for encrypting data packets because their content cannot be accessed until they are decrypted. Only the content of the data packets is encrypted; header information (generally TCP or UDP information) is not encrypted.

Encryption or decryption of data packets happens at the source and destination Cisco routers known as *peer routers* because neither is subordinate to the other. In most cases, such routers are configured on the outer boundary of the organization's network so they can provide a secure connection between networks (or between the in-house network and the Internet). Cisco Encryption Technology (CET) is implemented at the level of these routers.

Any other routers that the data packets encounter during transit are used only to transmit the packets on their way to the next router. Data is first transmitted from the source computer to the source peer router. At the router, the contents of the data packets are encrypted and then transmitted over the network; the destination peer router decrypts the arriving data before transmitting it to the destination computer. The specific interface of the source peer router that sends the encrypted data is the *outbound interface*; that which the destination peer router uses to decrypt the data is the *inbound interface*.

Before a peer router can begin encrypting data packets, it must establish an encrypted session. When a session is established, the router can securely transmit data on the network. When a session ends, the router has to create another session before it can continue transmitting the data.

When a new session begins, both peer routers authenticate each other before they transmit data — which ensures that only authenticated peer routers have access to the transmitted data. Cisco routers use several high-level algorithms to create public keys for encrypted data packets: the Data-Encryption Standard (DES), Digital Signature Standard (DSS), and Diffie-Hellman (DH) algorithms. Peer routers use the DH algorithm and the DES standards to create secure sessions between them.

Routers use encryption to provide the following services:

✦ **Maintaining privacy of data:** Before transmitting data to the destination, network routers convert the data at the source peer router. Until the data is decrypted at the other end, it appears as bytes of seemingly unrelated text. This ensures the privacy of data during transit.

✦ **Maintaining integrity of data:** The integrity of data is ensured during transit because both the source and destination peer routers are authenticated before the transmission of the data. This ensures the security of the data packets. Maintaining integrity of data also implies that hackers are not able to intercept the data packets in between transit and alter their content. The authenticity of data is verified using encryption technologies like peer authentication and CET. Besides these technologies, authentication of data can also be ensured using security algorithms such as the Digital Signature Standard (DSS).

✦ **Maintaining authenticity of data:** Routers can ensure the authenticity of transmitted data by requesting receipts for sent and received data. These receipts can be in the form of a digital signature that contains information regarding the messages (such as information regarding a packet's sender, date, and time of the transmission). Routers use CET to ensure authentication.

Implementing encryption

You can implement encryption by following these general steps:

1. Enable peer router authentication by using DSS key encryption.

2. Establish an encrypted session with a peer router.

3. Encrypt and decrypt data by using peer routers.

As already discussed, the first step before establishing an encrypted session is authentication of both the peer routers. To do so, create a pair of DSS keys for both peer routers. The pair includes both a public and a private DSS key. Exchange and verify the DSS keys between both the peer routers. This process is performed only once; after validation, the keys can be used to create further sessions.

Each pair of generated DSS keys is unique in itself, which means a unique DSS public and private key. The private DSS key is stored on a private location on the router's NVRAM. However, if you are using a router with an Encryption Service Adapter (ESA), the DSS key will be stored in a secure area of the ESA's memory. Although the DSS private key is not accessible to any other device, the public DSS key is available to all the peer routers for exchange. Network administrators must use *voice authentication* (verbalized verification of the DSS public key) to authenticate these keys. When the session starts, authenticated peer routers use each other's DSS public keys to authenticate each other, as shown in Figure 7-2.

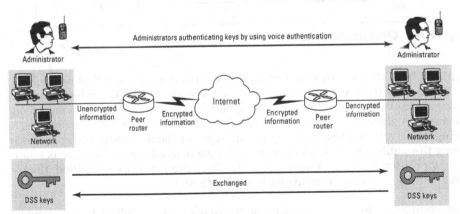

Figure 7-2: Trading DSS keys for mutual authentication

Before a peer router can transmit data safely to another router, it must establish an encryption session (such as that shown in Figure 7-3). A router starts such a session whenever it receives data packets for encryption — but before a new encryption session can begin, any previous session must end.

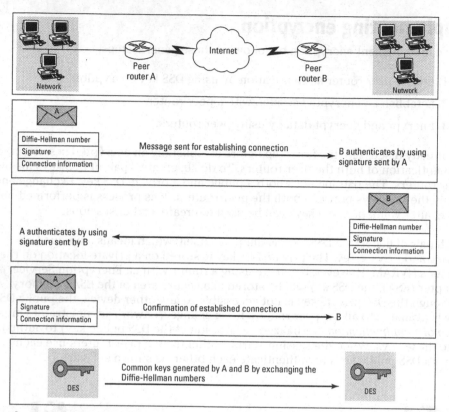

Figure 7-3: Creating an encryption session

Initially, both the peer routers exchange a connection message that not only authenticates the routers but also creates a temporary DES key, which is referred to as a *session key*. In authentication, *signatures* are attached to the connection message. A signature is a piece of coded text that each peer router generates by using its private DSS key. This key is confirmed at the destination peer router by using the public DSS key, which was earlier exchanged. Each signature is unique to its own router and cannot be duplicated. When the signature is verified, the router that sent the signature is considered authenticated.

The connection message also generates a session key, which is the key used to encrypt data in the course of the encryption session. The process of creating the session key involves exchanging Diffie-Hellman (DH) numbers in the connection message. These numbers then derive a common session key, which is shared by both the routers.

After the authentication of both the routers and generation of the session key, the router can start encrypting the data. The routers use an encryption algorithm to convert the plaintext data into encrypted text, as shown in Figure 7-4. In case the session times out, the encrypted session ends and the DES key and the DH numbers are lost. A new DES key and new DH numbers must be created every time the peer routers establish a new session.

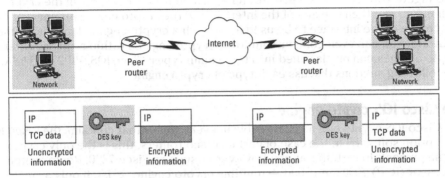

Figure 7-4: The process of encrypting data

Before you configure your routers for CET, make sure you have taken these three general steps:

✦ Ascertain which peer routers to use.

✦ Identify the network topology to use.

✦ Ascertain which crypto engines to use with each router.

Note   A *crypto engine* is a software program that performs the actual encryption.

After these steps have been incorporated, identify the peer routers between which the encryption process will take place. These routers pass data over unsecured networks, such as the Internet. If routers that participate in the encryption session are not within your administrative control, make sure that you share a trusted relationship with other routers' administrator.

Note   Only trusted routers should be allowed to be a part of encryption sessions.

Take extra care when you choose a network topology to use between routers. Encrypted data must always pass between a single pair of encrypted routers — no more; no additional encryption routers should exist between any pair of encrypted routers. If multiple peer routers exist, such as for the purpose of load balancing, then a chance exists that the data packets might be lost during transit. This doesn't mean that load balancing should not take place. You can set up devices between the peer routers to perform load balancing. One of the most common network topologies is the hub-and-spoke topology created between the peer routers at the corporate office and the peer routers at the branch offices. You can also configure the Internet firewall routers as peer routers for encryption.

Because the crypto-engine program does the actual encryption, your first step is to configure your router as a peer router — which means configuring the crypto engine. You can then use any of the interfaces of the crypto engine for encryption. The choice of the interface to be used along with a crypto engine depends on the hardware. You can even configure multiple crypto engines within a single router. Crypto engines can be classified into three main types: Cisco IOS, VIP2, and ESA. The following sections discuss each type of crypto engine.

The Cisco IOS crypto engine

The Cisco IOS crypto engine is available in every router that contains the Cisco IOS encryption software. In the case of certain Cisco routers, this is the only crypto engine present. In certain routers, however — such as Cisco 7200, Route Switch Processor (RSP) 7000, and 7500 — multiple crypto engines exist. If only a single crypto engine exists, the Cisco IOS crypto engine must be configured before you configure any other router interfaces. The identification mark of the Cisco IOS crypto engine is the chassis slot number of the RSP. If no RSP number occurs, then the Cisco IOS crypto engine is the default option during configuration.

The VIP2 crypto engine

The VIP2 crypto engine is available only in the Cisco RSP7000 and 7500 series routers. Both the Cisco RSP7000 and 7500 series routers consist of two crypto engines: the Cisco IOS crypto engine and the Versatile Interface Processor (VIP2) crypto engine. The VIP2 crypto engine manages the VIP2 port interfaces; the Cisco IOS crypto engine manages the other interfaces. The identification mark of the VIP2 crypto engine is the chassis slot number of the VIP2 port interface.

The Encryption Service Adapter (ESA) crypto engine

The ESA crypto engine is available with the Cisco 7200, RSP7000, and 7500 series of Cisco routers that contain an Encryption Service Adapter (ESA). In a Cisco 7200 router, you can activate either the Cisco IOS engine or Cisco ESA engine. However, only one engine is active at any given point in time. It is the active engine that actually manages the router interfaces. The identification mark of the ESA crypto engine is the chassis slot number of the VIP2.

Applications using encryption

Some examples of where encryption can be used to secure communication are shown in Figure 7-5. These applications perform the following services:

✦ Securing network traffic on WANs that use a leased line or on the Internet

✦ Securing VPNs created over the Internet between partner organizations

✦ Securing traffic moving between Web browsers and the corporate servers

✦ Securing VPN gateways created between remote branches or locations and the corporate network on the Internet

✦ Securing communication between a remote location and the corporate network, using dial-up communication

Note   To ensure secure communication, a secured router should be configured at the remote location.

✦ Securing confidential information against hackers as it passes through the corporate network

Encryption is not always the best solution to solve the security problems associated with communication and transfer of data over the corporate network. Encryption puts additional strain on the CPU usage and also reduces the speed of transmitting data. Before you implement encryption, analyze the technical capacities of your network and research the security needs of your organization; a solution that overtaxes your technology is not the best solution. When you have made that determination, define an explicit security policy that defines the location, time, and the specific methods for implementing encryption. Figure 7-5 offers a starting point for this assessment.

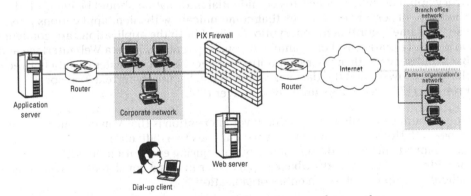

Figure 7-5: These applications can benefit from the use of encryption

Where should you implement encryption?

Network administrators have the choice of implementing encryption on the Application, Network, and Data Link layers of the OSI model, as shown in Figure 7-6. Implementing encryption at any of these layers has its own benefits, implementation problems, and associated costs.

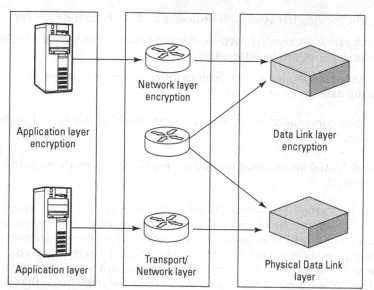

Figure 7-6: Encryption implemented at three layers of the OSI model

Encryption at the Application layer

Every application that generates confidential information should be encrypted. Similarly, all server applications that communicate with client applications must use the same algorithm for encryption, even if both the applications are configured on separate platforms. For example, if your applications have a Web interface and back-end servers, then your best option for securing the transfer of data between the Web browser and the data servers is to use Secure Hypertext Transport Protocol (HTTPS) and Secured Socket Layer (SSL).

One advantage of using Application-layer encryption is that you can encrypt data as needed. However, such convenience imposes two difficulties — delegation of user control and the additional labor of configuring encryption on each server individually. (The latter drawback in particular makes a consistent security policy difficult to implement for an entire organization.)

Encryption at the Network layer

You can implement Network-layer encryption anywhere on the network. Moreover, you need not upgrade any of the host applications to encrypt network traffic. The information stored on the third and fourth layers is not encrypted and is for routing the data packets. Therefore not only is network security ensured but also the users are also able to use QoS at both ends of the network.

One advantage of using Network-layer encryption is that the data packets travel invisibly between subnets — and security is relatively easy to implement at this level. One example of Network-layer encryption is CET, which is implemented on Cisco routers by using Cisco IOS software and IPSec encryption.

CET helps a network administrator to implement network security by using encryption. Because the implementation of encryption is done on the peer routers, it is transparent to the end users, in-between routers, and the network devices, as shown in Figure 7-7. The best location for configuring encryption is on the edge of the network, which is the source of data entry or exit from the network. When the data is encrypted at the source, it is decrypted only at the end or at the destination router.

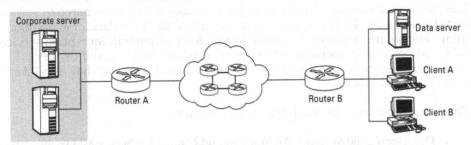

Figure 7-7: Network-layer encryption

By using Network-layer encryption, the network administrator can implement encryption at any point of the network. Because, the packet header information contains TCP or UDP information, only the contents of the data packets are encrypted. In this way, the encrypted data packets are transmitted over the network like any other IP data packet. Because only the contents of the data packets are encrypted, the packets can be switched like normal unencrypted data packets. In this way, secure data is transmitted undetected over the Internet.

Some characteristics of Network-layer encryption are as follows:

✦ It is supported by Cisco IOS software.

✦ It is not dependent on the type of topology implemented on the network.

✦ It is dependent on the interface used to implement encryption (but not on the protocol used).

✦ It does not require support from in-between routers or any other devices on the network.

✦ It encrypts according to user, application, or subnet.

Encryption at the Data Link layer

Data Link-layer encryption is performed on devices beyond the scope of routers. In data link encryption, information like the Network-layer header and the type of protocol used is also encrypted. The encryption depends on the type of network topology implemented on the network. Every weak point on the network must be secured by encryption. Because, even the header information is encrypted, the process of encryption, decryption, and routing of information is repeated several times. This leads to holdups in the network and security lapses.

AIM modules

Use Advance Interface Module (AIM) to perform hardware-based encryption of the data transmitted through the serial interface of Cisco 2600 and 3600 series routers. Cisco AIM modules are attached directly to the motherboard of the Cisco routers. The performance of these modules is about 10 times more as compared to software-based encryption. This is because these modules offload the data for encryption from the main processor of the router. In addition to providing encryption services, AIM modules can also perform other functions related to IPSec, such as key exchange, hashing, and storing security associations. In this way they help take the load off the processor.

The two most commonly used AIMs are as follows:

✦ **The Cisco 2600 Series AIM:** You can add Cisco 2600 Series AIM to all models of Cisco 2600. It provides encryption with up to 10-Mbps 3DES performance for a packet size not exceeding 1400 bytes.

✦ **The Cisco 3600 Series AIM:** You can add Cisco 3600 Series AIM to all models of Cisco 3600. It provides encryption with up to 40-Mbps 3DES performance for a packet size not exceeding 1400 bytes.

Cisco IOS cryptosystem — an overview

Cisco Encryption Technology actually comprises five distinct encryption technologies:

✦ **Digital-Encryption Standard (DES)** is the most widely accepted encryption standard for data encryption and decryption.

✦ **Triple DES** is a variation of DES that encrypts data three different times before sending.

✦ **Message Digest 5 (MD5)** converts data of different lengths into encrypted data of fixed length. It combines with DSS to create digital certificates.

✦ **Digital Signature Standard (DSS)** uses an algorithm to create a piece of code attached as a signature to the message. DSS is also used for authenticating peer routers.

✦ **Diffie-Hellman key agreement** helps in the authentication of the public keys used to create the session key. This session key is for the DES session and also helps in authenticating peer routers.

When combined, these technologies form a *cryptosystem* that can take advantage of their best features, as shown in Figure 7-8.

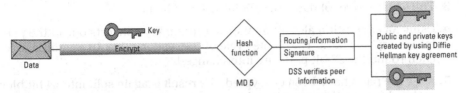

Figure 7-8: Cisco Encryption Technology cryptosystem

Many methods exist to ensure the privacy of encryption keys and to create these keys. One such method is DSS, which uses the concept of public and private keys to authenticate hosts and users during the process of encryption. By using the Diffie-Hellman key agreement, routers can exchange encryption keys without any actual physical exchange; only the information about the keys is exchanged and not the physical keys. Though it is most commonly used for encryption, the Diffie-Hellman method does not completely ensure the authenticity of the peer router. Cisco 11.2 and later versions contain three encryption technologies and therefore enable support for CET.

DES encryption

A commonly used encryption standard, DES converts plaintext into encrypted text by using an encryption algorithm. On the remote peer router, the encrypted data is then converted back to unencrypted text. As discussed before, the encryption technology uses keys for the purpose of encrypting and decrypting the data. The keys for encryption are available at both the peer routers, but neither of the routers transfers the keys over the network. The process of DES encryption is shown in Figure 7-9.

Figure 7-9: DES encryption

DES encrypts data by converting the plaintext into 64-bit blocks and then encrypts the data, after which it further encrypts the resultant text into 64-bit blocks. (Although the data is converted into blocks of 64-bit, the data can also be converted into blocks of 8-bits.) The default length of a DES key is 56 bits, and Cisco creates DES keys at random by using the Diffie-Hellman encryption method. The process of encrypting text by using DES comprises five steps:

1. DES breaks down the total text into fixed blocks, which helps simplify the management and encryption of the data.

2. A basic encryption algorithm serves to encrypt the DES key.

3. The 64-bit blocks of data are split into two 32-bit parts.

4. Using an encryption algorithm, the encryption key converts one of the parts into encrypted data. The whole cycle of encryption takes 16 rounds, and after each round the 32-bit parts are interchanged.

5. After the parts have been encrypted, the result is again split into 64-bit blocks of data by using the encryption key.

DES provides an advantage in that the encryption algorithm that serves to encrypt the data is also used to decrypt it. Similarly, the same encryption key is also used for both encryption and decryption of data. DES can be implemented both on hardware and on software.

Triple Data-Encryption Standard (3DES)

Triple DES (3DES) is a minor variation of DES. Because DES is easy to break with the help of advanced technology, Triple DES is implemented more widely than DES. Even though Triple DES is three times slower than DES, it has proved to be an extremely reliable solution because of the longer key length that it uses. This extended length of key plays an important role in eliminating many of the shortcut attacks you can use to reduce the amount of time it takes to break DES.

Triple DES is simply another mode of DES operation. It takes three 64-bit keys, for an overall key length of 192 bits. The procedure for data encryption in 3DES is exactly the same as DES. The only difference between the two mechanisms is that data encryption uses three steps: The data is encrypted with the first key, decrypted with the second key, and finally encrypted again with the third key (which is why this method is called *Triple* DES).

Although the input key for DES is 64 bits long, the actual key used by DES is only 56 bits in length. The reason behind this is that the least significant (right-most) bit in each byte is a parity bit. These parity bits are ignored during encryption. Therefore only the seven most significant bits of each byte are used, resulting in a key length of 56 bits; the eight parity bits contained by the three keys are not used in encryption. As a result, the effective key length of 3DES is 168 bits instead of 256 bits.

Because a 3DES key is three times the length of a standard DES key, the speed of 3DES-based encryptions is three times slower than standard DES. Although data is still encrypted and decrypted in 64-bit chunks (as with DES,), 3DES offers greater security than DES. The procedure for decrypting a message in 3DES is executed in reverse.

However, one inherent weakness of 3DES is that if any two of the three keys match each other, then the encryption procedure is essentially the same as standard DES. This situation should be avoided.

Note   Triple-DES has been adopted by ANSI as standard X9.52 and is a proposed revision to FIPS 46 as draft FIPS 46-3. Refer to RFCs 1828 and 2420 for more information on 3DES.

MD5 message hashing

Message hashing ensures the authenticity of transmitted data packets. The algorithm used in message hashing takes unencrypted text (such as user name and password) as input and converts it into encrypted text. The encrypted text is of a fixed length of 128 bits. This process is displayed in Figure 7-10. The MD5 encryption algorithm is also used for creating digital signatures; Cisco IOS Software uses it for message hashing.

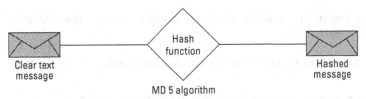

Figure 7-10: Encryption by message hashing

DSS encryption

The DSS encryption mechanism ensures the security of data from any changes made by hackers. By using a private key, an encryption algorithm is created and whoever has the public key can access this digital signature, but only the person who has created the digital signature can generate it again. DSS serves to authenticate the client computer or the client who must be contacted.

DSS creates public and private keys for encryption where the public key is a derivative of the private key. All the users share a pair of public and private keys, and the MD5 hash function serves to verify the authenticity of the transmitted data. The *hash function* matches the digital signature of the encrypted text with the copy of the signature kept with itself, as with in the case of fingerprint matching. The private key then serves to sign the message after being assured of its authenticity. The data can only be decrypted at the destination router, if it contains a copy of the public key. Here again, the process of authentication is repeated.

DSS ensures the authenticity of data transmitted over the network by verifying the identity of both the sender and the receiver. In addition, the public keys are shared and the private keys are not; hackers cannot decrypt the data even if they can intercept a public key. Entities such as certificate authorities (CA) keep the public keys secure.

Generating a DSS signature (as shown in Figure 7-11) entails these steps:

1. The first router uses MD5 to hash the routing information.

2. The router then further encrypts the routing information by using a private key, thereby creating digital signatures.

3. The signature is then attached to the message and transmitted to the destination Cisco peer router.

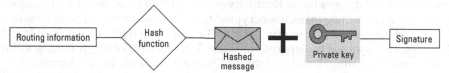

Figure 7-11: Generation of digital signatures

On the destination router, the digital signature is verified by using the following steps (as shown in Figure 7-12):

1. The destination router extracts the digital signature from the transmitted message.

2. The destination router decrypts the signature by using the first router's public key and derives the hash algorithm created by the first router.

3. The destination router uses the derived hash algorithm to decrypt the routing information.

4. The router compares both hashes. If the hashes match, the router is confident that the message is free of tampering.

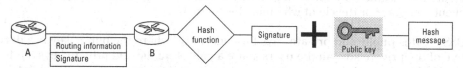

Figure 7-12: Signature verification by using DSS

Diffie-Hellman key agreement

Diffie-Hellman is an encryption technology that serves to ensure that the public keys are exchanged securely and helps in the creation of DES keys. When DSS authenticates both the peer routers, users must ensure the secure creation and generation of the session key. Because the security of the session key is of vital importance, the Diffie-Hellman encryption method serves to ensure that a hacker is not able to access the key. Not only is this protocol the oldest, it is also widely trusted for exchanging keys. One reason for this is that the keys are not physically exchanged, making them more difficult for hackers to hack. Diffie-Hellman uses two prime numbers, which are randomly selected but which have a special link with each other. These numbers are used to derive a session key, which prevents hackers from intercepting the key. This technology is used in Cisco Encryption Technology to secure data.

The secret key generated by the Diffie-Hellman algorithm is available with both the peer routers but is never transmitted over the network. Even if the hackers can get access to the public key, they will not be able to decrypt the data without the corresponding private key. One advantage of using the Diffie-Hellman key agreement is that since the users never enter the keys, hackers cannot intercept the keys. But the use of Diffie-Hellman also has a disadvantage associated with it: An administrator is always required at each peer router to authenticate the exchange of keys.

Note   The use of IPSec automates the process of exchanging keys in the Diffie-Hellman encryption method.

Configuring Cisco Encryption

Encryption must be configured at both the peer routers to transfer encrypted data between them. The Flash, RAM and IOS requirements for implementing encryption differ from one router to another. Table 7-1 gives the Flash and RAM requirements for configuring encryption on Cisco 1601–1604 routers.

Table 7-1 Flash and RAM Requirements for Cisco 1601–1604 (run from Flash)		
Feature Set	Flash	RAM
IP Plus	6MB	4MB
IP Plus 40	6MB	4MB
IP Plus 56	6MB	4MB
IP/IPX	6MB	2MB
IP/IPX Plus	6MB	4MB

Tip   The Plus feature sets include features, such as NAT, data encryption, and Network Timing Protocol (NTP).

Table 7-2 describes the Flash and RAM requirements for Cisco 1605 routers for Cisco IOS Release 11.3.

Table 7-2
Flash and RAM Requirements for Cisco 1605 (run from RAM)

Feature Set	Flash	RAM
IP Plus	4MB	8MB
IP Plus 40	4MB	8MB
IP Plus 56	4MB	8MB
IP/IPX	2MB	8MB
IP/IPX Plus	4MB	8MB

Table 7-3 depicts the Cisco 1750 feature sets and Flash and DRAM requirements for Cisco IOS Release 12.0.

Table 7-3
Cisco 1750 Feature Sets with Flash and DRAM Requirements for Cisco IOS Release 12.0

Feature Sets	Flash	DRAM
IP Plus	4MB	16MB
IP Plus 40	4MB	20MB
IP Plus 56	4MB	20MB
IP Plus IPSec 56	4MB	20MB
IP Plus IPSec 3DES	4MB	20MB
IP/Firewall Plus IPSec 56	4MB	20MB
IP/Firewall Plus IPSec 3DES	4MB	20MB
IP/IPX	4MB	16MB
IP/IPX/Firewall Plus	4MB	20MB

Note   You can get detailed information on Flash, RAM, and IOS requirements for Cisco routers at www.cisco.com.

Use the following checklist to organize encryption on one of your peer routers. Then duplicate these measures on the other router:

✦ Create public and private keys by using DSS

✦ Have your peer routers exchange DSS public keys

✦ Use the DES encryption algorithm

✦ Classify your crypto maps and assign them to specific interfaces

✦ Make a backup of the configuration

✦ Test and verify encryption

Creating public and private keys by using DSS

The DSS keys must be created for each crypto engine; however, if multiple crypto engines are used, a pair of DSS keys must be separately generated for each engine. The pair of DSS keys is employed by the peer routers for establishing authentication before the creation of the encrypted sessions. When a pair of DSS keys is created, it can be used to create any number of encrypted sessions.

Table 7-4 describes the commands used to generate DSS keys for a crypto engine.

Table 7-4 Commands That Generate DSS Keys for a Crypto Engine	
Command	Description
crypto key generate dss key-name [slot]	Use this command to generate DSS public and private keys.
show crypto key mypubkey dss [slot]	Use this command to view the DSS public key.
copy system:running-confignvram:startup-config	Use this command to save DSS keys to private NVRAM.

While creating DSS keys for routers using an ESA crypto engine, you are prompted for a password. The default location where the DSS keys are saved is at a secure location in the ESA memory.

Exchanging DSS public keys

The DSS public keys must be available with all the routers and therefore must be authenticated. In this way both the peer routers authenticate themselves before initiating an encrypted session. If multiple peer routers exist on the network, the process of authentication must be repeated for each router. When a router is authenticated, it has access to the data for the rest of the sessions. Any time a new peer router is added to the network, the router must be authenticated before it gets access to the encrypted data. The DSS keys must also be exchanged with every crypto engine used on the network. The following steps must be performed to exchange DSS public keys:

1. Phone the administrator of the remote peer router; stay in communication until the whole process of encryption ends.

2. Both administrators must decide which peer router serves as host and which serves as client.

3. The client router facilitates a DSS exchange connection by using the `crypto key exchange` command.

4. The host router commences a DSS exchange connection and transmits a DNS public key by using the `crypto key exchange` command.

5. Both the administrators must communicate for authenticating the serial numbers that appear on their respective monitors.

6. If numbers match, the client peer router acknowledges the host peer router's DSS key and types y where asked. Here y signifies the acceptance of the DSS key.

7. The client peer router then sends a public DSS key to the host router and selects the appropriate crypto engine at the prompt.

8. The DSS serial number of the client machine is displayed on both the monitors.

9. Once again both the administrators must communicate for authenticating the serial numbers and match the signatures on their respective screens.

10. The host router now accepts the client router's DSS public key.

11. The DSS keys are now exchanged, and the telephonic communication can now end.

Using the DES encryption algorithm

The peer routers use the DES algorithm for encrypting and decrypting data. All DES algorithms used by the router must be enabled — a router not enabled cannot be used. At least one DES algorithm must be enabled for creating and encrypting a session with a peer router. CET supports the following types of DES encryption algorithms:

✦ 40-bit variation of DES with 8-bit Cipher FeedBack (CFB)

✦ 40-bit variation of DES with 64-bit CFB

✦ DES with 8-bit CFB

✦ DES with 64-bit CFB

By default, one DES algorithm is allowed on a peer router. You can disable the default option and enable another algorithm in its place.

Table 7-5 describes the commands that you use in the global configuration mode to globally enable DES algorithms.

Table 7-5
Commands Used for Globally Enabling DES Algorithms

Command	Description
`crypto cisco algorithm des [cfb-8| cfb-64]`	Use this command to enable DES with 8-bit or 64-bit CFB.
`crypto cisco algorithm 40-bit-des [cfb-8| cfb-64]`	Use this command to enable 40-bit DES with 8-bit or 64-bit CFB.
`show crypto cisco algorithm`	Use this command to view all the DES algorithms that have been enabled.

Classifying crypto maps and assigning them to interfaces

Crypto maps identify the DES encryption algorithms that can be used with access lists. They can also be used to pinpoint peer routers providing encryption services. Crypto maps with the same name can be categorized together as *crypto map sets*. These crypto map sets are applied to interfaces, which compare the network traffic against the policies specified in the crypto map sets. These interfaces detect data packets that require security. Then the crypto map uses security associations to secure the data.

For every interface that transmits encrypted data to peer routers only one crypto map can be created. Moreover, every interface can have only one crypto map set applied to it. A *crypto map set* contains a mixture of IPSec, IKE, and manually configured SA entries using IPSec. You can implement a single crypto map set to more than one interface to apply the same policy to all the interfaces. The conditions under which you can create multiple crypto maps are as follows:

✦ Different types of IPSec security must be applied to diverse types of traffic.

✦ Different IPSec peers must handle different forms of data flows.

✦ IKE is not being used to implement a specific set of security associations; therefore you want to implement more than one entry from access lists.

Identify the interfaces used to encrypt or decrypt data transmitted over the network, the IP packets that will be encrypted or decrypted, and also the algorithm that performs this encryption. To do so, follow these steps:

1. **Configure an encryption access list:**

   Encryption access lists identify which IP packets will be encrypted and which will not be encrypted. Use extended IP access lists to create encryption access lists. Although IP lists are generally used to filter network traffic, encryption access lists are not used for this purpose. They are used to classify which data packets can be encrypted and which cannot be encrypted. You can use either of the commands shown in Table 7-6 to configure an encryption access list.

Table 7-6
Commands Used to Configure an Encryption Access List

Command	Description
`access-list access-list-number [dynamic dynamic-name [timeout minutes]] {deny|permit} protocol source source-wildcard destination destination-wildcard [precedence precedence] [tos tos][log]`	Use this command to specify the IP packets you want to encrypt.
`ip access-list extended name`	After this command, give the appropriate permit or deny statements.

2. **Classify your crypto maps:**

   Crypto maps are used to identify the type of DES encryption algorithm that can be used while configuring access lists. It also provides information regarding routers that provide remote encryption services. Each interface requires its own crypto map for sending data to a peer encryption router. Therefore be sure to define a crypto map for each interface; Table 7-7 shows the commands you can use for this purpose.

Table 7-7
Commands Used to Define a Crypto Map

Command	Description
`Crypto map map-name seq-num [cisco]`	Use this command (in global configuration mode) to assign a name to a crypto map.
`Set peer key-name`	Use this command to specify the remote peer router.

Command	Description
`Match address [access-list-number|name]`	Use this command to specify an encryption access list.
`Set algorithm des [cfb-8|cfb-64]` Or `Set algorithm 40-bit-des [cfb-8|cfb-64]`	Use this command to specify a DES encryption algorithm already enabled.

Note   If the same policy must be applied to all interfaces, more than one interface can use the same crypto map.

3. **Attach the crypto maps to your interfaces.**

This step implements the crypto maps created in the previous step. A crypto map encrypts all the data going out of the network and decrypts all data entering the network. To apply a crypto map to an interface, use the following command:

```
crypto map map-name
```

Caution   Once configuration is over, it is advisable to make a backup of the configuration. This backup must be secured against hackers.

Configuring encryption by using GRE tunnels

You can configure encryption by using GRE tunnels. The GRE tunnels are configured on the peer routers and should be configured to encrypt all traffic passing through the tunnel. However, you cannot configure the GRE tunnels to encrypt data selectively. Data can be configured for encryption by using GRE tunnels in two ways.

Encrypting only GRE tunnel traffic

To encrypt only the data transmitted through the GRE tunnel, follow these steps:

✦ The encryption access list should only contain one criterion.

✦ The crypto map must be applied to both the physical as well as tunnel interfaces.

Encrypting GRE tunnel traffic along with other traffic

Follow these steps to encrypt data transmitted through either a GRE tunnel or a non-GRE tunnel:

✦ Make two encryption access lists, one that contains only a criterion and a second that contains an encryption access list. This list contains information about the other types of non-GRE traffic.

✦ Make separate crypto-map sets; the first one contains a single crypto map including the initial encryption access list and the other containing another crypto map that includes two subdefinitions.

✦ The first crypto-map set pertains to the tunnel interface, and the second crypto-map set to the physical interface.

Testing and verifying encryption

You can use a number of Cisco IOS commands to test and verify the process of encryption.

Testing encryption

You can use the following command to initiate a session between two peers for testing the process of encryption:

```
test crypto initiate-session src-ip-addr dst-ip-addr map-name seq-number
```

where

✦ `src-ip-addr` denotes the IP address of the source computer. This IP address should be a valid source IP address in the access list's definition.

✦ `dst-ip-addr` denotes the IP address of the destination computer. This IP address should be a valid IP address destination address in the access list definition.

✦ `map-name` denotes the name of the crypto map.

✦ `seq-name` denotes the sequence number of the crypto map.

After you have given this command, you can check the status of the connection by using the following command:

```
show crypto cisco connections
```

Verifying encryption

You can verify the process of encryption at two levels: the local router's crypto engine and the local router's encrypted-session connections.

You can use the following commands to verify encryption at a local router's crypto engine:

```
show crypto engine brief
```

To view the configuration of all crypto engines within a router, use the following command:

```
show crypto engine configuration
```

If you want to display the status of both current and pending crypto connections, you can use the following command to verify encryption at the local router's encrypted-session connections:

```
show crypto cisco connections
```

To view the encrypted-session connections presently active for all crypto engines on a router, use the following command:

```
show crypto engine connections active
```

 Note   The show crypto cisco connections command has replaced the show crypto connections command that was used in Cisco IOS Release 11.2.

When you issue a show crypto cisco connections command, the output appears in tabular form and has the following command fields:

✦ *PE*: Refers to protected entity. This command field shows a representative of the source IP address as defined in the access list.

✦ *UPE*: Refers to unprotected entity. This field shows a representative of the destination IP address as defined in the access list.

✦ *Time*: Shows the time at which the connection was initiated for pending connections.

✦ *Timestamp*: Shows the time at which the connection was initiated for completed connections.

✦ Conn_id shows a number that serves to refer and track a connection. Conn_id can range from 1 to 299. It can also have any negative integer value. However, negative integer values are assigned when the connection is pending.

✦ New_id shows a number assigned to the connection after the connection has been set up.

✦ Alg shows the DES encryption algorithm that was used for the connection.

✦ Time shows the time at which the connection was established.

✦ Flags shows details of the connection state. It can have the following values.

  • BAD_CONN specifies no pending or existing connections for the table entry.

  • PEND_CONN specifies that the table entry is a pending connection.

  • TIME_KEYS specifies that the encrypted communication session be in progress.

  • UNK_STATUS specifies the status as invalid. This flag is also used when the connection status cannot be determined.

  • XCHG_KEYS specifies that the connection has timed out.

Troubleshooting Cisco Encryption Technology

You can use the `show` and `debug` commands for troubleshooting Cisco Encryption Technology. The reasons for most common problems can be found by determining the state of the connection. Use the following commands to determine the state of a connection.

✦ The `show crypto cisco connections` command checks the connection ID.

✦ The `show crypto map` command checks the status of the crypto maps.

To trace the packet flow and the occurrence of events, use the following commands:

✦ The `debug crypto key-exchange` command displays the debugging messages associated with DSS public-key exchange.

✦ The `debug key-exchange` command displays Diffie-Hellman key exchange messages.

✦ The `debug crypto sesmgmt` command displays connection setup messages.

Options for customizing encryption

No single encryption scheme can possibly protect all networks equally; sooner or later, you're likely to customize Cisco encryption to suit the specific needs of your network. To do so on a router, you can configure the following options:

✦ Modify encryption access list limits

✦ Decrease session-setup time

✦ Specify duration of encrypted sessions

Modify the limits of your encryption access lists

Configuring your encryption access lists also involves configuring the source and destination pair *in the criteria statements*. When a data packet reaches a device configured to encrypt access lists, the source and destination information of that data packet must be matched with the source and destination information in the criteria statements. The data is encrypted only in the event of a complete match.

By default, you can define up to 100 hosts (and 10 destinations per host) in an encryption access list. For example, if you have defined 4 hosts, then you can set no more than 40 criteria in your access list (up to 10 destinations per host). Thus setting encryption-access limits helps you preallocate memory for potential connections.

Although normally you need not change the default settings (which specify a maximum of 100 hosts and no more than 10 destinations per host), sometimes you may have to change these settings. For example, if you have 15 remote hosts and each one must connect to the host server, then the situation calls for 15 destination addresses to configure the encrypted access list. In such a case, change the encryption access list's maximum destinations-per-host from 10 to 15.

> **Note**   Changing maximum limits affects the memory of your system. Every addition you make to a limit requires a corresponding (additional) memory allocation.

Decrease session-setup time

The process of generating Diffie-Hellman numbers is CPU-intensive enough to slow down the setup of a session. You can shorten that interval by generating the Diffie-Hellman numbers beforehand. To do so, issue the following command in the global configuration mode:

```
Router (config)# crypto cisco pregen-dh-pairs count[slot]
```

Specify duration of encrypted sessions

By default, the duration of each encrypted session is 30 minutes. When the duration of the encrypted session expires, the session must be renegotiated if the session must be extended. However, you can change this default duration according to your requirements to shorten or extend the duration of the encrypted sessions. To change the time duration of the encrypted sessions, use the following commands.

```
Router (config)# crpto cisco key-timeout minutes
Router (config)# show crypto cisco key-timeout
```

The `Router (config)# crpto cisco key-timeout minutes` command defines the maximum time duration of encrypted sessions.

The `Router (config)# show crypto cisco key-timeout` command displays the defined duration of encrypted sessions.

Summary

This chapter provided a general outline of encryption, listed some common methods used to disrupt network security — such as IP spoofing, system-backdoor exploitation, and brute-force password attacks — and described the steps needed to implement encryption. The chapter described various crypto engines, some applications that use encryption, and Cisco Encryption Technology — concluding with instructions for configuring encryption on Cisco routers.

✦   ✦   ✦

Security Using Firewalls

Part III examines and evaluates the vital role that firewalls play in ensuring the security of a network that uses Internet connectivity. An overview of two Cisco firewall products — IOS Firewall and PIX Firewall — explains the best uses of firewall products and includes steps for configuring PIX Firewall.

Cisco IOS Firewall

C H A P T E R

8

♦ ♦ ♦ ♦

In This Chapter

Considering Cisco
IOS Firewall and
related products

Selecting Cisco IOS
firewall components

Implementing
Context-Based
Access Control

♦ ♦ ♦ ♦

Networked organizations require connectivity, not just between their own computers but also with the Internet. Employees have become more mobile, working from home is more widely accepted, and more employees can connect to their office networks from remote locations. All these factors expose an organization's network to the outside world — which also means exposure to hostile entities that can harm the network. A mechanism that denies network access to hostile or unauthorized traffic is an absolute must.

This chapter details Cisco IOS Firewall and its components — in particular, Context-Based Access Control (CBAC), which is a crucial security tool. The chapter covers configuring CBAC on a router, evaluating the benefits and limitations of CBAC, and applying CBAC in a typical practical scenario.

Cisco IOS Firewall Overview

Today, all *campus networks* (groups of interconnected LANs) are exposed to the Internet in one way or another, which increases the risk of attack. A single loophole in network security is enough to provide a way in for expert hackers — and for a successful attack on network resources. In the absence of unlimited security budgets, you still want to provide strong security on your boundary routers without investing in additional hardware — which makes Cisco IOS Firewall an indispensable part of your solution. As a security-specific option for Cisco IOS software, Cisco IOS Firewall adds application-based filtering, dynamic (and user-specific) authentication and authorization, detection and prevention of common network attacks, filtering of Java applets, and a number of other security enhancements.

In addition to its firewall technology, Cisco IOS Firewall provides the CBAC feature. Hardware compatibility is considerable; Cisco 1600,2500, 2600, 3600, 7100, 7200, 7500, and RSM series routers support all Cisco IOS firewall features. Table 8-1 lists the flash and RAM requirements for implementing IOS Firewall version 12.0 on various Cisco router series.

Table 8-1 Flash and RAM Requirements for Implementing IOS Firewall v. 12.0		
Router Series	Flash Requirements	RAM Requirements
1600	6MB	4MB
2500	8MB	4MB
2600	4MB	20MB

Cisco IOS Firewall is also scalable and versatile. You can use it to configure a Cisco IOS router to function as

✦ A firewall between two organizations' networks

✦ A firewall between two user groups in a network

✦ A firewall between branch offices

✦ An Internet firewall

✦ A part of an Internet firewall

Cisco IOS Firewall is part of a larger family of Cisco IOS software; the upcoming section examines the characteristics of this family so you can use its applications efficiently.

Features of Cisco IOS software

As the *Internetworking Operating System* (IOS) that provides network services and facilitates networked applications, Cisco IOS software works well with Cisco networking equipment such as access servers, routers, and switches. It uses a suite of technologies to provide internetworking intelligence, enable interoperable connections between otherwise-incompatible hardware devices (across a variety of protocols), and offers the flexibility and scalability needed to accommodate changes and expansion in networks.

Cisco IOS software offers a variety of capabilities, which include

✦ **Security features:** Cisco IOS software offers authentication, authorization, and encryption features to ensure network security. Authentication involves validating a user's identity and can be implemented by using a variety of techniques, such as password scheme, digital signatures, token cards, and biological systems. Authorization controls the action that an authorized user can perform on the network resources. Confidentiality of the information is achieved by encryption.

Cross-Reference
For more information on authentication and authorization, refer to Chapter 10.

✦ **QoS management:** A communication network is an integral part of any up-to-speed organization. Because almost all activities in an organization depend on the network, it is important that the performance of network is optimum at any given point in time. Because these networks transmit important and confidential data on which most business decisions are based, there should be minimal packet loss and delay. A cost-effective network must provide secure, predictable, measurable, and guaranteed services. QoS (Quality of Service) is a set of techniques for managing network resources (such as bandwidth) for the best possible network performance.

✦ **VPN support:** Cisco IOS software supports VPN services. VPNs create dynamic connections across shared networks, such as the Internet. VPNs can also be used as an alternative to dedicated leased lines, providing a cost-effective method of accessing or transmitting data over public networks.

Cross-Reference
For more information on VPNs, refer Chapter 12.

✦ **Load balancing:** This feature distributes processing activities evenly in a network so no single device is overburdened. The more heavily an organization depends on its network services, the more vital the servers are — especially those that store data. To ensure uninterrupted access to information, this feature treats an unusually high number of requests as a signal to redistribute the processing load among several servers.

✦ **Caching:** Heavy Internet traffic can challenge ISPs (and the organizations they serve) to overcome bandwidth congestion, maximize network service quality, maximize availability of the Internet, and reduce transmission costs. *Caching* provides one answer: When a user sends a request, a copy of the information received as an answer to the request is stored on a local device in anticipation of similar requests. When another user sends the same request, the information stored on the local device is retrieved and sent to the user. By reducing the number of times a browser must refresh from a faraway and heavily used source, caching helps reduce Internet traffic — and can also reduce transmission costs (not all requests have to go to the servers on the Internet).

Vulnerabilities in Cisco IOS software

Although Cisco IOS software offers a variety of security services, some inherent vulnerabilities in the software exist. Crucial among these vulnerabilities are the following:

✦ **Cisco IOS HTTP server:** This vulnerability is defined as Cisco bug ID CSCdr36952 and affects almost all Cisco routers and switches that run Cisco IOS software releases 11.1 to 12.1. This defect causes halting and reloading of Cisco routers or switches that have IOS HTTP service enabled and attempt to browse `http://<router-ip>/%%`. The defect makes the network prone to denial-of-service attacks.

✦ **TELNET option handling:** This vulnerability is due to a defect, which causes unexpected reloading of Cisco routers when they are tested for security vulnerabilities by using security-scanning software. Hackers can use this defect to launch denial-of-service attacks. The IOS software releases vulnerable to this defect are 11.33AA and 12.0(2) to 12.0(6). However, 12.0(7)S, 12.0(7)T, 12.0(7)XE are not vulnerable to this defect.

✦ **SYSLOG denial-of-service:** This vulnerability is due to a defect, which causes devices implementing Cisco IOS software to hang or crash when invalid UDP packets are sent to their SYSLOG port. The IOS software releases vulnerable to this defect are 11.33AA, 11.3DB and 12.0.

However, for all these vulnerabilities, Cisco has developed fixes and upgrades. You can refer to `www.cisco.com` to know more about the vulnerabilities in Cisco IOS software and their fixes.

Benefits of Cisco IOS Firewall

Cisco IOS Firewall enhances the security features of Cisco IOS software by adding application-based filtering, dynamic user-specific authentication and authorization, detection and prevention of common network attacks, Java applets filtering, and a number of other features.

The Cisco IOS Firewall can integrate with Cisco IOS software while providing maximum security. The benefits of the Cisco IOS Firewall are

✦ **Flexibility:** It is an integrated solution that provides secure Internet access, multiprotocol routing, and enhanced security features, such as per user and application protocol-based filtering. Due to these capabilities, it provides scope for applying security policies in exactly the same manner as they are defined.

✦ **Low cost and investment protection:** No need to add new hardware. The Cisco IOS Firewall integrates with the existing Cisco IOS software and can work with the routers already deployed.

✦ **Support for VPNs:** Cisco IOS Firewall is compatible with IPSec, Cisco IOS encryption, and QoS features required for a secure VPN.

✦ **Easier management:** You can implement security features remotely by using Cisco ConfigMaker from a central console.

Cisco IOS Firewall Components

Cisco IOS Firewall provides integrated security features for protecting a network against attacks and intrusion. The components of the Cisco IOS Firewall are

✦ **Context-Based Access List:** This is an enhanced access list that allows packets of only valid sessions initiated by hosts on the internal network to enter the internal network. It detects and prevents denial-of-service attacks and network intrusion.

✦ **Intrusion detection:** This includes real-time monitoring of the network traffic, detecting any unauthorized user sending traffic into the network, and detecting any misuse of the network by internal users. It actually detects inappropriate, incorrect, or anomalous activities in the network.

✦ **Denial-of-service detection and prevention:** This includes protecting the servers and routers from attacks of denial-of-service. It checks the Transport-layer headers for any suspicious information and keeps track of the number of half-open sessions to hosts.

✦ **Blocking of Java applets:** This includes blocking the unintentional download-ing of malicious Java applets by internal users. The users can download Java applets only from the so-called "friendly" sites.

✦ **Real-time alerts and audit trails:** These include logging of alert messages for attacks on the network or any misuse of network resources. Audit trails include logging of details of the transactions on the network along with the timestamp and other details for each event. You can also configure alerts and audit trails to log messages according to specific Application-layer protocols.

✦ **Event logging:** This includes keeping track of potential security breaches or any misuse of network resources. System error messages are logged to a SYSLOG server or some terminal.

✦ **Firewall management:** This is a network configuration tool that runs a wizard for network design, assigning addresses to the network resources and firewall implementation.

✦ **Standard and extended access lists:** These provide basic traffic filtering according to criteria set by the administrator. You configure the access lists and set the criteria for the packets that should be allowed and blocked. The criteria are different for standard and extended access lists. The standard IP access lists can filter packets according to source IP address; extended IP access lists can only filter traffic by source and destination IP address. IP address lists also filter traffic by TCP/UDP port number.

✦ **Dynamic access lists:** These create entries in the access list dynamically after authenticating the user who wants to access resources. These entries allow the user to access the resources temporarily. You can also define the duration for which the user accesses the resource by configuring a timeout for these entries. After the time expires, the temporary entry is deleted and the user is again denied access to those resources. The user has to be authenticated once again to access the resources. It provides a better control over the traffic than with the static access lists.

✦ **Reflexive access lists:** These grant access to the internal network selectively; traffic from external, untrusted networks may enter only if it is a part of a session initiated from an internal host. The idea is to provide network access to only those packets that internal users require — which blocks any external host from initiating a session with an internal host.

✦ **Network Address Translation (NAT):** This allows a network with private IP addresses to connect to the Internet by translating these addresses into registered IP addresses. If your internal network has been configured with private IP addresses, your internal hosts cannot directly communicate with any host on the Internet because the hosts do not have valid IP addresses. You can solve this problem by using Network Address Translation (NAT) to translate these invalid or unregistered IP addresses into valid, registered IP addresses at the boundary of your network. With NAT, you can use one or more registered IP addresses to provide Internet connection to all your internal hosts that do not have registered IP addresses. The Internet world knows your network by these valid IP addresses. This provides additional security by hiding the addresses of your network from attackers.

For more information on NAT, refer to Chapter 6.

✦ **Time-based access list:** You can implement access lists by time of day if you first create a time range — whether of the day or the week — and assign a name to it. While configuring an access list that will be applied on an interface, specify this name as a parameter in the statements as required. A parameter in the named access lists where you can specify the name of the time range. However, it is available for only IP and IPX.

✦ **IPSec encryption:** IPSec is a set of standards that provides security to data while being transported over untrusted networks, such as the Internet. It operates at the network and protects and authenticates IP packets between two IPSec supporting devices.

✦ **VPN and QOS support:** Cisco IOS Firewall supports Cisco IOS software encryption, tunneling, and QoS features to provide support to secure VPNs. It supports advanced bandwidth management and service-level validation.

For information on VPNs, refer to Chapter 12.

✦ **Peer router authentication:** The firewall authenticates all the peer routers before accepting routing updates from them. This prevents incorrect updates sent by untrusted sources from updating the routing table.

✦ **Authentication Proxy:** The firewall can be configured to support user authentication by using TACACS+, RADIUS, and other security servers. You can also set individual, per-user security policies.

You can configure all these components to protect the network and prevent network attacks. Cisco IOS Firewall can be configured by using Cisco ConfigMaker, which is a Windows 95, 98, NT 4.0-based software tool. The guidelines for configuring a firewall are

✦ **Decide access control *before* you connect the console port to the network.** A hacker who can gain control of the console port can also break into the firewall. If the firewall is compromised, the entire network is compromised.

✦ **Password-protect the console.** If the network is configured for AAA, use the same authentication method for the console. However, if the network is not configured for AAA, you should at least configure the `login` and `password` commands.

✦ **Use the correct command to set privileged access to the firewall.** Use the `enable secret` command (which offers encryption) instead of the `enable secret` command to set the privileged access to the firewall.

✦ **Apply access lists to all virtual terminal ports.** Also, password-protect the virtual terminal ports.

✦ **Limit Telnet access.** Apply access lists to limit the number of users who can telnet to the router.

✦ **Disable all local services that you do not use.** Turn off Cisco Discovery Protocol (CDP) and Network Time Protocol (NTP) if you do not need them.

✦ **Configure interfaces and routers to prevent spoofing.** Set up an input access list at every interface and disable source routing at all routers.

✦ **Configure the access lists at asynchronous Telnet ports.** Doing so keeps the firewall from being used as relay.

✦ **Hide internal addresses from external users.** Use the `no proxy-arp` command to prevent the advertisement of internal addresses to the outside world.

✦ **Disable direct broadcast messages on the firewall and routers.** This will protect the network from denial-of-service attacks that can be launched by using direct broadcast messages.

Using Context-Based Access Control

Context-Based Access Control (CBAC) is an important component of Cisco IOS Firewall; other features of the firewall are built on CBAC to provide security. CBAC is a stateful packet-inspection system. A router using CBAC constantly maintains a state table containing entries based on all inspected packets. This state table serves to determine the return traffic that should be allowed into the network. Using CBAC, a router can also examine headers above the Network layer, which makes the router capable of keeping track of specific applications.

CBAC functions

CBAC filters and inspects network traffic, issuing alerts and establishing audit trails to keep tabs on not only the network transactions themselves, but also their contexts.

Traffic filtering

In normal access lists, the traffic can be filtered according to information in the Network-layer header or the Transport-layer header. However, CBAC can examine the protocols above the Transport-layer header inside a packet, which makes it capable of filtering TCP and UDP packets based on specific application protocols. It can keep track of the state of specific TCP or UDP sessions. As a result, CBAC can also support protocols that use multiple ports. For example, FTP uses two ports, port 21 for control messages and port 20 for data transfer. When an FTP client from inside the internal network issues commands that require a data connection to be set up, CBAC opens a channel to allow that connection to be initiated from the FTP server located on an external network. This channel is a part of the overall FTP conversation. After the data transfer is complete, the CBAC deletes the data channel.

CBACs can inspect packets for the sessions initiated from one side of the firewall. As a result, you can configure the CBAC to allow packets to travel only if they are part of a session that originated from the internal network. Also, your CBAC can restrict traffic from entering the internal network unless the users of your internal network have a legitimate need for it to be admitted.

You can configure CBAC to filter Java applets at the firewall itself, which prevents destructive Java applets from entering your network. The internal users can download applets residing inside the firewall and from trusted sites outside the firewall. You can either configure the filtering based on the specific server addresses or block Java applets embedded in an archived or compressed file.

Traffic inspection

The packets traveling through the firewall are inspected by CBAC. It then records and maintains information about the state of each TCP and UDP session in a state table. CBAC creates temporary openings in the firewall for the return traffic and any additional channels required by the application based on the information in the state table.

CBAC inspects packets at the Application layer and keeps track of each TCP and UDP session, which makes it capable of preventing SYN flooding, which is a type of denial-of-service attack.

Note   In SYN flooding, a network attacker floods a server with a continuous stream of requests of connection without completing the connection. The server becomes so busy in serving the requests from this host that it cannot service any other host. As a result, the server is unable to handle the large number of half-open connections.

When inspecting traffic, CBAC inspects packet sequence numbers in the TCP header, and if these sequence numbers are beyond a reasonable range, the packets are dropped at the firewall itself. CBAC can also detect unusually high rates of new connections forming — and send the appropriate alert messages.

Alerts and audit trails

You can configure CBAC to send information about the events occurring at the firewall. CBAC sends this information by sending audit trails and alerts. For advanced session-based reporting, audit trails can send the messages to the SYSLOG server with timestamps, information about source and destination hosts, ports used, and total number bytes transmitted. On detecting any unusual activity, real-time alerts can be configured to send SYSLOG error messages to management consoles. In addition, you can configure CBAC to generate alerts and audit trails on a per-application basis.

CBAC operation

CBAC operates by inspecting the packets that pass through the firewall. It creates entries in a table, called a state table, for the inspected packets. CBAC then creates temporary entries in the access lists applied in the opposite direction. These temporary entries allow the returning traffic to proceed. Without temporary entries, the returning traffic is blocked.

CBAC operates in three phases:

- ✦ Inspecting data packets
- ✦ Creating entries for a state table
- ✦ Creating and deleting dynamic temporary entries in an access list

The following sections discuss these phases in more detail.

Packet inspection

As administrator, you specify the protocols that CBAC monitors. When you apply CBAC to an interface, you specify the direction in which the packets must be moving (either inbound or outbound) when CBAC inspects them. Only the packets of a specified protocol, passing through the specified interface in the specified direction, receive CBAC scrutiny.

The packets entering the firewall interface are tested against any access list applied on the interface and then inspected by CBAC. Thus if the packet is denied by the access list, it would be dropped without being inspected by CBAC.

If you want specific types of packets inspected by CBAC, use an access list applied on the same interface (and in the same direction) to grant network access to those packets.

CBAC inspects only the control channels of connections. It does not check the data channels. However, both channels are monitored for state changes so each can be blocked after the task is completed. In FTP, CBAC monitors the control and data channels. However, CBAC inspects only the control channel for FTP commands and responses. After the data transfer, the temporary entry allowing data channel is deleted. However, the control channel might still be allowed. The control channel is blocked only after the hosts terminate the FTP session. While inspecting packets at the Application layer, CBAC recognizes application-specific commands in the control channel. Thus it can detect and prevent certain application-level attacks. It also keeps track of sequence numbers of TCP packets and drops the packets that have sequence numbers falling in an unexpected range.

Creating entries for a state table

When CBAC inspects a packet, it creates an entry for the state of the packet connection in the state table. The packets returning through the interface are then allowed only if they are a part of a session for which there is an entry in the state table. After detecting the return packet, the corresponding entry of the state of the packet connection is updated (if necessary).

UDP does not have any sessions such as TCP because it is a connectionless protocol. For UDP, the CBAC adopts the method that evaluates the following two criteria:

✦ The return packet should have the same source and destination addresses and port numbers as the packets sent. However, the source and destination addresses and ports are swapped.

✦ The return packet should arrive within a certain time period after the similar initial packets are sent.

If both these conditions are met, the returning UDP packets are forwarded.

Creating and deleting dynamic temporary entries in an access list

As soon as a packet is inspected and the state entry is updated, CBAC creates a temporary statement entry in the access list to test the returning packets. This temporary statement identifies the returning packets and allows them to enter the network. These temporary statements provide temporary openings in the firewall, allowing only traffic generated in sessions initiated inside the network.

The CBAC process

CBAC can be configured on an internal or external interface. To understand the process of CBAC, consider an example where CBAC is configured at an internal interface to inspect the packets going from the internal network to the external network. An internal interface is one that connects to the internal network. Another interface is connected to the Internet. In the example, an internal host initiates a Telnet session with an external host. The internal host sends the first TCP packet of the Telnet session that arrives at the internal interface of the firewall.

An inbound access list, applied to the internal interface, permits all required traffic — including traffic that must be inspected by CBAC (for example, Telnet traffic). An outbound access list, applied to the internal interface, blocks unwanted traffic, along with the return traffic of the Telnet session. If the outbound access list permitted all Telnet traffic, CBAC would have no reason to create a temporary entry in the same access list to permit such traffic — but that would also mean that CBAC would have no power to protect the network against spurious Telnet traffic.

The sequence of events that occur in the CBAC process looks like this:

1. The packet arrives at the internal interface of the firewall. This packet is the inbound packet for the internal interface.

2. The router tests the packet against the inbound access list applied to the internal interface. The packet must be permitted for any further processing of the packet to occur. Otherwise the packet would be dropped at this point. The packet is permitted and sent to CBAC inspection.

3. CBAC inspects the packet and records the information about the state of the connection of the packet in its state table as a new entry. If CBAC were not configured, the packet would be sent to the outbound interface without any inspection.

4. CBAC adds a temporary statement (based on the entry in the state table) to the outbound access list on the same interface. This statement is added at the top of the access list. It is defined such that it permits the packets entering the internal network, which are a part of the same connection as the first packet inspected by CBAC.

5. The destination sends a response packet. The packets arriving from the destination in response to the packets sent by an internal host are called return packets. This return packet enters the router and arrives at the internal interface facing the internal network. This return packet is the outbound packet for the internal interface.

6. The router would test the return packet against the outbound access list on the internal interface. The return packet is a part of the same Telnet connection, which was initiated by an internal host by sending the first packet of this connection. Because the temporary statement created in the outbound access list is defined to permit such a packet, the packet would be permitted to enter the internal network.

7. CBAC inspects the packet and updates the state-table entry for the connection accordingly. Due to the changes in the state table, CBAC might make the necessary modifications in the temporary statement in the outbound access list, such that only the packets matching the current state of the connection are permitted.

8. After the connection times out, the CBAC deletes the entry in the state table. To reflect this change, it also deletes the temporary statement in the outbound access list.

You can configure CBAC to generically inspect all TCP and UDP sessions regardless of the Application-layer protocol. However, there are selective Application-layer protocols for which you can configure specific CBAC inspection. The Application-layer protocols that can be configured for CBAC are FTP, H.323, HTTP, Java, Microsoft Netshow, Unix r-commands such as rlogin, rexec, Real audio, Sun RPC, Microsoft RPC, SMTP, SQL* Net, Stream Works, TFTP, VDOLive, and CU-SeeMe. CBAC understands the control commands of all these Application-layer protocols.

Configuring CBAC

Before configuring CBAC, you choose the interface on which it is to be configured. You can configure CBAC on an internal or external interface of the firewall. The internal interface is directly connected to your internal network while the external interface is connected to the untrusted network, such as the Internet. The objective is to enable sessions to originate from the internal interface and to block any sessions originating from the external interface.

The interface that serves to configure CBAC depends on how the internal network is connected to the external network. If no demilitarized zone (DMZ) is present (as shown in Figure 8-1), you should configure CBAC on the external interface. Doing so prevents the traffic from the external network from entering the router unless the traffic is a part of a session initiated by an internal host.

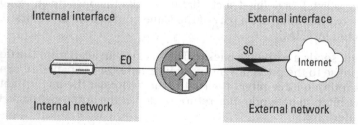

Figure 8-1: Network without DMZ

However, if a DMZ is present (as shown in Figure 8-2), you configure CBAC on the internal interface. This is because you want to allow the external hosts to initiate sessions with the hosts on DMZ. However, you also want to prevent them from initiating sessions with any host on the internal network.

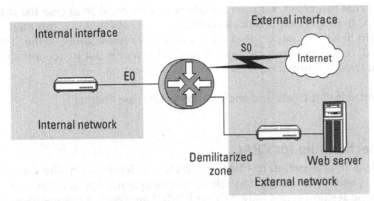

Figure 8-2: Network with DMZ

CBAC is usually configured in only one direction. However, in scenarios when you want to configure a firewall between two networks that require protection from each other, configure CBAC in both directions. After you have chosen the interface on which to configure CBAC, you can complete the configuration by following these general steps:

1. Create IP access lists and apply them to the interface.

2. Define an inspection rule for CBAC and apply it to the interface.

3. Configure global timeouts and thresholds.

4. Configure logging and audit trails.

Upcoming sections provide details and instructions for each of these tasks.

Create IP access lists and apply them to the interface

When you configure CBAC in a system that uses IP access lists on outbound and inbound interfaces, make sure you define the traffic types appropriately so they don't hinder CBAC. For example, if you use the IP access list to block outgoing traffic that you wanted CBAC to inspect, the traffic never reaches CBAC for inspection. In such a case, the definition of outgoing traffic includes *all* traffic going from the internal network to the external network; the session can never be established. Similarly, if you configure an IP access list to block incoming traffic that should be sent to CBAC for inspection, the same problem exists: The definition of incoming traffic includes *all* traffic coming from the external network to the internal network, and CBAC can't do its work. To avoid such problems, set up your IP access lists as follows:

✦ **On the internal interface, set up an extended IP access list to handle outbound traffic and block all return traffic.** You want to deny specific packets; CBAC can create a temporary entry for traffic that meets a criterion you specify (for example, a particular protocol, source or destination address, or port number). Access lists that test outbound traffic should permit any packet you want CBAC to inspect; denied packets are dropped (thus never inspected).

✦ **On the external interface, set up a standard or extended IP access list that allows CBAC to inspect all inbound traffic.** Access lists that test inbound traffic should block any packet that comes as a reply to outgoing traffic. You can set CBAC to create temporary openings in the access list to accommodate such return traffic — provided it passes CBAC inspection.

For the commands that create and apply IP access lists, see Chapter 5.

Define an inspection rule for CBAC

An *inspection rule* is an instruction to CBAC in which you define the traffic you want CBAC to inspect — using (for example) such details as specific Application-layer protocols or generic session types (say, TCP or UDP). You assign a unique name to each inspection rule; all statements grouped under the same name form a part of the same inspection rule. CBAC inspects packets against each of these statements, in the sequence in which they were entered. To define an inspection rule, the command is

```
Router(config)#ip inspect name inspection-name {test-condition}
```

where

✦ `inspection-name` specifies the name assigned to the inspection rule.

✦ `test-condition` specifies the parameters and other conditions that a packet should match for CBAC to create a temporary entry in the access list to allow the corresponding return packets to enter the internal network.

The upcoming sections provide specific commands that define inspection rules for different protocols.

Inspection of Java applets

Any unprotected user of the Internet risks exposure to destructive Java applets. Although administrative practicality discourages setting (and enforcing) a policy that requires users to disable Java in their browsers, you still must protect the network against destructive applets. CBAC can filter Java applets at the firewall itself, such that your users can download applets only from trusted external sites or sites actually within the firewall. You have two general ways of configuring CBAC appropriately for this purpose:

✦ **Define (and tell CBAC how to recognize) "friendly" external sites.** The firewall should allow Java applets only from friendly sites and block those from other sites.

✦ **Define (and tell CBAC how to recognize) "unfriendly" external sites.** The firewall should block Java applets only from unfriendly sites and permit those from other sites.

CBAC cannot detect encapsulated Java applets (such as those contained in .ZIP files) or applets loaded from nonstandard ports (such as those for FTP and gopher) — and as you may expect, CBAC can't block what it can't detect.

To filter Java applets by CBAC, use the following command:

```
Router(config)#ip inspect name inspection-name
http [java-list access-list] [timeout seconds]
```

where

+ *access-list* specifies the name or number of the standard access list that defines the friendly and unfriendly sites.

+ *seconds* specifies idle timeout in seconds.

 If you do not create the standard access list before specifying its name or number in this command, all Java applets are blocked.

Inspection of Application-layer protocols

The Application-layer protocols, which would be inspected by CBAC, are permitted to go out from the internal network to the external network. The return packets, coming from the external network to the internal network for this protocol are permitted to enter the internal network if they are a part of a session initiated from inside. This implies that they are a part of a session for which CBAC has created a temporary opening in the access list.

To create an inspection rule to inspect Application-layer protocols, use the following command:

```
Router(config)#ip inspect name inspection-name
protocol [timeout seconds]
```

where

+ *protocol* specifies a protocol keyword.

+ *seconds* specifies the idle timeout in seconds. If the CBAC does not detect a packet for the protocol for the specified number of seconds, the temporary entry in the access list would be removed — which overrides the global TCP/UDP timeouts for the specific protocols.

The protocols that can be specified in the command are listed in the Table 8-2. The table also lists the keywords to be used.

Table 8-2
Application-Layer Protocols Supported by CBAC

Application-Layer Protocol	Keyword to be Used	Port Number
CU-SeeMe	cuseeme	7648
RPE	exec	512
FTP	ftp	21
HTP	http	80
H.323	h323	1720
Microsoft Remote Procedure Call	msrpc	135
Microsoft Netshow	netshow	1755
Remote login	login	513
RealAudio and Real Video	real-audio-video	7070
SMTP	smtp	25
SQL-Net	sql-net	1521
StreamWorks	streamworks	1558
SUN RPC	sunrpc	111
TFTP	tftp	69
VDOLive	Vdolive	7000

To define a CBAC inspection rule for an RPC Application-layer protocol, you should use the following command:

```
Router(config)#ip inspect name inspection-name rpc
program-number number [wait-time minutes] [timeout seconds]
```

where

- ✦ *number* specifies the specific program number to be permitted.
- ✦ *minutes* specifies the number of minutes to keep the temporary opening in the access list to allow the subsequent connections for the same source and destination address and port pairs. The default value is zero minutes.
- ✦ *seconds* specifies the idle timeout.

You can configure inspection for various program numbers by creating multiple entries with different program numbers. All traffic for the specific program number is permitted; traffic for other program numbers is blocked.

In SMTP inspection, CBAC inspects the SMTP packets for commands. Any packet with illegal commands (if they are not in the list of legal commands) is dropped and the session times out. The legal commands are `DATA`, `EHLO`, `EXPN`, `HELO`, `HELP`, `MAIL`, `NOOP`, `QUIT`, `RCPT`, `RSET`, `SAML`, `SEND`, `SOML`, and `VRFY`.

Inspection of generic TCP and UDP sessions

You can also configure generic inspection of TCP and UDP sessions without inspecting specific Application-layer protocols. However, generic inspection of TCP and UDP cannot recognize application-specific commands. Therefore, it does not permit all return packets for an application. This is true for particular applications that use different port numbers for return packets, such as FTP.

Inspection of TCP and UDP sessions requires that the return packets have exactly the same source and destination addresses and source and destination ports. The only difference should be that the source and destination addresses and port numbers are reversed. The packets that violate this condition are dropped. CBAC also checks the sequence number. It drops a TCP packet having sequence number, which is outside the range of the window.

In UDP, no acknowledgment packets are received and no sequence number is checked. Therefore, if return packets are not received within a certain time period after the first packet is sent from the internal network to the external network, the session is considered terminated and all the returning packets after the timeout are dropped.

To configure generic inspection for TCP/UDP sessions, use the following command:

```
Router(config)#ip inspect name inspection-name {tcp|udp} [timeout seconds]
```

where `seconds` specifies the idle timeout for the session.

If return packets are not received within the configured timeout, the session is considered terminated and the temporary opening in the access list is removed.

Applying an inspection rule to an interface

After creating the inspection rule, you apply it to an interface to make it operational. You can apply it to an interface as inbound or outbound.

✦ **Inbound:** An inspection rule applied as inbound inspects inbound packets and creates a temporary opening in the outbound extended access list applied on the interface. You usually apply the inspection rule inbound on an internal interface.

✦ **Outbound:** An inspection rule applied as outbound inspects outbound packets and creates a temporary opening in the inbound extended access list applied on the interface. You usually apply the inspection rule outbound on an external interface.

To apply an inspection rule to an interface, use the following command:

```
Router(config-if)#ip inspect inspection-name [in|out]
```

where

✦ `inspection-name` specifies the name of the inspection rule to be applied to the interface.

✦ `[in|out]` specifies whether the rule is applied inbound or outbound.

Configuring global timeouts and thresholds

In addition to the specific idle timeouts and thresholds for each protocol while configuring them by using specific commands, configure global timeouts and thresholds. These apply only if the specific timeouts and thresholds for the protocols are not specified. If you do not set a specific timeout for any protocol, CBAC uses globally configured timeouts and thresholds.

Configuring global timeouts

CBAC waits for a certain period of time for a TCP session to reach an established state before dropping it. To configure this wait time, use the following command:

```
Router(config)#ip inspect tcp synwait-time seconds
```

where *seconds* is the time in seconds. The default value is 30 seconds. Thus if the TCP session is not established within 30 seconds of the first packet detection, the temporary opening in the access list for the return packets would be removed by CBAC.

CBAC does not delete the temporary entry in the access list immediately after the FIN packet is detected. It waits a period of time that you configure using the following command:

```
Router(config)#ip inspect tcp finwait-time seconds
```

The default value of *seconds* is 5. Thus CBAC manages a TCP session for five seconds after it detects a FIN exchange, after which it deletes the temporary entry in the access list.

TCP idle timeout is the time for which CBAC waits after no TCP activity is detected before deleting the temporary entry from the access list. To configure idle timeout for a TCP session, use the following command:

```
Router(config)#ip inspect tcp idle-time seconds
```

The default value of *seconds* is 3600 or 1 hour. Thus if CBAC does not detect any activity for an established TCP session for an hour, it deletes the temporary entry from the access list.

UDP idle timeout is the time for which CBAC waits after no UDP activity is detected before deleting the temporary entry from the access list. To configure idle timeout for a UDP session, use the command

```
Router(config)#ip inspect udp idle-time seconds
```

The default value of *seconds* is 30. Thus if CBAC does not detect any activity for a UDP session for 30 seconds, it deletes the temporary entry from the access list.

A DNS session is a short session. CBAC treats the DNS sessions differently. For them, idle timeout has to be defined separately. The command to do so is

```
Router(config)#ip inspect dns-timeout seconds
```

The default value of *seconds* is 5. Thus, if CBAC detects no activity in a DNS session continuously for five seconds, it deletes the temporary entry from the access list. After the temporary entry is deleted, no packets of DNS are permitted to enter the network.

Configuring global thresholds

Thresholds are defined in terms of the number of sessions above or following a value. Before configuring thresholds, however, consider the matter of *half-open sessions* — which can be defined differently for connection-oriented and connectionless protocols:

✦ For TCP, a half-open session is an initiated session that has not yet completed the three-way handshake — which means that a TCP session is not yet established.

✦ For UDP, a half-open session means no return packets were received after the first packet was sent.

CBAC keeps track of the number of half-open sessions and the number of session-establishment attempts per minute. As the number of half-open sessions exceeds a threshold, CBAC starts deleting half-open sessions — and continues to do so until the number of half-open sessions falls below another threshold value. CBAC does so to accommodate new connection requests. Otherwise no new sessions could be made — in effect, denying service to new connections.

The command to configure the upper threshold, which is the number of existing half-open sessions that causes CBAC to start deleting the half-open sessions, is

```
Router(config)#ip inspect max-incomplete high number
```

where *number* specifies the value of the threshold. The default value is 500. Thus if the number of half-open sessions reaches 500, CBAC starts deleting the existing half-open sessions — which happens until the number of existing half-open sessions drops below the lower threshold value. This lower threshold value is configured by the command

```
Router(config)#ip inspect max-incomplete low number
```

where *number* specifies the value of the lower threshold. The default value is 400. Thus CBAC continues to delete the half-open sessions until the number of existing half-open sessions reaches 400. As the existing number of half-open sessions reaches 400, CBAC stops deleting the half-open sessions until the number of half-open sessions rises to the upper threshold, which is 500.

The thresholds discussed above are for a complete firewall. The firewall does not keep track of the number of half-open TCP sessions to a host. It might happen that a host might become non-functional due to the number of half-open sessions on it even though the threshold configured at the firewall is not crossed. To deal with such a situation, Cisco has provided a provision for specifying a threshold for the number of half-open sessions to each host. The command to configure this threshold is

```
Router(config)#ip inspect tcp max-incomplete host number block-time seconds
```

where

✦ *number* is the threshold number of half-open sessions for a host. The default value is 50. Thus if the number of half-open TCP sessions for a host reaches 50, CBAC starts deleting half-open sessions for the same host.

✦ *seconds* specifies the block time for new sessions. If the block time is 0 seconds, CBAC drops the oldest half-open session for each new connection that requests the same host. On the other hand, if the block time is a finite value greater than 0, CBAC deletes all the existing half sessions for the host and blocks any new sessions establishment attempt to that host for the number of seconds configured in block time. New sessions can be established with the host only after the block time has expired. The default value of this parameter is 0 seconds.

Similarly, CBAC has threshold values for the rate of session-establishment attempts per minute. As the rate of attempted new sessions exceeds a certain threshold value, CBAC deletes half-open sessions and continues to delete them until the rate of attempts falls below another threshold. This feature is a way to accommodate new sessions and block deliberate overflows.

The command to configure the upper threshold, the rate of session-establishment attempts that causes CBAC to start deleting half-open sessions, is

```
Router(config)#ip inspect one-minute high number
```

where *number* is the number of session-establishment attempts per minute, the upper threshold. The default value is 500. Thus, if the number of session-establishment attempts per minute exceeds 500, CBAC starts deleting the existing half-open sessions until the rate of new session-establishment attempts falls below a threshold value configured by the following command:

```
Router(config)#ip inspect one-minute low number
```

where *number* is the number of new session establishment attempts per minute, the lower threshold. The default value is 400. Thus CBAC continues to delete the half-open sessions until the rate of new session-establishment attempts drops to 400 per minute.

Configuring logging and audit trail

It is not enough to configure the firewall to protect your network. To understand the pattern of attacks and evaluate whether the current firewall offers sufficient protection, monitor the network continuously; keep a record of all attempted attacks and intrusions that your firewall prevented. Continuous monitoring (with occasional upgrades dictated by the records of monitoring) is necessary to deter future attacks. To keep a record of network access through the firewall, turn on logging and audit trails on the firewall.

By default, audit-trail messages are not displayed. To turn on CBAC audit-trail messages, use the following command:

```
Router(config)#ip inspect audit-trail
```

This command must be issued in the global configuration mode. The *ip audit trail* command does not have any arguments. After you turn on audit trails, the audit-trail messages are displayed on the console.

You can use the no form of this command to turn off audit-trail messages. When written in that form, the command looks like this:

```
Router(config)#no ip inspect audit-trail
```

By default, the router sends all logging messages to the console. These messages include the debug messages and error messages. However, these messages can be configured to be stored at other destinations (such as the SYSLOG server, buffer, or host). You can also define the category of messages that should be logged.

To enable logging of messages to all destinations except the console terminal, use the following command:

```
Router(config)#logging on
```

To store the logging messages to an internal buffer on the router, use the following command:

```
Router(config)#logging buffered
```

When the buffer is full, the older messages are replaced with newer messages as they are generated.

You can also configure to store all logging messages on a SYSLOG server. The command to do so is

```
Router(config)#logging ip-address
```

where *ip-address* specifies the IP address of the SYSLOG server where the messages should be sent.

Errors are assigned severity levels from 0 to 7. The error messages with severity level 0 need greater attention than messages with higher severity levels. The lower the severity level, the more serious the problem. You can control messages that should be sent to the SYSLOG server. The command to control this is

```
Router(config)#logging trap level
```

where *level* specifies the severity level of the messages. Error messages with the specified severity level (or higher levels) can only be sent to the SYSLOG server. The default level is 7. Thus all messages would be sent to the SYSLOG server.

Verifying CBAC

To view all CBAC configurations and all existing sessions being inspected by CBAC, use following the command:

```
Router#show ip inspect all
```

To view the a specific inspection rule, use the following command:

```
Router#show ip inspect name inspection-name
```

where *inspection-name* specifies the name of the inspection rule that should be displayed.

To view the entire CBAC inspection configuration including the timeout and threshold values, use the following command:

```
Router#show ip inspect config
```

To view the inspection rules and access lists applied to the interfaces, use the following command:

```
Router#show ip inspect interfaces
```

To view the sessions being tracked and inspected by CBAC, use the following command:

```
Router#show ip inspect session [detail]
```

If you use the optional keyword detail, the command displays additional statistics about the sessions also.

Debugging CBAC

You can use the debug command to obtain information about the events on the router — for example, packets received (and their content), replies sent (and their content), and the actions taken by the router. Gathering this data helps you judge the effectiveness of the router configuration and can spotlight some areas in need of improvement.

CBAC uses software functions to perform its various activities, such as adding a temporary entry to the access list or removing the entry.

The CBAC debug commands can be broadly classified as three types:

✦ Generic debug commands
✦ Transport-level debug commands
✦ Application-level debug commands

All debug commands must be issued in the privileged EXEC mode. The following sections discuss the debug commands.

Generic debug commands

To display the software functions being called by CBAC as and when they are called during session inspection, use the following command:

```
Router#debug ip inspect function-trace
```

To display the software objects being created and deleted as and when they are created and deleted, use the following command:

```
Router#debug ip inspect object-{creation|deletion}
```

Object creation indicates the beginning of a CBAC-inspected session while object deletion indicates the end of a CBAC-inspected session.

To display the information about the CBAC software events as they happen, use the following command:

```
Router#debug ip inspect events
```

This command also displays the information about packet processing by CBAC.

CBAC uses several timers to determine the expiration times of different sessions. To display messages about the timer events, such as start and termination of a timer or as these happen, use the following command:

```
Router#debug ip inspect timers
```

To enable the display of the detailed information for all the other CBAC debugging, use the following command in conjunction with other debug commands:

```
Router#debug ip inspect detail
```

Transport-level debug commands

To display the messages about the TCP or UDP packet inspection events including the details of the TCP or UDP packets, use the following command:

```
Router#debug ip inspect {tcp|udp}
```

You must issue this command from execution mode.

Application-protocol debug commands

To display messages that indicate the inspection of Application-layer protocols (including the details of the packets that use a particular protocol), use the following command:

```
Router#debug ip inspect protocol
```

where *protocol* specifies the Application-layer protocol(s) to be debugged. You need to use protocol keywords to specify the protocol to be inspected.

Note   Refer to Table 8-2 for the protocol keywords that you can use with the `Router#debug ip inspect protocol` command.

Turning off CBAC

You can use the *no ip inspect* global configuration command to turn off CBAC. When you turn off CBAC, SMTP commands and Java applets are not blocked — which means they might pass through the firewall.

Caution

> Be careful when using the no ip inspect command because *it removes all CBAC configuration entries.* It also resets CBAC timeouts and thresholds to default values. Turning off CBAC also leads to the deletion of all existing sessions and their access lists.

Interpreting messages generated by CBAC

CBAC generates SYSLOG and console error messages to alert the network administrator to attempted network attacks. CBAC can generate five types of alerts, which the following sections discuss in detail.

Audit-trail error messages

Audit-trail messages contain the details of the inspected messages. You can determine the protocol examined by using the port number of the responder. A sample audit-trail error message looks like this.

```
%FW-6-SESS_AUDIT_TRAIL: tcp session
initiator (192.168.2.14:31192) sent 32 bytes - -
responder (192.168.126.214:25) sent 208 bytes
```

DoS attack-detection error messages

CBAC generates these error messages when it detects denial-of-service attacks. A sample DoS attack-detection error message looks like this.

```
%FW-4-ALERT_ON: getting aggressive, count (500/450) current 1-min rate: 260
%FW-4-ALERT_OFF: calming down, count (0/450) current 1-min rate: 0
```

A getting aggressive statement followed by a calming down statement represents a single attack.

For the denial-of-service attack that occurs at a specific TCP host, the messages may display %FW-4-HOST_TCP_ALERT_ON statement. A sample DoS attack-detection error message that pinpoints the attack at a specific TCP host looks like this:

```
%FW-4-HOST_TCP_ALERT_ON: Max tcp half-open connections (50)
exceeded for host 172.21.124.104
%FW-4-BLOCK_TCP_ALERT_ON: Blocking new TCP connections to host
 172.21.124.104 for 4 minutes (half-open count 50 exceeded)
%FW-4-UNBLOCK_HOST: New TCP connections to host 172.21.124.104
 no longer blocked
```

FTP error messages

These error messages are generated when FTP attacks are detected. A sample FTP error message looks like this:

```
%FW-3-FTP_PRIV_PORT: Privileged port 1000 used in
PORT command - FTP client 10.0.0.2 FTP server 10.1.0.2
%FW-3-FTP-SESSION_NOT_AUTHENTICATED: Command issued before
the session is authenticated - FTP client 10.0.0.2
%FW-3-FTP_NON_MATCHING_IP_ADDR: Non-matching address
172.19.148.154 used in PORT command - FTP client
172.19.54.143 FTP server 172.16.127.242
```

Java-blocking error messages

These error messages are generated when CBAC detects and selectively blocks Java applets. A sample Java-blocking error message looks like this:

```
%FW-4-HTTP_JAVA_BLOCK: JAVA applet is blocked
  from (172.21.124.216:80) to (172.16.54.40:44767)
```

SMTP attack-detection error messages

These messages are generated when CBAC detects and blocks illegal SMTP commands. A sample SMTP attack-detection error message looks like this:

```
%FW-4-SMTP_INVALID_COMMAND: Invalid SMTP command from
  initiator (192.158.12.4:52419)
```

Although CBAC is an effective feature, it has (as does any feature of any program) a range of advantages and disadvantages — as explained in the next two sections.

Advantages of CBAC

CBAC provides some distinctive benefits to network security:

✦ It can enhance security options on the basis of specific Application-layer protocols. It understands the commands of the application protocols and can support the filtering of Application-layer protocols that use multiple channels. This capability helps you apply complex security policies with relative ease.

✦ It keeps track of how many sessions and half-open sessions are going on. Hence, it can detect and prevent denial-of-Service attacks.

✦ It protects against Java-applet attack and provides safer Internet browsing.

✦ It integrates the firewall with other Cisco IOS software features and provides seamless interoperability.

✦ It monitors and sends messages to chronicle any events in the system and provides detailed information about network usage (including any suspicious activity).

✦ It supports a range of platforms (from Cisco 800-series routers to 7200-series routers).

Limitations of CBAC

Although CBAC offers an attractive capability — the intelligent filtering of TCP and UDP packets — it has a few limitations that you should consider before you implement it:

✦ CBAC inspects only IP protocol packets. It can inspect only TCP or UDP packets. It cannot be used for filtering other IP traffic, such as ICMP. The other packets have to be filtered using the other existing access lists only.

✦ As with normal access lists, CBAC cannot inspect packets having source or destination addresses of the firewall itself.

✦ Unlike normal access lists, CBAC requires that you specify the protocols for which you want to enable filtering. If you do not specify a certain protocol, no temporary openings would be created and the existing access list on the interface would determine the filtering of the packets for that protocol. In normal access lists, if a protocol is not specified, the packets for that protocol are dropped (as per the implicit deny all statement specified in the access list).

✦ Unless a packet travels through the firewall, CBAC cannot act on the packet. Thus CBAC cannot protect the network from the attacks originating from inside the network. It can protect the network against those attacks that traverse the router on which the firewall is configured.

✦ CBAC should not be taken to be perfect protection against all attacks. It cannot detect all types of attacks.

✦ If the router or the interface on the router fails, the CBAC conversations are lost. CBAC does not support redundant firewall routers.

✦ If an access list applied on an interface has not been created, it normally permits all traffic since it is empty. However, on inspecting the traffic, CBAC defines a temporary statement in the access list. After CBAC adds this statement, the access list does not remain empty. The implicit deny statement becomes active, and all traffic except the one allowed by the temporary entry is denied. This could terminate the rest of the existing sessions for the duration for which the temporary entry is active.

✦ If an access list is deleted and then re-created, CBAC temporary entries are lost. All CBAC channels on that interface would be terminated.

✦ If the traffic received by the firewall is encrypted, CBAC might not work as expected. This is because CBAC cannot accurately inspect the payload to determine the commands of the Application-layer protocol. It poses problems with those Application-layer protocols that use multiple channels for their operation.

✦ If IPSec and CBAC are configured on the same router, IPSec and CBAC are compatible. CBAC can inspect the packets arriving at the router. This is because the firewall router is an endpoint for IPSec. However, if IPSec and CBAC are not on the same router, CBAC receives the packet having protocol numbers in the IP header and not that of TCP and UDP. Therefore CBAC does not inspect these packets. CBAC inspects only TCP/UDP packets.

✦ CBAC uses 600 bytes of memory per connection, which is a hardware limitation. Thus as the number of connections increases, the performance of the router deteriorates. It uses more CPU resources when it is inspecting packets. Thus the router in which you install Cisco IOS Firewall should be well equipped with high CPU resources and high memory space.

Compatibility issues

Although CBAC can be used with all firewall features, you should consider some of its intrinsic compatibility issues when you implement it. The most important of these issues are as follows:

✦ **Compatibility with protocols:** CBAC does not work for all protocols. In fact, it works only for IP protocol traffic and examines only TCP and UDP packets. CBAC cannot filter IP traffic, such as ICMP. Also, CBAC cannot filter packets that have the address of firewall as their source or destination address.

✦ **Compatibility with FTP:** CBAC does not allow three-way FTP traffic. For FTP traffic, CBAC only allows data channels that have a destination port in the range of 1024 to 65,535. If FTP client-server authentication fails, CBAC does not open data channels.

✦ **Compatibility with Cisco encryption technology:** CBAC cannot effectively examine encrypted data packets. If encryption and CBAC are configured on the same firewall, CBAC does not work for multichannel protocols (except StreamWorks and CU-SeeMe). However, CBAC does work with single-channel TCP and UDP. Therefore, if you decide to configure CBAC on a firewall that has encryption configured on it, you should configure CBAC only for generic TCP and UDP, CU-SeeMe, and StreamWorks.

✦ **Compatibility with IPSec:** When CBAC and IPSec are configured on the same router, CBAC is compatible with IPSec, but only when the destination router is the endpoint for IPSec. However, if the router is not an endpoint for IPSec and the packet is not an IPSec packet, CBAC does not examine the packets. This is because the protocol number in the IPSec packet's IP header does not specify TCP or UDP.

Cisco IOS Firewall administration

You can administer the Cisco IOS Firewall either by using the router's command-line interface or by using ConfigMaker.

As you may expect, the command-line interface (CLI) is less user-friendly than the GUI-based ConfigMaker — but CLI is a more powerful and flexible tool. ConfigMaker, for its part, offers only limited product support and equally limited configuration parameters — but it can reduce the administrative burden.

CBAC configuration

To understand CBAC configuration better, consider the example of an organizational network shown in Figure 8-3. In this network, the following partial security policy must be implemented:

✦ The users on the network should be allowed to access the Internet. They should be able to download Java applets only from the friendly sites, which are 172.16.0.1 and 172.16.0.2.

✦ The users should be only allowed to browse the Internet, use FTP to download information, and use SMTP to send mails. The rest of the protocols should be blocked.

✦ Only the internal users should be able to initiate a session. Block any sessions initiated by an external host unless these are required by the same Application-level protocol.

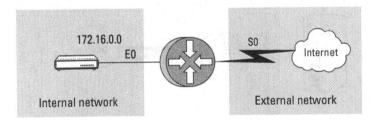

```
Router (config) #ip inspect name testcbac http java-list 10 timeout 30
Router (config) #ip inspect name testcbac ftp timeout 30
Router (config) #ip inspect name testcbac smtp timeout 30
Router (config) #access-list 10 permit host 172.16.0.1
Router (config) #access-list 10 permit host 172.16.0.2
Router (config) #int s0
Router (config-if) #ip inspect inspection-name out
```

Figure 8-3: Network diagram of a typical CBAC configuration

For implementing the partial security policy in the network, the commands to be given on the router are also shown in Figure 8-3.

Case Study

The following scenario illustrates how to configure CBAC.

Scenario

AllSolv, Inc., an IT solution provider, is based in Boston and has branch offices in New York, Connecticut, and Washington, D.C. Part of the network-security policy of AllSolv, Inc. highlights the following points:

✦ Internal hosts should be able to download Java applets from the friendly sites: 172.16.0.0 and 172.16.1.1.

✦ The internal users should be able to FTP other sites and also use RealAudio. The timeout for these protocols should be 30 seconds.

Keeping the preceding points in mind, the network administrator of AllSolv, Inc. has decided to configure CBAC to implement the security policy.

The network diagram of AllSolv, Inc. is shown in Figure 8-4.

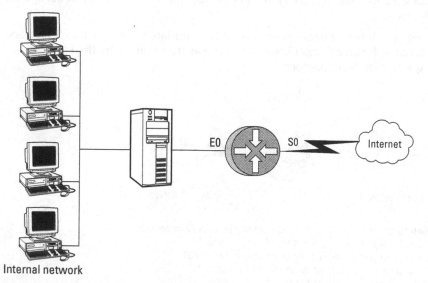

Internal network

Figure 8-4: Network diagram of AllSolv, Inc.

Sample configuration

The following sample configuration can be used to configure CBAC:

```
Router(config)#ip inspect name scenariotest http java-list 20 timeout 30
Router(config)#ip inspect name scenariotest ftp timeout 30
Router(config)#ip inspect name scenariotest realaudio timeout 30
```

The preceding commands configure the inspection rule; the next step is to apply the rule like this:

```
Router(config)#interface ethernet 0
Router(config-if)#ip inspect scenariotest in
```

The preceding commands apply the rule to interface E0:

```
Router(config)#access-list 20 permit 172.16.0.0
```

```
Router(config)#access-list 20 permit 172.16.1.1
```

The preceding commands create access list 20.

Summary

This chapter introduced Cisco IOS Firewall and its components. The main component of Cisco IOS Firewall, Context-Based Access Control (CBAC), offers a way to fine-tune the packet-filtering functions of access lists. Configuring CBAC on a router requires careful matching of interface directions (inbound or outbound) with either standard or extended IP access lists. As with any individual security measure, CBAC offers benefits at the cost of imposing some limitations (in this case, on the speed with which packets can reach their destinations). An example illustrated the application of CBAC to a practical networking scenario.

✦   ✦   ✦

Cisco PIX Firewall

There is a growing need for dedicated security systems to provide impenetrable security to the network and its resources. To counter the sophisticated tools and strategies used by intruders, network administrators require security tools of matching capabilities. Using access lists or firewalls installed on routers are not sufficient to protect network resources and data on the network. Losses in businesses due to security breaches outweigh the cost of providing security. Thus, it is essential to use dedicated firewalls, such as PIX Firewall, to ensure security of networks.

This chapter covers the basics of PIX Firewall and its components. It also covers the basic configuration of the firewall, such as interface configuration. The chapter describes the advanced configuration of PIX Firewall to provide security in different scenarios.

Introducing Cisco PIX Firewall

Cisco PIX stands for Cisco Private Internet Exchange Firewall, an integrated hardware/software product that offers excellent enterprise-wide security. Available in various models to meet the requirements of different networks, PIX Firewall manages to attain a difficult goal: maximum security with almost no effect on network performance.

PIX Firewall hides the internal network completely from the external world, acting as a gatekeeper to prevent intruders from entering the network. The result is that an internal network can connect to the Internet and other external networks safely and securely.

Note *Stateful filtering* is a secure method of checking data packets that stores information about packets in a *session-state table,* well away from external prying eyes. Before a session can be successfully established, any identifying information about the session must match that stored in the table.

Although various earlier methods—such as access lists configured on boundary routers and proxy servers—offer some protection to networks, customarily that protection comes at the cost of reduced network performance. Routers, for example, are designed primarily to provide connectivity services; burdening them with providing security as well can degrade their performance. A more desirable approach is to use a separate, dedicated device to handle network-security tasks. One such solution is the *proxy server*, which allows a user to gain access to an external network only after the user is authenticated and authorized. Proxy servers also maintain session states and provide strong security for the Application layer of the OSI networking model. The downside is that operations at the Application layer are process-intensive. Tying up the server's processor—even on a dedicated machine—can degrade network performance when large numbers of users connect to external networks. Thus proxy servers are not scalable solutions.

PIX Firewall has features that sidestep such limitations:

✦ It uses stateful filtering.

✦ Its operating system is designed with security as the primary mission. It does not suffer from the loopholes in general-purpose operating systems such as Unix and Windows NT.

✦ It can handle multiple simultaneous connections at wire speed (in fact, more than any software-based firewall) because of two features: the Adaptive Security Algorithm (ASA) and a cut-through proxy option.

✦ Its two-tiered security model uses a perimeter router, a demilitarized zone (DMZ), PIX Firewall itself, and an internal router.

✦ It makes sessions extremely difficult to hijack, using a randomizing algorithm to generate sequence numbers in TCP packets.

A firewall must allow movement of traffic on a network — but in a secure and manageable way. PIX Firewall allows traffic to travel through it in three ways:

✦ PIX Adaptive Security Algorithm (ASA) keeps track of the traffic passing through the firewall. ASA establishes and maintains a state session table, basing it on information from packets received and sent by the firewall. This table consists of session-state information for each connection. A packet that fails to match any entry in the table is blocked.

✦ Cut-through proxy authentication uses a database (either RADIUS or TACACS+) to grant users access to the Internet or external networks.

✦ Statics and conduits bypass ASA and provide an access tunnel through the firewall.

Upcoming sections take a closer look at each of these methods of providing access.

PIX ASA

To protect sensitive internal network resources, PIX Firewall uses an Adaptive Security Algorithm (ASA) to provide stateful security for all TCP/IP sessions. When an internal host initiates a connection, it sends the first packet of the connection to the firewall. This packet contains information such as source and destination addresses, source and destination ports, and the TCP sequence number. ASA records all such information and uses it to create an encrypted signature, which PIX Firewall uses to identify this particular host from then on — but only for the duration of the actual connection. The signature becomes invalid after the connection terminates; ASA creates a new signature every time a host initiates a session. This mechanism minimizes the time that any would-be intruder would have for mounting an attack.

The ASA process rests on the concept of *security values* — in effect, hierarchical numbers that you assign to the interfaces of a firewall (using the `nameif` command) to identify how secure they are. Interfaces that connect to a firewall-protected network are the most secure; they should receive higher security values than interfaces that connect to external (and/or untrusted) networks or the Internet. Security values provide a consistent way to establish connectivity rules. Normally, a firewall denies connectivity to interfaces that have low security values — and allows interfaces with higher security values to connect. (If necessary, you can override this rule — by creating conduits and statics in PIX Firewall, as explained later in this chapter.)

To understand the operation of PIX ASA, consider a situation where PIX Firewall connects an internal network to the Internet. The internal network is the protected network with a high security value. The interface connected to the Internet is assigned a low security value. The default rule in PIX Firewall is that a connection is allowed only if the destination has a lower security than the source. The steps in the ASA process are as follows:

1. To communicate with a site on the Internet, a host sends a first packet to establish a connection to the firewall.

2. PIX Firewall receives the packet, determines that it's destined for the external network, and checks the interface on which the packet is received to determine whether the interface through which it would exit has a lower security value. If so, PIX Firewall allows this connection.

Note   Connections are always allowed if the source has a higher security value than the destination.

3. PIX Firewall determines whether to translate the addresses on the packet — and whether to do so statically or dynamically.

4. PIX Firewall determines whether the packet is the first one of the connection (or of the session) and whether the packet already has an entry in the session-state table.

If the packet is the first, PIX Firewall makes a new entry for the corresponding session in the session-state table. PIX Firewall then creates an encrypted unique signature (based on the session information) for the host sending the packet.

5. PIX Firewall translates the internal, unregistered IP address in the packet into a registered IP address from its global address pool (which hides the internal IP addresses from the outside world), strips the packet of its unregistered IP address, assigns the registered IP address, and sends the packet out via the outbound interface.

6. The destination host (which hosts the destination site) receives the readdressed packet and sends a response packet.

7. PIX Firewall receives the response packet at the external interface (which has a lower security value than the internal interface), processes the packet with ASA, compares the characteristics of the response packet against the entries in the session-state table, and checks for a match with the signature.

8. If the packet matches any entry in the session-state table, PIX Firewall does the necessary address translation (back to the original unregistered IP address), sending the packet out of the internal interface. The host receives the packet, and the transaction is complete.

This entire PIX ASA process is extremely fast and offers some unique advantages:

✦ All outbound connections are allowed until the outbound access list denies a connection.

✦ All inbound connections are blocked unless the administrator configures conduits to allow specific connections.

The administrator can configure the external hosts to initiate sessions only to a few selected internal machines.

✦ No packet can arrive from an interface with a lower security value than that of the internal destination interface — *unless* it matches an entry maintained by ASA in the session-state table.

✦ Any attempt to violate any of the preceding three rules triggers alert messages and promptly terminates the connection.

✦ PIX Firewall normally drops all ICMP packets unless the administrator has specifically configured conduits to accommodate them.

Cut-through proxy authentication

Serving a function similar to that of a proxy server, the *cut-through proxy* authentication mechanism of PIX Firewall authenticates users at the Application layer — but the similarity ends here. After the user is authenticated and a security policy is applied, PIX Firewall transfers control of the transaction to the ASA engine. Operating at the Network layer, the ASA engine performs better than a proxy server.

PIX Firewall can also be configured to authenticate users by working with security database servers such as TACACS+ and RADIUS. In addition, PIX Firewall sets an unauth timer command for each authenticated session. Until this timer expires, the user can continue working without any intervention; after the timer expires, PIX Firewall prompts again for user authentication.

When a user tries to gain access to a resource on the protected side of PIX Firewall, the following sequence of events takes place:

1. The user initiates a connection setup with the protected resource.

2. PIX Firewall receives the packet and compares its session-state table in ASA to determine whether the user has logged in previously and whether the unauth timer has timed out.

3. If the unauth timer for the user has expired, PIX Firewall prompts the user for authentication. The user enters username and the password; authentication occurs at the Application layer.

   This authentication information is sent to the security database servers. The session can continue only if the security database servers send back the message that the user exists in their database and authentication is successful.

4. If the user is authenticated successfully, PIX Firewall hands over the session to the Network-layer ASA engine.

This process happens faster than the analogous process in other firewalls (which require all packets to travel up to the Application layer even after authentication). The result is an increase in the overall packet flow — and some related advantages of cut-through proxy authentication:

✦ **PIX Firewall can use security databases to authenticate users.** This feature is not available in most proxy-server implementations.

✦ **PIX Firewall can authenticate inbound and outbound sessions in a stateful manner.**

✦ **PIX Firewall authenticates at the Application layer.** After authentication, however, the session flow is transferred to the Network-layer ASA, which leaves room for more Application-layer authentications.

Conduits and statics

To enable any host on the external network to initiate a session with an internal host, you must create a tunnel through the firewall by creating conduits and statics. This access tunnel is required (for example) when you are using a VPN concentrator on the internal network. The users from the external network must connect to this

VPN concentrator to securely send and receive data. In this situation, you would create conduits and statics to permit the IPSec traffic inside the network:

✦ A *static* (that is, a static access list) maps the IP address of the VPN concentrator to a specific global registered IP address. This global IP address is reserved for the VPN concentrator.

✦ A *conduit* is an access list that permits selected IPSec traffic through the firewall. Although the conduits and statics provide an access tunnel to outside hosts to initiate a session to the internal hosts, ASA provides stateful security to VPN traffic through the conduit.

Consider the typical network shown in Figure 9-1.

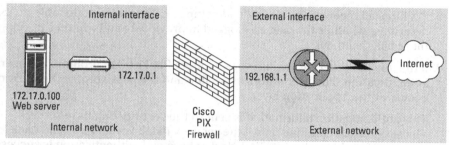

Figure 9-1: A sample network for conduits and statics

The internal network has a Web server, which must be accessed by the hosts on the external network. The Web server is assigned the internal IP address of 172.17.0.100. External users are to be granted access to this Web server over the Internet. The following steps are used to configure statics and conduits for the Web server on the firewall.

1. When an external user must connect to a Web server over the Internet, it sends a packet. This packet arrives at the external interface of the firewall with the destination address of the Web server, 192.168.1.100.

2. At the firewall, a static mapping of the IP address 192.168.1.100 to the IP address 172.17.0.100 needs to be configured. This can be done by the command

   ```
   PIXFW(config)#static (inside, outside) 192.168.1.100
   172.17.0.100
   ```

   This static conveys to the firewall that if a packet with the destination address 192.168.1.100 enters from outside the network, the destination address has to be replaced with 172.17.0.100. This static also conveys to the firewall that if a packet with source address 172.17.0.100 arrives from the network for going out to the Internet, the source address has to be replaced with 192.168.1.100. Using this information, the firewall determines if the packet is destined for 172.17.0.100 inside the network.

3. PIX Firewall determines that the interface on which the packet arrives has a lower security value than the internal interface. Therefore, the packet would be dropped and the connection attempt would be terminated. However, to allow the packet to enter the internal network, a conduit needs to be configured on the firewall. This can be done by the command

```
PIXFW(config)#conduit permit tcp host 192.168.1.100 eq 80 any
```

This conduit is meant to indicate to the firewall to allow packets from any external host to proceed if the packet is destined for the Web server on the HTTP port (TCP port number 80).

4. The firewall determines that a conduit has been created to allow access to the packets. Therefore, the firewall translates the IP address of the packet and sends it to the network to the Web server at the IP address `172.17.0.100`.

5. Now the user can load the Web page successfully.

PIX Firewall Models

Cisco PIX Firewall offers strong security and scalability to meet the needs of your network. Cisco PIX Firewall is available in the following five models:

✦ Cisco Secure PIX 535

✦ Cisco Secure PIX 525

✦ Cisco Secure PIX 515

✦ Cisco Secure PIX 506

✦ Cisco Secure PIX 501

As the model numbers increase, the capacity of PIX Firewall to handle concurrent connections also increases — along with the number and type of ports it supports. One vital constant is that all models of Cisco PIX Firewall support IPSec encryption; you can use any of the models listed here for remote deployment of a VPN or for site-to-site deployment. You can choose a PIX Firewall model whose capacity matches your security requirements and network size.

From an administrator's point of view, a highly significant aspect of Cisco PIX Firewall is licensing. Licenses for PIX Firewalls spell out (in terms specific to each model) such particulars as level of service, memory supported, maximum number of interfaces supported, and functions. In addition, these licenses allow a single PIX software image to be used across several PIX Firewall platforms. The three configurations of Cisco PIX Firewall licenses are

✦ **Unrestricted:** The unrestricted license does not restrict the number of interfaces and RAM available to the PIX Firewall. You can opt for this license if you want to implement a "hot standby" system to reduce network downtime.

Note A *hot standby* is the system (with the same configuration as the main system), which is kept running, ready to take over the load immediately if there is any failure in the main system.

✦ **Restricted:** The restricted license limits the number of interfaces and RAM available within the system. In contrast to the unrestricted license, the restricted license does not allow a redundant system for failover configurations.

✦ **Failover:** The failover license enables the Cisco PIX Firewall as a "hot standby." The hot standby firewall can take over the working when an unrestricted licensed PIX Firewall fails. The failover-licensed firewall must be connected to a firewall with an unrestricted license, using a dedicated failover cable. (This will be discussed in further detail later in the chapter.)

Note The feature set of unrestricted and failover license has the same performance and characteristics.

Table 9-1 gives an overview of the features available in each licensing option.

Table 9-1 Features Available with Each Licensing Option			
Features	*Unrestricted*	*Restricted*	*Failover*
Firewall services	Supports all firewall services	Supports all firewall services	Supports all firewall services
RAM support	Maximum	Limited	Maximum
Number of interfaces	Maximum	Limited	Maximum
DES	Requires zero cost option to enable DES support	Requires zero-cost option to enable DES support	Requires zero-cost option to enable DES support
3DES	Requires additional license to enable 3DES support	Requires additional license to enable 3DES support	Requires additional license to enable 3DES support
Failover support	Yes	No	Not available
Additional hardware requirement	Requires no additional hardware	Requires no additional hardware	Requires failover cable

The upcoming section discusses the different licensing conditions available for different models of Cisco PIX Firewalls and their associated licenses.

Cisco Secure PIX 535 Firewall

Cisco Secure PIX 535 Firewall is used mainly for large enterprise networks and service providers. It allows up to 500,000 concurrent connections and has a throughput of 1.0 Gbps. This PIX Firewall includes a VPN gateway that provides a secure transmission of data. In addition, it provides site-to-site and remote VPN applications with a 56-bit DES and 168-bit 3DES.

Features of restricted license

The restricted license for Cisco Secure PIX Firewall 535 has the following features:

✦ Includes 512MB RAM

✦ Supports a maximum of 8GB Ethernet or 10/100 Fast Ethernet interfaces

✦ Supports a single VAC

Features of unrestricted license

The unrestricted license for Cisco Secure PIX 535 has the following features:

✦ Includes 1GB RAM

✦ Supports a maximum of 8GB Ethernet or 10/100 Fast Ethernet interfaces

✦ Supports a single VAC

✦ Allows a stateful connection for sharing information with a hot-standby PIX

Features of failover license

The failover license for Cisco Secure PIX 535 has the following features:

✦ With a failover license, the Cisco Secure PIX Firewall 535 works in a hot-standby mode

✦ Maintains current sessions and acts as a redundant system

Table 9-2 describes the features of the Cisco Secure PIX Firewall 535.

Table 9-2 Cisco Secure PIX Firewall 535	
Features	**Description**
Concurrent connections	Supports 500,000 concurrent connections
Connections per second	Allows 7,000 connections per second
168-bit 3DES IPSec VPN throughput	Gives a throughput of 100 Mbps

Continued

Table 9-2 *(continued)*	
Features	*Description*
VPN tunnels supported	Supports 2,000 VPN tunnels
Cleartext throughput	Gives a cleartext throughput of 1.0 Gbps
Processor	Has a 1.0-Ghz Intel Pentium III processor
RAM	Has a 512MB or 1GB (SDRAM)
Flash Memory	Has a 16MB flash memory
Cache	Has a 256KB cache

Cisco Secure PIX Firewall 525

Cisco Secure PIX Firewall 525 is also used for enterprise networks and service providers. This PIX Firewall provides an enhanced level of security as it is based on the Adaptive Security Algorithm (AGA), which keeps a track of the source and destination addresses, port numbers, and TCP sequence numbers. In addition, this algorithm provides a stateful connection-oriented firewall.

Features of restricted license

The restricted license for Cisco Secure PIX 525 has the following features:

✦ Includes 128MB RAM

✦ Supports a maximum of six 10/100 Fast Ethernet interfaces

✦ Offers enterprise-level security

Features of unrestricted license

The unrestricted license for Cisco Secure PIX 525 includes all the features of restricted license of the Cisco Secure PIX Firewall 525. In addition, it has the following features:

✦ Gives a cleartext throughput of up to 370 Mbps

✦ Supports a maximum of 8GB Ethernet or 10/100 Fast Ethernet interfaces

✦ Allows Stateful failover to a backup PIX Firewall

✦ Allows more than 280,000 concurrent connections

Table 9-3 gives a few features of the Cisco Secure PIX Firewall 525.

Table 9-3 Cisco Secure PIX Firewall 525	
Features	**Description**
Concurrent connections	Supports 280,000 concurrent connections
Cleartext throughput	Gives a cleartext throughput of 370 Gbps
Processor	Has a 600-Ghz Intel Pentium III processor
RAM	Up to 256 MB RAM
Flash Memory	Has a 16MB flash memory
Interfaces	Supports dual integrated 10/100Base T Fast Ethernet and RJ 45 interfaces

Cisco Secure PIX Firewall 515

Cisco Secure PIX Firewall 515 is used mainly for small to medium enterprise networks. The Cisco Secure PIX Firewall 515 allows up to 125,000 concurrent connections and has a throughput of 120 Mbps.

Features of restricted license

The restricted license for Cisco Secure PIX Firewall 515 has the following features:

✦ Allows an organization to deploy a high level of security along with a basic firewall

✦ Allows for more than 50,000 connections

✦ Provides up to 170 Mbps throughput

✦ Supports a maximum of three Ethernet interfaces

Table 9-4 gives a few features of the Cisco Secure PIX Firewall 515with a restricted license.

Table 9-4 Cisco Secure PIX Firewall 515 with a Restricted License	
Features	**Description**
Concurrent connections	Supports 100,000 concurrent connections
Cleartext throughput	Gives a cleartext throughput of 170 Mbps

Continued

Table 9-4 (continued)	
Features	**Description**
RAM	Has 64MB RAM
Flash Memory	Has 16MB flash memory
Console port	RJ-45
Boot/Update	TFTP only
Failover port	Disabled

Features of unrestricted license

The unrestricted license for Cisco Secure PIX 515 includes all the features of restricted license of the Cisco Secure PIX Firewall 515. In addition, it has the following features:

✦ Supports failover functions

✦ Supports a maximum of six 10/100 Ethernet ports

✦ Allows 100,000 concurrent connections

Table 9-5 describes some features of the Cisco Secure PIX Firewall 515 with an unrestricted license.

Table 9-5 Cisco Secure PIX Firewall 515 with an Unrestricted License	
Features	**Description**
Concurrent connections	Supports 50,000 concurrent connections
Cleartext throughput	Gives a cleartext throughput 170 Mbps
RAM	32MB
Flash Memory	16MB
Console port	RJ-45
Boot/Update	TFTP
Failover port	DB-25 EIA/TIA-232

Features of failover license

The failover license allows firewall redundancy. This redundancy plays an important part in controlling costs. A breakdown of the firewall can result in a major loss of revenue as well as lead to increased security threats. In case a firewall is running in the failover mode, the failover package developed by Cisco for Cisco Secure PIX Firewall 515 provides you with a second firewall.

Cisco Secure PIX Firewall 506

Cisco Secure PIX Firewall 506 offers not only complete firewall features, but also IPSec and VPN capabilities. This firewall includes some common features of VPN, such as tunneling, encryption, and security. In addition, this firewall supports both 56-bit DES and 168-bit 3DES algorithms. Cisco Secure PIX Firewall is used by remote office and branch office organizations.

Table 9-6 describes some features of Cisco Secure PIX Firewall 506.

Table 9-6 Cisco Secure PIX Firewall 506	
Features	**Description**
Processor	200MHz Intel Pentium MMX
RAM	32MB
Flash Memory	8MB
Cleartext throughput	8 Mbps
56-bit DES throughput	6 Mbps
168-bit 3DES throughput	6 Mbps
Console Port	RJ-45
Interfaces	Dual integrated 10Base–T ports, RJ45

Cisco Secure PIX Firewall 501

Cisco Secure PIX Firewall 501 is mostly used for small offices. You use this firewall to secure network communications over the Internet. The standard-based IKE/IPSec form the basis of security provided by this firewall. In addition, it supports 56-bit DES and 168-bit data-encryption techniques.

This firewall provides the following software licenses:

✦ **10-user license:** This license allows a maximum of 10 concurrent source IP addresses to pass through the Cisco Secure PIX Firewall 501 from your internal network. In addition, the DHCP server, which is integrated with this firewall, can support up to 32 DHCP connections.

✦ **50-user license:** This license allows a maximum of 50 concurrent source IP addresses to pass through the Cisco Secure PIX Firewall 501 from your internal network. In addition, the DHCP server, which is integrated with this firewall, can support up to 128 DHCP connections.

Note

In addition to the 10-user and 50-user licenses, Cisco Secure PIX Firewall also provides two optional encryption licenses, DES and 3DES licenses. Because these are encryption licenses, the U.S. encryption laws might apply to these laws.

Table 9-7 provides some essential figures for the features of Cisco Secure PIX Firewall 501.

Table 9-7	
Cisco Secure PIX Firewall 501	
Features	*Description*
Processor	133-Mhz AMD SC520
RAM	16MB SDRAM
Flash Memory	8MB
Cleartext throughput	10 Mbps
56-bit DES throughput	6 Mbps
168-bit 3DES throughput	3 Mbps
Concurrent connections	3500
Console Port	RJ-45
Interfaces	Dual integrated 10Base –T ports, RJ45

PIX Firewall Failover

You use the PIX Firewall Failover in case the primary firewall breaks down. In case of a failover, the secondary firewall takes over the role of the primary firewall and thus the network downtime decreases. In the event of a breakdown of the primary firewall, the secondary unit assumes the IP and MAC addresses of the primary unit and starts filtering the data packets.

Note   You can configure failover on all Ethernet interfaces. However, for configuring stateful failover, the interface should be at least 100 Mbps or GB Ethernet.

To configure failover, you must have both PIX Firewalls of the same model and running on the same software version. In addition they should have identical flash memory and available RAM.

Before you start configuring for failover, review the following principles and keep them in mind:

✦ The time on both PIX Firewalls should be in sync. To synchronize the time, you can use the `clock set` *time* command on the active PIX Firewall.

✦ Both PIX Firewalls should be connected by a failover cable. The primary end of the cable should be attached to the primary firewall and the secondary end to the secondary firewall.

✦ Configure only the primary firewall. When the primary firewall automatically updates the configuration of the secondary firewall. However, it can perform this update only when you issue the `write memory` command and save your configuration to the flash memory. The primary firewall uses this saved configuration to update the secondary firewall.

✦ Power on the secondary firewall only after configuring the primary firewall.

✦ Assign IP addresses to each interface of the primary firewall by using the `ip address` command.

After you have taken note of all these points, you can configure failover by following these steps:

1. Issue the `configure terminal` command to enter the configuration mode (on the primary firewall).

2. Issue the `failover` command statement. This statement enables failover on the primary firewall.

3. Issue the `show failover` command to verify that the primary firewall has been enabled.

4. Issue the `failover ip address` command statement for each interface. This command specifies the interface addresses of the secondary firewall. Remember that the addresses of both the primary and the secondary firewalls are in the same subnet.

5. If you want to configure Stateful Failover, you can use the `failover link` command to give the name of the interface being used. To verify that the Stateful Failover has been enabled, you can use the `show failover` command.

6. You can use the `failover poll` command to set the time for both firewalls to exchange "hello" packets and confirm the availability of each other. By default, the time taken for both firewalls to exchange "hello" packets is 15 seconds. However, you can change it to a minimum of 3 seconds and a maximum of 15 seconds.

The primary firewall is now configured.

7. Power on the secondary firewall. As soon as the secondary firewall starts, it is recognized and synchronized by the primary firewall. When the process of synchronization starts, a message (`Sync Started`) appears. When synchronization is complete, another message (`Sync Completed`) appears.

8. Use the `show failover` command to verify whether the failover was successful.

9. Save the configuration to flash memory by issuing the `write memory` command.

Configuring PIX Firewall

You must configure PIX Firewall so only the specified traffic is allowed to enter or leave the internal network. For the Proxy Firewall version 4.2 and later versions, you have two options for configuring the firewall. You can use a Windows-based PC to configure the firewall. One option is to plug in the console cable into the serial cable of a PC and configure PIX Firewall by using the command-line interface (CLI). The other option is to install the PIX Firewall setup wizard on the computer and use it to configure the PIX Firewall. The PIX Firewall versions earlier than 4.2 can be configured only through CLI.

The command-line interface of the PIX Firewall is the same as CLI of Cisco IOS. This similarity is both in structure as well as appearance. PIX CLI also has different configuration modes, and each mode provides different levels of configuration options and commands. The three modes of CLI of PIX Firewall are as follows:

✦ **Unprivileged mode**: In this mode, you can view a limited number of current settings on PIX Firewall. This mode is also called the user mode.

✦ **Privileged mode**: It enables you to view settings related to configuration, monitoring, and troubleshooting. It is a gateway to the configuration mode. This mode provides limited configuration options. This mode is also called as the enable mode.

✦ **Configuration mode**: In this mode, you can change the physical structure of PIX Firewall. This mode is also called the config mode.

The following sections describe these three command modes.

Unprivileged mode

This is the first command mode that appears when you log in to PIX Firewall. It is the default mode and has a low security level. To revert to this mode from any other command mode, you must press the key combination Ctrl + Z. The characteristics of the unprivileged mode are as follows:

✦ The prompt for this mode is hostname followed by the greater than sign (>). An example is PIXFW>.

✦ This mode provides limited capability of viewing only certain settings of the firewall.

✦ This mode does not provide the facility for changing the configuration of the firewall.

✦ By default, this mode does not require any password authentication. However, you can configure a login password for this level.

You can also connect to PIX Firewall by using Telnet to configure the firewall. However, you can connect to the firewall through Telnet only from the inside interface. A password for Telnet is necessary for providing Telnet connection to the firewall. PIX Firewall has the default Telnet password `cisco`. You can use the `passwd` command in the privileged command mode to change the password for Telnet. This password is stored by the firewall in an encrypted manner and cannot be retrieved. Even the blank spaces are encrypted.

Privileged mode

You enter the privileged mode by entering the `enable` command at the unprivileged mode. This mode is the gateway to the configuration mode. All the commands can access the privileged mode to configure PIX Firewall. Hence, it is important that you set a password to enter this command mode. You can set the password for this mode by using the following command

```
PIXFW#enable password password
```

where `password` specifies the password that the user must enter before entering the privileged mode. This password is stored in an encrypted form in the firewall.

The characteristics of the privileged mode are as follows:

✦ The prompt for this command mode is hostname followed by a hash mark (#). An example is `PIXFW#`.

✦ The privileged mode provides the facility for changing the settings of the firewall and writing these changes to flash.

✦ All commands of unprivileged mode are available in this mode.

✦ You can revert to unprivileged mode by typing the `disable` command.

Configuration mode

Configuration mode is the most powerful mode. You can make changes in the configuration of the firewall by using this mode. To enter the configuration mode from the privileged mode, enter the command `config t` at the privileged mode prompt. The characteristics of the configuration mode are as follows:

✦ The prompt for this mode is hostname followed by `(config)#`. An example is `PIXFW(config)#`.

✦ This command mode provides all the commands that allow a user to make the configuration changes in PIX Firewall.

✦ This command mode does not provide the commands of the unprivileged mode. However, it provides all the privileged mode commands.

Caution   Only authorized users should be allowed to use this command mode, which provides crucial and powerful commands. Be sure of the implications of a command before executing it.

Implementing security on an interface

Defining the security level at network interfaces is essential to define the rules of communication that take place between two interfaces. Communication is allowed between two interfaces only if the connection is set up from a higher security side to the lower security side. You can implement a segmented security model having various levels of security.

PIX Firewall can be purchased with more than two interfaces. You can implement security levels at each interface and provide protection to each internal network from the other. You can assign a name and security level to an interface on PIX Firewall by using the following command

```
PIXFW(config)#nameif hardware_id if_name security_level
```

where

✦ `hardware_id` specifies the interface type, such as Ethernet, Token Ring, and FDDI and number for the interface whose characteristics are being defined in this command.

✦ `if_name` specifies the network interface name assigned to the interface. The interface name can contain up to 255 characters.

✦ `security_level` specifies the security level of the interface. This parameter is entered as `securityn,` where *n* specifies a number between 0 and 100.

By default, the first two interfaces of the PIX Firewall are assigned the name outside and inside. The security value assigned to the inside interface is 100. The security value assigned to the outside interface is 0. However, you can change these settings by using the `nameif` command.

In terms of their security requirements, the PIX Firewall does not consider all networks equal. It recognizes the fact that some networks require more security than others. Thus, you must determine the security risk faced by each network. Depending on the security risk faced by each network, you must assign security levels to the interfaces, which are connected to these networks. A higher security risk network requires a higher security level on the firewall.

The rules for communication between the interfaces that have security levels assigned to them are as follows:

✦ The only packets allowed would originate from an inside network with security level 100 and attempt travel to an outside network with security level 0. However, if any access list, authentication, or authorization is defined, then the packets would be permitted only if allowed by these restrictions.

✦ The only packets dropped would originate from an outside network that has security level 0 and attempt travel to an inside network with security level 100. However, if conduits are configured to allow the packets, PIX Firewall allows those packets to override this rule. In addition, if authentication or authorization is configured, the packet would be allowed only if permitted by these restrictions.

✦ Packets originating from one network to another network of equal security level would be dropped. However, if conduits are configured to allow the packets, PIX Firewall allows the packets to override this rule.

Security level 100 is normally allotted to an interface connected to an inside network. Security level 0 is normally allotted to an outside network or the Internet connected interface. If a command requires two interfaces to be specified, you must specify the interface with a higher security level before the other.

An interface is considered an outside interface if it has a lower security value than the interface it is being compared to. Similarly, an inside interface is the one that has a higher security value than the interface it is being compared to. An inside interface can be visualized to be behind the firewall while the outside interface can be visualized to be outside the firewall.

Configuring interface settings

Networks connect to the interfaces of the firewall. Therefore, interfaces must be configured to communicate with the hosts on the network. In addition, an interface must be configured for speed and duplexity. It must be assigned an IP address and other parameters. To configure speed and duplexity settings on an interface, issue the following command:

```
PIXFW(config)#interface hardware_id [hardware_speed] [shutdown]
```

where

+ *hardware_id* specifies the interface type, such as Ethernet, Token Ring, Fddi, and number of the interface.

+ *hardware_speed* specifies the speed for accessing the network. It can have values such as 10baset, 100basetx, 100full, aui, and bnc for Ethernet interfaces. For a Token Ring, it can have values, such as 4 Mbps and 16 Mbps.

+ *shutdown* deactivate the interface.

To configure the interface Ethernet 1 for auto speed and duplexity, the command is

```
PIXFW(config)#interface Ethernet1 auto
```

After setting the speed and duplexity, you must assign an IP address to the interface. The command to do so is

```
PIXFW(config)#interface if_name ip_address [netmask]
```

where

+ if_*name* specifies the name assigned by the nameif command for the network interface.

+ *ip_address* specifies the IP address assigned to the interface.

+ *netmask* specifies the network mask of the IP address assigned to the interface.

Saving the configuration

After all configurations have been set, you must save the configuration. You can store, observe, and erase the current configuration by using the write command. The options available with the write command are listed:

+ To erase the flash memory configuration, use the following command:

```
Router#write erase
```

+ To save the current configuration on a floppy disk, use the following command:

```
Router#write floppy
```

The destination floppy disk must be formatted with DoS or a PIX 520 boot disk.

+ To save the current configuration in the flash memory, use the following command:

```
Router#write memory
```

✦ To merge the current configuration with the configuration saved in flash, use the following command:

```
Router#configure memory
```

✦ To save the configuration to the failover standby unit from ROM or RAM, use the following command:

```
Router#write standby
```

The configuration is automatically written to the secondary unit as soon as the primary unit starts. However, if they have different copies, use the `write standby` command.

✦ To view the present configurations on the terminal, use the following command:

```
Router#write terminal
```

✦ To view the image stored in flash, use the following command:

```
Router#show configure
```

✦ To save the current configuration to a host on the network, use the following command

```
Router#write net [[server_ip]:[filename]]
```

where `server_ip` and `filename` specify the IP address of the host and the file in which you want to save the current configuration.

Tip If you have specified the filename in the `tftp-server` command, specify a colon after the IP address.

Advanced PIX Firewall Features

It is important to control traffic flow from outside the firewall into the internal network. It is also important to control the traffic flowing out of the secured internal network. In short, the entire traffic flow should be controlled by the firewall.

Network engineers have to bring about a balance between the strictness of the security policy and user inconvenience in accessing network resources. The design of the network and its security should provide enough protection, in practical balance with easy and flexible user access to resources.

Controlling outbound access through the firewall

The PIX Firewall provides features to control the hosts on the inside network, which communicate with the hosts on the outside network. These features are Network Address Translation (NAT) and Port Address Translation (PAT), conduit statements, and the ability to grant a multimedia application dynamic access through the firewall.

PIX NAT

If you have a network that uses private unregistered IP addresses, you cannot directly connect to the Internet because your IP addresses are not valid for external use. To enable the hosts on this network to connect to the Internet, you must assign one or more valid registered IP addresses at the exit point or the interface connected to the Internet. Then, you must configure the exit point to translate the IP address of all the packets traveling out of the network to these valid IP addresses.

When the source IP address of the packets coming from the inside network is stripped off and a global IP address is assigned to the packet before it is sent out on the Internet, it is called *translation*. Translation allows unregistered clients to access the Internet without changing their IP addresses. It also provides the organization with the scope of using the complete range of private IP addresses. Thus the organization can have any number of nodes and networks. This also hides the internal IP addresses from the external world, thereby increasing security.

In NAT, mapping is done between internal IP addresses and external registered IP addresses. This mapping is done on PIX Firewall. PIX Firewall supports three types of NAT:

✦ **Static NAT:** In static NAT, the administrator configures the address mapping statically on the firewall. Each host address of the internal network is permanently mapped to an address on the external network.

✦ **Dynamic NAT:** In dynamic NAT, the administrator creates a pool of valid registered IP addresses. PIX Firewall intercepts the traffic coming from the internal network and translates the internal IP addresses with an IP address from the pool of global IP addresses. These translations are stored in a table, which is referred to when the returning packets from the Internet are forwarded to internal hosts.

✦ **PAT:** It is a modified version of NAT. In PAT, only one external registered IP address is assigned to the outside interface of the firewall. This IP address is mapped to all internal unregistered IP addresses. PIX Firewall selects and assigns an external IP address and a TCP/UDP source port number to each internal IP address. Thus, it is actually a combination of an external IP address and a port number that uniquely maps to an internal IP address. This mapping is again recorded by the firewall for forwarding the returning packets to the internal hosts.

To configure NAT, you first must define the global pool of outside registered IP addresses that will be mapped to the internal IP addresses. To define this address pool, you use the following command:

```
PIXFW(config)# global [if_name] nat_id global_ip[-global_ip]
[netmask global_mask]
```

where

- ✦ *if_name* specifies the network name of the interface where the pool of addresses would be used.

- ✦ nat_id specifies a positive number that groups the nat command and global command. It can have a value up to 2,147,483,647.

- ✦ *global_ip* is one IP address or a range of IP addresses globally registered. It is the pool of addresses that would be used for mapping.

- ✦ *global_mask* is the network mask for the global pool of addresses.

The next step is to configure NAT. This configuration would specify the addresses that would be mapped the global address pool by the firewall. To configure NAT, use the following command:

```
PIXFW(config)#nat [if_name] nat_id local_ip
[netmask [max_cons [em_limit]]] [norandomseq]
```

where

- ✦ *if_name* specifies the interface name of the internal network.

- ✦ *nat_id* specifies the positive identifier that binds all nat statements. All nat and global statements that have the same nat_id are also bound with each other.

- ✦ *local_ip* specifies the internal IP address that has to be translated.

- ✦ *netmask* specifies the local IP network mask. To allow all hosts to be eligible for translation, specify 0 as the local_ip and 0 as the netmask.

- ✦ *max_cons* specifies the maximum TCP connections allowed from the particular interface.

- ✦ *em_limit* sets the embryonic connection limit. The default is 0, indicating unlimited connections.

Note

An *embryonic connection* refers to a partially completed connection or half-open session. An embryonic connection is made when a host initiates a connection but does not receive any reply or acknowledgment. The em_limit helps prevent denial-of-service attacks. The maximum number of embryonic connections should be less than or equal to the connection licenses. The rule of thumb is to keep this value to a maximum of 70 percent of the licensed connections. The minimum practical value is 1.

- ✦ norandomseq specifies not to randomize the sequence number of the TCP packet. Use this option if another firewall in the same line is randomizing the sequence number. However, if you use this key word, it opens a security hole in the firewall.

To understand the entire operation of translation, consider an example of a network shown in Figure 9-2.

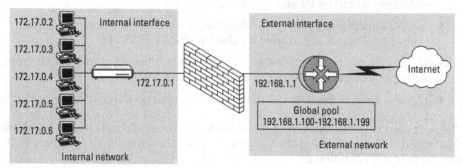

Figure 9-2: A sample network for address translation

At the firewall, create a global registered address pool by using the following command:

```
PIXFW(config)#global (outside) 1 192.168.1.100-192.168.1.199
```

The global pool of addresses is the range of IP addresses from `192.168.1.100` to `192.168.1.199`, which are configured on the outside interface of the firewall.

Then, NAT is configured on the firewall to specify the internal IP addresses that would map to the global IP address pool by using the following command:

```
PIXFW(config)#nat (inside) 1 172.17.0.0 255.255.255.0
```

This command specifies that any IP address of the network `172.17.0.0/24` would be mapped to the global IP address pool with `global_id` 1 configured with the previous command.

The sequence of events at the firewall is as follows:

1. A user on a host with the IP address `172.17.0.10` sends a packet to a host on the Internet to start a session. The packet has the source address `172.17.0.10`.

2. It reaches the inside interface of the firewall. The firewall determines translation instructions for the packet because of the `nat` command configured on the interface. The `nat` command conveys to the firewall to pick an address from the global address pool with `global_id` 1 and translate the internal IP address of the packet to this global IP address.

3. The firewall strips the packet of its original IP address and assigns `192.168.1.100` to the packet.

4. The packet leaves the outside interface of the firewall with the source address `192.168.1.100`.

5. The mapping is also stored by the firewall in a table. So, when the return packets from the host on the Internet arrive with the destination address `192.168.1.100`, the firewall translates the destination address of these packets to `172.17.0.10`.

While implementing NAT, you might require the addresses of a few internal host addresses to be visible to the outside world (such as registered IP addresses to one or more hosts on the internal network). So, the source IP address on the packet originating from these hosts should not be translated. These hosts (for example, a Web server or a mail server) may have to be accessed by the external users on the Internet. Be sure to disable NAT for such addresses.

To disable NAT for one IP address or a range of IP addresses, use the `nat 0` command. If you want to disable address translation for the internal address `172.17.0.100`, use the following command:

```
PIXFW(config)#nat (inside) 0 172.17.0.100 255.255.255.255
```

This command informs the firewall to reveal the address `172.17.0.100` to the outside world.

Port Address Translation

Port Address Translation (PAT) maps all internal IP addresses to one external global registered IP address. It is also called *many-to-one address translation*. In PAT, the firewall translates the IP address and port number of the internal host and adds an entry in the mapping table. The entry consists of the mapping of IP addresses and the port numbers. PIX Firewall uses this mapping table entry until the session is functioning. After the session terminates, the entry is deleted.

Note   The PAT feature increases the address pool of an organization; one IP address can be used to translate 64000 internal hosts. (Normally the practical limit is 4000.)

Consider an example of a network shown in Figure 9-3. The organization has one registered IP address `192.168.1.100`, and the internal network number is `172.17.0.0/24`. To connect to the Internet using the registered IP address for all the hosts, the configuration is done using the following sequence of commands:

```
PIXFW(config)#nat (inside) 2 172.17.0.0 255.255.255.0

PIXFW(config)#global (outside) 2 192.168.1.100
```

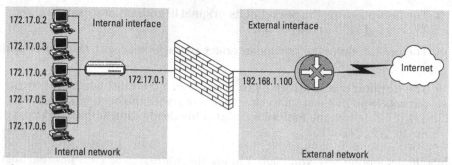

Figure 9-3: A sample network for Port Address Translation

You can also use multiple nat statements to specify multiple network numbers, and they should be mapped to the global pool of IP addresses. In the previous example, if the internal network has three networks (172.17.0.0/24, 172.17.5.0/24, and 172.17.6.0/24), then the following sequence of commands would be executed:

```
PIXFW(config)#nat (inside) 2 172.17.0.0 255.255.255.0
PIXFW(config)#nat (inside) 2 172.17.5.0 255.255.255.0
PIXFW(config)#nat (inside) 2 172.17.6.0 255.255.255.0
PIXFW(config)#global (outside) 2 192.168.1.100
```

The three nat statements form part of the same nat group that have to be translated to the global pool. Because both the nat statements and the global statement have the same nat_id, they are associated — which implies that these nat statements would use the global pool of IP addresses having the same nat_id.

NetBIOS translation

NetBIOS is a nonroutable protocol that uses the naming conventions of the English language to identify a computer. To route the NetBIOS traffic over IP networks, it must be encapsulated in IP. Thus the complete NetBIOS packet forms the data portion of the packet after encapsulation. In addition, the IP source address is a part of both the IP header and the NetBIOS header.

As shown in Figure 9-4, the IP source and destination addresses are a part of the NetBIOS header. The IP packet in which this packet would be encapsulated also has the IP source and destination addresses. In a network that allows NetBIOS over IP, PIX Firewall changes the IP address in the NetBIOS header and the IP header. When a user (in a network which is configured to allow NetBIOS over IP) sends the data packets to an outside server, the packet gets routed through PIX Firewall. The PIX Firewall changes the source address on both the IP header and the NetBIOS header and then sends the packet to the outside server. If any of the IP or NetBIOS packets gets corrupted during transportation, the destination host rejects the packet.

Len	XxEFFF	Command	Data1	Data2	Xmit/response correlator	Destination Address	Source Address

NetBIOS packet header

Figure 9-4: NetBIOS packet header

If the firewall does not use built-in NetBIOS support, it translates the IP address in the IP packet header. However, if the PIX Firewall is configured to perform NetBIOS translations, it replaces the original source address with the address from the pool. This operation usually does not pose any problems. However, some operating systems (such as Windows NT) can have problems with customized packets. A security concern with NetBIOS is that it is susceptible to hacking. Therefore, NetBIOS should be deployed carefully.

Multimedia applications

Some multimedia applications supported by the PIX Firewall are as follows:

✦ Intel Internet Video Phone

✦ Microsoft NetMeeting

✦ Microsoft NetShow

✦ Oracle SQL*Net

✦ Real Network RealAudio

✦ VDOnet VDOLive

✦ Vocal Tec Internet Phone

✦ Vxtreme Web Theatre 2

✦ White Pine CU-SeeMe

✦ Xing Technologies Stream Works

Multimedia applications pose various problems for firewalls. First, the multimedia applications use UDP, which is a connectionless transport protocol. Second, a few of these applications use several UDP ports for sending data to their clients. All firewalls are not well-equipped to handle such complex traffic. However, PIX Firewall can handle these applications by dynamically opening and closing UDP ports and provides secure multimedia connections.

Some firewalls adopt the method of opening a large number of UDP ports for multimedia applications. However, this increases the security risk. In addition, some firewalls cannot support multimedia with NAT — which restricts the benefits of multi-media to only the registered IP addresses. Otherwise all the inside IP addresses have to be exposed. However, the PIX Firewall also supports multimedia with NAT.

Multimedia applications also pose problems when used along with PAT. The multi-media applications expect the data to arrive on specific ports, and any changes in the port can confuse them. However, the use of specific ports by these applications can differentiate with the port mappings of PAT. Multimedia applications might fail to work because of such conflicts.

If Web Theatre2 and NetShow fail to work properly, you can use the established command to examine the problem. The established command enables debugging of an application that uses multiple TCP/UDP ports. The syntax of this command is

```
PIXFW(config)#established protocol dst_port_1
[permitto protocol [dst_port_2[.dst_port_2]]]
[permitfrom protocol [src_port[.src_port]]]
```

where

+ *protocol* specifies the protocol type in the IP header, which is TCP or UDP.

+ *dst_port_1* specifies the destination port to which the connection is required.

+ *dst_port_2* specifies the destination port to be permitted by PIX Firewall for return packets.

+ *src_port* specifies the source port on the server. The server would send data on this port. Therefore, it should be allowed by the firewall.

+ permitto *protocol* permits an inbound connection to the specified protocol and the port number.

+ permitfrom *protocol* permits inbound connections from the specified protocol and the port number.

Controlling inbound access through the firewall

If you must allow external users to access resources on the internal network—in particular, the Web server—configure PIX Firewall to allow selective inbound access to the Web server. Your network security strategy should incorporate a careful design for this procedure.

To allow the external hosts to access the internal hosts of the protected network, you use the two commands static and conduit in conjunction. The static command specifies the IP address available to the external hosts, and the conduit command allows or rejects access to those hosts based on the protocol, the port number, and the IP address.

The static command

To access an internal host, the external host must know the IP address of the internal host—which implies that the internal host should have a static IP address. If address translation occurs, there should be static mapping between the static IP address of the internal host and a global registered IP address. The static command does this job. This command permanently maps a static address to a registered IP address. It is somewhat similar to a static route in the routing table. As a result of the permanent nature of address mapping, PIX Firewall does not need to maintain a session-state database for the corresponding sessions — which reduces the load on the firewall.

You can use the `static` command for the following purposes at the firewall:

✦ **Define static mapping of an internal host so the traffic from that host always has the same translated IP address when leaving the firewall.** This action might be necessary in situations such as when the destination network also has a firewall that has been configured to allow traffic to enter from only a specific IP address. In such a situation, you must statically map the IP address of the internal host to the IP address required by the destination firewall.

✦ **Control external hosts trying to connect to an internal host.** In this situation, the `static` command has to be used in conjunction with the `conduit` command. With the `static` command, you translate the external advertised IP address to a specific internal host IP address. With the `conduit` command, you specify permissions based on certain criteria. This action might be required if you have a Web server placed inside the internal network that must be accessed by external hosts.

✦ **Map a range of internal IP addresses to a range of registered IP addresses.** This is called a *net static*; it can create 256 statics with the same command. You can make this happen by entering the `global_ip` and `local_ip` values as 0.

The syntax for the *static* command is

```
PIXFW(config)#static [internal_if_name external_if_name]
 global_ip local_ip [netmask network_mask]
 [max_conns [em_limit]] [norandomseq]
```

where

✦ `internal_if_name` specifies the interface name of the internal network. It is the higher-security-level interface.

✦ `external_if_name` specifies the interface name of the external network. It is the lower-security-level interface.

✦ `global_ip` gives the global registered IP address for the outside interface. It is the IP address on the lower-security-level interface.

✦ `local_ip` specifies the local unregistered IP address of the inside network. It is the IP address on the higher-security-level interface.

✦ `network_mask` specifies the network mask for both `global_ip` and `local_ip`. For host addresses, the netmask would be 255.255.255.255. For any network, the netmask would be 0.0.0.0 with the `global_ip` and/or `local_ip` as 0.0.0.0. This command with the netmask parameter determines the scope of addresses that would be permanently mapped between the `local_ip` and `global_ip` ranges.

✦ *max_conns* specifies the maximum number of simultaneous connections permitted through the use of `static`. This number must be equal to or less than the number of connection licenses bought with the firewall.

✦ *em_limit* specifies the limit for embryonic connections.

✦ `norandomseq` is a keyword that tells the firewall not to randomize the TCP sequence number.

The `static` command has a higher preference than the `nat` and `global` commands pair. Thus, NAT can translate addresses of only those hosts that have not been mentioned in the `static` command. If IP of any host has been statically mapped using `static` command, NAT would not translate its IP address. The rules of thumb rules to determine the commands to be used in different situations are as follows:

✦ Use `nat` and `global` commands when you want to permit traffic from higher security interface to a lower security interface.

✦ Use the `static` and `conduit` command when you want to permit traffic from a lower security interface to a higher security interface.

Consider an example of static mapping to understand how it operates. In the network shown in Figure 9-5, the inside interface address of PIX Firewall is 172.17.0.1/24, and the outside interface address is 192.168.1.10/24. The NAT is implemented such that the IP address 172.17.0.100 is translated to the global IP address 192.168.1.10.

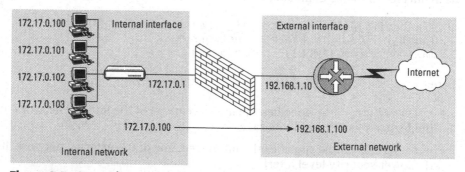

Figure 9-5: A sample network for static mapping

Now, you want to define static mapping of this IP address such that the IP address 172.17.0.100 is translated to 192.168.1.100. The command to do so is

```
PIXFW(config)#static (inside, outside) 192.168.1.100 172.17.0.100
```

Packets from the host 172.17.0.100 would have the source IPO address 192.168.1.100 as they travel out of the firewall.

In net static, you can use the `static` command to statically map a range of internal unregistered IP addresses to a range of global registered IP addresses. With net static, you can create 256 mappings of addresses with the same command. While defining net static for an entire class of IP addresses, specify major network numbers as the `global_ip` and `local_ip` as the network mask. Consider an example of the network in Figure 9-6.

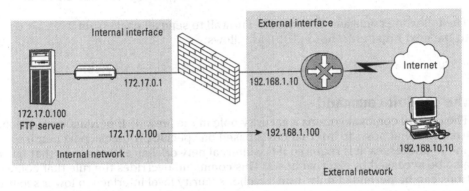

Figure 9-6: A sample network for access tunnel

The internal network has the network number `172.17.0.0/24`. The organization holds a range of outside global IP addresses from `192.168.5.1` to `192.168.5.254`. Instead of mapping each host with a statement separately, you can do this using just one `static` command. The command is

```
PIXFW(config)#static (inside, outside) 192.168.5.0 172.17.0.0
netmask 255.255.255.0
```

Each address of the inside network `172.17.0.0/24` is statically mapped to each address of the outside network `192.168.5.0/24`. The only essential difference between the `static` and `net static` commands is that `net static` sets the host bits of the `global_ip` and `local_ip` to 0, indicating a range of hosts.

The `static` command maps a specific internal IP address to a global IP address. You can also define a static route to reach a specific IP address — done with the route command (whose functionality is similar to that of `static` command). The `route` command informs the firewall about the address of the specified gateway for sending a packet to a destination IP address.

The syntax of the `route` command is

```
PIXFW(config)#route if-name ip_address netmask gateway_ip [metric]
```

where

✦ `if_name` specifies the network interface name.

✦ *ip_address*   specifies the destination IP address. It might be a host or a network address. To specify a default route, specify this argument as 0.0.0.0 or 0.

✦ *netmask* specifies the network mask to apply to the IP address. To specify a default route, specify the netmask as 0.0.0.0 or 0.

✦ *gateway_ip* specifies the IP address of the gateway or the next hop address.

✦ *metric* specifies the number of hops to the gateway. The default value is 1.

The following command tells the PIX Firewall to send all packets for 172.17.0.100 to the next hop (192.168.1.100), as follows:

```
PIXFW(config)#route internal 172.17.0.100 255.255.255.0 192.168.1.100
```

The conduit command

The *conduit* command opens a security hole in the firewall. It permits connections from external hosts to internal hosts based on specific protocols, port numbers, and IP addresses. It is required if the internal network has a Web server that must also be accessed by external hosts. This command overrides the rule that connections can be permitted only from a higher security level interface to lower security level interfaces. It creates an exception by permitting a connection from lower security level interface to a higher security level interface.

You can link the conduit command with a global command or a static command. If you associate it with a global command, the security hole would be created for the range of hosts specified in the global command. If you associate it with the static command, the security hole is created for the specific hosts defined in the *static* command.

The syntax for the conduit command is

```
PIXFW(config)#conduit {permit|deny} protocol
  global_ip global_mask [operator port [port]]
  foreign_ip foreign_mask [operator port [port]]
```

where

✦ permit|deny specify whether the matching packets should be permitted or blocked.

✦ *protocol*   specifies the protocol for the connection. The protocols can be tcp, udp, eigrp, gre, igmp, icmp, grp, ip, nos, ospf, ipinip, or an integer representing a protocol. To specify all the protocols of TCP/IP suite, specify this as ip.

✦ *global_ip* specifies a global IP address that has been defined by a global or *static* command.

✦ *operator* and *port* specify a port or port range. Operator can have eq, lt, any, gt, neq, and range as values. The port can have values that can be the port number or the port name. If you want to specify an SNMP service, the operator port pair would be eq snmp.

+ *global_mask* specifies the network mask for *global_ip*.

+ *foreign_ip* specifies the IP address of external hosts allowed or not allowed to access the internal resources.

+ *foreign_mask* specifies the network mask for foreign_ip.

There are a few similarities between access lists and conduit. Both define permissions and conditions for matching packets. If you want to specify all IP addresses, the keyword any can be used in the access list and the conduit command. In the conduit command, if you want to specify 0.0.0.0 0.0.0.0 for global_ip global_mask, you can specify the keyword any instead. Similarly, if you want to specify 0.0.0.0 0.0.0.0 for foreign_ip foreign_mask, you can specify the keyword any instead. To allow any external host to access the Web server whose global address is 192.168.10.100, the command is

```
PIXFW(config)#conduit permit tcp 192.168.10.100
255.255.255.255 eq http any
```

If you want to specify the IP address of a specific host, you specify 0.0.0.0 0.0.0.0 in global_ip global_mask or foreign_ip foreign_mask. Instead of this, you can specify the keyword host followed by the host IP address. Taking the previous example, the command can be written as:

```
PIXFW(config)#conduit permit tcp host 192.168.10.100 eq http any
```

Similar to the access list, conduit commands also follow the "rule of implicit deny." Packets that do not match what the conduit command specifies are dropped.

If you specify icmp as the protocol in the conduit command, the command changes to

```
PIXFW(config)#conduit {permit|deny} icmp global_ip
global_mask foreign_ip foreign_mask icmp_type
```

where *icmp_type* specifies the type of ICMP message to allow or block.

Consider an example for using both static and conduit commands. In the network shown in Figure 9-6, the external host is to be allowed access to the FTP server on the internal network. The address of the FTP server is 172.17.0.100, and the global address mapped to it is 192.168.1.100. The external host to be given access to the FTP server has the IP address 192.168.10.10. The command sequence to configure the firewall for this situation is

```
PIXFW(config)#static 192.168.1.100 172.17.0.100
```

```
PIXFW(config)#conduit permit tcp host 192.168.1.100 eq ftp host 192.16.10.10
```

You cannot use the conduit command with PAT. This is because PAT randomizes the port numbers that cause conduit statements to act inaccurately.

Permitting ping from outside

By default, PIX Firewall does not permit pinging from an external host to an internal host. However, you require this to test connectivity with the external network. The solution is to use the `conduit` command. To allow inbound pinging, you must configure a conduit so it allows `icmp echo-reply` traffic to enter the internal network. The following command performs the required task:

```
PIXFW(config)#conduit permit icmp any any echo-reply
```

This command tells the firewall to allow all `echo-type icmp` responses from outside the network to enter the internal network.

Configuring PIX Mail Guard

You do not require external mail relay in the perimeter or the DMZ network if you have installed PIX Firewall. PIX Mail Guard, a component of PIX Firewall, permits only seven SMTP commands to be used when the host accesses the SMTP server. These seven commands are `HELO`, `MAIL`, `RCPT`, `DATA`, `RSET`, `NOOP`, and `QUIT`. The Mail Guard rejects all other commands. Moreover, no alert message is sent to the sender. The sender only receives the OK message. This eliminates the possibility of break-in by using any other command.

PIX Mail Guard is enabled by default in PIX Firewall. If it is disabled, you use the following command to enable it:

```
PIXFW(config)#fixup protocol smtp 25
```

Consider an example of a network having an SMTP server on the internal network, which must be accessed by external users. The IP address of the server is 172.17.0.50, and it is mapped to the global address 192.168.1.15. To allow external hosts to access an SMTP server located in the internal network, the following sequence of commands is used.

```
PIXFW(config)#static (inside, outside) 192.168.1.15 172.17.0.50
```

```
PIXFW(config)#conduit permit tcp host 192.168.1.15 eq smtp any
```

```
PIXFW(config)#fixup protocol smtp 25
```

The fixup protocol command

This is a useful feature of PIX Firewall that enables you to tell the firewall how it should deal with different Application-layer protocols. This command enables you to observe, change, enable, or disable Application-level protocol analysis by using the firewall. Using this command, you can tell the firewall to change the packet contents to suit the needs of a security policy.

The syntax of the command is

```
PIXFW(config)#fixup protocol protocol [port[-port]]
```

where

+ *protocol* specifies the specific protocol. By default, it can have only the following six values: smtp, ftp, http, rsh, sqlnet, and h.323.

+ *port* gives the port number or range of port numbers for the Application-layer protocol. You can also specify multiple ports for a protocol. If you do not specify the port number, the default port number of the specified protocol is assumed by PIX Firewall.

Denial-of-service attack

A *denial-of-service* (or DoS) attack occurs when a server does not provide services to genuine clients because it is too busy servicing the attacker client's requests. This happens because the attacking client continuously sends requests for service without completing the sessions.

A popular form of DoS attack is SYN flooding. In SYN flooding, a hacker sends session requests (SYN packet) with a fictitious source address to a port of the target host. The target host sends back a reply (SYN ACK packet) to this request to the same fictitious destination address. Because this destination address does not exist, the connection is not set up. The target host waits for a reply from the fictitious host to complete the connection (ACK packet). It waits till the connection timeout occurs. The hacker keeps sending these session request packets in huge numbers. The target host queues these requests and tries to respond to each request. This queue keeps the target host so busy that it cannot respond to genuine requests. As a result, genuine hosts are denied the service.

PIX Firewall prevents such DoS attacks. It uses em_limit as a component of static and nat commands. This places a restriction on the number of half-open sessions that can exist through the firewall. When the number of half-open sessions reaches the threshold, PIX Firewall does not accept any more sessions.

Consider an example where you want to limit the total number of half-open sessions to a server to 50. The server is on the internal network and has the IP address 172.17.0.200 and the global address 192.168.1.200. The command to limit the number of half-open sessions is

```
PIXFW(config)#static (inside, outside) 192.168.1.200
  172.17.0.200 netmask 255.255.255.255 20 50
```

This command indicates the firewall will limit the total number of completed connections to 20.

PIX DNS Guard feature

The PIX DNS Guard feature of PIX Firewall prevents DNS denial-of-service (DoS) attacks. A hacker launches a DNS DoS attack by hijacking the session between a client and a DNS server. The hacker then floods the client with DNS replies, making it dysfunctional.

DNS Guard identifies outbound DNS resolve request and allows reply only from one DNS server. To understand how DNS Guard prevents a DNS DoS attack, consider the example of a network, as shown in Figure 9-7.

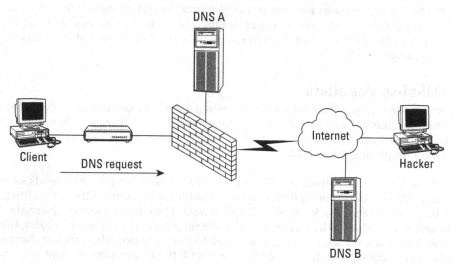

Figure 9-7: A sample network for DNS DoS attack

The client sends a DNS request to the DNS servers, DNS A and DNS B. This request reaches the firewall, which forwards the request to the DNS servers. The hacker monitors the traffic from DNS B on port 53 (DNS port). The hacker detects traffic on this port and hijacks the DNS reply session of DNS B. The hacker then floods the external interface of the firewall with replies. The firewall receives the reply from DNS A and forwards it to the client. The firewall also matches the packets from the hacker with the session-state database and determines that these are bogus DNS replies and drops them — which prevents the DoS attack.

Hijacking UDP is a popular form of DoS attack. PIX Firewall prevents it by opening dynamic conduits to permit UDP packets from the requesting client. After the request is completed, the firewall closes the dynamic conduit even if the UDP timer has not expired. This prevents UDP port from remaining open after the request has been completed.

Monitoring the PIX Firewall Configuration

After configuring PIX Firewall, verify the configuration. You should test and verify different sections of the configuration and find any drawbacks in the configuration.

To ensure that the interfaces are functioning properly and that the cables are connected correctly, use the command

```
PIXFW#show interface
```

A sample output of the *show interface* command is shown in Figure 9-8.

PIXFW#show interface

interface ethernet0 "outside" is up, line protocol is up
Hardware is i82555 ethernet, address is 0011.0050.130b
IP address 192.168.1.1, subnetmask 255.255.255.0
MTU 1500 bytes, BW 100000 Kbithalfduplex
        221142 packets input, 114477011 bytes, 0 no buffer
        Received 30 broadcasts, 10runts, 2giants
        5 inputerrors,0 CRC,4 frame,0 overrun,0 underruns,0 unicastrpidrops
        0 outputerrors,10000 collisions, 0 interface resets
        0 babbles, 0 late collisions, 111150 deferred
        0 lost carrier, 0 no carrier

Figure 9-8: A sample output of the `show interface` **command**

In the output of the show interface command, notice the first line of the output. It describes two entities, the interface status and the line protocol status. In an operational interface, both these entities should be working.

To view the IP addresses configured on the interfaces, use the command

```
PIXFW#show ip address
```

A sample output of this command is

```
PIXFW#show ip address
inside ip address 172.17.0.1 mask 255.255.255.0
outside ip address 192.168.10.1 mask 255.255.255.0
```

To view the ARP cache for verifying the connectivity of PIX Firewall, use the following command:

```
PIXFW#show arp
```

A sample output of this command is

```
PIXFW#show arp
Inside 172.17.0.100 001a.11ab.001b
```

To verify whether new `arp` entries are being formed, clear the ARP cache with the `clear arp` command. Then, after some time, view the ARP cache with the `show arp` command again. The network should be operational; otherwise no entries show up in the ARP cache.

You can test the connectivity to the interfaces with the `ping` command. You can ping interfaces of PIX Firewall by using the name of the interfaces. A sample output of `ping` is

```
PIXFW#ping inside 172.17.0.1
Inside 172.17.0.1 response received - 25Ms
Inside 172.17.0.1 response received - 25Ms
Inside 172.17.0.1 response received - 25Ms
```

You can view ICMP, TCP, and UDP packet traffic by using the `debug packet` command from the console port. The command looks like this

```
PIXFW#debug packet if_name [src source_ip [netmask mask]]
[dst dest_ip [netmask mask]]
[[proto icmp] | [proto tcp [sport src_port] [dport dest_port]]
| [proto udp [sport src_port] [dport dest_port]] [rx | tx | both]
```

where

- ✦ `if_name` specifies the interface name. The packets coming from the specified interface are to be monitored.
- ✦ `source_ip` specifies the source IP address.
- ✦ `mask` specifies the network mask for the corresponding source or destination IP address.
- ✦ `dest_ip` specifies the destination IP address.
- ✦ `proto icmp` instructs the firewall to display only ICMP packets.
- ✦ `proto tcp` instructs the firewall to display only TCP packets.
- ✦ `src_port` specifies the source port.
- ✦ `dest_port` specifies the destination port.
- ✦ `proto udp` instructs the firewall to display only UDP packets.
- ✦ `rx` instructs the firewall to display only the packets received at the PIX Firewall.
- ✦ `tx` instructs the firewall to display only the packets that were transmitted from PIX Firewall.
- ✦ `both` instructs the firewall to display both received and transmitted packets.

Caution

This command generates a large amount of output and places excessive load on the CPU of the firewall. Therefore this command should be used with caution.

To view the `conduits` configured on the PIX Firewall, use the following command:

```
PIXFW#show conduit
```

A sample output of this command is

```
PIXFW#show conduit
Conduit 192.168.5.100 23 tcp 192.168.1.10
```

To display a detailed list of the address translations occurring at the firewall and the connection information related to those translations, use the following command:

```
PIXFW#show xlate [global_ip [local_ip]]
```

where *global_ip* and *local_ip* specify the registered and local unregistered IP addresses, respectively.

A sample output of the command is

```
PIXFW#show xlate
Global 192.168.1.100 Local 172.17.0.100 static nconns 0 econns 0 flags s
Global 192.168.1.50 Local 172.17.0.10 static nconns 0 econns 0 flags s
```

To clear the translation table at a particular moment, use the command

```
PIXFW#clear xlate
```

Case Study

In the AllSolv Inc.'s network shown in Figure 9-9, the task is to configure the firewall according to the following criteria:

✦ Any external host can access the Web server 172.17.0.200. The external world knows the address of the Web server as 192.168.0.10.

✦ The valid addresses available with the organization range from 192.168.0.10 to 192.168.1.60.

✦ The IP addresses of the hosts inside the network should be translated when their packets are destined for the outside hosts.

✦ For the security of the Web server, the number of completed connections should not exceed 50 and the number of incomplete connections should not exceed 100.

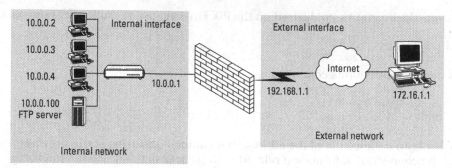

Figure 9-9: A sample network diagram of AllSolv, Inc.

Configure the interfaces using the following sequence of commands:

```
PIXFW(config)#nameif ethernet0 outside security0
PIXFW(config)#interface ethernet0 auto
PIXFW(config)#ip address outside 192.168.0.1 255.255.255.0

PIXFW(config)#nameif ethernet1 inside security100

PIXFW(config)#interface ethernet1 auto

PIXFW(config)#ip address inside 172.17.1.1 255.255.255.0
```

To define default routes on the inside and outside network interfaces, use the following sequence of commands.

```
PIXFW(config)#route outside 0 0 192.168.0.2

PIXFW(config)#route inside 0 0 172.17.1.2
```

Since the Web server 172.17.0.200 should be accessible to external hosts, there must be a static mapping of the addresses from 172.17.0.200 to 192.168.0.10. The IP address 192.168.0.10 is the destination address, which the external hosts would use to access this server. To allow the external hosts to access the server, there should be a *conduit* that creates a limited security hole, allowing only http access from external hosts to the Web server. For the security of the Web server, the maximum number of complete connections should be 50 and the maximum number of incomplete connections should be 100. The following sequence of commands performs all these tasks:

```
PIXFW(config)#static (inside, outside) 192.168.0.10 172.17.0.200 50 100

PIXFW(config)#conduit permit tcp host 192.168.0.10 eq http any
```

Since the valid IP addresses of the organization range from 192.168.0.10 to 192.168.0.60, there should be a global pool of addresses defined on PIX Firewall. The internal hosts' addresses should be translated to these global addresses. The following sequence of commands performs these tasks:

```
PIXFW(config)#global (outside) 1 192.168.0.11-192.168.0.60
 netmask 255.255.255.0

PIXFW(config)#nat (inside) 1 0 0
```

Summary

This chapter described Cisco PIX Firewall and its features. Cisco PIX Firewall offers a strong security and scalability to meet the needs of your network, in five models:

✦ Cisco Secure PIX 535

✦ Cisco Secure PIX 525

✦ Cisco Secure PIX 515

✦ Cisco Secure PIX 506

✦ Cisco Secure PIX 501

Each model has its own licensing requirements; one is likely to fit the needs of your network. The steps involved in configuring a PIX Firewall remain consistent from one model to the next, and if necessary, you can control access to internal resources through PIX Firewall. As an additional security measure (especially where active connections to outside networks exist), you can use various commands to monitor PIX Firewall.

✦   ✦   ✦

Understanding and Implementing AAA

P A R T

IV

◆ ◆ ◆ ◆

In This Part

Chapter 10
Cisco AAA Security
Technology

Chapter 11
Configuring the
Network-Access
Server for AAA
Security

◆ ◆ ◆ ◆

The three *As* for good security are *authentication, authorization,* and *accounting* (also known as the *AAA* standard). Network security services that measure up to AAA establish a better-than-industry-standard level of security. Part IV shows you how to secure your network access, using AAA as your guide to the best methods of authentication, authorization, and accounting. A brief overview of Cisco AAA products is followed by a description of an ideal AAA security server, which leads into the steps that configure your network access server for AAA security.

Cisco AAA Security Technology

CHAPTER 10

◆   ◆   ◆   ◆

In This Chapter

Securing network access by using AAA

Comparing authentication methods

Defining authorization methods

Listing accounting methods

Understanding authentication proxy

Configuring authentication proxy

◆   ◆   ◆   ◆

The first step toward ensuring network security is to validate any client that requests access to network resources. The main goal of such *access control* is to prevent unauthorized users from gaining access to the network server and its resources. An equally vital security goal, however, is to control the use of network services by users who already have access. You can approach both goals by implementing network-security services according to the Authentication, Authorization, and Accounting (AAA) concept of network architecture — and control access on both the network server and the router.

This chapter provides an overview of the mechanisms that make up AAA architecture — as well as the security technologies associated with each component and some appropriate ways to enforce AAA-based policies. Specifically, the chapter describes the technology and implementation of security protocols supported by Cisco products — and provides preliminary steps to take before you configure and implement AAA security for local or remote security databases. Finally, the chapter covers the mechanism and configuration issues involved in proxy authentication.

Securing Network Access by Using AAA

Any network that provides remote access to clients runs the risk of unauthorized access and denial-of-service attacks.

Hackers can gain access to sensitive information by exploiting any insecure implementation of access control. Thus network designers and administrators must devise and implement an excellent access-control policy; fortunately, an appropriate standard exists: AAA.

Authentication, Authorization, and Accounting (AAA) is an access-control concept based on coordinated network-security technologies; the goal is to control access to the router or the network access server by using a consistent approach to configuring network services.

AAA security services

You can use AAA-based architecture for secure network access. The components of AAA security service architecture are discussed following.

✦ **Authentication:** This process of identifying not only an individual user, but also the level of privileges assigned to that user, regulates the access and use of network resources and services. Users must be authenticated before they are allowed access. The authentication service validates the online identity of an end user or a device, such as host, server, switch, router, and other networking components. This is achieved by utilizing the login and password dialog boxes and challenge and response, messaging support, and security protocols.

Tip   The most effective AAA implementation uses multiple authentication methods instead of relying only on local line passwords.

To configure AAA authentication, follow these general steps:

1. Create a *named list* of authentication methods — defining not only the methods of authentication, but also the sequence in which they must be performed.

2. Apply the named list to various interfaces.

Caution   Before any interface can perform AAA authentication, it must have this named list applied. If you do not apply the list to an interface, a default method list is applied to *all* interfaces — in effect, negating AAA implementation.

✦ **Authorization:** This process of determining specific services and network resources that an individual may access also defines the operations that the individual may perform on the resources. Authorization provides the method for controlling network access remotely. This includes one-time authorization (or authorization for each service, per-user account list, and profile), user-group support, and support for IP, IPX, ARA, and Telnet.

AAA authorization uses sets of attributes and privileges to describe the resources each user is authorized to access — and the actions each user may legitimately perform on those resources. Depending on what works best for your network, you can store these sets of attributes and privileges in a database — either locally (on the access server or router) or remotely (on a security server). Remote security servers, such as RADIUS and TACACS+, authorize by associating pairs of attribute values (AVs), matching the listed users to their listed access rights.

✦ **Accounting:** This process is, for the most part, collecting information to determine who is using which resources. On a network, an accounting service also sends the collected access information — such as user identities, start and stop times, executed commands (such as PPP), number of packets, and number of bytes — to the security server.

On a remote-access network, accounting also serves billing purposes (as with ISPs and other organizations that provide customer services). The crucial tool that an accounting service contributes to security is the *audit trail* — a list of transactions that helps an organization track the patterns of usage (which helps in gauging the network bandwidth and service utilization) and spot suspicious activities.

The network's access server reports user activities, storing accounting records (each with a pair of attribute values) and sending them to the TACACS+ or RADIUS security server. An administrator can analyze the records for the purposes of network management, client billing, and auditing.

TACACS and RADIUS

Broadly speaking, Terminal Access Controller Access Control System (TACACS) and Remote Authentication Dial-In User Service (RADIUS) are security server protocols that are used for AAA with firewalls, NAS, and routers. Servers that implement TACACS are at times referred to as TACACS servers. Also, servers that implement RADIUS are at times referred to as RADIUS servers.

Terminal Access Controller Access Control System (TACACS) is both a security-server application and a protocol designed to implement AAA as three distinct functions (Authentication, Authorization, and Accounting) by providing centralized control of user access. A single application-control server, running a TACACS+ daemon, can support all AAA services. Networks that use TACACS+ typically host its services and user information in a database (often running on a Windows NT or Unix system).

Remote Access Dial-In User Services (RADIUS) was originally developed by Livingston Enterprises to control its network access servers and prevent unauthorized access. It is an open Internet standard, and many third-party security products support it. RADIUS is a distributed client server protocol and can be integrated with other security protocols, such as TACACS+, Kerberos, and local security databases.

To manage its security functions, AAA uses the standard protocols of RADIUS, TACACS+, and Kerberos. In a remote-access internetwork, the router or access server can be configured to act as a network access server. Implementing AAA helps establish communication between the network's access server and the RADIUS, TACACS+, or Kerberos security server. A properly set up AAA system can configure the type of authentication and authorization dynamically, on a per-user or per-service basis.

AAA and access traffic

Remote access is an important way for traveling executives, salespeople, and remote offices to gain access to central office resources. Because most remote-access connections are carried over asynchronous lines, remote access is vulnerable to security attacks.

To accomplish a remote-access session, the remote user requires appropriate application software, a network protocol, and Data Link-layer drivers. The client can use FTP or Telnet client software to initiate a remote session by using TCP/IP or IPX/SPX protocol stacks. The application software and protocol stacks encapsulate the higher-layer data and protocols in Link-layer protocols, such as SLIP and PPP. The encapsulated packets are transmitted across the analog or digital asynchronous line.

A typical AAA setup used to secure usual remote-access process consists of a remote client system, the communication service provider, a network access server, and a remote security database running security server software. Cisco offers a security server software product called Cisco Secure Access Control Server. A typical AAA-based secure network-access scenario is illustrated in Figure 10-1.

AAA technologies help protect all modes of remote access to a network's access servers; they allow only two such modes:

✦ **Character-mode:** An AAA security mechanism secures traffic generated by access that uses auxiliary, console, asynchronous lines (TTYs), or virtual terminal lines (VTYs).

✦ **Packet mode:** An AAA security mechanism protects dial-up access to a particular packet or interface by using `async`, `group-async`, BRI ISDN, or PRI ISDN interfaces on Cisco routers. Some protocols that generate packet-mode traffic are PPP, ARAP, and NASI.

AAA security servers

Central to the implementation of AAA security is the *AAA security server*—which stores access-control information for enforcing AAA security policy—and is thus considered a database. This database can be stored as a local database on the network access server or on a remote security database running an AAA security protocol.

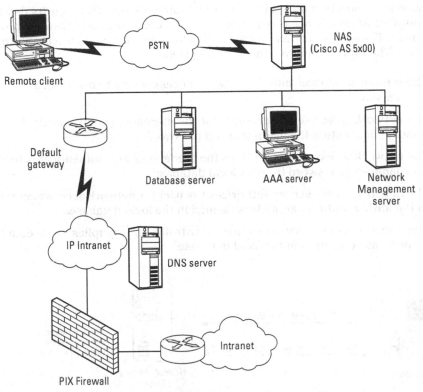

Figure 10-1: A typical AAA-based secure network access setup

AAA with local security database

In a local security database, the username and password information is stored on the network access server itself if few remote users are accessing the network. This is referred to as local authentication on a local security database. A network can have multiple network access servers. A few characteristics of AAA on a local security database are as follows:

◆ It is ideal for small networks having few remote users accessing network access servers.

◆ All security credentials, including the username and password and the authorization parameters, are stored in the local security database of the Cisco network access server.

◆ Remote users are authenticated and authorized against the local security database on the network access server.

◆ The authorization and accounting features have limited support from the local security database.

To provide authentication from a local security database, the local security database on the network access device is populated with the username and password profiles of each user. The authentication process with a local security database is shown in Figure 10-2. The process involves the following steps:

1. The remote client dials into the network access server to establish a PPP session.

2. The network access server prompts for the username and password. The remote client enters the username and password.

3. The network access server receives the credentials and authenticates the username and password from its local database.

4. The network access server authorizes the user for network access according to the authentication parameters defined in the local database.

5. The network access server monitors user traffic and compiles the accounting records, as configured in the local database.

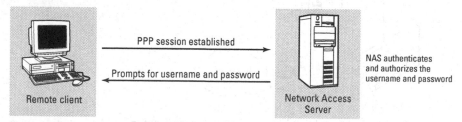

Figure 10-2: AAA with local security database

By using the local security database, AAA security is advantageous for small networks in terms of implementing and minimizing the cost of installation and maintenance.

AAA with a remote security database

Using a remote security database for implementing AAA security is best suited for networks that have a vast network infrastructure with multiple remote users accessing network access servers. The remote security database resides on a special security server on the network. The username and password along with other parameters for each of the network access server and router are stored on this remote security database.

The remote security database provides central management of remote user profiles. It eliminates the need for updating each network access server and router to modify a username and a password whenever a change is requested. It helps in enforcing consistent remote-access policies throughout the organization. The primary characteristics of AAA on a remote security database are as follows:

✦ The remote security database implementation is ideal for medium to large size enterprise networks consisting of many remote clients and network access servers. The implementation cost of remote security database is higher than that of a local security database.

✦ The security credentials, including the username, passwords and authorization parameters, are centrally stored in the remote security database. This provides a better control of network-access policies.

✦ The remote clients are authenticated and authorized against the remote security database.

✦ The remote security database supports all the features of authorization and accounting through the network access server and the security server.

✦ The remote security database can control network access to or from the network access server. The remote security database protocols support access control to routers, Ethernet switches, and firewalls.

The authentication process with a remote security database is shown in Figure 10-3. The remote security database must first be populated with individual user profiles, which are expected to access the network remotely. The network access server must be configured to interoperate with the remote security database for validating remote clients.

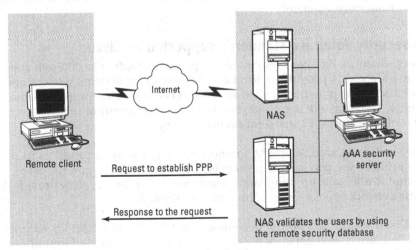

Figure 10-3: AAA with remote security database

The authentication process with a remote security database involves the following steps:

1. The remote client establishes a PPP connection with the network access server.

   Note   If a Unix Server is used for dial-up, the remote client establishes a Serial Line Internet Protocol (SLIP) connection.

2. The network access server prompts for username and password. The remote client enters the username and password.

3. The network access server receives the credentials from the client and forwards the information to the security server. The information exchanged between the network access server and the remote security database server depends on security protocols.

4. The remote security database authenticates and authorizes the remote client for network access. The security database configures the network- access server with appropriate authentication parameters. It also activates the access lists in the network access server for authorization purposes.

5. The network access server compiles all accounting records as configured in the remote security database and sends these records to the security server.

An advantage of implementing a remote security database is that it provides centralized management and control of network-access policies. Besides simplifying management, it also ensures consistent access policies for remote access, dial-up access, and router management.

Remote security database standards supported by Cisco

Many remote-security database applications operate according to different standards. These standards provide uniform access control for network devices and remote clients. The applications called security servers are shareware or commercial products. These products provide centralized management of security and database tools to enforce a consistent security policy.

Cisco has developed Cisco Secure ACS remote-security database products to support three primary security server protocols: TACACS+, RADIUS, and Kerberos. TACACS+ and RADIUS are predominant security-server protocols; they provide AAA security for network access servers, routers, and firewalls.

Primarily, Cisco Secure ACS products support the TACACS+ and RADIUS security protocols. Similarly, Cisco network access servers, routers, and PIX Firewall—as well as the Cisco IOS itself—support the integration of an existing network with security servers that run TACACS+ and RADIUS protocols. These protocols govern the flow of access-control information between the security server and network devices.

The network access server acts as a proxy agent for a remote client by posing as a TACACS+ or RADIUS client — in effect, "fooling" the security server. Figure 10-4 shows such a setup in action.

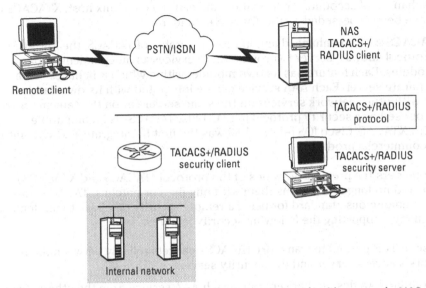

Figure 10-4: TACACS+ or RADIUS support on a network with servers in NAS, router, and security roles

The TACACS+, RADIUS, and Kerberos protocols all have distinct features that can influence the direction of security policy, as outlined in the upcoming sections.

TACACS+

Terminal Access Controller Access Control System (TACACS) is both a security-server application and a protocol. Both are designed to implement AAA as three distinct functions (Authentication, Authorization, and Accounting) by providing centralized control of user access. A single application-control server running a TACACS+ daemon can support all AAA services. Networks that use TACACS+ typically host its services and user information in a database (often running on a Windows NT or Unix system).

Currently, three versions of TACACS security-server applications exist:

✦ **TACACS:** As an industry-standard protocol described in RFC 1492, TACACS specifies forwarding security credentials (such as username and password) to a centralized security database server. Such a server can host a TACACS database (or a database such as the Unix standard password file with TACACS protocol support).

✦ **XTACACS:** Cisco has added extensions to the TACACS protocol to support new, advanced features. Extended TACACS (or XTACACS) is a multiprotocol standard that calls for authorization of connections that use SLIP, PPP (IP or IPX), ARA, EXEC, and Telnet. XTACACS supports multiple TACACS and SYSLOG exchanges of accounting information and can run on a Unix host. XTACACS has since been superseded by the TACACS+ standard.

✦ **TACACS+:** As an enhanced and improved version of TACACS, the TACACS+ protocol allows a server to provide AAA services as independent, separate modules. Each feature has its own module, within which it behaves like a separate server. Each AAA service can be integrated with its own database or with other network services on the same server (or on the same network). Proposed as a security protocol in RFC 1492, TACACS+ is incompatible with XTACAC. Cisco IOS release 10.3 was the first to integrate TACACS+ into a commercial product.

Cisco considers the previous versions of the protocol (TACACS and XTACACS) obsolete and no longer maintains them with bug fixes or patches. TACACS+ has become a unanimous standard for using a remote security database to implement AAA security, supporting the following security features:

✦ Use of TCP port 49 to transport TACACS+ packets reliably between the network's access server and the security server.

✦ Modular AAA design that separates each AAA service from the others. Each service has its own database, but the services integrate to function as a single security server.

✦ Encryption of data payloads (in TCP packets containing TACACS+ protocol values) enhances security between network access server and security server.

✦ Complete control of authentication, using PAP and CHAP challenge-and-response methods. It also secures authentication through the login and password dialog boxes.

✦ Support for encapsulation protocols used to secure dial-up access for SLIP, PPP, and ARAP. In addition, TACACS+ supports the TN3270 and X.121 addresses of the X.25 e-mail-encoding standard.

✦ Ensuring authenticity by forcing the remote client to terminate the call; the server itself calls the remote client back to verify its identity. This feature can also be a cost-saving measure, especially over leased lines.

✦ Filtering user access during authorization. The TACACS+ database on the security server can instruct the network access server to assign a previously configured access list during authorization.

✦ Support for remote dial-up and LAN access is automatic for any network access servers, routers, or other internetwork devices that have built-in support for the protocol.

TACACS+ supports all modules of AAA—Authentication, Authorization, and Accounting. (The process for each of these is discussed in subsequent sections that cover other methods of Authentication, Authorization, and Accounting.)

RADIUS

Remote Access Dial-In User Services (RADIUS) was originally developed by Livingston Enterprises to control its network access servers and prevent unauthorized access. It is an open Internet standard, and many third-party security products support it. RADIUS is a distributed client server protocol and can be integrated with other security protocols, such as TACACS+, Kerberos, and local security databases.

Some major versions of RADIUS (each with its own range of special features) are as follows:

✦ IETF implementation: This was developed and proposed by Livingston Enterprises, which is presently a division of Lucent technologies. The IETF implementation of the RADIUS protocol is specified in RFC 2865. It supports nearly 63 attributes.

✦ Cisco implementation: This was introduced in Cisco IOS release 11.2. The number of attributes and functionality are increased with each version of IOS software and Cisco Secure ACS.

✦ Ascend implementation: Ascend is constantly improving the protocol by adding vendor-specific attributes such as token caching and password changing. It uses an Application Programming Interface (API) for rapid development of new extensions. Ascend has catalyzed the development and deployment of RADIUS. It supports more than 254 attributes.

✦ Other vendors: Many versions of RADIUS come from other vendors such as Merit, Funk Software, and Microsoft. Each has its own versions that support AAA security modules.

The specific authentication, authorization, and configuration information are contained in RADIUS attributes. These attributes are appended at the end of each RADIUS packet. RADIUS attributes consist of a type, length, and value triplet with their own functions. The overall length of the RADIUS packet identifies the end of the list of attributes.

RADIUS is a versatile and popular protocol. Its popularity is one result of its useful features:

✦ RADIUS uses UDP port 1812 to transport RADIUS packets between the network access server and the security server. However, this mode of transmission of packets is unreliable. Variations in deployment of RADIUS and differences in UDP ports exist. UDP simplifies the implementation of RADIUS client/server architecture.

✦ The RADIUS protocol does not provide integrated AAA support. The RADIUS server provides an authentication and authorization mechanism while the RADIUS accounting server performs the accounting procedure separately.

✦ The RADIUS protocol only encrypts passwords in RADIUS packets by using an MD5 hashing algorithm.

✦ Similar to TACACS+, it also provides control of authentication through PAP and CHAP challenge and response mechanisms.

✦ RADIUS supports SLIP, PPP, and ARAP framed protocols along with Telnet, rlogin, and LAT.

✦ RADIUS provides additional security by forcing the remote client to terminate the call; the server itself calls back to ensure authenticity. It is often used as a cost-saving feature.

✦ All packet transactions in RADIUS use variable length AV pairs. It allows easy addition of attributes without affecting the existing implementation of the protocol. Besides using the existing vendor-specific attributes, the vendors can develop their own attributes.

RADIUS supports all modules of AAA – Authentication, Authorization, and Accounting. Although the authentication and authorization processes are supported collectively, the accounting process is separate.

TACACS+ and RADIUS operation are similar. However, several differences exist between these security protocols; Table 10-1 summarizes the major differences.

Table 10-1
A Comparison of RADIUS and TACACS+ Protocols

RADIUS	TACACS+
RADIUS uses UDP as transport protocol.	TACACS+ uses TCP as transport protocol.
RADIUS is less secure because it encrypts only the password in the access-request packet.	TACACS+ is more secure because it encrypts the entire body of the packet.
RADIUS combines authentication and authorization mechanisms. It uses a separate mechanism for accounting.	TACACS+ uses the AAA architecture, which separates authentication, authorization, and accounting.
RADIUS does not support ARA access, Net BIOS Frame Protocol Control protocol, NASI, and X.25 PAD connections.	TACACS+ supports multiprotocol access.
It does not allow users to control which commands can be executed on a router.	TACACS+ provides two ways to control the authorization of router commands, on a per-user or per-group basis.
The challenge and response is unidirectional.	The challenge and response is bi-directional.

Kerberos

Developed by MIT, Kerberos is strictly an authentication protocol and does not offer any authorization feature. It is just meant to validate requests for network services. Kerberos uses the 40- or 56-bit DES Encryption algorithm for encryption and authentication purposes. Kerberos enforces single-login mechanisms that require authenticating the user only once — and allow secure communication thereafter. The password is not encrypted wherever that user must be validated for other network services after the initial login.

Kerberos uses third-party applications called Key Distribution Center (KDC) to perform secure validation of clients and services. It is a Kerberos server and a database program that keeps information of its clients in KDC. On the client side, client software called KINIT is required that authenticates the user to KDC. Kerberos consists of many software components to achieve secure authentication. The main Kerberos authentication components are as follows:

✦ The KDC that contains the user information database

✦ The Kerberos application server software for supporting the server side of the Kerberos protocol

✦ Kerberos client KINIT and the utilities software for remote access

✦ Specific applications and services modified to support the Kerberos credential infrastructure. These applications are termed as *Kerberized* products.

The latest version of Kerberos released by MIT is version 5. Kerberos is also supported and implemented by other vendors such as CyberSafe Corporation and WRQ Inc. Microsoft has a built-in Kerberos server in its Windows 2000 and XP products. Cisco has added the flexibility in its routers that they can be easily integrated with a Kerberos system. Some key features of Kerberos are as follows:

✦ It uses a secret-key authentication protocol.

✦ It authenticates users and their network services by using the single-login mechanism.

✦ It uses 40- or 56-bit DES encryption mechanism for authentication.

✦ Its administration is labor-intensive.

Kerberos provides authentication for PPP and login access to network access servers. The authentication methods that use Kerberos are described in the Authentication Methods section.

Cisco Secure Access Control Server

Cisco Secure Access Control Server (Cisco Secure ACS) was developed by Cisco to address remote security database requirements of enterprises and service providers. Different versions of Cisco Secure ACS work on Windows NT Server or Solaris to control network access. All these versions support the industry-standard

TACACS+ and RADIUS security server protocols. Cisco Secure ACS has a central database that stores user and group profiles and their authentication, authorization, and accounting information.

Cisco Secure ACS can be used to control network access at the following locations:

✦ Router or Ethernet switch console and VTY port access

✦ PIX Firewall

✦ Routers and Cisco network access servers

Interoperability of Cisco Secure ACS with network access server, PIX Firewall, and Cisco router helps it to implement a complete and extensive security policy by using the AAA architecture. You can also use Cisco Secure ACS to control access of non-Cisco specific equipment that supports RADIUS and TACACS+ protocols.

 Cross-Reference   For more information on Cisco Secure ACS, refer to Chapter 15.

Since Cisco Secure ACS products are platform-independent, they support a number of operating systems. According to the operating systems they support, Cisco Secure ACS includes the following products:

✦ Cisco Secure ACS for Windows NT

✦ Cisco Secure ACS for Unix

✦ Cisco Secure Global Roaming Server (GRS)

The following sections discuss each one of these products in detail.

Cisco Secure ACS for Windows NT

You can use Cisco Secure ACS for Windows NT to implement a scalable security policy in a Windows NT environment. It offers a secure remote database for workgroups and enterprises. Due to its scalability features, it successfully caters to the needs of large Windows NT-based networks, workgroups, and also smaller networks. Some powerful features of Cisco Secure ACS for Windows NT are as follows:

✦ Offers interoperability with network access servers, routers, and firewalls.

✦ Provides simultaneous support to RADIUS and TACACS+ protocols.

✦ Provides a remote security database for Windows NT server.

✦ Allows single login since it supports Windows NT user database.

✦ Provides a Web-based interface, which you can use to easily configure user and group profiles.

✦ Provides support to Windows NT performance monitor to view statistics about real-time applications.

✦ Uses MS-CHAP to authenticate Windows NT user database.

Following are some areas where Cisco Secure ACS for Windows NT can be used to provide application solutions:

✦ Service providers can use Cisco Secure ACS as an advanced outsourcing solution for an organization.

✦ It can be used as an accounting and centralized access-control solution for servers with multiple access that run TACACS+ and RADIUS.

✦ It can also be used for controlling access to firewalls, routers, and network access servers.

✦ Due to its scalability, it can be used as a solution for networks supporting multiple network access servers.

Cisco Secure ACS for Unix

Cisco Secure ACS for Unix can be used for both small and large networks. Due to its powerful AAA features, many service providers can use it to provide outsourcing services to organizations for securing sensitive information and resources of these organizations. Cisco Secure ACS for Unix has some powerful features:

✦ Provides AAA support to firewalls, routers, and network access servers.

✦ For bigger networks, it provides support to several relational databases, such as Sybase and Oracle.

✦ Allows import of an existing RADIUS database.

✦ For Sun Solaris, it acts as a remote security database.

✦ Provides a Web-based interface, which you can use to easily configure user and group profiles.

✦ Provides support for a dial-up VPN at the Layer 2 Forwarding tunnel points.

Following are some areas where Cisco Secure ACS for Unix can provide application solutions:

✦ Service providers can use Cisco Secure ACS as an advanced outsourcing solution for an organization.

✦ It can be used as a centralized access-control solution for servers with multiple access that run TACACS+ and RADIUS.

✦ It can be used as a remote-access-control server in organizations that use relational databases, such as Oracle and Sybase.

Cisco Secure GRS

You can use the Cisco Secure GRS software to transmit data packets between network access servers and multiple Cisco Secure ACS systems. By using network access and RADIUS and TACACS+ servers, you connect to a global roaming network that comprises the Internet and regional service providers.

By using a Cisco Secure GRS, a regional service provider can distribute its Points of Presence (POPs) to various ISPs. ISPs can also provide global roaming service and connectivity external to their local region or territory by collaborating with other ISPs. Cisco Secure GRS not only saves costs for the users but also for the ISPs (as they do not have to purchase any additional resources for providing services outside their local territories).

Authentication Methods

Authentication provides the first check on any user who is trying to access network resources. It provides a mechanism to identify the legitimate user for network access based upon several conditions, which in turn depend on the technique used for authentication. Authentication can be provided using several techniques. Some major authentication mechanisms are the username and password, S/key, security cards and server, Password Authentication Protocol (PAP), TACACS, RADIUS, Kerberos, and Challenge Handshake Authentication Protocol (CHAP). Each of these authentication mechanisms is discussed ahead.

Username/password authentication

The username and password-based authentication method is the most common and widely used authentication mechanism. The username and password authentication range from easy-to-guess passwords with weak authentication strength to OTP (One-Time Password) -based strong authentication methods. Using strong authentication methods provides better resistance to any attempt for unauthorized access. Weaker authentication methods like using static username and passwords are easy to implement and do not guarantee adequate security. A comparison of authentication techniques vis-à-vis security strength is given in Figure 10-5.

Each authentication method outlined in Figure 10-5 has distinctive characteristics:

✦ **No username or password:** System administrators of organizations with few resources and employees often take the risk of not implementing username and password-based authentication mechanisms. This method does not require users to submit any security credentials for accessing network resources. This is the least-secure method, and any hacker can gain access to network resources.

✦ **Username/Password:** This is the basic authentication mechanism that ensures primary identification of the user. The user is authenticated from a preconfigured database of user accounts, and the passwords do not change. The password only changes whenever the system administrator or user wishes to change it. This authentication method is not secure and is susceptible to password-cracking applications and playback attacks.

Note   Playback attacks are also commonly known as replay attacks.

✦ **Policy-based Username/Password:** Most network-security policies demand password expiration policies. The password expires according to a preset policy. This period may be from one to eight weeks. The password can be changed by the user himself and does not require any intervention from the administrator. This authentication is still not secure from playback attacks and password-cracking programs but is a better way to avoid attacks.

✦ **S/Key one-time passwords (OTP):-** S/Key protects the network from unauthorized access by preventing password replay attack. S/key uses a secret passphrase to generate the first password, and subsequent passwords are generated from the first password by encrypting it.

✦ **One-time passwords (OTP):** This method is based on a secret passphrase that generates a list of passwords. These passphrases are valid for one-time login and thus do not provide any opportunity to an eavesdropper who manages to capture the passphrase. S/Key is typically an OTP method used for terminal access.

✦ **Security cards:** Security cards (or token cards) meet the twin security criteria of providing users with "something you have and something you know." The security card is in possession of the user, who also knows a special personal identification number (PIN) of alphanumeric characters. The security server running token security software validates this PIN. The user is requested to enter the security card and the PIN number to access resources. Another implementation of security cards uses mathematical algorithms to compute random PIN numbers only known to the user. This is the most secure authentication mechanism.

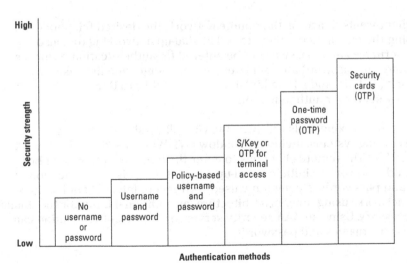

Figure 10-5: Authentication methods and their relative security strength

The network security policy should address the issue of secure authentication based upon network architecture and requirements. The network managers should evaluate the risk components and achieve balance between security strength and authentication methods.

A typical dial-up remote-access method involves the dial-up networking component at the client end supported by appropriate access devices and a dial-up server, called Remote Access Server (RAS) or network access server (NAS), at the peer end. The remote network end may have an additional security server to authenticate the remote client, as shown in Figure 10-6.

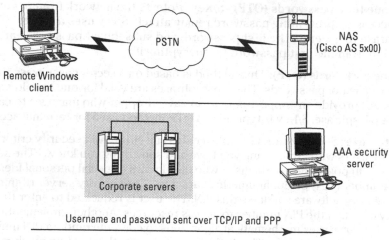

Figure 10-6: A remote client accessing a network access server (NAS)

When the client wants to access the remote network, the desired telephone number is dialed using the dial-up networking tool. The dial-up networking tool also requires a username and a password to be entered for authentication purposes. This username and password are sent over the communication line, using a protocol stack (TCP/IP) and a Data Link-layer driver (PPP) to RAS or NAS, coupled with a security server for authentication.

Similar dial-up networking tools are available with all versions of Microsoft Windows operating systems, including Windows NT, Windows 2000, Windows XP, and Windows ME. The remote client has to enter the target telephone number, username, and password to initiate a dial-up connection. This authentication of usernames and passwords is commonly used with secure Internet applications. For remote networks using domain architecture, an additional input for the domain might be necessary. Using an AAA security server for secure authentication can validate these usernames and passwords.

S/Key authentication

Remote-access scenarios where the username and passwords are sent over the communication line in cleartext are vulnerable to security threats. The hackers use eavesdropping techniques to capture the username and passwords used in remote logins. They use the captured information and use password replay attack mechanisms to gain unauthorized access to the network. This situation is compounded by the fact that passwords are not changed frequently, which provides the hacker sufficient time to analyze the captured data.

Bellcore and his associates devised the S/Key authentication system to generate one-time passwords that can be securely used over remote connections. This protects the network from hackers who might want to eavesdrop and replay attacks. The S/Key authentication system uses an OTP obtained from the hash of the remote user's secret password. The remote user's secret password is never used and does not cross the network boundary.

The S/Key does not require any modification in the remote client software and imposes minimum inconvenience to the users. S/Key is widely accepted and implemented because it integrates easily with existing remote-access mechanisms; the S/Key client and host do not store any secret information. The S/Key system consists of three main components:

✦ The remote client system used by the user to access the peer network's resources.

✦ The S/Key client software installed on the remote client system that will generate the OTP for authentication. (Using the hash of the secret key generates this OTP.)

✦ The S/Key host software is installed on the remote security server for validating the authentication request.

The S/Key components mentioned above are integrated with the existing access mechanism, such as the Dial-up networking component, to send the OTP. Figure 10-7 illustrates a typical S/Key setup and its components.

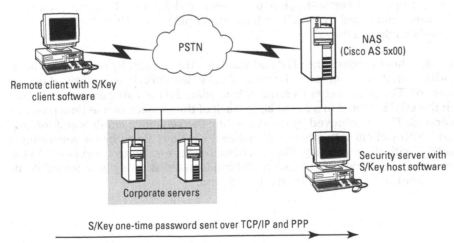

Figure 10-7: S/Key authentication: components

S/Key client software

The purpose of the client software is to generate the OTP for authentication. This piece of software is installed on the remote client system. The remote client will require the OTP before it can access the remote network.

To generate this OTP, the user enters a password in the S/Key client interface box. The S/key client software generates the OTP by performing a one-way hashing algorithm on the secret password from the user and a seed value sent by the host. S/Key uses MD4 or MD5 one-way hashing algorithms to generate the OTP. This password generated by the S/Key client software consists of six short words. An example of such a OTP (generated by an S/Key client) is KURT BLOB DRAM SON YEAR SURE. The S/Key client software can have a command-line or a graphical user interface. A popular S/Key program for Windows-based systems is keyapp.exe.

The keyapp.exe program has a graphical user interface. It allows the user to enter the secret password according to which the OTP is calculated and displayed. This OTP can be copied to the clipboard and pasted in an authentication screen of dial-up networking for remote login. The authentication software, such as dial-up networking, sends this authentication information to the remote network in cleartext for authentication. After this OTP is used for validation, this information is of no use to any hacker who eavesdrops the communication link. Some S/Key client programs generate a list of OTPs that can be saved or printed for manual entry into the authentication dialog box. As the printed or saved version of the file containing the list of passwords can be used for playback attacks, this feature should be avoided.

S/Key hosts

The S/Key host validates the authentication request from the S/Key remote client. After receiving the authentication request from the remote client, it sends a challenge and response key with S/Key parameters (which include a sequence number and a seed value used by the client hash algorithm). Then the S/Key client responds back with the OTP.

The S/Key host receives the OTP and validates the request by running the hash algorithm on it and compares the hashed value with previously received one-time password. The remote client's request is validated if the two values match, and then the OTP is stored in a file to keep track of the number of one-time passwords generated. This is achieved by decrementing the sequence number and forcing the remote S/Key client software to reinitialize the S/Key calculator for generating a new OTP with the secret key. The Cisco Secure Access Control Server (ACS) for Unix supports S/Key authentication and can be used as S/Key host for validating the authentication requests from S/Key clients.

Security cards

Security cards (or *token cards*) enhance traditional OTP security by integrating security servers with OTP generators. These security cards are in possession of the users. The self-containment of the security card makes it resistant to attacks. Because of this characteristic, security cards are often used in different applications that require strong security protection and authentication.

The security card is programmed to contain information for a specific user. It stores this information on a magnetic strip or EPROM/EEPROM embedded onto them. The user is assigned a unique Personal Identification Number (PIN) that generates a password unique to the security card. The generated password is for remote authentication. This is one of the highest commercially available security mechanisms used for authentication. It offers an extra level of security by increasing the OTP functionality and leveraging the use of security cards. The OTP authentication takes place between the specified token server maintaining the token card database and the remote client's authentication package.

Security cards offer a high level of security, but they are also vulnerable to logical attacks. Nowadays most security cards store the key material in an EEPROM. Because an EEPROM write operation can be affected by unusual voltages and temperatures, raising or dropping the voltage supplied to the microchip can trap the information residing on a security card. However, security cards that have magnetic strips are only vulnerable to special deciphering equipment.

Security card and server operation

A security card generates a one-time password validated by the token server. A token card and server system consists of a remote client system (which is able to process the token card), a token card, a network access server and a token server. A typical setup for a security card and server is shown in Figure 10-8.

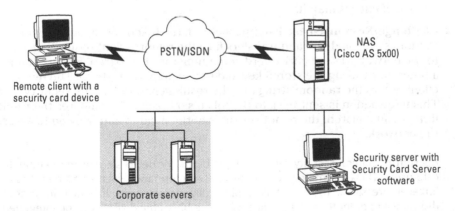

Figure 10-8: A typical setup for a security card and server

The security card containing the user information works with the security or token server as follows:

1. The user inserts the security card in the device and inputs the PIN known only to him/her.

2. A one-time password is generated with the token card by using a security algorithm. This algorithm may vary for different vendors.

3. The remote user copies the one-time password into the authentication dialog box, (as with dial-up networking), for initiating the connection and requesting validation.

4. The one-time password is sent to the token server through the network access server.

5. The token server receives the authentication request from the client and uses the same algorithm to validate the password from the security database. If appropriate entries are located, the remote client is authenticated.

The method mentioned above is a general method of how a security card and its server software interact for validation. The method to generate PIN and one-time password may vary for different vendors but the interactions between the client and security remains the same. Vendors use two common systems that incorporate a security card and server:

✦ **Time-based:** The time-based security card system uses a mathematical algorithm according to time. The generation of passwords or token is performed using this algorithm and almost synchronized with the token server. The security card usually has an LCD display that displays the password and contains a cryptographic key. The remote client sends the generated password to the token server. Because of the algorithm, the token server expects the same password. The server compares the received password or token with the internally expected result. The remote client is authenticated, and access is allowed if entries match.

✦ **Challenge/Response-based**: In this method, the token server itself generates a random string of digits and transfers it to the remote client requesting access to the network. The security card containing the cryptographic key computes a function by using the stored key and received random string. The remote client enters the random string and the result generated by the security card. This information is sent back to the token server, which compares the result. If the results match, the remote client is authenticated and allowed to access the network.

Note   Apart from general security cards, multiple biometric devices are used to authenticate users. These biometric devices store user information such as retina scans or finger impressions. The user has to physically identify himself/herself in front of the device in order to be authenticated. These biometric devices can be integrated with security servers to maintain the user information database and provide consistent authentication.

Tip   Security cards are also implemented in software for any installations on a remote client. Software programs such as SofToken (for example) also generate one-time passwords and eliminate the cost of setting up the hardware.

Cisco token card and server support

Cisco supports token card authentication within Cisco Secure ACS software. The token card servers supported by Cisco are as follows:

✦ SecurID ACE/Server from RSA Security Inc. (www.rsasecurity.com)

✦ CRYPTOCard RB-1 from CRYPTOCard Corporation (www.cryptocard.com)

✦ SafeWord from Secure Computing Corporation (www.securecomputing.com)

✦ Axent Technologies token server in Cisco Secure ACS version 2.4 for Windows NT (www.axent.com)

PAP and CHAP authentication over PPP

The Internet community has adopted two schemes for the transmission of IP datagrams over serial point-to-point links such as PSTN or ISDN. These two schemes are Serial Line Internet Protocol (SLIP) and Point-to-Point Protocol (PPP). PPP is the successor of SLIP and is the most widely used WAN protocol over asynchronous lines. PPP has the following features:

✦ Control of data-link setup

✦ Assignment and management of IP addresses

✦ Network-protocol multiplexing

✦ Link-configuration and link-quality testing

✦ Error detection

✦ Optional negotiation for capabilities such as Network-layer address and data compression negotiation

PPP supports authentication. However, the authentication phase of a PPP session is optional. After the link has been established and the authentication protocol is agreed, the peer can be authenticated. If authentication is enabled, it takes precedence over the Network-layer protocol configuration phase. The authentication option requires that the calling side of the link enter authentication information to ensure that the user has adequate network permissions to make the call. PPP enables authentication between remote clients and servers by using either PAP or CHAP.

PAP authentication over PPP

The PPP uses Password Authentication Protocol (PAP) and is the basic authentication mechanism used for remote access. It uses a two-way handshake mechanism for a remote node to establish its identity and access the network. The handshake occurs only after the initial PPP link is established, as shown in Figure 10-9.

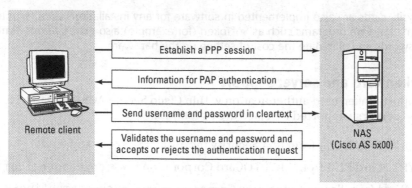

Figure 10-9: PAP authentication over PPP

After link establishment is complete, the remote client sends a username-and-password combination repeatedly to the authentication server until the authentication is acknowledged. The connection is terminated if the call is not authenticated. Messages exchanged between the remote client and the authenticating sever during PAP authentication includes the following:

1. The remote client initiates the dial-up connection to establish a PPP session with the peer server.

2. The remote client informs the peer network access server that it is using PPP and negotiates for PPP link layer drivers.

3. The network access server configured for PAP authentication over PPP informs the remote client to use PAP to enable this session.

4. The remote client sends the username and password in the specified PAP format. This information is sent in cleartext over the communication link.

5. The network access server validates the received username/password after comparing it to the security database. If the NAS does not find any match, the session is terminated.

Because the security credentials are sent in cleartext over the communication link, PAP is not recognized as a secure authentication protocol. Any hacker can eavesdrop and use an analyzer to extract usernames and passwords from the captured packets. No protection from playback or repeated trial-and-error attacks exists. The remote node controls the frequency and timing of the login attempts.

CHAP authentication over PPP

Challenge Handshake Authentication Protocol (CHAP) provides a stronger security than PAP; actual passwords are never sent over the communication link. This prevents any eavesdropping activity and protects against playback attacks.

CHAP uses a three-way handshake mechanism to validate the identity of the remote client. The authentication handshake is performed only after the initial link establishment. This handshake might be periodically repeated to ensure the authenticity of the peer. The initialization of CHAP sequence by using the three-way handshake is illustrated in Figure 10-10.

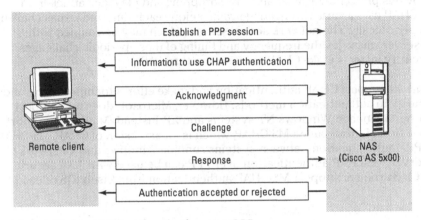

Figure 10-10: CHAP authentication over PPP

As shown in Figure 10-10, the initialization of CHAP sequence is described in the following:

1. The remote client initializes the dial-up connection and establishes the PPP connection.

2. The remote client informs the peer network access server that it is using PPP and negotiates for PPP Link-layer drivers.

3. The network access server configured for CHAP authentication over PPP instructs the remote client to use CHAP to enable this session.

4. The remote client replies to the request with positive acknowledgment.

When the acknowledgment is received, the three-way handshake process for CHAP authentication begins. It follows these steps:

1. The network access server sends a challenge message to the remote client. This challenge message consists of a challenge ID and a random number. The random number is unique and unpredictable.

2. The remote client applies a one-way hash function, such as MD5, on the challenge ID, random number, and the password. The remote client sends the value generated from this process in response to the challenge.

3. The network access server receives the response. It then applies the one-way hash function to the random number and challenge sent by it earlier and the password expected from the client. If the calculated value matches with the value sent by the client, the authentication is acknowledged. Note, however, that the actual passwords are never transacted over the communication link.

CHAP provides protection against any eavesdropping and playback attack from hackers. CHAP uses a variable challenge value unique each time and issues challenge requests periodically. The network access server (which may be coupled with a security server) manages the frequency and timing of these periodic challenges. These security features make CHAP more secure than PAP.

Most vendors support CHAP authentication and make efforts to improve the underlying security in authentication methods. However, Microsoft does not support CHAP authentication in Windows NT systems and XP. Instead, Microsoft supports its own version of CHAP called MS-CHAP, which is an extension of CHAP. MS-CHAP enables PPP authentication between systems running Windows and a network access server. MS-CHAP authentication over PPP can be used with AAA security servers. Cisco routers support MS-CHAP authentication from Cisco IOS release 11.3 onward.

TACACS+ authentication

The type field within the header of the TACACS+ packet identifies the AAA process. TACACS+ uses three packet types for authentication. They are START, CONTINUE, and REPLY. Figure 10-11 illustrates a typical TACACS+ authentication process, in which the network access server exchanges user-authentication information with the TACACS+ security server.

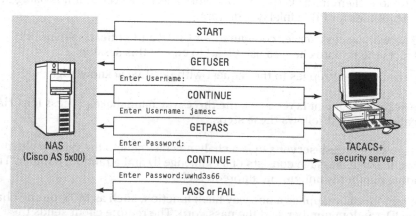

Figure 10-11: TACACS+ authentication process

1. The network access server receives authentication request from the client. The network access server configured for TACACS+ sends a START authentication packet to the TACACS+ server to initiate the authentication process.

2. The authentication engine on the TACACS+ security server sends a GETUSER packet with a username prompt back to the network access server.

3. The network access server prompts the user for the username. The user enters the username. This username information is sent back within a CONTINUE packet to the TACACS+ server.

4. The TACACS+ server sends a GETPASS packet to the network access server with a prompt for password.

5. The network access server displays the password prompt to the user for input. The user enters the password. Then, the network access server sends the password in a CONTINUE packet to the TACACS+ server.

6. The TACACS+ server compares the password with the information stored in the TACACS+ configuration file. If the entries match, the user is authenticated; a PASS packet goes to the network access server. If the passwords do not match, a FAIL packet goes to the network access server.

TACACS+ provides a secure authentication method that encrypts the data payload (TCP packets that contain the TACACS+ protocol values) to maintain security between the network access server and the TACACS+ security server. The body of each TACACS+ packet is encrypted and stored in the TACACS+ server in an encrypted form.

RADIUS authentication

The RADIUS server receives user requests, authenticates users, and provides configuration information to the remote client. RADIUS supports secure authentication process by using Access-Request, Access-Accept, Access-Reject, and Access-Challenge packets between the RADIUS client and the RADIUS security server. The steps involved in RADIUS authentication are shown in Figure 10-12.

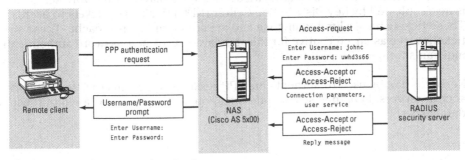

Figure 10-12: RADIUS authentication process

The RADIUS authentication is described in the following:

1. The remote client establishes a PPP session and sends a PPP authentication request to the network access server.

2. The network access server sends a prompt for the username and password to the user. The user enters the username and password.

3. The network access server receives the username and password from the client and sends this information with other attributes in an Access-Request packet to the RADIUS security server. The password is encrypted before sending.

4. The RADIUS security server validates the client and authenticates the user. Depending on the outcome of the comparison between the username and the password provided by the user and the username/password database, the RADIUS server sends either of the following responses:

   • **Access-Reject:** The remote client is not authenticated because the results do not match. The network access server prompts the client to resend the username and password. On successive failures, the client is denied access.

   • **Access-Accept:** The remote client is authenticated because the results match.

   • **Access-Challenge:** The RADIUS server issues this response to verify the user. The network access server prompts the client for additional data and sends it to the RADIUS security server. This packet can be sent periodically to the network access server for the user to resubmit his username and password.

Note   In RADIUS, using MD5 for hashing security encrypts user passwords sent during the authentication process.

Kerberos authentication

The components involved in Kerberos authentication are shown in Figure 10-13. Kerberos ensures that only legitimate users are validated for network services. This is accomplished by Key Distribution Center (KDC) that issues tickets to users. These tickets have a limited lifetime and are stored in the user cache. These stored tickets serve as an alternative for the standard username/password authentication mechanism.

Kerberos can be used to authenticate PPP sessions and logins to Cisco network access servers. In both cases of authentication, KDC operates as a remote security database.

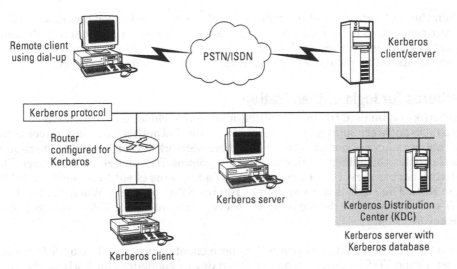

Figure 10-13: Kerberos authentication: components

Kerberos for PPP authentication

Kerberos authenticates PPP sessions to a network access server in the same way as TACACS+ and RADIUS. In fact, Kerberos can be used in combination with TACACS+ that allows a greater level of flexibility. The remote user is not required to run the KINIT application. The network access server itself behaves as a proxy authentication server for the remote client by acting as a Kerberos client to the KDC. The remote client dials into the network access server to access network resources. The Kerberos authentication process is given:

1. The remote client establishes a dial up connection with the network access server and initiates a PPP session.

2. The network access server prompts the remote client for the username and password. The user enters the username and password.

3. The network access server is configured for PPP authentication by using Kerberos. The network access server acts as a proxy and requests Ticket Granting Ticket (TGT) from KDC to authenticate the remote client request. TGT is a credential issued by KDC to authenticated users only. TGT allows the users to be authenticated to other network services within the Kerberos realm represented by KDC.

4. KDC sends an encrypted TGT back to the network access server that consists of the remote clients identity.

5. The network access server decrypts TGT by using the password from the remote client. The remote client is authenticated if the decryption process is successful. Otherwise the remote client is denied access.

When the authentication of the remote client is successful, the network access server recognizes that KDC is valid and the remote client's computer also becomes a part of the Kerberos realm. A Kerberos realm is a logical domain consisting of users, hosts, and network services registered with the Kerberos server.

Kerberos for login authentication

Kerberos can be used to secure authentication of login access to Cisco devices. Cisco IOS software supports the Kerberos method of authentication for access to any network access server. The intermediate network access server or the router itself proxies the authentication request for gaining TGT on behalf of the user. The network access server or the router acts as a Kerberos client to request a valid TGT from KDC. The client is not required to run the KINIT program. When the valid TGT is decrypted, the device requests service credentials for Telnet access from the actual client.

Cisco IOS 12.0 supports Kerberos 5. A remote client does not require a KINIT program to get a valid TGT for authenticating a Cisco device configured for Kerberos because KINIT is integrated within the login procedure of Cisco IOS implementation of Kerberos. The telnet, rlogin, rsh, and rcp services in Cisco IOS software are already Kerberized.

Authorization Methods

AAA authorization limits the type of services available to any user. This feature can define access by restricting or permitting access to network resources and specify specific Cisco IOS commands a user can exercise on network devices. When an access server authenticates a user, the privileges are assigned to him/her on the services. These privileges are in effect until the user disconnects. The Cisco IOS software supports three different types of authorization:

✦ **EXEC**: Applies to the attributes associated with a user's EXEC terminal session and the ability to log in to Cisco router's command-line interface (CLI). This is helpful in avoiding a manual update of enabled passwords on every network device on the internetwork.

✦ **Command**: Indicates the commands that the user can use after logging in to CLI. The command authorization attempts authorization for all EXEC mode commands, including global configuration commands, associated with a specific privilege level. Cisco IOS provides 15 levels of privileges within the CLI.

✦ **Network**: Gives users permission to log in to framed services, such as PPP, SLIP, and ARAP. It is associated with the network connection.

AAA authorization limits the services available to a user. When AAA authorization is enabled, the network access server uses information retrieved from the user's profile, which is located either in the local user database or on the security server to configure the user's session

The network access server can be configured to control user access to the network, so that the users can only perform certain functions after authentication. Authorization can be used with either the local security database on the network or remote security database, as shown in Figure 10-14. The remote security database can apply access lists configured in the network access server to be applied to an authenticated user.

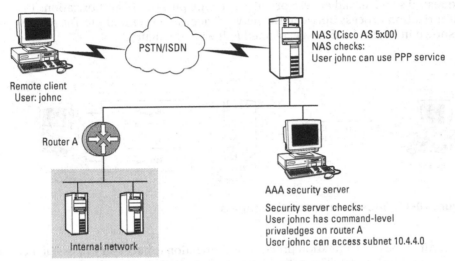

Figure 10-14: Controlling network services using authorization

An authorization policy is implemented by compiling a set of attributes defining the privileges for a specific user. This policy defines what the user is allowed to perform on the network. After authentication, the network access server determines and applies the user's capabilities and restrictions from the database containing the authorization policies. You can configure authorization to run for all network-related services requests, including IP, IPX, SLIP, PPP, Telnet, and ARAP. Authorization can also control access to hosts and network when associated with dynamically assigned access lists. AAA supports several methods of authorization. Some of these methods are as follows:

✦ **Local:** The network access server uses its local database to authorize specific privileges for users defined by using the `username` command. This local database method offers only a limited set of control functions.

✦ **TACACS+:** The network access server enforces the authorization information obtained from the TACACS+ security daemon. TACACS+ authorization defines specific rights for users by associating attribute-value pairs, which are stored in a database on the TACACS+ security server.

✦ **RADIUS:** To enforce authorization, the network access server requests authorization information from the RADIUS security server. RADIUS authorization defines specific rights for users by associating attributes, which are stored in a database on the RADIUS server.

TACACS+ authorization

TACACS+ can be used for authorization and control of network resources and user privileges. The TACACS+ authorization process uses two types of packets: REQUEST and RESPONSE. The user-authorization process is controlled by exchanging attribute/value (AV) pairs between the network access server and TACACS+ security server. The AV pairs usually contain the username, network address of the user, requested service, and access privileges for the purpose of authorization. The authorization process between the network access server and the TACACS+ server is shown in Figure 10-15 and explained following the figure.

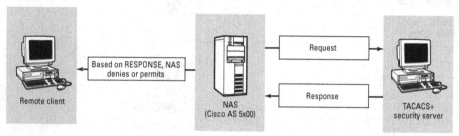

Figure 10-15: TACACS+ authorization process

1. After the authentication process, authorization is necessary to assign network access privileges. The network access server sends an authorization request packet to the TACACS+ security server. The REQUEST packet type is for this process. This packet contains a fixed set of fields that describe the authenticity of the client or network process and a set of arguments defining the services and options for requested authorization.

2. The TACACS+ server processes the request from network access server. The TACACS+ security server responds back with a RESPONSE packet containing a set of arguments defined by AV pairs. These values within AV pairs are according to the previously configured permissions and privileges for an individual user on the TACACS+ server.

3. The network access server uses the AV pairs contained in the RESPONSE packet to deny, permit, or modify the services requested by the client.

The authorization RESPONSE from the TACACS+ security server contains AV pairs that decide the permissions and privileges for the client. A few examples of AV pairs are as follows:

✦ **Service = ppp**: The primary service allowed for the client.

✦ **Protocol = ip**: The protocol allowed for the service parameter.

✦ **Addr = 10.5.5.1**: A valid and authorized network address.

The values depend on the arguments within the REQUEST packet sent by the network access server to the TACACS+ server for a specific user.

RADIUS authorization

The authorization process in RADIUS is easier than TACACS+. The authorization process in RADIUS occurs simultaneously with the authentication process. RADIUS combines authentication and authorization. The packets sent by the RADIUS server to the client contain authorization information, making it difficult to decouple authentication and authorization. When the RADIUS server validates the client, it authenticates the client, looks up the authorization parameters for the user, and responds with Access-Accept, Access-Reject, or Accept-Challenge response packets.

The network access server receives the authentication parameters from the RADIUS security server and acts accordingly, thus permitting selected services for the client. The Access-Accept or Access-Reject response from RADIUS server contains AV pairs for network authorization. AV pairs decide the services that the user can access, including Telnet, rlogin, or LAT connections and PPP. The AV pair also defines the connection parameters such as host or client IP addresses, access lists, and timeout values. A few examples of RADUIS AV pairs are as follows:

✦ User-Name = jamesc: The username of the client.

✦ CHAP-Password = uwj39992k092m: The CHAP password used for authentication.

✦ Client-Id = 10.5.5.1: The IP address assigned to the client.

✦ Login Service – 540: An integer value identifying the requested network service.

✦ Login-TCP-Port = 21: An integer value to identify the application port for service.

Accounting Methods

The accounting policy for any network is implemented to analyze the network usage and traffic pattern. The accounting data provide enough information to keep track of network resources and the types of services being accessed by users. The information can also be used for creating baselines and capacity planning. For organizations providing online customer services, the accounting info can be used to bill clients for connection time or the resources accessed on the network. The accounting information can also be used to detect suspicious intrusion activities on the network.

The network access server creates accounting records according to per-user activities. These accounting records can be configured to be stored on the network access server or can be sent to any remote security database. These accounting records are similar to SYSLOG records. These accounting records can also be configured to be stored on a database server. These records can be imported in any spreadsheet application of special reporting applications, such as Seagate Crystal Reports. This information can be used for network management, billing, and auditing purposes. Figure 10-16 shows AAA accounting implemented in a network.

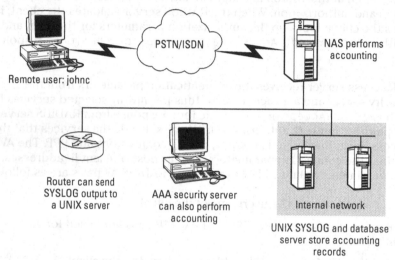

Figure 10-16: AAA accounting

The accounting records are also based on AV pairs that contain specific accounting values such as the type of service accessed, start and stop timestamps, amount of data transacted, network server accessed, and the source of the network records. Both TACACS+ and RADIUS security protocols can record and transmit accounting records to remote security database. Cisco routers and access devices can be configured to perform accounting by capturing and displaying accounting information.

TACACS+ accounting

The TACACS+ accounting process is similar to its authorization process and uses REQUEST and RESPONSE packet types. The accounting method provides records that can be used to audit user activities and access the pattern of specific network devices. The accounting process is not embedded into TACACS+ as a security feature. It is mostly used for billing and management activities. The TACACS+ accounting process between the network access server and the TACACS+ security server is shown in Figure 10-17.

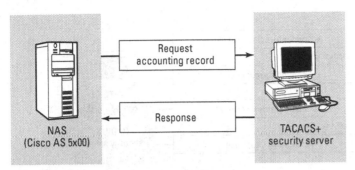

Figure 10-17: TACACS+ accounting

The TACAS+ accounting process is the following:

1. The network access server sends a REQUEST packet to the TACACS+ security server containing accounting information. The packet contains a fixed set of fields that identifies the authenticity of the user or process. The REQUEST packet includes an accounting record consisting of AV pairs that define the services for which accounting information is being compiled. This is according to the selected event and the accounting method.

2. The TACACS+ security server responds with a RESPONSE packet to the access server to acknowledge the receipt of the accounting record. The RESPONSE packet indicates to the network access server that the record has been stored and recorded and the accounting function on the TACACS+ security server is complete.

The accounting process in TACACS+ stores accounting records in a database typically running on Unix or Windows NT operating systems.

RADIUS accounting

Although TACACS+ is considered to be more versatile, RADIUS is more popular. RADIUS is an AAA protocol of choice for enterprise ISPs because it uses fewer CPU cycles and is less memory intensive. RADIUS is a client/server protocol and the communication between a network access server and a RADIUS server is according to User Datagram Protocol (UDP). The RADIUS protocol has been modified to include delivery of accounting information between a RADIUS client and a RADIUS server by using UDP port 1813.

The RADIUS client sends the user accounting information to its designated RADIUS accounting server by using an Accounting-Request packet with accounting AV values. The RADIUS accounting server receives the request and responds with a response packet Accounting-response, indicating that it has received the request successfully. The RADIUS accounting process is shown in Figure 10-18.

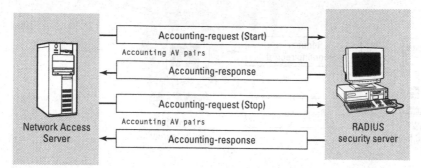

Figure 10-18: RADIUS accounting

The steps that occur in RADIUS accounting between a network access server and a RADIUS client when a user tries to log in to a network access server are as follows:

1. The network access server sends an `Accounting-Request` start packet to the RADIUS security server by using UDP port 1813. This packet is sent only when the initial authentication is completed.

2. The RADIUS security server sends an `Accounting-Response` packet to acknowledge the receipt of the `Accounting-Request` start packet.

3. After the network access server has sent all the accounting information it wanted to send, it sends an `Accounting-Request` stop packet. This stop packet describes the type of service delivered and other optional values.

4. The RADIUS server acknowledges receipt of the `Accounting-Request` stop packet by sending an `Accounting-Response` packet.

Understanding Proxy Authentication

Proxy authentication provides dynamic, per-user authentication, and authorization of clients making an attempt to access network resources. Proxy authentication process makes use of industry-standard implementation of TACACS+ and RADIUS authentication protocols.

The authentication proxy feature supported in Cisco IOS Firewall allows network administrators to enforce specific security policies on a per-user basis. Prior to this technique, the user identity and related authorization information was typically associated with the user's IP address, or a single security policy was applied to an entire user group or subnetwork. However, with authentication proxy, the users can be identified and authorized on the basis of their per-user policy. In addition, access privileges for users can be tailored on per-individual basis.

Using the authentication proxy feature, Cisco IOS Firewall enables users to log in to the network or access the Internet through HTTP. Cisco IOS Firewall automatically retrieves specific access profiles from a security server and applies them. Specific user access profiles are active only when there is active traffic from the authenticated user. The authentication proxy feature is compatible with other Cisco IOS security features such as Network Address Translation (NAT), Context-Based Access Control (CBAC), IP Security (IPSec) encryption, and Cisco Secure VPN Client software.

Discussing authentication proxy

Authentication proxy mechanism is triggered whenever a user initiates an HTTP session through a firewall. The authentication proxy first checks whether the user has already been authenticated. If the user has already been authenticated, the connection is completed without any further intervention by the authentication proxy mechanism. Otherwise the authentication proxy prompts the user for authentication credentials, which are the username and password.

To access the desired device or network, users must be successfully authenticated by the authentication server — which means they must provide valid usernames and passwords. If a user is successfully authenticated, the authentication proxy retrieves the user's authorization profile from the AAA security server. The authentication proxy uses the information in the profile to create and apply dynamic Access Control Entries (ACE) to allow the user access to appropriate network resources. The authentication proxy modifies each of the access list entries in the user profile by replacing the source IP addresses in the downloaded access list with the source IP address of the authenticated host. Using this method, the firewall allows authenticated users only access to the network as configured in the authorization profile.

The authentication proxy notifies the user of failure in case the authentication of the user fails. It then prompts the user for multiple retries. However, if the user cannot be successfully authenticated within five retries, the authentication proxy stops prompting the user for a username and password. The user has to wait for two minutes and again initiate an HTTP session to trigger authentication proxy.

The authentication proxy also sets up an idle timer for each user profile. The authentication proxy is not triggered as long as activity through the firewall and authorized user traffic is permitted access through the firewall. However, if the idle timer expires, the authentication proxy removes the dynamic access lists entries that allowed user access to resources. This leads to blocking of all traffic from the user's host. To start accessing network resources again, the user has to trigger the authentication proxy and get successfully authenticated by initiating another HTTP connection.

Authentication proxy can be used to provide an additional level of security for a network. A few situations call for the implementation of authentication proxy:

✦ **Managing access privileges on a per-user basis.** Use the services provided by the authentication servers instead of configuring access control by host IP address or global access policies.

✦ **Requiring local users to be authenticated and authorized before they may gain through-the-firewall access to the intranet, to Internet services, or to hosts.** The authentication proxy can also be implemented to authenticate and authorize remote users before permitting them access to local services or hosts through the firewall. It can also be used to control access for specific extranet users.

✦ **Using authentication proxy in conjunction with VPN client software to validate users and to assign specific access privileges.**

The authentication proxy is compatible with Cisco IOS security features, such as

✦ Cisco IOS Firewall Intrusion Detection System (IDS)

✦ NAT

✦ CBAC

✦ IPSec encryption

✦ VPN client software

Configuring authentication proxy

The authentication proxy triggers only in response to HTTP connections; it requires that HTTP services run on the standard HTTP port 80. The remote client must have JavaScript enabled on the Web browser for secure access. Before configuring an authentication proxy, the following points should be ensured for successful implementation of the authentication proxy:

✦ The browser should support JavaScript, but only after it's enabled for secure authentication. The client host must run the browser software with JavaScript enabled; the client itself can use Internet Explorer or Netscape Navigator (versions 3.0 or later).

✦ Authentication proxy offers an option for using standard access lists. Before configuring authentication proxy, have a good understanding of access lists.

✦ Authentication proxy follows Cisco's AAA architecture in performing user authentication and authorization. An administrator should be thoroughly familiar with the configurations that support AAA user authentication and authorization before configuring authentication proxy.

✦ Configure CBAC on the firewall to run the authentication proxy successfully with Cisco IOS Firewall.

✦ Configure the authentication proxy for AAA services. In addition to configuring AAA on the firewall router, the authentication proxy requires a per-user access profile configuration on the AAA server. Configure the AAA authorization service `auth-proxy` on the AAA server to support the authentication proxy.

✦ To use the authentication proxy, enable the HTTP server on the firewall, and the HTTP server authentication method should be configured to use AAA.

After configuring the earlier prerequisites and verifying the services, you can configure the authentication proxy by following these general steps:

1. Configure the global authentication proxy idle timeout. If the timeout expires, the authentication proxy removes access-control entries (along with any associated dynamic access lists that allowed the user access to resources). The user has to get authenticated after the idle-timeout expires to access resources. The following command sets the global idle-timeout value:

   ```
   router(config)# ip auth-proxy auth-cache-time min
   ```

   In this command, min is the timeout value in minutes. The default value is 60 minutes.

2. Configure the firewall router to display the name of the firewall router in the authentication proxy login page by using the following command:

   ```
   router(config)# ip auth-proxy auth-proxy-banner
   ```

   The `banner` feature is disabled by default.

3. Create an authentication proxy rule, which defines how to apply the authentication proxy. The rule associates HTTP connections with an authentication proxy name. You can give the rule a sharper degree of fine-tuning by associating it with a standard access list. Using the access list, you can control which hosts can use the proxy authentication feature. By default, the rule intercepts HTTP traffic from all hosts whose connection initiating packets are received at the configured interface.

   ```
   router(config)# ip auth-proxy name auth-proxy-name
    http[auth-cache-time min] [list std-access-list]
   ```

   The `auth-cache-time` is optional, and it defines the idle-timeout value for the rule. If both idle-timeout and global authentication proxy cache timer are configured, it overrides the global authentication proxy cache timer. If you do not specify this option, the global idle-timeout value is used.

   The `list` is optional. It associates a standard access list to the named authentication proxy rule. The authentication proxy intercepts HTTP connections initiated from hosts in the access list.

4. Apply the rule to an interface by using the following command in the interface-configuration mode of the specific interface:

   ```
   router(config-if)# ip auth-proxy auth-proxy-name
   ```

After configuring the authentication proxy, it is recommended to verify the configuration of authentication proxy by re-checking the configuration and establishing user connections with JavaScript in both enabled and disabled mode. To check the current authentication proxy configuration, use the `show ip auth-proxy configuration` command in privileged EXEC mode.

Summary

This chapter explained how to secure the network access by using AAA (Authentication, Authorization, and Accounting) services. Effective methods of implementation include authentication proxy, for which the chapter provided configuration instructions.

✦   ✦   ✦

Configuring the Network Access Server for AAA Security

You can use the concept of *AAA-based network access security* to consistently configure your network's authentication, authorization, and accounting security features. This chapter explains AAA security, shows how to implement it on your servers, describes how AAA can help make remote access easier to secure, and examines AAA configuration on your network access server (NAS).

AAA Security Servers

Cisco products support AAA access control by using either a local server database in your network's NAS or a remote security database that runs an AAA security protocol. Both methods have advantages and disadvantages. This chapter presents AAA in relation to both local and remote security databases.

AAA in relation to a local security database

If your network has relatively few users in need of authentication or access via your Cisco network access server(s), you can configure your NAS to store username and password information—which is known as *local authentication*. A local security database with an AAA configuration offers some clear advantages:

✦ Provides remote user authentication

✦ Provides limited support for accounting and authentication services

✦ Gives the local NAS an additional task that is appropriate to small networks

Caution   Avoid using local authentication on your NAS if it's part of a large network; the additional demands on the NAS processor would impair performance.

✦ Saves all information about usernames, passwords, and user rights

✦ Avoids the cost of setting up and maintaining a remote security database by controlling user access

Figure 11-1 shows the authentication of a remote user at the network access server—which is possible because every NAS in a network contains a copy of the local security database, listing all usernames, their profiles, and their network privileges.

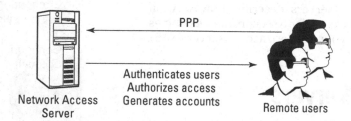

Figure 11-1: Authenticating remote users by using a local security database

The process of authenticating users by using AAA services is as follows:

1. Using PPP, a remote user connects to the network access server.

2. When prompted, the user provides username and password.

3. The server validates the username and password against entries stored in the local database.

4. After validation, the server grants the user access to specific network services, according to information stored in the local database.

5. The network access server monitors network traffic and processes the accounting records as instructed in the local database.

AAA in relation to a remote security database

As the size of the network increases, so does the number of users requiring validation. Eventually a *remote security database* is necessary. This database contains usernames and passwords for all network access servers and routers on the network.

Note   Although customarily stored on a local security server, a security database may eventually become too large to keep there — especially if multiple network access servers are in use.

As a separate element of the network, a remote security database allows centralized management of remote users, saves space on network access servers by relieving them of redundant entries, and facilitates the updating of all network access servers when user profiles and privileges change. Implementing remote security databases can improve AAA services in the following ways:

✦ Network access servers share accounting and authorization tasks with the remote security database.

✦ Information such as usernames, passwords, and user rights can be stored in a central location.

✦ All remote users are authenticated against the same entries (stored in the remote security database), regardless of which NAS handles the initial connection.

✦ Large networks can provide access to remote users (and to network access servers) with minimal degradation of server performance.

Tip   As you design your AAA implementation, make allowance for the cost of maintaining a security server.

✦ The administrator has more ways to establish necessary controls. For example, a network access server can control user access to the remote security database(s). Some databases can also control access to routers, switches, firewalls, and virtually any other network device that supports remote-access protocols.

✦ Using a remote security database can give you centralized control of all the network devices.

Tip   A remote security database can save you the cost of individually administering each network access server — provided the remote security database itself is secure (which makes it worth some extra-careful administrative attention).

Figure 11-2 shows how a remote security database authenticates remote users.

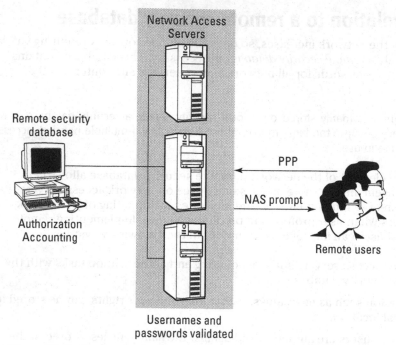

Figure 11-2: Authenticating remote users by using a remote security database

The database should contain the user profiles of all remote users, and you should configure a network device to help the remote security database implement AAA services. The steps involved in the process are as follows:

1. Using PPP, a remote user connects to the network access server.

2. When prompted by a network access server, the user provides username and password.

3. The security server receives the user's information from the network access server.

4. The remote security database authenticates the user's information using download commands and access lists to provide authentication parameters to the network access server.

5. The network access server grants the user access to the network and processes the accounting records as instructed by the remote security database.

6. The network access server sends the user's records to the security server, which can also process accounting records

A remote security database can make the management of network access servers simpler by ensuring consistent enforcement of security policies for remote users, providing dial-up access, and centrally managing routers.

Cisco support for remote security database standards

Remote security database servers provide a standardized level of access for network equipment and routers. Many applications have been created according to these standards. As explained in Chapter 10, Cisco devices use three types of security-server protocols: TACACS+, RADIUS, and Kerberos. TACACS+ and RADIUS are the most commonly used, providing AAA for network devices such as routers, network access servers, and firewalls (as shown in Figure 11-3).

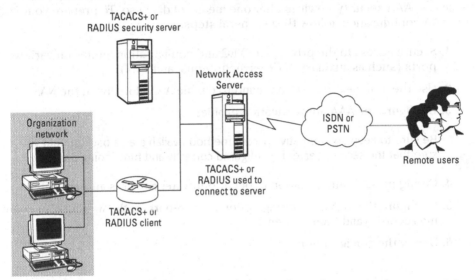

Figure 11-3: Cisco supports TACACS+ and RADIUS for various network components, including remote security databases

Challenges of securing remote access

To provide remote users with access to your organization's network, you use remote-access facilities provided by the network access servers. First, however, make sure that your security policies are properly defined — and applied on the network as consistently as possible. If this is not the case, your network can face multiple security problems when it provides remote access. Hackers can remotely access the network by using any of the following methods:

✦ They could consider the absence of an effective security policy as an "authorization" to access the network's resources by any means available to them.

✦ They could access any improperly secured device console.

✦ They could guess the passwords to access network devices (especially if they can get access to dial-up tools).

You can secure remote access by configuring the remote-access components to compensate for any known security weaknesses. As you do so, weigh the probable threats to network security against the available protective measures. For example, you can secure the entry points to your NAS by using passwords — and use the NAS to authenticate dial-up access.

Configuring AAA on your NAS

A primary security goal for configuring your network server is to control user access — AAA security services offer one means of doing so. To prepare your NAS for AAA configuration, follow these general steps:

1. Secure access to the privileged EXEC and configuration modes on various ports (such as auxiliary, VTY, asynchronous, and TTY).

2. Use the `aaa new-model` command to enable AAA globally on the NAS.

3. Configure the AAA authentication profiles.

Tip

Be sure to keep an alternative access method available as a backup until you are sure that the security server is configured correctly and functioning properly.

4. Configure AAA authorization to occur only after a user is authenticated.

5. Configure the AAA accounting options that report on the writing of accounting records (and their content).

6. Debug the configuration.

Securing Privileged EXEC and Configuration Mode

This is the first step where you secure user access to the privileged EXEC mode. This mode gives user access to the configuration mode (where changes can be made to the access server).

To gain access to the configuration mode, you have to provide an *enabled password* — that is, a password with the following characteristics:

✦ Contains a maximum of 25 characters.

✦ Cannot be blank.

✦ Contains both uppercase and lowercase alphanumeric characters.

✦ Cannot contain a number as the first character.

✦ Can contain leading spaces, intermediate spaces, and trailing spaces. However, all the leading spaces are ignored.

You can use the console port to access the privileged EXEC mode without using an enabled password—which is why your NAS can't be remotely administered.

Following Cisco guidelines, use the `enable secret` command to provide additional security to the Message Digest 5 (MD5) hashing function. You can ensure the security of passwords and prevent them from being visible on the screen by using the `service password-encryption` command. You use the `enable` and `service` commands to further secure the EXEC mode. The syntax of the `enable` command is

```
enable password [level level]{password|[encryption type]encrypted password}
```

where

- ✦ `level level` specifies the privilege level to which the password would apply. You can use numbers through 0 to 15 to specify the privilege level. This argument is optional. If this argument is not specified in the command, the privilege level is taken as 15.

- ✦ `password` specifies the password that a user must provide in order to enter the `enable` mode.

- ✦ `encryption type` specifies the algorithm used to encrypt the password. The encryption type available currently is 7. (This argument is optional.)

- ✦ `encrypted password` specifies the encrypted password that the user enters.

The syntax for the `service` command is

```
service password-encryption
```

The `service password-encryption` command takes no arguments, but you can use the `password-encryption` command (along with the `service-password encryption` command) to encrypt passwords. You can reverse the effects of these commands by using `no` along with them.

Caution   You cannot retrieve an encrypted password when it's lost—but you can implement a password-recovery program and specify a *new* `enable` password. Note, however, that if the program is not executed properly, you might spoil the configuration file. Make sure your security policy spells out the measures used to secure password encryption for network services.

After securing user access to NAS, create an AAA segment in the configuration file and then use the following steps to enable AAA globally on NAS:

1. Configure NAS and authenticate users for accessing the privileged command level.

2. Create a character string that contains the list of authentication methods triggered when a user logs in. Also, allocate a dedicated username database for authentication. You can have more than one database.

The command aaa new-model creates a new AAA configuration. Another command—aaa authentication login default enable—automatically provides security to all protocols except for PPP. In the next step configure and analyze the AAA commands and their implementation.

Configuring AAA Authentication Profiles

Authentication refers to verifying a user's identity. You configure AAA authentication profiles to define the parameters that would be used to verify a user's identity. To configure AAA authentication profiles, you define the *authentication method lists*. Authentication method lists are profiles that specify logins and authentication methods. You use the aaa authentication command to define an authentication method list. After defining authentication method lists, apply them to your network's interfaces. To define an AAA authentication methods list, proceed as follows:

1. Specify login authentication.

2. Assign a list name (a unique combination of alphanumeric characters).

Note   You can also specify the list name as default to apply the authentication method to all interfaces. Different authentication methods must be assigned to different named lists.

3. Specify the authentication methods (no more than four).

Note   Authentication methods check whether a user can access the privileged command level. If an authentication method encounters any error, the next method in the sequence is tried.

To enable AAA authentication, use the aaa authentication command in the global configuration mode. The syntax is

```
aaa authentication {arap|enable|login|nasi|ppp}
{default|listname} method1 [method2] [method3] [method4]
```

where

✦ arap specifies that an AAA authentication method would be used for AppleTalk Remote Access (ARA).

If arap is a command parameter, the method argument can take the following parameters:

• guest allows guest logins.

• autho-guest allows guest logins if the user is already logged in (EXEC mode).

- `line` specifies the use of line password for authentication.

- `local` specifies use of the local username database for authentication.

- `tacacs+` specifies the use of TACACS+ authentication.

- `radius` specifies the use of RADIUS authentication.

✦ `enable` is the command that creates authentication methods. If you use `enable` as a command parameter, then the `method` argument can take the following parameters.

- `enable` specifies the use of the `enable` password for authentication.

- `line` specifies the use of the line password for authentication.

- `none` specifies no use of any authentication method.

- `tacacs+` specifies the use of TACACS+ authentication.

- `radius` specifies the use of RADIUS authentication.

✦ `login` can set AAA authentication at login. If `login` is used as a command parameter, the `method` argument can take following parameters.

- `enable` specifies the use of the `enable` password for authentication.

- `krb5` specifies the use of Kerberos 5 for authentication.

- `line` specifies the use of the line password for authentication.

- `local` specifies the use of the line password for authentication.

- `none` specifies no authentication method.

- `radius` specifies the use of RADIUS authentication.

- `tacacs+` specifies the use of TACACS+ authentication.

- `krb5-telnet` specifies the use of Kerberos 5 Telnet authentication protocol for authentication if Telnet serves to connect to the router.

✦ `nasi` specifies the use of AAA authentication for NASI clients who connect through the access server. If `nasi` is used as a command parameter, the `method` argument can take following parameters:

- `enable` specifies the use of the enable password for authentication.

- `line` specifies the use of the line password for authentication.

- `local` specifies the use of the local username password for authentication.

- `none` specifies no authentication method.

- `tacacs+` specifies the use of TACACS+ authentication.

✦ ppp: indicates that one or more specified authentication methods can be used on serial interfaces that run PPP and TACACS+. If ppp is used as a command parameter, the method argument can take following parameters:

- if-needed specifies that the user need not be authenticated if he or she is already authenticated on the TTY line.

- krb5 specifies the use of Kerberos 5 for PAP authentication.

- local specifies the use of the line password for authentication.

- none specifies no authentication method.

- radius specifies the use of RADIUS authentication.

- tacacs+ specifies the use of TACACS+ authentication.

✦ default indicates that when a user logs in, the specified methods serve as the default list of methods.

✦ listname refers to the name you assign to the list of authentication methods.

Enabling AAA Authorization

After you have configured AAA authentication profiles, the next step is to configure AAA authorization. You configure AAA authorization to specify the services that should be available to a specific user. After you enable AAA authorization, NAS configures a user's session by allowing access to only the services specified in the user profile. To configure AAA authorization, you issue the aaa authorization command in global configuration mode. The syntax is as follows:

```
aaa authorization {network|exec|commands level|reverse-access}
{default|listname}{if-authenticated |local|none|radius|tacacs+|krb5-instance}
```

where

✦ network specifies that a user can access network services, such as PPP and SLIP.

✦ exec specifies that a user can start EXEC shells.

✦ commands specifies the commands for EXEC shells.

✦ level specifies the command level that should be authorized.

✦ reverse-access specifies authorization for reverse-access connections.

✦ default indicates that the specified authorization methods serve as the default list of authorization methods.

✦ *listname* refers to the name you assign to the list of authorization methods.

✦ if-authenticated specifies that the user can use the requested service only if he or she is authenticated.

✦ local specifies use of the local database for authentication.

✦ none specifies no authorization.

✦ radius specifies the use of RADIUS authorization.

✦ tacacs+ specifies the use of TACACS+ authorization.

✦ krb5-instance specifies the use of the instance defined by Kerberos instance map command.

Configuring AAA Accounting

The accounting service keeps track of applications, services, and network resources that users access and use. To configure AAA accounting, you set the accounting parameters in the global configuration mode, according to the following syntax:

```
aaa accounting {system|network|exec|connection|commands level}
{default|listname}
 {start-stop|wait-start| stop-only|none} [tacacs+/radius]
```

where

✦ system specifies that all system events must be audited.

✦ network specifies that all network service requests (such as PPP and SLIP) must be audited.

✦ exec specifies that EXEC commands must be audited.

✦ connection specifies that all outbound connections (such as Telnet) must be audited.

✦ *commands level* indicates the commands and the level at which they should be audited.

✦ default indicates that specified accounting methods serve as the default list of accounting methods.

✦ *listname* refers to the name you assign to the list of accounting methods.

✦ start-stop indicates that a start accounting notice would be sent when the process starts. Also, at the end of the process, a stop accounting notice is sent.

✦ `wait-start` indicates that the accounting would start only when the user acknowledges the `start accounting` message. Also, at the end of the process a `stop accounting` notice is sent.

✦ `stop-only` indicates that a `stop accounting` notice would be sent at the end of a user-requested process.

✦ `none` specifies that no accounting be performed on the interface.

✦ `tacacs+` or `radius` specifies the use of TACACS+ or RADIUS accounting.

After you have configured NAS, the next step is to debug the configuration to ensure that NAS has been configured properly. To view the methods of authentication and authorization that have been configured, you use the following `debug aaa` commands:

✦ Use the `debug aaa authentication` command to view AAA/TACACS+ authentication information.

✦ Use the `debug aaa authorization` command to view AAA/TACACS+ authorization information.

✦ Use the `debug aaa accounting` command to view accounting information about the processes that occur.

Case Study

The following scenario illustrates how to configure AAA services on a network access server.

Scenario

AllSolv, Inc., an IT solution provider, is based in Boston and has branch offices in New York, Connecticut, and Washington, D.C. According to their network-security policy, the dial-up access for the remote users must be secured. The policy also highlights the following points:

✦ Dial-up access must be controlled by password authentication in a local database.

✦ Network devices should be configured with access passwords at NAS access points.

Keeping these points in mind, the network administrator decides to configure AAA security on the NAS with local security database. The network diagram of AllSolv, Inc. is shown in Figure 11-4.

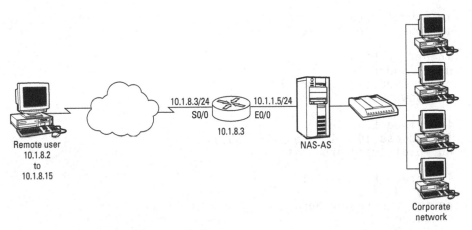

Figure 11-4: Network diagram of AllSolv, Inc.

Sample configuration

Suppose you configure the NAS in the network of AllSolv, Inc. with the following commands, starting with the time reference for messages:

```
service timestamps debug datetime msec

service timestamps log uptime
no service password-encryption
hostname NAS-AS
```

Then you establish a new AAA configuration as follows:

```
aaa new-model
```

You specify secure access to all lines except PPP:

```
aaa authentication login default enable
```

Finally, you issue the following commands to configure authentication on the NAS:

```
aaa authentication login console-in local
aaa authentication login vty-in local
aaa authentication login tty-in line
aaa authentication ppp dial-in if-needed

enable secret 5 $4$G6NM$5T2.GFRJKLF5ESR1RFGJK
enable password 7 A003ERTY89

username admin password 0 vbnmgh
username user1 password 0 tyryuirr
username user2 password 0 frwsdted
clock timezone PST -5
```

```
ip subnet-zero
ip host modem 2097 10.1.1.5

interface BRI0/0
no ip address
no ip directed-broadcast
shutdown

interface Ethernet0/0
ip address 10.1.1.5 255.255.255.0
no ip directed-broadcast

interface Ethernet0/1
no ip address
no ip directed-broadcast
shutdown

interface Serial0/0
physical-layer async
ip address 10.1.8.1 255.255.255.0
no ip directed-broadcast
encapsulation ppp
ip tcp header-compression passive
async mode dedicated
peer default ip address pool classpool
no fair-queue
no cdp enable
ppp authentication chap dial-in

interface Serial0/1
no ip address
no ip directed-broadcast
shutdown

interface Serial1/0
no ip address
no ip directed-broadcast
shutdown

interface Serial1/1
no ip address
no ip directed-broadcast
shutdown

router rip
network 10.0.0.0

ip local pool classpool 10.1.8.2 10.1.8.15
ip classless
```

```
ip route 0.0.0.0 0.0.0.0 10.1.1.3
no ip http server

line console 0
exec-timeout 0 0

password 7 PGHT78U0
logging synchronous
login authentication console-in
transport input none
line 65 70
line 97
no exec
password 7 U9PHJ56DWD
login authentication tty-in

modem InOut
modem autoconfigure type usr_sportster
transport input all
stopbits 1
speed 115200
flowcontrol hardware
line aux 0
password 7 W2ERGTH
login authentication is-in
end
```

Summary

This chapter outlined the types of AAA security servers, the steps involved in implementing AAA on these servers, and the challenge of securing access by remote users. The chapter presented techniques for configuring AAA on NAS, such as securing the privileged EXEC and configuration modes, configuring AAA authentication profiles, configuring AAA authorization, configuring AAA accounting options, and debugging the resulting NAS configuration.

✦   ✦   ✦

Virtual Private Networks

Today, in light of the prohibitive cost of setting up a large private network, most organizations implement *virtual private networks* (VPNs) to ensure secure and reliable transmission of information across the Internet. But even VPNs are prone to security threats; Part V explains the fundamentals of VPN technology and offers criteria for deciding which security measures can best protect your organization's VPN. In addition to providing implementation scenarios, Part V discusses how to use and configure IPSec in the process of securing your VPN.

Fundamentals of Virtual Private Networks

Until relatively recently, organizations were localized and had a limited area of operation; today, most large organizations have a global presence. More mergers and acquisitions mean more branch offices and clients in scattered geographic locations — hence the need for fast, secure transmission of information to employees, business associates, and clients. Most organizations are implementing virtual private networks (VPNs) to ensure secure and reliable information transmission.

This chapter introduces you to virtual private networks. It discusses the need for VPNs. It also discusses the types of VPNs and various tunneling protocols. Finally, the chapter discusses the scenarios in which VPNs can be implemented.

Introducing VPNs

Employees of highly competitive, global organizations need access to information from remote locations, whether they work from their homes or work with remote branch offices. To ensure an effective transfer of information over the corporate network, however far-flung its subnetworks may be, organizations can use VPNs — *virtual private networks* that use public networks (such as the Internet) to allow network connectivity over a large geographical area.

Tip   Sometimes VPNs are still called *wide-area networks* (WANs).

VPNs are IP-based networks that use dedicated channels called *tunnels* (in effect, channels guarded with encryption and other security measures) to transfer data. VPNs provide a secure connection between distributed units of a corporate network over public networks without requiring expensive leased lines.

A VPN allows remote employees working in branch offices to communicate securely with the network at corporate headquarters — using the same network (and addressing scheme) as the employees at the home office. Even remote users connecting to the corporate VPN by using the Internet can be validated at the corporate VPN. What secures the data transmitted between the remote locations and the corporate VPN is a tunneling protocol through the Internet.

In effect, a VPN is a shared infrastructure that provides security benefits similar to a private network at a reduced cost. However, in contrast to private networks that use leased lines, VPNs utilize IP networks including the Internet. VPNs are more flexible and cost-effective as they can use different technologies (such as the Internet, ISPs, and ATMs) and do not need dedicated leased lines. A typical VPN is shown in Figure 12-1.

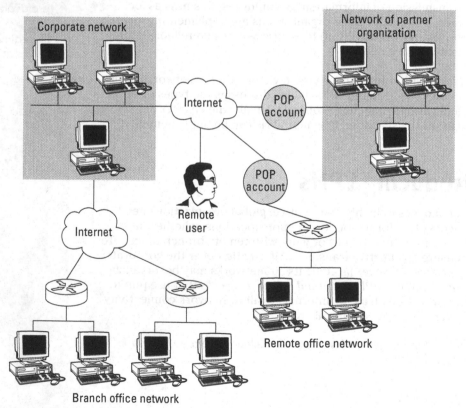

Figure 12-1: A typical virtual private network

Figure 12-2 shows a variation of a VPN, with the corporate office at one location and remote clients at the other.

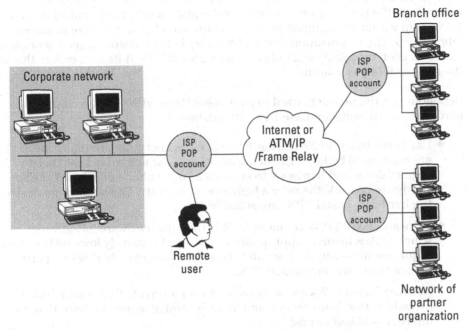

Figure 12-2: VPN in a corporate office scenario with remote clients

You can use VPNs to connect all (or some) branch offices to a home-office corporate network. Only certain branch offices might require secure access; you can set up a VPN connection with these offices and provide standard Internet-based connections to the remaining branch offices. Whether to implement a VPN also depends on the applications used on your network. For example, if all branch offices and mobile users connect to corporate headquarters for e-mail services only, you can set up a single VPN that handles only the e-mail servers and clients of that particular branch office. Other factors that can affect your VPN decision are as follows:

✦ Amount of data that must shared on the network

✦ Type of application(s) expected to run while the VPN is in use

✦ Security policy (or policies) applied to the VPN

✦ Type(s) of business models in use

✦ Level of user access required for the application server

✦ Level of user access required for the Internet server

A VPN is basically platform-independent; any existing IP-based network can be converted to a VPN by installing the software that enables secure remote access. A VPN can also be set up between two corporate networks; such a multi-network setup is called an *extranet*. The only difference between these two types of networks is the way they are managed or the place where their control lies. For a VPN setup within an organization or in an intranet, all resources are managed internally by the organization. For a VPN set up between two companies or on an extranet, each organization handles its own port of VPN at its own end. In this way, the responsibility is shared.

Depending on the products used to implement them, VPNs can be classified as hardware-based, software-based, or network-based.

✦ Hardware-based VPNs use hardware such as encrypting routers. These VPNs are often used by large global organizations — which is because these VPNs require dedicated hardware to support a large volume of network traffic. Hardware-based VPNs offer a high level of security. The standalone devices of the hardware-based VPNs are scalable.

✦ Software-based VPNs are more flexible than the hardware-based variety — which makes them an appropriate way to meet relatively low-level security requirements — but they are also difficult to manage, offering less performance than hardware-based VPNs.

✦ Network-based VPNs are implemented over a private IP. Network-based VPNs provide better, more secure, and more controllable performance than the Internet — at higher cost.

As always, no one solution resolves all possible problems. Software-based VPN solutions can help keep costs down; hardware-based VPN solutions provide increased performance and security.

Methods of implementing VPNs

The basic aim of all VPNs is to ensure secure and reliable transmission of data over public networks. VPNs are implemented using IP tunnels or ISDNs, Frame Relay, ATM connections. These VPNs work in one of the following ways:

✦ By creating IP tunnels between various sites over the Internet or service providers' network

✦ By creating IP tunnels between an ISP and the corporate firewall, where tunnel creation and termination are procedures managed by the ISP

✦ By creating IP tunnels between a remote user and the corporate firewall, where tunnel creation and termination are procedures managed by the client computer and the firewall

✦ By using ISDN, ATM, or Frame Relay connections between various sites

IP tunnel-based VPNs

In IP tunnel-based VPNs, the data packets are encapsulated within an IP packet before being transmitted over an IP-based network. Organizations usually install, configure, and manage these VPNs on their own. Hence they rely on an ISP only for physical connections.

Note ISPs and other service providers also offer their own IP tunnel-based VPN services.

An IP tunnel-based VPN offers the following benefits.

✦ Dedicated and long-distance connections are replaced with local connections; telecom costs diminish significantly.

✦ Flexibility in implementing branch-office networking and remote computing.

✦ A single secure connection provides intranet, Internet, and extranet access.

Caution One major drawback of IP tunnel-based VPNs is that a consistent service level is not guaranteed.

ISDN, Frame Relay, or ATM-based VPNs

ISDN, Frame Relay, or ATM-based VPNs use public-switched data-network services. These VPNs use ISDN B channels, PVCs, or SVCs to separate the traffic from that of other users. These VPNs are usually provided and managed by service providers (SPs); various additional services are available as QoS. These VPNs offer the following benefits.

✦ It is convenient to obtain international connections for ISDN, Frame Relay, or ATM-based VPNs.

✦ The billing and accounting information is easily available.

✦ Security is not a major concern for the organizations that implement these VPNs — which is due to the fact that the data is usually carried over the SP's network.

However, because ISDN, Frame Relay, and ATM services are not widely available and are expensive, these VPNs are expensive.

Features of a complete VPN solution

As discussed earlier, VPNs use tunnels to transmit data between two networks over an intermediate network. In tunneling, the data packets are enclosed in a packet that can travel under another protocol. However, in VPN tunneling, the data packets are encrypted before being encapsulated to ensure security of data.

A complete VPN solution should incorporate following features:

✦ **Adherence to IPSec features:** IPSec is a set of standards developed by Internet Engineering Task Force (IETF). Products that abide to these standards can interoperate seamlessly. A VPN solution should be designed in accordance to the IPSec standards so that it can seamlessly integrate with the existing (as well as future) network infrastructure of an organization.

✦ **Firewalling:** A firewall acts as a boundary that controls the flow of traffic traveling from one network to another. It also protects an organization's network from external attacks. A VPN solution should include a firewall that is interoperable with other components of the VPN.

✦ **Tunneling:** A VPN solution should provide complete tunneling. Most VPN solutions do not allow encryption of *entire* packets (data as well as IP headers). Since hackers can find the source of a data packet in the header (and target that host), these solutions are insecure.

✦ **Confidentiality:** The basic aim of implementing a VPN is to ensure secure remote access. VPNs support a variety of encryption methods to ensure confidentiality of the data being transmitted. A good VPN solution should include multiple encryption algorithms, which support key lengths longer than the recommended minimum bit length. This increases the level of security provided by the VPN.

✦ **Authentication:** In VPNs, authentication ensures that the tunnels are established only between those peers who have a proven identity. A secure VPN solution can authenticate encryption devices as well as users. Doing so ensures that only authenticated users can establish a tunnel. Although password-protection is the most commonly used authentication method, it is inherently insecure as passwords can be easily broken or hacked. For VPNs, X.509 digital certificates have become the default authentication method — which is because digital certificates provide stronger authentication over password protection. A good VPN solution should integrate X.509 certificates to provide enhanced security.

✦ **Automated key management:** A good VPN solution should have automated key management. Automated key management defines the validity or lifetime of session keys. Most VPN solutions require these keys to be entered on each network device manually. However, as the number of network devices increase, manually entering keys on each device becomes cumbersome. In addition, manual entry of keys is insecure. A VPN solution that has the ability to set lifetime or validity of the keys is preferred as the keys are recycled at definite intervals of time. When the keys are recycled at set time intervals, the hackers get less time to break the keys and thus gain access to the information.

✦ **Remote management:** A VPN solution should support remote management. It should also support centralized logging and auditing of events, such as individual connections, attempted security attacks, and failed key negotiations, on a central SYSLOG host. The VPN solution should also configure and filter logs according to your requirements and specifications for better manageability.

Note   The extent of security provided by the VPN increases if it uses multiple encryption algorithms that support key lengths longer than the recommended minimum bit length. The reason is simple: The amount of time a hacker needs for breaking a key is directly proportional to the bit length of the key. Longer keys take longer to break.

Why Implement VPNs?

Underlying the basic concept of a VPN is the fundamental rationale for its implementation — including such questions as these: What problems can a VPN solve? What are the advantages of a VPN over other technologies? The upcoming sections examine some answers to these questions.

Problems addressed by VPNs

When the Internet was designed, the basic aim was to provide access to a nearly unlimited pool of information. However, as the usage of the Internet expanded to various areas such as business, it was realized that there were certain inherent problems in the Internet. The Internet does not ensure reliable and secure transmission of data. As a result, the organizations that want to use the Internet to transmit sensitive data securely must implement special technologies—such as VPNs.

Ever since the emergence of the VPN technology, secure remote access has been the strongest reason for implementing VPNs. For organizations that have varied connectivity needs, VPNs address the following issues:

✦ Providing remote, mobile, and telecommuting users with access to corporate network resources

✦ Connecting connect remote offices securely to corporate intranet

✦ Providing controlled access of corporate network resources to business partners, clients, and suppliers

When implementing a VPN solution, the same network infrastructure can be used to address all issues mentioned above. Besides providing secure remote access, VPNs are also used to build extranets and site-to-site intranets.

An organization would definitely consider the cost benefits that it can achieve if it implements a particular technology. Usually, the cost savings that can be achieved by implementing VPNs range from 30 percent to 70 percent when compared to other competing technologies. However, this range is not fixed; it varies from one organization to another, depending on the networking requirements of an organization.

VPN is one technology that utilized the features of the Internet to provide effective sharing of information to provide economical, faster, and reliable sharing of information. Besides enabling fast and reliable transfer of data, VPNs provide significant benefits to organizations and ISPs. The following sections discuss these benefits.

Benefits to organizations

Most organizations are considering or implementing VPNs to solve the problem of fast, secure, and reliable methods of sharing information. VPNs also offer the following benefits to organizations:

✦ **VPNs are flexible and scalable networks.** Therefore, organizations can conveniently extend their networks to provide connectivity to remote offices, business partners, and clients, based on their business requirements.

✦ **VPNs utilize the IP backbone for connectivity purposes.** This helps in a considerable simplification of network topologies. Because the IP backbone is owned by an ISP or Application Service Provider (ASP) who is responsible for administration, this ultimately leads to reduction in management burden.

✦ **VPNs are cost-effective as compared to private networks.** This is the case because VPNs do not require dedicated leased lines. The total cost of operation for VPNs is also lower because they use low-cost transport bandwidth and backbone devices.

Benefit to ISPs

Today, most ISPs aim toward providing services to small corporations that provide higher margins. However, this requires expanding capacity and coverage of large geographical areas. VPNs can be used to add these new services without major capital investments. To add VPNs to an existing network, you need software or broad-level upgrade VPNs. These can be used for multiple VPN applications, which offer substantial financial benefits.

Besides these financial benefits, VPNs have the following advantages:

✦ VPNs not only provide Internet access but also provide remote-access outsourcing and branch-office connectivity. Using VPN technologies, ISPs can also capture information related to tunnel users for itemized billings.

✦ VPNs enable coverage of large geographical areas with low capital investments. ISPs and the Network Service Providers (NSPs) can provide value-added services and geographic expansion by using any of the three applications of VPNs:

• Dial-access outsourcing

• Virtual leased line

• Virtual Point of Presence

Dial-access outsourcing

Outsourcing enables organizations to build high-margin businesses while reducing the investments on line charges, equipment, and technical staff. In dial-access outsourcing, as shown in Figure 12-3, an access connector at the ISP's POP initiates the tunnel. On the premises of a customer organization, a device or a tunnel switch terminates the tunnel.

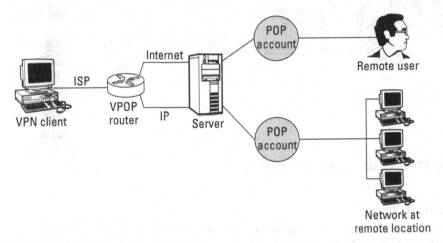

Figure 12-3: Dial-access outsourcing

In this system, the organization has complete control over user authentication and network access; the tunnel carries with it the required information about end-users. Therefore ISPs need deliver only the tunnels themselves; the organizations using the service handle issues of network access.

| Note | If an organization is using a VPN-enabled router to connect to an ISP, the tunnel can be extended to the network of the enterprise. |

Virtual leased lines

VPNs are useful for the NSPs that provide connectivity over the value-added IP networks. This makes the network management simpler and reduces the cost of providing these services to the enterprise customers.

VPNs are useful because all traffic from the enterprise customers can pass through the same network in different tunnels. This balances the load on the network. At the same time, NSPs do not make the network more complex; they can leverage the existing network. They also provide connectivity over the Internet to expand their services. ISPs and NSPs that do not have an infrastructure to offer branch connectivity services can also support branch connectivity having their own IP network. To do so, they simply tunnel the traffic between the branch offices of an enterprise over the Internet. Figure 12-4 illustrates the use of virtual leased lines in a VPN.

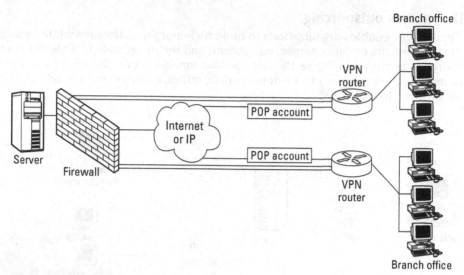

Figure 12-4: Virtual leased lines in a VPN

Virtual POPs

ISPs that prefer not to spend money on infrastructure can use Virtual POPs (VPOPs) to expand their geographical reach. In such an application, the dial-access outsource receives calls at its POP and then POP sends the traffic to the ISP over the VPN. These calls are sent based on the user information. VPOPs are also useful for those ISPs that do not have tunneling-enabled equipment. Figure 12-5 shows a typical Virtual POP network.

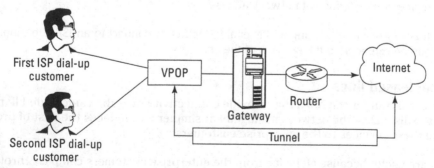

Figure 12-5: Virtual POP

Among all the benefits that a VPN solution offers to the organizations and service providers, cost benefit is the most significant. The cost-analysis sample in Table 12-1 illustrates how to find the cost benefits that a VPN can offer to an organization. This cost-analysis sample shows the capital costs and operational costs of a private leased line, compared to those of a VPN for the same organization.

	Table 12-1	
	Capital and Monthly Operating Costs for Private Leased Lines and VPN	
Type of Cost	**Private Leased Line**	**VPN**
Capital costs	$16,000	$61,500
Monthly operating cost	$28,250	$13,000

As an exercise, you can use the details given in Table 12-1 to calculate the percent of operational cost savings, the payback period, and the Return On Investment (ROI) for the VPN scenario.

```
% Operational cost saving = ((28,250 - 13,000)/28,250) * 100% = 53.98%
```

The formula for calculating the payback period for VPN scenario looks like this:

```
Payback period = Capital cost of VPN scenario /
(operating cost of private leased line scenario - operating cost of VPN
scenario)
```

The payback period is as follows:

```
  Payback period = 61,500 / (28,250 - 13,000) = 4.03 months
```

The formula for calculating the ROI looks like this:

```
ROI = ((Monthly operational savings)*12 - capital cost of VPN scenario)
 / capital cost of VPN scenario) * 100%
```

The ROI is as follows:

```
  ROI = ((15250*12) - 61500) / 61500) * 100% = 197.56%
```

Note

The VPN calculator is available at the following Web site: www.enterasys.com/ aurorean/vpn_calculator/vpncalculator.html

For cost analysis, visit this site: www.cisco.com/warp/public/779/largeent/ learn/technologies/vpn/vpn_calc/vpnstart.html

Deployment considerations for VPNs

Before deploying a VPN solution, you must clearly define what you expect to get from it. Such expectations generally fall into three categories:

✦ Security

✦ Interoperability

✦ Ease of use

The following sections discuss these categories.

Security

The organization's security expectations define the kind of security you expect to get from the VPN. While determining those security expectations, you need answers to the following questions.

✦ What kind of authentication should the VPN solution provide? The authentication methods that can be used are token cards, biometrics, digital certificates, and Kerberos.

✦ What kind of encryption and what key sizes should be supported by the VPN solution?

✦ Should the VPN filter data streams to block viruses, Java applets, and ActiveX controls?

✦ Should the VPN support *role-based* access control? (Such access control uses parameters such as type of authentication, user identity, time of day, source address, and destination address.)

✦ Should the VPN monitor, log, and audit all the traffic that flows on the network?

✦ Should the VPN use alarms to notify the network administrator of specific events that occur on the network?

Interoperability

To determine realistic expectations for interoperability, you need answers to the following questions:

✦ Should the VPN be based on public standards?

✦ Should the VPN be able to integrate with firewalls and routers?

✦ Should the VPN be compatible with PPTP, L2TP, IPSec, and IPv4?

✦ Should the VPN be able to work across multiple platforms?

✦ Should the VPN support all kinds of applications?

✦ Should the VPN support multiple load-balancing methods?

Ease of use

To estimate the expectations of the VPN's end-users, you need answers to the following questions:

✦ Should the client be transparent to the end-user?

✦ Should the VPN allow single sign-on for the user?

✦ What is the number of users that the VPN should be able to support?

✦ Should the VPN support the centralized management of security systems?

When you get answers to all the preceding questions, it will be easy to decide whether you should proceed with deploying of a VPN solution.

Note Most organizations simply deploy a VPN without clearly defining their requirements and later regret this decision when the VPN does not meet their expectations. Hence, it is important that you define your expectations of a VPN and make sure your VPN solution can meet them before you deploy it.

After an organization decides to implement a VPN, the issue that must addressed is who should build the VPN. Two options are available: Network managers can implement their own VPNs or outsource the job.

A few years ago, only the network manager could do the task of implementing a VPN; no service providers with the required expertise were available. Today, managed VPN services are gaining popularity. Service providers not only implement VPNs for an organization but also provide value-added services, such as security consulting, security policy formulation, VPN management, and other after-sales services. An organization must weigh the pros and cons of both options before deciding who should build the VPN.

The deployment considerations that must be kept in mind when implementing a VPN are as follows:

✦ **Protocol support:** Layer 2 VPNs can tunnel any network protocol carried by PPP; IPSec tunnels IP in particular. Layer 2 and IPSec VPNs differ in the impact they have on network addressing, firewall configurations, and routing. When you decide on which protocols to support, also consider whether existing network devices support the VPN you choose.

✦ **Integration:** You must decide what type of user authentication would be required. Although most VPN products can be integrated with external authentication servers, their features vary to a great extent. Also decide whether your VPN should support Network Address Port Translation (NAPT). If the VPN should, then you must configure NAPT before your VPN starts working.

✦ **Client software:** Although operating systems such as Windows 2000, Windows XP, and Solaris have embedded IPSec remote-access clients, Windows 95/98/NT/ME, Mac OS, and Linux require add-on IPSec clients. Check to determine whether you require client software for your VPN.

✦ **Performance:** The performance of a VPN is determined by the speed of transmission over the public network and the efficiency of VPN processing at the endpoints. In the process of encapsulation, additional information is added to each packet, which increases the packet size. As a result of encapsulation, if packets become oversized, the internetwork routers fragment them before transmitting. This further degrades the performance. Also as VPN technologies encrypt data packets before transmitting them, the process time increases. However, using ASICs or coprocessor cards can minimize the impact of encryption and authentication on performance.

Tip

Before purchasing VPN products, consider not only the performance requirements but also throughput, number of concurrent tunnels, and number of client licenses for a VPN product before purchasing.

✦ **Flexibility:** It is important to determine the message integrity and encryption algorithm requirements before purchasing a VPN product. Many VPN products support a variety of authentication methods and algorithms and thus offer flexible deployment. However, these products are more expensive. You must determine the importance of flexibility of deployment in your network before purchasing a VPN product.

✦ **Manageability:** Before deploying a VPN solution, you must consider whether end-user security must be configured at the desktop. It is advisable to use VPN products with client features that can be centrally managed.

Cisco provides a variety of VPN-enabled router series, such as Cisco 1000, 1600, 1700, 2500, 4500, and 4700 series. You can refer www.cisco.com for the flash and memory requirements for implementing IPSec and encryption technologies on these routers. Table 12-2 shows the flash and RAM requirements for implementing IPSec—and how, with Cisco IOS Release 12.0XA, you can use encryption technologies such as IPSec 56 and 3DES on Cisco 1720 routers.

Table 12-2 Flash and Memory Requirements for Cisco 1720 Routers		
Feature Set	*Flash Requirement*	*Memory Requirement*
IP plus IPSec 56	4MB	20MB
IP plus IPSec 3DES	4MB	20MB

Transmitting Data in a VPN Scenario

As discussed earlier in the chapter, a VPN connection is established over a shared network. VPNs transmit data packets over a public network (such as the Internet) via dedicated, secured channels called *tunnels*. These tunnels simulate point-to-point connection between remote users and the corporate network.

Before discussing how data is transmitted in a VPN scenario, it is important to know the components of a VPN connection. A typical VPN connection consists of a VPN server, VPN client, and tunnels. In a VPN connection, a tunnel is established between a VPN client and a VPN server. It is through this tunnel that the VPN traffic flows. VPN traffic falls into two categories.

✦ **Member traffic:** IP traffic that flows between two workstations, both of which are within the VPN.

✦ **Non-member traffic:** All other IP traffic.

To understand the working of a VPN, consider the following situation: A global organization has implemented a VPN as a faster and more secure way of sharing information with sales representatives at remote locations. To gain access to the organization's network, a sales representative dials in to the local ISP and logs in to the ISP network, as shown in Figure 12-6.

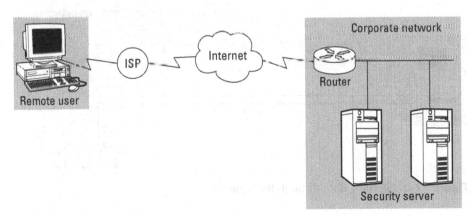

Figure 12-6: Dialing in to the ISP

To establish connectivity with the corporate network, a request to create a tunnel is sent to the security server on the corporate network. This server authenticates the user and creates the other end of the tunnel, as shown in Figure 12-7.

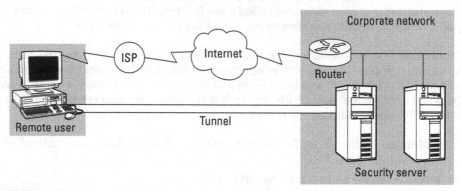

Figure 12-7: Connecting to the corporate network

When the tunnel is established, the VPN software encrypts the data and then sends it through the tunnel over the ISP connection, as shown in Figure 12-8.

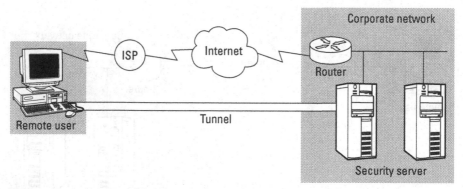

Figure 12-8: Sending data through the tunnel

The security server receives encrypted data, decrypts it, and then sends the decrypted data to the corporate network, as shown in Figure 12-9. Any information sent back to the remote user is encrypted.

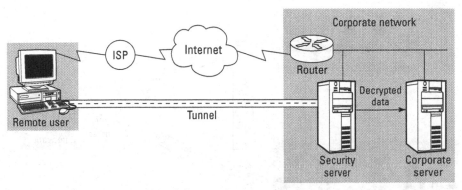

Figure 12-9: Sending decrypted data to the corporate network via the security server

Types of VPN

Any current VPNs fall into one of three categories:

✦ Intranet VPNs

✦ Extranet VPNs

✦ Remote-access VPNs

A VPN's category depends on the purpose for which it's deployed, as explained in the following sections.

Intranet VPNs

Intranet VPNs connect branch offices and corporate departments. Intranet VPNs can improve or replace private lines by utilizing the shared infrastructure provided by service providers. They ensure secure information transmission between various departments of an organization and the branch offices. As sensitive information is transmitted between different departments, intranet VPNs provide strong encryption services. You can create intranet VPNs by using the Internet, ATM network, or Frame Relay. Figure 12-10 shows an intranet VPN.

Intranet VPNs built on a WAN IP infrastructure use IPSec to establish secure tunnels over the Internet. These VPNs along with service providers' QoS mechanisms ensure optimum usage of WAN bandwidth.

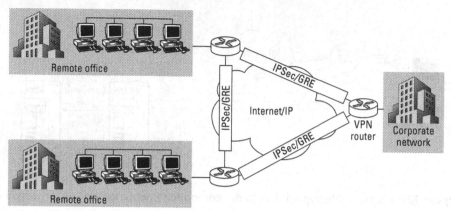

Figure 12-10: An intranet VPN

An intranet VPN offers some distinctive advantages:

✦ Convenient and quick connectivity to new sites

✦ Reduction in the bandwidth cost

✦ Increased network uptime

Note   Deploying intranet VPNs using the Internet is a cost-effective method of implementing VPN technology. However, the throughput levels are not guaranteed. It is important for the organizations to consider the service level they require when deploying VPNs. Organizations that need guaranteed throughput levels should opt for Frame Relay, ATM, or service providers' end-to-end network to deploy VPNs.

Extranet VPNs

In a private network environment, it is not only expensive but also difficult to extend the connectivity to corporate suppliers and partners — which is due to the fact that you must extend dedicated lines to the suppliers and partners to establish connectivity. Also, define and manage the network-access policies; extranet VPNs connect an organization with its business associates, suppliers, and customers. These VPNs are based on open, standard-based solutions to ensure interoperability with different networks at business partners and customer ends. To organize extranet connectivity, you utilize the same architecture and protocols you would use to implement an intranet VPN or a remote-access VPN. With extranet VPNs, however, external users are granted access permissions only after they have connected to the organization's network. Figure 12-11 shows an extranet VPN.

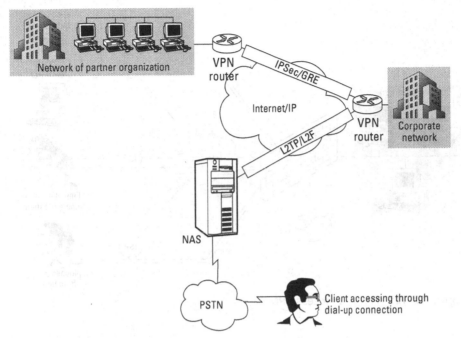

Figure 12-11: An extranet VPN

Remote-access VPNs

A remote-access VPN establishes a secured connection between a remote location and the corporate network. It helps to reduce communication expenses by using the dial-up infrastructures of the ISP for establishing the connection. A remote-access VPN allows the users to connect to their intranet or extranets over the shared infrastructure as they would connect to the private network. Centralized management and scalability are required by a remote-access VPN. Figure 12-12 shows a typical remote-access VPN.

The advantages of remote-access VPNs over the private dial-up network are as follows:

✦ Cost reduction

✦ Increase in scalability

✦ Better focus on business objectives

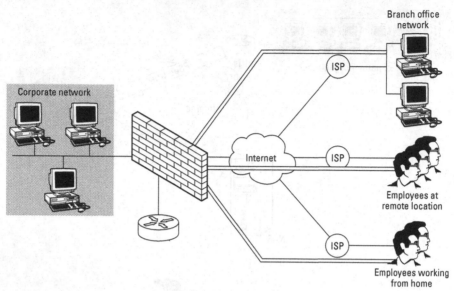

Figure 12-12: A remote-access VPN

Note

Since the organizations that use remote-access VPNs do not need to manage the dial-up network, they can concentrate more on their business objectives.

When implementing a remote-access VPN, you must decide whether tunneling and encryption should be initiated from the client side or from NAS.

In a *client-initiated model*, an encrypted tunnel is initiated at the client end by using PPTP, L2TP, or IPSec. Thus, in this case, the service provider's network acts just as a transport medium to the corporate network. In a client-initiated model, the service provider's network, which is for dialing to Point to Presence (POP), is secured. In such a model, each client end that accesses VPN must have tunneling and encryption software.

In a *NAS-initiated model*, the remote user dials in a service provider POP by using the Point-to-Point Protocol/Serial Line Internet Protocol (PPP/SLIP) connection. The service provider authenticates the user and then starts a secure tunnel from POP to the corporate network. The benefit of using a NAS-initiated model is that the organization does not maintain any end-user client software. Figure 12-13 shows NAS remote-access VPN.

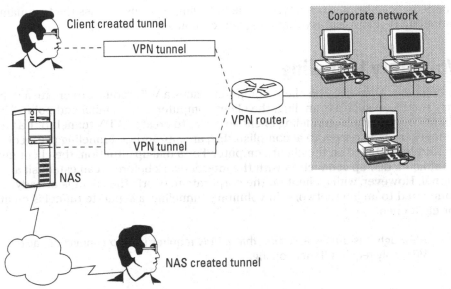

Figure 12-13: Client-initiated and NAS remote-access VPNs

Tunneling Protocols

VPNs use tunneling technology to transfer data. Tunneling is a method of transmitting data in a hidden form by encapsulating data packets into a tunneling protocol. These encapsulated data packets are then transferred from one network to another via dedicated tunnels. As a result, remote users become virtual nodes into which users have tunneled on the network.

The tunneling process involves three basic steps. In the first step, data packets are encapsulated within a tunneling protocol packet. Next, these encapsulated packets are transmitted across the network. When these encapsulated data packets reach the end of the tunnel, the final step is to extract the original data from the encapsulated packet and forward it to its final destination. Each tunneling protocol, has a slight variation in the way the process of tunneling takes place — but these basic steps remain the same. The tunneling protocols can act at either Layer 2 or Layer 3 of the OSI model. The Layer 2 and Layer 3 protocols are implemented differently.

GRE (Generic Routing Encapsulation) is the common tunneling method configured between a source and a destination router. The source routers are known as ingress, and the destination routers are known as egress. The packet assigned to be forwarded across the tunnel is further encapsulated within a new GRE tunnel and with the destination address of the tunnel end-point. When the packet arrives at the tunnel endpoint, the GRE header stripes away and the packet moves forward to the destination, which was assigned in the original IP packet header. GRE tunnels are typically point-to-point.

Tunneling can be of various types. The following sections discuss the two main tunneling types, voluntary tunneling and compulsory tunneling.

Voluntary tunneling

In *voluntary tunneling,* the client computer issues a VPN request to create a voluntary tunnel. In such a tunneling, the client computer is the tunnel end-point. The client computer uses tunneling client software to create a VPN tunnel to the target tunnel server. However, to accomplish this, an appropriate tunneling protocol should be installed on the client computer. For a dial-up situation, the client must establish a dial-up connection with the internetwork before it can establish a tunnel. However, with a client on the corporate network, the client is already connected to an internetwork. In voluntary tunneling, a separate tunnel is created for each client.

Note   Although it is usually assumed that a VPN requires dial-up connection, actually a VPN only requires IP networking.

Compulsory tunneling

In *compulsory tunneling,* a computer between the client computer and the server or a network device creates a secure tunnel on behalf of the client computer. As a result, the client computer is not the tunnel end-point. Also, the client computer does not require the tunneling software. The computer or the network device that creates a tunnel on behalf of the client computer is called as Front End Processor (FEP). To create a tunnel, an appropriate protocol must be installed on the FEP.

Compulsory tunneling derives its name from the fact that the client computer must use a tunnel created by the FEP. Multiple dial-up clients can use the same tunnel between the FEP and the tunnel server; the tunnel is terminated only after the last client disconnects.

VPNs can be configured to use any (or a combination of) these tunneling protocols:

✦ **Point-to-Point Tunneling Protocol (PPTP):** An extension of PPP and inherits its features and limitations. PPP is a remote-access protocol that was developed to handle secure dial-up connections. PPTP supports multiprotocol networking over public networks, such as the Internet.

✦ **Layer 2 Forwarding (L2F):** A tunneling protocol that encapsulates the data packets into PPP before transmitting them to an L2F server. The L2F server then de-encapsulates these packets before forwarding them to the destination. It supports multiple tunnel connections from the same virtual private dial-up network (VPDN) client.

✦ **Layer 2 Tunneling Protocol (L2TP):** Combines the best features of PPTP and L2F and incorporates them for use over PPP. L2TP supports a variety of routed protocols, such as IP, IPX, and AppleTalk. It also supports a variety of backbone technologies, such as Frame Relay, ATM, SONET, and X.25.

✦ **Internet Security Protocol (IPSec):** A Layer 3 tunneling protocol that provides encryption security services to ensure integrity and authenticity of the data packets that travel over the Internet.

The following sections discuss these tunneling protocols in detail.

PPTP

Point-to-Point Tunneling Protocol (PPTP) is an established tunneling technique. The PPTP specifications were developed by the PPTP forum, which consists of Microsoft Corporation and a group of several leading manufacturers of networking equipment used by the ISPs, including Ascend Communications, 3Com, ECI-Telematics, and US Robotics.

PPTP was released in Microsoft Windows NT 4.0 Beta 2 in April 1996 and has been constantly upgraded since then. PPTP is an extension of Point-to-Point Protocol (PPP), which is one of the commonly used Data Link-layer protocol used over wide-area networks. PPTP adds a new level of security and multi-protocol communications over the Internet. Figure 12-14 shows PPTP as an extension of PPP.

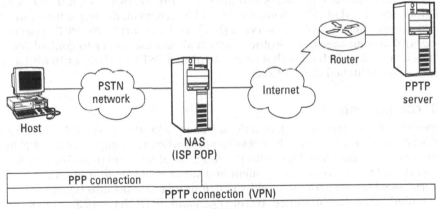

Figure 12-14: PPTP as an extension of PPP

PPTP, with the extensions or modifications made in PPP, provides implementation of VPNs through public data networks such as the Internet, which are secure and also support multiple protocols. PPTP enables the remote users to access their corporate networks and applications by dialing or connecting into the local ISP's Point of Presence (POP), instead of dialing directly into the organization's network.

Point-to-Point Tunneling Protocol (PPTP) as an open standard protocol allows users to take advantage of the vast Internet infrastructure or other public networks to provide secure connectivity between remote clients and private networks.

Where the remote users access the corporate network over the Internet or any public network using VPNs, the user does not require local remote-access servers, modem banks, and related WAN infrastructure at the corporate office—which is because with PPTP, Front-End Processors (FEP) equipment (such as modem banks) remains at the ISP's nationwide locations.

Consider a network consisting of Windows NT 4.0 servers. You can configure these servers to continue performing NT domain security authentication before the user gains access to the organization's network. If required, each remote connection is administered, logged, or monitored on an individual basis. With slight adjustments at both the client and administrator end, you can achieve the same functionality as a direct call to the organization's network. The only difference is that the network session takes place over the Internet, rather than over the organization's private dial-up network. In the Windows NT 4.0 network mentioned above, private dial-up networks, which have been the obvious choice for remote access at present, would only be necessary when dedicated bandwidth must be available, or when the implementation does not support PPTP. Eliminating the cost of setup and maintaining the private organization-owned dial-up network, particularly in situations where nationwide links are necessary, will create a substantial savings for the typical IS department.

PPTP does not specify any changes to the PPP protocol. However, it describes a new mode for carrying PPP. Client/server architecture can decouple functions, that exist in current network access servers (NAS) and support VPNs. PPTP specifies a call-control and management protocol, which allows the server to control access for dial-in circuit, switch calls that originate from a PSTN or ISDN, or to initiate outbound circuit-switched connections.

PPTP components

A network access server (NAS), as a device usually located at the ISP end, provides temporary, on-demand network access to users who are using PSTN or ISDN lines. Client/server architecture decouples the function of NAS and provides benefits such as flexible IP address management and support of Non-IP protocols for dial-up networks — which is accomplished by distributing the tasks into two major components called PPTP Access Concentrator (PAC) and PPTP Network Server (PNS).

✦ **PPTP Access Concentrator (PAC):** PAC is a device attached to one or more PSTN or ISDN lines capable of PPP operation and of handling the PPTP protocol. It provides physical native interfacing to PSTN or ISDN lines and provides control of external modems or terminal adapters. It can also participate in PPP authentication. The PAC must implement TCP/IP to pass traffic to one or more PNSs. It may also tunnel non-IP protocols, which are supported by PPTP.

✦ **PPTP Network Server (PNS):** The PNS handles the server side of the PPTP protocol. A PNS is assumed to operate on general-purpose computing/server platforms. The PNS also provides multiprotocol routing and bridging between NAS interfaces. If PAC does not support it, PNS might also provide PPP authentication.

PPTP tunneling

When the Point-to-Point Tunneling Protocol (PPTP) server receives a packet from the routing network, it obtains the necessary information (such as private network computer name or address information) in the encapsulated PPP packet and sends it across the private network to the destination computer. PPTP allows only IP, IPX, or NetBEUI datagrams to be encapsulated inside an IP packet. Multi-protocol support with PPTP is shown in Figure 12-15.

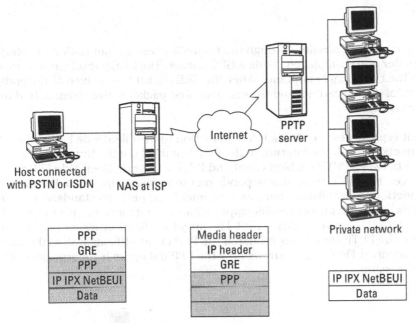

Figure 12-15: A PPTP client connected to the private network

Where the Internet is used as the intermediate public network, PPTP encapsulates the encrypted and compressed PPP frames into IP datagrams for transmission over the Internet. These IP datagrams are routed over the Internet until they reach the PPTP server connected to the Internet and the private network. The PPTP server disassembles the IP datagram into a PPP frame and then decrypts the PPP frame using the network protocol of the private network.

After the PPTP control session has been established, Generic Routing Encapsulation (GRE) Protocol serves to encapsulate the data or payload in a secure manner. A typical PPTP packet encapsulated using the Internet Generic Routing Encapsulation Protocol is shown in Figure 12-16.

GRE has been defined in RFC 1701 and 1702.

Media header
IP header
GRE header
PPP packet

Figure 12-16: Typical PPTP packet structure with GRE

The data or payload passing through the tunnel is given a Point-to-Point Protocol (PPP) header and then placed inside a GRE packet. The GRE packet carries the data between the two tunnel endpoints. After the GRE packet has arrived at the endpoint of the tunnel it is discarded, and the encapsulated packet is then transmitted to its final destination.

The client typically establishes a PPP connection to the client-side FEP at the ISP and connects through the Internet to the PPTP-enabled destination. PPTP can operate either between PPTP-enabled client and PPTP server or client side FEP and PPTP server. How PPTP operates depends on the tunneling modes being used. After the connection is established, one can implement and perform standard network validations, and all protocol-specific applications operate as if the user had dialed directly into a RAS server utilizing PPP. The target application server is reached only when the PPTP server has validated the PPP client utilizing RAS authentication as initial security. Figure 12-17 shows how the PPP datagram is incorporated into the PPTP session.

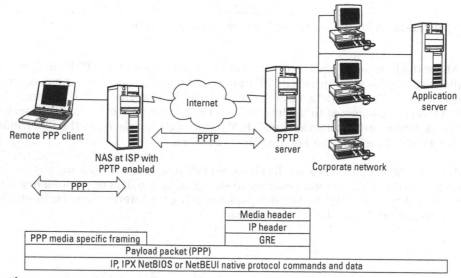

Figure 12-17: PPTP tunneling

PPTP architecture

The PPTP protocol specifies two basic types of packets:

✦ **Control packets:** This type of packet, found in the fixed-length packet header, performs two functions: It specifies how often to send status queries and it manages the signals between the PPTP-enabled client or FEP and the destination server. Control packets communicate through a TCP connection between a pair of PPTP server and PPTP client or PPTP server and FEP.

✦ **Data packets:** This type of packet, which resides in the data portion of a packet, can vary in length. It consists of the normal user data and application commands.

Control connection

A series of control messages are exchanged between the tunnel endpoints, the PPTP client, and the PPTP server. The control connection is a standard TCP session over which PPTP call control and management information is exchanged. For each PAC-PNS pair, both the tunnel and control connections exist. The control connection establishes, manages, and releases or tears down the PPTP tunnel. Control messages notify a PAC of the incoming calls from PNSs. They also instruct the PAC to transfer outgoing calls to PNSs.

The PPTP protocol specifies a series of control messages sent between the PPTP-enabled clients and the PPTP server. Table 12-3 describes the primary control messages used to establish and maintain the PPTP tunnel.

Table 12-3 Message Types	
Message Types	**Description**
Start-Control-Connection-Request	Starts PPTP session
Start-Control-Connection-Reply	Replies to start session request
Stop-Control-Connection-Request	Ends PPTP session
Stop-Control-Connection-Reply	Replies to stop session request
Echo-Request	Maintains session
Echo-Reply	Replies to maintain session request
WAN-Error-Notify	Reports an error on the PPP connection
Set-Link-Info	Configures the connection between client and PPTP server

Caution   Each of these PPTP control messages has a packet format that varies slightly.

The control messages are sent in TCP datagrams. The PPTP control message is generally summarized to have the format shown in Figure 12-18.

| Media header |
| IP header |
| TCP header |
| PPTP control message |

Figure 12-18: PPTP TCP datagram with control messages

Either PAC or PNS can initiate a control connection for the PPTP tunnel. When the TCP session between the PAC and PNS is established, the control connection is initiated by using the control connection messages. To initiate the connection `Start_Control_Connection_Request` and `Start_Control_Connection_Reply` messages are used. The control messages are also used to negotiate information about basic operating status of the PAC and PNS.

After the control connection is established, the PAC or PNS may initiate sessions by using control connection messages for outbound calls or inbound requests. The `Set_Link_Info` control messages communicate any changes in the individual user sessions to the PAC and PNS. For the PPTP tunnel to be up, the control connection must be alive. To keep the control connection alive, periodic keep-alive echo messages are sent. This ensures that a connectivity failure between the PNS and the PAC can be detected in time. Other failures can be reported via the `Wan_Error_Notify` message, which is on the control connection.

Data transmission

After the PPTP tunnel is established, user data is transmitted between the client and PPTP server. Data is transmitted in IP datagrams containing PPP packets. The IP datagrams are created using the GRE protocol. The IP Datagram created by PPTP is shown in Figure 12-19.

| PPP delivery header |
| IP header |
| GRE header |
| PPP header |
| IP header |
| TCP header |
| Data |

Figure 12-19: IP datagram containing encrypted PPP packet, as created by PPTP

Since the datagram has to travel over the shared or public network, it must carry the necessary routing information along with it. The IP delivery header provides the information necessary for the datagram to traverse the Internet. The GRE header serves to encapsulate the PPP packet within the IP datagram. The PPP packet inside the IP datagram is in the encrypted form. Thus, even if the IP datagrams are intercepted during their journey to the destination, it is impossible to read the data.

The PPTP tunnel serves to carry all user-session PPP packets for sessions involving a given PNS-PAC pair. This imposes the need for a mechanism, which would indicate the session to which a particular packet belongs. A key, present in the GRE header, indicates the session to which a particular PPP packet belongs.

The GRE header, which contains acknowledgment and sequencing information, performs congestion control and error detection over the tunnel. The control connection serves to determine rate and buffering parameters, which regulate the flow control of PPP packets for a particular session over the tunnel.

Sequence of events during a PPTP session

A typical sequence of events during a PPTP session is shown in Figure 12-20. The sequence is identical for both compulsory and voluntary tunneling modes. The only difference is that the PPTP control connection commands would be initiated at the client end if voluntary tunneling mode is in effect; under tunneling mode, these commands are issued at the ISP FEP end.

The sequence of events during a PPTP session is:

1. The client establishes a PPP connection to the Internet, via an Internet Service Provider (ISP).

2. The client "dials" again, using another entry, to connect to the VPN in a session that runs concurrent to the PPP session.

   The process of dialing for PPTP connection is different for each tunneling mode. When the FEP is PPTP-enabled, a simple connection requesting a connection to the target PPTP server would alert the ISP FEP to initiate the PPTP session. But when the client is PPTP-enabled, the client will dial again through the dial-up networking utility by specifying an IP address and VPN port of the target server instead of a phone number.

3. A `Start_Control_Connection_Request` message is sent by the FEP or the PPTP client to the PPTP server to initiate a control connection with the target PPTP server. The target PPTP server sends back `Start_Control_Connection_Reply`. The control connection is established.

4. When the reply is received by the FEP or the PPTP-enabled client, a PPTP channel is initiated by sending `Incoming_Call_Request` to the PPTP server. The PPTP server sends back an `Incoming_Call_Reply` to which the FEP or the PPTP client sends an `Incoming_Call_Connected` message and the tunnel is established. The user authentication of the client occurs through this tunneled channel.

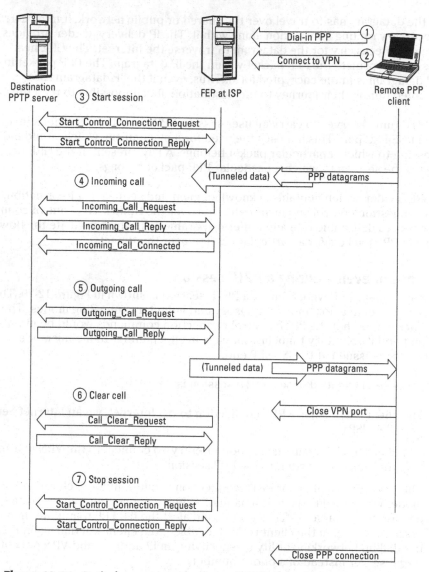

Figure 12-20: Typical sequence of events of PPTP tunneling

5. PPTP server might also initiate establishment of the PPTP tunnel by sending `Outgoing_Call_Request` to the FEP. FEP sends back `Outgoing_Call_Reply` to confirm the tunnel formation.

6. FEP or the PPTP client and PPTP server start exchanging data over the tunnel.

7. After the data exchange is completed, client sends a message to the FEP to close the VPN port. The FEP or the PPTP client sends `Call_Clear_Request` message to request termination of the tunnel. PPTP server sends `Call_Disconnect_Notify` message in reply and the call is disconnected.

8. To disconnect the control connection, FEP or the PPTP client sends a `Stop_Control_Connection_Request` message to the PPTP server. PPTP server sends a `Stop_Control_Connection_Reply` in reply, and the control connection is also terminated. After this, if the client wants to disconnect from the FEP, it can close the PPP connection and disconnect the call to the ISP.

PPTP benefits

PPTP solves many problems for the network administrator who must accommodate remote users and avoid building and maintaining a relatively costly WAN through private lines. Because PPTP "tunnels" or encapsulates IP, IPX, and NetBEUI protocols inside IP packets, users can run applications dependent upon certain network protocols. The "tunnel" also allows the target server to perform the security checks and validations and enables administrators and clients to encrypt data. This would ensure the safety of the data transmitted over nonsecure networks. If the ISP equipment supports PPTP, no additional software or hardware is required on the client end. It requires only standard PPP connection support. The benefits of PPTP are as follows:

✦ It centralizes Front-End Processors such as Internet routers and modem banks at the ISP's Points of Presence.

✦ It tunnels the most common network protocols: IP, IPX, and NetBEUI.

✦ It allows users to run protocol-specific applications through the Internet, without editing applications or user interfaces.

✦ It allows secure authentication of users, by using Password Authentication Protocol (PAP), Challenge Handshake Authentication Protocol (CHAP), and MS-CHAP.

✦ It accepts RSA RC-4 encrypted data embedded in the tunneled packets, as well as DES encryption. It uses a 40-bit session key, which is negotiated between the RAS server and client when they initialize their PPP connection.

✦ It terminates the client's PPP connection directly at the server, rather than at the Front-End Processor, through a PPTP channel.

PPTP is worth implementing if you are looking for a low-cost alternative to building a private network for WAN and remote dial-in applications. However, compared to dialing directly into the RAS server, there will be a drop in performance. Essentially one has to look into the trade-off between the advantages such as low cost and security with the slight drop in the performance. But the overhead involved in slipping an IPX, NetBEUI, or TCP/IP protocol inside a TCP/IP "envelope" has proven to be minimal.

Microsoft has consistently supported PPTP in Windows NT 4.0. However, tunnel implementations using MS Windows 2000 and Windows XP also use the Layer 2 Tunneling Protocol (L2TP) — indicating that L2TP is replacing PPTP.

Layer 2 Forwarding Protocol

Layer 2 Forwarding (L2F) is a tunneling protocol developed by Cisco Systems. Cisco submitted the draft to the Internet Engineering Task Force (IETF) for approval as a standard.

Note   L2F has been defined in RFC 2341.

As L2Frequires only local dial-up capability, it reduces user costs and provides the same level of security as that of a private network. An L2F tunnel can support more than one connection. It is able to do so because it defines connections within the tunnel using Multiplex IDs (MIDs). Each new connection is identified by a unique MID within the tunnel — which is especially useful when more than one remote user connects (only one dial-up connection is required).

Once the tunnel is established, the ISP is transparent to the user and the enterprise customer. The tunnel creates a secure connection between the user and the enterprise customer's network over the generally insecure public network. L2F is a Layer-2 protocol, which makes it capable of supporting other protocols apart from IP, such as IPX and NetBEUI.

L2F tunneling is not dependent on an IP network backbone (as is PPTP). Rather, it can work with other WAN-backbone technologies — such as Frame Relay, ATM, or FDDI. L2F uses PPP for client authentication (and also supports TACACS+ and RADIUS in that role). L2F authentication happens at two levels, first when the remote user connects to the ISP, and second when a connection is established to the enterprise customer's home gateway.

L2F components

The L2F specifications rest on two basic definitions of components — the network access server (NAS), through which all external access to the internal network must pass, and the Home Gateway (the entryway to which external traffic first connects, and through which validated traffic may pass). Virtual private dial-up network allows private networks to span from the client directly to the Home Gateway. Typically, a Home Gateway is the tunnel endpoint located at the corporate or enterprise network.

The initial dial-up server at the ISP is referred as network access server (NAS). For example, mobile users of an enterprise customer must connect to the organization's home gateway of choice anywhere, anytime. To do so, they typically connect to the NAS at the ISP, which then automatically connects the remote users to the corporate Home Gateway.

L2F protocol architecture

The protocol definition for virtual dial-up services requires two areas of standardization:

✦ **Encapsulation of SLIP/PPP packets within L2F:** The ISP NAS and the Home Gateway must have a common understanding of the encapsulation protocol so that SLIP/PPP packets can be successfully transmitted and received across the Internet. Authentication is provided via dial-up PPP, CHAP, or PAP, or through SLIP (without authentication). This can include TACACS+ and RADIUS as well as support for smart cards and one-time passwords.

✦ **Connection Management of L2F and MIDs:** The tunnel is created between two endpoints. As discussed earlier, MIDs have been defined for identifying specific connections within a tunnel. Connection management handles the initiation and termination of the tunnel. Termination of a tunnel includes diagnostic codes that help identify possible causes of termination and support accounting.

L2F packet format

L2F can encapsulate PPP or SLIP packets — which would ready them for secure transmission over a physical medium such as network cabling. Frames from the remote user are received at the NAS; any linked framing/transparency bytes are removed before the message is encapsulated in L2F and forwarded through the appropriate tunnel. The Home Gateway accepts these frames, de-encapsulates the message, and processes the incoming frame for the appropriate interface and protocol values. Figure 12-21 shows the entire encapsulation packet.

L2F header
Payload packet (SLIP/PPP)
L2F Checksum (optional)

Figure 12-21: L2F encapsulation packet

L2F tunneling operation

The L2F protocol is, in effect, a tunneling mechanism based on specific standards for transporting link-layer frames (such as HDLC, async PPP, SLIP, and PPP ISDN). The protocol specifies the use of a *virtual private dial-up network* (VPDN) to provide mobile users with a connection to the Home Gateway of choice. Whenever the users dial in to the company's ISP, they are connected to the Home Gateway. The ISP's task is reduced to maintaining IP connectivity to the Home Gateway. The ISP configures its network access servers to receive calls from users and forward the calls to the enterprise customer's Home Gateway. The ISP only maintains information about the Home Gateway (in effect, the tunnel endpoint located at the enterprise network). Figure 12-22 shows the L2F tunneling process.

The L2F tunneling process has three phases: Protocol negotiation, tunnel authentication, and tunnel teardown. The following sections describe of the sequence of events that establish an L2F tunnel.

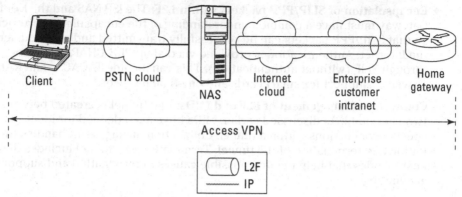

Figure 12-22: L2F tunneling process

Protocol negotiation

When a user wants to connect to the enterprise customer's Home Gateway, a PPP connection is established with the ISP's NAS. The NAS then establishes an L2F tunnel with the Home Gateway, which then authenticates the client's username and password, and establishes the PPP connection with the client.

Figure 12-23 shows the protocol negotiation events between the ISP's NAS and the enterprise customer's Home Gateway.

After the standard negotiation phase of the PPP Link Control Protocol (LCP), the NAS starts PPP authentication by sending a CHAP challenge to the client. The client, in turn, responds with a CHAP response. NAS receives the CHAP response and matches the configuration (either configured locally or obtained from its AAA server). This AAA server could be either a TACACS+ or a RADIUS server; the configuration designates the NAS to initiate a VPDN connection, which would forward the PPP session to the Home Gateway, using an L2F tunnel.

To establish the L2F session with the Home Gateway, the NAS and the Home Gateway exchange the L2F management messages. At the first place, they exchange L2F_CONF packets to create the tunnel. Then they exchange L2F_OPEN packets to open the L2F tunnel. When the L2F tunnel is open, the NAS and Home Gateway exchange L2F session packets.

The NAS and Home Gateway exchange L2F session (MID) packets. The L2F_OPEN (MID) includes the client's information from the LCP negotiation, the CHAP challenge, and the CHAP response. The Home Gateway responds to the NAS with an L2F_OPEN (MID) packet. The Home Gateway authenticates the CHAP challenge and response (using either local or remote AAA) and sends a CHAP Auth-OK packet to the client. This completes the three-way CHAP authentication.

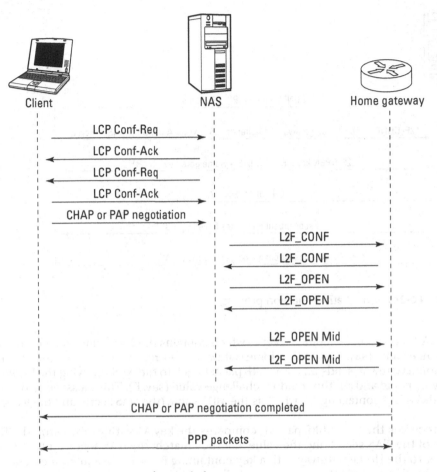

Figure 12-23: L2F protocol negotiation

When the client receives the CHAP Auth-OK packet, it understands that PPP has been through the LCP authentication phase. The client and the Home Gateway can now exchange I/O PPP-encapsulated packets.

Tunnel-authentication process

Before the NAS and Home Gateway open up an L2F tunnel, they authenticate each other via a common *tunnel secret* — a pair of usernames with the same password, configured on both the NAS and the Home Gateway. The tunnel secret is combined with random-value algorithms, which encrypt the tunnel secret. The NAS and Home Gateway authenticate each other using the resulting value and establish the L2F tunnel. Figure 12-24 describes the tunnel-authentication process.

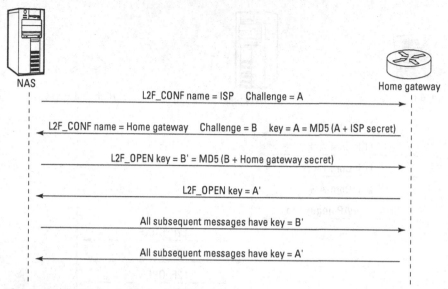

Figure 12-24: Tunnel-authentication process

The NAS sends an L2F_CONF packet—which contains the NAS name and a random challenge value (say, A)—to the Home Gateway. After receiving the L2F_CONF packet, the Home Gateway sends an L2F_CONF packet back to the NAS, carrying the Home Gateway name and another random challenge value (say, B). This message also includes a key containing A', which is the MD5 value (the NAS secret and the value A).

NAS receives the L2F_CONF packet, compares the key A' with its own stored MD5 value of the NAS secret and the value A. If they match, the NAS sends an L2F_OPEN packet to the Home Gateway with a key containing B'. All subsequent messages from the NAS include the key B'—and all subsequent messages from the Home Gateway include the key A'.

After the Home Gateway authenticates the client, the access VPN tunnel is established. The L2F tunnel creates a *virtual point-to-point connection* between the client and the Home Gateway. The NAS acts as a transparent packet forwarder. For subsequent clients who must connect to the Home Gateway, the L2F session negotiation need not be repeated because the L2F tunnel is already open.

Tunnel teardown

Either side of the tunnel can initiate the tunnel teardown process by sending an L2F_CLOSE message at any time. The MID parameter or value decides the termination of the entire tunnel or a client within the tunnel. When sent with MID of 0, it indicates the termination of the entire tunnel and all clients within it. When sent with a non-zero MID, it indicates the termination of that client within the tunnel. When sent from the Home Gateway in response to an L2F_OPEN packet, it indicates that the Home Gateway has declined the connection.

Protocol considerations

You must consider several factors while deciding to use L2F. These factors affect the functioning of L2F tunnels and must be contemplated for a better understanding of L2F operation in certain situations. Some of these factors include the features of PPP, the method of authentication; whether PPP hangs up the PPP session, and the operation of L2F over IP and UDP.

PPP features

L2F permits operation of features of the protocols, such as PPP, without explicit knowledge of these features — which is due to the fact that it simply transmits the datagrams between the tunnel's endpoints. For example, in a PPP session, L2F simply transports HDLC frames. The two PPP endpoints can negotiate higher-level features related to PPP protocol. These include reliable link, compression, multilink, encryption, NCP configuration negotiation, and termination request. These features operate between the dial-in client and the Home Gateway and are transparent to L2F, which continues to transfer HDLC frames between the endpoints.

Extended authentication

PPP has two methods or protocols for the authentication purpose. When used with PPP, L2F supports both the PPP authentication modes (PAP and CHAP). However, when used with SLIP (which does not have any such authentication feature in itself), an ASCII exchange of username and password is required before L2F is started.

Termination

L2F simply tunnels link-layer frames and does not interpret the messages related to the other protocols, such as PPP. Due to this fact, L2F does not detect frames like TERMREQ. Typically, a TERMREQ message refers to hanging up the PPP session. Hence, if the Home Gateway receives a TERMREQ message, its response will be to "hang up" the PPP session. This PPP session is actually carried over the L2F tunnel; it has to be related to the appropriate L2F message type. In such a situation, the L2F implementation at the Home Gateway converts this "hang up" into an L2F_CLOSE message, which will shut down a client's session in the tunnel.

Operation over IP and UDP

L2F uses the UDP port 1701. The entire L2F packet, including payload and L2F header, is sent within a UDP datagram. UDP uses port numbers for higher-layer protocol identification purposes. For L2F, port 1701 acts as the source as well as the destination port. Hence, all L2F information is sent using the same port number. This imposes the need for a mechanism to de-multiplex the received datagrams. This de-mulplexing is achieved using Client ID (CLID) values.

The CLID serves to assist endpoints in de-multiplexing tunnels when the underlying point-to-point substrate lacks an efficient or dependable technique for doing so directly. Using the CLID, it is possible to de-multiplex multiple tunnels whose packets arrive over the point-to-point media interleaved without requiring media-specific mechanisms. Packets with an unknown CLID are discarded.

Layer 2 Tunneling Protocol

Layer 2 Tunneling Protocol combines the best features of the two tunneling protocols, Point-to-Point Tunneling Protocol (PPTP) and Layer 2 Forwarding (L2F). This protocol is documented in RFC 2661. It encapsulates PPP frames to be transported over IP, X.25, Frame Relay, or ATM networks. Thus, L2TP can reliably transport all network-layer protocols supported by PPP. You can even use L2TP as a tunneling protocol over the Internet.

In L2TP, the PPP tunnel connection extends to the destination access gateway, instead of being terminated at the ISP's Point of Presence (POP). The tunnel can be initiated from either the remote system or the ISP's gateway access. In traditional dial-up networking services, the hosts connecting to the ISP are given registered IP addresses, which are used for communicating. This limits the applications that can be implemented in VPN. Because L2TP extends the PPP tunnels to the destination access gateway, it supports unregistered and privately administered IP addresses over the Internet. This provides flexibility in the use of the existing access infrastructure, such as the Internet, modems, access servers, and ISDN terminal adapters.

L2TP components

The main L2TP components involved in forming L2TP tunnel are as follows:

✦ **L2TP Access Concentrator (LAC):** LAC is situated at the ISP's POP where the remote system dials to initiate the L2TP tunnel. It provides the physical connection to the remote system. In the LAC, the physical media can be connected to numerous PSTN lines or ISDN lines. The client directly connects to LAC, which tunnels the PPP frames to the L2TP network server (LNS). LAC initiates the incoming calls and receives the outgoing calls.

✦ **L2TP Network Server (LNS):** LNS constitutes the other side of the L2TP tunnel endpoint. PPP sessions being tunneled through the Internet from the remote system are logically terminated by LNS. In effect, it terminates the calls received from the remote systems. It can also terminate multiple calls, placed on different media such as ISDN, and PSTN, using a single connection. It processes PPP frames and passes them to higher-layer protocols. LNS initiates the outgoing calls and receives the incoming calls.

✦ **LAC Client:** LAC is a host running L2TP natively. In effect it is an L2TP enabled client, which is capable of encapsulating L2TP.

L2TP tunneling

When a remote-system user wants to access the corporate network, the remote system initiates a PPP connection through PSTN to the LAC situated at POP of the service provider. The LAC then tunnels the PPP connection across the Internet,

Frame Relay, or ATM cloud to LNS, which provides access to the corporate network. The L2TP tunnel has two endpoints, LAC and LNS. The user datagrams are sent within the L2TP tunnel. The LAC and LNS keep track of the connected computer's status.

A LAC client might tunnel to the corporate network without using a separate LAC. In this case, the host containing the LAC client software already has a connection to the Internet. It creates a virtual PPP connection, and the local L2TP LAC Client software creates a tunnel to LNS. The user on the remote system is authenticated by the LNS gateway before accepting the tunnel connection. Authorization and accounting are provided by a network access server at the corporate office.

In the configurations where only PPP is used, the Layer 2 termination point and PPP session endpoint reside on the same physical devices. However, Layer 2 and PPP endpoints can be terminated at different devices. The L2TP tunnel is between the LAC and LNS while the PPP connection is between the LNS of the corporate network and the remote system. Figure 12-25 shows the typical scenario where L2TP is applied.

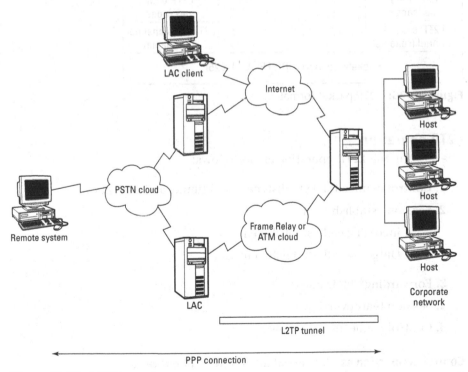

Figure 12-25: L2TP tunnel

L2TP architecture

L2TP uses two types of messages:

✦ **Control messages:** These messages are used in establishment, maintenance, and teardown of tunnels and calls. Control messages use a reliable control channel within L2TP for guaranteed delivery. Sequence numbers are used in control messages to provide reliability. The packets lost are retransmitted.

✦ **Data messages:** These messages carry PPP frames over the tunnel. Data messages are not transmitted reliably, and they are not retransmitted when packet loss occurs. Data messages might use sequence numbers, which reorder packets and are not for retransmission.

As shown in Figure 12-26, the PPP frames are passed over an unreliable data channel encapsulated first by an L2TP header and then by a packet transport such as UDP, Frame Relay, ATM, or X.25. Control messages are sent over a reliable L2TP control channel that sends packets in-band over the same packet transport.

Figure 12-26: L2TP packet format

L2TP operation

The steps in the L2TP operation are as follows:

1. Control connection establishment and tunnel authentication
2. Session establishment
   a. Incoming call establishment
   b. Outgoing call establishment
3. Forwarding PPP frames
4. Session teardown
5. Control connection teardown

Control connection establishment and tunnel authentication

Before a session can be initiated, control connection must be established between LAC and LNS. This includes establishing the identity of the peer and the peer's L2TP version number. The process of establishing the connection and authenticating the tunnel is shown in Figure 12-27.

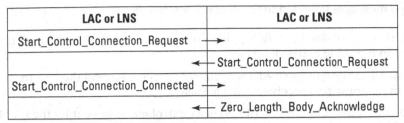

LAC or LNS	LAC or LNS
Start_Control_Connection_Request →	
	← Start_Control_Connection_Request
Start_Control_Connection_Connected →	
	← Zero_Length_Body_Acknowledge

Figure 12-27: L2TP connection establishment

The various messages involved in the process are as follows:

✦ Start_Control_Connection_Request (SCCRQ) is a control message sent by either LAC or LNS to initiate a tunnel.

✦ Start_Control_Connection_Reply (SCCRP) is a control message sent in reply to a received SCCRQ message. It indicates that the request was accepted.

✦ Start_Control_Connection_Connected (SCCCN) is a control message sent in reply to SCCRP to complete the tunnel establishment.

✦ Zero_Length_Body_Acknowledge (ZLB_Acknowledge) simply acknowledges the receipt of the last message.

During the establishment of the connection, the optional authentication of the tunnel occurs. The challenge might be sent by either LAC or LNS. If the challenge is sent in SCCRQ, the challenge response is sent in the SCCRP. If the challenge is sent in SCCRP, the challenge response is sent in SCCCN. The tunnel establishment is allowed only if the expected response and the actual challenge response match.

Session establishment

A separate session must be established for each PPP stream. LAC initiates the session with LNS for an incoming call, while LNS initiates the session with LAC for an outgoing call.

The sequence of events in establishing an incoming call is shown in Figure 12-28.

LAC	LNS
(Call detected)	
Incoming_Call_Request →	
	← Incoming_Call_Reply
Incoming_Call_Connected →	
	← ZLB_Acknowledge

Figure 12-28: L2TP incoming call establishment

The various messages involved in the process are as follows:

✦ `Incoming_Call_Request` (ICRQ) is a control message sent by the LAC to LNS when an incoming call is detected.

✦ `Incoming-Call-Reply` (ICRP) is a control message sent by the LNS to the LAC in response to a received ICRQ message.

✦ `Incoming-Call-Connected` (ICCN) is a control message sent by the LAC to the LNS in response to a received ICRP message.

The sequence of events followed in establishing an outgoing call is shown in Figure 12-29.

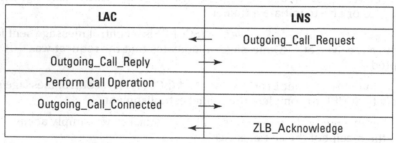

LAC	LNS
←	Outgoing_Call_Request
Outgoing_Call_Reply →	
Perform Call Operation	
Outgoing_Call_Connected →	
←	ZLB_Acknowledge

Figure 12-29: L2TP outgoing call establishment

The various messages involved in the process are as follows:

✦ `Outgoing_Call_Request` (OCRQ) is a control message sent by LNS to LAC to indicate that an outbound call connection from LAC is to be established.

✦ `Outgoing-Call-Reply` (OCRP) is a control message sent by LAC to LNS in response to a received OCRQ message.

✦ `Outgoing-Call-Connected` (OCCN) is a control message sent by LAC to LNS following the OCRP and after the outgoing call has been completed.

Forwarding PPP frames

After the tunnel has been established, the remote system (which is accessing the corporate network) sends PPP frames to LAC. LAC encapsulates the PPP with L2TP and forwards them to LNS over the appropriate tunnel. LNS receives the L2TP frames, strips L2TP, and processes them as normal PPP frames. LNS then uses PPP authentication to validate the user and then assigns the network address, if required.

There can be multiple sessions in a tunnel. Also, multiple tunnels can exist between a pair of LAC and LNS. Each tunnel is given an ID called Tunnel ID, which identifies the tunnel. Similarly each session is also given an ID called Session ID, which identifies the session inside a tunnel. These IDs are present in the packet header.

Session teardown

Session teardown can be initiated by either LAC or LNS. Figure 12-30 shows the sequence of events in session teardown.

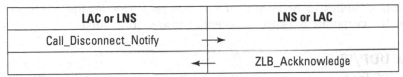

LAC or LNS	LNS or LAC
Call_Disconnect_Notify ⟶	
⟵	ZLB_Ackknowledge

Figure 12-30: L2TP session teardown

In session teardown, `Call_Disconnect_Notify` (CDN) is a control message sent by the initiator of the teardown to request disconnection of a specific call in the tunnel.

Control connection teardown

Control disconnection teardown may also be initiated by either LAC or LNS; Figure 12-31 shows the sequence of events.

LAC or LNS	LNS or LAC
Stop_Control_Connection_Notification ⟶	
⟵	ZLB_Ackknowledge (Clean up)

Figure 12-31: L2TP control connection teardown

The message `Stop_Control_Connection_Notification` (StopCCN) is sent by either LAC or LNS, whoever wants to initiate the termination of the control connection. It is not necessary to clear all sessions individually when tearing down the tunnel. An implementation might shut down an entire tunnel — and all sessions on the tunnel — by sending the StopCCN. The sender of StopCCN waits for a finite period for the acknowledgment of the message before releasing the control information for the tunnel.

L2TP tunnel modes

L2TP supports two types of tunnels — actually two *modes* of tunnel operation — compulsory and voluntary:

✦ **Compulsory mode:** The L2TP tunnel is established between LAC at the ISP's POP and LNS at the corporate network. In this mode, the service provider should support L2TP. Based on authentication, it should also determine whether L2TP should be used for a specific session and with which destination should the tunnel be formed. This does not require any changes at the remote client end.

✦ **Voluntary mode:** The L2TP tunnel is established between the remote client (which is the LAC Client) and the LNS at the corporate network. It is similar to PPTP and is transparent to ISP. But the client must support L2TP for this mode to operate. Thus the client can have Internet access and one or more VPN connections at the same time — but such an arrangement can lead to multiple IP addresses being assigned to the client. The resulting ambiguity opens the corporate network to potential attacks from outside.

L2TP over UDP/IP

L2TP uses UDP for transport over IP networks. It uses the registered UDP port 1701. Figure 12-32 shows the implementation of L2TP over UDP/IP.

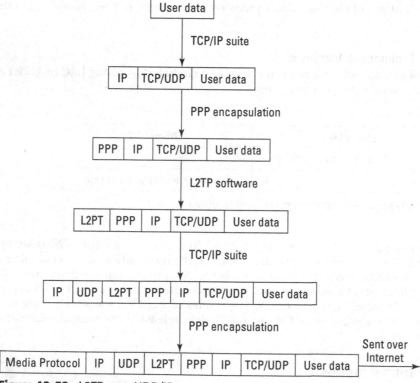

Figure 12-32: L2TP over UDP/IP

A remote system can communicate with the destination server by following this series of steps:

1. The remote system encapsulates user data in TCP/UDP header.

2. The system attaches IP header to this TCP/UDP segment.

3. To transport it over the PSTN to LAC, this IP packet is encapsulated in PPP.

4. At LAC, the PPP packet is encapsulated in L2TP header.

5. This L2TP packet is encapsulated in UDP segment.

6. LAC attaches its IP header to the segment and encapsulates the packet in the specific media protocol header of the media in use.

A LAC client has the L2TP software installed on it. Therefore, if a LAC client wants to communicate with a destination over VPN, then all the steps just listed will occur at LAC client only.

Comparison of PPTP, L2F, and L2TP

The tunneling protocols PPTP, L2F, and L2TP have different characteristics and operations. A comparison between the three tunneling protocols is given in Table 12-4.

Table 12-4
Comparison Between Tunneling Protocols

Feature	PPTP	L2F	L2TP
Standard	RFC 2637	RFC 2341	RFC 2661
Carrier	IP/GRE	UDP/IP, FR, ATM, X.25	UDP/IP, FR, ATM, X.25
Multiprotocol support	Yes	Yes	Yes
Call type supported	Incoming and outgoing	Incoming	Incoming and outgoing
Port	TCP port 1723	UDP port 1701	UDP port 1701
Tunnel modes	Voluntary tunneling mode	Compulsory tunneling mode	Compulsory and voluntary tunneling mode
Encryption	Microsoft PPP Encryption (MPPE)	MPPE, IPSEC (optional)	MPPE/ECP, IPSEC (optional)
Authentication	PPP authentication (user)	PPP authentication (user), IPSEC optional (packet)	PPP authentication (user), IPSEC optional (packet)
Multiple tunnels to a destination	No	No	Yes
PPP Multilink support	No	Yes	Yes

Tip   L2TP combines the best characteristics of both PPTP and L2F, which is why it is being widely implemented.

The tunneling protocols address various VPN requirements:

✦ **Authentication:** Although Layer 2 protocols support user authentication via the user-authentication methods of PPP, most Layer 3 tunneling protocols assume that the endpoints are authenticated before the tunnel is established. As a Layer 3 protocol, IPSec is an exception; it authenticates the endpoint computers.

Note   IPSec ensures computer authentication instead of specific user authentication; any user who has access to the endpoint can use a tunnel.

Tunneling protocols also support a variety of authentication methods. Layer 2 protocols support authentication methods, such as one-time passwords and smart cards. IPSec uses methods such as public-key certificate authentication.

✦ **Dynamic address allocation:** Although Layer 2 protocols support dynamic address allocation to the clients, Layer 3 tunneling protocols work with an assumption that the clients have been allocated addresses before the tunnel is initiated.

✦ **Data compression:** Layer 2 protocols support a variety of PPP-based data compression schemes. Although Layer 3 protocols do not support data compression schemes, IETF is trying for similar methods for Layer 3 protocols.

✦ **Multiprotocol support:** Although Layer 2 protocols support multiple payload protocols that enable users to access their corporate networks by using protocols such as IPX and NetBEUI, Layer 3 protocols support the target networks that use the IP protocol.

VPN Scenarios

This section discusses three basic VPN scenarios: branch office connection network, business partner and office network, and remote-access network.

Branch office connection network

In a branch office connection network scenario, two trusted intranets of an organization are connected. Security of data (as well as intranets) is a major concern. You not only must secure sensitive data while it's being transmitted over the public network, but also protect the organization's intranet from external intruders.

Consider a situation where an organization uses leased lines to securely communicate with its branch offices. However, it wants to use a technology that would help in minimizing the cost incurred from communicating with the branch offices. To do so, the organization can implement an intranet VPN. The organization can implement the VPN connection between the corporate office and its branch offices. To implement a VPN, the organization must obtain Internet access from an ISP. Also, a router with IPSec firewall functionality should be placed at the boundary of each intranet. This would secure the transmitted data from external intruders. The IPSec firewall would also be providing data packet encryption and authentication. Hence, by using an intranet VPN, the organization's corporate office can communicate cost-effectively and securely with its branch offices.

A network to link business partners and suppliers

Consider the following situation: An organization that routinely uses its network to transact business with its business partners, suppliers, and clients can use Frame Relay or leased lines to secure interactions with partners. This method is expensive and relatively limited geographically. Therefore the organization and its business partners decide to implement an extranet VPN.

Naturally the first stage of the process is to design the VPN itself. Two major design considerations are as follows:

✦ All data being transmitted should travel encrypted.

✦ All network devices on the VPN of the organization should either use public address in the intranet or use a network access server. Doing so avoids routing collisions.

To implement an extranet VPN, the organization must obtain Internet access from an ISP. The organization also must deploy a firewall to protect against intruders. This VPN can be deployed between a client workstation (at a business partner's end) and a server (on the organization's intranet). In such a VPN, the remote clients can be authenticated either at the firewall that protects the intranet or at the organization's server. The point at which client authentication happens depends on the security policy of the organization.

Remote-access network

Consider the following remote-access network scenario: A connection is established between a remote user and an organization's intranet; this user must have frequent access to important files located on the home-office server of his organization's intranet. To enable secure and cost-effective access to these files, the organization can implement a remote-access VPN: The remote user's computer (client) connects to the Internet by dialing in to an ISP. The client then gets authenticated and establishes a tunnel between itself and the firewall at the boundary of the organization's intranet. The organization can apply IPSec authentication to protect its intranet from malicious data packets; encrypting the data packets guards against their being easily used if intercepted.

In a remote-access scenario, the following design considerations govern the deployment of a VPN:

✦ The clients accessing the organization's intranet should support IPSec protocols.

✦ Dynamic tunnels must be established (the addresses of remote clients are dynamic).

✦ The firewall should reject all dial-in traffic that cannot be authenticated.

Summary

This chapter reviewed the basics of virtual private network technology — including the need for implementing VPNs, the benefits that VPNs offer, the types of VPNs, and the tunneling protocols that make them possible. Implementation scenarios illustrated VPNs in action.

✦   ✦   ✦

Securing a Virtual Private Network

The last couple of decades have seen major changes in the scope and speed of business: Global markets and e-business, once speculative concepts, are now buzzwords. As organizations move toward globalization, they require fast, reliable, and secure methods of transmitting information to branch offices anywhere in the world. Virtual private networks (VPNs) have become a common, cost-effective way to avoid the expense of leased lines while still giving remote users secure, multiprotocol access to corporate intranets. VPN technology is presently the most cost-effective and practical way to secure data transmitted over the convenient (but risky) medium of the Internet. The convenience of the Internet imposes an added responsibility on organizations that use it: They must ensure that their VPNs are secure from hackers.

This chapter covers basic VPN technologies, outlines the Internet Security Protocol (IPSec), and describes how to configure IPSec. As a further step, the chapter discusses Cisco Secure VPN Client, an integral part of Cisco Secure VPN Software.

Basic VPN Technologies

Although VPNs provide a secure way to transfer information, they are prone to security attacks (in particular, the man-in-the-middle variety). The technologies that implement VPNs — named and known by the protocols they use — have distinctive characteristics that support specific features of a VPN (for example, tunneling, encryption, and authentication). Upcoming sections define and describe these technologies.

Point-to-Point Tunneling Protocol

Point-to-Point Tunneling Protocol (PPTP) is an extension of Point-to-Point Protocol (PPP), which is one of the most commonly used Data Link-layer protocols over wide-area networks. PPTP secures transmitted data by creating a VPN through public data networks, such as the Internet. It supports enhanced security and multiprotocol communications over the Internet. PPTP uses the authentication mechanisms of PPP (CHAP and PAP). It encapsulates the PPP packets into IP datagrams before transmitting them over the TCP/IP-based networks.

Note   PPTP is described in RFC 2637.

As an open-standard protocol, PPTP provides secure connectivity between remote users and private networks. PPTP enables remote users to access the corporate networks by dialing into the local ISP's network, instead of dialing directly into the company network. PPTP is a cost-effective way to provide remote access to users. It does not require a leased line or dedicated servers, as it can be used over public-switched telephone networks (PSTNs). However, PPTP does not follow a single standard for encryption and authentication. As a result, two applications compatible with PPTP might not be compatible with each other if they encrypt data differently.

The client end Internet service provider (ISP) might require initial dial-in authentication. This authentication is only for the ISP NAS and not meant for the private network. The PPTP server can provide additional authentication as it acts as the gateway to a private network.

As an extension of PPP, PPTP authenticates remote PPTP clients by using PAP and CHAP. You can provide authentication over PPP by implementing an enhanced version of CHAP (such as MS-CHAP) in addition to CHAP and PAP.

The PPTP control messages and GRE packets that establish the tunnel are not secured; they do not require authentication or encryption — a serious (and classic) security shortcoming. Any hacker can capture the connection-sequence packets and change them to take control of the secure channel using false packets. The PPP payload data is not cryptographically protected, so it too can be captured.

Fortunately, the security aspects of a VPN (in any competent implementation) can't be damaged by such attacks. To provide additional security to the corporate VPN, deploy a firewall deployment at either end — customer premises (or ISP premises) as well as your home office. This firewall implementation can be either hardware- or software-based.

Cross-Reference   For more about implementing firewalls, see Chapters 8 and 9.

Layer 2 Forwarding

Layer 2 Forwarding (commonly known as *L2F*) is an open-tunneling Layer 2 protocol developed by Cisco. L2F requires a local dial-up capability for tunneling. It supports multiple protocols, such as IP, IPX, and NetBEUI. L2F is similar to PPTP, as it allows users to establish tunnels between routers, servers, and/or clients over the Internet. L2F uses PPP for authenticating the remote server. Besides this, L2F also supports TACACS+ and RADIUS for authentication. However, unlike PPTP, L2F tunneling is *not* dependent on IP and can work with other media, such as Frame Relay and asynchronous transfer mode (ATM).

Note   L2F is described in RFC 2341.

An L2F tunnel can support more than one connection—because it defines the connections in a tunnel by using *Multiplex IDs* (MIDs). Each connection within a tunnel has a unique MID. This enables multiple users at a remote site to access the corporate network using a single dial-up connection.

Layer 2 Tunneling Protocol

Layer 2 Tunneling Protocol (L2TP), developed jointly by Microsoft, Cisco, 3Com, and others, combines the best features of PPTP and L2F. It encapsulates PPP frames transported over IP, X.25, Frame Relay, or ATM networks. Thus, L2TP supports all Network-layer protocols, which are supported by PPP.

Note   L2TP is described in RFC 2661.

In L2TP, the PPP tunnel connection extends into the destination's gateway. This PPP tunnel can be initiated from either the remote computer or the ISP's gateway. L2TP uses CHAP and PAP as authentication methods but also supports such methods as RADIUS.

Because L2TP extends the PPP tunnels to the destination access gateway, it supports unregistered and privately administered IP addresses over the Internet. This provides flexibility in the use of existing access infrastructure, such as the Internet, modems, access servers, and ISDN terminal adapters. Besides supporting multiple protocols, L2TP also supports interoperability with other L2TP applications.

Using L2TP with IPSec in L2TP operations gives rise to some specific security concerns—for example, maintaining security at (and between) the ends of a tunnel and securing the data packets themselves. Upcoming sections examine these concerns.

Tunnel-endpoint security

When a tunnel is being established, the tunnel endpoints might perform authentication. But this method does not provide any authentication beyond tunnel establishment. After the authentication has been successfully performed, any unauthorized user can detect the tunnel stream and send packets on the tunnel.

Avoid selecting an easy-to-guess session ID — and avoid selecting it in a predictable manner. The idea is to make your packets difficult for hackers to trace between LAC and LNS.

Packet-level security and end-to-end security

L2TP is concerned only with the confidentiality, authenticity, and integrity of L2TP packets traveling through its tunnel. Protecting the L2TP packet stream with secure transport also protects the data carried in the tunneled PPP packets as they travel from LAC to LNS. Despite this protection, one should not ignore the need for end-to-end security between the hosts.

IPSec

IP Security (IPSec) is a protocol suite developed by Internet Engineering Task Force (IETF) to support the secure transmission of data over a network at the OSI Network layer. IPSec provides encryption services that ensure the integrity and authenticity of data packets traveling over the Internet. IPSec is a Layer 3 protocol and supports multiple protocols.

IPSec can be used as a VPN technology or can be used as an encryption method with L2TP and PPTP. IPSec is based on encryption methods compatible with the existing IP standard (IPv4). The following section discusses IPSec in detail.

Introducing IPSec

Internet and large corporate networks have been using the Internet Protocol (IP) to transmit data. IP transmits data in the form of manageable chunks called packets. However, these packets are susceptible to security threats, such as spoofing, sniffing, session hijacking, and man-in-the middle attacks. To take care of these security threats, IP Security (IPSec) protocol suite was developed by IETF. IPSec is an extension of IP that takes care of the security issues at the network level. Hence, IPSec ensures the security of the network rather than the security of applications that use it. As IPSec provides security to the network, all applications that use the network are also secured.

To ensure authenticity, integrity, and confidentiality, IPSec uses the following protocols:

✦ **Authentication Header (AH):** This protocol adds a header to the IP datagram. This header ensures the integrity and authenticity of the data.

✦ **Encapsulated Security Payload (ESP):** This protocol provides data confidentiality by encrypting the data (as well as the IP address in the IP datagram). ESP also ensures data integrity and authenticity.

✦ **Internet Key Exchange (IKE):** This protocol ensures secure and authenticated transmission of data packets. It defines a *security association* between two peer devices. A security association is a policy that outlines the data-handling mechanism between any two devices. IKE consists of Internet Security Association and Key Management Protocol (ISAKMP) and Oakley. ISAKMP and Oakley are the protocols that manage the creation of encryption keys.

Creating authentication headers

An *authentication header* (AH) is the part of a data packet that serves as its network credentials, vouching for the source of the data packet as its true origin. The AH also ensures the integrity of data (by using a shared secret key) and protects against replay attacks (by using a sequence-number field to ensure that any replay of the message would have a different number and so be easier to spot). As a further protection of data integrity, the AH uses a *checksum* — a value generated by a message-authentication code such as MD5. Taken together, all these functions of the AH make up the process called *authentication*.

The AH applies a one-way hash function to a data packet, which generates a *message digest* (MD), a summary of the packet's information that serves as a miniature "payload" for the AH. With the AH in place, the packet is transmitted to the IPSec peer device. The receiver peer applies its own hash function (previously agreed upon with the sender), extracts the transmitted hash value received from the sender, and compares the two hashes. If they match, authentication is complete. If even one bit does not match, then the hash output changes — and is detected.

 An AH does not provide data encryption; any data in the header is sent as cleartext.

Figure 13-1 shows the working of a typical AH.

 Authentication header is described in RFC 2402.

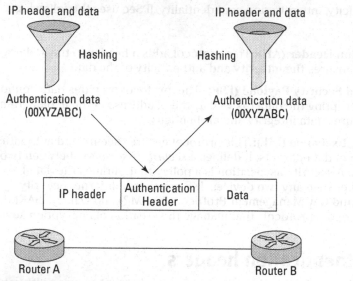

Figure 13-1: How an authentication header works

AH can be used in two modes, transport mode and tunnel mode.

✦ **Transport mode:** In this mode, the entire data packet (except the *mutable fields*) is authenticated. Mutable fields refers to the fields in the IP header that cannot be predicted by the receiver, such as the type of service and header checksum.

✦ **Tunnel mode:** In this mode, a new header is created and used as the outermost header of the data packet. It is after this new header that the authentication header is placed. The original data packet (the payload and the IP header) is placed after the authentication header. In the tunnel mode, AH authenticates the entire data packet; hence any changes made to the data packet during transition can be easily identified.

As both payload and datagram are authenticated, this mode is more secure as compared to the transport mode. As the header is also authenticated, the hackers cannot trace the actual source and destination of the packets. Therefore, hackers cannot perform traffic analysis.

Encapsulated Security Payload

As discussed earlier, ESP provides confidentiality by encrypting the payload as well as the IP address. ESP supports various symmetric encryption algorithms, the default being 56-bit data-encryption Standard (DES). Implement this encryption standard to ensure interoperability among IPSec devices. ESP also provides optional services, such as anti-replay, data origin authentication, and connection-less integrity. The options selected at the time of IPSec configuration determine the services that ESP provides.

Note   ESP is described in the Requests for Comments posted online by the programming community (specifically, RFC 2406).

Like AH, ESP can also be used in two modes, the transport mode and the tunnel mode. In the transport mode, ESP encrypts and optionally authenticates only the payload. However, in the tunnel mode, ESP encrypts and optionally authenticates the entire original data packet.

Significant differences between AH and ESP include the following:

✦ ESP encrypts the data packet (whole or in part); AH does not encrypt data.

✦ In the transport mode, ESP authenticates only the data and not the IP header. However, AH in the transport mode authenticates the entire data packet except the mutable fields.

✦ In the tunnel mode, ESP authenticates the entire original data packet (without the newly added outer IP header). However, AH in the tunnel mode authenticates the entire packet.

Internet Key Exchange

In an IPSec framework, IKE authenticates peers and handles the creation and management of encryption keys. IKE also manages the hashing algorithms between the peer devices and outlines the Security Association (SA).

Note   Although you can configure IPSec without IKE, it is preferable to configure IPSec with IKE, as IKE provides enhanced features and flexibility.

Using IKE, you can specify the lifetime of an IPSec SA. Also, when you use IKE, you do not need to manually specify the IPSec SA parameters for the peer devices. IKE offers some uniquely useful capabilities:

✦ Provides anti-replay services

✦ Allows encryption keys to change during an IPSec session

✦ Enables dynamic authentication of peer devices

✦ Generates session keys used by the peer devices

IKE uses the following algorithms and mechanisms:

✦ **DES:** An encryption algorithm that serves to encrypt data in the packets. IKE uses 56-bit DES and 3DES.

✦ **MD5:** A hash algorithm that serves to authenticate the data in packets.

✦ **SHA:** A hash algorithm used during IKE exchanges to authenticate packet data.

✦ **Diffie-Hellman:** A protocol for creating shared secret keys over an insecure channel. IKE uses this protocol to generate session keys.

✦ **RSA signatures and encrypted nonces:** Used to authenticate the peer devices. RSA signatures provide non-repudiation; nonces provide repudiation.

Note   A *nonce* is a random value used in encryption algorithms.

Security association

As mentioned earlier, a security association (SA) outlines the ways in which the management of data packets would be handled between two peer IPSec devices. When security provisions are decided for the devices communicating with each other, determine the algorithms that would be used for providing security, encryption, and integrity. An SA manages all this information. It specifies the:

✦ Authentication algorithm used in AH

✦ Keys of the authentication algorithm of AH

✦ Authentication algorithm used in ESP

✦ Keys of the authentication algorithm of ESP

✦ Protocol used to authenticate the communication between the peer devices

✦ Lifetime of the keys

✦ Lifetime of SA

✦ Source address of SA

A security association is identified by a unique number called the Security Parameter Index (SPI) and the destination IP address. Before sending a packet, a host checks the SA database and applies appropriate security to the packet. It also inserts the SPI to the IPSec header. When the IPSec peer device receives the packet, it checks the SA database and matches the SPI and the destination IP address. If these values match, the packet is processed per the request.

Note   Both IPSec and IKE use SAs to specify security parameters.

At the heart of IPSec is the Diffie-Hellman protocol; the upcoming section explains it.

Diffie-Hellman key agreement

The Diffie-Hellman key arrangement is a public-key encryption protocol that was developed in 1976 by Whitfield Diffie and Martin Hellman. This protocol enables two IPSec peer devices to establish a shared secret key on an insecure channel. In this key arrangement, each IPSec peer generates a private key and then a public key. The public key is a derivate of the private key. The peers then exchange their public keys over the insecure channel. Each peer now has its private key and the other peer's public key. Each peer now runs an algorithm to generate a secret value. The secret value generated by the peers is same. This secret value serves to generate a shared secret key, which then serves to encrypt the data, using the encryption algorithms specified in IPSec SA. The following steps are involved in the creation of a shared secret key:

1. Each peer device generates a large prime number (p or q) and sends its prime number to the other peer over an insecure channel. For example, consider peer devices A and B. A generates a prime number p; B generates another prime number q. A sends p to B while B sends q to A over an insecure channel. A and B use p and q to generate a root value called g.

2. The peers then generate a Diffie-Hellman key. Each peer combines this key with the p and q values to generate a public key. These public keys are then exchanged.

3. Using the other peer's public key and its own private key, each peer generates a secret value.

    This secret value — identical for both peers — then serves to derive a shared secret key.

RSA cryptosystem

IKE uses the RSA cryptosystem to provide authentication. RSA was developed by Rivest, Shamir, and Adleman in 1977. IKE uses RSA signatures as well as RSA encrypted nonces. Each IPSec peer device generates a pair of public/private keys. Although the public key can be shared and transmitted over an insecure network, the private key is known only to the peer and serves to decrypt the data. The RSA algorithm encrypts the message and the receiver's public key. The encrypted data is then sent to the peer device. The receiving peer device uses the RSA algorithm and its private key to decrypt the encrypted data.

Hashed Message Authentication Codes

Hashed Message Authentication Codes (HMACs) ensure integrity and authenticity of data. To authenticate data, HMAC uses cryptographic hash algorithms and a private key. A hash algorithm converts variable length data into a fixed-length hash message. This hash message then serves as a signature, which is sent with the message. The HMAC, on the receiving peer's end, uses the private key to hash the received message. It then compares the resultant hash with the received hash value.

Note   To ensure authenticity, the values of both hashes should match exactly.

As IPSec is an open Internet standard, various vendors and service providers offer IPSec-capable equipment. Cisco also provides a range of IPSec devices, such as Cisco routers, Cisco Secure PIX Firewall, Cisco Secure VPN Client software, and Cisco VPN concentrators (which act as building blocks for its VPN solutions).

Working of IPSec

As discussed earlier, IPSec ensures secure transmission of data over the Network layer by using a variety of protocols and technologies. IPSec follows these steps:

1. Process initiation

2. IKE Phase 1

3. IKE Phase 2

4. Data transfer

5. Tunnel termination

Process initiation

In this step, the traffic that needs to be sent through the IPSec client is checked for the type of security it needs. The access lists in Cisco routers and PIX Firewall determine the data packets that need to be encrypted. If the packets need to be encrypted, the IPSec client initiates the next step in the process.

Tip

When deciding a security policy for VPN, first decide on the traffic that needs to be protected by IPSec. It is based on this decision that the IPSec devices are configured.

IKE Phase 1

In this phase, the IPSec peer devices are authenticated. Then, an IKE SA policy is negotiated between the IPSec peers to secure the IKE exchange. In this phase, an authenticated Diffie-Hellman exchange is performed. Diffie-Hellman exchange is a secure method of creating public keys further used to create shared secret keys, which the IPSec encryption algorithms then use. This phase is complete when a secure channel is set up for the exchange of IKE parameters.

There are two modes of IKE: main and aggressive.

✦ **Main mode:** Three two-way exchanges take place between the sender and the receiver. In the first exchange, each IPSec peer agrees upon the algorithms that will be used to secure the IKE transactions. In the second exchange, using Diffie-Hellman exchange generates shared keys. In the third exchange, identities of the sender and the receiver are verified. Checking the identity value, which is the IP address of the IPSec peer in an encrypted form, completes the verification.

The final result of the main mode is matching IKE SAs between the IPSec peer devices. These IKE SAs are bi-directional and specify the authentication methods used, encryption algorithms, the lifetime of SA in seconds, and the shared keys.

✦ **Aggressive mode:** The establishment of an IPSec session takes comparatively less time as fewer exchanges take place. Thus, this mode is faster than the main mode. In the first exchange, the Diffie-Hellman public key, an identity packet, and the nonces are put into the proposed IKE SA and sent to the destination device. The destination device sends back all information required to complete the transaction. After this step, the source device just needs to confirm the exchange.

The exchange of information between the source and the destination devices takes place without setting up of a secure channel. Consequently, a threat of hackers discovering the source of SA exists.

IKE Phase 2

In IKE Phase 2, IPSec SAs are negotiated and established to create an IPSec tunnel. After IKE establishes a secure tunnel in Phase 1, the IKE Phase 2 enters the quick mode. In this mode, IPSec policy is negotiated. The keying material for creating the IPSec security algorithm is also derived. Finally, IPSec SAs are established. Then, nonces are exchanged. These nonces ensure protection against replays. It is the quick mode that renegotiates an IPSec SA when the lifetime of an IPSec SA is over.

Note   To ensure the security of the keying material, specify the Perfect Forward Secrecy (PFS) option in the IPSec policy.

Data transfer

In the data transfer phase, the IPSec tunnel that was created in the IKE Phase 2 serves to transfer the data between the IPSec peer devices. This data is transferred in the form of packets, which are encrypted and decrypted by using encryption algorithms and keys. These encryption algorithms and keys are specified in the IPSec SA.

Tunnel termination

An IPSec SA terminates when it is deleted or when its lifetime is over. With the termination of IPSec SAs, the IPSec tunnel is also terminated. Usually, when the lifetime of an IPSec SA is about to expire, IKE renegotiates the SAs. This ensures that new SAs are established before the termination of the existing SAs. As a result, an uninterruptible data flow is maintained. With the termination of IPSec SA, the keys also terminate; the renegotiation results in a new SA and new keys.

Implementing IPSec

IPSec can be implemented on Cisco routers and PIX Firewall to ensure secure transmission of data between the networks. Cisco routers have Cisco IOS software that implements IPSec. Implementing of IPSec involves the following steps:

1. Planning for IPSec
2. Configuring IKE
3. Configuring IPSec
4. Verifying the configuration

The following sections discuss the entire process of configuring IPSec, from planning onward.

Planning for IPSec

To configure IPSec, defining the IPSec security policy is a prerequisite. The IPSec security policy specifies the following:

✦ The hosts and the networks that need to be protected

✦ The encryption policy

✦ Details of IPSec peers, such as their IP addresses

Using the IPSec security policy, determine the IPSec features you require. During this phase, also outline the IKE policy; make sure it takes into consideration the number and location of IPSec peer devices. Before configuring IPSec, ensure that the access lists that have been created for filtering the packets enable IPSec traffic.

Configuring IKE

After you have defined the IKE and IPSec security policy, the next step is to configure IKE. Configuring IKE involves the following steps in the following sections.

Enabling or disabling IKE

IKE is enabled for all interfaces at a router, by default. However, it is a good idea to disable IKE access for interfaces that would not be used by IPSec. This would secure the router from the denial-of-service attacks. To disable an interface that would not be used by IPSec, block the UDP port 500 on the interface by using an access list statement.

Note   To enable IKE globally, use the `crypto isakmp enable` command.

Creating IKE policy

After enabling or disabling IKE as per your requirements, the next step is to create an IKE policy. You create an IKE policy by using the `crypto isakmp policy` command. This command enables the IKE policy configuration mode, in which you set the IKE parameters, such as encryption algorithm and peer authentication method.

Note   Multiple IKE policies can be configured on each peer device.

Configuring preshared key

If you have specified a preshared key in your IKE policy, then your next step is to configure that key by using the `crypto isakmp key` command. The best approach is to configure a different preshared key on each pair of IPSec peers.

Verifying the IKE configuration

The final step is to verify the IKE configuration. You verify the IKE configuration by using the `show crypto isakmp policy` command. This command displays the IKE policy on the screen.

Configuring IPSec

After you have configured IKE, the next step is to configure IPSec. Configuring IPSec involves the following steps.

Configuring transform set

You use the IPSec security policy to define a *transform set*. A transform set defines a specific set of algorithms and security protocols. To define a transform set, use the `crypto ipsec transform-set` command. The syntax of this command is

```
crypto ipsec transform-set transform-set name transform 1
```

where

   ✦ `transform-set name` specifies the name of the transform set to be created.

   ✦ `transform 1` specifies the transform (such as AH transform or ESP transform).

Using the earlier command, you can set up to three transforms.

Configuring lifetimes of IPSec SAs

As discussed earlier, IPSec SAs have a pre-defined lifetime, as specified in a crypto map (which also specifies the other components of an IPSec policy). Cisco IOS software defines a global lifetime value for all crypto maps. However, you can change the global lifetime of IPSec SA by using the `crypto ipsec security-association lifetime` command.

 Note   The lifetime of an SA can be specified either in seconds or kilobytes. The default value of a SA lifetime is 3600 seconds or 4,608,000KB.

Creating crypto access lists

You create crypto access lists to define the traffic that needs to be protected by IPSec while being transmitted. To create a crypto access list, you should use the IP extended access list. The following syntax serves to create a crypto access list:

```
access-list access-list number {permit|deny} protocol
source source wildcard destination destination wildcard
```

where

- ✦ permit: Indicates that all packets that match the specified value should be encrypted.
- ✦ deny: Indicates that all packets that match the specified value should not be encrypted.
- ✦ protocol: Indicates the IP packet types that should be encrypted.

Creating crypto maps

After creating crypto access lists, the next step is to create crypto maps. These crypto maps would then be used by IPSec to create a security association. You can assign only one cryto-map name to an interface. However, you can create multiple crypto-map statements for a crypto-map name by using a sequence number for each crypto-map entry. To enter the crypto-map configuration mode and create a crypto-map entry, use the crypto map command. The syntax is

```
crypto map mapname sequencenumber {cisco| ipsec-manual}
```

where

- ✦ mapname specifies the name that you want to assign to the crypto map.
- ✦ sequencenumber specifies the number that you want to assign to the crypto-map entry. The sequence number ranks the crypto-map entries according to their priority. The lower the sequence number, the higher the priority.
- ✦ cisco specifies that Cisco Encryption Technology would be used to secure the traffic, which is specified in the crypto-map entry — which is the default value.
- ✦ ipsec-manual specifies that IKE would not be used to create IPSec SAs to secure the traffic, which is specified in the crypto-map entry.

You can create only one crypto-map set for an interface. However, multiple interfaces can have a single crypto-map set.

Applying crypto maps to interfaces

The last step in configuring IPSec is to apply crypto maps to your interfaces by using the `crypto map` command in the configuration mode of the router interface. The syntax is

```
crypto map mapname
```

where *mapname* specifies the name of the crypto map. You can assign only one crypto-map set to an interface. When you apply a crypto map to an interface, security associations are set up in the security association database.

Verifying IPSec

After configuring IPSec, the final step is to verify the configuration. You can verify IKE and IPSec configuration by using the following commands.

✦ The `show crypto isakmp sa` command displays the current IKE security authorities at a peer device.

✦ The `show crypto isakmp policy` command displays the parameters of the IKE policy.

✦ The `debug crypto isakmp` command enables you to view messages about all IKE events.

✦ The `clear crypto isakmp` command clears the currently active IKE connections.

✦ The `show crypto ipsec transform set` command displays the transform sets that have been configured.

✦ The `show crypto map` command displays the configuration details of a crypto map.

✦ The `show crypto ipsec security-association lifetime` command displays the lifetime value specified in a particular crypto-map entry.

✦ The `show crypto ipsec sa` command displays the settings of the existing security associations.

✦ The `clear crypto sa` command clears the currently active IPSec SAs.

✦ The `debug crypto ipsec` command enables you to view the IPSec events.

Cisco Secure VPN Client

Cisco Secure VPN Client is a component of Cisco Secure VPN Software and serves to implement IPSec VPN solutions. By using Cisco Secure VPN Client, remote users can create secure and reliable tunnels to access data stored on the corporate network.

Tasks performed by Cisco Secure VPN Client

Cisco Secure VPN Client enables users to perform the following tasks.

✦ **Establish a security policy:** The users can use Cisco Secure VPN to establish a security policy directly from their desktop. The security policy defines how a network would be prevented from security breaches. It includes policies that define how the integrity of data would be maintained and what methods would be used to determine the identity of the users and to detect network intrusions.

For more about creating an effective security policy, see Chapter 1.

✦ **Use public/private key:** You can use IKE to configure Cisco Secure VPN Client to use public/private key system. A public/private key system is for encrypting and decrypting data traffic. This key system uses an encryption algorithm, such as 3DES and an encryption key, which the sender and the receiver use to communicate with each other.

For more information on encryption algorithms, refer to Chapter 7.

✦ **Use digital certificate:** You can configure Cisco Secure VPN Client with IPSec to use digital certificates. Created for authentication purposes, a *digital certificate* is an electronic file that contains the credentials of the user and is issued by a Certificate Authority (CA).

Features of Cisco Secure VPN Client

The features of Cisco Secure VPN Client are as follows:

✦ It is compatible with Windows-based communication devices, such as modems, LAN adapters, and comm port drivers.

✦ It supports IPSec.

✦ It supports DES, MD5, and SHA-1 algorithms.

✦ It is compatible with X.509 CAs, such as VeriSign Onsite and Windows 2000 Certificate Services.

✦ It provides a graphical user interface to configure security policy.

System requirements for installing Cisco Secure VPN Client

Apart from the features mentioned above, Cisco Secure VPN Client is easy to install. The following sections discuss the server-side and client-side system requirements for installing Cisco Secure VPN Client.

Server-side system requirements

The server-side requirements to install Cisco router for interoperability with Cisco Secure VPN Client are as follows:

✦ A Cisco router that matches your network's needs:

- Cisco 1700 series routers are recommended for small networks.
- Cisco 2600 or 3600 series routers are recommended for medium-sized networks.
- Cisco 7100 VPN routers are recommended for large networks.

✦ Cisco IOS IPSec software. The specific Cisco IOS IPSec software image to use depends on the router you choose:

- For Cisco 1700 series router and Cisco 7100 VPN router, use Cisco IOS software image from Cisco IOS Release 12.0(4)XE or later. You can also use Cisco IOS Release 12.0(5)T.
- For other Cisco routers, such as 2600 and 3600 series, use Cisco IOS Release 12.0(5)T.

Client-side system requirements

The client-side requirements for installing and operating Cisco Secure VPN Client are as follows:

✦ Windows 95, 98, or Windows NT 4.0 operating system. If the operating system is Windows NT, also apply Service Pack 3 or above.

✦ Pentium processor

✦ Minimum 9MB of available hard disk space

✦ Minimum 16MB RAM for Windows 95 and minimum 32MB RAM for Windows 98 or Windows NT

✦ CD-ROM drive

✦ Cisco IOS Release 12.0(4)XE or later release

✦ TCP/IP protocol should be enabled on the computer

✦ Modem for dial-up connection

✦ Ethernet

✦ Interoperability

Cisco Secure VPN Client is interoperable with all Cisco routers that support IPSec. The following Cisco router models support IPSec:

✦ Cisco AS5300 universal access

✦ Cisco 1600 series

✦ Cisco 1740 series

✦ Cisco 2500 series

✦ Cisco 2600 series

✦ Cisco 3600 series

✦ Cisco 4000 series

✦ Cisco 7100 series

✦ Cisco 7200 series

✦ Cisco 7500 series

However, Cisco recommends the use of the following VPN-based routers when setting up Cisco Secure VPN Client:

✦ Cisco 17200 VPN routers for small offices

✦ Cisco 2600 or Cisco 3600 series routers for medium-size organizations

✦ Cisco 7100 VPN routers for large organizations

Cisco supports the following configurations to ensure interoperability between Cisco Secure VPN Client and Cisco routers:

✦ Static or dynamic client IP addresses with pre-shared keys

✦ Static or dynamic client IP addresses with digital certificates

You can enable a router to dynamically allocate IP addresses to clients by configuring IKE mode configuration before establishing the IPSec tunnel. After configuring IKE mode, the peers are authenticated by using pre-shared keys or digital certificates to establish tunnels.

IKE mode configuration is also known as dynamic IP addressing. Dynamic IP address refers to a temporary address assigned during the log in session and is returned to the address pool at the end of the session. Dynamic IP addressing occurs between IKE Phase 1 and IKE Phase 2 and is initiated by the gateway. The gateway assigns a dynamic address to the VPN client.

The following sections discuss these configurations.

Static or dynamic client IP addresses with pre-shared keys

You can generate pre-shared keys by using pre-defined, static IP addresses for Cisco Secure VPN Client. This configuration is recommended for small networks that have up to 10 clients.

 Note   Although pre-shared keys are easy to implement, they are not scalable.

The advantages of using pre-shared keys are as follows:

✦ Pre-shared keys are easy to implement.

✦ Implementation of pre-shared keys does not require the services of a CA for security.

The disadvantage of using pre-shared keys is that the network is less scalable, as the router must be reconfigured whenever a new client is added.

Static IP addressing is also known as Manual configuration. The tasks involved in configuring static IP addressing between a VPN client and Cisco routers are as follows:

1. Specifying an internal network address on the VPN client

2. Configuring a new gateway for a security policy

3. Specifying the VPN client's identity

The following sections discuss these tasks.

Specifying an internal network address on the VPN client

To specify an internal network address on the VPN client, follow these steps:

1. Click Start ➪ Programs ➪ Cisco Secure VPN Client ➪ Security Policy Editor to open the Security Policy Editor.

2. From the Options menu, click Global Policy Settings to open the Global Policy Settings window.

3. Select the Enable to Specify Internal Network Address check box. Click OK. The Network Security Policy window opens. Under My Identity, in the Internal Network IP Address box, specify the IP address.

Configuring a new gateway for a security policy

To configure a new gateway for a security policy, follow these steps:

1. In the left pane of the Security Policy Editor window, click Other Connections.

2. From the File menu, select New Connection.

   In the left pane of the Security Policy Editor window, the default New Connection placeholder appears.

3. Rename New Connection with a name appropriate for your network.

4. In the left pane of the Security Policy Editor window, click the new connection that you have created.

   The new connection pane appears.

5. In the right pane under Connection Security, click Secure.

6. In the right pane, under Remote Party Identity and Addressing, choose IP Subnet from the ID Type list.

7. Under Remote Party Identity and Addressing, in the Subnet box, enter the IP address of your subnet.

8. Under Remote Party Identity and Addressing, in the Mask box, enter the subnet mask of the IP address of your network.

9. From the Protocol list, select All.

10. Select the Connection using Secure Gateway Tunnel check box.

11. In the ID_Type list, click IP Address.

12. In the ID_Type box, enter the IP address of the secure gateway.

Specifying the VPN client's identity

To specify the identity of a VPN client, follow these steps:

1. In the left pane of the Security Policy Editor window, double-click the new connection that you have created.

   The new connection expands, and My Identity and Security Policy appear.

2. Click My Identity.

3. In the right pane under My Identity, from the ID_Type list, select IP Address.

4. In the Internal Network IP Address box, enter the VPN Client static IP address.

5. In the Port list, click All.

6. From the Name list, select Any.

7. Click Pre-Shared Key and enter the key that would be used during the authentication phase.

Static or dynamic client IP addresses with digital certificates

You can request a CA to issue a digital certificate by using Cisco Secure VPN Client with pre-defined IP addresses. As compared to the static or dynamic client IP addresses with pre-shared keys configuration, this configuration can be used for larger networks. In addition, digital certificates can be scaled to meet your requirements.

Note   You can support Cisco Secure VPN Client with Cisco routers that use digital certificates issued by VeriSign and Entrust.

The advantages of using digital certificates are as follows:

✦ The network is scalable (whereas pre-shared keys are not) and new clients can be easily configured.

✦ Digital certificates provide better authentication for each device.

The disadvantage of this configuration is that the organizations have to purchase digital certificates from a CA.

Cisco Secure VPN Client software is available in a CD. To install Cisco Secure VPN Client software on a computer, insert this CD in the CD-ROM drive. The installation wizard starts and guides you through the installation process. After you have installed Cisco Secure VPN Client on a computer, the Cisco Secure VPN Client starts automatically each time you start the computer.

Summary

This chapter examined the standard methods of securing virtual private networks with technologies such as PPTP, L2TP, and IPSec. Chief among these is IPSec; the chapter outlined the steps involved in configuring it: planning for implementation, configuring IKE, configuring IPSec itself, and verifying the configuration. The chapter also described Cisco Secure VPN Client, an integral part of Cisco Secure VPN Software.

✦　　✦　　✦

Cisco Technologies and Security Products

P art VI provides a closer look at Cisco technologies and Cisco security products. It describes Cisco IOS IPSec, an internetworking system that uses a secure version of Internet Protocol. A summary of various Cisco network-security tools — including firewalls and VPN-management products — describes the features and components of CiscoWorks 2000 ACL, Cisco PIX Firewall Manager, VPN/Security Management Solution, and Cisco Secure Policy Manager.

Cisco IOS IPSec

IPSec uses several technologies to ensure the authenticity, confidentiality, and integrity of data transmitted over open (insecure) networks such as the Internet. In particular, IPSec uses Internet Key Exchange (IKE), RSA security, Triple digital-encryption Standard (3DES), authentication header (AH), and Encapsulated Security Payload (ESP) to accomplish its mission.

This chapter outlines the process of configuring Cisco IOS by using pre-shared keys and RSA-encryption nonces. Familiarity with this process is especially useful if you plan to expand the scope of your Cisco VPN.

◆ ◆ ◆ ◆

In This Chapter

Understanding the use of pre-shared keys in Cisco IOS IPSec configuration

Using RSA-encryption nonces in Cisco IOS IPSec configuration

Expanding the scope of a Cisco VPN

◆ ◆ ◆ ◆

Configuring Cisco IPSec by Using Pre-shared Keys

To enable authentication on Cisco routers, you can configure Cisco IOS by using pre-shared keys. A router configured for authentication can act as an IPSec gateway and can manage and monitor the flow of traffic to and from a network. Enabling authentication on Cisco IPSec by using pre-shared keys is a four-stage process:

   ◆ Planning for implementing IPSec

   ◆ Configuring IKE

   ◆ Configuring IPSec

   ◆ Verifying IPSec configuration

Upcoming sections discuss each of these stages.

Planning for implementing IPSec

Before configuring IPSec on a router, first of all have a well-defined IPSec security policy, which is in sync with your overall organization's security policy. This calls for some planning before actually getting on with the task of configuring each router. Your plans can include the following steps:

1. Determining an IKE policy between IPSec peers on the basis of their location and number.

2. Determining an IPSec policy, which includes details of IPSec peers such as IP addresses and IPSec modes.

3. Verify the current configuration of each router. To do so, you can use various show commands such as `show crypto map` or `show crypto isakmp policy`.

4. Verify whether unencrypted traffic can pass through the network or not. In effect, ensure that the network is working even without any encryption. You can use the `ping` command to check whether the network is working or not.

5. Verify whether IPSec traffic is permitted to pass through access lists that have been created for filtering data packets.

Configuring IKE

After you have planned for IPSec, configure Internet Key Exchange (IKE). Follow these steps to configure IKE:

1. **Enabling or disabling IKE:** To globally enable IKE, issue the `crypto isakmp enable` command. By default, IKE is always globally enabled for all the interfaces of a router. If you run into situations for which IKE should be disabled (especially for those interfaces that never process IPSec traffic), you can do so by issuing the `no crypto isakmp enable` command (or by using access-list statements to block UDP port 500 on the interfaces).

2. **Formulating IKE policies:** After you have enabled IKE, formulate IKE policies for establishing IKE between IPSec peers. An IKE policy specifies some parameters used while an IKE session is established between two IPSec peers. Some parameters defined by an IKE policy are

   • Message-encryption algorithms such as DES

   • Peer-authentication methods such as pre-shared keys

   • Message-integrity algorithms such as MD5

   • IP addresses of IPSec peer machines

   • Lifetime of an established SA

   • Internet Security Association and Key Management Protocol (ISAKMP)

   • Parameters of key exchange (Diffie-Hellman group identifiers) such as 768-bit Diffie-Hellman group 1

The first step in defining an IKE policy is to issue the `crypto isakmp policy` command, including an appropriate `priority` value to reflect the assigned priority and identify the IKE policy uniquely. The priority value can be any integer from 1 to 10,000, where 1 is the highest priority and 10,000 the lowest priority. The syntax for the command is

```
crypto isakmp policy priority
```

Issuing the `crypto isakmp policy` command sets up the command mode for IKE configuration. In `config-isakmp` mode, you can use the keywords described in Table 14-1 to specify parameters in your `isakmp` policy.

Table 14-1
ISAKMP Policy Parameters

Keyword	Default Values	Range of Values Accepted	Description
des	des	56-bit DES-CBC	A message-encryption algorithm
sha	sha	SHA-1	A message-integrity algorithm
md5	sha	MD5	A message-integrity algorithm
rsa-sig	rsa-sig	RSA signatures	A method for peer authentication
rsa-encr	rsa-sig	RSA-encrypted nonces	A method for peer authentication
pre-share	rsa-sig	Pre-shared keys	A method for peer authentication
1	1	768- or 1024-bit Diffie-Hellman	A key-exchange parameter
2	1	768- or 1024-bit Diffie-Hellman	A key-exchange parameter
Lifetime seconds	86400	Any number	The lifetime of an SA established by an IKE
exit	(none)	(none)	Ends config-isakmp mode

Note   You can configure more than one IKE policy on each IPSec peer .

3. **Configuring pre-shared keys:** After you have formulated IKE policies, configure the pre-shared keys and, if necessary, invoke the IKE identity mode. You use the configuration command `crypto isakmp key` to configure a pre-shared authentication key. To delete a pre-shared authentication key, you use the `no crypto isakmp key`. The syntax for `crypto isakmp key` is as follows:

```
crypto isakmp key key-string address peer-address
crypto isakmp key key-string hostname peer-hostname
```

Table 14-2 describes the parameters in the code shown in Step 3.

Table 14-2
Crypto ISAKMP Key Command Parameters

Parameter	Description
key-string	This parameter indicates the pre-shared key. It can take any alphanumeric character up to 128 bytes. Both IPSec peers should have the same pre-shared key.
address	This parameter is used in case the IKE identity of the remote peer has been set with its IP address.
peer-address	This parameter indicates the IP address of the remote peer.
hostname	This parameter is used in case the remote IKE identity has been set with its host name.
peer-hostname	Indicates the remote peer's host name.

4. **Verifying IKE configuration:** To verify whether the policies have been configured correctly, use the `show crypto isakmp policy` command as demonstrated in the following example (the IKE policy for a router):

```
Router# show crypto isakmp policy
Protection suite of priority 50
encryption algorithm:      DES-Data Encryption Standard (50 bit
keys).
hash algorithm:            Message Digest 5
authentication method:     Pre-shared Key
Diffie-hellman group:      #1 (768 bit)
Lifetime:                  86400 seconds, no volume limit
Default protection suite
encryption algorithm:      DES-Data Encryption Standard (50 bit
keys).
hash algorithm:            Secure Hash Standard
authentication method:     Rivest-Shamir-Adleman Signature
Diffie-hellman group:      #1 (768 bit)
Lifetime:                  86400 seconds, no volume limit
```

Using transform sets while configuring IPSec

After you configure IKE, the next step is to configure IPSec, beginning with the *transform set*—a group of individual IPSec *transforms* (or generic cryptographic operations) that establish what happens to IPSec traffic (according to an established security policy). For example, in a security association between IPSec and IKE (during a transaction in the IKE Phase quick mode), IPSec peers agree upon a transform set for protecting data transmission.

Cross-Reference   For more information on using transform sets, refer to Chapter 13.

The IPSec default mode for each transform is tunnel mode. The following IPSec transforms are supported by Cisco IOS:

✦ ESP transforms are as follows:

  • esp-des: Makes use of DES cipher (56 bits).

  • esp-3des: Makes use of 3DES cipher (168 bits).

  • esp-md5-hmac: Provides data integrity to ESP packets. Makes use of esp-des or esp-3des transform and supports HMAC-MD5 authentication.

  • esp-sha-hmac: Provides data integrity to ESP packets. Makes use of esp-des or esp-3des transform and supports HMAC-SHA authentication.

  • esp-null: You can use this transform in conjunction with esp-md5-hmac or esp-sha-hmac for authenticating ESP without encryption. This transform does not have a cipher. This transform should not be used alone as it does not provide any security to the data transmission.

  • esp-rfc1829: This transform is mostly used with previously implemented IPSec.

✦ AH transforms are as follows:

  • ah-md5-hmac: Refers to the AH-HMAC-MD5 transform.

  • ah-sha-hmac: Refers to the AH-HMAC-SHA transform.

  • ah-rfc1828: This transform is mostly used with a previously implemented IPSec.

Tip   You can have no more than one AH transform and two ESP transforms in a transform set. If you try to specify more than one AH transform, the Cisco IOS command parser won't let you do so.

Changing transform sets

You can change a transform set by following these steps:

1. From the crypto map, delete the transform set.

2. From global configuration, delete the transform set.

3. Configure the transform set after making corrections to the transforms.

4. In the crypto map, allocate the transform set.

5. Empty the SA database.

Tip   You can also change the transform set by reentering the transform with new transforms.

Configuring lifetimes for global IPSec Security Associations

Renegotiate IPSec SAs as they have a fixed validity period or lifetime. For all crypto maps, Cisco IOS defines a global lifetime value. You can override this value by using the global configuration command `crypto ipsec security-association lifetime`. You can reset the default value by using the `no crypto ipsec security-association lifetime`. To ensure that no break occurs in data transmission, a new SA is negotiated before the expiry of the previous one.

The syntax for crypto ipsec security-association lifetime is

```
crypto ipsec security-association
lifetime {seconds seconds | kilobytes kilobytes}
```

Table 14-3 describes the parameters in the preceding code.

Table 14-3 Crypto IPSec Security-Association Lifetime Command Parameters	
Parameters	**Description**
`seconds seconds`	This gives the time (in seconds) after which an SA will expire. By default, this is 3600 seconds.
`kilobytes kilobytes`	This gives the amount of traffic (in kilobytes) transmitted between IPSec peers by using an SA during a lifetime of the SA. By default, this is 4,608,000KB.

Creating crypto access lists

You configure crypto access lists to define non-IPSec protected IP data. To create crypto access lists you should use IP extended lists. You can use crypto access lists to determine the data to be protected by IPSec. The syntax for creating crypto access lists is similar to the one that is for creating IP extended lists. The syntax is

```
access-list access-list-number {permit | deny} protocol
source source-wildcard destination destination-wildcard
[precedence precedence] [tos tos] [log]
```

Table 14-4 describes the parameters in the preceding code.

Table 14-4 Crypto Access Lists Command Parameters	
Parameter	**Description**
permit	This command specifies that all data packets that match with the conditions specified in the crypto access lists be encrypted.
deny	This command specifies that all data packets that match with the conditions specified in the crypto access list need not be encrypted.
source	This command specifies the hosts, networks, or subnets.
destination	This command specifies the hosts, networks, or subnets.
protocol	This command determines the type of IP packet to be encrypted.

The following functions are performed by crypto access lists:

✦ Determine the outbound data, which is to be IPSec secured.

✦ Select the IPSec secured data from the inbound data.

✦ Segregate and discard from the inbound data, the data that should have been IPSec secured.

Note   It is recommended that for IPSec usage, you configure symmetrical crypto access lists. The access list for outbound traffic should evaluate both the inbound and outbound data. The conditions in the access list apply to the outbound data in the forward direction while these conditions are in the reverse order for the inbound data. In addition, the same access list is for determining which inbound data packets need to be encrypted.

Creating crypto maps

Crypto maps help you create security associations for data to be encrypted. To configure, alter, or enter configuration mode of a crypto map, issue the global configuration command crypto map. To delete a crypto map entry you use the no crypto map command. Syntax for the crypto map command is

```
crypto map map-name seq-num cisco
crypto map map-name seq-name ipsec-manual
crypto map map-name seq-num ipsec-isakmp [dynamic dynamic-map-name]
no crypto map map-name [seq-num]
```

Table 14-5 describes the parameters in the preceding code.

Table 14-5
Crypto Map Command Parameter

Parameter	Description
cisco	This is a default value and shows the CET to be used in place of IPSec. This CET is specified in the new crypto map entry.
map-name	This gives the name of the crypto map set.
seq-num	This gives the number assigned to the crypto map entry. The sequence numbers for crypto maps that refer to dynamic maps should have lower-priority entries and thus should have highest sequence numbers.
ipsec-manual	This specifies that IPSec security associations will not be established by using IKE.
ipsec-isakmp	This specifies that IPSec security associations will be established by using IKE.
dynamic	This is an optional command and indicates that an already existing static crypto map is being referenced by this crypto map entry.
dynamic-map-name	This is also an optional command and shows the dynamic crypto map name to be used as the policy template.

As discussed earlier, the `crypto map` command also invokes the crypto map configuration mode. The crypto map configuration mode has the following command options:

```
match address [access-list-id |name]
set peer [hostname | ip-address]
set pfs [group1 | group2]
set security-association level per-host
set security-association lifetime {seconds seconds | kilobytes kilobytes}
set transform-set transform-set-time [transform-set-name2......transform-set-name6]
set session-key {inbound | outbound} ah| esp
exit
```

Table 14-6 describes the parameters in the preceding code.

Table 14-6
Crypto Map Configuration Mode Parameters

Parameter	Description
access-list-id | name	Specifies the extended access list that the crypto map uses.
hostname | ip-address	Indicates the IP address or host name of the permitted IPSec peer.
group1 | group2	Specifies the Diffie-Hellman group to be used when a new Diffie-Hellman exchange takes place. group1 indicates 768-bit Diffie-Hellman prime modulus group; group2 indicates 1024-bit Diffie-Hellman prime modulus group.
set security-association level per-host	Indicates that for every host pair of source and destination in a crypto access list, there should be a separate security association.
seconds seconds	Specifies the lifetime of a security association.
kilobytes kilobytes	Gives the amount of traffic (in kilobytes) transmitted between IPSec peers by using an SA during a lifetime of the SA.
transform-set-name [transform-set-name2...... transform-set-name6]	Indicates the available transform sets according to their priority. A maximum of six transform sets can be specified for an IPSec-ISAKMP or a dynamic crypto map entry. You should set lowest-priority numbers for your strongest transform sets.
set session-key {inbound | outbound} ah | esp	Enables you to manually set passwords for AH and ESP and also manually set SA parameters.
exit	Ends the crypto-map configuration-mode session.

Applying crypto maps to interfaces

To apply a crypto map to a router interface you use the crypto map (interface configuration) command. To remove the crypto map from the interface you use the no crypto map command. The syntax for crypto map (interface configuration) command is

```
crypto map map-name
```

In this command the map-name command parameter specifies the crypto map set. When you apply the crypto map, the SAs are invoked and are set up in the SA database. To view the SAs you can issue the command show crypto ipsec sa.

Verifying IPSec configuration

After you have configured IPSec you should verify its successful configuration. You can do so by using various Cisco IOS commands, such as show, clear, and debug. Because IKE was configured first, let's start by first verifying IKE configurations.

Verifying your IKE configuration

The following commands verify and test for a successful IKE configuration:

✦ show crypto isakmp policy: This command enables you to view IKE policy parameters. Consider this example:

```
Router# show crypto isakmp policy
Protection suite of priority 50
encryption algorithm:      DES-Data Encryption Standard (50
bit
keys).
hash algorithm:      Message Digest 5
authentication method:      Pre-shared Key
Diffie-hellman group:      #1 (768 bit)
Lifetime:      86400 seconds, no volume limit
Default protection suite
encryption algorithm:      DES-Data Encryption Standard (50 bit
keys).
hash algorithm:      Secure Hash Standard
authentication method:      Rivest-Shamir-Adleman Signature
Diffie-hellman group:      #1 (768 bit)
Lifetime:      86400 seconds, no volume limit
```

✦ show crypto isakmp sa: This command enables you to examine all current IKE SAs at a peer. Consider this example:

```
Router# show crypto isakmp sa
Dst      src      state      conn-id      slot
172.17.49.243      172.17.50.243      QM_IDLE      42      0
```

✦ clear crypto isakmp: This command enables you to clear IKE active connections. The syntax for this command is

```
clear crypto isakmp [connection-id]
```

The connection-id parameter indicates the connection to be clear. If the connection-id parameter is not specified, then all active connections are cleared. The following example shows the clear crypto isakmp command in action:

```
Router# show crypto isakmp sa
Dst      src      state      conn-id      slot
172.17.49.243      172.17.50.243      QM_IDLE      42      0
Router# clear crypto isakmp 42
2w4d: ISADB: reaper checking SA,
Router# show crypto isakmp sa
Dst      src      state      conn-id      slot
```

Verifying your IPSec configuration

To test and verify successful IPSec configuration, you can use the following commands:

✦ show crypto ipsec transform-set: To examine transform sets you issue the show crypto IPSec transform-set command. The syntax for this command is

```
show crypto ipsec transform-set [tag transform-set-name]
```

The tag transform-set-name is an optional command parameter that displays only those transform sets that have specified names.

✦ show crypto map: To examine the configuration of the crypto map you issue the show crypto map command. The syntax for this command is

```
show crypto map [interface interface | tag map-name]
```

Table 14-7 describes the parameters in the preceding code.

Table 14-7
Show Crypto Map Command Parameters

Parameter	Description
interface interface	Shows only the crypto map set which has been applied to the specified interface
tag map-name	Shows only the crypto map set whose name has been specified

✦ show crypto ipsec sa: This command displays the current SA's configuration settings. The syntax for this command is

```
show crypto ipsec sa [map map-name | address | identity]
[detail]
```

Table 14-8 describes the parameters in the preceding code.

Table 14-8
Show Crypto IPSec SA Command Parameters

Parameter	Description
map map-name	Shows all SAs configured for the crypto map
address	Displays all sorted SAs, first by destination address and then by protocol
identity	Displays only the information relating to the information flow
detail	Displays the details of information gathered by error counters

✦ `show crypto ipsec security-association lifetime`: This shows the lifetime of a security association, which is associated with a specific crypto map entry.

✦ `debug crypto ipsec`: This command shows all the events of IPSec. You can issue the `no debug crypto ipsec` command to disable the debug output option.

✦ `clear crypto sa`: This command clears the security associations of IPSec. The syntax for this command is

```
clear crypto sa peer {ip-address | peer-name}
clear crypto sa map map-name
clear crypto sa entry destination-address protocol spi
clear crypto sa counters
```

Table 14-9 describes the parameters in the preceding code.

Table 14-9
Clear Crypto SA Command Parameters

Parameter	Description
ip-address	The IP address of the remote IPSec peer
peer-name	The name of the remote IPSec peer as a fully qualified domain name
map-name	The crypto map set's name
destination-address	The peer's (or remote peer's) IP address
protocol	The protocol (either AH or ESP)
spi	The Security Parameter Index (SPI)

You can also configure Cisco IOS IPSec for authentication by using RSA-encryption nonces. The following section discusses Configuring Cisco IOS IPSec by using RSA-Encryption Nonces in detail.

Configuring Cisco IOS IPSec by Using RSA-Encryption Nonces

You can use RSA nonces to authenticate IPSec peers and the Diffie-Hellman key exchange. Configuring Cisco IOS for RSA (actually similar to configuring Cisco IOS by using pre-shared keys) entails five steps:

1. Planning for IPSec
2. Configuring IPSec

3. Configuring IKE for RSA-encrypted nonces

4. Configuring IPSec

5. Verifying IPSec configuration

The following sections discuss the first three of these steps in detail.

Note   The last two of the five steps (configuring IPSec and verifying its configuration) are identical to those you would use to configure Cisco IOS with pre-shared keys.

Preparing for IPSec

The first step before using RSA encryption is to prepare for IPSec. This step involves specifying a security policy for using RSA encryption. To prepare an IPSec policy tailored to RSA encryption, follow these general steps:

1. **Determine methods for distributing RSA public keys:** Determine the methods for distributing RSA public keys on the basis of the location and number of IPSec peers. RSA encryption is used when the IPSec peers are not large in number and RSA public key can be distributed out-of-band.

2. **Determine the method of authentication:** Based on your requirements, you can select a strong encryption method such as RSA encryption. RSA encryption provides more powerful encryption than pre-shared keys.

3. **Determine IKE policies:** For RSA encryption, host names form the basis for IKE identity. Specify an IKE policy for each peer that identifies its host names and fully qualified domain name.

4. **Verifying RSA public key configuration:** Verify the configuration of the RSA public key for your router and peer routers.

Configuring RSA encryption

Configuring RSA encryption is a five-step process, involving the following tasks:

1. **Planning for RSA keys:** Planning for RSA involves the following steps:
   - Specify which IPSec peers will use RSA encryption.
   - Specify the size of RSA key modulus. It can be anywhere between 360 and 2048 bits.
   - Get the keystrings for RSA public keys

2. **Configuring domain name and host name of the router:** As discussed, domain and host names form the basis for IKE identity. RSA uses this IKE identity and the nonce value for encryption. You can issue the `hostname name` command to specify a host name for the router. Similarly, to specify the default domain name, issue the `ip domain-name name` command. (You can use the `no ip domain-name name` command to disable DNS usage.)

3. **Generating RSA keys:** To generate RSA keys you can issue the command `crypto key generate rsa [usage-keys]`. RSA provides you with two types of keys, namely special-usage keys and general-purpose keys. The special-usage key generation results in the creation of two key pairs, of which the first key pair is used when the authentication method specified in the IKE policy is RSA signatures and the second key pair is used when the authentication method specified in the IKE policy is RSA-encrypted nonces. On the other hand, general-purpose key generation involves only one key pair, which can be used with any authentication method that the IKE policy specifies. You can issue the `crypto key generate rsa [usage-keys]` command to view the RSA keys you generated.

4. **Entering RSA public keys of the peers:** To enter RSA public keys of the peers follow these steps:

   a. Issue the command `crypto key pubkey-chain rsa` to enter public-key configuration mode and invoke the `config-pubkey-chain` mode. The configuration mode enables you to specify the RSA public keys of the peers. In addition, indicate whether the RSA public key is a named key or an addresses key. When the IKE identity of the remote peer is its host name, then you use the named-key command. If the IKE identity of the remote peer is its IP address, then you use the addressed-key command. The syntax for named-key command is

      `named-key key-name [encryption | signature]`

      The syntax for addressed-key command is

      `addressed-key key-address [encryption | signature]`

   b. Issue the command `key-string` to invoke config-pubkey-mode. This mode enables you to specify the remote peer's RSA public key. Enter the RSA public-key string of the peer. Exit the config-pubkey-mode mode to return to the `config-pubkey-chain-mode`.

   c. Exit the `config-pubkey-chain-mode` after you have specified the RSA public keys for all IPSec peers whose authentication mode in the IKE policy is RSA-encrypted nonces.

   d. Press Ctrl+Z to return to the global configuration mode.

Tip   You can issue the show crypto key *pubkey-chain* rsa [name *key-name* | address *key-address*] command to view all the RSA public keys.

5. **Deleting RSA keys:** You can use the global configuration command `crypto key zeroize rsa` to erase all the RSA keys of your router.

Configuring IKE for RSA-encrypted nonces

To configure IKE for RSA-encrypted nonces, you issue the command `crypto isakmp policy` to choose RSA encryption as the method of authentication. This command invokes the `config-isakmp` model; while in that mode, you specify RSA encryption. The following code snippet illustrates this process:

```
Router(config)# crypto isakmp policy 50
Router (config-isakmp)# authentication rsa-encr
Router (config-isakmp)# exit
```

In the crypto policy, this specification would be displayed as follows:

```
Router# show crypto isakmp policy
Protection suite of priority 50
encryption algorithm: DES-Data Encryption Standard (50 bit
keys).
hash algorithm:     Message Digest 5
authentication method:    Rivset-Shamir-Adleman Encryption
Diffie-Hellman group:    #1 (768 bit)
Lifetime:    86400 seconds, no volume limit
```

In addition to configuring Cisco IOS IPSec for authentication, you can also use various features of Cisco IOS IPSec to expand the scope of your Cisco VPN, as detailed next.

Expanding the Scope of Cisco VPNs

You can create remote access VPNs by using various features of IPSec, such as IKE mode configuration, dynamic crypto map, and IPSec extended configuration. In addition to creating remote access VPNs, you can create site-to-site VPNs that offer greater scalability features. The following section discusses how you can use the various IPSec features to create remote access VPNs.

Using dynamic crypto maps

Dynamic crypto maps are only supported by IKE. You can use these in situations where the IPSec peers cannot be determined beforehand and who obtain their assigned IP addresses dynamically.

A dynamic crypto map entry is similar to a crypto map entry except that in a dynamic crypto map entry all the parameters are not configured. The parameters are configured dynamically after an IPSec negotiation takes place.

Configuring a dynamic crypto map for a router

You can configure a dynamic crypto map for a router by following these steps:

1. Invoke the `config-dynamic-crypto-map` mode by issuing the `crypto dynamic-map` command.

2. Set the parameters for the dynamic crypto map. To do so, issue the `set transform-set` command for each entry in the dynamic crypto map.

3. Use the command `crypto map map-name seq-num ipsec-isakmp [dynamic dynamic-map-name]` to allocate the dynamic crypto map to a static crypto map.

4. Enter the interface configuration mode to assign the crypto map to an interface. In the interface mode, issue the command `crypto map map-name`.

Configuring a dynamic crypto map for a PIX Firewall

You can configure a dynamic crypto map for a PIX Firewall by following these steps:

1. Specify the transform sets permitted for the dynamic crypto map entry.

   For example, issue the command `crypto dynamic-map dynamic-map-name dynamic-seq-num set transform-set transform-set1, [transform-set name 9]`. In addition, you can use the set of `crypto dynamic map` commands to configure parameters such as `access list`, `IPSec lifetime`, and `PFS`.

2. Issue the command `crypto map map-name seq-num ipsec-isakmp dynamic dynamic-map-name` to assign the dynamic crypto map to a static crypto map set.

3. Issue the command `crypto map map-name interface interface-name` to assign the crypto map to an interface.

Implementing IKE Mode Configuration

By using the IKE Mode Configuration, a Cisco router or a PIX Firewall can download a network configuration, such as IP address, to a VPN client during an IKE negotiation. IKE mode configuration is of two types:

✦ **Client initiation:** The client invokes the gateway.

✦ **Gateway initiation:** The gateway invokes the client.

The upcoming section discusses configuring IKE mode config for a router and a PIX Firewall.

Configuring IKE mode config for a router

Follow these steps to configure IKE mode for a router:

1. Assign a pool of IP addresses to the VPN client; do so by issuing the following command:

   ```
   ip local pool pool-name start address end-address
   ```

2. Refer to the local address pool in the IKE policy by issuing the following command:

   ```
   crypto isakmp client configuration address-pool local pool-name
   ```

3. Invoke the `config-dynamic-crypto-map` mode and set the dynamic crypto map for IKE mode configuration; issue the following command:

   ```
   crypto dynamic-map dynamic-map-name dynamic-seq-num
   ```

4. Set the parameters for the dynamic crypto map.

5. Exit the `config-dynamic-crypto-map` mode.

6. Configure IKE mode configuration by issuing the following command:

   ```
   crypto map tag client-configuration address {initiate | respond}
   ```

7. Add the dynamic crypto map (with its configured IKE mode) to a global IPSec crypto map by issuing the following command:

   ```
   crypto map map-name seq-num ipsec-isakmp [dynamic dynamic-map-name]
   ```

8. Issue the `crypto map map-name` command to assign the crypto map to an interface.

Configuring IKE mode config for a router

Follow these steps to configure IKE mode for a PIX Firewall:

1. Assign a pool of IP addresses to the VPN client. To do so, issue the following command:

   ```
   ip local pool pool-name start address [end-address]
   ```

2. Refer to the local address pool in the IKE policy by issuing the following command:

   ```
   crypto isakmp client configuration address-pool local pool-name [interface-name]
   ```

3. Set dynamic crypto map for IKE mode config by issuing the following command:

   ```
   crypto dynamic-map dynamic-map-name dynamic-seq-num
   ```

4. Configure a dynamic crypto map by using the following command:

   ```
   crypto dynamic-map dynamic-map-name dynamic-seq-num set
   transform-set transform-set1, [transform-set name 9]
   ```

5. Specify the crypto maps that will configure clients; to do so, use the following command:

   ```
   crypto map map-name client-configuration address {initiate |
   respond}
   ```

6. Add the dynamic crypto map (with its configured IKE mod) to a global IPSec crypto map by issuing the following command:

   ```
   crypto map map-name seq-num ipsec-isakmp [dynamic
   dynamic-map-name]
   ```

7. Use the `crypto map map-name` command to assign the crypto map to an interface.

IPSec extended authentication on PIX Firewall

IPSec extended authentication enables IPSec VPNs to authenticate users by obtaining user information stored in remote security databases that run TACACS+ and RADIUS.

Only VPN clients support IPSec extended authentication. Configuring PIX Firewall for such authentication is the most effective implementation of this functionality. Before you do so, however, first configure IKE as outlined in the previous section of the chapter. After you have configured IKE, follow these steps:

1. Configure an AAA server by issuing the following command:

   ```
   aaa-server group_tag (if_name) host server_ip key
   ```

2. To invoke extended authentication, issue the command

   ```
   crypto map map-name client authentication aaa-group-tag.
   ```

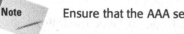 **Note** Ensure that the AAA server group tag is the same for Steps 1 and 2.

3. If PIX Firewall is already configured to use pre-shared keys or RSA signatures, set the remote IPSec clients to ignore the option of IPSec extended authentication.

   If it uses pre-shared keys, issue the following command:

   ```
   isakmp key keystring address ip-address [no-xauth].
   ```

   If it uses RSA signatures, issue this command instead:

   ```
   isakmp peer fqdn fqdn [no-xauth]
   ```

Configuring Tunnel Endpoint Discovery

Tunnel Endpoint Discovery (TED) enables IPSec sessions to be initiated between Cisco routers configured with dynamic crypto maps — and IPSec peers that are not preconfigured. To create a dynamic crypto map with configured TED, follow these steps:

1. Invoke the `config-dynamic-crypto-map` mode and configure a dynamic crypto map; issue the following command:

   ```
   crypto dynamic-map map-name
   ```

2. Set parameters for the dynamic crypto map; then define the transform set and create an access list (which you can do by using the command `match address`).

3. Exit the `config-dynamic-crypto-map` mode.

4. Assign the dynamic crypto map to a static crypto map set. To do so, issue the following command:

   ```
   crypto map map-name seq-number ipsec-isakmp dynamic
   dynamic-map-name [discover]
   ```

   The `discover` keyword is what enables TED.

Summary

This chapter examined the use of pre-shared keys to configure Cisco IOS for authentication — a four-stage process (planning for IPSec, configuring IKE, configuring IPSec, and verifying IPSec configuration). In addition, it introduced RSA-encryption nonces as a means of authenticating IPSec peers:

1. Planning for IPSec

2. Configuring IPSec

3. Configuring IKE for RSA-encrypted nonces

4. Configuring IPSec

5. Verifying IPSec configuration

The chapter also described the Diffie-Hellman key exchange and the use of IPSec features (such as IKE mode configuration, dynamic crypto maps, and IPSec extended configuration) to create remote-access VPNs. One further method, Tunnel Endpoint Discovery (TED), enables IPSec sessions to occur between Cisco routers that have been configured with dynamic crypto maps (as well as between IPSec peers that have not been preconfigured).

✦   ✦   ✦

Cisco's Network-Security Management Products

Cisco ACL Manager (Cisco Access-Control List Manager) is an add-on application that provides a consistent Web interface for the applications that govern access rights to the Cisco devices in an enterprise-scale network environment. ACL Manager reduces the time required to create new filters. It is also used for maintaining existing filters in Cisco devices.

Note In the context of ACL Manager, the terms *access-control list* and *ACL* are exactly equivalent to *access list* as used throughout this book.

This chapter describes three Cisco security products that any network administrator who runs a Cisco-compliant network should know about: CiscoWorks2000 ACL Manager, Cisco Secure Policy Manager, and Cisco Secure Access Control Server (ACS).

CiscoWorks2000 ACL Manager

As a component of the CW2000 Routed WAN Management solution, CiscoWorks2000 ACL Manager should be installed on the same computer as the Resource Manager Essentials when you set up Routed WAN solution. You can define the ACL Manager on Cisco devices and can configure it to recognize any access list that a user can view and/or modify.

The ACL Manager serves to set up and manage IP and IPX filtering and device access control. It uses the role-based security implemented in the CiscoWorks2000 server. One of its available security tools is a range of predefined roles that the administrator can assign in an ACL Manager application. For example, a help-desk user can view the access list but cannot modify it, whereas an administrator can view the access list as well as modify it.

The ACL Manager is a multiuser application. However, there might be a situation where many users are running the ACL Manager at the same time; all of them use the same device for changing access lists. Consider a situation where the first user who makes changes to the Cisco device invalidates the changes made by other users. To validate their respective changes, other users would need to refresh the Cisco device and make changes once again. A better policy would give multiple users access the ACL Manager only when they need to view the access lists — and not allow them to make any modifications to it.

An administrator can use the ACL Manager to identify all the changes made by users. The ACL Manager ensures that the deployment of ACL filters is accurate and consistent. (An access list implemented on a router to filter data packets is known as an *ACL filter*.) ACL Manager helps to remove redundant entries in the access list. In addition, the ACL Manager also helps to consolidate and merge the access-list entries. This reduces the device-search processor cycle and increases the speed of packet forwarding.

The ACL Manager establishes a link with the CiscoWorks2000 Management Server security system (a member of CiscoWorks2000 family of products). CiscoWorks2000 Management Server enables the administrator to control user access to ACL Manager tools.

The ACL Manager provides various access list management tools, which help monitoring of devices, traffic, and response time. It also provides other features related to WAN. Therefore, the ACL Manager solution is complementary to the Routed WAN Management solution.

Features of ACL Manager

ACL Manager provides the following features:

✦ It is used along with the Web-based CiscoWorks2000 desktop, which includes a GUI, easier navigation among access lists, and printing. It also helps make backups of ACLM data.

✦ It contains the ACL Use Wizard, which helps in uniform implementation of access lists.

✦ It contains interfaces that can be used for implementing an access list.

✦ It provides facilities for managing the network to maintain scalability and increase efficiency.

✦ It contains a downloadable component that can be used to download any ACL changes uniformly.

✦ It consists of a Template Manager that helps to filter policies.

✦ It contains a component called a DiffViewer, which helps review and recognize the changes made to access lists.

✦ It helps reduce the size of the access list and improve the performance of the devices.

✦ It provides the facility to graphically create, modify, and manipulate access lists for Cisco devices.

✦ It provides the facility of printing access lists, ACEs, and optimization details to the client's printer.

✦ It uses integrated CiscoWorks2000 backup tasks,with which users can make a backup of ACL Manager data.

✦ It supports the system's clipboard; users can cut, copy, and paste data to or from any ACL Manager browser field and those in other applications.

ACL Manager provides a Cisco device with features, which help in maintaining IOS devices. The device model retrieves the configuration files from the Config Archive and filters the important information. ACL Manager consists of a GUI combined with the Essentials front-end. You can create, view, and edit the access lists by using this interface. The interface appears in the form of a tree having panels. The network devices are represented in its left pane. When a node in the left pane is selected, the contents and features of the selected node appear in the right pane.

Tools of ACL Manager

ACL Manager offers the following tools:

✦ **Class Manager:** Enables you to create and modify services, networks, service classes, and network classes.

✦ **Template Manager:** Enables you to create and modify the ACL templates.

✦ **ACL Use Wizard:** Enables you to choose a use type (such as line access or packet filtering), device(s), a template to apply to the device(s), and an interface.

✦ **ACL Optimizer:** Examines the access list to see whether creating or modifying an access list has also optimized it.

✦ **Diff Viewer:** Shows any modifications made to the configuration while creating the scenario.

✦ **Downloader:** Enables an administrator to set up network update tasks.

✦ **Job Browser:** Shows the status of the downloaded tasks.

✦ **Hits Optimizer:** Allows reordering the access-control entries (ACEs). An ACE is an ordered list of fields that is checked against the contents of each data packet. Each ACE also has an associated action that explains the steps to be performed when a match between the packet contents and the ACE is found.

The following sections discuss each of these tools in more detail.

Class Manager

The Class Manager provides information regarding networks, services, service classes, and network classes. These classes are used to define templates, which filter policies, and define access lists.

Class Manager maintains the consistency and accuracy of an access list. Any changes made to an ACL are uniformly applied across the network, which increases the productivity of the ACL. For example, to provide access to a new file server, the administrator just needs to update the file server class, and the ACL Manager automatically updates the access list containing the specified class. The Class Manager defines the network, which contains the IP address, the network mask, and its subnets.

A list of host addresses, host address ranges, or networks is known as a *network class*. For example, a class called data server might contain all the information about the data servers existing on a network. The scope of such a class can be further expanded during the creation of an access list for a specific device. While creating filter policies for particular access lists, an administrator can use these classes instead of using network or user addresses. This is an advantage when an administrator adds or removes users — the administrator only needs to make changes to the appropriate class and the ACL Manager replicates the changes.

The ACL Manager contains not only a list of known TCP and UDP ports (also called services), but also the new TCP and UDP services. These new services are added to the list when they are implemented in the network. To simplify the process of configuring access lists, users can create service classes. These classes consist of standards or ranges of TCP or UDP ports that a user defines. These standards help in reducing the time taken to define individual ACL entries for certain services. The service class can be used by an ACL administrator to grant or refuse access to specific users based on the application mentioned in the service class.

The benefits of Class Manager include

✦ Minimizing the time taken to make ACL changes

✦ Minimizing the time taken to implement new access lists

✦ Improving the consistency of ACL usage in a network

Template Manager

The Template Manager serves to create ACL templates, which help improve the performance of the network. These templates include classes that help increase the accuracy and maintain the consistency of an access list after implementing changes. Any change in filtering policy requires the network administrator to modify these templates. The ACL Manager informs the network administrator of any changes made to the template—and whether the change affects any devices.

The benefits of the Template Manager include

✦ Helping to minimize the time required to implement changes in access lists

✦ Minimizing the time taken in identifying the devices affected when ACL filtering policies change

✦ Improving the consistency of ACL usage in a network

ACL Use Wizard

The ACL Use Wizard serves to apply certain templates to the network. You can apply a single template to multiple devices by selecting all the devices simultaneously. The administrator can either choose a single interface or multiple interfaces. In the case of a single interface, the template is applied to a single device; within multiple interfaces, the same template is applied to all devices that support the interfaces.

Because ACL Use Wizard applies specific templates to the entire network, it minimizes the time required to deploy access lists to multiple devices.

ACL Optimizer

ACL Optimizer shows an exhaustive report of optimizations made to the access list. The ACL Optimizer consists of three levels of optimization that help in these tasks:

✦ Keeping track of frequently used ACL entries

✦ Minimizing redundancy in ACL entries over a period of time

✦ Converting network and port addresses to ranges wherever the Cisco software provides this facility

ACL Optimizer benefits the network by enhancing device performance in two ways:

✦ It reduces the number of ACL entries that a device has to process.

✦ It gives ACL entries in an efficient order.

Diff Viewer

The Diff Viewer allows an administrator to inspect the changes before they are actually implemented on the network. The navigation interface of the viewer is the same as that of the tool used to author access lists; it displays only the interfaces, ACLs, and devices that have changed.

Downloader

The downloader helps a network administrator in updating ACL changes on the network. The administrator can also save the changes and job processing. An administrator can also use the Downloader to specify job-control features — and then can use them for recovery in the event of job failure.

Job Browser

The Job Browser provides information on the job status. It also displays all scheduled jobs along with their details (such as description, time at which the job was scheduled, status, the name of the user who created the job, and the name of the approver who approved — or has to approve — the job).

Hits Optimizer

The Hits Optimizer orders ACEs by number of hits. ACEs that are hit more are arranged above the ones that are hit less. A *hit* occurs when an access-control entry matches the contents of a packet.

Benefits of ACL Manager

If the number of routers increases, their configurations also become more complex. As a result, configuration problems become harder to detect and avoid. The ACL Manager provides solutions to these problems by using the inventory and making changes to audit features.

    Inventory is a list of all devices in a Resource Manager Essentials database.

ACL Manager has the following benefits:

✦ Minimizes the cost of installation

✦ Is user-friendly and increases productivity

✦ Provides an interface that makes differences of access-list features transparent to the users

✦ Minimizes the time taken for configuring routers

✦ Can be implemented on most of the operating-system platforms, such as Windows NT, HP UX, Solaris, and AIX

✦ Uses features, such as inventory, transport facilities, Config Archive, and Change Audit Service

✦ Assists automatic deployment of access lists

✦ Provides support to use ACL features used in IOS

✦ Minimizes time required to implement access lists on multiple devices

✦ Helps create templates for developing policies to standardize the use of access lists

✦ Helps users implement complex access lists by using templates

✦ Increases network output by optimizing access lists

✦ Uses classes to reduce errors that can appear due to multiple ACEs

✦ Provides a clipboard facility, which simplifies entering the ACL configuration on many devices

✦ Enhances the productivity of the administrator

✦ Saves information regarding comments and templates

✦ Minimizes time required to solve ACL problems

✦ Can be used along with other products used in a Routed WAN

Tasks performed by ACL Manager

The ACL Manager needs certain rights to perform tasks. The network administrator assigns these rights depending on the task that must be performed by each user. In most cases, users who have the access rights of a network administrator or network operator can perform the ACL Manager tasks. The essential navigation tree lists the tasks that each user can perform.

Network operators can use ACL Manager for the following operations:

✦ Examining access lists

✦ Viewing and canceling downloaded jobs

✦ Creating and editing access lists

✦ Using ACL templates

A network administrator can use ACL Manager to perform the following tasks:

✦ All tasks performed by network operators

✦ Decide when to download changes and remove scenarios

✦ Change class definitions, modify ACL templates, and view downloaded jobs

System requirements for installing ACL Manager

ACL Manager can be installed on Windows 2000 Server, Windows NT, and Solaris. However, ACL Manager must be installed on a computer running Essentials Release 3.0 or later. The following sections discuss the system requirements for Windows 2000 Server, Windows NT, and Solaris.

Server requirements for Windows 2000 and Windows NT

The server requirements for installing ACL Manager on Windows 2000 Server and Windows NT are as follows:

✦ 450 MHz or faster Pentium III processor

✦ Minimum 128MB RAM

✦ Minimum 70MB of available hard drive space

✦ Service Pack 6 is required for Windows NT 4.0 Server and Workstation.

Server requirements for Solaris

Before installing ACL Manager for Solaris, ensure that the computer is running Solaris 2.6 or later. The server requirements for installing ACL Manager on Solaris are as follows:

✦ Minimum 128MB RAM

✦ Minimum 50MB of available hard drive space

Installing ACL Manager

As discussed earlier, you can install ACL Manager on Windows NT, Windows 2000 Server, or Solaris. The following sections discuss the installation procedure for Windows NT or Windows 2000 Server and Solaris.

Installing ACL Manager on Windows NT or Windows 2000 Server

Follow the steps given to install ACL Manager on Windows NT and Windows 2000 Server:

1. Close all applications and insert the CD into the CD-ROM drive.

2. Launch Windows Explorer and double-click the CD-ROM drive icon.

3. Double-click setup.exe to start the setup wizard.

4. Follow the instructions provided by the setup wizard to complete the installation.

5. After the installation is complete, remove the CD from the CD-ROM drive.

Installing ACL Manager on Windows NT or Windows 2000 Server

To install ACL Manager on a Solaris system, follow these steps:

1. Log in as root or enter su (and then the root password) at the command prompt to log in as the system superuser.

2. Insert the CD into the CD-ROM drive.

3. At the command prompt, type the following:

```
# cd/cdrom/cdrom0
# ./setup.sh
```

4. To accept the copyright terms, press **Y** and then press Return or Enter.

A message appears on the screen asking you to select the components that you want to install.

5. To install all components, type `all` and then press Enter.

6. After the installation is complete, remove the CD from the CD-ROM drive.

Devices supported by ACL Manager

The devices supported by ACL Manager include

✦ Cisco IOS routers

✦ Access servers

✦ Hubs

✦ Catalyst 6000 V.5.3

ACL Manager supports Cisco IOS release 10.3 through 12.1.

Cisco Secure Policy Manager

The *Cisco Secure Policy Manager* (CSPM) is a system that implements security based on policies applied to the Cisco Firewall Virtual Private Network, IP security, and Intrusion Detection system sensors. This helps the network administrator to explain, implement, and audit security policies for the VPN routers and the PIX Firewall.

This manager can be used for centralized management of defining, distributing, enforcing, and auditing security policies across the network. It provides an in-depth system for managing security on Cisco Security devices, such as Cisco IDS sensors. The Secure Policy Manager helps the administrator to create different policies for managing access to network resources. The Secure Policy Manager converts these policies into the corresponding configuration demands and allocates them to the network devices. Administrators use CSPM for auditing, for logging, and for analyzing events.

Since the Security Policy Manager has a graphical user interface, the administrator can graphically display security policies implemented on Cisco firewalls and VPN gateways. Due to centralized management, you save both the time and cost of securing each device individually. Besides this, CSPM also provides functions for monitoring events and Web-based reporting. It also simplifies the process of implementation of security products and services on Cisco networks.

Feature sets of CSPM

The feature sets of CSPM include CSPM GUI and Distributed CSPM server. Depending on the way the CSPM is installed, these feature sets might reside on the same host or multiple hosts. The following sections discuss these feature sets.

CSPM graphical user interface

The graphical user interface of Cisco Secure Policy Manager is user-friendly. It has the following components:

✦ **View pane:** This pane displays the security polices, configuration panels, message check for consistency—as well as summaries of security policies in a graphical form (based on the action currently being performed and the node selected in the Navigation pane).

✦ **Navigation pane:** This pane contains five tree-like shapes that display the network topologies and the other components of Cisco Security Policy Manager, such as summaries of security policies, templates of tunnels, network services, and administrator accounts. These "trees" can be expanded or collapsed based on your needs. You can do so by clicking on the plus or minus signs displayed along the side of the required branch. You can call up additional menus by right-clicking a node in the Navigation pane.

✦ **Navigation toolbar:** This toolbar serves to select the "tree" to be used or viewed in the Navigation pane. All the trees can also be selected and viewed simultaneously.

✦ **Status bar:** The Status bar appears at the bottom of the screen and displays information about objects and tool tips for menu items.

✦ **Main toolbar:** The main toolbar serves to access frequently used actions, such as saving, updating, or examining information. It also contains tools such as the Topology Wizard (only available in the main toolbar or from the list that appears when you right-click a node).

The CSPM GUI is included in the CSPM Server feature set. The CSPM Server feature set includes the following subsystems:

✦ **Database:** This subsystem stores the system configuration information and the audit information.

✦ **Generation:** This subsystem collects all intermediate device-specific polices. It also modifies addresses for NAT.

✦ **Reporting:** This subsystem generates scheduled reports. It also generates reports on demand.

Distributed CSPM server

The distributed CSPM server has a set of features that help in controlling and monitoring the managed devices. It enables you to offload processes to multiple servers.

This feature set includes CSPM GUI feature set and exchanges the audit and status with the CSPM server.

Versions of Cisco Secure Policy Manager

The following versions of Cisco Secure Policy Manager are available:

✦ CSPM Version 3.0

✦ CSPM Version 2.3f

✦ CSPM Version 2.3i

✦ CSPM Version 2.2

✦ CSPM Version 2.1

✦ CSPM Version 2.0

 Note The basic features of CSPM remain the same in each version.

You can upgrade CSPM from one release to another. However, you cannot upgrade between *i* and *f* versions because they are incompatible. You should keep the following points in mind when upgrading from one version to another:

✦ Backup the database before performing the upgrade.

✦ Export a copy of your latest .CPM file.

✦ Upgrade the CSPM server before upgrading CSPM GUI or distributed system, when you are upgrading a client/server or a distributed server.

 Note To get detailed information on how to upgrade CSPM from one version to another, visit www.cisco.com.

Licensing options for CSPM

There are two licensing options available for Cisco Secure Policy Manager:

✦ **Evaluation license**: If you download CSPM, you obtain an evaluation license for CSPM. This license is valid for a time period of 90 days. After 90 days, you can upgrade the evaluation license to the permanent license by using the Update License command. The Update License command is available in the Help menu of CSPM GUI. To update the evaluation license, proceed as follows:

    1. Log in to the CSPM GUI as administrator with full-access privileges.

    2. Choose Help ➪ Product Updates ➪ Update License to open the Update Product License dialog box.

    3. In the License filename and path box, enter the filename and the path of the license.

4. In the Password box, enter the password that you want to specify for the license.

5. Click OK to update the product license and close the Update Product License dialog box.

✦ **Permanent license**: If you obtain CSPM on a CD-ROM, you get a permanent license disk for CSPM. During installation, provide the password for the license.

Features of CSPM

The features of Cisco Secure Policy Manager are as follows:

✦ It facilitates centralized management of Cisco firewalls.

✦ It facilitates creation of policies.

✦ It provides VPN tunnel templates.

✦ It supports offline configuration of security policies.

✦ It facilitates convenient configuration of NAT policies for firewalls.

✦ It enables role-based administration by providing three access levels.

✦ It has a built-in auditing and reporting system.

✦ It facilitates centralized management of Cisco VPN routers.

✦ It facilitates centralized management of Cisco IDS sensors.

✦ It enables automated configuration rollback.

✦ It is scalable and provides management support for up to 500 Cisco devices.

✦ It has a distributed architecture; supports intranet, extranet, and the Internet environment.

✦ It supports secure communications.

✦ It facilitates high-level policy definition and management.

✦ It ensures policy integrity and consistency before distributing a policy to the network.

Benefits of Cisco Secure Policy Manager

The benefits offered by Cisco Secure Policy Manager are the following:

✦ It enables convenient firewall and NAT management.

✦ It enables administrators to implement a real-time IDS; provides strong security against network intrusions.

✦ It simplifies the management of a VPN gateway by enabling centralized management of VPNs.

✦ It is scalable, which enables an organization to expand its network.

✦ It supports deployment of Cisco firewall and VPN routers on multiple topologies; enables flexible deployment over multiple topologies.

✦ It facilitates convenient management, which does not require technical expertise.

✦ It providers preestablished templates that contain common configuration.

✦ It ensures the integrity of the policies defined in the network and protects the network from security breaches.

✦ It enables network administrators to configure and verify security policies offline without connecting to the network.

✦ It provides templates that enable a network administrator to conveniently create policies.

✦ It provides updated information on network and system events.

✦ It enables network administrators to configure alarm notifications according to their requirements.

✦ It stores previous system configurations as a backup measure.

✦ It minimizes configuration and syntax errors in the network.

✦ It reduces the policy and configuration conflicts in a network.

✦ It enables a network administrator to assign different administrative access levels to different people in the IS department.

✦ It is convenient to manage, which reduces the dependency of the organization on technical experts.

Configuration tasks

Before you actually configure the Cisco Secure Policy Manager, some additional tasks (called *preconfiguration* tasks) are necessary:

1. **Defining network topology:** The first step is to define the network topology that you will use in the network topology tree. While doing so, you need not depict the entire network. Only those objects required for implementing security policies, should be depicted.

2. **Defining and applying network policy:** The second task is to define the network policy that allows services between two peers and contains features that help secure network sessions (such as Java blocking and tunneling). The Cisco Secure Policy Manager creates these rules.

3. Generating, verifying, and publishing commands: The final task is to create, verify, and publish commands generated by the Cisco Secure Policy Manager. They are then interpreted by the devices. The bases of these commands are the network topology, the organization, and the assigned security policies.

System requirements for installing CSPM

The system requirements for CSPM version 3.0 are as follows:

✦ Minimum 600MHz Pentium II processor

✦ Minimum 512MB RAM

✦ Minimum 4GB free hard disk space

✦ Video display with 1024 × 768 resolution and 64K color support

✦ CD-ROM disk drive

✦ Windows NT Server 4.0 with Service Pack 6a

Note The computer on which you would install CSPM should be partitioned using NTFS.

✦ Microsoft Internet Explorer 5.5

Note If it is installed in a client/server mode, the policy administrator GUI can also run on Windows 95, 98, 2000, or NT 4.0.

The software requirements for a target host are as follows:

✦ Microsoft Internet Explorer 5.5

✦ NTFS file partition

✦ TCP/IP protocol stack

✦ Microsoft XML Parser

Installing CSPM

You can install CSPM as one of the following:

✦ Standalone system

✦ Client/server system

✦ Distributed system

When deciding on how to install CSPM, consider the topology of your network, the number of devices that need to be managed, and the security requirements of the network. The following sections discuss these installation options.

Standalone system

In this installation option, the CSPM server set is installed on a single host. This standalone system then performs database, distribution, generation, monitoring, and reporting functions. A standalone CSPM system is ideal for a small office setup where internal networks have access to the Internet.

To install a standalone system or the CSPM Server feature set on a computer, follow these steps:

1. Insert the CSPM CD-ROM into the CD-ROM drive to start the Autostart program.

2. Under Options, select Install Product and click Next. The License Agreement window appears. Select the *I accept the agreement* option and click Next to proceed.

3. In the Location box, specify the location of the CSPM license disk. In the Password box, enter the password. (The password is printed on the license disk label.)

4. Under Installation Option, select Stand-alone CSPM.

5. In the Installation Folder box, specify the location where you want to install CSPM and then click Next.

6. In the Password field, enter the password. In the Confirm Password field, enter the password and select Next.

7. From the Local IP Address list, select the IP address configured on the computer.

8. Check the Export this key check box to export the database key. In the File Destination box, specify the location where you want to store the database key. Click Next. The Verify Install Settings dialog box appears.

9. Verify the settings and click Copy Files to copy files on the disk. When the necessary files have been copied, the Setup is complete dialog box appears. Click Finish to close the dialog box.

Client/server system

In this installation option, the CSPM server set is installed on a single host, while the CSPM GUI feature set is installed on one or more clients. The client/server installation option allows remote administration; you can administer the hosts from any other CSPM GUI host in the network. This installation option is well suited for a multi-office environment with multiple networks.

Distributed system

In this installation option, the CSPM server set is installed on a single computer while the CSPM GUI feature set and the distributed CSPM server is installed on one or more computers. In this installation type, each distributed CSPM server in the network manager is a part of the network. The CSPM GUI feature set is for remote administration. This type of installation is suited for a multi-office environment where the network is spread across various locations.

To install a client/server or distributed server on a computer, follow these steps:

1. Install CSPM server feature set.

2. Insert the CSPM CD-ROM in the CD-ROM drive of the target computer to start the Autostart program.

3. Under Options, select Install Product and click Next. The License Agreement window appears. Select the *I accept the agreement* option and click Next to proceed.

4. In the Location box, specify the location of the CSPM license disk. In the Password box, enter the password. (The password is printed on the license disk's label.)

5. Under Installation Option, select Client/Server CSPM for installing client/server system. If you want to install a distributed system, select Distributed CSPM.

6. From the Feature Set list, select the feature set you want to install.

7. In the Installation Folder box, specify the location where you want to install CSPM and then click Next.

8. In the CSPM server Key box, specify the location of the database key. Click Next. The Verify Install Settings dialog box appears.

Note   If the CSPM Server is on a private network that has a managed device to perform NAT, you must override the IP address specified in the database key. To override the IP address, check the *Use these parameters* check box. In the Server IP Address box, specify the IP address to which you had mapped the CSPM server. To override the port number, in the Port box, enter the port number.

9. Verify the settings and click Copy Files to copy files on the disk. When the necessary files have been copied, the Setup is complete dialog box appears. Click Finish to close the dialog box.

You can convert a standalone system to a client/server or a distributed system. To convert a standalone system to a client/server or a distributed system, perform the following steps:

1. Right-click the CSPM server icon and select Properties. In the Properties window, click the Database tab to open the Database panel.

2. Under General Settings, click Export Key to export the database key from the computer where the standalone system is running.

3. The Export Key To dialog box opens. In the Save in box, specify the location where you want to export the database key.

4. In the File name box, enter the name of the key file.

5. Click Save to export the file to the specified location.

After you have exported the database key from the stand-alone system, you can install the client/server or distributed system on the target host by using this database key.

Logging in to CSPM

After you have installed CSPM, log in to connect to the database on the CSPM server. To log in to CSPM server, perform the following steps:

1. Choose Start ⇨ Programs ⇨ Cisco Systems ⇨ Cisco Secure Policy Manager. Click Cisco Secure Policy Manager.

2. In the Log on to Cisco Secure Policy Manager dialog box, under Authorization, enter the username and password in the appropriate fields.

3. If you are logging in from the CSPM server, click the Connect button to connect to the database. If you are logging from CSPM GUI or distributed CSPM server, click Options. Select Remote. Under Database Server, specify the port number.

4. Click OK.

5. Click Connect (which connects you to the database on CSPM server) and open CSPM GUI.

Implementation of CSPM

Cisco Secure Policy Manager serves to implement, configure, and maintain networking products and security in an organization. It is user-friendly and graphical and helps a network administrator in implementing network security. It is the most common network management tool for products created by Cisco and provides a solution to both the security and networking needs of an organization. It can be implemented on network firewalls, VPNs, or IDS sensors.

Devices supported by CSPM

CSPM supports the following Cisco devices:

✦ Cisco Secure PIX Firewalls versions 4.2.4, 4.2.5, 4.4.x, 5.1.2, 5.2.x, 5.3.x, and 6.0x1

✦ Cisco Secure IDS sensors versions 2.2, 2.5, and 2.6

✦ Cisco IOS routers with any of the following IOS versions: 12.0(5)T, 12.0(5)XE5, 12.0(7)T, 12.1(1), 12.1(2), 12.1(2)T, 12.1(2) XH12.1(3), 12.1(3)T, 12.1(3)XI12.1(4), 12.1(4)E12.1(5), or 12.1(5)T

Cisco Secure ACS

Cisco Secure ACS, software designed for Windows NT and Unix, serves to track the activities of the users who are logged in the network. The Access Control Server (ACS) serves to identify the users who have access to the network and the rights assigned to them. The ACS can store the authentication and authorization information of users.

Since all the network devices are configured to the Internet directly with ACS, it is easy to centrally control dial-up access and secure the access to network devices. By using Cisco Secure ACS, the network administrator can use different authentication methods and assign different levels of rights to users.

The ACS also acts as a central location for storing account information. Every user session authenticated by ACS is stored on the server. This information is for preparing bills, planning capabilities, and securing audits.

Cisco Secure ACS has a Web browser interface that allows the following tasks:

✦ Supporting unlimited Cisco Network Access Servers

✦ Supporting token cards and token-card servers

✦ Managing Cisco Secure ACS and NAS clients (RADIUS and TACACS+ enabled)

✦ Managing Telnet access to routers and switches

✦ Managing remote connections to VPDNs

✦ Configuring token caching for all users who use a token server to log in

✦ Administering Secure Computing token-card users

✦ Assigning group-level absolute attributes

✦ Centralizing AAA for access through routers, switches, firewalls, and NAS

Cisco Secure ACS for Windows NT

The Cisco Secure ACS controls the dial-in access to Cisco's NAS server by authenticating users. It uses a Windows NT service to manage authentication, authorization, and accounting of users on the network. Cisco Secure ACS supports centralized control of user access, dial-up access servers, and firewalls. It also helps in managing the access ability of user accounts and the global implementation of changes on the network, which help in providing dial-up service to the entire organization. Because the ACS is integrated with Windows NT, organizations can (to some extent) exploit the investment made in deploying Windows NT networks.

The Cisco Secure ACS provides support for Cisco NAS and the PIX Firewall. It uses protocols, such as Remote Access Dial-In User Services (RADIUS) and Terminal Access Controller Access Control System (TACACS+), for providing services, such as Authentication, Authorization, and Accounting, for the purpose of authenticating users. Cisco uses the Windows NT Users database, the Token Server database, or the Cisco Secure User database.

By using NAS, all the dial-in users are redirected to the Cisco Secure ACS for authentication of users and assigning appropriate permissions. NAS uses either of the two protocols, TACACS+ and RADIUS, for authenticating the remote user from the Cisco Secure Server. This server authenticates the username and password and returns a success or failure status to the NAS. Based on the result of the authentication, NAS allows or denies access to the remote user. After a user is authenticated, the Cisco Secure ACS sends the associated authorization attributes to the NAS.

Versions of CSNT

At present, the following versions of Cisco Secure ACS for Windows NT (CSNT) are available:

- ✦ Cisco Secure ACS 2.0
- ✦ Cisco Secure ACS 2.1
- ✦ Cisco Secure ACS 2.1(4)
- ✦ Cisco Secure ACS 2.3
- ✦ Cisco Secure ACS 2.4
- ✦ Cisco Secure ACS 2.5
- ✦ Cisco Secure ACS 2.6

Cisco Secure ACS versions 2.5 and 2.6 work with Windows NT as well as Windows 2000.

Interface design

The design of the Cisco Secure ACS Interface is based on the interface of Microsoft Internet Explorer 3.0 and Netscape Navigator 3.0. The design is an integration of HTML and Java functions, which provides an interface with a quick response and simplicity of use. Enable Java support on your browser to use this interface. By using the Cisco Secure ACS interface, you can easily observe and modify details about individual users or groups of users. You can also resume service after stopping it, add administrator for remote administrator, modify details of NAS, and review reports. These reports list both the users currently connected to the network and unsuccessful attempts by users to connect to the network.

Features

Cisco Secure ACS provides practical networking advantages through various features:

- ✦ Provides the maximum amount of flexibility to user groups and helps implement changes to the security policy

✦ Uses HTML/Java GUI to simplify the configuration of user and group profiles and to configure ACS

✦ Provides online documentation that facilitates quick problem solving

✦ Supports both TACACS+ and RADIUS simultaneously

✦ Uses a method to import a vast number of users

✦ Provides support for Virtual Private Networks both at the beginning and the end of the tunnels

✦ Provides support for processing transactions at high speed

✦ Provides a facility for a single log in as provided in Windows NT

✦ Provides support for managing the Windows NT database that contains usernames and passwords

✦ Runs on any type of NT server, a PDC, BDC, or a standalone server

✦ Provides support for protocols, such as Challenge Handshake Authentic Protocol (CHAP), Apple Talk Remote Access (ARA), and Password Authentication Protocol (PAP)

✦ Provides support for token-card servers that implement Security Dynamics and Axent

✦ Assigns user restrictions based on Caller Line Identification (CLI)

✦ Can be configured to disable user accounts after a specified number of incorrect login attempts

✦ Can be configured to disable user accounts by date

✦ Can be used to view the list of users who have logged into the network

✦ Uses the Performance Monitor, which is a part of Windows NT for reviewing statistical data

✦ Provides an upgrade from an earlier version of Cisco Secure ACS

✦ Stores additional accounting information in CSV file formats so it can be used in billing applications

Besides the features mentioned above, Cisco Secure ACS Release 2.4 has the following additional features:

✦ It has enhanced database-replication features.

✦ It offers stronger encryption for Cisco Secure ACS database.

✦ It authenticates all supported versions of LDAP directory service.

✦ It allows authentication of external users by using an enabled password.

✦ It supports the Microsoft callback feature.

✦ It supports both month/day/year and day/month/year date formats.

✦ It can be used to assign users to Network Device Groups (NDGs).

✦ It synchronizes NAS, AAA, NDGs, and proxy table entries.

✦ It supports CSV- and OBDC-compatible accounting and administrative logging.

Functions of ACS

ACS functions can be divided into three categories (which should be familiar if you have implemented AAA security):

✦ Authentication

✦ Authorization

✦ Accounting

Cross-Reference   For the details of AAA security, see Chapter 11.

The upcoming sections provide details of these functions.

Authentication

Authentication helps in establishing a user identity and can be performed in various ways. The most common method is by using fixed usernames and passwords. Other authentication methods include CHAP, token cards, and one-time passwords (OTPs). OTP is a method by which the password need be provided only once — after that, the user is authenticated until the session ends. Cisco supports all these methods of authentication.

The check for username and password is the most common method of authentication; it is the most inexpensive. Another reason for its popularity is that it does not require any upgrade or new hardware. However, it has a major disadvantage in that the hackers can gain access to the network if they find the password for a user's account. Therefore, it is not a secure method of authentication; it should be used only where a low level of authentication is required (for example, chatting on the Internet).

You can encrypt the password to minimize the danger of its capture by hackers. You can also use certain client and server access-control protocols, such as TACACS+ and RADIUS, to encrypt the passwords. TACACS+ and RADIUS can only be implemented between NAS and ACS; the passwords vulnerable to hackers while in transit from a client (hackers can connect to NAS by using an ISDN line). The ISPs provide an additional level of security by using OTP.

Token cards are the most secure authentication mechanism used on networks. Cisco Secure ACS supports two manufacturers of token cards, Axent and Security Dynamics Inc. (SDI). The client computers that use SDI connect to the server for authenticating token cards. However, in case of Axent, the authentication server uses Cisco Secure ACS (along with an associated address and secret key) for authentication.

Password authentication

Cisco Secure ACS for Windows NT supports all commonly used authentication protocols. These protocols are as follows:

- ✦ Windows NT User Database
- ✦ ARAP
- ✦ ASCII/ PAP
- ✦ External Token-Card Server
- ✦ CHAP

These protocols process the passwords according to the type of protocol, its version, and how NAS and its client have been configured. The following sections discuss how passwords are processed under various conditions.

CiscoSecure provides support for two types of passwords:

- ✦ **Inbound passwords:** This type of password is mostly used by Cisco Secure ACS to authenticate Windows NT users. These passwords are supported by both TACACS+ and Radius protocols. They are stored in the Cisco Secure User database.

- ✦ **Outbound passwords:** This type of password is also used in TACACS+. For example, if a NAS server needs to authenticate another NAS server and client. In this case, the Cisco Secure User database passes the password back to the NAS server and client.

To ensure security on Cisco Secure ACS, you should specify separate passwords as inbound and outbound passwords.

Fundamental password configurations

Under Cisco Secure ACS, most users create their passwords with one of four fundamental password configurations:

- ✦ **ASCII login with token card:** For using this type of configuration, the password is not required to be stored in the Cisco Secure User database.

- ✦ **Windows NT User database:** Just as in the case of ASCII login with token card, here too the password is not stored in the Cisco Secure User database, though only ASCII/PAP authentication protocols are supported.

✦ **Common passwords for ASCII/PAP/CHAP/ARAP:** This is generally the most suitable method for creating user accounts and getting authentication. However, as the password is transmitted in clear text formats during the process of ASCII/PAP login, hackers can easily exploit the situation to get hold of the password.

✦ **Individual passwords for ASCII/PAP/CHAP/ARAP:** If users need more security, they can be assigned a set of two passwords: one for ASCII/PAP and other CHAP/ARAP. Thus at least one password is always safe to use, even if the other one is hacked.

Advanced password configurations

Besides the four fundamental password configurations, Cisco Secure ACS also offers two advanced password configurations:

✦ **Token caching:** In token caching, an ISDN user connects to a location by using the same OTP that was entered the first time the user was authenticated. For more security NAS is requested to include the OTP along with the username, whereas the password would contain an ASCII/PAP/CHAP/ARAP password.

✦ **TACACS+ SENDAUTH:** NAS can use the TACACS+ protocol to authenticate the server with another NAS or client by using outbound authentication. This authentication could be either by CHAP, PAP, or ARAP. Generally either a user's ASCII/PAP or CHAP/ARAP password is used, depending on the protocol that has been configured. The best practice is to require users to utilize a separate SENDAUTH password so hackers can never detect or expose the inbound password.

Authorization

The level of authentication is directly proportional to authorization. Hence, the higher the level of authorization, the stronger the authentication needs to be. The Cisco ACS determines the level of user rights by sending user profiles to network devices. By using authorization, you can assign different levels of rights to individual users or to a group of users. For example, remote users that connect to the corporate network by using dial-up access would have different rights and privileges on the network from internal users of the corporate network. Users can be assigned different levels of rights with respect to services, security, and the time limit within which they can log in to the network.

Another important service used by organizations is the authorization of service implemented on VPNs. You can use Cisco Secure ACS to provide information about users for establishing a tunnel between the corporate network and the Internet. Cisco Secure ACS can be implemented at either of the peer routers in a VPN.

Access to a specific user or to a group of users can be allowed or denied based on the day, date, or time. For example, an administrator can configure the network to allow remote users to log in only after a specific time or a specific day. Similarly, temporary accounts (which expire after a specific date) can also be created.

You can also restrict user or group access according to the protocols and services implemented. After a service has been configured, you can restrict access to the other services by using ACL. An access list that assigns rights to a user on an individual or group basis can restrict a user's access to confidential information. ACL can also be used to restrict a user's access to services such as Simple Network Management Protocol (SNMP) and File Transfer Protocol (FTP).

Accounting

Accounting refers to keeping track of activities performed by a user. An ACS maintains this list in a CVS log file. The log file can be integrated with common databases and spreadsheet applications. The integrated data helps in creating bills, auditing security, and creating reports.

Modules of Cisco Secure ACS on Windows NT

The Cisco Secure ACS consists of the following modules:

✦ CSAdmin

✦ CSAuth

✦ CSTacacs

✦ CSRadius

✦ CSLog

✦ CSDBSynch

✦ CSMon

You can control each of the service modules from the Microsoft Service Control panel or the Cisco Secure ACS browser interface.

CSAdmin

Since it has an internal Web server, Cisco does not need a separate Web server. All services are implemented on an internal Web server. Therefore, as part of configuring Cisco Secure ACS, configure the HTML/Java interface—and make sure you enable the CSAdmin service and run it on the Web server.

Although you can use the Cisco Secure ACS browser interface to manage the start up and shut down of most services, you cannot use the browser to start or stop the CSAdmin service. The correct tool for this purpose is the Windows NT Service menu. Bottom line: If the service is stopped for any reason, no other machine on the network (besides the NT machine on which the server is running) can access the Cisco Secure ACS.

You can use `CSAdmin` to configure the following administrative capabilities:

✦ **Windows NT/2000 event log:** By default, `CSMon` logs events in the Windows NT/2000 event log. However, you can disable this feature by using `CSAdmin`.

✦ **Scripts to be executed when an event fails:** You can use `CSAdmin` to specify the scripts that would be used when an event fails. Although the scripts normally used are Windows NT/2000 batch files, you can also use executable files as scripts.

✦ **SMTP server and administrator e-mail account details:** You can configure the SMTP server and administrator e-mail account details by using the `CSAdmin` to enable Cisco Secure ACS to send notifications via e-mail.

✦ **Frequency of test logins:** CSMon attempts test logins after every 60 seconds. However, you can specify the frequency at which you want `CSMon` to attempt test logins. You can also disable this feature if you want to disallow test logins.

CSAuth

`CSAuth` provides authentication and authorization services. The principle function of Cisco Secure ACS is providing authentication and authorization services for requests received from network devices and notifying users about the level of their rights and privileges for the device. Based on information provided by the Cisco Secure ACS, users are allowed or denied access to specific network devices. All the information about the rights assigned to users is shared in a database, which is managed by `CSAuth`.

Cisco Secure ACS can access a single database at a time. When Cisco Secure ACS receives a request to provide authentication, the Cisco Secure ACS User Database requests the `CSAuth` Manager to store the data in its own database. The paths for storage of user passwords used for authentication are saved in this database. Based on where the username is saved, `CSAuth` decides on the database to be used. `CSAuth` consists of three databases used for authentication. They are as follows:

✦ **Cisco Secure ACS User Database:** This is the first database, and it takes the least amount of time to authenticate users. Because the usernames and passwords are stored here and the search is carried out at the same location, the process only consists of a single stage.

✦ **Windows NT User Database:** The second database reuses the existing user profiles created on Windows NT. When the NT database is linked with the Cisco Secure User Database, `CSAuth` can be used to compare the client's username against the list of usernames stored in the Windows NT User Database. It then connects to Windows NT by using the client's username and password. Using the Microsoft login API that accepts or denies the request, it processes the request of authentication. If the API accepts the requests, `CSAuth` provides client access to the resources and logs out of the Windows NT login.

✦ **Third-party databases using token-card servers:** You can obtain these from third-party vendors such as Security Dynamics and Axent. Cisco ACS is a client of the token-card server. Cisco compares the username with the list of users maintained on the token-card server in a similar way as it does in the case of the Windows NT User Database. The server validates the requests and either accepts or rejects the authentication request. If the token-card server validates the request, CSAuth provides the user the right to access the network resources between the Cisco Secure ACS and token-card server. The token server might support TACACS+ or RADIUS. The Cisco Secure ACS handles all communication between the token server and CSAuth.

After a user name has been validated from any of the three databases, information regarding the rights assigned to the user or to the group is obtained from the Cisco Secure User Database. The information obtained is about all the services that the users can access, such as IP port authorization and IP over PPP. These lists govern the user's access to protocols. The authorization information is sent to the CSTacacs or CSRadius modules, which then passes on this information to the device that had requested the authentication.

CSRadius and CSTacacs

CSAuth modules use the CSRadius and CSTacacs services to communicate with any network device that requests authentication. Certain conditions must be met, however, before these services can run effectively:

✦ The type of protocol used must be defined in the Cisco Secure ACS.

✦ A special key is required to connect to access devices.

✦ Must be configured by using the CSAdmin service.

✦ Needs the IP address of the access device.

✦ Needs to connect to access devices, such as routers, firewalls, switches, and access servers.

✦ The type of protocol used must be defined in the Cisco Secure ACS.

Basically, the CSRadius protocol serves to connect with RADIUS devices and CSTacas protocol serves to connect to TACACS+ devices. In case only a single protocol is used, the type of service depends on the device that uses it.

CSLog

CSLog service involves obtaining and logging user information. This information is obtained by the CSLog from the RADIUS and TACACS+ data packets and stored in a CSV file, which is created daily. If you are using Cisco Secure ACS v 2.0, the default location where the CSV files are saved is \Program Files\Cisco Secure ACS v2.0\Logs\. This folder contains the following three subdirectories:

✦ Tacacs Accounting

✦ Audit

✦ Radius Accounting

Information about all the unsuccessful login attempts is stored in the Audit directory. Information about the successful login attempts is stored in the other two subdirectories based on the protocols used.

However, if you are using Cisco secure ACS v2.6, CVS flies are stored in \Program Files\Cisco Secure ACS v2.6\Logs\. Ten subdirectories in which the CVS files are stored are the following:

✦ AdminAudit: Stores log files containing information about administrator activities.

✦ Backup and Restore: Stores log files containing information about ACS system backup and restore activity.

✦ DBReplicate: Stores the log files containing information about database replication activity.

✦ DBSync: Stores the log files containing information about RDBS synchronization activity.

✦ Failed Attempts: Stores the log files containing information about failed authentication attempts.

✦ RADIUS Accounting: Stores the log files containing information about successful authentication and authorization for RADIUS users.

✦ TACACS+ Accounting: Stores the log files containing information about successful authentication and authorization for TACACS+ users.

✦ TACACS+ Administration: Stores the log files containing information about TACACS+ administration events.

✦ Service Monitoring: Stores the log files containing information about service activities.

✦ VoIP Accounting: Stores the log files containing information about successful authentication and authorization for Voice over IP (VoIP) users.

CSDBSynch

The CSDBSynch module serves to manage automated user and group services for Cisco Secure ACS. It synchronizes the Cisco Secure ACS database with other RDBMS systems. It also synchronizes AAA server, NAS, and NDGs.

CSMon

The `CSMon` module serves to monitor Cisco Secure ACS and to correct system problems. `CSMon` serves to monitor the following system parameters:

✦ **Application-specific performance:** `CSMon` monitors application viability by performing test logins. To do so, it uses a built-in test account. `CSMon` also monitors the time taken by each test authentication to receive a positive response. It then updates the average response time value to determine the application performance thresholds.

✦ **Generic host system state:** `CSMon` monitors system thresholds, such as available space on the system hard drive, processor utilization, physical memory utilization, and space available on Cisco Secure ACS installation drive.

✦ **System resource consumption:** `CSMon` records the system resource usage by Cisco Secure ACS and compares it with predefined thresholds. It monitors memory and processor utilization, threads used, and failed login attempts.

`CSMon` also records abnormal events in logs, which can be later used to diagnose problems. To record abnormal events, `CSMon` uses two logs:

✦ **Windows NT/2000 event log:** `CSMon` logs all messages to Windows NT/2000 event log, which is enabled by default.

✦ **CSMon log:** `CSMon` has a CSV log to keep track of errors and abnormal activities. CSMon logging cannot be disabled.

You can configure `CSMon` to send notifications when abnormal events occur. These notifications are sent in the form of e-mails. However, you create scripts to send notifications by other means.

`CSMon` takes the following actions when an action fails:

✦ **Predefined actions:** These actions are predefined in the program and occur when `CSMon` detects a triggering event. Because these actions are predefined in the program, they do not need to be configured.

✦ **User-defined actions:** The users define these actions by creating scripts or external programs. User-defined actions can also be configured by using the sample scripts that come with `CSMon`. The sample scripts available with `CSMon` are as follows:

- `RESTART_ALL_SERVICES.BAT`: Used to restart all Cisco Secure ACS services.

- `RESTART_PROTOCOL_MODULES.BAT`: Serves to restart `CSRadius` and `CSTacacs`.

- `REBOOT.BAT`: Serves to reboot the Cisco Secure ACS system.

System requirements for installing CSNT

To ensure successful installation and operation of CSNT, make sure your system meets (or, preferably, *exceeds*) the following minimum requirements:

✦ 200 MHz processor.

✦ Minimum 64MB RAM (128MB recommended).

✦ CD-ROM drive.

✦ Minimum 300MB free hard drive space for typical installation.

✦ Windows NT Server 4.0 with Service Pack 5 or Service Pack 6.

✦ Minimum monitor resolution of 256 colors at 800 × 600.

✦ Cisco IOS Software Release 11.1 or later on NAS. For Radius support, Cisco IOS Software Release 11.1 is required.

✦ PIX Firewall version 4.24 or later.

Configuring CSNT

You can install CSNT after you have authenticated a PPP dial-up user against CSNT by using the Windows NT User Database through the TACACS+ protocol. The tasks involved in installing and configuring CSNT are as follows:

1. **Configuring the Windows NT Server to operate with CSNT**. To configure the Windows NT Server to operate with CSNT, follow these general steps:

   a. Configure Windows NT User Manager.

   b. Use Windows NT Services to control ACS.

2. **Verifying the basic network connections.** The next step is to verify the network connections between the dial-up client, NAS, PIX Firewall, and the Windows NT Server. Verifying the basic network connections can eliminate the connectivity problems often encountered when configuring CSNT.

3. **Installing CSNT on Windows NT Server.** Before installing CSNT on the Windows NT Server, you must have NAS information such as hostname, IP address, and TACACS+ key. CSNT is installed by using an InstallShield-based setup program. The general steps for installing CSNT are as follows:

   a. Choosing and configuring the database

   b. Configuring CSNT for NAS by using the Web browser

   c. Configuring NAS and PIX Firewall for CSNT

   d. Configuring CSNT by using the Web browser

4. **Configuring CSNT through Web browser interface.** If the CSNT installation is successful, the ACSNT Admin icon appears on the Windows NT desktop. You should initially configure CSNT with the Web browser interface; to launch the browser, use one of the following commands:

   `http://127.0.0.1:2002, http://<host name>:2002,`

   or

   `http://<ip address>:2002`

5. **Configure NAS, PIX, and the client for AAA.** The last step is to configure NAS, PIX Firewall, and the client for AAA. Begin by configuring the following operations to work with CSNT:

   - Dial up by using the Windows NT User Database with TACACS+

   - Dial up by using a token-card server with TACACS+

   - Dial up by using the CSNT User Database with TACACS+

   - Dial up by using the CSNT User Database with RADIUS

   - VPDN by using the CSNT User Database with TACACS+

   - Dial up for the ARAP client by using the CSNT User Database with TACACS+

   - Router management by using the CSNT User Database with TACACS+

   - PIX Firewall authentication and authorization by using Windows NT User Database with TACACS+

Managing CSNT

As discussed earlier, the Web browser interface serves to administer the CSNT. The navigational bar has nine buttons, which help in managing various functions of CSNT. These buttons in their default order are listed:

- **User Setup:** This button serves to add, edit, and delete the user accounts. The button is also used to display the users in the database.

- **Group Setup:** This button serves to create, edit, and rename groups. The button is also used to display all users in a group.

- **Network Configuration:** This button serves to configure and edit the NAS parameters and AAA server distribution. It is also used to add and delete NASs.

- **System Configuration:** This button serves to start and stop CSNT services, configure logging and TACACS+ and RADIUS options. It is also used to control RDBMS synchronization.

- **Interface Configuration:** This button serves to specify the user-defined fields that should be recorded in the accounting logs. It is also used to configure TACACS+ and RADIUS options and specify the options displayed on the user interface.

✦ **Administration Control:** This button serves to administer CSNT from any workstation on the network.

✦ **External User Databases:** This button serves to configure unknown-user policy and specify authorization privileges for unknown users. It is also used to configure external database types.

✦ **Reports and Activity:** This button serves to display RADIUS Accounting Reports, Failed Attempts Report, List Logged in Users, List Disabled Accounts, Admin Accounting Reports, and TACACS+ Accounting Reports. These reports and lists can be imported to database and spreadsheet applications.

✦ **Online Documentation:** This button serves to display detailed information about the configuration and operation of CSNT.

Administering CSNT

As discussed earlier, you use the Administration Control button on the navigation bar to enable administration from a remote client. You can also use the Administration Control button to add or modify remote administrator information, by proceeding as follows:

1. On the navigation bar, click Administration Control.

2. Click Add new administrator.

3. In the Administrator Name box, enter the user name of the administrator.

4. In the Password box, enter the password used by the administrator to log in.

5. In the Confirm Password box, re-enter the administrator password.

6. In the Administrator Privileges section, select the privileges that you want to give to the administrator. Also, select the Reports and Activity items that the administrator can access.

7. Click Submit to save the settings.

Troubleshooting CSNT

To troubleshoot AAA problems related to CSNT, it is advisable to look at Failed Attempts Reports. This report gives information on a variety of failures. You can also use the debug commands to troubleshoot CSNT. The commands frequently used to troubleshoot CSNT are as follows:

✦ You can enable the debug aaa authentication command to display authentication information with TACACS+ and RADIUS client/server interaction.

✦ You can enable the debug aaa authorization command to display authorization information with TACACS+ and RADIUS client/server interaction.

✦ You can enable the `debug radius` command to display RADIUS interactions between the AAA server and the IOS client.

✦ You can enable the `debug tacacs` command to display TACACS+ interactions between the AAA server and the IOS client.

Cisco Secure ACS for Unix

Cisco Secure ACS 2.3 for Unix (CSUNIX) secures the network from unauthorized users by authenticating users against user and group profile database. CSUNIX GUI supports Microsoft Internet Explorer and Netscape navigator. This multiplatform support also incorporates a Web-based tool for configuring and managing Java — which in turn allows convenient server management from multiple locations. CSUNIX also provides CryptoCard token-card server software (and its strong authentication capability). CSUNIX also supports relational database technologies from Sybase and Oracle — which can greatly simplify the management of user and group profiles.

Versions of CSUNIX

The following versions of CSUNIX are available:

✦ Cisco Secure ACS 2.1

✦ Cisco Secure ACS 2.1.2

✦ Cisco Secure ACS 2.2.2

✦ Cisco Secure ACS 2.2(3)

✦ Cisco Secure ACS 2.3

✦ Cisco Secure ACS 2.3(2)

✦ Cisco Secure ACS 2.3(5)

✦ Cisco Secure ACS 2.3(5.1)

Note   Although features differ slightly in different versions of Cisco Secure ACS, the basic features of the product remain the same.

Features of CSUNIX

CSUNIX ensures network security and tracks the activities of users who logged in to the network by using the TACACS+ protocol. As mentioned earlier, TACACS+ enables you to control network access from a central location; CSUNIX extends this capability to include the following tasks:

✦ Managing RADIUS-enabled and TACACS+-enabled NAS clients on the same network as Cisco Secure ACSs

✦ Managing remote connections to VPDNs

✦ Assigning mid-level group administration privileges

✦ Configuring token-caching capability for all users who use the token server to log in

✦ Assigning group-level attributes

✦ Administering Secure Computing token-card users

The features of CSUNIX include

✦ Support for managing sessions

✦ Support for Unix command-line interface

✦ Support for profile data caching

✦ Support for data replication

System requirements for installing CSUNIX

To ensure successful installation and operation of CSNT, make sure your system meets (or, preferably, *exceeds*) the following minimum requirements:

✦ UltraSPARC 1 or compatible (without DSM)

✦ UltraSPARC 10 or compatible (with DSM and Oracle or Sybase)

✦ Minimum 128MB RAM (minimum 256MB RAM for Oracle or Sybase)

✦ 256MB swap space. 512MB for Oracle and Sybase

✦ Minimum 256MB free hard drive space for SQL Anywhere (minimum 2GB of free hard drive space for Oracle or Sybase)

✦ CD-ROM drive

✦ Solaris 2.6 or Solaris 2.5.1 with patches

Summary

This chapter explained CiscoWorks 2000 ACL Manager — its features, components, built-in tools, and benefits to a network — and described the features of Cisco Secure Policy Manager (as well as the steps that prepare it for configuration). The chapter also explained how to implement Cisco Secure Policy Manager and outlined the features and functions of Cisco Secure ACS.

✦   ✦   ✦

Cisco Firewall and VPN Management Products

Most organizations implement networks to get convenient, fast, and reliable access to the information their business requires—the very capability most threatened by a security breach. To counter such threats, Cisco provides several powerful tools:

◆ PIX Firewall, a dedicated firewall to ensure the security of internal networks

◆ PIX Firewall Manager, a tool for getting the most out of PIX Firewall

◆ VPN/Security Management Solution, a tool for optimizing secure control of your company's virtual private network

This chapter discusses the features and system requirements of Cisco PIX Firewall Manager and lays out the installation procedure for PIX Firewall. For organizations that run virtual private networks, the chapter covers the features, components, and installation of VPN/Security Management Solution.

Cisco PIX Firewall Manager

In organizations that deploy multiple PIX Firewall units, the configuration and management of those units is a major concern. Fortunately, Cisco PIX Firewall comes with its own management tool—PIX Firewall Manager—that you can use to manage and configure multiple PIX Firewall units from a single location. Among the network tasks you can centralize with this tool are these essential functions:

✦ Modify the configuration of PIX Firewall units

✦ View SYSLOG messages

✦ Define customized alarms for each type of SYSLOG message

Components of PIX Firewall Manager

PIX Firewall Manager software consists of two major components that perform specialized client/server tasks:

✦ **Management Server:** This Windows NT service runs in the background. It receives requests from the Management Client. These requests are then sent to the specified PIX Firewall unit. The PIX Firewall unit sends the response to the Management Server, which then forwards the responses to the Management Client.

✦ **Management Client:** This Java applet provides a graphical user interface (accessed from a network browser) to enhance the efficiency of managing the firewall.

 Note   Any network browser you use with the Management Client must be Java 1.02-compliant.

Benefits of PIX Firewall Manager

PIX Firewall Manager enables an administrator to configure and manage PIX Firewalls from a single source, which benefits the network in various ways:

✦ Allows configuration and management of up to 10 PIX Firewall units

✦ Allows creation of common configurations for multiple PIX Firewall units

✦ Encrypts all communication between the PIX Firewall and the PIX Firewall Manager

✦ Generates reports by using the Report Wizard

✦ Generates a 3-D bar-chart report to show network traffic through the PIX Firewall

✦ Can provide information on network traffic passing through up to 50 hosts

✦ Generates reports of FTP and HTTP file-transfer activities performed by the host, showing source IP addresses and filenames

✦ Generates the initial inbound and outbound connection statements in the PIX Firewall configuration

✦ Allows setting the time interval for updating SYSLOG message files

Note   At present, many versions of PIX Firewall Manager are available. The most commonly used is Version 4.2, which you are likely to find installed as release 1, 2, 3, 4, or 5.

Installing PIX Firewall Manager

Before installing the PIX Firewall Manager, make sure your host hardware fulfills the system requirements. PIX Firewall Manager also imposes its own installation requirements; make sure that the version of PIX Firewall software on your system meets them.

System requirements for installing Management Server

Before you install the Management Server component of PIX Firewall Manager on a Windows NT computer, make sure the computer meets or exceeds the following requirements:

✦ Source computer must have Windows NT Workstation or Windows NT Server (version 4.0 or later) installed, with Service Pack 3.0.

✦ Source computer should have a Pentium processor and a minimum of 32MB RAM.

✦ TCP/IP protocol must be enabled on the computer.

✦ IP address of the source computer should not be dynamically allocated.

✦ Source computer that runs Management Server must be inside the firewall.

✦ The user must be registered as a PIX Administrator or PIX User on the Windows NT system.

System requirements for installing Management Client

The system requirements for installing the Management Client component are as follows:

✦ The network browser in use with Management Client must be compliant with Java 1.02 or 1.1. Management Client provides specific support for the following browsers:

- Microsoft Internet Explorer 4.0 version 4.72.3110.8
- Netscape Navigator version 3.0 or later
- Netscape Navigator Gold version 3.0 or later
- Netscape Navigator (standalone) version 4.0 or later
- Netscape Communicator version 4.0 or later

✦ The operating system must be one of the following: Windows 95, Solaris, Windows NT 4.0 Workstation, or Windows NT Server.

✦ The computer that runs Management Client must be inside the PIX Firewall and within the network.

PIX Firewall Manager system requirements

PIX Firewall Manager is not backward-compatible with all versions of PIX Firewall. It can manage only those units that run PIX Firewall software versions 4.3(2), 4.4, 5.0, or later. You can identify the version of the PIX Firewall software by typing the show version command at the firewall console. Also, the local PIX Firewall must be configured to communicate with foreign Private Link firewalls. If you want to manage a PIX Firewall unit outside the local network, then all foreign units — and at least one firewall on the local network — must run a Private Link.

Information required for installing PIX Firewall Manager

Have the following information ready and available before installing PIX Firewall Manager:

✦ **Passwords**: You must know the passwords of the PIX Firewall privileged mode, Telnet, and Windows NT Administrator.

✦ **Configuration**: You must configure the PIX Firewall in advance to determine its IP address. The show ip address console command serves to view the IP address.

✦ **Port number**: You must know the port number of the built-in Web server running on the PIX Firewall Manager.

✦ **IP address**: You must know the IP address of the Windows NT system running PIX Firewall Manager. To view the IP address of Windows NT system running PIX Firewall Manager, follow these steps:

1. Choose Start ➪ Settings ➪ Control Panel.

2. Double-click the Network icon.

3. Click the Protocols tab and select the TCP/IP Protocols ➪ Properties.

4. Select the IP Address tab of the Microsoft TCP/IP Properties dialog box.

Installation process

If you have the prerequisites in place for installing PIX Firewall Manager, you can proceed with installation.

Note Make sure you have Windows NT Administrator privileges before you install PIX Firewall Manager.

To install the PIX Firewall Manager, follow these steps:

1. Insert the first PIX Firewall Manager CD into the Windows NT system's CD-ROM drive.

   PIX Firewall Manager software gives you the following installation options:

   - Choose Control Panel ⇨ Add/Remove Programs.
   - Type **a:\setup.exe** in the Run dialog box.
   - Double-click the diskette icon in the My Computer window and then double-click the miniature computer Setup icon.

2. The Installation Wizard starts and guides you through the rest of the installation process.

   During installation, you need to specify the port number of your Web server.

   Though the default port is 8080, you can specify any port between 1025 and 64000. After you have specified the port number, the installation program starts copying all its files and prompts you to insert the second diskette in the diskette drive.

3. In the final dialog box, click the Finish button.

   The Management Server starts automatically.

After the setup of PIX Firewall Manager is complete, you should change the default passwords of the pixadmin and pixuser users. This is because the default Pix Firewall Manager passwords are set to expire after 42 days. To change the default passwords of the pixadmin and pixuser user accounts, you need to perform the following steps:

1. Choose Start ⇨ Programs ⇨ Administrative Tools ⇨ User Manager.

2. After the User Manager starts, select the pixadmin username from the Username section of the screen and then choose User ⇨ Properties. This will open User Properties dialog box.

3. Specify the new password in the Password and Confirm Password fields. Also select the Password Never Expires option from the User Properties dialog box.

4. Select the pixuser username from the Username section of the screen and then choose User ⇨ Properties to open the User Properties dialog box.

5. Specify the new password in the Password and Confirm Password fields.

6. Select the Password Never Expires option from the User Properties dialog box.

7. Click OK to exit.

You can verify that the Management Server is running by:

1. Choose Start ➪ Settings ➪ Control Panel.

2. Double-click the Services icon. The names of PIX Firewall Management Server services and their status appear. A server is running if its status appears as Started. If the status field is blank, the server can be started by selecting its name and then clicking the Start button.

You can stop a management server by following these steps:

1. Choose Start ➪ Settings ➪ Control Panel ➪ Services.

2. In the Services dialog box, from the Service list, select the PIX Firewall Management Server. To stop this service, click the Stop button.

After you have installed PIX Firewall Manager, the next step is to start the Management Client. Before starting the Management Client, you need to restart the network browser and disable all the proxies. After you have disabled browser proxies, the home page of the Management Client appears. When the Management Client is loaded, you are prompted for a username and password. For read-write access, specify `pixadmin`, and for read-only access you can specify `pixuser`. Specify the username and password and click OK. This will start the Management Client.

The Management Client window

The Management Client window consists of tabs, buttons, the Contents area, the PIX Firewall IP Addresses area, and the Main Tree. The tabs available in the Management Client are as follows:

✦ **Administrator tab:** Enables you to view and change information for a firewall unit.

✦ **Alarm and Report tab:** Enables you to receive notification when errors occur. It also displays system usage reports.

✦ **Common Configuration tab:** Enables you to configure specific authentication and administration information for multiple PIX Firewall units at the same time.

✦ **SYSLOG Notification Settings tab:** Enables you to set the information, which is used by the Alarm and Report tab.

The Management Client window also has buttons, such as the "Tasks" button and the "Save to Flash Mem of PIX" button. The Tasks button provides you with a wizard-like function that enables you to generate inbound and outbound connection statements in the PIX Firewall configuration. The "Save to Flash Mem of PIX" button saves the configuration changes to flash memory in the PIX Firewall.

The Contents area has buttons that can be used to view or modify the configuration, depending on the task selected. The Contents area displays the task information of the selected PIX Firewall folder. The Contents area also displays the configuration for the current task.

Limiting access to Management Client

To specify the users who can access the Management Client, you should create user accounts on the computer on which PIX Firewall Manager is installed. You can give users either administrative or read-only access privileges.

When the Management Client starts, users need to enter their login ID and password. To limit access to the Management Client, follow these steps:

1. Start the User Manager.

2. In the User Manager dialog box add new users to the Windows NT system by selecting User ➪ New User. Specify the information for the user including the user's login name, full name, and password.

3. In the Groups area, double-click PIX Admins to allow the user to change PIX Firewall settings. However, if you want to give the read-only access to the user, double-click PIX Users. The Local Group Properties dialog box opens.

4. Click Add to add an existing user to the selected group. The Add Users and Groups dialog box appears.

5. From the Names field, select the name of the user, click Add, and then click OK to add the user.

6. Click OK to go back to the User Manager dialog box.

7. Click OK to exit the User Manager dialog box.

It is advisable not to assign a user to both the PIX Admins and PIX Users groups.

SYSLOG reports

The PIX Firewall logs the SYSLOG messages for system events, such as security alerts. These messages are stored in log files. The PIX Firewall Manager enables you to use these messages to generate alerts and reports.

Generating SYSLOG reports

PIX Firewall generates SYSLOG messages for a variety of system events, such as security alerts. These messages are stored in the log files and are used for creating reports. You need to configure PIX Firewall to generate SYSLOG messages. The Windows NT system running the PIX Firewall Manager stores these messages in the log files.

SYSLOG messages can also be sent to a SYSLOG server. The SYSLOG server listens to these messages from the PIX Firewall on UDP port number 514.

After the messages are stored in the Windows NT system, the PIX Firewall Manager uses the information stored in the daily log files to generate reports. For example, PIX Firewall SYSLOG messages for Friday are saved in the friday.log file. All the log files are located in the computer that has PIX Firewall Manager; you get to them via the following path:

```
\PIX Firewall Manager\protect\<weekday>.log
```

Each log file is retained on the Windows NT system for one week. You can configure SYSLOG host and message information settings on each PIX Firewall unit from the Management Client by selecting the Administrator-SYSLOG option.

Viewing SYSLOG reports

You can either use the PIX Firewall Management Client GUI or the Microsoft Excel macro to view the SYSLOG reports. Microsoft Excel macro is a feature of PIX Firewall Manager that serves to generate SYSLOG reports in Excel. However, you can print the reports by using Microsoft Excel only.

To view SYSLOG reports from PIX Firewall Management Client GUI, click the Alarm and Report tab. To view and print SYSLOG reports by using the Microsoft Excel macro, navigate to the PIX Firewall Manager homepage. Then follow the instructions given on the homepage to view the reports.

Troubleshooting reporting problems

If you face any problems while generating SYSLOG reports, it may mean that the configuration settings of the SYSLOG host or Message type are not correct. There can also be problems in SYSLOG reporting if the data does not reach the SYSLOG host. When attempting to generate SYSLOG reports, if you have problems displaying SYSLOG information or you get a "Database Empty" error message, you should

✦ Check the configuration requirements. If there is a need, reconfigure the SYSLOG Host and Message Types settings.

✦ Make sure that the SYSLOG messages are generated by the PIX Firewall.

✦ Make sure that the Message Type is set to capture Level 7 messages.

✦ Make sure that the SYSLOG reports display the host names as well as the IP addresses.

Limitations of PIX Firewall Manager

Although PIX Firewall Manager provides you with the ability to configure and manage multiple PIX Firewall units, it has some limitations. The limitations of PIX Firewall Manager are as follows:

✦ When installing the PIX Firewall Manager on a backup domain controller, if connectivity between the backup domain controller and the primary domain controller breaks, the PIX Firewall Manager users and groups are not added to the Windows NT Security Account Manager database. As a result, you will not be able to use the PIX Firewall Manager.

✦ PIX Firewall does not support all PIX Firewall commands. For example, it does not support `ping`, `clock set`, and `hostname` commands. Hence, if you want to change the configuration of the PIX Firewall by using these commands, you need to type them at the console port of the PIX Firewall.

VPN/Security Management Solution

With increasing number of business transactions happening over the net, the need for reliable and secure transmission of information over public networks has increased. As a result, many organizations have started deploying IPSec-based VPNs. However, as these VPNs become complex, managing and monitoring them becomes difficult. For effective management and monitoring of VPNs, Cisco provides VPN/Security Management Solution (VMS).

The VPN/Security Management Solution (VMS) provides a Web-based interface for monitoring and troubleshooting VPNs. It also provides an application for configuring and monitoring firewall security. It has an integrated set of Web applications with features that assist in deploying and monitoring security devices. Cisco VMS also optimizes VPN performance and security administration resulting in reduced cost of operation.

Benefits of VMS

The Cisco VPN/Security Management Solution (VMS) has the following benefits:

✦ Assists in the deployment and management of perimeter security for networks using the Cisco PIX Firewall products.

✦ Sends alerts to security threats in real time through Cisco Intrusion Detection Sensors.

✦ Assists in the deployment of the Cisco VPN 3000 Concentrator Series, Cisco VPN 7100, Cisco 7200 Series devices, Cisco PIX Firewall, and Cisco Intrusion Detection Sensors.

✦ Displays a view of VPN resources and their performance related to device usage, throughput, Internet Key Exchange errors, and exceeded performance thresholds.

✦ Monitors L2TP and PPTP remote access and IPSec-based site-to-site VPNs.

✦ Allows a graphical view of VPN device configurations.

✦ Performs software upgrade planning for VPN-capable devices and troubleshoots IPSec errors using the SYSLOG Analyzer.

✦ Allows deployment of perimeter security polices.

Components of VMS

VMS consists of various components that together provide VPN and security management features. The components included in VMS are as follows:

✦ VPN Monitor

✦ Resource Manager Essentials

✦ CiscoWorks2000 Management Server

✦ Cisco Secure Policy Manager Lite

✦ CiscoWorks2000 Inventory Services

✦ CiscoView

These components are discussed in detail in the following sections.

VPN Monitor

VPN Monitor is a Web-based VMS component that allows viewing and storing of information on site-to-site and remote-access VPNs. It enables graphical monitoring of devices. VPN Monitor also provides real-time graphs for problem analysis. It also supports Cisco VPN Concentrator 3000 Series, Cisco 7100 Series VPN routers, and Cisco 7200 Series routers. You can view data related to system resources from a dashboard, which is configured on a Web browser. This dashboard provides data, such as percent CPU usage per device, real-time memory usage, and active sessions. The dashboard also displays the percentage of packets dropped during transactions. This helps in identifying the bottlenecks in the network.

For devices you want to monitor, you need to add the devices to the device dashboard. To add a device to the dashboard, follow these steps:

1. Choose VPN Management Solution ➪ Administration ➪ Monitor ➪ Dashboard ➪ Device List to open the Device List window.

2. Select the device that you need to monitor from Available Devices, and click Add. The device is added to Dashboard Devices.

Tip   If you have difficulty in adding a device to the dashboard, ping the device to check whether it is on the network.

To remove a device from the dashboard, select the device from Dashboard Devices, and then click Remove. The device is removed from Dashboard Devices and is returned to Available Devices.

Resource Manager Essentials

Resource Manager Essentials (RME) provides the operational management features, such as software distribution, device inventory and credentials management, and

SYSLOG analysis for problem solving. It notifies VPN and security problems. RME serves to monitor and manage LAN and WAN resources. It can be used to implement configuration changes and software updates on multiple devices. RME can also be used to create customized SYSLOG reports to segregate problems related to IPSec.

CiscoWorks2000 Management Server

CiscoWorks2000 Management Server provides services, such as common database, Web, and desktop that enable integration of VMS with other Cisco and third-party tools.

Cisco Secure Policy Manager Lite

Cisco Secure Policy Manager Lite (CSPM-Lite) provides guidelines for implementing security on Cisco PIX Firewalls. CSPM-Lite is usually used with Cisco PIX Firewalls and IDS to improve the security of the network. In cases where Cisco Intrusion Detection Sensors are implemented, CSPM-Lite notifies and reports intrusions. It also monitors the events generated by VPN routers and PIX Firewalls.

CiscoWorks2000 Inventory Services

CiscoWorks2000 Inventory Services tracks the activities of network devices. It also reports hardware and software characteristics and allows device credentials management. It also aids Resource Manager Essentials (a suite of applications used for network administrations) in enabling the network managers to quickly build network inventory.

CiscoView

CiscoView is a Web-based, graphical device-management application. It provides real-time device status reports, as well as operational and configuration functions. It provides a view of device chassis, with color-coding of modules and ports. This helps in evaluation of status of the device. It allows multi-user access to the CiscoView server in Web-based applications. You can use CiscoView to change the settings of the network devices.

Installing and updating Cisco Works2000 VMS

Before you start installing Cisco Works2000 VMS, it is important that you know the system requirements for installing VMS. It is available as VMS bundle CDs. You need to install VMS on the server as well as the client side.

Server requirements

You can install VMS bundle CDs only on the computers that have Windows 2000, Windows NT, and Solaris operating systems. The server requirements for installing VMS bundle CDs on Windows 2000, Windows 2000 Professional, Windows 2000

Server, Windows 2000 Advanced Server, Windows NT Workstation 4.0, and Windows NT Server 4.0 are as follows:

✦ Computer with 500 MHz or faster Pentium processor

✦ Color monitor with video card capable of displaying 256 or more colors

✦ CD-ROM drive

✦ 10 Mbps or faster network connection

✦ At least 512MB RAM

✦ Minimum 9GB of available hard drive space

✦ 1GB virtual memory

It is recommended that the computer should have the NTFS file system. If the computer has the Windows 2000 operating system, one of the following versions should be installed with Service Pack 1:

✦ Windows 2000 Professional

✦ Windows 2000 Server

✦ Windows 2000 Advanced Server

However, if the computer has the Windows NT operating system, one of the following should be installed with Service Pack 6a:

✦ Windows NT Workstation 4.0

✦ Windows NT Server 4.0

Client requirements

The requirements for installing VMS bundle CDs on the client side are as follows:

✦ Computer with 266 MHz or faster Pentium processor running Windows 2000, Windows NT 4.0, or Windows 95/98 or Solaris SPARCstation or Sun Ultra 10 running Solaris 2.7

✦ Minimum 2GB available hard drive space

✦ 400MB virtual memory for Windows

✦ Minimum 64MB RAM

To install VMS, you need to install two CDs. Then, you need to install VPN Monitor. The following sections discuss the installation procedure for both the CDs and VPN Monitor on Windows 2000 and Windows NT.

Installing CD One on Windows 2000 and Windows NT

To install the CD One on Windows 2000 and Windows NT, you need to perform the following steps:

1. Log in as a local administrator on the computer on which you want to install CD One.

2. Insert the CD One into the CD-ROM drive.

   • If the Autorun feature is enabled in the computer, the Installer window opens automatically.

   • If Autorun is not enabled, complete Steps 3 through 11.

3. Choose Start ➪ Run to open the Run dialog box.

4. In the Open box, type the following command:

   `e:\autorun.exe`

   where *e* is the CD-ROM drive. The Installer window opens, ready to proceed with installation.

5. In the Installer window, click the Install button. The Welcome screen appears.

6. Click the Next button. The Setup Type dialog box appears.

7. Choose the Typical option and then click Next.

   The installation script checks dependencies and verifies the available disk space; the Start Copying File dialog box appears.

8. Click Next. The installation proceeds and the Integration Utility dialog box appears.

9. Select Later and then click the Next button. The Requirements Verification screen appears.

10. Click OK.

    When the installation is complete, the Restart Windows dialog box appears, asking if you want to restart your system.

    If you are installing CD One on Windows 2000, the Restart Windows dialog box might not appear. To complete the installation, you must restart your system manually. CD One is installed in the default directory, `c:\Program Files\CSCOpx`.

11. After the installation is complete, configure the Web browser on the client system.

Installing CD Two on Windows 2000 and Windows NT

After installing CD One, you must either install CD Two or Resource Manager Essentials. By default, the program installs CD Two in the same location as CD One.

To install CD Two on Windows 2000 and Windows NT systems, perform the following steps:

1. Log in as the local administrator on the computer on which you have installed CD One.

2. Insert the CD Two in the CD-ROM drive. If the Autorun feature is enabled on the computer, the Installer window opens automatically. However, if the Autorun feature is not enabled on the computer, to open the Installer window in the Run dialog box, type the following command:

   `e:\autorun.exe`

   where *e* represents the CD-ROM drive.

3. Click Install. The Welcome screen appears.

4. Click Next. The Start Copying Files dialog box appears.

5. Click Next. The installation program now checks dependencies and system requirements. The Requirements Verification dialog box displays the results of the requirements checking and indicates whether the installation can continue.

6. If the minimum recommended requirements are met, click OK. The Setup screen appears, displaying installation progress while files are copied and applications are configured. Then the Setup Complete dialog box appears.

7. Click the Finish button to finish the installation.

   If minimum system requirements are not met, an error message appears. Cancel the installation by clicking OK in the error-message box. Then check your system, make sure that all minimum requirements are met, and restart the installation.

Tip

After the installation is complete, remove the CD-ROM from the drive. If you did not restart the computer after installing CD One, restart it now.

Installing VPN Monitor on Windows 2000 and Windows NT

To install VPN Monitor, you first need to install both the CDs. To install VPN Monitor on Windows 2000 and Windows NT, perform the following steps:

1. Log in as the local administrator on the computer on which you installed CD One and CD Two.

2. Insert the VPN Monitor CD-ROM into the CD-ROM drive.

   If the Autorun feature is enabled on the computer system, the Installer window opens automatically.

Note

If the Autorun feature is not enabled, issue the `autorun.exe` command to open the Installer window.

3. Click Install. The Welcome screen appears.

4. Click Next. The Start Copying Files dialog box appears.

5. Click Next. The installation program checks dependencies and system requirements.

   The Requirements Verification dialog box displays the results of the requirements checking and shows whether the installation can continue. If minimum requirements are not met, an error message appears.

6. Click OK. The files are copied and applications are configured. Then the Setup Complete dialog box appears.

7. Click the Finish button and remove the CD-ROM from the drive.

Logging in for the first time after installing CD One, CD Two, and VPN Monitor

The CiscoWorks2000 Server desktop is the interface for CiscoWorks2000 network-management applications, including VPN Monitor. When you log in for the first time after installing CD One and Two and Installing the Monitor, make sure that the browser is configured correctly for CiscoWorks2000. To log in, follow these steps:

1. Connect to the CiscoWorks2000 Server from the Web browser.

2. Enter **admin** in both the User Name and Password fields of the Login Manager.

3. Click Connect or press Enter.

Adding devices in inventory

After installing VMS, you can add or update devices in the inventory. To add devices in inventory, follow the steps given here:

1. Log in to CiscoWorks2000 server. The CiscoWorks2000 Server desktop appears.

2. Choose Resource Manager Essentials ➪ Administration ➪ Inventory ➪ Add Devices to add a device.

3. The Add a Single Device dialog box appears. Enter the access information and annotations for one device.

4. In the Device Name box, enter the device name or its IP address.

5. Click Next. The Enter Login Authentication Information dialog box opens.

6. In the Read Community String box, enter an appropriate value. Click Next.

7. Click Finish. The Single Device Add dialog box shows that the device has been added to the Pending list.

8. Click Add Another if you want to add another device.

Updating devices in inventory

To update a device in inventory, follow these steps.

1. Log in to CiscoWorks2000 server. The CiscoWorks2000 Server desktop appears.
2. Choose Resource Manager Essentials ➪ Administration ➪ Inventory ➪ Update Inventory.
3. The Update Device dialog box appears. Enter the access information and annotations for one device.
4. In the Device Name box, enter the device name or its IP address.
5. Click Next. The Enter Login Authentication Information dialog box opens.
6. In the Read Community String box, enter an appropriate value. Click Next.
7. Click Finish.

Verifying installation

To verify that all the CDs in the bundle have been successfully installed, make sure that the following drawers appear on the CiscoWorks2000 desktop:

✦ Server Configuration
✦ Device Manager
✦ Management Connection
✦ Resource Manager Essentials (appears if you have installed CD Two)
✦ VPN Management Solution

Summary

This chapter explained the features of Cisco PIX Firewall Manager, the system requirements for implementing PIX Firewall Manager, and the installation procedure for PIX Firewall. A review of the features and components of VPN/Security Management Solution led into the installation procedure for VPN/Security Management Solution on Windows 2000 and Windows NT.

✦   ✦   ✦

A Networking Primer

To aid in the selection and deployment of network-security measures, Part VII refreshes your knowledge of basic networking concepts. It reviews standard types of networks, networking models, and topologies (as well as network cabling and devices). For those new to network administration (or interested in targeting a particular network layer for security enhancement), Chapter 18 reviews the OSI networking model and standard networking protocols.

Networking Basics

As computers have become indispensable communications tools, one understandable result is a persistent quest to achieve consistently high standards of data transfer. The predominant business advantage that computers presently offer is the capability to operate and share data as linked, mutually interacting systems — a *network*. With the use of networks, high-speed data transfer within a company — no matter how geographically scattered its offices — becomes not only possible, but also cost-effective.

This chapter throws light on the concepts any new network administrator must master in order to tackle the job. The chapter introduces the types of networks, the standard networking models and layouts (topologies), as well as the brass tacks of network cabling, leased lines, network architecture, hardware devices, and management concerns.

Introduction to Networks

Two basic tools are essential for understanding networks: the standard terminology of the industry and the accepted models for network design. Networks are classified on the basis of how many computers they connect, the relationship between those computers, and the specific hardware, software, and layout used to connect them.

Although this book includes a glossary with a more extensive collection of networking terms, the following list is a good starting point:

+ **Networking hardware:** All hardware devices used for networking — in effect, any physical medium (such as cable) or device (such as a router) that interconnects computers on a network.

✦ **Networking software:** Applications whose purpose and function is to operate and implement a network — typically, such software would include the network operating system and the specialized client/server applications that coordinate the operation of the computers on a network.

✦ **Network Operating System (NOS):** A software program that enables computers on a network to exchange data and communicate with each other. Examples are Windows 2000 Server, Linux, Unix, and Solaris.

✦ **Network Interface Card (NIC):** Also known as a *network card*, this circuit board is dedicated to networking tasks and located on the motherboard. Using its NIC, a computer connects to the network and can communicate with other computers on the network.

✦ **Server:** A computer that provides services to the client computers based on the requests placed by them.

✦ **Client:** A computer that requests services from the server or from other clients.

✦ **Peer:** A computer that requests from (and provides services to) other computers on the network. A peer can act as a server as well as a client.

Networking Models

Two networking models predominate: *client/server* and *peer-to-peer*. Depending on the requirements of your organization (as well as factors such as network size, design, and cost), you can decide to implement either model; upcoming sections provide details of their respective advantages and limitations.

Client/server model

This model consists of a server that answers the requests of multiple client computers, either accepting or rejecting the requests according to factors such as the clients' established privilege levels. After a request is accepted, the server processes it and returns a result to the client. The client/server network model is suitable for networks that have a large number of computers. The server stores all necessary resources that the client computers are configured and permitted to use. Figure 17-1 depicts the client/server model.

Tip

Use a client/server design when your network has more than 25 client computers.

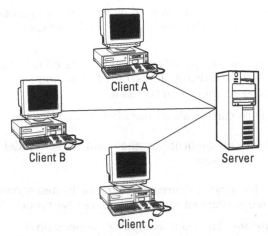

Figure 17-1: The client/server model

If a large number of clients connect to the server, you may want to establish one or more servers to handle specific types of transactions and provide specialized services to the client computers. Examples of such *dedicated* servers are

✦ **File server:** Shares data with and among the client computers.

✦ **Print server:** Connected to a printer, this server treats the printer as a resource that the clients share. The client computers can request print jobs; the server processes them and sends them to the printer.

✦ **Web server:** Provides regulated access to the Internet (and sometimes also displays content such as the company Web page on the Internet). Client computers can connect to the Internet through the Web server and through browse-approved sites.

✦ **Database server:** Maintains a database of useful information and regulates access to the information, providing read/write privileges to client accounts depending on their established privilege levels and legitimate need for stored data.

✦ **Remote-access server:** Supports remote connections. The client computers can dial in from remote locations and access resources on the server. The connection is established using the public telephone system.

The client/server model offers certain practical advantages:

✦ **Ease of management:** The power to manage resources on each computer on the network lies with the system administrator who operates the server. Management of resources is centralized; individuals using the client computers need not be trained to perform advanced administrative tasks.

✦ **Security:** The server is the focal point of centralized network-security measures. Client computers can be secured largely by securing the server computer.

✦ **Permissions for shared resources:** The permissions on the shared resources on the server can be customized. As a result of this, only the person who is authorized to access a particular resource can access it.

✦ **Ease of backups:** Regular backups can be taken centrally to securely store data.

No one model of networking is right for all applications; the client/server model is no exception. It has two general disadvantages:

✦ **Hardware requirements:** The hardware requirements for a dedicated server are high-end; buying a dedicated server can easily be an expensive proposition.

✦ **Dependency on the administrator:** The client computers depend on the administrator to perform all administrative tasks. An inefficient or careless administrator can have an adverse impact on the performance of the network.

Peer-to-peer network model

The peer-to-peer network model is often appropriate for smaller networks. In this model each computer is required to act as both a client and a server. All computers on the peer-to-peer network can share resources amongst themselves. Figure 17-2 depicts the peer-to-peer model.

Figure 17-2: The peer-to-peer model

For networks of appropriate size, the peer-to-peer model offers the following advantages:

✦ **Cost-effectiveness:** Peer-to-peer networks are cost-effective because none of the computers must have a superior hardware configuration.

✦ **Shared administrative work:** Because the computers in a peer-to-peer network can act as clients as well as servers, they don't depend on the system administrator to perform administrative tasks.

✦ **Ease of setup:** Peer-to peer networks can be configured with ease.

However, peer-to-peer networks suffer from the following disadvantages:

✦ **Uneven security:** Each individual on a peer-to-peer network is responsible for the security of his/her computer. Thus the security of the network suffers even if one of the peer computers on the network doesn't take adequate precautionary measures.

✦ **High training requirements:** Each user on the network must be trained to be capable enough to manage his or her computer. Thus the cost of training could be high.

✦ **Lack of central administration:** Without central administration, managing the resources can be difficult and relatively inefficient.

Types of Networks

Networks can be classified by number of users, geographical scope, and the technologies on which they are based. Some commonly used types of networks are as follows:

✦ LANs (local-area networks)

✦ WANs (wide-area networks)

✦ Public networks

✦ Intranets

✦ Extranets

Local-area network

Two or more computers connected to share information form a network. A privately owned network that spans a building or a campus with a size of a few kilometers is referred to as a local-area network (LAN).

Designing a LAN involves selecting an appropriate topology, appropriate cabling, and appropriate network architecture.

Note   Network topologies, network cabling, and LAN architectures will be discussed later in this chapter.

Wide-area network

In response to new needs for communication and reduced communication costs, wide-area networks (WANs) are growing in popularity. A WAN is a network spread over wide areas, such as across cities, states, or countries. The geographic dispersal of offices, increasing numbers of telecommuters, and the growth of client/server applications have increased the demand for WAN connections to remote sites. In constructing WANs to meet this rising demand, IT professionals struggle with a variety of issues, such as evolving services, emerging applications, and mobile users.

Selecting an appropriate WAN service is becoming increasingly complex. The number of WAN services to choose from continues to grow, but no single service has emerged as the solution for all situations. One must make constant trade-offs between cost, performance, and availability.

It might be advantageous to change or reconfigure WAN services frequently to adapt to changing tariffs and minimize WAN charges, but the process of reconfiguring, or even replacing a piece of equipment to handle a different WAN service can be a problem. If the process is complex and costly, organizations may actually find it easier and less expensive to keep their existing configuration and absorb the tariff increases, rather than change services. It is only when the premise equipment allows flexibility that organizations can truly design their WANs to best meet both their business needs and budgetary requirements.

The following standards and services are integral to a WAN:

✦ **X.25:** This standard was developed during the 1970s to provide an interface between public packet switched networks and their customers. X.25 defines the packet-switched data network protocols to be followed for the exchange of data and control information between Data Terminal Equipment (DTE) — usually a computer — and Data Circuit Terminating Equipment (DCE) — switching node. All devices that conform to this standard can communicate with each other. To make sure that the packets are transmitted in order, X.25 uses an acknowledged connection-oriented service. Acknowledgment is sent from each hop, which makes it rather slow but reliable. X.25 specifies a structure of three layers based on the first three layers of the OSI model — the Physical, Data Link, and Network layers.

OSI layers are discussed in detail in Chapter 18.

✦ **Frame Relay:** Frame Relay is a standards-based technology defined by both American National Standards Institute (ANSI) and International Telecommunication Union (ITU). Transmission rates range from 56/64 Kbps to 45 Mbps. Frame Relay is a Data Link-layer protocol (OSI level 2) that provides signaling, data transfer, and switching to route data to a desired destination at higher speeds and throughput rates. Frame Relay defines a DTE/DCE interface that can multiplex many virtual circuits over a single physical transmission link. Frame Relay is a Data Link-layer protocol.

✦ **Integrated Services Digital Network (ISDN):** The most common telecommunication network is the public circuit-switched telephone system. This system was designed for carrying analog voice and is not suitable for modern communication needs. With the need for end-to-end digital data transmission increasing, the world's telephone companies met in 1984 and agreed to build a new, fully digital, circuit-switched telephone system by the early part of the 21st century. This new service (called ISDN) integrates voice and other services. ISDN brings the digital network to the customer. The twisted-pair copper telephone line that could traditionally carry only one voice, one computer, or one fax communication can now carry as many as three separate communications at the same time through the same line by using ISDN.

✦ **Switched Multimegabit Data Services (SMDS):** This is a high-speed packet-switched datagram-based data communication service offered by telephone companies to subscribers. The speeds vary from 1 to 34 Mbps. It supports all major networking protocols and can interconnect Ethernet, Token Ring, and FDDI networks. SMDS, also called *Connectionless Broadband Data Service* (CBDS), is a packet-switched datagram service designed for high-speed WAN data communications. SMDS is described in a series of specifications produced by the Bellcore organization.

✦ **Digital Subscriber Line (DSL):** Services include ADSL (Asymmetric Digital Subscriber Line), HDSL (High Bit-Rate Digital Subscriber Line), SDSL (Single-Line Digital Subscriber Line), and VDSL (Very High Bit-Rate Digital Subscriber Line). DSL technologies use sophisticated modulation schemes to pack data onto copper wires. xDSL (Extended DSL) operates over existing copper telephone lines and requires short runs of cable to a central telephone office; it can also operate on local loops created either intra-building or intra-campus. xDSL supports high-speed Internet/intranet access, online services, video-on-demand, TV signal delivery, interactive entertainment, and voice transmission to all consumer markets. The major advantage of high-speed xDSL services is that they can all be supported on existing copper phone lines. The data-transfer rate varies; *downstream* traffic (from the service provider to the customer site) can travel at a minimum of 786 Kbps (for SDSL), up to a maximum of 52 Mbps (for a VDSL). For upstream traffic (from the customer to the service provider), it varies from a minimum of 786 Kbps for SDSL to 13 Mbps for VDSL. Digital connectivity uses digital modems to accomplish the task of data transfer.

✦ **Synchronous Optical Network (SONET):** Most of today's telecommunication networks in advanced countries make use of fiber-optic cables. In the mid-1980s, a number of companies got together along with the CCITT (now ITU-T) to standardize the optical systems. This resulted in a standard called SONET. In Europe, the same CCITT recommendations are referred to as Synchronous Digital Hierarchy (SDH). Most present networks in Europe and the United States use trunks running SDH/SONET in the Physical layer. With the advent of SONET interface boards, customers can plug their computers directly into telephone networks over conditioned leased lines.

Public networks

Public networks, though unsecured and relatively indiscriminate in the activities they support, are generally cheaper to use than private networks. The three basic types of public networks — PSTN, PSDN, and PPDN — are detailed in upcoming sections.

PSTN

Public Switched Telephone Networks (PSTN) is a worldwide system of separately owned and operated networks. This system provides customers with a variety of high-quality voice and data services. The different components of PSTN are as follows:

✦ Local exchanges that provide telephone services in a specific local area

✦ National Exchanges that provide long-distance services between regions

✦ Recognized Private Operating Agencies (RPOAs) that provide other telecommunication services like cellular mobile telephone networks and packet networks for data communications

PSTN offers two types of services:

✦ **Switched services:** Provided through shared lines and facilities of PSTN

✦ **Dedicated services:** Provides the same facilities as switched services through separate lines or routing patterns

The media used can be twisted-pair, coax, or fiber-optic cable. Using PSTN, the current network media can be extended. The service is often much cheaper than installing a new, long-distance transmission media. The customers install their own wiring and equipment on their premises and connect it to the wiring of the telephone company.

As a PSTN is a circuit-switched network, the circuit links between any two points and the line quality may vary from one call to another causing variations in transmission quality. This may show up as differences in modem speed, throughput, or loss of carrier. Availability and reliability are other problems associated with PSTN.

PSDN

PSDN or *Packet Switched Data Network* is a form of public data network in which messages are transmitted in one or more fixed-length data packets by finding the best route for each packet.

In *packet switching*, messages are divided into fixed-length segments, or "packets" and then sent through the network from the source to the destination. At each intermediate node of the switch, the packet is buffered, examined, and queued (the store-and-forward method is used). However, each node can dispatch a packet without waiting for the rest of the message; thus, the technique achieves high throughput using a form of time-division multiplexing. Good line utilization is achievable, with a high degree of reliability and flexibility. The mode of working is to deliver packets without the virtual-circuit distinction between phases for setting up and tearing down calls and data transfers.

Since the packets travel from the source to the destination through various nodes, they are likely to reach their destination at different times. To help reassemble the packets into the original information structure, each packet is attached with a sequence number.

PPDN

A *Public Packet Data Network* (PPDN) is a network of separate packet networks. Unlike PSTN, these networks use packet-switching to transmit data. In some countries, private companies are also allowed to operate PPDN. ARPAnet and Telnet are examples of PPDN. PPDN offers the same service as PSTN, but uses the packet-switching method instead of circuit switching.

 Packet-switching and circuit-switching methods are discussed in detail in Chapter 18.

The packet-switching method of transmission offers certain advantages:

✦ Better bandwidth utilization as the data is split across different routes.

✦ Alternate routes can be defined in case of problems with one route.

These advantages can be used to offer services more reliable than PSTN.

Intranets

An *intranet* is a private, corporate network that implements the protocols, standards, and processes found on the Internet. It also provides the security privileges of a private LAN. The term *intranet* was coined in 1995. A combination of *intra* and *network*, the term means an internal network. An intranet is a non-public Web site devoted to one organization. Although an intranet can function on its own, it can be linked to the Internet for greater accessibility of information. Refer to Figure 17-3, which illustrates a corporate intranet also connected to the Internet.

The network infrastructure of an organization can be greatly enhanced by the power of a corporate intranet. Intranets allow organizations to deploy enterprise-wide applications. These applications can run in heterogeneous environments. They can also interact with a variety of legacy data sources like mainframe databases and client/server databases.

An intranet is based upon open standards and protocols. Consequently, intranets provide a framework for applications highly interoperable, portable cross-platform, and scalable. Intranets also offer access to all resources via an intuitive, easy-to-use, browser-based software interface. They provide authenticated and encrypted access to sensitive information. Intranets allow common access to crucial information across organizational, geographic, and platform boundaries.

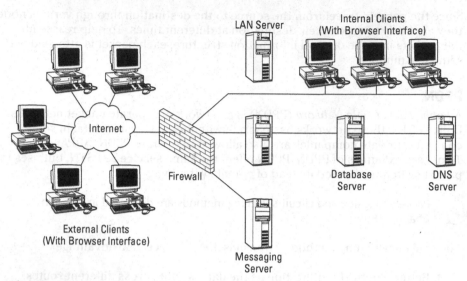

Figure 17-3: An intranet with a connection to the Internet

Having looked at the design issues of an intranet, the building blocks of an intranet are as follows:

✦ TCP/IP protocol suite

✦ Web-server software

✦ Web-database server

✦ Software tools for creating HTML documents

✦ WWW browser software

✦ DNS server

✦ Firewall

✦ Helper applications that work along with browser software

✦ Collaborative computing technologies

TCP/IP Protocol Suite

Just as TCP/IP is the primary protocol of the Internet, it's also the primary protocol of intranets. TCP/IP should be active on every machine that participates in the corporate intranet. Despite its known security loopholes, TCP/IP is still the ideal protocol for intranets for the following reasons:

✦ **Reliable data delivery:** TCP/IP provides reliable delivery of data, even when inoperable links are encountered. The dynamic routing procedure that TCP/IP provides makes this possible.

✦ **Scalability:** TCP/IP can support up to 20 million users.

✦ **Compatibility:** TCP/IP is entirely compatible with almost every network operating system.

✦ **Encryption and compression support:** TCP/IP supports compression methods and encryption, thereby increasing the speed at which data is delivered, while maintaining the privacy of data.

Web-server software

At the heart of the intranet is the Web server. This software runs on the central computer and provides access to the information located on the intranet. When a user requests any type of information, it must first pass through the Web server before it is sent to a user. The most commonly used Web servers are as follows:

✦ Microsoft Internet Information Server

✦ Netscape SuiteSpot

✦ Apache

✦ WebSite Professional

✦ Lotus Domino

Many of these Web servers are available for multiple operating systems, such as Unix, Windows NT, SUN Solaris, and so on.

Web database server

A Web database, like any other database, is a repository of information. This repository can be accessed either using a query language like SQL or by a set of programming APIs. Access to a Web database is not achieved through commands typed in at the command line or by using software designed for a particular platform.

Instead, a Web database is accessed through other Web applications (for example, forms developed using HTML tags). Using server-side CGI scripts, applications can be designed for the purpose of querying a database produce specific results based on user requirements.

A Web database can be integrated into applications accessed only through a Web browser. A corporate intranet would typically maintain a number of such Web databases. Information from various parts of an organization can be integrated using Web-based applications and presented to users as though they were from a single source. Internal and external users of the intranet can also manage information better for faster access.

End-users access information in a Web database through a browser interface. Access to data can be provided through hyperlinks. This process helps to optimize bandwidth usage. This process differs from other database systems that give the results through an SQL query.

Some of the popular database servers that have support for the Web are as follows:

✦ Oracle

✦ Sybase SQL Server

✦ Microsoft SQL Server

These databases are relational and support OLTP (OnLine Transaction Processing) and scalability.

Software tools for creating HTML documents

HTML is used for creating the Web pages that comprise the content of the intranet. There are a number of tools available for creating HTML code. You can create Web pages using a text editor such as vi in Unix, or use graphical editors such as Microsoft Windows Notepad, MS-DOS edit, or any word processor. Specialized HTML editors are also available. These tools can be categorized as follows:

✦ **Word-processor add-ons** allow a standard word processor to be used for creating and modifying HTML pages.

✦ **Standalone HTML editors** can provide WYSIWYG (What You See Is What You Get) capability.

✦ **Conversion tools** allow conversion from a specific document format into HTML.

WWW browser software

The browser software is an application that gives the user flexible options to browse the Web. Some browser software packages available are as follows:

✦ Netscape Navigator

✦ Microsoft Internet Explorer

✦ HotJava

✦ WebSurfer

✦ NCSA Mosaic for Windows and Windows NT

DNS

Like the Internet, any intranet uses the IP addressing scheme. Each server has an IP address assigned to it. A corporate intranet may consist of a number of servers with IP addresses. It is difficult for a user to remember the IP address of each machine. Thus each IP address is mapped to a domain name. For example, the

Human Resource Department may have a domain name of `www.hro.com`. Research and Development may have a domain name of `www.rnd.com`. The domain name of `www.rnd.com` may correspond to an IP address of `172.17.8.242`.

Mapping a given domain name to the respective IP address is the task of the DNS (Domain Name Server). Earlier networks used a text file to map the IP address to the respective domain name. However, a larger network could make maintenance of the text file difficult and error-prone. A DNS server maintains a table that helps the DNS server in mapping the domain name to the IP address.

Firewall

A corporate intranet provides a wealth of information when connected to the Internet. However, along with the easy access to information comes the risk of unauthorized access. Unauthorized external users can easily access confidential information on the intranet. If the corporate intranet is linked to the Internet, users can also go to sites restricted by corporate policies. To safeguard the security of corporate information, a corporate intranet can implement a firewall.

A firewall is a combination of hardware and software that acts as a secure line of defense against external attacks. The software that performs the task of defending against external attacks and preventing confidential information from traveling outside is referred to as the proxy service. The hardware or computer on which this software runs is referred to as the application-level gateway.

 For more information on firewalls, refer to Chapter 8 and Chapter 9.

Helper applications

Typically, a Web browser can display graphical images and play standard sound files. The Web server and the browser use a mechanism called *Multipurpose Internet Mail Extensions* (MIME) to match data sent between the browser and the server. However, other kinds of data require the use of helper applications, also referred to as *external viewers*. If the required file is of a data type that MIME does not support, the browser hands over control to a helper application that handles the respective file. For example, helper applications may be required to execute MPEG files.

Secure/MIME (S/MIME) is an extension of the MIME protocol. Developed in response to the widespread interception and forgery of e-mail, this protocol supports message encryption. Any two packets that support S/MIME can communicate securely over the Internet. S/MIME ensures cryptographic security features, such as confidentiality and authenticity for e-mails.

Collaborative computing

Networking has introduced innumerable communication possibilities within the corporate network. *Collaborative computing* is a system that provides platforms for group discussions and conferencing and training to the employees, irrespective of the geographical location of the users. Collaborative computing can be categorized as follows:

✦ **Synchronous (real-time) collaborative computing:** These computing technologies involve real-time interaction between people.

✦ **Asynchronous (non-real-time) collaborative computing:** This type of computing does not require simultaneous presence of the employees. An example of asynchronous collaborative computing is e-mail (electronic mail).

Extranet

An *extranet* is an intranet partially accessible to authorized outsiders. Typically, an intranet is accessible only to employees of the same organization. On the other hand, an extranet provides various levels of accessibility to outsiders. Like the intranet, the extranet implements the standards and processes found on the Internet. Yet, it securely shares an organization's business information with customers, suppliers, vendors, and partners. The benefits that HTML (HyperText Markup Language), HTTP (HyperText Transfer Protocol), and other Internet technologies have brought to the Internet and intranets can be implemented in extranets.

Companies can use an extranet to perform various vital business tasks:

✦ Share product catalogs with business partners

✦ Collaborate with other companies on joint development and training efforts

✦ Provide access to services provided by one company to a group of other companies, such as an online banking application managed by one company on behalf of affiliated banks

✦ Exchange information of mutual interest exclusively with partner companies

Network Topologies

Designing a LAN involves selecting an appropriate topology. The selection of the topology influences the type of equipment required, network growth, network management, and the cost involved in setting up and maintaining the network. The upcoming sections detail the three basic topologies — Bus, Ring, and Star.

Bus topology

Bus topology consists of a single cable that connects all the computers in the network. Refer to Figure 17-4 to get a better idea of the Bus topology. It is also known as linear Bus because all the computers are connected in a single line. The single cable that connects the computers is also known as the backbone or the segment. The computers, also called nodes, are connected in a linear fashion with each node being connected to two nodes on either side. The nodes on either end are connected to only one node. This is the simplest topology and serves commonly for smaller networks.

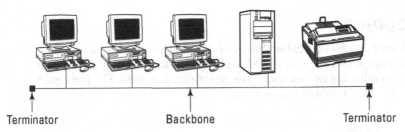

Figure 17-4: Bus topology

The information sent over the network has the address of the destination computer. The information, along with the destination address, is put on the cable in the form of electronic signals. All the computers on the network receive this information, but disregard it unless their address matches the destination address. Only one computer can send data at a time.

The data travels from one end of the cable to the other. If the signal is not terminated at the other end of the cable, it bounces back. This condition is known as *ringing*. To stop the signals from ringing, they must be terminated with the help of special devices called *terminators*. The terminators are attached at both the ends of the cable to stop the signals from ringing.

The number of users is one of the main factors that affect the performance of a Bus network. An increase in the number of users leads to an increase in the time a computer must wait before it can transmit data.

Bus is a passive topology; the nodes do not participate in boosting the signal and passing it to the next node. A special device called a *repeater* must boost the signals.

The advantages of using the Bus topology are as follows:

✦ It is a simple, reliable, and easy-to-implement topology.

✦ It requires the least cabling (compared to other topologies) and therefore is cost-efficient.

The disadvantages of using the Bus topology are as follows:

✦ The network performance is negatively affected with an increase in the number of users.

✦ If more than one computer decides to send data at the same time, they will interrupt each other's signals and none of them can send data. In such a situation, data must be sent again, wasting time and bandwidth.

✦ Troubleshooting a Bus network is difficult because a loose or broken cable is difficult to trace.

Ring topology

Ring topology consists of a cable that connects all the computers in a ring. Figure 17-5 shows how computers are connected if a Ring topology is used. Each node is connected to two adjacent nodes; there are no terminated ends. The information travels in a ring, without a must-terminate signal.

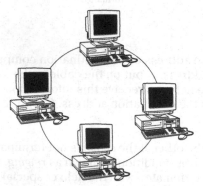

Figure 17-5: Ring topology

Sometimes ring topology uses token passing as the transmission method: A special packet called a token is passed around the network, and a computer must have the token before it can send data. The computer modifies the token, gives it the electronic address of a destination computer, and puts the token on the network. The modified token is passed around the ring, through all the other computers, until it finds a computer with an address that matches the address on the data.

Subsequently, the destination computer sends back a message to the sender stating that it has received the data. Finally, the sending computer releases the token on the network for another computer to send the data.

The number of users affects the performance of a Ring network too. In this topology, however, more than one token can be active at a time — and more than one computer at a time can send data.

A Ring topology, unlike the Bus topology, is active: Each node on the ring boosts the signal before passing it to the next node.

The advantages of using a Ring network are as follows:

✦ Each computer gets equal access to the token; no single computer can monopolize the network.

✦ No bandwidth is wasted because signals from different computers don't interrupt each other.

✦ The bandwidth saved can be used for time-sensitive features like audio and video.

The disadvantages of using a Ring network are as follows:

✦ If one node on the network is malfunctioning, it can bring down the whole network.

✦ A Ring network is not easy to extend.

✦ A Ring network is difficult to troubleshoot because flaws in a cable are difficult to trace.

Star topology

Star topology consists of various computers connected to one central component called the hub. Figure 17-6 is an example of Star topology. It is easy to expand a Star network because a new node can be added to the hub and the other nodes on the network are not affected.

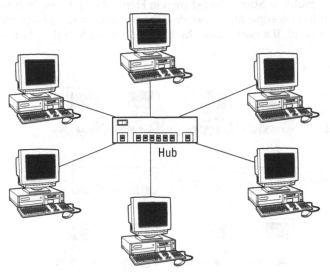

Figure 17-6: Star topology

Each node sends the data to a hub, which resends the data to the destination node.

The hubs can be active or passive. An active hub or multiport repeater regenerates the signal and sends signals to all the nodes connected to it. It requires electrical power to function. A passive hub is merely a connection point and does not regenerate the signal. It does not require electrical power to function.

The advantages of using a Star network are as follows:

✦ It is easy to add nodes to a Star network without disturbing the other nodes on the network.

✦ It is easy to detect cable faults.

✦ One faulty node does not affect the performance of the other nodes.

The disadvantages of using the Star topology are as follows:

✦ If the hub fails the whole network comes to a standstill.

✦ The cable usage is higher because each node is directly connected to the hub.

✦ The cost of implementing a Star network is higher because of an additional component (the hub).

Star Bus topology

Star Bus topology is a combination of Star and Bus topologies. It consists of one Bus segment connecting multiple Star hubs (shown in Figure 17-7). If one hub fails, the network is divided into two separate networks that cannot communicate with each other. On the other hand, if a node fails, the hub can detect it and isolate it from the network.

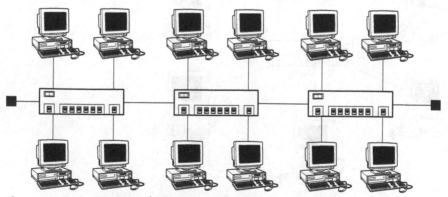

Figure 17-7: Star Bus topology

Star Ring topology

The Star Ring topology is a combination of Star topology and Ring topology. The nodes are connected to a central hub, much like a Star network (shown in Figure 17-8). The ring is implemented within the hub.

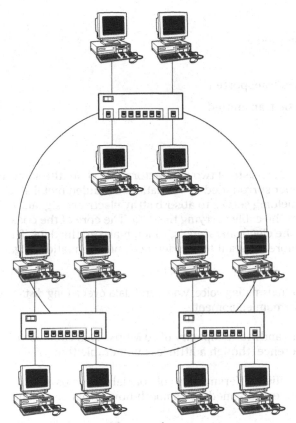

Figure 17-8: Star Ring topology

Network Media: Cabling and Wireless

Computers must be connected to exchange data. Physical media (such as cables) and wireless media (such as radio waves) can provide the necessary connection. Though physical media are preferable (from a security standpoint), wireless media are acceptable if physical cabling is not feasible. Keep in mind these two general principles regarding network media:

✦ The standard types of physical media currently deployed in networks are all varieties of cable — coaxial, twisted-pair, and fiber-optic — each with its own appropriate uses.

✦ The three types of wireless media are in current use: infrared waves, radio, and satellite-assisted microwaves. Often these are relatively costly and hard to secure.

When you choose a particular type of connection medium for your network, consider the following factors:

✦ Cost of equipment

✦ Type of data to be transmitted

✦ Distance to be covered

✦ Speed at which the data is transported

✦ Criticality of the data to be transmitted

Coaxial cable

A *coaxial cable*, also called coax, consists of two conductors that share the same axis. It has a core made of solid copper surrounded by insulation, a braided metal shielding, and an outer cover. The shielding serves to absorb stray electronic signals, called noise, so that they do not affect the cable carrying the data. The core of the coax is made of copper and carries the electronic signals, which make up the data. This shielding makes a coax cable more resistant to interference and attenuation (signal loss).

Tip   Coaxial cables are good for transmitting voice, video, and data over a long distance, at a high rate, and with minimum equipment.

A coaxial cable typically has a bandwidth capacity of 10 Mbps. This cable is vulnerable to electromagnetic interference, though a little less vulnerable than UTP.

Cable manufacturers have classified different types of coaxial cables based on the size, impedance — resistance of the media to smooth flow of signals — and the type of the core of a cable.

Types of coaxial cables

The two types of coaxial cables are *thinnet* and *thicknet*.

Thinnet

Thinnet is a .25-inch-thick cable. It is flexible and easy to install and maintain. The thinnet cable is directly attached to the network card of the computer. Thinnet cables can carry a signal up to about 185 meters before the signal suffers attenuation.

Thicknet

The thicknet cable is thicker — about .5 inches in diameter and is referred to as Standard Ethernet. As the copper core is thicker, it can carry signals farther than the thinnet cable. A thicknet cable can carry data over a distance of 500 meters before it suffers attenuation. It is sometimes used as a backbone to connect several smaller thinnet-based networks.

A thicknet cable is less flexible than a thinnet cable, and this might make it difficult to install. It is also more costly than a thinnet cable.

Tip   A thicknet cable segment can be connected to a thinnet with the help of a device called the *transceiver*.

Connectors

Coaxial cables are connected to computers using the BNC connectors (see Figure 17-9). This connector is mounted with pins at each end of a cable. It has a center pin connected to the center cable conductor and a metal tube connected to the outer cable shield. A rotating ring outside the tube locks the cable to any connector with holes in it.

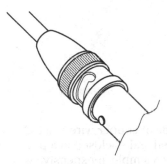

Figure 17-9: A BNC connector

BNC T-connectors (shown in Figure 17-10) are used for connecting two cables to a network interface card (NIC).

Figure 17-10: A BNC T connector

If small segments of a coax are available, they can be connected using a BNC barrel connector (shown in Figure 17-11).

Figure 17-11: A BNC barrel connector

A BNC terminator is attached to the end of a Bus cable to absorb any stray signals (see Figure 17-12). A Bus network must have BNC terminators.

Figure 17-12: A BNC terminator

Twisted-pair

A *twisted-pair cable* consists of two insulated strands of copper wire twisted around each other. A number of such twisted pairs, gathered and enclosed in a protective sheath, form a larger cable. This twisting of wires is a simple, inexpensive way to help minimize interference from other sources. Twisted-pair cables can be used where cost and ease of installation are the main criteria.

Caution   Twisted-pair cable cannot always guarantee the integrity of data transmitted over a long range.

Twisted-pair cable can be either unshielded (UTP) or shielded (STP). Each type has its characteristic dimensions and uses, as detailed in the upcoming sections.

Unshielded twisted-pair

UTP consists of two insulated copper wires twisted around each other (shown in Figure 17-13). The maximum cable length per segment is approximately 100 meters.

Figure 17-13: Unshielded twisted-pair (UTP) cable

UTP supports a bandwidth of 1 to 155 Mbps, though in actual use, its bandwidth capacity is about 10 Mbps. As compared to other cables, the UTP cable is most vulnerable to electromagnetic interference. UTP is generally used for telephone networks. There are five standards for UTP cables (refer to Table 17-1).

Table 17-1 Categories of UTP		
Category	**Transmission**	**Transmission Speed**
1	Voice	Up to 4 Mbps
2	Voice	Up to 4 Mbps
3	Data	Up to 16 Mbps
4	Data	Up to 20 Mbps
5	Data	Up to 100 Mbps

Categories 3, 4, and 5 are data-grade cables. They consist of either four or eight wires enclosed in a jacket. A cable with four wires is referred to as two-pair wire, or a four-core cable, and a cable with eight wires is referred to as four-pair wire or an eight-core cable.

Category 3 cables became popular because they were already installed in almost all buildings as telephone connections. Category 5 cables are an enhancement over Category 3 cables. The Teflon outer-cover and the increased number of twists per centimeter make Category 5 cable less susceptible to crosstalk. This also allows the Category 5 cable to carry data farther.

Note

UTP cables use *RJ-11* and *RJ-45* connectors. RJ-11 (telephone jack) connectors are used for two-pair wires while RJ-45 connectors are used for four-pair wires. These connectors are attached at both ends of the patch cables. One end of the patch cable is attached to the computer while the other end is connected to the wall jack. The wall jack connects the drop cable to a punch-down block, which in turn is connected to a patch panel. The patch panel has patch cables that provide connectivity to other devices.

Shielded twisted-pair

STP consists of a copper braid jacket and a foil wrap between and around the wires (see Figure 17-14). This makes the signals less susceptible to outside interference. The maximum length of an STP segment is 100 meters.

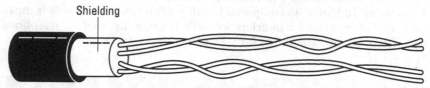

Figure 17-14: Shielded twisted-pair (STP) cable

 STP is easy to install. It supports a bandwidth of 1 to 155 Mbps (typically 16 Mbps). It is less vulnerable to electromagnetic interference than UTP and coaxial cables.

Fiber-optic cable

A fiber-optic cable consists of a core of ultra-thin fiber of glass or fused silica (see Figure 17-15). This core conducts light. The core is surrounded by another layer of glass (*cladding*) that reflects the light back into the core. The core and cladding are enclosed in a plastic sheath.

 The diameter of an optical fiber is the same as the diameter of a human hair.

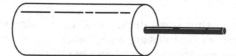

Figure 17-15: Fiber-optic cable

At one end of the cable, a light source, typically a *light-emitting diode* (LED) or a laser diode emits pulses of light. On the other end of the cable, a light detector — a photodiode — emits electrical signals when light falls on it.

Advantages of fiber-optic cables are as follows:

✦ They can transmit data safely at a much higher rate than other kinds of cables. This rate can vary from 100 Mbps to 2 Gbps.

✦ They are much lighter and thinner than copper cables.

✦ They are more resistant to attenuation and outside interference.

Fiber-optic cables have two general disadvantages:

✦ Fiber, being a new technology, requires skilled people to handle it.

✦ Optical transmission is one-way only; two-way transmissions require two fibers (or different frequencies on one fiber).

Fiber-optic cables are of two types: multimode and single-mode.

Multimode fiber

Multimode fiber allows multiple paths of light (as shown in Figure 17-16). Light waves bounce inside the fiber until they reach the detector, which uses light-emitting diodes (LEDs) for signaling. Although multimode provides less bandwidth than single-mode fiber, it is more affordable.

Signal bouncing off the walls

Figure 17-16: Multimode fiber

Single-mode fiber

In a single-mode fiber, the diameter of the fiber is reduced to one wavelength of light, propagating the light to travel in a straight line without any bouncing (see Figure 17-17). Single-mode fiber requires laser diodes to operate, which are costlier than the LEDs. However, they are more efficient and travel a longer distance.

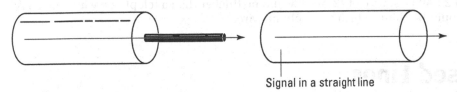

Signal in a straight line

Figure 17-17: Single-mode fiber

IBM cabling system

IBM defined its own cable types in 1984, setting its own standards and specifications. The IBM system classifies cables into the labeled types shown in Table 17-2.

Table 17-2
IBM Cabling Types

IBM Type	Label	Description
Type 1	STP	Two pairs of 22 AWG wires surrounded by an outer braided shield.
Type 2	Voice and data cable	Two STP cables of 22 AWG for data, a shield and four pairs of 26 AWG for voice.
Type 3	Voice-grade cable	Four UTP cables of 22 or 24 AWG. Used for cable runs within walls.
Type 4	Not defined	
Type 5	Fiber-optic cable	Two 62.5/125 micron multimode optical fibers.
Type 6	Data patch cable	Two 26 AWG STP cables. Used to connect devices with wall jacks.
Type 7	Not defined	
Type 8	Carpet cable	Two STP 26 AWG cables, in a flat jacket. For use under carpets.
Type 9	Plenum	Two STP cables, fire-resistant.

The preceding classification of cable types is defined to specify which cable type would be appropriate for a given environment. These cable types conform to the *American Wire Gauge* (AWG) standards.

The AWG system serves to indicate the thickness of the wire. The AWG number decreases as the thickness of the wire increases. A telephone wire has a thickness of 22 AWG. A wire of 12 AWG would be thicker than a telephone wire, and 24 AWG would be thinner than a telephone wire.

Leased Lines

Leased lines — permanent telephone lines used to connect two distant locations — are different from dial-up connections. With dial-up connections, you must establish a connection before you can browse the Internet; if you are using leased lines, the connection is always active. Five types of leased lines are available: conventional, T1 links, T2 links, T3 links, and T4 links.

Conventional leased lines

Conventional leased lines work on a single pair of telephone lines and offer a reliable media for information transfer. They offer a speed ranging from 2.4 Kbps to 19.2 Kbps and work on analog signals. However, as the distance between the source and the destination stations increases, the leased line has to pass through a series of intermediate telephone exchanges, which reduces the reliability of data transfer.

With the advancement in technology, analog telephone exchanges have been upgraded to digital exchanges. This ensures a high degree of reliability on data transfers in the conventional leased lines when compared to high-speed digital lines. Today 9.6-Kbps leased lines are also provided as digitized leased lines by means of using multiplexers in the telephone exchanges.

T1 link

One of the most popular methods of interconnecting offices is a T1 link. This is a 1.544 Mbps dedicated link that consists of 24 multiplexed channels. The analog signals from the 24 channels are fed into a *codec* (coder/decoder) one at a time. The T1 link uses time division multiplexing.

Each channel inserts seven data bits and one control bit into the frame (thus a frame consists of 192 bits and an extra bit for framing). The analog signals are digitized using *Pulse Code Modulation* (PCM) at a rate of 8000 samples per second, resulting in a data-transfer rate of up to 1.544 Mbps. When a T1 link is used, 23 channels transfer the data; one channel carries a special synchronization pattern that allows faster recovery if errors occur during transmission.

A variation of the T1 link is the T1-C link, which operates at 3.152 Mbps. Another variation of the T1 link is the Fractional T1 link, where the customer uses only a portion of the 24 channels available in a T1 link. This not only provides less bandwidth, but it is also cheaper because a customer is charged only for the channels used.

The CCITT has a recommendation for PCM carriers at 2.048 Mbps called E1. This carrier has 32 8-bit data samples. Thirty of these channels are used for information and two are used for signaling.

E1 is a link commonly used in European countries and is considered the European standard. Both E1 and T1 use PCM carriers and provide clear and discrete channels. The only difference between E1 and T1 is that T1 uses 24 channels for transmission and E1 uses 32 channels.

Under a standard given by AT&T, T1 links are most commonly used in North America and Japan.

T2 link

Many T1 lines can be multiplexed together using time-division multiplexing (TDM). Four lines of T1 are multiplexed to give a T2 link. Four T1 links generate a data rate of 6.176 Mbps. The effective data rate, when the bits for framing and recovery are added, is 6.312 Mbps.

T3 link

Six T2 links are combined to produce a T3 stream. T3 streams operate at a speed of 44.736 Mbps. T3 links are either used by Internet Service Providers (ISPs) for their link to the Internet or used by large corporations for their link to the ISP. The operating speed of a T3 is approximately 45 Mbps.

T4 link

Seven T3 links combine to produce a T4 stream. A T4 stream operates at 274.176 Mbps.

LAN Network Architecture

Network architecture is defined as the overall structure of a network. Some important components of a network architecture are cables, topology, and *access methods*.

Tip   A set of rules that specify how a computer puts data on the network and reads data from the network is referred to as the access method.

The most common LAN network architectures in use today are Ethernet, Token Ring, FDDI, and ATM.

Ethernet

Ethernet is currently the most widely installed LAN architecture. In the early 1960s, the University of Hawaii developed a WAN called ALOHA to connect its computers spread across the Hawaiian Islands. This laid the foundation for today's Ethernet. In 1975, Xerox introduced the first Ethernet product. This version of Ethernet was designed to connect about a hundred computers on a 1-kilometer cable. The speed of transmission was about 2.94 Mbps.

Initially, the access method that Ethernet used was the ALOHA access method. In this access method, a computer could transmit whenever it wanted to do so. After transmission, it would wait for an acknowledgment. If the acknowledgment was not received within a short period of time, the transmitting station would assume that a collision had occurred. Collision results from two or more devices sending data along the same channel at the same time. After the collision, the respective stations would choose a random backoff time and would then retransmit the data. This access method, also referred to as *pure ALOHA*, actually used only about 18 percent of a channel; the high rate of collisions took up all the rest.

Another system, *slotted ALOHA*, was then developed: Transmission slots were assigned to each station. A station could transmit only during the allotted slot.

This significantly reduced the collision rate. Network utilization increased to almost 37 percent.

To overcome the problems of ALOHA, Ethernet now uses Carrier Sense Multiple Access with Collision Detection (CSMA/CD). In this access method, a computer first "senses" to find if the communication channel is busy. If so, it waits until the channel becomes idle and then tries again. Table 17-3 lists the features of Ethernet.

Table 17-3
Features of Ethernet

Feature	Description
Topology Used	Logically uses Linear Bus
Other Topologies	Star Bus
Access Method	CSMA/CD
Transfer Speed	10Mbps or 100Mbps
Cable Types	Thicknet, thinnet, unshielded twisted-pair, STP, fiber optic
Specifications	IEEE 802.3

IEEE is one of the Standards Organizations that brought the IEEE 802 series standards for LANs. 802.1 introduced the standards. The 802.3 standard lays a set of conventions for a 1-Persistent CSMA/CD LAN. As Ethernet implements the 802.3 standard, it is important to know about IEEE naming standards and 100 Mbps IEEE standards to understand Ethernet better.

IEEE naming standards

IEEE follows a naming convention for the specified LAN standards. The IEEE naming convention can be divided into three parts. Each part has a significance of its own. The names have three parts as listed in Table 17-4.

Table 17-4
IEEE Standard Naming Convention

Name	Description
X	The first part of a number depicts the speed of transmission. For example, 10 would depict a speed of 10 Mbps.
Base	The word "Base" indicates that baseband signaling is being used.
Y	The third part specifies the segment type or length.

An Ethernet network can transfer data at one of two speeds: 10 Mbps or 100 Mbps: The IEEE standards for 10 Mbps Ethernet networks are as follows:

✦ **10Base5:** 10Base5 uses thick coaxial, or thicknet, cabling and Bus topology. The 10Base5 standard imposes a restriction on the maximum number of segments and repeaters in a single network. A segment is a portion of a network bounded by bridges, repeaters, hubs, or switches. The transmission speed for this type of Ethernet is 10 Mbps, the type of signaling used is baseband, and the maximum segment length can be up to 500 meters.

✦ **10Base2:** 10Base2 uses thin coaxial, or thinnet and Bus topology. The 5-4-3 rule in the case of 10Base5 applies for 10Base2 also. Each segment can have a maximum of 30 computers. To increase the length of the cable, BNC barrel connectors can be used. For example, you require a cable length of 50 meters and have two cable segments of length 30 meters and 20 meters, respectively. You can connect the two using a BNC barrel connector. Nevertheless, the use of connectors should be kept to a minimum since a connector reduces the signal quality (unlike a repeater that increases the signal strength).

✦ **10BaseT:** In a 10Base5 or a 10Base2 topology, if a cable break occurred in the backbone, tracking it down would be difficult. Further, the entire network would be "down" in such a situation. This problem has driven systems toward the Star topology. However, within the hub, the signaling system used is still that of the Bus topology. The transmission speed for 10BaseT is 10 Mbps, the type of signaling used is baseband, the maximum segment length is 100 meters, and the type of cable used is UTP.

Tip Maintenance of a 10BaseT network is easier than maintaining 10Base5 or 10Base2. A computer can be added on to the network without affecting the rest of the network. Organizations are increasingly going in for 10BaseT due to the ease of maintenance.

✦ **10BaseF:** Used when the distance between repeaters is large, for example, between buildings. In 10BaseF, the type of cable used is fiber-optic and the link is point-to-point. The type of signaling used is baseband. The maximum segment length in 10BaseF is 2000 meters.

100 Mbps IEEE standards

Client/server computing and multimedia have been accelerating the rate of development in communication networks. Mainframe processing is slowly dying out and is being replaced by decentralized computer processing. Computer capabilities have also increased rapidly. 10 Mbps Ethernet has been unable to keep pace with these changes.

This situation made the IEEE instruct the 802.3 committee in 1992 to come up with a faster LAN. To be backward-compatible with the thousands of existing LANs, one proposal was to keep the 10 Mbps Ethernet as it was, but make it faster. The other proposal was to revamp the entire 10 Mbps system. The IEEE worked quickly on the first proposal, and the 802.3u standard was officially approved in June 1995. (802.3u was not a new standard. It was merely an extension of the existing 802.3 standard.) This set of specifications, referred to as *fast Ethernet,* was a low-cost, Ethernet-compatible LAN operating at 100 Mbps. The committee defined a number of alternatives that could be used with different transmission media.

✦ **100Base-X:** Uses two physical links between nodes, one link for transmission, the other for reception.

✦ **100Base-TX:** Uses Category 5 UTP or STP.

✦ **100Base-FX:** Uses optical fiber.

✦ **100Base-T4:** Uses Category 3 UTP, the cabling system used by 10 Mbps Ethernet. Consequently, no major rewiring is required. However, to achieve the 100 Mbps rate over the lower-quality cable, 100Base-T4 uses four twisted-pair lines between nodes.

The main advantage of the 10 Mbps standard, 10BaseT, is the use of the star-wired Bus. All computers are connected to a central hub, and maintenance is extremely simple. This advantage is carried down to the Fast Ethernet also.

Token Ring

Token Ring uses the *token-passing* access method: A small frame called a *token* (in effect, a special bit pattern) is circulated around the ring. If a computer wishes to transmit, it has to wait until the token reaches it. The computer waiting to transmit seizes the token and changes one bit in the token. This process transforms the token to a *start-of-frame sequence.*

At this point in time, there is no token on the ring. The other stations wishing to transmit data must wait. The frame travels around the ring. The receiving station copies the frame. The frame then returns to the transmitting station, which absorbs or "drains" the frame of all data. Subsequently, the transmitting station inserts a new token on the ring when the following conditions have been met.

When a new token has been inserted into the ring, the next station waiting to transmit can seize it and transmit the data. For example, assume that all stations are idle. Computer A wishes to send data to computer C. Computer A seizes the token. It changes a bit and appends all other fields to this token. It then sends the data to Computer C. Refer to Figure 17-18, which illustrates the token-passing access method.

At this point, no other station can use the token. There is no question of contention or collision, because no two stations can transmit at the same time.

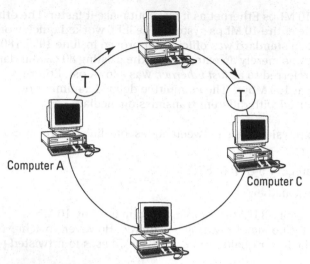

Computer A

Computer C

Figure 17-18: Token-passing access method

When Computer A has transmitted the last of the frames, it regenerates the token, and the token is in circulation once more. Every station gets an equal opportunity to put its data on the network. This access method is not efficient under conditions of light loads; although all stations are idle, a computer will have to wait for the token to reach it. However, under conditions of heavy traffic, network efficiency increases to almost 100 percent. The IEEE 802.5 specifications standardize the token-passing access method.

Token Ring architecture uses a *Star Ring topology*. In the traditional Ring topology, if the cable breaks at some point in the network, the entire ring fails. To avoid this flaw, a Star Ring topology connects its stations physically to a central hub by a cable containing at least two twisted pairs. The stations are part of a logical ring — the path of the token between computers.

Every computer belonging to the token architecture is connected to a central hub. However, the token is circulated through the logical ring only. This is made possible because of the internal ring located in the central hub. The hub is equipped with a certain number of ports, depending on the vendor and the hub model. When all the ports in the hub have been utilized for connecting stations, more rings can be added to extend the network. The ring is equipped with a ring-in and ring-out connection point that serves to connect other hubs to it. A maximum of 12 hubs can be connected to each other.

Tip   Since this architecture uses the token-passing access method, if one station fails, the entire network is "down." However, hubs have in-built fault tolerance. If one of the computers fails, the hub automatically detects the failure and isolates the machine from the network. The failed computer is consequently bypassed, and the token can continue through the network.

FDDI

The Fiber-Distributed Data Interface (FDDI) standard was produced by ANSI in the mid-1980s. It was a period when Fast Ethernet had not emerged as a high-speed networking technology. Network reliability had become an important issue. Today, though not as common as Ethernet, FDDI is being increasingly used for LAN backbones and for connecting high-speed computers in a local area.

The FDDI specifications are for a 100 Mbps, token-passing, dual-ring LAN using fiber optics as the transmission medium. FDDI allows a maximum segment length of 2 km, with a maximum of 1000 stations per segment.

FDDI token-passing uses two rings instead of one. Figure 17-19 illustrates the FDDI token-passing method. The two rings rotate in the opposite directions and are often referred to as dual counter-rotating rings. The primary ring serves to transfer data. The secondary ring serves as a backup.

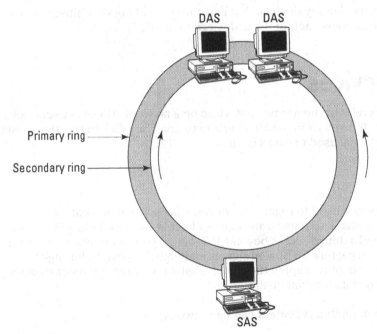

Figure 17-19: FDDI token passing

FDDI has the following advantages:

- ✦ Provides physical durability
- ✦ Uses multiple tokens to improve network speed
- ✦ Provides added security because it does not use electrical signals, which can be tapped

ATM

As LAN technology grew rapidly, the need grew for a worldwide standard that would provide interoperability of information. The development of high-speed applications like teleconferencing, video-on-demand, and distance learning required high-speed networks with high bandwidth. Asynchronous Transfer Mode (ATM), also referred to as cell relay, is a technology that can be implemented in a WAN. Further, its power and flexibility make it efficient as a high-speed LAN backbone as well. The features of ATM are as follows:

✦ **ATM transmits data as small, fixed-size packets called cells.** The size of each cell is 53 bytes. Of these, 5 bytes consist of the header information. The remaining 48 bytes are user data, also referred to as payload.

✦ **Networks using ATM technology are connection-oriented.** This feature can be explained using the concept of virtual channel connections and virtual paths, discussed in the next section.

A network consists of many devices that make up the network architecture. The following section discusses each of these devices in detail.

Network Devices

Network devices refer to the hardware devices on a network. These network devices ensure a smooth transmission of data over a network. The following sections discuss some most commonly used network devices.

Repeater

A repeater is a device used to regenerate or replicate a signal. Repeaters are used in transmission systems to regenerate signals affected by attenuation. For example, if you must extend a thinnet cable beyond 185 meters you will require a repeater. There are analog repeaters for analog signals and digital repeaters for digital signals. Analog repeaters can only amplify the signal; digital repeaters can reconstruct a signal and send it at its original quality.

Whether analog or digital, repeaters can be of two types:

✦ **Amplifiers:** These amplify the incoming signal along with the noise.

✦ **Signal-regenerating repeaters:** These filter the signal from the noise and retransmit only the amplified signal.

Hub

In a Star network, all computers are connected to a central component. This central component can be a computer or a hub. The *hub* (or *concentrator*) has cables connecting it to all the other machines on the network, as well as ports to which the cables from various computers are attached. A hub is referred to as 8-port or 16-port depending on the number of ports (see Figure 17-20).

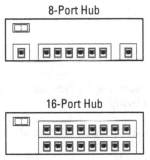

Figure 17-20: Hub

Hubs can be classified as active, passive, and hybrid, depending on what they do to the signals they receive.

Active hubs

Active hubs regenerate the signal before retransmitting it, much like the repeater. Hubs are also known as multiport repeaters because they have 8, 12, or 16 ports. They require electrical power to function.

Passive hubs

Passive hubs do not regenerate the signal before retransmitting it. They act as connection points. They do not require electrical power to run. Examples of passive hubs are punchdown blocks and wiring panels.

Hybrid hubs

Hybrid hubs can be used for connecting more than one type of cable. This allows different type of cables to be connected to one common hub.

Bridge

A bridge is a device that connects two similar or dissimilar LANs. For example, a bridge can connect an Ethernet with a Token-Ring network. Bridges rely heavily on broadcasting to transmit the data to the destination machine.

Bridges work at the Data Link layer of the OSI model and control data flow, handle transmission errors, provide physical addressing, and manage access to the physical medium. To achieve these goals, bridges use various Data Link-layer protocols. Figure 17-21 displays a bridge.

Figure 17-21: Bridge

Bridges analyze incoming frames, decide on how to forward the frames, and forward the frames to their destinations. There are two types of bridges:

✦ **Source-routing bridges:** The entire path to the destination is contained in each frame.

✦ **Transparent bridges:** Frames are forwarded one hop at a time toward the destination.

Note   Local bridges connect LANs in the same area; remote bridges connect LANs in different areas, usually over telecommunication lines.

Router

A router is a device that connects two or more segments (see Figure 17-22). The router works at the Network layer of the OSI model. For each segment being interconnected, a network interface card (NIC) is included in the router. Some computer systems, like Windows NT, can be configured to act as routers.

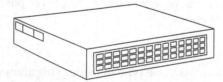

Figure 17-22: Router

The role of the routers is similar to the role of the bridges. Routers, however, provide additional functionality, such as forwarding packets based on addresses and filtering them based on a condition. A bridge just forwards the packets from one LAN to another.

Routing assumes that the address contained in the frames contains some information about where the host is located. This enables the router to forward packets without broadcasting or having to rely on a table containing all the destination addresses.

Switches and routers extend a small network into larger networks, thus creating a LAN, MAN, or WAN with less traffic congestion. Because switches and routers divide the network into small segments, the local broadcast traffic is blocked at the local port of the Router/Switch. This enables segments of the network to remain unaffected by the heavy traffic on other segments of the network.

Brouter

A *brouter* is a device that combines a bridge and a router. A bridge connects two segments that use the same protocol. A router on the other hand can connect dissimilar networks. A bridge and a router both can route the packets to their destination dynamically. A brouter examines all the packets and, depending on whether they belong to a different network or the source network, routes them to their destination.

A brouter tries to deliver a packet using the protocol information in the packet. If this fails, it bridges the packet, using the physical address.

Gateway

A *gateway* is a hardware-and-software combination that connects two different systems. For example, a gateway can be used to connect two different types of LANs or enable users on two different mail systems to interact with each other. It can convert packets of one type into another type. A gateway works at Layers 4 to 7 (Transport layer to Application layer) of the OSI model.

The gateway accepts data from one environment and strips off the old protocol suite. It then puts the data into the format of the protocol suite of the destination network. A gateway must convert data from one type to another. This might slow down the gateway.

Modem

A *modem* — by now a familiar device to most computer users — enables a computer to transmit and receive data over telephone lines as changes in voltage. Modems can be internal or external. An external modem is a stand connected to a computer through a port. An internal modem is fitted inside the computer in one of the expansion slots.

Apart from converting the type of signals, a modem can also perform the following functions:

✦ **Voice/data:** Some modems can switch between voice and data modes. In data mode, the modem acts like a regular modem. In voice mode, the modem acts like a regular telephone. Modems that support a voice/data switch have a built-in loudspeaker and microphone for voice communication.

✦ **Auto-answer:** An auto-answer modem acts as an answering machine for the computer.

✦ **Data compression:** In compressed form, data can be transmitted at faster rates. Some modems support data compression.

Note   The modem at the receiving end must be able to decompress the data using the same compression algorithm.

✦ **Fax capability:** Some modems can also send and receive faxes.

Switch

Switches are a combination of hubs and bridges. They consist of several RJ45 connectors, which are used to connect network systems. A switch doesn't merely amplify the signals; it also acts as if a bridge were attached to each port. A switch, typically, keeps track of the MAC addresses associated with each of the ports attached to it. As a result, it can route traffic depending on the MAC address. Figure 17-23 shows what a switch looks like.

Figure 17-23: Switch

Tip   Network devices (such as repeaters, bridges, switches, and hubs) are used primarily to improve the *performance* of the network. They are not a means for improving *security* on a network.

Network Management

The increasing use of communication networks has led to a greater need for initializing and optimizing the performance of these networks. Surveys prove that network downtime results in enormous loss to businesses. Reliability, reduction of recurring costs, and the ability to manage an entire network from a centralized location are factors that must be considered to reduce network downtime. Several standards have been framed as to what network management should accomplish.

In general, *network management* is the process of controlling a complex data network to maximize its efficiency and productivity.

Network-Management System

A *network-management system* (NMS) is a set of software programs available to network engineers, with features and functionality designed especially for managing data networks. Various network-management products are available, but every NMS has three major elements designed specifically for its task: its platform, its applications, and its protocols. The upcoming sections review each of these elements.

Network-management platform

The network-management platform is software that provides the generic functionality for managing a variety of network devices. This functionality includes

- ✦ A GUI that conforms to a standard interface
- ✦ A Network map that indicates the location and status of network devices
- ✦ A DBMS that stores information
- ✦ A customizable menu system for easy addition of new applications to the existing interfaces
- ✦ An event log that records network events chronologically

Network-management applications

Apart from the generic functionality provided by the network-management platform, a network-management system may require special functionality to manage certain devices. Network-management applications are developed by vendors of network devices to help customers in managing their devices effectively.

For example, the manufacturer of a modem or a hub builds a suite of applications. One application could show the physical connectors on the hub when the engineer clicks on the hub on a network map. The application could also allow the engineer to configure the different features of the hub.

Some of the goals of a network-management application are to:

- ✦ Manage a specific set of devices
- ✦ Avoid functionality overlap with the network-management platform
- ✦ Integrate with the network-management platform through the menu

Network-management protocols

For optimum functioning of a network, the devices on the network must be monitored and fine-tuned. Fine-tuning of a network is only possible if data is available on network performance.

Engineers must answer the following questions by querying the network devices:

✦ Is a specific hub functioning?

✦ Is the connectivity between any two points on a network alive?

✦ Is one hub being overloaded while the other hub is lying idle?

✦ Is one segment of a network overused while the other segment is underutilized?

Until recently, the different manufactures of network devices bundled their own proprietary network-management applications that used specific protocols and had specific interfaces. For a network with two hubs manufactured by different vendors, there is a possibility that the engineer has to learn two different ways to query these two hubs. There is a possibility that one hub supports a Graphical User Interface, while the other supports a Character User Interface.

In addition, the protocols used would not provide sufficient data on network performance. For example, the `ping` utility serves to check connectivity between point A and point B (on IP networks). This utility sends a packet to the destination and listens for the echo to establish connectivity. If a packet fails to reach the destination, it does not clearly indicate whether the connection is down or the packet has been lost. (Such loss is due to an overload on the network, or to the dropping of the packet by a particular hub that lacks buffer space for storage).

Due to these shortcomings in the existing protocols, there is a need for developing protocols that support information required by the network engineer. These protocols must support queries on the device name, network interface address, the number of interfaces in the device, the number of packets per second that the network would have received. The user should also be able to reconfigure the protocol based on the requirements. The parameters that can be configured include the device name and the network interface address.

Many network-management protocols have been developed. Some of them are as follows:

✦ High-level Entity Management System (HEMS)

✦ Simple Gateway Monitoring Protocol (SGMP)

✦ Common Management Information Protocol (CMIP) over TCP

✦ Simple Network-Management Protocol (SNMP)

HEMS is a network-management protocol that evolved to SGMP, which further evolved to SNMP. SNMP was developed specifically for use by IP devices; CMIP was meant to be protocol-independent and supports a large number of network devices. Although more powerful than SNMP, CMIP has not become popular because of the complex network configuration it needs to function. Many organizations now use SNMP in all areas of network management. Some of these areas get further consideration later in this chapter.

Choosing a Network-Management System

An ideal network-management system would, in simple terms, make the network engineer's life extremely simple. Steps should be taken to ensure that the right network management system is chosen. The steps involved in this important process are as follows:

1. **Perform device inventory:** Identify the devices present on the network — workstations, PCs, gateways, switches, hubs, modems, and so on. After the list of devices is ready, the mission-critical devices should be identified. For example, an organization's timely communication with overseas offices might be more important than smooth functioning of the network printers. The bridges, routers, and gateways should consequently be given a higher priority than the network printers.

2. **Prioritize the functional areas of network management:** Identify the most important of the five functional areas. This, again, is organization-specific. For organizations that allow external users to access their corporate network, security management may be the most crucial area.

3. **Survey network-management applications:** Find the application that corresponds to the identified key areas of network management.

4. **Choose the network-management platform:** Identify the network-management platform that runs the applications you have chosen for the management of your network.

Network-management architectures

A network-management platform can have various architectures, depending on the needs of the data network. The three most common network management architectures are centralized, hierarchical, and distributed. Although no single architecture that can be called "the best" without reservation, each does have features that work well in specific environments. The following sections discuss these architectures in detail.

Centralized architecture

In the *centralized* architecture (as shown in Figure 17-24), the network-management platform is located on a single computer with a centralized database. This computer periodically queries the other computers on the network and then writes the status onto the centralized database. This database is backed up regularly, for recovery in case of breakdown.

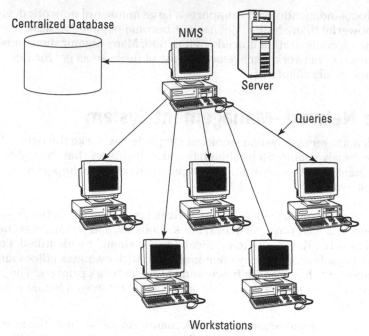

Figure 17-24: Centralized architecture

A network engineer with centralized architecture can monitor all network events from one location. This helps in troubleshooting and problem solving. Accessibility, security, and convenience are the main advantages of the centralized approach.

Nevertheless, as the scope of the network-management process widens, it may be difficult (as well as expensive) to scale a single system for the additional load. Further, if the connection from the management station to the network is severed then all management capabilities will be lost.

Hierarchical architecture

Hierarchical network-management architecture (as shown in figure 17-25) uses multiple computers. One computer acts as the central server and the others function as clients. The management functions are distributed between the server and the clients. For example, each client system can monitor a different portion of the network.

Some of the key features of this approach are as follows:

✦ NMS is not dependent on a single system

✦ Management tasks are distributed

✦ Information storage is centralized

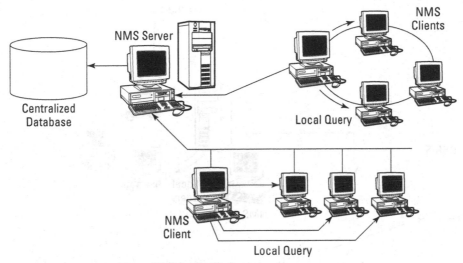

Figure 17-25: Hierarchical architecture

The NMS clients query the respective local devices that they are responsible for and use the NMS server only for information storage. Consequently, precious bandwidth resources can be saved with hierarchical architecture.

On the other hand, since there is no single centralized location for management of the entire network, information gathering will become more difficult and time-consuming for the network engineer. Further, if there is duplication in the list of devices managed by each client, twice as much bandwidth may be consumed.

Distributed architecture

This architecture combines the centralized and the distributed approaches, as shown in Figure 17-26. This approach uses multiple peer platforms. Each peer platform has a complete database of its own for devices on the particular network segment. Any report can be sent to the central computer.

Some of the key features of this approach include:

✦ Single location to access all management information

✦ Not dependent on a single system

✦ Distribution of network-management tasks

The distributed approach is made possible through a replication service. This service running on any server keeps the multiple databases on different systems synchronized.

The main disadvantage of the distributed architecture is that the overhead associated with the synchronization can consume a significant amount of network resources.

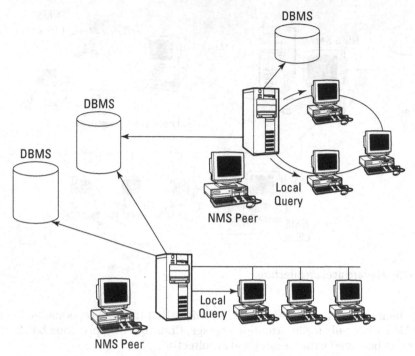

Figure 17-26: Distributed architecture

Functional areas of network management

The International Organization for Standardization (ISO) has defined the scope of network management by dividing it into the following five functional areas:

✦ Fault management

✦ Configuration management

✦ Accounting management

✦ Performance management

✦ Security management

The following sections discuss each of these functional areas in detail.

Fault management

Fault management is defined as the process of locating and correcting network problems, or faults. Among the five functional areas of network management, fault management is the most critical for the smooth functioning of a network.

The main purpose behind fault management is to increase the reliability of the network. This is achieved by giving the network engineer tools to quickly detect and start recovery procedures. Rather than spending time "fire-fighting," or fixing one crisis after another, fault management aims at working on a fault in such a way that users will not even note it existed.

There are three steps involved in the process of fault management. They are as follows:

1. Identifying the fault
2. Isolating the cause of the fault
3. Correcting the fault

These steps can be understood with an example. Consider the following situation, shown in Figure 17-27. If the link between node A at the Boston office of AllSolv, Inc. and the Boston switch fails, the NMS should be able to identify that node A is no longer reachable. It should isolate the cause of the fault, that node A is unreachable because the link is down. To correct the fault, it should try to establish another connection or link between node A and the central switch through available means — possibly using a dial-up connection through the Internet.

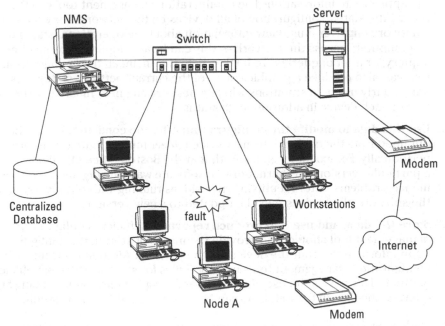

Figure 17-27: Fault between node A and switch

Configuration management

Configuration management is the process of obtaining data from the network to accomplish three vital tasks:

✦ Manage the current network configuration

✦ Store the data to maintain an up-to-date inventory of all network devices

✦ Produce reports based on the configuration information collected

The control that a network engineer has over network devices is significantly enhanced when the network engineer has rapid access to configuration information about these devices. Reconfiguring these devices and tracking the location as well as number of these devices becomes simpler with effective configuration management.

Configuration management involves the following steps:

1. **Gather information about the current network environment:** Gathering information about the network configuration manually can be monotonous, time-consuming, and error-prone. The process can be automated by using a configuration-management tool that will perform this task automatically. The configuration-management tool can send queries from the management station to the other devices on the network. Each device then responds with the appropriate information. The configuration-management tool can then record the status/configuration of all devices on the network. For example, a network engineer must view information about the operational status of all computers across the network — this can be accomplished by sending a query, or a set of queries. To further help the engineer, the configuration tool can also produce a graphical map of the current network status. It is particularly useful in situations where a network engineer must view the location of each device in addition to its status.

2. **Use this data to modify the configuration:** After the configuration has been obtained from the devices, the network engineer must update this information periodically. For example, consider that at the Boston office of AllSolv, Inc., a particular version of Ethernet bridge software was causing network performance problems. After identifying the bridges running with older version of the software, the bridges must be updated to a new version.

3. **Store the data, and use it to produce reports:** An efficient configuration-management tool should also provide the means of storing the configuration information about the devices in the network. Although certain configuration-management tools use ASCII files for storage, the most efficient method of storage is the use of a DBMS for storage of information. Using SQL queries, the data in the database can be easily queried for information.

SQL queries can be used to generate reports on the network usage, peak-time usage, uptime and downtime, software version, status, and inventory. For example, for a network device, the inventory information should include

✦ Serial number

✦ Make and model

✦ Operating system

✦ RAM capacity

✦ Network address

Configuration management helps the network manager keep track of the devices on the network and also helps to fine-tune and optimize the network based on data.

Performance management

With fault management, configuration management, and security management in place, the performance of a network may still not reflect peak efficiency. The reason: These tools cannot ensure that a network is free from congestion and overloading. That problem can be tackled by the continuous monitoring of network performance.

Performance management is the process of monitoring network devices and their associated links to determine utilization and error rates. It also involves providing a consistent level of service to users.

Performance management involves the following steps:

1. **Collect data on current network utilization:** To monitor the performance of the data network, the first step would be to identify the current utilization of the network resources. The amount of usage of a network device (hub, router, bridge, or a network link) is referred to as utilization. The utilization of a file server, for example, can be measured by processor load, disk access rate, and network interface card utilization. The utilization of a bridge or a router can be measured by processor load, percentage of dropped packets on each device, or the number of packets being held in a queue.

2. **Analyze the relevant data:** Analysis of the corresponding data results in a graphical representation of the utilization. Graphs can be plotted to represent historical data to view weekly, monthly, quarterly, and yearly trends. For example, a network engineer notices that the amount of processing power of a network increases over time. In this case, the engineer may decide to reduce the traffic flow through the device before the processor power reaches a critical level. Another alternative would be to upgrade the device to a more powerful processor.

3. **Set threshold values:** A network engineer can set thresholds on a variety of values that affect network performance. For a network device, threshold values can be set for process utilization or disk capacity usage. Performance-management tools can then report to the network engineer when the performance reaches the threshold value. The method of reporting can be simple, such as ringing a bell or flashing a light.

4. **Use simulation to determine how the network can be altered to maximize performance:** A network engineer can use simulations to determine how to alter a network for more efficient use and better performance. For example, assume that users at the Kansas office of AllSolv, Inc. are experiencing performance problems while using a new application that communicates across the WAN to the central data center. The network engineer examines the link utilization and finds that it averages over 80 percent utilization. The network engineer decides to upgrade the bandwidth of the link. In spite of the upgrade, performance is as poor as before. After investigating further, the network engineer finds that the Transport layer used by the new application implements a stop-and-wait protocol. The protocol sends a single packet at a time for each session and waits for the packet to be acknowledged before sending the next packet. Consequently, upgrading the link has not solved the problem of poor performance — it just resulted in a waste of resources. This waste could have been avoided if the network conditions after implementing the solution had been simulated. This could have saved time and helped the network engineer detect the problem. The appropriate solution to this problem would have been to make the new application use a protocol that would have a window size greater than one.

Accounting management

Accounting management is the process of measuring the usage of network resources by users to accomplish three tasks:

✦ Determine costs

✦ Bill the users

✦ Set quotas

Accounting management also involves granting or removing permissions for access to the network.

Billing users is essential when expenses involved in building and maintaining the data networks have to be recovered. Accounting management can also help extensively in budget and personnel planning.

Accounting management involves the following steps:

1. **Gather data about the utilization of network resources:** Assume that the file server of a department has a network interface card that has reached its peak packet-processing capacity. In the absence of a network-management tool, a network engineer would have to spend a considerable amount of time finding out the percentage of users accessing the file server. Assume that the network engineer finds that the users from the Documentation department contribute significantly to the file server usage. The network engineer would then probably decide to provide a file server dedicated to the Documentation group to optimize the performance of the network. An accounting-management tool

would have helped the network engineer handle the situation sooner. An instant report that gave the percentage usage of the file server could have helped the network engineer in the same way.

2. **Set usage quotas and bill users for their network use:** Quotas can be set on a network to ensure that each user gets a "fair share" of network resources. For example, AllSolv, Inc. may be providing external users dial-up access to a database of information on the network. Users pay an access fee for the same. Each dial-up user is allowed to use the facility for 10 hours a week. A user exceeding this quota may have to pay an additional monthly amount based on the additional hours that the user has accessed the service.

Security management

Security management is a process of implementing and managing security in an enterprise network. To build a secure enterprise network, four primary areas should be taken into consideration:

✦ **Authentication:** This is the process of identifying an individual, usually based on a username and password. Before revealing sensitive information or striking a business deal, the identity of the person or process is first established.

✦ **Access control:** This is a set of mechanisms and policies that restrict access to computer resources.

✦ **Data integrity:** This is a process of preventing the tampering of data during transmission and maintaining its validity and correctness.

✦ **Confidentiality:** This is the process of safeguarding information from unauthorized users.

 To know more about network security and security management, refer to Chapters1, 2, and 3.

Network-Management Protocols

Network-management protocols provide a standard way of accessing any network device made by any manufacturer. Irrespective of the vendor, any network device can be queried for management information. This information could be the operational status of the network device or the name of the device.

Some of the protocols designed specifically for network management are as follows:

✦ Simple Network-Management Protocol (SNMP)

✦ Simple Network-Management Protocol version 2 (SNMPv2)

✦ Common Management Information Protocol (CMIP)

✦ Remote Monitoring Protocol (RMON)

The SNMP Model

The SNMP model consists of four components:

✦ Managed nodes

✦ Management stations

✦ Management information base

✦ Management protocol

Figure 17-28 shows the components of the SNMP model.

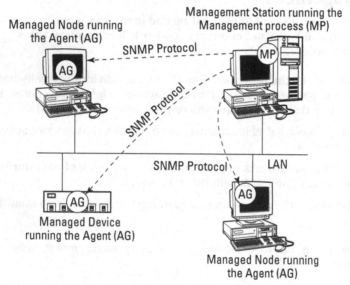

Figure 17-28: Components of the SNMP model

Managed nodes

A *managed node* is any device capable of communicating status information. A managed node can fall into any of three categories:

✦ A host system, which includes workstations, mainframes, terminal servers, or printers

✦ Router systems

✦ Media devices, which include bridges, repeaters, hubs, or analyzers

A managed node can run a management process referred to as an SNMP agent. Devices designed for network use have this as an in-built ability. Many of these devices may have limited capability to run management software. Consequently, management software should be designed in such a way that it has minimal impact on the managed device.

Every agent maintains a set of variables that describe its state. For example, the agent in a router may maintain its packet-loss rate as one of the variables. In SNMP literature, this variable is also referred to as an object. Examples of such variables include:

✦ Number of particular kinds of error messages received

✦ Broadcast messages received and sent

✦ Number of packets and bytes in and out of the device

Management stations

The actual management of network activities takes place at *management stations* — general-purpose computers that contain two specialized tools:

✦ Network-management protocol

✦ One or more network-management applications

The special management processes running in the management stations communicate with the agents in the managed devices over the network. This task is entirely a matter of issuing commands and getting responses. Typically, the management station is also equipped with a user interface that allows the network manager to view the status of the network.

Management information base

The agent maintains a collection of variables in a database — the *management information base* (MIB). The management process requiring this information makes a request to the agent. The agent responds by querying its database and sending the information to the manager. Using a hierarchical format, the MIB defines the information available from a device.

The first version of the MIB designed for use with the TCP/IP protocol suite is known as MIB-1. MIB-2 expands the set of objects defined in MIB-1.

In addition, vendor-specific enhancements are available for the MIB. For example, an organization might want to make the CPU utilization of its Ethernet bridge available as a resource, using a network management protocol. MIB-2 does not contain any object that corresponds to CPU utilization — but the vendor of the Ethernet bridge can define a new object for CPU utilization.

Management protocol

The exact information that an agent should support (and the format in which it should supply the information) is defined by SNMP. The process in the management station and the agent in the managed device interact using the SNMP management protocol.

Protocol data units and their message types

Every agent maintains a set of variables that describe its state; the management station may query this set of variables. The management station and the managed device interact by exchanging message units called *protocol data units* (PDUs). These units are always one of four types:

✦ **Reads:** By reading the value in the variables maintained by an agent, the manager monitors the managed device. It uses the Get-Request PDU. For example, a manager may want to know the number of packets sent through a network device such as a switch. The manager will send a Get-Request PDU to the agent in the managed device, requesting the information.

✦ **Writes:** The manager controls the agent by writing onto the variables. It uses the Set-Request PDU that allows a network engineer to configure a number of parameters on a remote device. For example, a network engineer might want to remotely shut down a network device for administrative purposes or configure the name of a remote network device. You can use the Set-Request PDU to accomplish this task.

✦ **Responses:** After reception of a GetRequest, GetNextRequest or a SetRequest, the SNMP entity on the agent's side responds with a Response PDU. Either this PDU carries the requested information or it indicates failure of the previous request.

For example, a management station might want to find whether a specific terminal is running. The management station sends a Read PDU to the specific agent. If the terminal is up, a suitable response is sent back by the agent in the managed device. If the terminal has been shut down, the agent in the managed device responds with a Trap PDU, indicating that an abnormal event has occurred.

✦ **Traversal operations:** Every managed device is capable of performing different functions. Consequently, each device can also maintain management variables. All variables related to a particular functionality are grouped together. SNMP also provides traversal commands that allow the management station to gather information from the managed device sequentially.

For example, a network engineer must look up the entries in the IP routing table in a network device. The IP routing table is dynamic. Consequently, the network engineer will not be aware of the number of entries in the routing table. The management station sends a GetRequest to the agent on the device, asking for the IP address in the first row of the table. This request is followed by a series of `GetNextRequest` PDUs from the NMS to the agent until the end of the table is reached (see Figure 17-29).

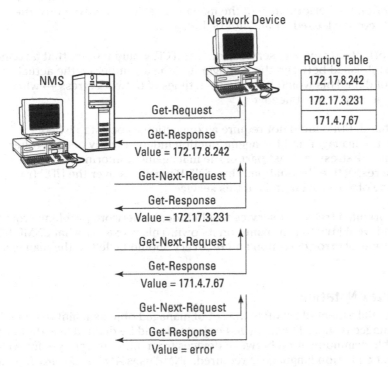

Figure 17-29: Traversal operations

Traps

Sometimes unplanned events such as congestion may force managed devices to reboot. A managed device might try to report an abnormal event to the management station under its own initiative. When a significant event occurs, the agent at the side of the managed device sends a `Trap` PDU to the management station. For example, a device may wish to inform an NMS that its disk space is nearing capacity. However, the PDU merely states that an event of significance has occurred. It is the responsibility of the management station to issue further requests to the managed device and get further information. One factor to keep in mind is that *the management station does not acknowledge* `Trap` *PDUs*. As an alternative, the management station can periodically poll the managed node and check for unusual events. The polling would be accelerated on receipt of a trap. This method is called *trap-directed polling*.

Transport mappings

One of the primary goals of network management is that the impact of adding network management to managed devices should be minimal. In keeping with this primary goal, the transport service used by the SNMP protocol should have a minimal impact on the performance of the managed device. Consequently, the transport protocol stack used should not be bulky.

A connection-oriented transport service, such as TCP, would require that a connection first be established between the manager and the agent before the actual transmission of data. This would be difficult in times of network stress — when network management is most needed.

On the other hand, UDP would not require a connection to be established. Consequently, the manager and the agent function independently of each other. In times of network stress, at least part of the management information would get through to the respective destination. Thus SNMP functions over the UDP transport service because of lower overheads of this service.

A connection-oriented transport service would hide the network problems from the application and would try to retransmit on its own. This is exactly what SNMP tries to avoid. The onus of error detection and recovery should be left to the manager and the agent.

Abstract Syntax Notation

The most essential aspect of SNMP is the set of managed objects maintained in the MIB of the managed device. The managed objects should be defined in a standard format to enable communication between devices from different vendors for which standard object definition language is required. SNMP uses *Abstract Syntax Notation One* (ASN 1). ASN 1 variables are converted into bytes for transmission by encoding rules called *Basic Encoding Rules* (BERs) or the *ASN 1 Transfer Syntax*.

Community strings

A minimal amount of security is implemented in SNMP through the usage of *community strings*. When an NMS wishes to query a managed device, it sends a `GetRequest` PDU to the device. This PDU contains a community string. The SNMP agent in the managed device uses this community string to verify if the NMS is authorized to access the MIB information.

Some implementations of SNMP agents allow for various levels of security using the community string. For example, a set of NMSs could have read-only access to the information in the MIB. The agent could define a community string that would allow only `GetRequest` and `GetNextRequest` messages from this set of NMSs.

Caution

Community strings are sent in clear ASCII text, which makes them easily accessible to intruders.

Simple Network-Management Protocol provides a number of advantages:

✦ SNMP is a relatively simple protocol that does not place a major processing load on the existing network.

✦ It is in wide use today. Major vendors of internetworking hardware (such as bridges and routers) design their products to support SNMP, making it easy to implement.

The simplicity of SNMP creates problems as well as advantages. Some of its disadvantages are as follows:

✦ SNMP uses cleartext in its security measures, which makes the protocol insecure.

✦ If the response to a request exceeds the UDP packet size limit, the protocol does not provide for sending an alert or other such information to the management station. The result is reduced network performance.

✦ SNMP is officially standardized for use only on IP networks. Although most networks support IP, non-IP networks cannot use SNMP.

Tip   If your network must work with non-IP networks, you may want to implement SNMP *proxy agents*. These agents gather information from network devices that do not support IP, conveying the information to an NMS that supports SNMP.

In order to arrive at an answer to these problems, a new version of SNMP was published — SNMPv2.

SNMPv2

SNMPv2 differs from SNMP in the following areas:

✦ Performance

✦ Security

✦ Management hierarchy

✦ Multiprotocol support

Performance

Remember, if the response to a request exceeds the UDP packet size limit, no management information is made available to the management station. This reduces the performance of the protocol. However, to improve performance, SNMPv2 has introduced a PDU — `GetBulkRequest` — for bulk operations. The response to this PDU returns as much information as possible. If the information exceeds the maximum UDP packet size, it is truncated and only the part that fits into the packet is returned. This ensures that at least a part of the management information is transmitted.

Security

SNMP provides trivial authentication by exchanging a string in plaintext called the *community string*. This authentication is also based on the assumption that the message has not been tampered with on the way. The security features provided here are limited. SNMPv2 addresses these security shortcomings by using the concept of *parties* and *contexts*.

A *party* is a set of protocol entities that communicate through a management protocol and a transport service using authentication and privacy features. Each of these parties can be configured differently. For example, one party can be configured so it can communicate with every party in every other system. One party may be configured so it can communicate with a specific party in a remote system; this requires authentication of the remote system. Some parties can be configured so they can communicate with specific remote parties. In addition, these parties can be configured such that all management information being communicated should also be encrypted.

To determine which parties are allowed to perform operations on specific portions of the MIB, SNMP associates every agent with an Access-Control List (ACL), as shown in Table 17-5.

Table 17-5
Access-Control List

Remote Party	Local Party	Context	Operation
Remote Party 1 (RP1)	Local Party 1 (LP1)	Context 1 (C1)	get
Remote Party 2 (RP2)	Local Party 2 (LP2)	Context 1 (C1)	get + set
Remote Party 3 (RP3)	Local Party 3 (LP3)	Context 1 (C1)	get
Remote Party 3 (RP3)	Local Party 3 (LP3)	Context 2 (C2)	get

The first row of the table indicates that the party, RP1, in the manager system can perform the get operation on the C1 portion of the MIB through the local party LP1 in the agent. The other rows can be similarly interpreted.

Management hierarchy

The use of the single-manager concept in SNMP proved that a manager could not poll more than a hundred agent systems. To solve this problem, SNMPv2 introduced the concept of Intermediate Level Managers (ILM). First, the Top Level Manager (TLM) would instruct the ILM about the variables that must be polled and the agents in which these variables present. The TLM also informs the ILM about the events that it must be informed about. The ILM then begins the process of polling. When the ILM detects an event that the TLM has to be informed about, the ILM sends a special PDU, the `InformRequest` PDU, to the TLM. On reception of this PDU, the TLM directly operates upon the agent that caused this event. This new PDU provides a standard way for hierarchical or distributed network management systems to communicate. Figure 17-30 illustrates the SNMPv2 management hierarchy.

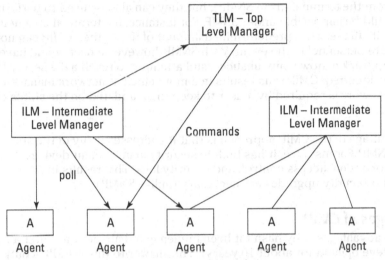

Figure 17-30: SNMPv2 management hierarchy

Multiprotocol support

SNMPv2 is standardized to work on the following major network protocol stacks — IP, Apple AppleTalk, and Novell IPX. Consequently, SNMPv2 messages can run on almost all networks of the world. Irrespective of the protocol that carries the SNMPv2 messages, the protocol operations remain the same. For example, if an agent received a `GetBulkRequest` from an NMS running Novell IPX, the message would be interpreted just as if it were sent over IP. The respective network protocols function at the Network layer of the OSI model. On the other hand, SNMPv2 functions at the Application layer. Protocols at the Network layer can be changed without modifying the SNMPv2 protocol in any way.

CMIP

Due to the drawbacks with SNMP, different governments and many large corporations got together and funded a project for a new network management protocol. With unlimited support and an unlimited development budget, people thought that Common Management Information Protocol (CMIP) would replace SNMP. Because of implementation problems, the availability of CMIP is restricted.

CMIP was designed to build on SNMP by making up for SNMP's shortcomings and becoming a bigger, more detailed network manager. Its basic design is similar to SNMP, whereby PDUs are employed as variables to monitor a network. CMIP contains 11 types of PDUs (compared to SNMP's 5).

Advantages of CMIP

The biggest feature of the CMIP protocol is that its variables not only relay information to and from the terminal (as in SNMP), but they can also be used to perform tasks that would be impossible under SNMP. For instance, if a terminal on a network cannot reach its file server a predetermined amount of times, then CMIP can notify the appropriate personnel of the event. With SNMP, however, a user would have to explicitly keep track of how many unsuccessful attempts to reach a file server that a terminal has incurred. CMIP thus results in a more efficient network management system, as less work is required by a user to keep them updated on the status of their network.

Another advantage to the CMIP approach is that it addresses many of the shortcomings of SNMP. For instance, it has built-in security-management devices that support authorization, access control, and security logs. This results in a safer system, and no security upgrades are necessary (unlike SNMP).

Disadvantages of CMIP

Based on the advantages, why hasn't it been implemented already (for after all, it has been in development for about 10 years). The answer to this is CMIP's only significant disadvantage: The CMIP protocol takes more system resources than SNMP by a factor of 10. In effect, few systems on this planet would be able to handle a full implementation of CMIP without massive network modifications (such as the installation of thousands of dollars worth of memory and the purchase of new protocol agents). This major disadvantage has no inexpensive workaround, and for this reason, many people believe that the CMIP protocol is doomed to fail. The only possible workaround is to decrease the size of the protocol by changing its specifications. Several protocols have been developed to run "on top" of CMIP and thus use fewer resources, but none of these has gathered enough momentum to challenge SNMP.

RMON

SNMP as a network management protocol allows management stations to periodically poll compatible managed devices and determine if they are still functioning. However, for traffic management and monitoring performance variations, an enhanced network management technology would be required — technology that would help to determine potential problems before they occurred. The solution to this problem was RMON (an abbreviation for Remote MONitoring). Two RMON standards exist, RMON and RMON2.

RMON standard

The RMON standard specifies a consistent method for monitoring networks with products from multiple vendors. Some features of RMON are as follows:

✦ RMON uses SNMP to monitor the basic operations. RMON also defines nine additional MIB groups, as shown in Table 17-6.

This arrangement provides a much richer set of data, enhancing the amount of information available to the management station. (A later section of the chapter details each of these groups.)

✦ RMON does not require IS Managers to travel to remote sites, nor does it require a dedicated technician on-site. It allows network managers to gather and analyze network data from remote sites at a centralized location.

✦ RMON allows a variety of management stations and agents from different vendors to communicate with each other over the same network.

✦ RMON allows history of performance to be maintained for each segment. This allows the network manager to look at key statistics of the past and predict potential trends.

✦ In SNMP, the management station had to periodically send read requests to the agent at the managed device to check its status. This increases the network traffic. Excessive network bandwidth was required as the number of LAN segments increased. RMON, on the other hand, provides the concept of threshold values at the agents' side. When this threshold value was exceeded, the agent at the managed device would automatically send a *trap* PDU to the manager.

✦ RMON replaces the expensive equipment referred to as *protocol analyzers*.

Table 17-6
The RMON MIB

Group	Description
Statistics	Collects traffic and error statistics — fragments, collisions, and so on — for the segment being monitored.
History	Allows the network manager to record network statistics at user-defined time intervals.
Alarm	Permits users to set threshold values, exceeding which alarms are generated.
Host table	Gathers traffic statistics for specified network nodes. The table maintained stores the MAC address and the corresponding statistics.

Continued

Table 17-6 *(continued)*	
Group	**Description**
Host top N	Lists the top network nodes and the corresponding statistics.
Matrix	Tracks traffic and errors occurring between pairs of hosts.
Filters	Enables packets that meet user-defined filtering rules to be captured.
Packet capture	Captures those packets that meet the filtering criteria. The management stations can then retrieve the packets and then decode them.
Event	Enables the logging of events that match parameters set in other areas of the MIB. The log entries can then be sent to the management stations.

The *RMON probe* is a device (a combination of hardware and software) that helps in monitoring network traffic. It has two components:

✦ **Embedded RMON probe:** Built into hubs, routers, and switches, this hardware device is sufficient to support one of the nine additional MIB groups.

✦ **Computer-based RMON agent:** This is software that runs on a workstation.

RMON2 standard

Although RMON facilitated remote monitoring, its benefit was limited to the Data Link layer. This meant that the RMON probe would only be able to identify traffic on the monitored segment. It would not be able to identify hosts beyond the router connection on a segment. Further, the type of traffic could not be monitored. This posed a serious limitation; an administrator would not be able to monitor the effect of Web browsing and other applications upon a network.

As an answer to these limitations, RMON2 was developed as an extension. Some features of RMON2 include the following:

✦ With RMON2, the network manager's visibility of the network is not restricted to the Data Link layer alone. The network manager can see traffic flowing right from the network through the Application layer. This capability will have a considerable impact on controlling and trouble-shooting client/server environments. Consequently, the network manager can obtain information on individual protocols such as IP, IPX, and so on. Information on individual network applications such as Notes, Internet Explorer, and others can also be obtained.

✦ RMON2 also provides Physical-layer correlation. It allows network problems to be tracked right down to individual ports on RMON compatible routers or switches.

RMON2, unlike RMON, monitors not just the network traffic, but also the applications and the related protocols that constitute that traffic. The scope of the network manager has increased from the Data Link layer to encompass the Network and Application layers as well. Such familiarity with the enterprise-wide view provides the network manager with knowledge and information to manage, troubleshoot, and monitor complex networks. RMON2 consequently facilitates a new class of applications for client/server analysis: Network and Application layer accounting and internetwork monitoring.

Implementing network management

In a network adopting a hierarchical network management topology, a central point of control has particular significance. It is logical to focus the operational functions of the network at the focal point of network; most members of technical staff who have networking expertise are housed in the data center. The central control entity is often referred to as the Network Operations Center (NOC), however, the definition has changed now with NOCs being referred to as Network Control Centers (NCCs), reflecting the point that enterprise-wide networks are not operated but controlled through some central contact point.

NCC may also be referred to as the Help Desk, Support Center, Management Center, or any other similar-sounding name. The NCC must do more in the total network environment than just keep the network operating. An enterprise network's NCC must also maintain levels of service to the users, plan future growth, and ensure user satisfaction. The six major functions that the NCC must use to attain these goals are as follows:

✦ **Ad-hoc information center:** Users should be able to call one telephone number when some part of the enterprise network suffers a lapse of function. Though many calls will be trivial (such as complaints of powered-off network equipment or wrong connections), the assurance must be there that all calls will be answered.

✦ **Network operations:** Enterprise networks need external triggering for their operation. Someone must initialize equipment, shut down servers, and so on.

✦ **Technical support:** Technical support specialists should be available around the clock to answer to any query pertaining to the smooth operation of the enterprise network, as and when needed.

✦ **Problem management:** The traditional network management function within an enterprise network with the objective of problem determination (short term as well as long term) should have procedures and methods in place to ensure reported user problems are resolved. Escalation procedures should be in place to ensure that the problem gets resolved at some level or the other.

✦ **Network configuration and inventory:** This is particularly relevant to an organization where there are different users and support groups that procure IT/Networking equipment independently. All the information about the equipment should be available with a central authority, the NCC, to ensure proper inventory management and reduce waste in the process of procuring additional network equipment.

✦ **End-user education and training:** End users must be trained, at least in basic network equipment operation, so they can attend to first-level (basic or trivial) problems themselves without having to call the NCC.

In the enterprise network, a user experiencing a problem with a network device would call a predefined telephone number at the NCC. (Each network device should be labeled with the NCC telephone numbers as well as its own network address.) The end user experiencing the problem would speak to an on-duty NCC network manager who would open a log for reporting the problem (the *trouble ticket*) and try to rule out any user-based causes for the problems (such as unfamiliarity with the device) to ascertain whether the device is operating properly.

The network manager may initiate this step by using a network management protocol to try to contact the faulty device and run a complete diagnostic check over the enterprise network. Ideally, the process should be proactive instead of reactive. The NCC manager may, depending on the nature of the problem, suggest a workaround such as setting up a dial-up connection in case of the primary link going down.

Once the trouble is logged, the problem should be handed over to the concerned personnel for resolution. For some type of problems, the network equipment vendor may be asked to provide the needed resolution, in case the NCC personnel cannot attend to it. For those involving WAN links, the service provider should be called to resolve the problem. In either case, there should be a firm escalation policy in place at the NCC. For example, if the first level of network management cannot resolve the problem, it should be escalated to the second level. The end user must be notified at regular intervals that the problem is being attended to; in this case, a little forethought can keep morale high and the network more efficient.

Network management tools

Many tools are currently available in the market to help the administrator manage the network. Before obtaining and implementing those tools, some basic assessment of some vital business factors is essential. These factors include the following:

✦ The problem areas of the customer

✦ The needs of the customer

✦ The products and solutions available

Some of the common problem areas that organizations face are as follows:

✦ High management cost of networks

✦ Separate time zones between the offices

✦ Slow response time between the network-management, application-management, and systems-management teams.

✦ High cost of maintaining personnel

✦ Inefficient use of specialized skills

✦ Lack of coordination between network teams working at different locations

✦ High mobility of administrators

✦ Unbalanced utilization of available resources

✦ Consistency and security of distributed information

There are tools available, which provide satisfactory solutions in all these three areas of network management. The most popular tool available in the market is OpenView from Hewlett Packard (HP). The other tools available are Unicenter TNG from Computer Associates (CA) and Spectrum from Cabletron.

Summary

This chapter reviewed and summarized the basics of networking. The two types of networking models — client/server and peer-to-peer — have strengths and weaknesses that suit each to its own range of best uses. The most common types of networks — local-area networks (LANs), wide-area networks (WANs), public networks, intranets, and extranets — commonly follow three basic network topologies (Bus, Ring, and Star). Though networks are generally more securable when their computers are connected by some physical media such as cables (whether coaxial, twisted-pair, or fiber-optic), wireless networks are becoming more common. Their computers link by means of infrared or radio waves and can involve satellite communications. Given the rapid pace of change in the business world, some companies with far-flung offices find a more efficient approach to network connections in leased lines (permanent telephone lines that belong to a telecom service provider and connect distant locations). Types of leased lines include standard phone lines, as well as the faster, more advanced lines used in T1, T2, T3, and T4 links.

On a somewhat smaller scale, local-area networks use four basic LAN architectures — Ethernet, Token-Ring, FDDI, and ATM — as the most efficient ways to connect hardware devices, such as repeaters, hubs, bridges, routers, brouters, gateways, modems, and switches. Given that the typical modern network has complex needs all its own, the discipline of network management has developed its own range of tools — including platforms, applications, and protocols specific to the tasks of managing a network. A network administrator must manage five areas of technical function on the network: faults, configurations, accounting, performance, and security.

No one maker or vendor can provide a single solution to the possible needs of all networks; an administrator always works with a mix of technologies. Network management protocols provide a standardized way to access any network device made by any manufacturer. Protocols designed specifically for network management include

✦ Simple Network-Management Protocol (SNMP)

✦ Simple Network-Management Protocol version 2 (SNMPv2)

✦ Common Management Information Protocol (CMIP)

✦ Remote Monitoring Protocol (RMON)

✦   ✦   ✦

OSI Model – An Overview

This chapter deals with the most basic elements of net-working. To have a better understanding of how a network operates, it is essential to understand the OSI model and its associated protocols.

This chapter begins with an introduction to organizations responsible for creating standards used worldwide. The chapter also discusses the layers of the OSI model and the protocols associated with OSI layers.

Standards Organizations

The number of hardware and software vendors is increasing every day. If all manufacturers produced hardware and software according to their own specifications, compatibility would be difficult to ensure unless you purchased the computers, peripherals, and networking components (both hardware and software) from the same maker. To prevent such an eventuality, several international organizations collaborated on specifying standards to ensure compatibility. All products conforming to these standards would be compatible — a concept known as an *open system*. Some of the agencies that helped to create the standards are

 ✦ **ITU-T:** The International Telecommunication Union (ITU) is the body that sets the standards for international telecommunications. The ITU-T wing is concerned with telephone and data communication systems. Before 1993, ITU-T was known as the Consulting Committee on Telegraph and Telephone (CCITT). Now all telecommuni-cation standards issued come under the ITU-T banner. For example, the X.400 standard for addressing and transporting e-mail messages has been set by ITU.

 ✦ **ISO:** The International Organization for Standardization (ISO) exists for the purpose of setting industrial standards. ISO is made up of the national standards organizations from around the world and issues standards on a wide range of topics. The Open Systems Interconnection (OSI) model is the standard issued by ISO for networking computers. ISO is also a member of ITU-T. Both of these organizations cooperate when producing telecommunication standards. The American National Standards Institute (ANSI) is the United States' representative in the ISO.

✦ **IEEE:** The Institute of Electrical and Electronics Engineers (IEEE) sets international standards in the fields of electrical engineering and computing. For LANs, the IEEE 802 standard is the main standard, which has been defined by IEEE.

✦ **EIA:** The Electronics Industries Association (EIA) sets standards in the field of telecommunication equipment. The standards for cables are also set by EIA.

OSI Networking Model

The OSI model, specified by the ISO, is the most widely accepted model for understanding network communication. The OSI model specifies the rules to be followed when two computers must communicate with each other. This model is a conceptual framework of how interaction takes place between computers over a network.

The OSI model consists of seven hierarchical layers, as illustrated in Figure 18-1.

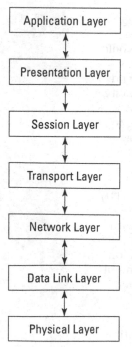

Figure 18-1: The seven layers of the OSI model

The OSI model explains the functions each layer performs, but it does not specify the exact services and protocols each layer uses. The specific implementation of each layer is left to individual protocol developers and hardware manufacturers.

Of these seven layers, the Application layer interacts with the user, and the Physical layer interacts with the hardware.

The Physical layer

As the first (and arguably the most concrete) layer of the OSI model, the Physical layer is concerned with the actual mechanisms that transmit and receive data as electrical impulses. The Physical layer performs the following functions:

✦ **It defines the physical transmission of data.** The events included in this definition are mechanical, electrical, and procedural (which refers to actions performed by a piece of hardware).

✦ **It defines the physical characteristics of the hardware.** The hardware can be network interface cards, wall jackets (wall jacks), or connectors. This layer also defines the physical characteristics of the actual medium (such as cable and airwaves) through which the signal must travel. In effect, the Physical layer is the nuts-and-bolts level of data transmission: It defines how a bit must be represented in terms of voltages, how a connection is established between computers, and how the connection is released.

✦ **It represents binary digits as voltages.** A computer stores data in binary form, but before physical transmission can take place the data is converted from binary form to signals. The conversion of data takes place in the Physical layer. The network card present in the Physical layer is responsible for converting the data from binary form to electrical, light, or radio signals.

Tip   Devices specified in the Physical layer follow a standard when encoding binary data or decoding electrical signals. One of the most common standards in local-area networks is the Manchester Encoding Method, which specifies the units of measurement and specific intervals at which the signals can be interpreted as binary digits.

✦ **It defines the devices responsible for transmitting signals on the network.** In addition to connectors, cables, and the network interface card, you can associate a device called a *repeater* (which re-amplifies a signal en route to a faraway destination) with the Physical layer.

Cross-Reference   Repeaters are discussed in more detail in Chapter 17.

The Data Link layer

Just above the Physical layer in the OSI hierarchy is the Data Link layer, where transmitted data finds its way through the network. This layer performs the following functions:

✦ Providing a service-interface to the Network layer

✦ Framing

✦ Switching

✦ Error detection and recovery

✦ Flow control

Services provided to the Network layer

The primary function of the Data Link layer is to support the functions of the Network layer by offering the following services:

✦ Unacknowledged connectionless service

✦ Unacknowledged connection-oriented service

✦ Acknowledged connectionless service

✦ Acknowledged connection-oriented service

Unacknowledged connectionless service

The unacknowledged connectionless service consists of the source computer sending data without establishing a connection with the data's destination. The sender does not receive an acknowledgment that the data was received. If a packet gets lost during transmission, no attempt is made to recover it. Sending letters by post is the typical example of such a service in the real world. Each letter is independent and travels to its destination without providing the sender any notification of whether or not the delivery was successful.

This service is used when the medium is reliable or when a loss of packets is preferable to investing time in re-transmitting the packets. Unacknowledged connectionless service is useful when transmitting real-time data, such as voice and video. In the case of voice and video, loss of a packet or two is acceptable, but the delay caused by retransmitting or providing acknowledgment is unacceptable. This service is implemented in Ethernet networks.

Unacknowledged connection-oriented service

Unacknowledged connection-oriented service is different from unacknowledged connection*less* service; in the latter case, a connection is established prior to the transmission of data.

An example of such communication is placing a phone call. First, you make a connection with the party that you are calling, and then you talk. While speaking with the other person, you may notice that the person at the other end is finding it difficult to understand what you are saying due to excessive noise on the line. No mechanism exists in the system to relay the lost conversation again. This is unacknowledged connection-oriented service. ATM and Frame Relay use this service for data transmission.

Acknowledged connectionless service

The acknowledged connectionless service consists of the source computer sending the data without establishing a connection. But in this case, the receiver sends back an acknowledgment for every frame that it receives. If the sender does not receive an acknowledgment within a stipulated time, the packet is retransmitted. In effect, this service compensates for unreliable media. A Token-Ring network implements acknowledged connectionless service.

Acknowledged connection-oriented service

The acknowledged connection-oriented service involves the sender establishing a connection with the recipient and then sending the frames. The receiver sends an acknowledgment of every frame received. This service is used when the reliability of data transfer and data integrity is extremely important. All frames are numbered, and this process ensures that they reach the destination in the right order and that duplicate frames are not sent to the destination computer.

Acknowledged connection-oriented service consists of three steps:

1. **Establishing the connection:** The source requests a connection from the destination. After establishing a connection, the source and destination computers initialize the variables and prepare to exchange data.

2. **Transmitting data:** The source and destination computers exchange data until one of them initiates a request to terminate the connection.

3. **Releasing the connection:** One of the participating computers initiates a request to release the connection, and the variables are cleared.

Acknowledged connection-oriented service is the type that TCP/IP networks implement. A typical example of such communication is Web browsing via dial-up connection: The user connects to the ISP server, establishing a path to communicate with the target server over the phone line during the period of connection.

Framing

The Data Link layer organizes data into frames to make the data more manageable and adds control information to the frames that is used for error detection and correction.

The Data Link layer computes a checksum for each frame, attaches the checksum to the trailer of the frame, and transmits the data. When the data arrives at its destination, the computer receiving the data computes the checksum again and compares it with the checksum in the frame. If they differ, an error is reported and the frames are re-transmitted.

> **Note**   A *checksum* is the count of the number of bits in a transmission unit. This count is included with the unit to confirm that the transmission was complete and no data corruption occurred. The sender computes a checksum before sending the data. The receiver computes the checksum when he receives the data. If the count matches, it indicates that the transmission was complete.

The size of the frame can vary depending on the framing method. Methods that are used to break data into frames include character count, character stuffing, and bit stuffing, as detailed in the upcoming sections.

Character count

The character count method includes the size of the frame in the header of the frame. The computer receiving data reads the header to determine the size of the frames. If the header is altered by noise bursts or interference along the transmission line, then the Data Link layer cannot identify the end of the frame. For example, if the frame size is 3 but interference on the line causes the entry in the header to change to 7, the receiving computer cannot detect the start of the new frame. Though checksum can help the receiver detect that an error has occurred in a frame, it has no way to detect where the next frame starts. This algorithm is not so popular because of these shortcomings.

Character stuffing

Character stuffing inserts an ASCII character sequence at the beginning and at the end of the frame. For example, FR ST may indicate the beginning of the frame, and FR EN may indicate the end of the frame. If the same character sequence (FR ST or FR EN) occurs as part of the message, the character sequence (that is the part of the message) is prefixed with FR. To reconstruct the data, the Data Link layer receiving the frames removes this FR when it opens them. The problem with this method is that it requires the use of ASCII character codes, which might not be feasible on some types of networks.

Bit stuffing

To avoid using ASCII characters, a method called *bit stuffing* was introduced. This process is similar to character stuffing. The difference is that bit stuffing adds a bit pattern called the *flag byte* at the beginning and end of each frame. If the same pattern occurs in the data, a zero is appended to the data.

Switching

Switching is the process of sending data from a source to a destination through a set of intermediate devices. These intermediate devices are referred to as switches.

Data is transmitted from one station to another by being routed through a network of nodes.

As shown in Figure 18-2, switched networks can be classified as follows:

✦ Circuit-switched network

✦ Message-switched network

✦ Packet-switched network

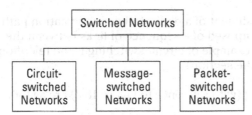

Figure 18-2: Switched networks

Figure 18-3 provides an illustration of a switched communication network. Suppose data must be transmitted from Computer A to Computer D. The data is first sent to Switch 1. From there, the data can be routed either through Switch 2 and Switch 6 or through Switch 5 and Switch 6, depending on the network traffic and length of the route.

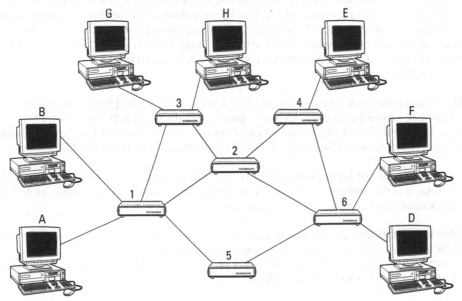

Figure 18-3: Switched communication network

Some switches on a switched communication network may not be connected to computers, but may be connected to other switching devices, such as routers and hubs. The task of these switches is limited to accepting data from a switching device and sending it to the appropriate receiving switching device. This is referred to as internal switching.

Normally, switch-to-switch links are shared multiplexed lines, either using TDM or FDM. These lines significantly reduce transmission costs. On the other hand, switch-station links are point-to-point, dedicated links.

Circuit switching

Circuit switching involves the establishment of a dedicated communication path between two stations. The path is composed of a sequence of links between the source and the destination. A typical example of circuit switching is the telephone network (which is explained later in the section).

The steps involved in circuit switching (with reference to Figure 18-3) are as follows:

1. Circuit establishment
2. Data transfer
3. Circuit disconnect

Consider the following situation. Computer A needs to send data to Computer D. Before the process of data transmission can begin, a station-to-station (A-D) circuit must be established. Station A sends a request to Switch 1, which asks for a connection to Station D. Switch 1 chooses the next leg in a route leading to Switch 6. Suppose that Switch 1 selects the link to Switch 2, after taking cost, traffic, and availability into consideration. Until now, a dedicated link has been maintained between Station A, Switch 1, and Switch 2. Next, Switch 2 selects a link to Switch 6, internally connecting Switch 1 to Switch 6. Finally, Switch 6 completes the connection to Computer D. Then Computer A performs a test to check whether Computer D is available.

The signals can now be propagated. The data may be analog (voice) or digital (client computer to server). After the process of data transfer, the connection can be terminated. Either of the two computers can initiate this action. Signals should also be transmitted to Switch 1, 2, and 6 to deallocate the dedicated links.

A connection must be established between the two computers before the actual process of data transfer can begin. This requires the destination computer to be available; otherwise the source would receive a busy signal.

After the circuit has been established, the channel is dedicated. The channel remains dedicated even if no data is transferred. Consequently, the channel may be idle. However, in a voice connection, utilization of the channel is 100 percent because in most cases there is a continuous flow of data.

There are minute and negligible delays at the switching nodes. However, after the circuit has been established, the network is quite fast and has a uniform transmission speed. The only delay would be the propagation delay through the transmission medium.

One example of circuit switching is the public telephone network. A number of national circuits are connected to form an international service. For any call made, national or international, a dedicated circuit is first established between the caller and the number that was dialed.

Note   Although it was developed to handle voice traffic, the public telephone network is increasingly being used for digital data transfer using modems.

Message switching

Circuit switching has some limitations. For example, the sending and the receiving stations must be available at the same time. Additionally, an entire set of links has to be dedicated to the connection. An alternative to this is message switching, which is used for digital data exchange. The intention of this approach is to exchange logical units of data, also referred to as messages. A dedicated communication path does not need to be established between the two computers. Instead, the link is established in steps, thereby establishing a virtual circuit. (Refer to Figure 18-3.) Assume that Computer A has a message to transmit to Computer D. Computer A appends Computer D's address to the message and then transmits the message to Switch 1. Switch 1 temporarily stores the message until the link to Switch 2 is available. After the link is available, Switch 1 transmits the message to Switch 2, which stores the message until a link is available. This process is also referred to as the store and forward mechanism.

The advantages of message switching are as follows:

✦ Messages can be temporarily stored on an intermediate node. Consequently, problems of network traffic can be alleviated.

✦ The receiver can be unavailable at the time of data transfer. The message can be temporarily stored and forwarded when the receiver is available.

✦ Message switching facilitates sending a single message to multiple destinations. Copies of the message can be made by the node and then forwarded.

✦ Messages can be prioritized. If a node has many messages to transmit, it can forward the higher-priority messages first.

The only disadvantage of the message switching process is that it is unsuitable for interactive applications, real-time traffic, or voice connections because of the delay.

Packet switching

Packet switching is a technique that attempts to combine the best features of circuit switching and message switching. Its advantages are most noticeable when it is used in a network where the volume of traffic is relatively high.

A packet is similar to the message in message switching. The only difference between packets and messages is that the size of a message is unrestricted. The size of a packet, however, is restricted to a few thousand bytes. This single difference has a significant impact on the performance of the network. Two types of packet switching are in common use on modern networks:

✦ **Datagram packet switching:** The following scenario refers to the network illustrated in Figure 18-3. Assume that Computer A has data to send to Computer D and that the data exceeds the maximum size for a packet. Computer A transmits the data to Node 1. Node 1 splits the data into three packets, P1, P2, and P3, and makes a routing decision for each packet. Suppose that Node 1 transmits P1 and P2 to Node 2. It then transmits P3 to Node 5. Consequently, the packets travel different routes, and it is even possible that P3 might reach Node 6 faster than P1 and P2. Each packet, treated independently, is referred to as a datagram.

✦ **Virtual-circuit packet switching:** Virtual-circuit packet switching differs from datagram packet switching in that a virtual circuit must be established between the two stations. When Computer A needs to transmit data to Computer D, Computer A asks for a connection to Computer D by sending a Call Request packet to Node 1 (see Figure 18-3). Node 1 decides to route the Call Request packet to Node 2. Instead of sending the data along different routes, as in datagram packet switching, Node 1 will send all subsequent data to Node 2. This is an important distinction between the two methods. Node 2 then decides to route the Call Request packet to Node 6. It will also route all subsequent data to Node 6. If Station D is prepared to receive the connection, it sends a Call Accept packet. The virtual circuit is now established. All data packets from A to D will travel the same path (A-1-2-6-D), and all data packets from D to A will travel the reverse path (D-6-2-1-A). The connection is terminated when one of the stations emits a Clear Request packet.

Superficially, virtual-circuit packet switching seems similar to circuit switching because a circuit is established in both cases. However, the difference lies in the fact that the link is not dedicated, so every packet is stored until the next link is available and then forwarded.

In virtual-circuit packet switching, a routing decision has to be made just once for every connection. This is different than datagram packet switching, which requires that a routing decision be made for each packet that must be transmitted.

Error detection and correction

Error detection and correction is another important service provided by the Data Link layer. Usually a frame consists of data and some additional bits that are used for error detection and error correction. If these bits are used for error detection, they are called error detection codes. If they are used to reconstruct a damaged message, they are referred to as error correction code.

Some common error detection methods are discussed in the following sections.

Parity Bit

The parity bit is one of the most common error detecting codes. A parity bit is appended to data so the number of ones in the frame is either even or odd. For example, if even parity is used, a message 101010101011 is transmitted as 1010101010111 to make the total number of 1s in the frame even. At the receiving end, the Data Link layer calculates the total number of ones in the frame and if the total is not even, it knows that an error has occurred. This parity bit can only be used to identify an error in a single bit. If two bit values have changed, this method cannot detect the error.

Cyclic redundancy code

Another common method of error detection is a polynomial code called the *cyclic redundancy code* (its use is called a *cyclic redundancy check* or *CRC*). The data that must be sent is treated as a series of polynomials that have coefficients of either 0 or 1. An *n*-bit frame is considered as the coefficient of a polynomial with *n* terms, from X^{n-1} to X^0. The *degree* of this polynomial is n-1. For example, 10011 has five bits and results in a five-term polynomial with the coefficients of 1, 0, 0, 1, and 1. Hence, the equation is $1^4 + 1^1 + 1^0$.

First the sender and the receiver agree upon a polynomial of *k* terms — for example, G (the *generator*). The high-order (leftmost) and low-order (rightmost) bits of the generator should both be 1 and the size of the frame should be greater than the size of the generator. The method is to append a checksum to the frame so the resulting frame is divisible by G. On receipt of the frame, the receiver will divide it by G. If this produces a remainder, an error has occurred during transmission.

Assume that the data to be transferred is 1101011011. Cyclic redundancy code can be used to detect errors in the transmission of this data as follows:

1. The sender and the receiver decide, in advance, on 10011 as the value of G. The degree of this number (n) is 4.

2. Append four zeros to the original frame. This results in the frame becoming 11010110110000.

3. Divide this by G to get the remainder. In this case, the remainder is 1110.

4. Append the remainder to the original frame. The frame now is 11010110111110. This is the checksummed frame and it will be transmitted.

5. At the receiving end, the receiver divides this frame by G. If no remainder is produced, it means no errors were made.

6. To get back the original data, the receiver removes the last *n* digits from the frame.

This is one of the most popular methods of error checking. This method can check for errors in *n* bit values. In this case, it can detect errors in 5 bits.

Three international standards (in the form of equations) are used to select G:

✦ CRC-12 = $X^{12} + X^{11} + X^3 + X^2 + X + 1$

✦ CRC-16 = $X^{16} + X^{15} + X^2 + 1$

✦ CRC-CCITT = $X^{16} + X^{12} + X^5 + 1$

The first equation is for 6-bit characters and the last two for 8-bit characters.

Flow control in the Data Link layer

The Data Link layer creates frames and passes them to the Physical layer for transmission. The Physical layer on the recipient's computer accepts the frame and passes it to the Data Link layer. The rate of data transfer can be different for the computer sending the data than for the computer receiving the data. The sender can flood the receiver with data that the receiver cannot handle, which can result in the loss of frames during transmission. If an acknowledgment is not received in the stipulated time, the frame is re-transmitted.

To solve problems that result from different data-transfer rates, a flow control mechanism is implemented in which the receiver and the sender monitor successful and failed transfers. One method of doing so is the *sliding window protocol*.

In the sliding window protocol, the sender maintains a sending window that keeps track of packets that have been sent but whose acknowledgments have not been received. Similarly, the recipient has a receiving window that keeps track of the packets it is going to receive. Both the sender and the receiver agree upon a window size, the number of frames that can be sent without waiting for an acknowledgment.

A long round-trip time for a packet can affect the efficiency of bandwidth utilization. For example, assume you are working with the following configuration: a network connection at 50 Kbps, a 600 milliseconds round-trip delay, window size of 1, and a frame size of 2000 bits. The sender starts transmitting the first frame at 0 milliseconds and completes sending the frame at 40 milliseconds. The frame reaches the receiver at 340 milliseconds, and the acknowledgment returns at 640 milliseconds (assuming no delay occurs at the receiving end and the acknowledgment frame is short). The sender starts transmission of the second frame at 640 milliseconds. The sender has been idle for (600/640 *100) 95 percent of the time. This problem arises because the sender is waiting for confirmation before sending the next frame. More bandwidth utilization can be achieved by relaxing this rule.

Bandwidth utilization can be maximized if the sender does not wait for the acknowledgment of every frame before sending the next packet. If the sender increases the number of outstanding packets (unacknowledged packets), using the time spent waiting for acknowledgment to send more packets can reduce idle time. In this case, the sender should have a maximum window size of 21. The sender transmits the first frame at 0 milliseconds, second at 40 milliseconds, and so on. At 640 milliseconds, when the first acknowledgment arrives, the sender has 21 frames unacknowledged. Every 40 milliseconds the sender receives an acknowledgment and the sender can transmit the next frame. This technique is called *pipelining*. Pipelining helps to increase the efficiency of the bandwidth utilization. To implement error detection and correction and pipelining, use any of the following algorithms:

✦ **Go back *n*:** Using this method, the receiver discards all frames received after it gets a packet containing an error — and sends no acknowledgments for those frames. All the packets, from the damaged packet onward, must be re-transmitted. For example, suppose the sender transmits packets one through ten continuously. The receiver gets packets one, two and three, but an error occurs in packet four. The receiver rejects packets four through ten. As a result, the sender does not get any acknowledgment for the final seven packets and retransmits them. If the communication channel is unreliable, this may result in the waste of a lot of bandwidth.

✦ **Selective repeat:** The other method for error handling during pipelining, is selective repeat. In this method the recipient's Data Link layer, ignores the flawed frame and stores all other frames. The sender does not get the acknowledgment for the flawed frame and retransmits it. If the window is large, this method uses a lot of memory for buffering the packets.

The Network layer

The Network layer is the third in the OSI model. It provides services to the Transport and Data Link layers, transmitting packets of information from senders to receivers. If sender and receiver are on different networks, this can mean going across routers. The Network layer must determine the best path through which it can receive the messages from the destination computer. This layer also ensures smooth flow of the traffic.

Routing — the primary function of the Network layer — is the process of determining the path a packet takes from its source to its destination. This path is decided with the aid of a routing algorithm. The routing algorithm should be correct, simple, stable, and optimal. The algorithm should also be robust and fair; it should be able to withstand changes in the network and should give all computers a chance to use the network.

Static routing

In static routing, the path between Computer A and Computer B is computed in advance and passed to the router when the network is started. No consideration is given to the current level of traffic on the network. Computer A can only communicate with Computer B through the pre-decided path. The relevant static algorithms use two different approaches:

✦ **Shortest-path routing:** The shortest-path routing algorithm is one of the simplest and most widely used algorithms for establishing a path between two computers. The shortest path could be in terms of physical distances (kilometers), hops (number of routers in between), or time that it takes a packet to reach another computer.

✦ **Flooding:** The flooding algorithm sends every packet received by the router on every line *except* the incoming line. The disadvantage of this method is that flooding can result in large numbers of duplicate packets and a glut of network traffic. A variation is *selective flooding*, which only sends packets onto lines that are going in approximately the right direction. The topology becomes a way to identify the approximate direction of the destination computer, and all packets are flooded in this direction.

Dynamic routing

In dynamic routing, each router chooses a path to reach another computer and updates it repeatedly. The router may access information from other routers or may study the network to assess the traffic, distance, and so on. Based on these factors, the routers periodically update the path to ensure that they are using the optimal one.

Many different algorithms can be used to select the best path. The dynamic routing algorithms are as follows:

✦ **Distance-vector routing:** The distance-vector routing algorithm is part of a routing method that maintains a table of best paths to various destinations. Routers exchange these tables. The measurement may be in terms of distance, delay, traffic, or similar factors.

✦ **Broadcast routing:** Broadcasting refers to sending packets to all hosts attached to the network.

✦ **Multicast routing:** *Multicasting* is the process of sending packets to a select group of computers. The algorithm used to achieve multicasting is called the multicasting algorithm. To implement multicasting, groups consisting of hosts are created. The number of hosts in a group is variable, and hosts may join or leave a group. Each host is running a number of processes. These processes inform the host about the group to which they belong. The hosts, in turn, inform the router about their groups — or the router may query the hosts periodically to determine which groups they belong to. Each router computes a spanning tree covering all the other routers in the subnet. The router gathers information from the other routers about which groups they are members of. When a packet that is meant for a group arrives at a router, the router examines the spanning tree and creates a route consisting of lines leading to hosts that belong to the group. To create this line the router may use the link state routing algorithm or the distance-vector routing algorithm. The router then passes the packet to only the routers found in the newly created line.

✦ **Routing for mobile computers:** With the number of portable computers increasing, the need arose to route for mobile hosts. The algorithm that routes for mobile computers divides the world into small cells. Each cell has two agents: One agent monitors all the mobile users who wander in that cell, and the other agent keeps track of the hosts based in that cell but not currently within the cell.

The Transport layer

The Transport layer is considered at the "top" of the lower layers of the OSI model—the Physical, Data Link, Network, and Transport layers. The role of this layer is to provide data transport from the sender computer to the destination computer. This layer provides its services to the layer above it—the Session layer. The services provided by the Transport layer include

✦ Addressing

✦ Connection management

✦ Multiplexing

✦ Congestion control

✦ Crash recovery

Addressing

Every frame sent out on the network must have the destination address. On a TCP/IP network, this address is a 32-bit number. Aside from the destination address, the sender must also specify a port number. There may be many processes executing on a computer. So, when the computer receives data over the network, it needs to know the process intended for this data. The port number serves to identify the process for which the data is addressed. The Transport layer takes care of this addressing.

Connection management

The Transport layer also provides connection management. After the connection has been established between the sender and the receiver, the Transport layer monitors the connection to check for lost or duplicated packets. If a packet is lost, the loss can be detected and the packet can be retransmitted using flow control algorithms. The bigger problem, however, is the handling of duplicate packets. For example, a customer connects to a bank through a network and asks the banker to transfer a large sum of money to another account. Unfortunately, this packet is stuck in the network. The sender does not receive an acknowledgment and retransmits the packet. This results in two packets in the network containing the same information. If both the packets arrive at the destination, the banker may end up transferring twice the intended amount. To avoid delaying the duplicates, a method called the *three-way handshake* was introduced. Its steps look like this:

1. A sequence number is attached to each packet sent. The sender, S, initiates the connection by sending a packet to the receiver, R. This packet contains a request for connection and the starting sequence number, x.

2. R endorses this sequence number and replies with its own sequence number, y, which is used in the acknowledgment packets.

3. S acknowledges y in the first data packet that it sends. Now each data packet that S transmits will be prefixed with $x+1$, $x+2$, $x+3$, and so on. Every acknowledgment that R sends will contain $y+1$, $y+2$, and so on. After the connection is established, any sliding window protocol can be used for data-flow control.

Multiplexing

The Transport layer can implement two types of multiplexing:

◆ **Downward multiplexing:** Many data-carrier companies charge their customers according to how many network connections they establish. Fewer connections mean a lower charge. The Transport layer can accept the packets from the layers above it; group the frames according to their destination, and establish one network connection for each group. As a result, there will be many processes on the sender's computer that use the same network connection to transmit information to the other computer. This type of multiplexing is referred to as downward multiplexing (refer to Figure 18-4).

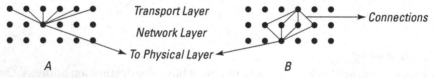

Figure 18-4: Multiplexing

◆ **Upward multiplexing:** In upward multiplexing, the goal is to transmit data at a faster rate. For example, Computer S implements a sliding window protocol. This leads to a slower data transmission rate because Computer S has to wait for acknowledgments before sending the packet again. By opening multiple network connections, data can be simultaneously transmitted along these lines, which leads to a faster rate of transmission.

Crash recovery

Another aspect of connection management is *crash recovery* during data transmission. In the case of a connectionless service, the computers know how to handle lost packets, and they know how to cope with it. If it is a connection-oriented service, a new connection is established and transmission begins with the packets that were not transmitted.

The problem is how to recover from a break in the network connection. If Computer S crashes while sending a large amount of data to Computer R, it would be optimal if Computer S started where it left off and did not retransmit all of the data. Because this problem cannot be handled effectively in this layer, the higher layers must deal with this situation. To solve this problem, the higher layer maintains information about its transactions.

The Session layer

The Session layer provides services to the layer above it, the Presentation layer. The primary services provided are the following:

- **Data exchange:** The exchange of data is the most important feature of the Session layer. The Session layer defines how the session between the users is established and released. Establishing a session is similar to establishing connections in the Transport layer. The Transport layer terminates the connection abruptly, which can result in loss of data. The Session layer ends the session only after both parties agree to disconnect.

- **Dialog management:** When a session is established between computers, the layers above the Session layer decide the mode of communication — full duplex or half duplex. During a *half-duplex* session, the sender and the receiver take turns communicating. This coordination of communication is called dialog management, which is orchestrated Token management. If half-duplex mode is chosen, the computer with the token sends the data. In *full-duplex* mode, no tokens are needed.

- **Synchronization:** The Session layer helps the system return to a previous state after an error by introducing *synchronization points* between sessions. If an error occurs, recovery can be made from a previous synchronized point. For example, a fax is being sent from a computer to a fax machine. At the receiving end, the fax has a paper jam. In this example, the Transport layer has moved the data from one machine to the other, and the error has occurred after the transfer, in one of the upper layers. If synchronization points are periodically introduced, it is possible to reset the state of the session to previous synchronization point, before the problem occurred.

- **Activity management:** This service involves breaking data that must be sent into units called activities. For example, in a multiple file transfer, transferring of one file constitutes one activity. Activity management can also be used to store incoming requests and to start processing them after all messages have been received.

- **Exception reporting:** This service informs the upper layers of any unexpected errors that arise in the Session layer.

The Presentation layer

The Presentation layer is the sixth layer in the OSI model. This layer provides services to the Application layer. The Presentation layer is concerned with the syntax and semantics of the message being transmitted (for example, the way characters are represented). Different computers may use different codes for representing characters, such as ASCII and EBCDIC. The Presentation layer abstracts this by defining the data structures that are used for network transmission. Data transmission is standardized so computers using different character coding can communicate. The Presentation layer will abstract the data structures and convert the data into network representation and vice versa.

The supported types of data are defined by ASN.1 (Abstract Syntax Notation 1). These data types, defined in the standard itself, are also called *built-in types*. Table 18-1 summarizes them.

Table 18-1
Data Types Supported by ASN

Data type	Description
Boolean	Represents logical data
Integer	Single whole number
Bit string	Binary data
Tagged	A new type derived from an old one
Real	For real values (example $M * B_e$, where M is the mantissa, B is base. and e the exponent)
Any	Data type is unrestricted and can be used with any valid type

The Application layer

The user's network applications fall into this category. The user interacts with the software present in this layer. All layers below this one exist to provide reliable transport for the information.

The Application layer contains four major protocols that are used by applications to communicate with other applications:

✦ ACSE (Association Control Service Element)

✦ RTSE (Reliable Transfer Service Element)

✦ ROSE (Remote Operations Service Element)

✦ CCR (Commitment, Concurrency, and Recovery)

This layer provides an application with the following features:

✦ **Network security:** Many concepts, such as cryptography and algorithms, are available that can be used to ensure network security.

✦ **Domain Name System (DNS):** This system is used in name resolution over the Internet.

✦ **Support protocols:** These protocols are used for network management, optimization, and fine-tuning.

Transmitting over the OSI

The network cable has a maximum amount of content that it can support at one point of time. The data to be transmitted is therefore broken into manageable chunks known as *frames*. Data is transmitted from one computer to the other in the form of frames. It is important to discuss the contents of the frame to understand how transmission of data takes place. The upcoming section discusses frames.

Frames

Though the contents of a frame depend on the network architecture and the protocol, the following elements are present in all frames, regardless of network architecture or protocol:

✦ **Header:** Contains the alert signal indicating that a frame is being transmitted. It also contains the source and destination address of the frame.

✦ **Data:** The raw information transmitted between computers — is the whole point of their interaction. The receiving computer removes the header and the trailer and retrieves the information from the data section of the frame.

✦ **Trailer:** The data must reach its destination without any errors. The *trailer* contains information (which varies depending on the type of frame) that aids the process of checking for errors.

Figure 18-5 illustrates the contents of a transmitted packet.

Figure 18-5: Contents of a packet

Transmitting data

Now that you know what comprises a frame, let's discuss how the transmission of data takes place. The data (in the form of frames) is sent from the Application layer. Each subsequent layer, except the Physical layer, adds header information to the data and passes it to the next layer. Each layer on the sending computer establishes a virtual connection with its counterpart on the receiving computer.

For example, if Sam wants to telnet to his friend Rita, the networking interaction looks like this:

1. The Telnet program works at the Application layer of the OSI model. The Application layer adds some information to the data and passes it to the Presentation layer (refer to Figure 18-6).

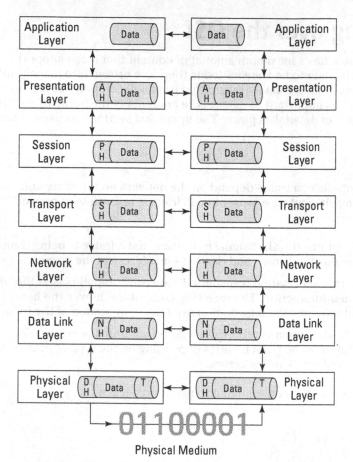

Figure 18-6: Transmission of data

2. The Presentation layer treats the original user data and the Application layer header information as equivalent data. The Presentation layer adds header information and passes it to the Session layer.

3. The data with the Application layer header is data for the Session layer. The Session layer adds the relevant header information and passes the packet to the Transport layer.

4. This process continues until the packet reaches the Data Link layer. The Data Link layer adds both header and trailer information to the packet before sending it to the Physical layer.

5. The Physical layer does not add any header information to the packet. It sends the data to the receiving computer in the form of bits (0s and 1s). The Physical layer is the only layer that interacts directly with its counterpart on the receiving computer.

6. The Physical layer on the receiving computer receives the data and passes it to the Data Link layer.

7. The Data Link layer reads the header information that was added by its counterpart on the sending computer. After reading the header information and removing it from the packet, the Data Link layer passes the packet to the Network layer.

8. Each subsequent layer reads the information relevant to it and passes the packet to the next higher layer.

9. The packet reaches the Application layer, and the Telnet operation is complete.

Although the data goes from the Application layer down to the Physical layer, a virtual connection exists between the peer layers. The header information added by a layer is meaningful only to its peer at the receiving end.

Protocols

The previous sections dealt with the functions of the seven layers of the OSI model, the algorithms that help these layers perform those functions, and the data transmission process. The algorithms are implemented in the form of *protocols* — sets of rules that put the algorithms into action to perform the required functions. Each layer of the OSI reference model has its own set of protocols that make the transfer of data possible.

This section covers the protocols that operate in Data Link, Network, and Transport layers (which play a significant role in network security).

Data Link-layer protocols

The Data Link layer gives network services an interface to the Network layer — in addition to performing such functions as framing, error detection and recovery, and flow control. These functions are performed by protocols.

Three major protocols operating at the Data Link layer are HDLC, SLIP, and PPP; the upcoming subsections provide details.

HDLC

The origin of the High-level Data Link Control (HDLC) protocol lies in SNA (Systems Network Architecture), a set of network protocols developed by IBM. SNA was originally designed in 1974 for IBM's mainframe computers. SDLC (Synchronous Data Link Control) protocol was the data link protocol that formed a part of SNA.

HDLC evolved from SDLC. LAP (Link Access Procedure) and LAPB (Link Access Procedure, balanced) are variations of HDLC for the X.25 networking standard.

HDLC is a bit-oriented protocol that uses the bit stuffing method to create frames. The frame structure that it uses is illustrated in Figure 18-7.

| 8 01111110 | 8 Address | 8 Control | >= 0 Data | 16 Checksum | 8 01111110 |

Figure 18-7: HDLC frame format

The HDLC protocol uses a sliding window with a 3-bit sequence number, giving a maximum of seven unacknowledged frames. Its individual parts have specific functions:

✦ The Address field serves to identify the terminal for which the frame is meant.

✦ The Control field is for acknowledgments, sequence numbers, and other purposes.

✦ The Data field contains user data.

✦ The Checksum field is for error detection and correction. The checksum is computed using the CRC-CCITT polynomial.

✦ The frame delimiter is 01111110.

SLIP

Serial Line IP (SLIP) and Point-to-Point protocol (PPP) are two communication protocols, which enable a node connected to a server to become an actual part of the Internet.

SLIP was devised in 1984 to connect Sun workstations to the Internet over a dial-up line using a modem. SLIP transmits raw IP packets with a flag byte (0xC0) for framing. If this pattern occurs within the frame, SLIP uses character stuffing to overcome the problem. Recent versions of SLIP provide header compression, and redundant fields in consecutive packets are omitted. Fields that differ are sent as increments to the previous value.

SLIP is used extensively. However, SLIP has some disadvantages:

✦ SLIP supports only IP traffic. Networks that do not use TCP/IP cannot be connected with SLIP.

✦ SLIP does not provide error detection. This task is left to the higher layers.

✦ IP addresses cannot be dynamically assigned.

✦ SLIP does not provide any methods of authentication.

✦ Because SLIP is not an approved Internet standard, several incompatible standards exist.

PPP

To solve the problems of SLIP and to arrive at an official Internet standard, the IETF set up a group that developed Point-to-Point Protocol (PPP). The three key features that PPP provides are as follows:

✦ A framing format that provides error detection

✦ A protocol for establishing the Data Link layer connection called Link Control Protocol (LCP)

✦ A protocol called Network Control Protocol (NCP) that configures each Network-layer protocol supported by PPP

To understand the how PPP works, consider an example. A user dials into an ISP to make a temporary connection. When the modem at the ISP's router responds, the physical connection is established. The next step is to establish the Data Link-layer connection. A series of LCP packets are sent to the ISP's router; they specify the PPP parameters and the responses from the router.

A set of NCP packets is sent from the sending computer to configure the Network layer. At this stage, the PC requires an IP address. The NCP serves to dynamically assign an IP address to the PC. This feature is not available in SLIP.

When the session is complete, NCP ends the Network-layer connection, and LCP ends the Data Link-layer connection. The modem disconnects the telephone, thereby ending the Physical-layer connection.

The PPP frame format is similar to the HDLC format. The difference between the two is that PPP is character-oriented, while HDLC is bit-oriented.

Some advantages that PPP provides are as follows:

✦ Error detection

✦ Support for multiple protocols, including IPX/SPX and DECnet

✦ Assignment of IP addresses at connection time

✦ Authentication

Network-layer protocols

As discussed previously, the Network layer concerns itself with routing and congestion control. Some protocols that function at the Network layer are as follows:

✦ Internet Protocol (IP)

✦ Internet Control Message Protocol (ICMP)

✦ Address Resolution Protocol (ARP)

✦ Reverse Address Resolution Protocol (RARP)

✦ Open Shortest Path First (OSPF)

✦ Border Gateway Protocol (BGP)

✦ Mobile IP

✦ IPv6/IPng

IP

Unlike the X.25 protocol, which is connection-oriented, the IP Network-layer proto-col is connectionless. It is based on the idea of IP datagrams transparently, but not necessarily reliably, transported from the source to the destination and possibly traversing several networks. The decision to enable the IP to provide an unreliable connectionless service evolved gradually and was facilitated by putting all the reliability mechanisms into the TCP. This way it was possible to have a reliable end-to-end connection, even when some underlying networks were not dependable.

The Transport layer takes messages and breaks them up into datagrams of 64KB each. Each datagram is transmitted through the IP, sometimes fragmenting into smaller units as it goes. When all the pieces finally get to the destination computer, a Transport-layer device reassembles them to form the original message.

Anatomy of an IP datagram

An IP datagram consists of a header part and a text part. The header has 20 bytes fixed part and a variable length optional part. This IP header has several parts that contain informa-tion such as the following:

✦ The version number of the IP protocol used

✦ IP header length

✦ The type of service

✦ Total length of the datagram (including header and text)

✦ Identification of the datagram

✦ Information related to the fragmentation of the datagram

✦ Time To Live (TTL), the "lifespan" of the datagram

✦ Header checksum

✦ Source and destination address

✦ Some optional fields

ICMP

Internet Control Message Protocol (ICMP) serves to monitor the operations of the Internet. Whenever an unexpected event occurs—a destination host cannot be located, for example—it is reported by the ICMP. Some important ICMP message types are summarized in Table 18-2.

Table 18-2
ICMP Message Types

Message Type	Description
Destination unreachable	The packet could not be delivered.
Time exceeded	The time to live field value reached zero.
Redirect	The packet has been sent to the wrong router.
Source quench	When a host begins sending too many packets, this message slows it down.

OSPF

The Internet is a collection of subnetworks. Each subnetwork that can also function by itself is called an *autonomous system* (AS). Each AS can follow a different routing algorithm. The process of communicating on the Internet is simplified by setting standards for routing between and within autonomous systems. A routing algorithm within an AS is referred to as an interior gateway protocol. A routing algorithm between autonomous systems is an *exterior gateway protocol*.

One of the most popular interior gateway routing protocols is the Open Shortest Path First (OSPF) protocol. This protocol is open, meaning it has been published in RFC.

An AS is divided into smaller units of contiguous networks called areas. These areas have participating routers known as area border routers. These routers maintain topological databases that contain information about the other routers in an AS. All the routers within an AS have identical topological databases.

An AS also contains an OSPF backbone that regulates inter-area traffic. It consists of area border routers that do not belong to a specific area but are common to the AS (as shown in Figure 18-8).

As shown earlier in Figure 18-4, routers D, E, F, J, K, and L form the backbone. If Computer 1 (C 1) in Area 1 wishes to communicate with Computer 2 (C 2) in Area 3, it has to go through Router M which in turn forwards the packet to Router L. Router L forwards the packet to Router K, which forwards the packet to Router J. The packet finally reaches Computer B via Router I and Router G, which belong to Area 3.

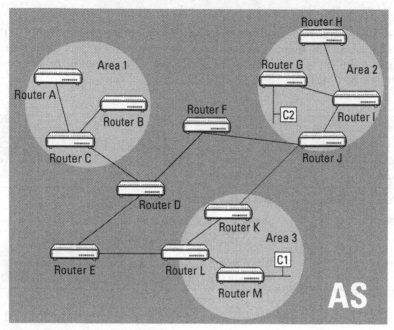

Figure 18-8: The OSPF network

OSPF supports three kinds of networks and connections: LANs, WANs, and point-to-point lines between routers. OSPF uses the link-state algorithm to decide the route to the receiver.

BGP

OSPF is for communicating within an AS. Between ASs, the protocol used for this purpose is the exterior gateway routing protocol. Border Gateway Protocol (BGP) is an example of such a protocol. Aside from the concern of moving data from the source to the destination, BGP has another priority — politics. This includes political, social, and economic considerations. For example, packets originating from a confidential location in a particular country should not travel through hostile nations. These policies are configured manually and are not part of the BGP.

The BGP protocol uses the distance-vector algorithm to arrive at a routing line.

Mobile IP

As the number of Internet users grows rapidly, the number of mobile users is also growing enormously. Many of them want to stay connected to the Internet even when they are in transit. The IETF established a Working Group to find a solution. Their goals were challenging:

✦ Mobile host should be able to use its home IP address anywhere

✦ No software changes to the fixed hosts

✦ No changes to the router software and tables

The solution was Mobile IP. Any site that wants to enable its users to roam creates a home agent. Any site that wishes to allow foreign users creates a foreign agent. When a user visits a foreign site, either by plugging into the foreign LAN or simply wandering into the wireless cellular network, the user account contacts the foreign agent and registers itself. The foreign agent contacts the home agent and sends it a care-of address — usually the IP address of the foreign agent. When packets arrive at the home agent, it redirects them to the foreign agent. Security is a concern. A home agent should be able to discern valid foreign-agent requests and block invalid ones. This can be accomplished by using authentication protocols.

Mobile Internet connectivity is still a new concept. However, several technological advancements are foreseen.

IPv6

The growth in the number of mobile users; the convergence of the computer, entertainment, and the communications industry; and the expansion of the Internet from governments, universities, and high-tech industry have all led to the need for a much more flexible IP. This led to the development of IPv6.

Some of the advancements that IPv6 provides, when compared to the current IPv4, are as follows:

✦ **Expanded routing and addressing capabilities:** IPv6 increases the IP address size from 32 bits to 128 bits. This supports more levels of addressing hierarchy and a much greater number of addressable nodes.

✦ **Anycast address:** *Anycasting* is a means of addressing a group of computers. It is similar to multicasting. The difference is that it delivers a packet to only one node instead of delivering a packet to all the nodes in a group. IPv6 identifies groups of nodes that can receive a packet sent to an *anycast address*. This achieves better traffic control.

✦ **Header format simplification:** Some IPv4 header fields have been dropped or made optional. This decreases the size of the header. Although the IPng addresses are four times longer than the IPv4 addresses, the IPng header is only twice the size of the IPv4 header.

✦ **Improved support for options:** More options are supported, and increased support for future options is provided.

✦ **Quality-of-service capabilities:** Packets can be labeled as belonging to particular traffic "flows" for which the sender requests special handling, such as nondefault quality of service.

✦ **Authentication and privacy capabilities:** IPv6 defines extensions that support data security and data integrity.

Transport-layer protocols

As discussed in the previous section, the Transport layer concerns itself with addressing packets and ensuring that they reach their destination safely. TCP and UDP use the algorithms discussed previously to perform these functions in the Transport layer.

Transmission Control Protocol

Transmission Control Protocol (TCP) is a protocol designed to provide reliable communication between pairs of processes using reliable and unreliable networks and Internets. TCP is a connection-oriented, acknowledged service that ensures the safe delivery of the packet (which keeps the protocol popular) and confirms delivery by sending an acknowledgment (which slows down the protocol, but not enough to hurt its popularity).

Some important features of TCP are as follows:

✦ TCP connections are full duplex and point-to-point. TCP does not support multicasting or broadcasting.

✦ TCP transmits data as a byte stream, not as a message stream. Consider, for example, a sending process that sends data as four 512-byte chunks. This data can be delivered to the receiving process as four 512-byte chunks, two 1024-byte chunks, or even one 2048-byte chunk. The receiver cannot detect the size of the units in which the data was written.

✦ TCP uses the process of buffering before transmitting data. When an application passes data to the Transport layer, TCP can buffer it until it has more data to send (or send the data immediately if necessary). However, if the application requires that some data be sent immediately without being buffered, it can use the PUSH flag. This flag signals TCP not to delay the transmission.

✦ TCP signals to the receiving process that urgent data is being sent by using the URGENT flag. When this data is received at the destination, the destination process is sent a signal. It is up to the process to interpret that the data is urgent based on the signal.

User Data Protocol

User Data Protocol (UDP) is a connectionless transport protocol. It does not guarantee delivery, nor does it guarantee duplicate protection. Raw IP datagrams can be transmitted without having to establish a connection. Client/server applications that require only a request and a response use UDP.

A single UDP segment consists of an 8-byte header followed by the data.

Summary

This chapter introduced the standards organizations that set consistent product standards for worldwide use. The major organizations that set standards for networks are ITU-T, ISO, IEEE, and EIA.

One such standard—the OSI reference model specified by the ISO—defines a seven-layer functional hierarchy that is now the most widely accepted model of network communication. The OSI model specifies rules that two computers must follow when they interact with each other at any of seven layers (Application, Presentation, Session, Transport, Network, Data Link, and Physical). Each layer has its own set of protocols that make the transfer of data possible:

✦ Protocols operating at the Data Link layer are HDLC, SLIP, and PPP.

✦ Protocols that function at the Network layer are as follows:

  • Internet Protocol (IP)

  • Internet Control Message Protocol (ICMP)

  • Address Resolution Protocol (ARP)

  • Reverse Address Resolution Protocol (RARP)

  • Open Shortest Path First (OSPF)

  • Border Gateway Protocol (BGP)

  • Mobile IP

  • IPv6/IPng

✦ Transport-layer protocols are TCP and UDP.

✦   ✦   ✦

Assessment Questions

The questions in this section test your knowledge of the content covered in the book. The questions are arranged by chapter and followed by answers. If you have any difficulty with a particular chapter, you can go directly to the questions and answers for that chapter for clarification.

Chapter 1 Questions

1. Why is security important for the network?

2. Who decides the network-security policy for an enterprise?

3. Name a few security products from Cisco Systems.

4. Which are the most common routes used for network intrusion?

5. Implementing a firewall at the network boundary provides no security at all. True or False?

6. What is denial of service?

7. What is a hacker?

8. What is data encryption?

9. A network-security policy decides the dress code of the employees. True or False?

10. Authentication of network users can be secured by using Cisco Secure Intrusion Detection Systems. True or False?

11. Vulnerabilities in which of the following areas constitute a threat to network security? (Select all that apply.)

    A. Configurations

    B. Protocols

    C. Flooring

    D. Operating systems

12. What is IP spoofing?

   A. A variant of the TCP/IP protocol that suppresses IP for internetwork communications.

   B. Masquerading as a packet from some other source IP address by modifying specific fields.

   C. Making TCP packets appear as UDP datagrams over the network.

   D. Implementing IP routing on nonrouting devices by manipulating the route table.

13. Which of the following are implementation flaws that can result in an intrusion? Assume all devices are Cisco products. (Select all that apply.)

   A. A router configured for IP routing with default access permissions.

   B. A network access server configured for remote dial-in and default Telnet settings.

   C. A network access server configured for remote dial-in with cleartext authentication.

   D. A client Web browser has Java applets and cookies disabled.

14. Which of the following TCP/IP protocols are vulnerable to security threats? (Select all that apply.)

   A. Telnet

   B. SMTP

   C. TFTP

   D. DTP

15. What are the major categories of security threats?

   A. Unauthorized access, physical assault, denial of service, and photo ID cards.

   B. Unauthorized access, physical assault, data diddling, and investigation.

   C. Photo ID cards, investigation, unauthorized access, and denial of service.

   D. Investigation, unauthorized access, denial of service, and data diddling.

16. What are the possible tools for locating the target of network intrusion? (Select all that apply.)

   A. TCP/IP tools such as `trace`, `ping`, and `finger`

   B. Port-scanning tools such as SATAN

   C. ICMP-flooding tools such as `pingflood`

   D. ICMP-sweeping tools such as `fping` and `gping`

17. Which TCP/IP protocol feature gives intruders the best information about an internetwork?

    A. POP3

    B. SNMP

    C. SMTP

    D. LDAP

18. Which of the following methods are employed by an intruder to gain unauthorized access to a network server? (Select all that apply.)

    A. Exploitation of TCP services

    B. Influencing the system administrator

    C. Exploiting Operating System loopholes

    D. Source address manipulation

19. What are the major components that constitute a network-security policy? (Select all that apply.)

    A. Access control

    B. Authentication and encryption

    C. Purchase of computer peripherals

    D. Auditing

20. Which of the following can be used to implement regular network monitoring and auditing? (Select all that apply.)

    A. WatchDogs

    B. Network intrusion-detection devices

    C. SNMP

    D. More PCs

21. Which of the following terms refers to hardware and software that no longer falls in the category of strategic software but is still functional in the organization's current computing environment?

    A. Strategic systems

    B. Tactical systems

    C. Legacy systems

    D. Unsupported systems

22. Which of the following terms refers to hardware and software that conform to the organization's computing standards?

    A. Strategic systems

    B. Tactical systems

    C. Legacy systems

    D. Unsupported systems

23. Which of the following terms refers to data meant for use strictly within the organization?

    A. Sensitive data

    B. Confidential data

    C. Private data

    D. Public data

24. Which of the following terms refers to information, such as the personal information about the employees, meant for use of specific departments within the organization falls under this category?

    A. Sensitive data

    B. Confidential data

    C. Private data

    D. Public data

Answers to Chapter 1 Questions

1. Security is important for the network to secure important data and devices from hackers. Due to increase in Internet usage, security of networks has become a major concern.

2. A network-security policy defines access policies and privilege levels. It decides how security has to be implemented across the network. This policy is designed and framed by the IT managers and senior officials of the company who are aware of the security techniques and technical intricacies of a network.

3. Cisco Systems has many security-related products. Cisco NetRanger is an Intrusion Detection Tool and Cisco PIX Firewall is flagship product from Cisco Systems.

4. Many vulnerable points within an internetwork allow intrusion. Network cables allow eavesdropping; an unprotected Internet connection offers a wide variety of options for breaching the security of an internetwork. Network devices (especially those that can control the network itself) are usually targeted for attack.

5. False. Implementing firewalls provides security by allowing packet level filtering and policy-based detection. It allows or disallows specific packets depending on protocol, ports, or even packet headers.

6. A denial-of-service (DoS) attack floods the network with unnecessary and spurious data (whether intentionally or as an unintended side effect), bringing down the servers or communication links. Such a flooding clogs the available bandwidth, preventing legitimate users from gaining access.

7. In its current common meaning, the term *hacker* denotes a person of diverse (and often sophisticated) computer skills who uses them to intrude into other people's networks as a prank, an act of industrial espionage, or malicious sabotage. Hackers who penetrate deeply enough into a network to take control of it can be aware of almost every detail of network operation.

8. Data encryption provides security and integrity of data by converting it into *ciphertext*—seemingly unintelligible form (difficult to decrypt without the proper key)—before sending it over unsecured links. Data encryption is one way to protect data from unauthorized use.

9. False. A network-security policy is a framework, which decides how the corporate assets can be secured in the best possible manner. It also decides what action and steps should be performed in the event of disaster or attack.

10. False. To secure authentication Cisco recommends the implementation of Cisco Secure Access Control Servers. It supports TACACS+, RADIUS, Kerberos, and SSL-based secure authentication. Cisco Secure Intrusion Detection System provides real-time monitoring by analyzing the network traffic and all layers of network communication.

11. A, B, and D. Many things can cause a threat to the network security system. Of the given choices all except flooring are possible flaws, which can cause network security threat.

12. B. IP spoofing is an attack where the primary intention of the intruder is to hide his identity. In a TCP/IP networked environment, this is achieved by masquerading or altering the source IP address. The intruder pretends to be sending data from an IP address other than its own by capturing and altering IP packets.

13. A and C. A router configured for IP routing with default access permits all traffic, providing no security check at all. A network access server (NAS) configured for remote dial-in but configured for cleartext authentication can allow any intruder to capture packets on the wire and analyze the packets to obtain security credentials.

14. A, B, and C. Telnet, SMTP, and TFTP are vulnerable to security threats. DTP refers to Data Transfer Process and is a part of a TCP/IP application. It is not a TCP/IP protocol.

15. D. The major categories of security threats are investigation, unauthorized access, denial of service, and data diddling.

16. A, B, and C. The target can be located by using TCP/IP command tools like `trace`, `ping`, `finger`, `whois`, and `nslookup`. Other methods include Port Scanning using SATAN and ICMP sweeps using `fping` and `gping`. ICMP flooding is a denial-of-service attack used to obstruct network services.

17. B. SNMP is by far the most vulnerable for intrusion and a favorite choice with the hacking community. SNMP exchanges community strings containing passwords in cleartext. By capturing SNMP queries an intruder can collect valuable information on network configuration. SNMP v2 has improved this security flaw by implementing MD5 algorithm to authenticate an SNMP server and agent. For Cisco configuration to prevent intruders, refer to `www.cisco.com/warp/public/614/9.html`.

18. A, B, and C. A network intruder can use methods, such as exploitation of TCP services by eavesdropping, using social engineering, or influencing the system administrator to gain privileged access to the network devices. But, the most popular method to obtain the administrative level security credentials for unauthorized access is exploiting the intrinsic vulnerabilities of the Operating System.

19. A, B, and D. A network-security policy is designed to provide optimum security by utilizing various components. The components that constitute a security policy are as follows: physical security, network security, access control, authentication, encryption, software security, auditing and review, security awareness, incident response, and disaster contingency plan.

20. B and C. Network monitoring and auditing are necessary to keep a check on the security policy to detect, respond, and perform actions when network intrusion is detected. It also provides an opportunity to improve upon existing security policy by regularly reviewing security logs and traffic patterns, using Network Intrusion-Detection devices and SNMP-capable technologies.

21. B. *Tactical systems* are hardware and software that no longer fit the category of strategic software but still function in the organization's current computing environment. These systems should be upgraded to or replaced with strategic systems.

22. A. *Strategic systems* are hardware and software that conform to the organization's current computing standards.

23. B. *Confidential data* refers to data meant for use strictly within the organization. Disclosure of confidential data can have adverse impact on the organization, its clients, and its business partners.

24. C. Private data refers to the information, such as the personal information about the employees, meant for use of specific departments within the organization that falls under this category. It is important that private data is *not* accessible to all the employees of the organization.

Chapter 2 Questions

1. A software application that uses a network adapter card in promiscuous mode to capture all network packets traversing across a network is _____.

2. The three major types of networks in context of security are _____.

3. What is an untrusted network?

4. What is a denial-of-service attack used for?

5. PPP supports _____, _____, and _____ authentication protocols.

6. Pretty Good Privacy (PGP) is an authentication mechanism not supported by TCP/IP protocol. True or False?

7. IPSec is a Network-layer security protocol. True or False?

8. What is the purpose of OSI Data Link layer?

9. Cisco PIX Firewall is a security product from Cisco. True or False?

10. A firewall cannot block traffic on the basis of application ports. True or False?

11. What is a packet sniffer?

    A. It is a hardware device that scans all the network devices for open ports.

    B. It encrypts the data packets to securely transport them over the network.

    C. It is a software application that captures all the packets on the network.

    D. It is a packet that attacks specific ports of network devices.

12. Which of the following is true for IP spoofing?

    A. A host sends packets to another host with another IP address, which is normally a trusted IP address.

    B. A host sends packets with IPX address rather than IP address.

    C. A hacker uses software that generates username and password combinations to get access to protected resources.

    D. A host sends a packet with its own IP address as the destination address.

13. Networks are divided into different categories based on perceived security risk. What are these categories? (Select all that apply.)

    A. Trusted networks

    B. Unprotected networks

    C. Untrusted networks

    D. Unknown networks

14. Which of the following statements are correct about network security? (Select all that apply.)

    A. VPNs form a part of trusted networks.

    B. VPNs are untrusted networks.

    C. Unknown networks are essentially untrusted networks lying within the trusted network.

    D. Untrusted networks are networks that belong to outside the organization's security perimeter and administrative control.

15. What is the MD5 algorithm?

    A. It is (along with a packet sniffer) a method of deciphering encrypted data on the network.

    B. It is a one-way hash function that takes any length of data and produces 128-bit fingerprint.

    C. It is a method used by hackers to break the username and password combination required to access resources on the network.

    D. It is a Data Link-layer encryption tool that uses private keys to decrypt data.

16. Which of the following are Transport-layer security protocols? (Select all that apply.)

    A. Secure Shell (SSH) protocol

    B. MD5

    C. IPSec

    D. Private Communication Technology (PCT) protocol

17. Which of the following are true about IPSec? (Select all that apply.)

    A. It provides security at the Application layer.

    B. Its main component protocols are AH and ESP.

    C. It provides security at the Network layer.

    D. Its main component protocols are SSH and TLS.

18. Which of the following provide security at the Data Link layer? (Select all that apply.)

    A. IPv6

    B. VLANs

    C. PPP

    D. SSH

19. Which of the following is true about CHAP?

    A. It is a secured authentication protocol that verifies the identity of the remote node using a three-way handshake.

    B. It is an authentication process in which the username and password are sent in cleartext form.

    C. It is a two-way handshake authentication process.

    D. It is an authentication protocol on the Network layer.

20. Which of the following are Cisco's security products? (Select all that apply.)

    A. Cisco Secure PIX Firewall

    B. CiscoWorks 2000

    C. Cisco Secure Policy Manager

    D. Cisco Secure Access Control Server

21. Which of the algorithms is used for digitally signed messages?

    A. DES

    B. DSA

    C. KEA

    D. MD5

22. Which of the algorithm is the 64-bit block cipher algorithm that uses variable-size keys?

    A. DES

    B. DSA

    C. RC2

    D. MD5

23. Which of the algorithms is used for both authentication as well as encryption?

    A. DES

    B. RSA

    C. RC2

    D. MD5

24. Which of the algorithm is a variation of Diffie-Hellman key exchange?

    A. KEA

    B. RSA

    C. RC2

    D. MD5

25. Which of the following is *not* true for VLANS?

    A. VLANs are implemented by using hardware.

    B. VLANs provide enhanced security to an organization.

    C. VLANs are used to increase the network performance.

    D. VLANs are easy to manage.

26. Which of the following is *not* a feature of CSPM?

    A. It provides huge scalability.

    B. It supports a centralized architecture.

    C. It enables the remote configuration of PIX Firewalls.

    D. It provides the facility of network address translation by using NAT.

27. Which of the following is a feature of Cisco Secure IDS? (Select all that apply.)

    A. It supports a range of interfaces, such as Ethernet, Token Ring, and FDDI.

    B. It is scalable to very large and distributed networks.

    C. It can detect a wide range of attacks.

    D. It allows the administrator to configure high-level policy for the IPSec environment.

28. Which of the following is *not* a feature of Cisco Secure ACS? (Select all that apply.)

    A. It uses Authentication, Authorization, and Accounting (AAA) to provide network security.

    B. Cisco Secure ACS uses security protocols, such as Terminal Access Controller Access Control Server + (TACACS+) or Remote Access Dial-In User Service (RADIUS).

    C. It supports an up to 10 Cisco NASs.

    D. It does not support third-party products.

Answers to Chapter 2 Questions

1. Packet sniffer. A packet sniffer is a program used to capture data traveling between two hosts on a network.

2. Trusted, untrusted, and unknown networks.

3. An untrusted network is a network external to the organization's security perimeter and the administrative control of the organization. They are the private, shared networks out of the security perimeter from which the internal network has to be protected.

4. Denial of service is a method used by attackers to flood the network with unnecessary and spurious data, intentionally or unintentionally bringing down the servers or communication links. Such a flooding clogs the available bandwidth or forces the system CPU to process many spurious packets. Hackers launch such attacks to destroy parts of the network and sometimes to alter network configurations.

5. Password Authentication Protocol (PAP), Challenge Handshake Authentication Protocol (CHAP), and MS-CHAP. The LCP component of PPP negotiates with the peer host for authentication and supports the PAP, CHAP, and MS-CHAP authentication protocols. MS-CHAP is a Microsoft implementation and is supported by Microsoft products only.

6. False. PGP is a cryptography mechanism supported by TCP/IP.

7. True. IPSec is a Network-layer security protocol. The cryptographically protected Network-layer packets are placed inside other network packets as payload.

8. The Data Link layer of the OSI model is responsible for the transmission of data over the physical medium and is also used for addressing devices on the network. The Data Link layer also provides reliable transit of data across a physical network link.

9. True. Cisco Secure PIX Firewall is a dedicated product for providing security to networks. It is a combination of hardware and software that acts as a firewall to the network.

10. False. A firewall can block traffic on the basis of application ports by using a policy. This policy will explicitly indicate the ports, which have to be blocked.

11. C. A packet sniffer is a software application that captures all the packets on the network. It puts the network adapter card in the promiscuous mode to listen to all the packets traveling through the network.

12. A. IP spoofing is when a host presents itself to another host as a trusted host of the network by manipulating the source IP address of the packets while sending them. This way the host on the network accepts the packets and sends a response to allow the session to continue.

13. A, C, and D. Networks are divided into three categories based on perceived security risk: trusted, untrusted, and unknown. Trusted networks are those inside the network security perimeter. The trusted networks comprise the computers, storage boxes, and application servers. An untrusted network is a network external to the organization's security perimeter and outside administrative control of the organization. The security policies for these networks cannot be defined. Unknown networks are networks neither trusted nor untrusted. They are identified as unknown elements to the firewall because the firewall cannot be explicitly configured to identify whether the network is trusted or untrusted.

14. A and D. Virtual private networks (VPNs) are trusted networks that transmit data across an untrusted network infrastructure and are an exception to the rule that trusted networks include the firewall and all networks behind it. The network packets that traverse a VPN are considered to originate from within the internal perimeter network. Untrusted networks are the networks that belong to agencies outside the organization's security perimeter (and outside its administrative control). The security policies for these networks cannot be defined.

15. B. MD5 is a one-way hash algorithm that takes any length of data and produces a 128-bit "fingerprint" or "message digest" that identifies it for network-security purposes. This fingerprint is "irreversible" — working backward from the fingerprint to determine the file is computationally infeasible. This technique effectively guarantees that no one can figure out network data on the basis of its MD5 fingerprint.

16. A and D. Transport-layer security protocols are Secure Shell (SSH) protocol, Secure Sockets Layer (SSL) protocol, Private Communications Technology (PCT) protocol, and Transport Layer Security (TLS) protocol.

17. B and C. IPSec is a security protocol that provides security at the Network layer. Its main component protocols are Authentication Header (AH) protocol and Encapsulation Security Payload (ESP) protocol.

18. B and C. VLANs and PPP operate at the Data Link layer and provide security to the network resources.

19. A. Challenge Handshake Protocol (CHAP) is a secure method of authentication that periodically verifies the identity of the remote node using a three-way handshake. Do so on the initial link establishment and repeat any time after the link has been established.

20. A, C, and D. Some Cisco security products include Cisco Secure PIX Firewall, Cisco IOS Firewall, Cisco Secure Scanner, Cisco Secure Policy Manager, and Cisco Secure ACS. CiscoWorks2000 is a network management software.

21. D. Message Digest Algorithm (5) or MD5 was released by RSA Laboratories. This algorithm is used for digitally signed messages.

22. C. Rivest's Cipher (RC2) is a 64-bit block cipher algorithm that uses variable-size keys.

23. B. RSA is a public-key algorithm, developed by Rivest, Shamir, and Adleman. RSA is used for authentication as well as encryption.

24. A. Key Exchange Algorithm (KEA) is a variation of Diffie-Hellman key exchange.

25. A. VLANs are implemented by using software rather than hardware devices. Hence, it is easier to manage relocation of a computer, which is a part of a VLAN. Also, it is easier to add nodes in a VLAN than adding nodes to a LAN.

26. B. CSPM supports a distributed architecture. This is the reason it can support PIX Firewalls on the Internet, intranet, and extranet.

27. A, B, and C. The key features of Cisco Secure Intrusion-Detection System include

> • It provides real-time detection of attempted intrusions.
>
> • Detection of a wide range of attacks. It can also detect content and context-based attacks.
>
> • Support for a range of interfaces, such as Ethernet, Token Ring, and FDDI.
>
> • It provides sensors that send alarms.
>
> • It is scalable to very large and distributed networks.

28. C and D. Cisco Secure ACS supports an unlimited number of Cisco NASs. It can support any third-party device that supports TACACS+ or RADIUS protocols. It also supports token cards and servers.

Chapter 3 Questions

1. What is IDS?

2. Who is an intruder?

3. What are the various types of IDSs?

4. Which type of IDS is better suited for a small network and why?

5. What are the two ways in which a detection agent can detect the presence of intruders on a network?

6. Is it possible for users to customize or create new signatures?

7. What is the disadvantage of using profile-based detection?

8. What are the advantage and the disadvantage of having all IDS from a single vendor?

9. Where are all the inherent security weaknesses of an operating system documented?

10. What are the weaknesses of the Transport layer?

11. Which are the three methods by which Cisco provides security?

12. What is a firewall?

13. What is the difference between the right to access network resources and the right not to access network resources?

14. What is the difference between the Network-layer firewall and Application-layer firewall?

15. What is cryptography?

16. Mention some advantages of encryption.

17. Which of the following are layers of the OSI model? (Select all that apply.)

    A. Physical layer and Data Link layer

    B. Network layer

    C. Transmission layer

    D. Transport layer and Application layer

18. What types of policies can you implement on the network?

    A. Access not specifically authorized is denied

    B. Access not specifically denied is authorized

    C. Access to monitor the network is authorized

    D. Access to monitor the network is denied

19. Select the types of firewalls. (Select all that apply.)

    A. Network-layer firewall

    B. Data Link-layer firewall

    C. Application-layer firewall

    D. Transport-layer firewall

20. What are the most common methods of securing information and resources on a network? (Select all that apply.)

    A. Encryption

    B. Authorization

    C. Authentication

    D. Accounting

21. Encryption of data provides which three services? (Select all that apply.)

    A. Maintaining the integrity of data

    B. Transmission of data

    C. Maintaining data privacy

    D. Ensuring the authenticity of the transaction

22. Which technologies are used for data authentication? (Select all that apply.)

    A. Digital Signature Standard

    B. Data Encryption Standard

    C. Open Systems Interconnection model

    D. Diffie-Hellman public-key algorithm

23. From the list given below, identify the flaws of not having a well-documented security policy. (Select all that apply.)

    A. Consistency in the deployment of security policies cannot be maintained.

    B. If network policies are not documented, they can be lost or forgotten.

    C. Backup measures to use in the event of a network attack must be known to everyone.

    D. Users require stepwise procedures about how software needs to be installed.

24. Which of the following is not true for a network-based IDS?

    A. It scans the content of data packets.

    B. It provides real-time alerts.

    C. It does not require software installation on all network devices.

    D. It depends on the operating system of the host computer.

25. Which of the following is not true for a host-based IDS?

    A. It uses event logs to verify whether a security attack was successful.

    B. It monitors user activities and file access operations.

    C. It can detect attempts made to manipulate system files.

    D. It is independent of the type of computer.

26. Which of the following technologies are used to build firewalls? (Select all that apply.)

    A. Static packet filtering

    B. ICMP tunneling

    C. Dynamic packet filtering

    D. Proxy

27. On which of the following layers of OSI model can you implement encryption? (Select all that apply.)

    A. Physical layer

    B. Application layer

    C. Network layer

    D. Data Link layer

28. Identify the security services offered by cryptography. (Select all that apply.)

    A. Confidentiality

    B. Integrity

    C. Authenticity

    D. Accounting

Answers to Chapter 3 Questions

1. IDS is an Intrusion-Detection System and is used for detecting intruders on the network and also for implementing measures to protect the network against intruders.

2. An intruder is an individual who attempts to gain unauthorized access to a network.

3. The two types of IDS are host-based and network-based.

4. A host-based IDS should be installed on a small network because its detection agent uses the resources of the computer on which it is installed for detection. This impacts the computer performance.

5. Through profile-based detection and signature-based detection.

6. Yes, users can customize the existing list of signatures and create new string-based signatures to detect intrusions.

7. Profile-based detection has two disadvantages: It is expensive to maintain and is unpredictable (since detection is based on a fixed user profile).

8. The advantage is that since all the IDSs belong to the same vendor they can be easily implemented on all types of processors. The disadvantage is that if a hacker finds a single weakness in the vendor product all the IDSs can be disabled.

9. All security weaknesses of operating systems are documented in the CERT archives.

10. The Transport layer is vulnerable to packet-storm denial-of-service (DoS) attack (in the case of UDP) and the session hijacking (in the case of TCP).

11. Cisco provides security by firewalls, encryption, authentication, and access-control lists (also known as access lists or ACLs).

12. A firewall is a mechanism that secures the transfer of data between two networks by testing and examining data packets and then either permitting them or denying them access to the network.

13. A user's rights to access network resources are those rights not specifically denied. Any rights to access network resources that a user does not have are those rights not specifically allowed.

14. At the Network layer, firewall decisions depend on source and destination addresses, as well as the ports used by individual IP packets. (Application-layer firewalls can act as hosts for running proxy servers, which do not allow traffic to pass directly between networks.)

15. Cryptography is a field of knowledge that encompasses encryption, decryption, and their implementation to ensure privacy of communication.

16. Proper encryption and decryption provide many advantages, such as confidentiality, entity authentication, data integrity, digital signatures, and PKI base.

17. A, C, and D. The different OSI layers are Physical, Data Link, Network, Transport, and Application layer.

18. A and B. You can implement two types of polices on the network:

    • Access not specifically authorized is denied.

    • Access not specifically denied is authorized.

19. A and C. Network-layer firewalls and Application-layer firewalls are the two types.

20. A and C. Encryption and authentication are the most common methods of securing information and resources on a network.

21. A, C, and D. Encryption of data provides three services: maintaining the integrity of data, maintaining data privacy, and ensuring the authenticity of the transaction.

22. A, B, and D. The technologies used for data authentication are Digital Signature Standard, the Diffie-Hellman public-key algorithm, and the Data-Encryption Standard.

23. A, B, and C. Failure to provide proper documentation for your network-security policy can lead to inconsistent deployment of policies that often cannot be maintained. Backup measures to use in case of network attacks should be known to everyone and well documented.

24. D. Network-based IDS is independent of the operating system of the host computer.

25. D. Most host-based IDS capabilities can monitor only specific types of computers. For example, a host-based IDS designed to protect just the Web server won't provide proper protection if the Web server runs multiple services (such as DNS and POP3).

26. A, C, and D. Firewalls can be built on a variety of technologies. Those most frequently used are static filtering, dynamic filtering, and proxy.

27. B, C, and D. Network administrators can implement encryption at any of the three layers of the Open Systems Interconnection (OSI) model: Application, Data Link, or Network.

28. A, B, and C. Cryptography provides the security services, such as confidentiality, entity authentication, data integrity, digital signatures, and PKI base.

Chapter 4 Questions

1. The total number of privilege levels is _____.

2. The `enable secret` command stores the password in cleartext. True or False?

3. By default, the number of virtual terminal lines on a Cisco router is _____.

4. Two examples of out-of-band access to the Cisco router are _____.

5. The default access level at the time of login to a Cisco device is _____.

6. When you `telnet` to a Cisco router, on which line do you connect?

7. What is a passive interface?

8. What is the difference between the `enable` password and the `enable secret` password?

9. Are IP permit lists enabled by default on Cisco switches?

10. What is the default console password on Cisco routers?

11. Which of the following correctly describes the use of a banner message?

    A. Welcome users to the system

    B. Warn of unauthorized access

    C. Tell users whom to contact in case of a problem

    D. Provide description of the router

12. Which prompt symbol indicates that the router is in privileged EXEC mode?

    A. Router>

    B. Router#

    C. Router$

    D. Router&

13. When you Telnet into a Cisco router, to which line do you connect?

    A. One of the console ports

    B. One of the EXEC lines

    C. One of the virtual-terminal lines

    D. One of the aux lines

14. To which level is the user-access mode changed when the `enable` command is used?

    A. 10

    B. 15

    C. 0

    D. 1

15. Which of the following commands do you use to configure a Cisco router so it requires a password before granting access to the EXEC command line through a console session? (Select all that apply.)

    A. `console password 0`

    B. `login`

    C. `password`

    D. login con 0

16. The `exec-timeout` command should be used to _____. (Select one.)

    A. Limit how many sessions a user can open

    B. Limit how long users can use the system

    C. Enable automatic logout of an unattended session

    D. All of the above

17. The default access level upon login to a Cisco device is _____. (Select one.)

    A. 5

    B. 1

    C. 0

    D. 15

18. In which router mode do you execute the command `passive-interface type number`?

    A. Privileged mode

    B. Global configuration mode

    C. Router configuration mode

    D. Interface configuration mode

19. Which command gives nonprivileged access to the routers via SNMP?

    A. `router (config)#snmp-server community private ro`

    B. `router# snmp-server community private ro`

    C. `router (config)# snmp-server community private rw`

    D. router# snmp-server community private rw

20. Port security provides which of the following?

    A. Login control

    B. MAC-address-based access control

    C. IP address-based access control

    D. Web security

21. Which of the following is true of SNMP? (Select all that apply.)

   A. Cisco IOS release 12.0 software supports SNMP v1 and SNMP v2.

   B. The `inform` message does not require acknowledgment.

   C. SNMP access level `read-only` (`ro`) is the privileged mode of access.

   D. SNMP v1 is described in RFC 1157.

22. Which of the following is true for the command `tacacs-server last-resort [password | succeed]`?

   A. The keyword `succeed` allows users to log in without passwords.

   B. The keyword `password` needs a standard login password for user authentication.

   C. Use this command only when no TACACS server is available.

   D. All of the above.

23. Consider the following IOS command: `Router(config)#banner motd`. What does the keyword `motd` mean?

   A. Method of terminal display

   B. Message of the display

   C. Message of the day

   D. Message on terminal daily

24. Which Cisco IOS command is used to enter privileged EXEC mode from user mode?

   A. `login`

   B. `privilege`

   C. `enable`

   D. `exec`

25. In port security, the default option in case of address violation is to do which of the following?

   A. Suspend

   B. Ignore

   C. Disable

   D. None of the above

26. Which of the following measures does not ensure the security of an administrative interface?

    A. Protecting console access

    B. Managing session timeouts

    C. Displaying banner messages

    D. Encrypting passwords

27. Which of the following is true for a console password? (Select all that apply.)

    A. It is case-sensitive.

    B. Its length can vary from 1 to 16 characters.

    C. The characters in the passwords can be alphanumeric.

    D. A console password can be set for both user-level mode and privileged-level mode.

28. Which of the following levels of user access provide a user with full rights for a device?

    A. 0

    B. 1

    C. 2

    D. 15

29. The SNMP Manager uses which of the following SNMP commands? (Select all that apply.)

    A. read

    B. trap

    C. transversal

    D. write

30. A managed device uses which of the following SNMP commands to asynchronously report events to the SNMP Manager?

    A. read

    B. trap

    C. transversal

    D. write

31. SNMP v1 does not support which of the following operations? (Select all that apply.)

    A. Get

    B. GetNext

    C. GetBulk

    D. Set

Answers to Chapter 4 Questions

1. 16. The total number of privilege levels is 16 (0 to 15).

2. False. The enable secret command stores the password in encrypted form.

3. Five. By default, a Cisco router has 5 virtual lines.

4. console and aux ports. The out-of-band access points are console and aux ports and the in-band access points are TFT and VTY access.

5. One. On a Cisco device, the default access level at login is 1, which has user-mode privileges.

6. Virtual terminal lines. Using telnet, you can connect to one of the virtual terminal lines.

7. A passive interface does not send routing updates that include hello messages — and can't form neighbor adjacencies in response to link-state routing protocols — but can still receive routing updates.

8. The enable password stores the password in cleartext while enable secret stores the password in encrypted form.

9. Yes. IP permit lists are by default disabled on Cisco switches.

10. By default, there is no console password.

11. B. The banner message warns the user against unauthorized access. It should not welcome the user in any way.

12. B. Privileged EXEC mode is indicated by the # symbol immediately after the router's hostname.

13. C. Using telnet, you connect to one of the virtual terminal lines.

14. B. The enable command changes the user access mode to privileged mode level 15.

15. B, C, and D. The following sequence of commands does the job:

```
router(config)# line con 0
router(config-line)# login
router(config-line)# password pwd
```

16. C. A timeout for an unattended session provides additional security. This can be done via the command `exec-timeout mm ss` where mm is minutes and ss is seconds.

17. B. The default access level upon log in to a Cisco device is 1, which has user mode privileges.

18. C. The correct syntax of this command is `router(config-route)# passive-interface type number`.

19. A. The `ro` keyword gives the non-privileged access, and the command is given on the global configuration mode.

20. B. Port security enables the switch to block packets that enter a port if the source MAC address does not match the allowed MAC address configured on the port.

21. A and D. Cisco IOS release 12.0 software supports SNMPv1 and SNMP v2. Also, SNMP v1 is described in RFC 1157. Choice B and C are incorrect because the `inform` message in SNMP is a reliable message and needs acknowledgment, and SNMP `ro` mode allows nonprivileged access (only reading of MIBs).

22. D. When no TACACS server is available, this command is used for authentication. The keyword `succeed` allows the user to log in without a password. The keyword `password` is used to force the user to supply the standard login password.

23. C. The keyword `motd` means *message of the day*.

24. C. The `enable` command is given to switch to the privileged mode from user mode.

25. A. The default value is to suspend, which means that the port will be enabled when it receives the configured MAC address.

26. C. Displaying banner messages does not ensure the security of an administrative interface. In fact, you should disable banner messages.

27. A, C, and D. For securing access through console port, passwords can be set for both user-level as well as privileged-level mode. Console passwords can range from 1 to 25 alphanumeric characters that can be either in uppercase or in lowercase.

28. D. Level 15, the privilege level, provides the user full rights to the device.

29. A and D. The `read` command monitors managed devices (such as routers) on which an SNMP agent is installed. The `write` command controls managed devices. The SNMP Manager uses both these commands.

30. B. Managed devices use the `trap` command to asynchronously report events to the SNMP Manager.

31. C. SNMP v1 does not support `Trap`, `GetBulk`, or `Inform` operations.

Chapter 5 Questions

1. Access lists can be applied to an interface as _____ or _____.

2. If a packet does not match any access list statement, the packet is _____.

3. What are the steps in access list configuration?

4. What are the two types of access lists?

5. The range for extended IP access list is _____ to _____.

6. The advantage of a named IP access over a numbered access list is that its statements can be selectively _____.

7. What is the sequence in which a routable packet is treated when it arrives at the interface of a router?

8. Where should you place an extended access list?

9. In a dynamic access list, a user can access resources on the network across the router only after _____.

10. You can configure _____ number of named access lists on a router.

11. Why do reflexive access lists provide greater security than normal access lists when an in-house user accesses the Internet?

12. You can configure ____ number of access list(s) per interface per protocol per direction.

13. Which command do you use when you want to view the contents of your access lists?

    A. `show ip interface access-lists`

    B. `show ip interface`

    C. `show access-lists`

    D. `show lists`

14. Which of the following is true of access lists? (Select all that apply.)

   A. A packet that does not match with any statement is allowed to proceed.

   B. A packet is first scanned with the routing table before it is tested against the inbound access list.

   C. A packet is first scanned with the routing table before it is tested against the outbound access list.

   D. You can have only one access list per interface per protocol per direction.

15. An extended IP access list filters packets according to which of the following parameters? (Select all that apply.)

   A. Source IP address

   B. Destination IP address

   C. MAC address

   D. Port number

16. Which of the following extended access lists blocks host 10.0.0.100 from sending information via `telnet` to host 10.0.1.100?

   A. `access-list 100 permit ip host 10.0.0.100 host 10.0.1.100 eq telnet`

   B. `access-list 100 deny  tcp host 10.0.0.100 host 10.0.1.100 eq telnet`

   C. `access-list 100 deny tcp host 10.0.1.100 host 10.0.0.100 eq telnet`

   D. `access-list 100 deny udp host 10.0.0.100 host 10.0.1.100 eq telnet`

17. Which of the following is the wildcard mask for checking the range of subnets 172.16.16.0/24 to 172.16.31.0/24?

   A. `255.255.240.0`

   B. `0.0.15.255`

   C. `0.0.0.255`

   D. `0.0.31.255`

18. Which of the following is a valid standard IP access list?

   A. `access-list 101 permit ip any any eq 20`

   B. `access-list 10 deny host 10.0.0.100 host 10.0.1.100`

   C. `access-list 10 permit 10.0.0.0 0.0.0.255`

   D. `access-list 110 permit 10.0.0.0 0.0.255.255`

19. Which of the following is a valid command to apply an access list to VTY lines?

   A. `router(config-if)#ip access-group 10 in`

   B. `router(config)#ip access-class 10 in`

   C. `router(config-line)#ip access-class 10 in`

   D. `router(config-line)#access-class 10 in`

20. Of the following, which correctly describe named access lists? (Select all that apply.)

   A. There is no limitation on the number of named access lists that can be created on a router.

   B. There can be more than one named access list per interface per protocol per direction.

   C. You can delete specific statements from a named access list.

   D. Named access lists can be used only with Cisco IOS 11.2 and later versions.

21. What is the function of the keyword `established` in extended IP access lists?

   A. It allows packets that are part of an already established session to proceed.

   B. It establishes a permanent path for a packet and then all the subsequent packets follow that path.

   C. It sets a higher priority for the packets matching the access-list statements.

   D. It denies packets that are part of an already established session.

22. Access List numbers indicate the protocol to be filtered. Which of the following protocol-to-range mappings are correct?

   A. Standard IP Access Lists: 1-199

   B. Standard IPX Access Lists: 800-899

   C. Extended IP Access Lists: 100-199

   D. Extended IPX Access Lists: 1000-1099

23. Of the following, identify the true statement(s) regarding the placement of access lists. (Select all that apply.)

   A. Place standard IP access list near the source

   B. Place extended IP access list near the source

   C. Place standard IP access list near the destination

   D. Place extended IP access list near the destination

24. Of the following access-list types, which employs user authentication before allowing access to resources?

    A. Extended IP Access Lists

    B. Dynamic Access Lists

    C. Reflexive Access Lists

    D. Standard Access Lists

25. Network `10.0.0.0/24` is connected to interface `Ethernet 0` (IP address `10.0.0.1`) of router `Router1` and network `10.0.1.0/24` is connected to interface `E1` (IP address `10.0.1.1`) of `Router1`. The requirement is that a user named `TEST` on network `10.0.0.0` should be able to access any host on network `10.0.1.0` for a maximum of 30 minutes at a stretch. The password of `TEST` is `TESTPWD` and only the host from which the user `TEST` does Telnet should be allowed access. Which of the following commands should be executed to accomplish the task?

    A. `login local, autocommand access-enable host,` followed by `username TEST password TESTPWD`

    B. `access-list 110 permit ip any any eq telnet,` followed by `access-list 110 dynamic dynacl timeout 30 permit ip 10.0.0.0 0.0.0.255 10.0.1.10 0.0.0.255`

    C. `login local, login local, autocommand access-enable host,` followed by `username TEST password TESTPWD, access-class 110`

    D. `access-list 110 permit tcp any host 10.0.0.1 eq telnet,` followed by `access-list 110 dynamic dynacl timeout 30 permit ip 10.0.0.0 0.0.0.255 10.0.1.0 0.0.0.255`

26. What is true about reflexive access lists? (Select all that apply.)

    A. Reflexive access lists allow access to all the packets that are part of an already established session.

    B. Reflexive access lists allow packets from external hosts to enter the internal network only if they are part of a session initiated by an internal host.

    C. Reflexive access lists require authentication of the user before allowing temporary access to resources.

    D. Reflexive access lists do not allow applications that change port numbers.

27. What is the command to nest the reflexive access list testreflex?

    A. `ip access-group testreflex`

    B. `access-class testreflex`

    C. `evaluate testreflex`

    D. `evaluate ip access-list testreflex`

28. Which of the following IP address classes are reserved for *multicasting* and experimentation?

   A. Class B

   B. Class C

   C. Class D

   D. Class E

29. The _____ addresses are usually reserved for governments worldwide.

   A. Class A

   B. Class B

   C. Class C

   D. Class D

30. Which of the following IP addresses is a loopback address?

   A. 0.0.0.0

   B. 1.0.0.0

   C. 126.0.0.0

   D. 127.0.0.0

31. In which of the following IP address categories do the IP addresses start with 10?

   A. Class A

   B. Class B

   C. Class C

   D. Class D

32. Identify the constituents of an IP address in a subnetted network. (Select all that apply.)

   A. Network address

   B. Port number

   C. Subnet address

   D. Host address

Answers to Chapter 5 Questions

1. Access Lists can be applied to an interface as inbound or outbound.

2. If a packet does not match any access-list statement, the packet is dropped.

3. The steps in access list configuration: create, define, and apply the access list.

4. Two types of access lists: Standard and Extended.

5. The range for IP extended access list is 100 to 199.

6. In a named access list, the advantage over numbered access list is that access list statements can be selectively deleted.

7. When a routable packet arrives at an interface of a router, the sequence in which it is treated is as follows:

    A. If an inbound access list is applied to the interface, then the packet is first tested against that inbound access list. The packet is allowed to proceed if the result of testing is `permit`, otherwise it is dropped.

    B. The packet's destination address is scanned for an entry in the routing table. If there is no entry and also no default route, the packet is dropped, otherwise the outbound interface is determined from the routing table.

    C. The packet is tested against the outbound access list (if one is applied) on the outbound interface. If the result of testing is `permit`, then the packet is sent out of the interface; otherwise it is dropped. If no outbound access list is applied to the interface, the packet is sent out of the interface.

8. An extended access list should be placed near the source.

9. In a dynamic access list, a user can access resources on the network across the router only after authentication.

10. You can configure an infinite number of named access lists on a router.

11. Reflexive access list provides greater security than normal access list while accessing the Internet because it does not allow any packets from the Internet to the internal network unless they are a part of a session initiated by an internal host. They protect against IP spoofing.

12. You can configure one access list per interface per protocol per direction.

13. C. The command to view the contents of your access lists is `show access-lists`.

14. C and D. A packet is first tested against an inbound access list, if any, then it is scanned for an entry for the destination network in the routing table, and then it is tested against outbound access list, if any. A guideline for configuring any access list is that you can have only one access list per protocol per interface per direction.

15. A, B, and D. Extended IP access lists filter traffic according to four factors: source IP address, destination IP address, specific protocol, and port numbers.

16. B. Telnet uses TCP as the transport protocol. The task is to block IP packets having source address 10.0.0.100 and destination 10.0.1.100 and with destination TCP port telnet. Therefore the command is

```
Router(config)#access-list 100 deny
 tcp host 10.0.0.100 host 10.0.1.100 eq telnet
```

17. B. If you represent the range of subnets 172.16.16.0/24 to 172.16.31.0/24 into binary form, the common bits would be the first two octets and the first 4 bits of the third octet. These bits will be checked; the rest will be ignored. Thus the wildcard mask is 0.0.15.255.

18. C. In options A and D, the number of the access list is from the range reserved for Extended IP access lists. In option B, the command mentions two IP addresses, one for host and one for destination. The standard access list checks only the source IP address. In option C, the number is 10 and the command contains only the source IP address and the rest of the syntax is also correct. Therefore it is the correct option.

19. D. To apply access list to vty line, the command `access-class access-list-number {in|out}` should be executed in the line configuration mode. Thus option D is correct.

20. A, C, and D. One advantage of a named access list is that you can configure an unlimited number of access lists on a router. Another advantage is that you can delete specific statements from a named access list. Numbered access lists do not provide any of these features. A limitation of the named access list is that only certain versions of Cisco IOS (ver 11.2 and later) support it.

21. A. The keyword `established` instructs the router to check the ACK bit of a packet. If these bits are set, the packet should be allowed to proceed. ACK bit is set in packets that are part of an already established session.

22. B, C. The range for Standard IP access lists is 1-99, Standard IPX access lists is 800-899, Extended IP access lists is 100-199, and Extended IPX access lists is 900-999. Thus choices B and C are correct.

23. B, C. The rule of thumb for placing access lists is to place standard IP access lists near the destination and extended IP access lists near the source.

24. B. Dynamic access lists allow access to resources only after the user is authenticated. The user first telnets to the router, the router authenticates the user through local username and password or through TACACS+ or some other method. After authentication, the user is logged out and is given permission to access the resources that were earlier blocked for him/her.

25. A and D. Remember four major points about this task:

   A. Login authentication should be local. Thus one of the commands should be
   ```
   login local
   ```

   B. To authenticate the user TEST with password TESTPWD, the command should be
   ```
   username TEST password TESTPWD
   ```

   C. To enable users to telnet to the router, the command should be
   ```
   access-list 110 permit tcp any host 10.0.0.1 eq telnet
   ```

D. To configure dynamic access list with a timeout of 30 minutes that allows access only to network `10.0.1.0`, the command should be

```
access-list 110 dynamic dynacl timeout 30
   permit ip 10.0.0.0 0.0.0.255 10.0.1.0 0.0.0.255
```

E. To automatically create temporary access lists after user authentication, the command should be

```
autocommand access-enable host
```

26. B and D. Reflexive access lists allow only those packets from the external network to enter internal network that are part of a session that was initiated by an internal host. This is how the reflexive access lists prevent IP spoof attacks. These access lists do not allow applications to change port numbers during communication; such applications as active FTP are disallowed.

27. C. The command to nest reflexive access list testreflex is `evaluate testreflex`.

28. C and D. Out of these five classes, Class D and Class E are reserved for *multicasting* and experimentation. The rest of the classes (such as Class A, B, and C) are assigned to public entities, schools, government, and organizations.

29. A. The Class A addresses are usually reserved for governments worldwide. Class A addresses always begin with a zero when written in a binary format.

30. D. `127.0.0.0` is assigned as a *loopback* address. The loopback addresses, such as ping, are used to diagnose the network.

31. B. In a binary format, a Class B address begins with 10. Due to this, the first octet of Class B has a minimum value of 128 and a maximum value of 191.

32. A, C, and D. In subnetting, the host address is split in two: the subnet address and the host address. Thus in a subnetted network, an IP address consists of three parts:

- Network address
- Subnet address
- Host address

Chapter 6 Questions

1. What is a perimeter router?

2. What is NAT?

3. In which RFC is NAT defined?

4. NAT is used to conserve IP addresses. True or False?

5. Where is a NAT router placed?

6. The dirty DMZ area is also known as _____.

7. What is PAT?

8. NAT increases the latency in packet forwarding. True or False?

9. What is the basic use of Network Address Translation?

10. What are the different types of NAT mappings?

11. Which command identifies an inside interface?

    A. `router(config-if)# ip nat inside`

    B. `router(config)# ip nat inside`

    C. `router(config-if)# ip nat inside ethernet0`

    D. `router(config)# ip nat ethernet0`

12. In which of the following situations would you use NAT? (Select all that apply.)

    A. When networks have overlapping IP addresses

    B. When globally unique IP addresses must be conserved

    C. When you must connect to remote sites

    D. When Internet traffic is heavy

13. Which keyword identifies if a dynamic pool is used for NAT overloading?

    A. `nat-overload`

    B. `overload`

    C. `overload-nat`

    D. `overload-dynamic`

14. What is the disadvantage of using NAT?

    A. Large routing-table entries

    B. Increase in latency due to translations

    C. Overlapping IP addresses

    D. Conservation of IP addresses

15. Which command is used to debug IP NAT translations?

    A. `debug ip nat statistics`

    B. `debug ip nat`

    C. `debug nat`

    D. `debug nat translation`

16. Which keyword identifies the NAT TCP load distribution?

    A. overload

    B. load-distribution

    C. rotary

    D. rotary-load

17. Which of the following accurately describes an outside global address?

    A. Locally and globally routable

    B. Must be a registered IP address

    C. Locally routable but not globally

    D. Globally but not locally routable

18. Which command is used to view current NAT mappings?

    A. show ip nat mapping

    B. show ip nat statistics

    C. show ip nat translation

    D. show ip nat

19. The network address 10.1.1.1/24 can be used in:

    A. Globally routable space

    B. Only for locally routable space

    C. Both locally and globally routable space

    D. Only the globally routable space

20. Which of the following attributes does TCP load distribution use to identify individual translations? (Select all that apply.)

    A. Destination IP address

    B. Port number

    C. Source IP address

    D. Host name

21. Which of the following commands is used to turn off minor TCP services that are normally available for the Echo, Chargen, Daytime, and Discard ports?

    A. no service tcp-small-servers

    B. no service udp-small-servers

    C. no ip tcp selective-ack

    D. no ip tcp path-mtu discovery

22. Which of the following commands is used to stop the specified interface from generating ICMP unreachable messages?

    A. `no service tcp-small-servers`

    B. `no service udp-small-servers`

    C. `no ip tcp selective-ack`

    D. `no ip unreachable`

23. Which of the following is not involved in hardening a bastion host?

    A. Physically securing the computer that would act as bastion host.

    B. Disabling all services that are not required.

    C. Establishing a security baseline by running security audit.

    D. Establishing a security policy.

Answers to Chapter 6 Questions

1. The perimeter router is the boundary router, which provides the first level of security to internal network from outer networks by acting as a demarcation point between the two.

2. NAT is Network Address Translation. NAT allows the use of one or more registered IP addresses for a group of computers. NAT takes advantage of the fact that only a few hosts in any given organization connect to the Internet at a specified time. As a result, the IP addresses of only a few internal networks have to be translated into globally unique IP addresses.

3. 1631. NAT has been defined in RFC 1631.

4. True. NAT conserves the IP addresses by using the mapping feature so fewer globally unique addresses are needed.

5. The NAT router is placed at the boundary between the inside and outside network.

6. The dirty DMZ area is also known as a semi-secured DMZ area because its only protection is the perimeter router; it has no proper firewall.

7. PAT is Port Address Translation. It is just similar to NAT except that it is a feature of Cisco 700 series routers.

8. True. NAT increases latency in packet forwarding; the packet header is changed according to entries in the NAT table.

9. The basic use of NAT is to allow the use of unregistered IP addresses in the public Internet.

10. The different types of NAT mappings are static and dynamic mappings.

11. A. The `ip nat inside` command is used to specify an inside interface, and it is given in interface configuration mode.

12. A and B. NAT is used as a solution to the overlapping networks and for conserving the registered IP addresses.

13. B. The `overload` keyword is used with the NAT overloading feature.

14. B. NAT table mappings result in increased latency (that is, more time needed to forward packets) — but NAT helps conserve IP addresses and is especially useful if networks overlap.

15. B. The `debug ip nat` command is used to troubleshoot NAT translations.

16. C. The `rotary` keyword signifies TCP load distribution.

17. D. The outside global address is globally routable but might or might not be locally routable.

18. C. The `show ip nat translation` command is used to view current NAT mappings.

19. B. This IP address belongs to the private address range, which can only be used for locally routable space.

20. B and C. The NAT table specifies a translation based on the source IP address and the port number.

21. A. The `no service tcp-small-servers` command is used to turn off minor TCP services available for the Echo, Chargen, Daytime, and Discard ports.

22. D. The `no ip unreachable` command is used to stop the specified interface from generating ICMP unreachable messages.

23. D. Hardening involves the following tasks:

- Physically securing the computer that would act as bastion host
- Disabling all services not required
- Installing all required services
- Configuring the bastion host as per your requirements
- Establishing a security baseline by running security audit
- Adding the bastion host to the network

Chapter 7 Questions

1. What is encryption?

2. What is a sniffer?

3. What are system backdoors?

4. How can hackers gain access to network resources using brute-force password attacks?

5. What are social engineering attacks?

6. Which is the only protocol used by Cisco routers to encrypt data packets?

7. How are non-IP data packets encrypted?

8. What are peer routers?

9. What does DES stand for?

10. Expand DSS.

11. What does DH stand for?

12. How are DSS keys authenticated by network administrators?

13. What is voice authentication?

14. What is a digital signature?

15. What is a crypto engine?

16. What are the three layers in the OSI model on which encryption can be implemented?

17. What are the two block sizes in which data can be broken down while using DES?

18. What is the default length of a DES key?

19. Which of the following is not a type of network attack?

    A. Misuse of system backdoor accounts

    B. Misuse of deleted data and default accounts

    C. Loss of data due to corrupted header information

    D. Misuse of unmonitored service

20. Of the following, identify the common network attacks. (Select all that apply.)

    A. Network packet sniffers

    B. Man-in-the-middle attacks

    C. UDP packet spoofing

    D. Brute-force password attacks

21. Which of the following services are provided by routers for the purpose of encryption? (Select all that apply.)

    A. Maintaining integrity of data

    B. Maintaining privacy of data

    C. Maintaining authenticity of data

    D. Maintaining authorization of data

22. Which steps are needed to implement encryption? (Select all that apply.)

    A. Configure router to handle encryption

    B. Enable peer router authentication by using DSS-key encryption

    C. Establish an encrypted session by using a peer router

    D. Encrypt and decrypt data by using peer routers

23. Identify the steps to perform before configuring CET on routers. (Select all that apply.)

    A. Identify the peer routers

    B. Identify the network topology

    C. Identify the size of data to be transmitted

    D. Identify which crypto engine to use with each router

24. Identify the different types of crypto engines. (Select all that apply.)

    A. Cisco IOS crypto engine

    B. VIP2 crypto engine

    C. ESA crypto engine

    D. EAS crypto engine

25. Which of the following services is *not* performed by an application that uses encryption for securing communication?

    A. Securing VPNs that connect partner organizations

    B. Securing VPNs that connect remote locations and the corporate network

    C. Securing connections between remote locations using leased lines

    D. Security information being transmitted over the network from hackers

26. Identify some characteristics of Network-layer encryption.

    A. It is supported by Cisco IOS software.

    B. It depends on the type of topology used on the network.

    C. It depends on the interface used to implement encryption.

    D. It depends on the protocol used to implement encryption.

27. Which one of the following is not an encryption technology?

    A. Digital Encryption Standard

    B. Message Digest Standard

    C. VIP2

    D. Diffie-Hellman key agreement

28. Which of the following encryption technologies does not involve physically exchanging keys?

A. Digital Encryption Standard

B. Message Digest Standard

C. VIP2

D. Diffie-Hellman key agreement

29. Which of the following encryption technology converts different length strings of data into encrypted data of fixed lengths?

A. Digital Encryption Standard

B. Message Digest Standard

C. Digital Signature Standard

D. Diffie-Hellman key agreement

30. Which of the following encryption technology uses an algorithm to create a signature and attach it to the message?

A. Digital Encryption Standard

B. Message Digest Standard

C. Digital Signature Standard

D. Diffie-Hellman key agreement

31. Which of the following is *not* a part of the steps for encrypting text-using DES?

A. Data is broken down into fixed blocks.

B. An algorithm is used to encrypt the DES key.

C. The 64-bit blocks are split into 32-bit ports.

D. Both ports are encrypted.

32. Which of the following are valid DES encryption algorithms? (Select all that apply.)

A. 40-bit variation of DES with 8-bit CFB

B. 10-bit variation of DES with 64-bit CFB

C. DES with 8-bit CFB

D. DES with 64-bit CFB

Answers to Chapter 7 Questions

1. Encryption is the process of converting cleartext data into in decipherable text by using an encryption algorithm.

2. A sniffer is an application or device that you can use to read, monitor, and capture data transmitted over the network.

3. System backdoors are accounts created by network administrators to gain access to the network in case the original accounts are corrupted.

4. In brute-force password attacks, hackers can gain access to the network by cracking a user's network password. Hackers do this by trying different combinations of the password until they find the correct password.

5. In a social engineering attack, hackers impersonate help desk staff or network administrator to gain access to passwords of valid network users.

6. Cisco routers use IP network protocol to encrypt all data packets transmitted over the network.

7. Data packets belonging to other network protocols are encapsulated in an IP packet before encryption.

8. Peer routers are Cisco routers configured at the beginning and the end of the network. All intermediate routers are used only for transmitting the packets to each other.

9. DES stands for Data-Encryption Standard. This is a standard encryption algorithm and is primarily used to encrypt and decrypt large amounts of data.

10. DSS stands for Digital Signature Standard. It is used to ensure data integrity.

11. DH stands for Diffie-Hellman key agreement. It is used for creating secure keys.

12. DSS keys are authenticated by network administrators, using voice authentication.

13. Voice authentication is the verbal verification of the DSS public key.

14. A digital signature is a piece of coded text used by peer routers to generate their own private DSS keys. Each digital signature is unique to a router and cannot be duplicated.

15. A crypto engine is a Cisco IOS software service used in Cisco Encryption Technology. Different crypto engines are used with different router interfaces.

16. Encryption can be implemented at the Application, Data Link, and Network layers.

17. While using DES, the data can be broken down in 8-bit blocks and 64-bit blocks.

18. The default length of a DES key is 56 bits.

19. C. Data lost due to corrupted header information is not a type of network attack.

20. A, B, and D. The most common network attacks are (respectively) network packet sniffers, man-in-the middle attacks, and brute-force password attacks.

21. A, B, and C. Routers offer services such as maintaining integrity, privacy, and authenticity of data.

22. B, C, and D. To implement encryption, enable peer router authentication by using DSS key encryption, establish an encrypted session by using a peer router, and then encrypt and decrypt data by using peer routers.

23. A, B, and D. Before configuring CET on routers, identify the peer routers to use, the network topology to use, and the crypto engine to be used with each router.

24. A, B, and C. Different types of crypto engines are Cisco IO crypto engine, VIP2 crypto engine, and ESA crypto engine.

25. C. Applications that use encryptions to secure communication between the corporate network and remote locations do not need to secure the communication if leased lines are used for establishing the connection.

26. B and D. Network-layer encryption depends on the type of topology used on the network.

27. C. VIP2 is not an encryption technology.

28. D. Diffie-Hellman key agreement does not involve the physical exchanging of keys.

29. B. The Digital Signature Standard converts variable-length data strings into encrypted data of fixed lengths.

30. C. VIP2 uses an algorithm to create a signature and attach it to the message.

31. D. While using DES, only one part is further encrypted — not both.

32. A, C, and D. Except for 10-bit variation of DES with 64-bit CFB, the rest are valid encryption algorithms.

Chapter 8 Questions

1. What type of product is a Cisco IOS Firewall?

2. Cisco IOS Firewall seamlessly integrates with Cisco IOS software on the router. True or False?

3. CBAC inspects only those packets that use IP at the Network layer. True or False?

4. A router using CBAC maintains a _____ table of the connection status of various sessions.

5. CBAC filters packets according to specific _____-layer protocols.

6. CBAC recognizes the application-specific commands when it inspects packets at the Application layer. True or False?

7. The inbound access list on the internal interface should _____ the packet if the packet is to be inspected by CBAC.

8. If CBAC is applied, the access list testing the packets coming from the external network to the internal network should be _____ access list.

9. CBAC can prevent users from downloading Java applets from Web sites even though they may be allowed to browse those sites. True or False?

10. What are half-open sessions?

11. Which of the following are true regarding Cisco IOS Firewall? (Select all that apply.)

    A. It's a combination of hardware and software.

    B. It integrates seamlessly with the Cisco IOS software.

    C. It cannot detect network intrusion.

    D. It's only a software product.

12. Which of the following are components of Cisco IOS Firewall? (Select all that apply.)

    A. Time-based access lists

    B. Context-based access lists

    C. PIX Firewall

    D. Cisco Secure ACS

13. Which of the following is the correct explanation of Network Address Translation?

    A. The user is authenticated on the router, and then a temporary entry is created in the access list that allows the user to access the network resources.

    B. You can use one registered IP address to give Internet connection to all the internal network hosts, which are using private IP addresses.

    C. It includes keeping track of potential security breaches and other suspicious activities and recording them.

    D. The packets coming from the external network to the internal network are allowed only if they are a part of a session that was initiated by an internal host.

14. Which of the following statements is true about Context-Based Access List?

    A. CBAC refers to the routing table to determine whether the packets received should be inspected by it or not.

    B. On an inbound interface, CBAC inspects the packets only after the routing table has been scanned for a route to the destination.

    C. CBAC maintains a state table for the packets inspected by it and keeps updating the table for each change in the status.

    D. CBAC inspects a packet only until the IP header.

15. If CBAC is configured on an internal interface, which of the following would you choose to configure?

    A. Configure outbound extended IP access list on the internal interface.

    B. Configure outbound standard IP access list on the internal interface.

    C. Permit the return traffic in the inbound access list configured on the internal interface.

    D. Configure the inbound access list on the internal interface to permit the traffic to be inspected by CBAC.

16. If CBAC is configured on an external interface, which of the following would you choose to configure?

    A. Configure inbound extended IP access list on the external interface.

    B. Configure outbound access list on the external interface to deny the traffic to be inspected by CBAC.

    C. Configure the inbound access list on the external interface to deny the return traffic.

    D. Configure the inbound access list on the external interface to permit the return traffic.

17. Which of the following commands would prevent the internal users from downloading Java applets from the unfriendly site 192.168.16.1? Assume that an access list 10, which denies IP address 192.168.16.1, has been already configured.

    A. `router(config-if)#ip inspect name test http java-list 10 timeout 30`

    B. `router(config)#ip inspect name test java 10 timeout 30`

    C. `router(config)#ip inspect name test http java-list 10 timeout 30`

    D. `router(config-if)#ip inspect name test http 10 timeout 30`

18. You are required to configure CBAC such that if the number of half-open sessions for the network exceeds 600, the CBAC should start deleting the half-open sessions until the half-open sessions reduce to 300. Choose the commands that you would use to accomplish this task. (Select all that apply.)

    A. `router(config)#ip inspect one-minute high 600`

    B. `router(config)#ip inspect max-incomplete high 600`

    C. `router(config)#ip inspect one-minute low 300`

    D. `router(config)#ip inspect max-incomplete low 300`

19. Which command would configure CBAC to wait for 30 seconds after hosts have closed the TCP session, before it deletes the temporary entry for the session in the access list?

    A. `router(config)#ip inspect tcp finwait-time30`

    B. `router(config)#ip inspect finwait-time 30`

    C. `router(config)#ip inspect tcp idle-timeout 30`

    D. `router(config)#ip inspect tcp finwait-time 0.5`

20. Which of the following is true for CBAC? (Select all that apply.)

    A. CBAC inspects the packets and creates a temporary entry in the access list to allow the return packets to enter the network.

    B. CBAC inspects the packets and creates temporary entry in the access list to block the return packets from entering the network.

    C. CBAC can inspect packets on per-application protocol basis.

    D. CBAC cannot support applications that use multiple channels for their session.

21. Which of the following is not a guideline for configuring a firewall?

    A. Password protect the console.

    B. Apply access lists to all virtual terminal ports.

    C. Apply access lists to limit users who can telnet to the router.

    D. Enable direct broadcast messages on the firewall and routers.

22. Which of the following commands will display the software functions being called by CBAC as (and when) they are called during session inspection?

    A. `Router#debug ip inspect function-trace`

    B. `Router#debug ip inspect object-{creation|deletion}`

    C. `Router#debug ip inspect events`

    D. `Router#debug ip inspect timers`

23. Which of the following commands will display the information about packet processing by CBAC?

    A. `Router#debug ip inspect function-trace`

    B. `Router#debug ip inspect object-{creation|deletion}`

    C. `Router#debug ip inspect events`

    D. `Router#debug ip inspect timers`

24. Which of the following is *not* true for CBAC?

   A. CBAC does not work for all protocols.

   B. CBAC does not allow three-way FTP traffic.

   C. CBAC can effectively examine encrypted data packets.

   D. CBAC integrates the firewall with other Cisco IOS software features and provides seamless interoperability.

Answers to Chapter 8 Questions

1. Cisco IOS Firewall is a software product that seamlessly integrates with Cisco IOS software to enhance the security capabilities of Cisco IOS software.

2. True. Cisco IOS Firewall seamlessly integrates with Cisco IOS software to enhance the security capabilities of Cisco IOS software.

3. True. CBAC inspects only those packets that use IP at the Network layer. It cannot inspect packets of ICMP and other Network-layer protocols.

4. A router using CBAC maintains state table of the connection status of various sessions.

5. CBAC filters packets according to specific Application-layer protocols.

6. True. CBAC recognizes the application-specific commands when it inspects packets at the Application layer.

7. The inbound access list on the internal interface should permit the packet if the packet has to be inspected by CBAC.

8. If CBAC is applied, the access list testing the packets coming from the external network to the internal network should be a(n) extended access list.

9. True. CBAC can prevent users from downloading java applets from Web sites even though they may be allowed to browse those sites.

10. For TCP, a half-open session means a session has been initiated, but the three-way handshake has not been completed; in effect, the TCP session is not yet established. For UDP, half-open session means no return packets have been received after the first packet was sent.

11. B and D. Cisco IOS Firewall is a software product that seamlessly integrates with the Cisco IOS software to enhance the security features of Cisco IOS software.

12. A and B. Time-based access lists and context-based access lists are two of the components of the Cisco IOS firewall. PIX Firewall is an entirely different product, which is a combination of software and hardware. Cisco Secure ACS is an AAA (Authentication, Authorization, and Accounting) Server from Cisco. It is an entirely different product from Cisco IOS Firewall.

13. B. Network Address Translation (NAT) allows a network with private IP addresses to connect to the Internet by translating these addresses into registered IP addresses. If your internal network has been configured with private IP addresses, your internal hosts cannot directly communicate with any host on the Internet because your hosts do not have valid IP addresses. You can solve this problem by using NAT. NAT translates these invalid or unregistered IP addresses into valid registered IP addresses at the boundary of router your network.

14. C. For packets inspected, CBAC maintains a state table with the information about the status of the session that packet belongs to. As soon as any change in the status of the session, the state table is updated.

15. A and D. The access list, which tests the return packets, should always be extended access list because CBAC creates entries, which include specific protocol and port numbers also. If the inbound access list on the internal interface denies the packets, they cannot be inspected by CBAC as they are dropped before reaching CBAC.

16. A and C. The access list, which tests the return packets, should always be extended access list because CBAC creates entries, which include specific protocol and port numbers also. If the inbound access list on the external interface permits the return packets, no point in CBAC creating temporary entries for them. Regardless of whether CBAC creates an entry for them, they are permitted.

17. C. The command for the task is `ip inspect name test http java-list 10 timeout 30` in the global configuration mode.

18. B and D. The command to configure an upper threshold of 600 half-open sessions is `ip inspect max-incomplete high 600` in the global configuration mode. The command to configure a lower threshold of 300 half-open sessions is `ip inspect max-incomplete low 300`. The other two commands configure upper and lower thresholds for how often (per minute) the establishment of a new session can be attempted.

19. A. A TCP session closes with the exchange of FIN packets. The command for task is `ip inspect tcp finwait-time 30`.

20. A and C. CBAC inspects the packets for which it is configured and makes entries in its state table that reflect the status of the corresponding sessions. It also creates a temporary entry in the access list for permitting return packet for those valid sessions initiated by an internal host. CBAC can be configured to inspect packets on the basis of their Application-layer protocols.

21. D. When configuring a firewall, you should disable direct broadcast messages on the firewall and routers. This would protect the network from denial-of-service attacks that can be launched by using direct broadcast messages.

22. A. The `Router#debug ip inspect function-trace` command is used to display the software functions being called by CBAC as and when they are called during session inspection.

23. C. The `Router#debug ip inspect events` command is used to display the information about the CBAC software events as they happen. This command also displays the information about the packet processing by CBAC.

24. C. CBAC cannot effectively examine encrypted data packets. If encryption and CBAC are configured on the same firewall, CBAC does not work for multichannel protocols, except for StreamWorks and CU-SeeMe.

Chapter 9 Questions

1. What type of product is PIX Firewall? Is it software, hardware, or a combination of software and hardware?

2. The PIX Firewall solution is better than the proxy server solution for security. Why?

3. PIX Firewall performs stateful filtering of traffic. True or False?

4. What is Adaptive Security Algorithm in PIX Firewall?

5. You use _____ to override a rule that allows connection only from a higher-security-value interface to a lower-security-value interface.

6. What are the available models of PIX Firewall?

7. PIX Firewall supports both NAT and PAT. True or False?

8. PIX Firewall can prevent denial-of-service attacks. True or False?

9. The component of PIX that prevents the DNS DoS attack is _____.

10. What is the difference between NAT and PAT?

11. Which of the following statements are correct about PIX Firewall? (Select all that apply.)

    A. PIX Firewall is a combination of software and hardware.

    B. PIX Firewall is installed on a router and it seamlessly integrates with the Cisco IOS.

    C. PIX Firewall does stateful filtering.

    D. PIX Firewall allows connections from lower-security interfaces to higher-security level interfaces.

12. Which of the following statements is true about PIX ASA?

    A. It records the information about the connection status of packets in a session state table and allows only the packets matching the table to enter the network.

    B. It creates security holes in the firewall to allow the external connections to enter the network.

C. It authenticates the users before allowing them access to the network.

D. It translates the internal IP address to the global IP addresses.

13. Which of the following command modes are supported by PIX Firewall? (Select all that apply.)

   A. Interface configuration mode

   B. Privileged mode

   C. Unprivileged mode

   D. Configuration mode

14. Which of the following commands assigns interface Ethernet 1 name inside and security level 50?

   A. `PIXFW(config)#nameif ethernet1 inside security50`

   B. `PIXFW#nameif ethernet1 inside security50`

   C. `PIXFW#interface ethernet1 name inside security50`

   D. `PIXFW(config)#interface ethernet1 name inside security50`

15. What command assigns IP address 172.17.0.100/24 to the inside interface?

   A. `PIXFW#ip address inside 172.17.0.100 255.255.255.0`

   B. `PIXFW(config)#ip address inside 172.17.0.100 255.255.255.0`

   C. `PIXFW(config)#interface inside ip address 172.17.0.100 netmask 255.255.255.0`

   D. `PIXFW(config)#ip address inside 172.17.0.100 netmask 255.255.255.0`

16. What are the functions of the global and nat commands?

   A. The global command opens a security hole in the firewall, and the nat command translates the internal IP address to global IP addresses.

   B. The global command translates the internal IP addresses to the global IP addresses, and the nat command opens a security hole in the firewall.

   C. The global command creates a pool of global registered IP addresses, and the nat command translates the internal IP addresses to the global IP addresses.

   D. The global command translates the internal IP addresses to the global IP addresses, and the nat command creates a pool of global registered IP addresses.

17. Which of the following sequence of commands would create a global pool of addresses 192.168.1.1 to 192.168.1.10 and translate the internal IP address to the global IP addresses?

A. `global outside 1 192.168.1.1-192.168.1.10 netmask 255.255.255.0, nat inside 1 0.0.0.0 0.0.0.0`

B. `global inside 1 192.168.1.1-192.168.1.10 netmask 255.255.255.0, nat outside 1 0.0.0.0 0.0.0.0`

C. `global outside 0.0.0.0 0.0.0.0, nat inside 1 192.168.1.1-192.168.1.10 netmask 192.168.1.1-192.168.1.10`

D. `global inside 0.0.0.0 0.0.0.0, nat outside 1 192.168.1.1-192.168.1.10 netmask 192.168.1.1-192.168.1.10`

18. Which of the following statements are true about the establishment of connections in PIX Firewall? (Select all that apply.)

A. PIX Firewall allows connection only from a lower-security level interface to a higher-security level interface.

B. PIX Firewall allows connection only from a higher-security level interface to a lower-security level interface.

C. PIX Firewall prompts the user for authentication only at the start of the connection.

D. PIX Firewall prompts the user for authentication when the `unauth` timer expires.

19. Which command specifies that the internal IP address of a host should be allowed to go out without translations? The IP address of the host is `192.168.1.100`.

A. `no nat 192.168.1.100 netmask 255.255.255.255`

B. `nat (inside) 0 192.168.1.100 255.255.255.255`

C. `nat(outside) 0 192.168.1.100 255.255.255.255`

D. `no nat (inside) 1 192.168.1.100 netmask 255.255.255.255`

20. Which command configures the PIX Firewall to always translate the internal IP address `172.17.0.100` to `192.168.1.100`?

A. `static (inside, outside) 192.168.1.100 172.17.0.100 netmask 255.255.255.255`

B. `static (outside, inside) 192.168.1.100 172.17.0.100 netmask 255.255.255.255`

C. `static (inside, outside) 172.17.0.100 192.168.1.100 netmask 255.255.255.255`

D. `static (outside, inside) 172.17.0.100 192.168.1.100 netmask 255.255.255.255`

21. Which command creates a security hole in the firewall to allow FTP connection from the outside hosts to the FTP server 172.17.0.10 on the internal network? The IP address 172.17.0.10 is translated to 192.168.1.10 at the firewall.

A. conduit permit ip 172.17.0.10 255.255.255.255 eq ftp 0.0.0.0 0.0.0.0

B. conduit permit tcp 192.168.1.10 255.255.255.255 eq ftp 0.0.0.0 0.0.0.0

C. conduit permit tcp 192.168.1.10 255.255.255.255 172.17.0.10 255.255.255.255 eq ftp

D. conduit permit ip 0.0.0.0 0.0.0.0 172.17.0.10 255.255.255.255 eq ftp

Answers to Chapter 9 Questions

1. The PIX Firewall is a combination of both software and hardware.

2. The proxy servers perform all their functions at the Application layer. The PIX Firewall performs only the authentication at the Application layer. After the user is authenticated, the Adaptive Security Algorithm (ASA) handles the session at the Network layer. Therefore it is faster than proxy servers.

3. True. The PIX Firewall maintains a session-state database and allows only those packets to enter the internal network that match an entry in this database.

4. The Adaptive Security Algorithm (ASA) records characteristics of the packets sent by a host on the internal network to a host on the external network. It then creates a signature using these characteristics, which is valid only for the same session. Using this session information, the ASA determines whether the packet coming from the external network should be allowed to enter the internal network or not. If the packet is determined to be a part of an already established valid session, it is allowed; otherwise, the packet is blocked.

5. You use a conduit to override the rule that allows connection only from a higher-security value interface to a lower-security value interface.

6. Available models of PIX Firewall are Cisco Secure PIX 506, Cisco Secure PIX 515, Cisco Secure PIX 520, Cisco Secure PIX 525, and Cisco Secure PIX 535.

7. True. PIX Firewall supports both NAT and PAT.

8. True. PIX Firewall can prevent denial-of-service attacks.

9. The component of PIX Firewall that prevents DNS DoS attacks is PIX DNS Guard.

10. NAT translates one internal IP address to one global registered IP address without changing the port number. PAT translates all the internal IP addresses to one global IP address. The sessions are given different port numbers to identify them. The source IP address of each packet that leaves the firewall is the same.

11. A and C. PIX Firewall is a combination of hardware and software, which is dedicated for security purposes. PIX Firewall stores the sessions status information in a database and filters packets using the entries in this database. If packets coming from outside the network are a part of a valid session having an entry in the database, only then they are allowed to enter the internal network. So, PIX Firewall does stateful filtering.

12. A. The PIX ASA records information about the connection status of packets in a session state table and allows only the packets matching the entries in the table to enter the network. This is stateful filtering. Creating a security hole is the job of the conduit command. The users are authenticated by cut-through authentication. The address translation is done by NAT and PAT.

13. B, C, and D. The interface configuration mode is not available in PIX Firewall. It is available in routers and switches. The PIX Firewall has three modes: Unprivileged mode, Privileged mode, and Configuration mode.

14. A. You configure the interface characteristics in the configuration mode with the command `nameif hardware_id if_name security_level`. Therefore choice A is correct.

15. B. You configure IP address on an interface in the configuration mode using the command `ip address if_name ip_address [netmask]`.

16. C. The global command creates a global pool of registered IP addresses that can be used for sending packets out of the network. The nat command translates the specified internal IP addresses to the global pool of registered IP addresses.

17. A. For translation of internal IP addresses to global registered IP addresses, first you create a global pool of the registered IP address using the global command and then use the nat command to translate the specified internal IP addresses to the global pool of IP addresses. The global command is executed for the outside interface, and the nat command is executed for the inside interface. Thus options B and D are wrong. In option C, the global pool of IP addresses is being defined using the nat command, which is wrong. Thus option C is also wrong.

18. B and D. The rule is that connection can be established only from a higher-security level interface to a lower-security level interface. PIX Firewall sets `unauth` timer after a user is authenticated. When the `unauth` timer expires, the cut-through authentication again prompts the user for authentication.

19. B. The `nat 0` command is used to specify that a specified IP address should be allowed to go without translation. Because the IP address is internal, the nat command is specified on the inside interface along with nat_id as 0.

20. A. The command that defines a static mapping of an internal IP address to a global registered IP address is as follows:

```
static [internal_if_name external_if_name] global_ip local_ip
[netmask network_mask] [max_conns [em_limit]] [norandomseq]
```

In options B and D, the interfaces have been incorrectly specified; in option C, the global and internal IP addresses are incorrectly specified.

21. B. The conduit command is used to create a security hole in the firewall. The syntax is as follows:

```
conduit {permit|deny} protocol global_ip global_mask [operator
port [port]] foreign_ip foreign_mask [operator port [port]]
```

FTP uses TCP as the transport protocol. Therefore options A and D are incorrect. In option C, both internal and global IP address of the FTP server are specified, which is incorrect.

Chapter 10 Questions

1. Authentication is a process of validating remote clients for network access. True or False?

2. AAA is the security architecture for _____, _____, and _____ mechanisms.

3. Authorization compiles reports on network usage and tracks user activities. True or False?

4. What is authorization?

5. What is accounting?

6. PAP and CHAP are _____ mechanisms.

7. PAP is more secure than CHAP. True or False?

8. Name the commonly used authentication methods.

9. What are RADIUS, TACACS+, and Kerberos used for?

10. Cisco products do not support RADIUS, TACACS+, and Kerberos. True or False?

11. Which of the following traffic modes are supported by AAA? (Select all that apply.)

    A. Character-mode traffic

    B. Packet-mode traffic

    C. Line-mode traffic

    D. AAA does not secure any traffic

12. What are major authentication methods? (Select all that apply.)

    A. S/key

    B. Visiting cards

    C. Security cards

    D. Security guards

13. What are two commonly used security-card methods? (Select all that apply.)

    A. Memory-based

    B. Time-based

    C. Challenge and response

    D. Client-based

14. Which authentication protocols are supported by PPP? (Select all that apply.)

    A. PAP

    B. PPTP

    C. CHAP

    D. VTP

15. Which of the following statements correctly describe a remote security database? (Select all that apply.)

    A. The security credentials are located on the network access server or router.

    B. It is ideal for medium to large-size networks with many remote clients.

    C The security credentials are stored centrally on the remote security database.

    D. It is ideal for small networks with few remote clients.

16. Which security server protocols are supported by Cisco for remote security database? (Select all that apply.)

    A. RADIUS

    B. MD5

    C. PPP

    D. TACACS+

17. What is true for TACACS+ protocol? (Select all that apply.)

    A. It uses a modular design that integrates each AAA service into a single database.

    B. It uses a modular design that separates each AAA service and has its own database.

    C. It uses UDP as a transport protocol.

    D. It encrypts the entire body of the packet.

18. Which authentication techniques should be used to avoid password playback attacks? (Select all that apply.)

    A. PAP

    B. CHAP

    C. S/Key

    D. No authentication

19. TACACS+ utilizes three packet types for authentication – START, CONTINUE, and REPLY. Which other packets are exchanged by TACACS+ during the authentication phase? (Select all that apply.)

    A. PAUSE

    B. GETUSER

    C. GETPASS

    D. GATEPASS

20. When does a RADIUS security server issue an access-challenge packet during the authentication phase?

    A. When the remote client is authenticated from the network access server cache

    B. When the security server wants to inform the network access server that it does not have the requested user profile in its database

    C. When the security server sends messages periodically to the network access server for the remote client to resubmit the username/password for verification

    D. When the remote client needs to be notified that the session has timed out

21. What is TGT in Kerberos?

    A. A credential issued by the network access server to an authenticated user.

    B. A protocol used by Kerberos to request a network access server for accounting records.

    C. A client software that authenticates the remote client to the KDC.

    D. A credential issued by KDC to authenticated users.

22. What are the different types of authorization supported by Cisco IOS? (Select all that apply.)

    A. Command

    B. Network

    C. Local

    D. EXEC

23. What does a Login-Service AV pair indicate during RADIUS authorization?

    A. It indicates to the network access server that it can run authorization services.

    B. It is an integer value to identify the requested network service.

    C. It is an integer value to identify the application port for a service.

    D. It indicates to the remote client that the network access server can handle RADIUS authorization services.

24. For what purpose would you implement an authentication proxy? (Select all that apply.)

    A. To authenticate and authorize local users before permitting access to an intranet, Internet services, or hosts through a firewall.

    B. To authenticate and authorize remote users before permitting access to local services or hosts through a firewall.

    C. To authenticate and authorize remote users before permitting access to an intranet, Internet services, or hosts through a firewall.

    D. To authenticate and authorize local users before permitting access to local services or hosts through a firewall.

25. On the firewall router, which command is used to display the name of the firewall in the authentication proxy login page?

    A. `router(config)# ip auth proxy auth-proxy-banner`

    B. `router(config)# ip auth-proxy auth proxy banner`

    C. `router(config)# ip auth-proxy auth-proxy-banner`

    D. `router(config-if)# ip auth-proxy auth-proxy-banner`

Answers to Chapter 10 Questions

1. True. Authentication is the process for identifying an individual who is entitled to access and use network resources and its services.

2. Authentication, Authorization, and Accounting.

3. False. Authorization is the process of determining the services and network resources that an individual is allowed to access.

4. Authorization is the process of determining the services and network resources that an individual is allowed to access.

5. Accounting is the process which an organization uses to determine who is using which resources. It provides the method for collecting and sending security server information used for billing, auditing, and reporting, such as user identities, start and stop times, executed commands (such as PPP), number of packets, and number of bytes.

6. Authentication. PAP and CHAP are authentication methods supported over dial-up PPP links.

7. False. PAP is not recognized as a secure authentication protocol, because the security credentials are sent in cleartext over the communication link that can be captured by any hacker. In CHAP the actual password is never sent over the communication link.

8. The authentication methods range from no username/password, policy-based username/passwords, S/key one-time passwords, one-time passwords, to security cards and security servers.

9. RADIUS, TACACS+, and Kerberos are security protocols used for implementing AAA security using remote security database. Cisco security servers support all the three protocols.

10. False. Cisco supports all the three security protocols.

11. A, B, and C. AAA technologies are useful in protecting remote access to the network access servers, whether character-mode or packet-mode. The character-mode traffic is also recognized as line-mode traffic.

12. A, C. The authentication methods range from no username/password, policy-based username/passwords, S/key one-time passwords, one-time passwords, to security cards and security servers.

13. B, C. The two common methods of implementing security-card-and-server systems are time-based and challenge/response-based. The time-based security card system uses a mathematical algorithm based on time. In the challenge/response method, the token server itself generates a random string of digits and transfers the string to the remote client requesting access.

14. A, C. PPP supports PAP, CHAP, and MS-CHAP. MS-CHAP is Microsoft's extension of CHAP and supported by Microsoft products only.

15. B, C. Security credentials — including usernames, passwords, and authorization parameters — are centrally stored in the remote security database. This database is stored on a security server. Medium-size and larger enterprise networks (consisting of many remote clients and network access servers) often find the remote security database an ideal implementation.

16. A, D. Cisco supports three primary security protocols – TACACS+, RADIUS, and Kerberos.

17. B, D. TACACS+ uses a modular framework that separates each AAA service and has its own databases. TACACS+ uses TCP packets and encrypts the entire body of the packet.

18. B, C. CHAP and S/Key OTP mechanisms can be used to prevent password playback attacks.

19. B, C. TACACS+ uses GETUSER and GETPASS packets for exchanging username and password information between network access server and security server.

20. C. The RADIUS server issues this response occasionally to verify the user. The network access server prompts the client for additional data and sends it to the RADIUS security server. This packet can be sent periodically to the network access server for the user to resubmit the username and password.

21. D. Ticket Granting Ticket (TGT) is a credential issued by the KDC to authenticated users only. TGT lets users authenticate to other network services within the Kerberos realm represented by the KDC.

22. A, B, D. The Cisco IOS software supports three different types of authorization – EXEC, Command, and Network.

23. B. Login-Service AV pair is an integer value identifying the requested network service.

24. A, B. The authentication proxy can be used to authenticate and authorize local users before permitting access to intranet or Internet services or hosts through the firewall. It can be implemented to authenticate and authorize remote users before permitting them access to local services or hosts through the firewall. It can also be used to control access for specific extranet users.

25. C. The correct command to configure the firewall router to display the name of the firewall router in the authentication proxy login page is

```
router(config)# ip auth-proxy auth-proxy-banner
```

Chapter 11 Questions

1. Why do you require a local security database?

2. When should you use remote security databases?

3. Which security protocols are supported by the Cisco IOS software?

4. Why is the `service password encryption` command used when implementing AAA configuration?

5. What two network access server modes can be secured by using AAA commands?

6. Mention the characteristics of an enabled password.

7. Which command is used to provide additional security to the MD5 hashing function?

8. Which command is used to create a new AAA configuration?

9. Why do you configure AAA authentication profile?

10. What is ARA?

11. When configuring NAS, what is the next step after configuring AAA authentication profiles?

Answers to Chapter 11 Questions

1. A local security database is used when the network consists of a small number of users and a single network access server.

2. You should use remote security databases to provide authentication and authorization services to remote users.

3. Cisco IOS software supports TACACS+, RADIUS, and Kerberos.

4. The `service password encryption` command is used to secure privileged EXEC mode on NAS.

5. The two network modes that can be secured by using AAA commands are character (line) mode and packet (interface) mode.

6. The characteristics of an enabled password are the following: contains a maximum of 25 characters, cannot be blank, can contain both uppercase and lowercase alphanumeric characters. An enabled password cannot contain a number as the first character and can contain leading spaces, intermediate spaces, and trailing spaces.

7. The `enable secret` command is used to provide additional security to the MD5 hashing function.

8. The `aaa new-model` command is used to create a new AAA configuration.

9. You configure AAA authentication profiles to define the parameters that would be used to verify a user's identity.

10. ARA stands for AppleTalk Remote Access.

11. The next task after configuring AAA authentication profiles is to configure AAA authorization on the network access server. The following are the steps involved in configuring your NAS:

    1. Secure access to privileged EXEC and configuration modes on various ports (such as auxiliary, VTY, asynchronous, and TTY).

    2. Use the `aanew-model` command to enable AAA globally on the NAS.

    3. Configure AAA authentication profiles.

    4. Configure AAA authorization to occur only after a user is authenticated.

    5. Configure the AAA accounting options that report on the writing of accounting records (and their content).

    6. Debug the configuration.

Chapter 12 Questions

1. What is a VPN?

2. How do VPNs differ from private networks?

3. Name the types of VPNs.

4. What is PPTP?

5. How does the control of a VPN differ between intranets and extranets?

6. What is L2F?

7. How is data secured when it passes over a VPN created between a corporate network and a remote location?

8. What is VPDN?

9. What is L2TP?

10. What are Layer 2 Tunneling Protocols?

11. What are the three major Layer 2 Tunneling Protocols?

12. Tunneling is a method of secure data transfer over public internetwork. True or False?

13. Which UDP port does L2F use?

14. Which mode(s) of tunneling are supported by L2TP?

15. Which of the following factors need to be considered while deciding to use VPN to connect to remote networks? (Select all that apply.)

    A. Type of security services used on the network

    B. Type of application running on the network

    C. Amount of data stored on the network

    D. Amount of administrative access required on the network

16. Which of the following is *not* a type of VPN?

    A. Extranet

    B. Secured

    C. Remote access

    D. Intranet

17. Which one of the following is *not* an advantage of intranet VPN?

    A. Helps reduce cost of transmitting data

    B. More users can connect to remote sites by using the Internet

    C. Provides faster connectivity to new locations

    D. Provides a stable connection

18. Which of the following protocols are supported by VPNs? (Select all that apply.)

    A. PPTP

    B. IPSec

    C. TCP/IP

    D. L2TP

19. Which of the following is *not* a consideration when deploying a VPN in a business partner's network?

    A. Security of data being transmitted on the business partner's network should be ensured.

    B. Transmitted data should always be decrypted.

    C. NAT should be used by network devices to avoid routing collision.

    D. No security measures are required on the business partner's network.

20. Which of the following considerations should be kept in mind when setting up a VPN in a remote location?

    A. Clients accessing the intranet should support IP Sec.

    B. Clients accessing the intranet should support TCP/IP.

    C. Dynamic tunnels are required to handle the dynamic remote client address.

    D. All unauthenticated traffic should be rejected by the firewall.

21. Which of the following RFC's define PPTP?

    A. RFC 1701

    B. RFC 2376

    C. RFC 2637

    D. RFC 2254

22. Which protocol does PPTP use to encapsulate the data or payload in a secure manner?

    A. HDLC

    B. GRE

    C. SNMP

    D. IGMP

23. Which PPTP component initiates the establishment of control connection?

    A. PAC

    B. PNS

    C. Either PAC or PNS

    D. It is not initiated at all.

24. Which of the following statements are true about PPTP?

    A. It supports multiple protocols.

    B. It works over PPP, X.25, and Frame Relay.

    C. It supports point-to-point connection only.

    D. It supports compulsory and voluntary tunneling modes.

25. Which two message types are used to create and open an L2F tunnel?

    A. L2F_CONF

    B. L2F_OPEN (MID)

    C. L2F_OPEN

    D. L2F_CLOSE

26. Which of the following is true about the L2F tunnel authentication process?

    A. Before opening up an L2F tunnel both the NAS and Home Gateway should authenticate with a common tunnel secret.

    B. The L2F session negotiation should repeat for each packet arrived at NAS from the client even if the tunnel is already open.

    C. Encryption is not done on the tunnel secret for the NAS and Home Gateway to authenticate each other.

    D. After the tunnel is authenticated, the NAS acts as a transparent packet forwarder.

27. In what conditions is the L2F tunnel terminated for a particular client?

    A. When the Home Gateway sends L2F_CLOSE packet with MID value 0 in response of an L2F_OPEN message

    B. When either side of the tunnel sends L2F_CLOSE message with MID value 0

    C. When either side of the tunnel sends L2F_CLOSE message with MID value non-zero

    D. When only the Home Gateway sends L2F_CLOSE packet with MID value non-zero

28. Which of the following are true for L2F? (Select all that apply.)

   A. An L2F tunnel can support only one connection.

   B. L2F can also work with ATM, Frame relay, and FDDI.

   C. L2F does not support IPX and NetBEUI.

   D. L2F supports TACACS+ and RADIUS apart from PPP for client authentication.

29. Which of the following are true about L2TP? (Select all that apply.)

   A. L2TP combines the features of PPTP and L2F.

   B. L2TP supports only one session per tunnel.

   C. The remote system directly connects to LNS, which then forms a tunnel with LAC.

   D. L2TP supports multiple sessions per tunnel.

30. Which of the following sequence of events is correct for L2TP operation?

   A. Session establishment, connection establishment, data transfer, session teardown

   B. Session establishment, session teardown, connection establishment, connection teardown, data transfer, data-transfer termination

   C. Connection establishment, session establishment, data transfer, session teardown, connection teardown

   D. Session establishment, connection establishment, data transfer, connection teardown, session teardown

31. Tunnel authentication in L2TP occurs during:

   A. Session establishment

   B. Data transfer

   C. Connection establishment

   D. Session teardown

32. Which of the following is true about an L2TP operation?

   A. Only LAC can initiate a connection for forming a tunnel.

   B. Session teardown brings down the tunnel carrying the session.

   C. Only LNS can initiate a connection for forming a tunnel.

   D. Tunnel teardown brings down all the sessions carried by the tunnel.

Answers to Chapter 12 Questions

1. VPN stands for virtual private network.

2. Unlike a private network that uses leased lines to connect networks, a VPN uses secured tunnels through IP networks such as Internet. VPNs are more flexible and cost-effective.

3. The types of VPNs are intranet VPNs, extranet VPNs, and remote-access VPNs.

4. PPTP is Point-to-Point Tunneling Protocol.

5. In the case of intranets, the control of VPN lies within the organization: in case of extranets, both companies share the management of VPNs.

6. L2F stands for Layer 2 Forwarding.

7. Although data is passed through a public network, such as the Internet, it is secured by creating a tunnel that connect the corporate network and the remote location.

8. VPDN stands for Virtual Private Dial-up Network.

9. L2TP stands for Layer 2 Tunneling Protocol.

10. Layer 2 Tunneling Protocols correspond to Data Link layer of OSI layer, and utilizes frames as their unit of exchange. Layer 2 tunneling protocols are independent of Network-layer transport.

11. The three major Layer 2 Tunneling Protocols are PPTP, L2F, and L2TP.

12. True. Tunneling is provided for secure data transfer of private networks over public internetwork.

13. The entire L2F packet, including payload and L2F header, is sent within a UDP datagram. L2F uses UDP port 1701.

14. Both compulsory and voluntary modes of tunneling are supported by L2TP.

15. B and C. The type of application running on the network and the amount of data stored on the network needs to be considered while deciding to use VPN to connect to remote networks.

16. B. Extranet, intranet, and remote access are the types of VPNs; *secure VPN* is not a distinct type.

17. B. One drawback of VPNs is that not many users can connect to remote sites by using the Internet.

18. A, B, and D. The PPTP, IPSec, and L2TP protocols can be used with VPN.

19. A. When deploying a VPN to a business partner's network, you do not need to ensure the security of data being transmitted on the business partner's network.

20. A, C, and D. When you set up a VPN to a remote location, the client that accesses the Internet should support IPSec, dynamic tunnels are required to handle the dynamic remote-client address, and all unauthenticated traffic should be rejected by the firewall.

21. C. PPTP is defined in RFC 2637, submitted by a collaboration forum of Microsoft, Ascend Communications, 3Com or Primary Access, ECI-Telematics, and US Robotics.

22. B. Generic Routing Encapsulation (GRE) protocol is used by PPTP to encapsulate data in a secure manner. The data or payload is given a PPP header and then placed inside a GRE packet. The GRE packet carries the data between the two tunnel endpoints.

23. C. The PPTP control connection can be initiated by either PAC or PNS to establish a tunnel between them. The *control connection* is a standard TCP session over which PPTP call control and management information traverses.

24. A, C, and D. PPTP supports multiple network protocols such as IP, IPX, and NetBEUI over PPP. Because it works over PPP, PPTP is not multipoint and provides only point-to-point connectivity.

25. A and C. L2F_CONF message is used to create a tunnel, and L2F_OPEN is used to open it. The MID packet is used after the L2F authentication phase is completed. L2F_CLOSE is used to terminate a tunnel session.

26. A and D. L2F session negotiation occurs only for the first packet arrived. When the tunnel is open, all subsequent packets are forwarded. The tunnel secret is encrypted using MD5 and a random value during NAS and Home Gateway authentication.

27. C. Either side of the tunnel can send a L2F_CLOSE command at any time. A MID value of 0 terminates the entire tunnel and all clients within it. A non-zero MID value terminates a particular client (identified by that MID) within the tunnel.

28. B and D. A L2F tunnel can support more than one connection using Multiplex Ids (MID). Because L2F is a layer-2 protocol, it can be used for protocols other than IP, such as IPX and NetBEUI.

29. A and D. L2TP has the best features of both PPTP and L2F. L2TP can have several sessions within a tunnel. Each tunnel is given a tunnel ID, and each session is also given a session ID to identify them.

30. C. The sequence of events in L2TP operation is connection establishment, session establishment, data transfer (forwarding of PPP frames), session teardown, and connection teardown.

31. C. Tunnel authentication in L2TP occurs during the establishment of the control connection; also during that time, the challenge might be sent by either LAC or LNS. If the challenge is sent in SCCRQ, the challenge response is sent in the SCCRP. If the challenge is sent in SCCRP, the challenge response is sent in SCCCN.

32. D. Sessions are carried within a tunnel. If the tunnel goes down, all the sessions in that tunnel also terminate.

Chapter 13 Questions

1. What authentication methods does PPTP use?

2. Name the protocol that combines the best features of PPTP and L2F.

3. Name the layer3 protocol suite that was developed by IETF to support secure transmission over the IP layer.

4. Name the symmetric encryption algorithm that ESP uses by default.

5. What is MD5?

6. What is SHA?

7. How is a security association identified?

8. What are the two modes of encryption supported by IPSec?

9. What is the difference between the transport and the tunnel mode?

10. Who developed the Diffie-Hellman key agreement?

11. Who developed RSA?

12. What is HMACs?

13. What are the steps involved in the working of IPSec?

14. What are the two modes of IKE?

15. What are the steps involved in configuring of IPSec?

16. What is a transform set?

17. Which command is used to define a transform set?

18. Which of the following protocols is an extension of IP and works at the Network layer?

    A. PPTP

    B. L2F

    C. L2TP

    D. IPSec

19. Which of the following protocols does the IP suite use to ensure authenticity, integrity, and confidentiality of data being transmitted? (Select all that apply.)

    A. AM

    B. ESP

    C. TCP

    D. IKE

20. Which of the following is not true for AH?

    A. It ensures data authenticity by applying a one-way hash function to the data packets.

    B. It is described in RFC 2402.

    C. It provides data encryption.

    D. It sends data in cleartext form.

21. Which of the following is *not* an optional service of ESP?

    A. Encryption of payload as well as of IP address

    B. Data-origin authentication

    C. Connectionless integrity

    D. Anti-replay

22. Which of the following is *not* true for IKE?

    A. It provides anti-replay services.

    B. It requires you to manually specify the IPSec SA parameters.

    C. It enables dynamic authentication of peer devices.

    D. It generates the session keys used by peer devices.

Answers to Chapter 13 Questions

    1. CHAP and PAP are the authentication methods of PPTP.

    2. Layer2 Tunneling Protocol (L2TP), which was developed jointly by Microsoft, Cisco, 3 Com, and others, combines the best features of PPTP and L2F.

    3. IPSec is the layer3 protocol suite that was developed by IETF to support secure transmission over the IP layer.

    4. 56-bit DES is the symmetric encryption algorithm that ESP uses by default.

    5. MD5 is a hash algorithm used to authenticate the data in packets.

    6. SHA is a hash algorithm used during IKE exchanges to authenticate packet data.

    7. A security association is identified by a unique number called the Security Parameter Index (SPI) and the destination IP address.

    8. The two modes of encryption are transport mode and tunnel mode.

    9. In the transport mode, only the data portion of the packet is encrypted; the IP headers are left unencrypted. In the tunnel mode, both the headers and payload are encrypted.

    10. Diffie-Hellman key agreement was developed by Whitfield Diffie and Martin Hellman in 1976.

11. RSA was developed by Rivest, Shamir, and Adleman in 1977.

12. HMAC stands for Hashed Message Authentication Codes.

13. The steps involved in the working of IPSec are as follows: process initiation, IKE phase 1, IKE Phase 2, data transfer, and tunnel termination.

14. The two modes of IKE are the main mode and the aggressive mode.

15. The steps involved in configuring IPSec are as follows: planning for IPSec, configuring IKE, and verifying the configuration.

16. A transform set defines a specific set of algorithms and security protocols.

17. To define a transform set, the `crypto ipsec transform-set` command is used.

18. D. IPSec is an extension of IP and works at the Network layer.

19. A, B, and D. The AH, ESP, and IKE are used by the IP suite to ensure authenticity, integrity, and confidentiality of data being transmitted.

20. C. AH does not provide data encryption.

21. A. Payload and IP address encryption is not an optional service of ESP.

22. B. IKE does not require dynamic authentication of peer devices.

Chapter 14 Questions

1. Which of the following keywords represents a message encryption algorithm?

    A. des

    B. sha

    C. md5

    D. rsa-sig

2. Which of the following keywords represents message integrity algorithm?

    A. des

    B. sha

    C. md5

    D. rsa-sig

3. Which of the following keywords represents a method for peer authentication?

    A. des

    B. sha

    C. md5

    D. rsa-sig

4. In the `crypto isakmp key` command, which of the following keywords is used in case remote IKE identity has been set with its host name?

   A. `peer-address`

   B. `hostname`

   C. `address`

   D. `peer-hostname`

5. What is the maximum number of transform sets that you can define when configuring IPSec?

   A. One

   B. Two

   C. Three

   D. Four

6. Which of the following transforms can be used in conjunction with `esp-md5-hmac` or `esp-sha-hmac` for authenticating ESP without encryption?

   A. `esp-des`

   B. `esp-null`

   C. `esp-rfc1829`

   D. `esp-3des`

Answers to Chapter 14 Questions

1. A. The keyword `des` represents a message encryption algorithm.

2. C. The keyword `md5` represents a message integrity algorithm.

3. D. The keyword `rsa-sig` represents a method for peer authentication.

4. B. The `hostname` parameter is used in case remote IKE identity has been set with its host name.

5. C. You can define a maximum of three transform sets when configuring IPSec.

6. B. The `esp-null` can use this transform in conjunction with `esp-md5-hmac` or `esp-md5-hmac` for authenticating ESP without encryption. This transform does not have a cipher. Since it does not provide any security to the data transmission, you should not use this transform alone.

Chapter 15 Questions

1. What is Cisco ACL Manager?

2. Is the ACL Manager a multiuser application?

3. List the tools of the ACL Manager.

4. What does the Class Manager provide?

5. Why is the Template Manager used?

6. What is the function of ACL Use Wizard?

7. What is the use of the Diff Viewer?

8. What is the Cisco Secure Policy Manager?

9. List the features of GUI of Cisco Secure Policy Manager.

10. What is RADIUS?

11. What is TACACS+?

12. Why is the Access Control Server used?

13. What does CHAP stand for?

14. Name the three categories of the ACS.

15. What are the services of the Cisco Secure ACS?

16. What are the two types of passwords provided by Cisco Secure?

17. What is the difference between inbound and outbound passwords?

18. What is meant by token caching?

19. Identify the tools of ACL Manager. (Select all that apply.)

    A. Class Manager

    B. Optimizer

    C. CSAuth

    D. Diff Viewer

20. Which of the following is *not* a feature of Class Manager?

    A. It minimizes the time taken to make ACL changes.

    B. It minimizes the time taken to implement new ACLs.

    C. It improves the consistency of ACL usage in a network.

    D. It minimizes the time taken in identifying the devices affected when ACL filtering policies change.

21. The _____ allows an administrator to inspect the changes before they are actually implemented on the network.

    A. Class Manager

    B. Optimizer

    C. Downloader

    D. Diff Viewer

22. The _____ helps a network administrator in updating ACL changes on the network.

    A. Class Manager

    B. Optimizer

    C. Downloader

    D. Diff Viewer

23. Identify the components of the Graphical User Interface of Cisco Secure Policy Manager. (Select all that apply.)

    A. View Pane

    B. Optimizer

    C. Navigation toolbar

    D. Navigation Pane

24. Which of the following subsystems of the CSPM Server feature set collects all intermediate device-specific polices?

    A. Database

    B. Optimizer

    C. Generation

    D. Reporting

25. CSPM can be installed as _____, _____, and _____ system. (Choose three options.)

    A. Stand-alone

    B. Client/server

    C. Distributed

    D. Peer-to-peer

26. Identify the tasks performed by the Web-browser interface of Cisco Secure ACS. (Select all that apply.)

   A. Supporting unlimited Cisco network access servers

   B. Managing Telnet access to routers and switches

   C. Storing the system configuration information and the audit information

   D. Supporting token cards and servers

Answers to Chapter 15 Questions

1. Cisco ACL Manager stands for Cisco Access Control List Manager. It is an extension of CiscoWorks2000.

2. Yes. The ACL Manager is a multiuser application.

3. The tools of the ACL Manager are as follows: Class Manager, Template Manager, Optimizer, Job Browser, Hits Optimizer, Diff Viewer, and ACL Use Wizard.

4. The Class Manager provides information regarding networks, services, service classes, and network classes.

5. The Template Manager is used to create ACL templates, which improve the performance of the network.

6. The ACL Use Wizard is used to apply certain templates to the network.

7. The Diff Viewer allows an administrator to inspect the changes before they are actually implemented on the network.

8. The Cisco Secure Policy Manager is a system that implements security measures based on policies applied to the Cisco Firewall Virtual Private Network, IP Security, and Intrusion-Detection system sensors.

9. The features of the Cisco Secure Policy Manager are the view pane, navigation pane, navigation toolbar, status bar, and the main toolbar.

10. RADIUS stands for Remote Access Dial-In User Services.

11. TACACS+ stands for Terminal Access Controller Access Control System.

12. The Access Control Server is used to identify the users who have access to the network and the rights assigned to the users.

13. CHAP stands for Challenge Handshake Authenticate Protocol.

14. The three categories of ACS are as follows: Authentication, Authorization, and Accounting.

15. The five services of the Cisco Secure ACS are as follows: CS Admin, CS Auth, CS TACACS, CS Radius, and CS Log.

16. Cisco Secure provides support for two types of passwords: inbound and outbound.

17. Inbound passwords are supported by TACACS+ and RADIUS and stored in the Cisco Secure User database. Outbound passwords are the passwords that the Cisco Secure User database passes back to the NAS server and client.

18. In token caching, an ISDN user connects to a location by using the same OTP entered the first time the user was authenticated.

19. A, B, and C. ACL Manager offers following tools:
- Class Manager
- Template Manager
- Optimizer
- Job Browser
- Hits Optimizer
- Diff Viewer
- ACL Use Wizard

20. D. The benefits of Class Manager include
- It minimizes the time taken to make ACL changes.
- It minimizes the time taken to implement new ACLs.
- It improves the consistency of ACL usage in a network.

A Template manager minimizes the time taken in identifying the devices affected when ACL filtering policies change.

21. D. The Diff Viewer allows an administrator to inspect the changes before they are actually implemented on the network.

22. C. The Downloader helps a network administrator update ACL changes on the network.

23. A, C, and D. The GUI of CSPM has the following components:
- View Pane
- Navigation Pane
- Navigation toolbar
- Status bar
- Main toolbar

24. C. The generation subsystem collects all intermediate device-specific polices. It also modifies addresses for NAT.

25. A, B, and C. You can install CSPM as one of the following:
- Stand-alone system
- Client/server system
- Distributed system

26. A, B, and D. A Web-browser interface allows a variety of tasks that include

- Supporting unlimited Cisco network access servers
- Supporting token cards and servers
- Managing Cisco Secure ACS and NAS clients RADIUS and TACACS+ enabled
- Managing Telnet access to routers and switches
- Managing remote connections to VPDNs

Chapter 16 Questions

1. Which management tool is used to manage the Cisco PIX Firewall?

2. What is a Management Server?

3. What is a Management Client?

4. What is the maximum number of PIX Firewall units that can be managed by a PIX Firewall Manager?

5. What is the maximum number of hosts on which the PIX Firewall Manager monitors network traffic?

6. Can the PIX Firewall manage all versions of PIX Firewalls?

7. Name some versions of PIX Firewalls that can be managed by the PIX Firewall Manager.

8. How can you find out the version of your firewall?

9. What is the default port number of a Web server?

10. What is the range of port numbers available for a Web server?

11. What are the components of the Management Client window?

12. Which UDP port does the SYSLOG server use for listening SYSLOG messages?

13. What are VPN/Security Management solutions (VSM)?

14. What is a VPN monitor used for?

15. What is RME?

16. What is CiscoView?

17. Before installing VSM, which version of Service Pack should be applied on Windows NT?

18. You want to install VSM on a computer running Windows 2000. What is the recommended file system?

19. What is the minimum hard drive requirement for installing VSM on Windows 2000 and Windows NT?

20. Which of the following are components of the PIX Firewall Manager? (Select all that apply.)

    A. Management Server

    B. Server Manager

    C. Management Client

    D. Client Manager

21. Which one of the following is *not* a feature of PIX Firewall Manager?

    A. Allows configuration and management of up to 10 PIX Firewalls

    B. Graphically displays network traffic through firewall

    C. Generates report of NNTP and HTTP file transfer by the host

    D. Generates initial inbound and outbound connection statements in the PIX Firewall configuration

22. Which tabs are available in the Management Client? (Select all that apply.)

    A. Administrator tab

    B. Alarm and Report tab

    C. Client tab

    D. SYSLOG- Notification Settings tab

23. Which of the following is *not* a feature of VMS?

    A. Sends security alerts by using Cisco IDS

    B. Monitors L2TP and PPP remote access and IPSec-based site-to-site VPNs

    C. Provides a graphical view of VPN device configuration

    D. Allows deployment of perimeter security policies

24. Which of the following is *not* a component of VMS?

    A. Cisco Security Policy Manager

    B. VPN Monitor

    C. Resource Manager Essentials

    D. Cisco Viewer

25. Which one of the following does *not* appear on the CiscoWorks2000 desktop?

    A. Server configuration

    B. Client configuration

    C. Device Manager

    D. VPN Management Solution

Answers to Chapter 16 Questions

1. PIX Firewall Manager is the firewall management tool provided by Cisco. It is used to manage and configure multiple PIX Firewalls from a central location.

2. A Management Server is a Windows NT service that runs in the background and processes requests sent by the Management Client.

3. A Management Client is the system used to send requests to the Management Server.

4. The PIX Firewall Manager can manage up to 10 PIX Firewall units.

5. The PIX Firewall Manager provides information about network traffic passing through up to 50 hosts.

6. No. The PIX Firewall cannot manage all versions of PIX Firewalls.

7. The PIX Firewall Manager can manage firewalls that have the PIX Firewall Software version 4.3 or later.

8. You can type the `show version` command at the firewall console to display the version of firewall used.

9. The default port number is 8080.

10. The range of port numbers is from 1024 to 64000.

11. The Management Client window consists of tabs, the contents area, the PIX Firewall IP address area, and the main tree.

12. The SYSLOG server uses UDP port number 514 to listen to SYSLOG messages.

13. The VPN/ Security Management Solution provides a Web-based interface for monitoring and troubleshooting VPNs.

14. A VPN monitor is a Web-based VMS component for viewing and sorting information on site-to-site and remote-access VPNs.

15. Resource Manager Essentials (RME) provides the operational-management application features, such as software distribution, credentials management, device management, and SYSLOG analysis.

16. CiscoView is a Web-based graphical device-management application providing real-time device status and configuration functions.

17. Before installing VSM, apply Service Pack 6 on Windows NT.

18. The recommended file system is NTFS.

19. The minimum disk drive space required for installing VSM on Windows 2000 and Windows NT is 9GB.

20. A and C. The Management Server and Management Client are the components of PIX Firewall.

21. C. PIX Firewall does not generate reports of NNTP and HTTP file transferred by the host.

22. A, B, and D. The tabs available in the Management Client are the Administrator tab, Alarm and Report tab, and the SYSLOG Notification Settings tab.

23. B. The VMS does not monitor L2TP and PPP remote access and IPSec-based site-to-site VPNs.

24. A and D. The Cisco Security Policy Manager and Cisco Viewer are not components of VMS.

25. B. Client configuration does not appear on the CiscoWorks2000 desktop.

Chapter 17 Questions

1. Which of the following is *not* true for a client/server model?

    A. Management of resources is centralized.

    B. Security of the network is centralized.

    C. Permissions for centralized resources can be customized.

    D. Client computers need not depend on the administrator to perform administrative tasks.

2. Which of the following is *not* true for a peer-to-peer model?

    A. It is cost-effective to implement.

    B. Security of the network is centralized.

    C. It is easy to configure.

    D. Client computers need not depend on the administrator to perform administrative tasks.

3. Which of the following is an OSI Level 2 protocol that provides signaling, data transfer, and switching to route data to a desired destination at higher speeds and throughput rate?

    A. X.25

    B. Frame Relay

    C. SMDS

    D. SONET

4. Which of the following is public data network in which messages are transmitted in one or more fixed-length data packets by finding the best route for each packet?

    A. PSTN

    B. PPDN

    C. PSDN

    D. ISDN

5. Which of the following is *not* true for TCP/IP?

    A. TCP/IP provides reliable delivery of data.

    B. TCP/IP can support up to 20 million users.

    C. TCP/IP is entirely compatible with only selected network operating system.

    D. TCP/IP provides support for compression methods and encryption.

6. Which of the following servers maps a domain name to its corresponding IP address?

    A. DNS

    B. Database server

    C. File server

    D. Web database server

7. Identify the purposes for which an extranet can be used. (Select all that apply.)

    A. Share product information with business partners.

    B. Access services provided by one company to a group of other companies.

    C. Access services within the organization's network provided by a centralized server.

    D. Exchange information of mutual interest exclusively with partner companies.

8. Which of the following topologies consists of a single cable that connects all the computers in the network?

    A. Bus

    B. Ring

    C. Token Ring

    D. Star

9. Which of the following is *not* a feature of the Bus topology?

   A. It is simple, reliable, and easy to implement.

   B. It requires the least amount of cable (as compared to other topologies) and therefore is cost-efficient.

   C. No bandwidth wastage in signals from different computers interrupting each other.

   D. One faulty node does not affect the performance of the other nodes.

10. Which of the following is *not* a feature of ring topology?

   A. Each computer is given equal access to the token, and therefore no single computer can monopolize the network.

   B. It requires the least amount of cable (compared to other topologies) and therefore is cost-efficient.

   C. No bandwidth wastage in signals from different computers interrupting each other.

   D. The bandwidth saved can be used for time-sensitive features like audio and video.

11. In which of the following topologies are all computers connected to a central computer called hub?

   A. Bus

   B. Ring

   C. Star

   D. Token Ring

12. Which of the following is *not* a feature of Star topology?

   A. It is easy to add nodes to a Star network.

   B. It is easy to detect cable faults.

   C. One faulty node does not affect the performance of the other nodes.

   D. A faulty hub does not affect the performance of the network.

13. Which of the following mediums consists of two conductors that share the same axis?

   A. Coaxial

   B. Twisted-pair

   C. Fiber-optic

   D. Infrared

14. Which of the following categories of UTP supports up to 20Mbps of transmission speed?

    A. Category 1

    B. Category 2

    C. Category 3

    D. Category 4

15. Which of the following categories of UTP are referred to as data-grade cables? (Select all that apply.)

    A. Category 2

    B. Category 3

    C. Category 4

    D. Category 5

16. Which of the following categories of UTP is least susceptible to crosstalk?

    A. Category 2

    B. Category 3

    C. Category 4

    D. Category 5

17. Which of the following is *not* a feature of fiber-optic cable?

    A. It can transmit data safely at a rate that can vary from around 100Mbps to 2Gbps.

    B. It does not require expertise to implement fiber-optic cable.

    C. It is much lighter and thinner than copper cables.

    D. It is more resistant to attenuation and outside interference.

18. Which of the following leased line link is a 1.544Mbps dedicated link and consists of 24 multiplexed channels?

    A. T1 link

    B. T2 link

    C. T3 link

    D. T4 link

19. Which of the following 10Mbps Ethernet uses thick coaxial, or thicknet, cabling and Bus topology?

    A. 10Base2

    B. 10Base5

    C. 10BaseT

    D. 10BaseF

20. Which 10Mbps Ethernet is primarily used when the distance between the repeaters is large?

    A. 10Base2

    B. 10Base5

    C. 10BaseT

    D. 10BaseF

21. Which technology is also referred to as cell relay?

    A. Ethernet

    B. Token Ring

    C. FDDI

    D. ATM

22. A _____ is a device that connects two LANs.

    A. Repeater

    B. Hub

    C. Bridge

    D. Modem

23. Which of the following is a combination of a hub and a bridge?

    A. Repeater

    B. Switch

    C. Gateway

    D. Modem

24. Which of the following is not supported by configuration management?

    A. Managing the current network configuration

    B. Storing the data to maintain an up-to-date inventory of all network devices

    C. Isolating the cause of the fault

    D. Generating reports based on the configuration information collected

25. The term _____ refers to any device capable of communicating status information.

    A. Managed nodes

    B. Management stations

    C. Management nodes

    D. Managed stations

26. Which of the following is *not* true for SNMP?

   A. SNMP is a relatively simple network management protocol and does not place a major load on the existing network.

   B. SNMP uses ciphertext for security.

   C. Major vendors of internetworking hardware, such as bridges and routers, design their products to support SNMP, making it very easy to implement.

   D. If the response to a request exceeds the UDP packet size limit, no management information is made available to the management station.

27. Which of the following is *not* true for RMON?

   A. RMON uses SNMP to monitor the basic operations.

   B. RMON requires a dedicated technician on-site.

   C. RMON allows a variety of management stations and agents from different vendors to communicate with each other over the same network.

   D. RMON allows history of performance to be maintained for each segment.

28. Which of the following is *not* a type of Protocol Data Unit?

   A. Reads

   B. Writes

   C. Traps

   D. Responses

Answers to Chapter 17 Questions

1. D. In a client/server model, the client computers depend on the administrator to perform administrative tasks.

2. B. In a peer-to-peer model, each individual on the network is responsible for the security of his/her computer. Therefore the security of the network suffers even if one of the peer computers on the network doesn't take adequate precautionary measures.

3. B. Frame Relay is a Data Link-layer protocol (OSI level 2), which provides signaling, data transfer, and switching to route data to a desired destination at higher speeds and throughput rate. Frame Relay defines a DTE/DCE interface that can multiplex many virtual circuits over a single physical transmission link.

4. C. Packet Switched Data Network is a public data network in which messages are transmitted in one or more fixed-length data packets by finding the best route for each packet.

5. C. TCP/IP is entirely compatible with almost every network operating system.

6. A. A Domain Name Server (DNS) maps the name of the domain with its corresponding IP address.

7. A, B, and D. Companies can use an extranet to

   • Share product catalogs with business partners

   • Collaborate with other companies on joint development and training efforts

   • Provide or access services provided by one company to a group of other companies (such as an online banking application managed by one company on behalf of affiliated banks)

   • Exchange information of mutual interest exclusively with partner companies

8. A. Bus topology consists of a single cable that connects all the computers in the network. It is also known as linear Bus because all the computers are connected in a single line. The single cable that connects the computers is also known as the backbone or the segment.

9. A and B. Bus topology is simple, reliable, easy to implement, and requires the least amount of cable (as compared to other topologies).

10. B. Ring topology consists of a cable that connects all the computers in a ring and requires more cable than the Bus topology.

11. C. Star topology consists of various computers connected to one central component called the hub.

12. D. Because Star topology consists of various computers connected to one central hub, a faulty hub brings the entire network to a halt.

13. A. A coaxial cable consists of two conductors that share the same axis.

14. D. Category 4 of UTP supports up to 20Mbps of transmission speed.

15. B, C, and D. Categories 3, 4, and 5 are data-grade cables. They consist of either four or eight wires enclosed in a jacket. A cable with four wires is referred to as two-pair wire or a four-core cable, and a cable with eight wires is referred to as four-pair wire or an eight-core cable.

16. D. The Teflon outer cover and the higher number of twists per centimeter make Category 5 cable less susceptible to crosstalk.

17. B. Fiber-optic cabling requires skilled people to handle it.

18. A. One of the most popular methods of interconnecting offices is a T1 link. This is a 1.544Mbps dedicated link that consists of 24 multiplexed channels. The analog signals from the 24 channels are fed into a codec (coder/decoder) one at a time. The T1 link uses time division multiplexing.

19. B. 10Base5 uses thick coaxial, or thicknet, cabling and Bus topology.

20. D. 10BaseF is primarily used when the distance between repeaters is large, for example, between buildings.

21. D. ATM, also referred to as cell relay, is a technology that can be implemented in a WAN.

22. C. A bridge is a device that connects two LANs.

23. B. Switches are a combination of hubs and bridges. Their appearance is similar to hubs.

24. C. Configuration management is the process of obtaining data from the network to manage the current network configuration, store the data to maintain an up-to-date inventory of all network devices, and produce reports based on the configuration information collected.

25. A. A *managed node* is a device capable of communicating status information. A managed node can fall into any of three categories:

- Host systems (which include workstations, mainframes, terminal servers, and printers)
- Router systems
- Media devices (which include bridges, repeaters, hubs, and analyzers)

26. B. SNMP uses cleartext for security. This makes the protocol quite insecure.

27. B. RMON does not require IS managers to travel to remote sites, nor does it require a dedicated technician on-site. It allows network managers to gather and analyze network data from remote sites at a centralized location.

28. C. The management station and the managed device interact by passing message units called Protocol Data Units (PDUs). These PDUs can be of the following types:

- Reads
- Writes
- Traversal operations
- Responses

Chapter 18 Questions

1. Which OSI layer interacts with the user?

    A. Application layer

    B. Presentation layer

    C. Session layer

    D. Physical layer

2. Which OSI layer interacts with the hardware?

    A. Application layer

    B. Presentation layer

    C. Session layer

    D. Physical layer

3. Which OSI layer provides a service-interface to the Network layer?

   A. Application layer

   B. Presentation layer

   C. Data Link layer

   D. Physical layer

4. Which topology implements acknowledged connectionless service?

   A. Bus

   B. Star

   C. Ring

   D. Token Ring

5. ATM and Frame Relay use _____ service for data transmission.

   A. Unacknowledged connectionless

   B. Unacknowledged connection-oriented

   C. Acknowledged connection-oriented

   D. Acknowledged connectionless

6. TCP/IP networks use _____ service for data transmission.

   A. Unacknowledged connectionless

   B. Unacknowledged connection-oriented

   C. Acknowledged connection-oriented

   D. Acknowledged connectionless

7. Which OSI layer computes a checksum for each frame and attaches the checksum to the trailer of the frame before transmitting it?

   A. Application layer

   B. Presentation layer

   C. Data Link layer

   D. Physical layer

8. Which of the following methods is *not* used for breaking data into frames?

   A. Character count

   B. Character stuffing

   C. Bit stuffing

   D. Bit count

9. In which of the following methods is the size of the frame included in the header of the frame?

    A. Character count

    B. Character stuffing

    C. Bit stuffing

    D. Bit count

10. Which of the following methods inserts an ASCII character sequence at the beginning and at the end of the frame?

    A. Character count

    B. Character stuffing

    C. Bit stuffing

    D. Bit count

11. Which of the following methods adds a flag byte at the beginning and end of the frame?

    A. Character count

    B. Character stuffing

    C. Bit stuffing

    D. Bit count

12. Which of the following is defined as the process of sending data from a source to a destination through a set of intermediate devices?

    A. Framing

    B. Character stuffing

    C. Bit stuffing

    D. Switching

13. Which of the following involves the establishment of a dedicated communication path between two stations?

    A. Framing

    B. Circuit switching

    C. Message switching

    D. Packet switching

14. Which of the following is *not* a feature of message switching?

    A. Messages can be temporarily stored on an intermediate node.

    B. Copies of the message can be made by the node and then forwarded.

    C. It is well suited for interactive applications or for real-time traffic.

    D. Priorities can be assigned to messages.

15. Which of the following is best suited for networks where the volume of traffic is relatively high?

    A. Framing

    B. Circuit switching

    C. Message switching

    D. Packet switching

16. The Data Link layer passes the frames to the _____ layer for transmission.

    A. Application layer

    B. Presentation layer

    C. Data Link layer

    D. Physical layer

17. Which of the following OSI layers provides its services to the Transport layer and the Data Link layer?

    A. Application layer

    B. Presentation layer

    C. Network layer

    D. Physical layer

18. In _____, each packet received by the router is sent on every outgoing line except the incoming line.

    A. Flooding

    B. Shortest Path Routing

    C. Distance vector routing

    D. Multicast routing

19. In _____, a table is maintained for giving the best path to reach the different destinations.

    A. Flooding

    B. Shortest Path Routing

    C. Distance vector routing

    D. Multicast routing

20. Which of the following methods involves sending packets to all hosts attached to the network?

    A. Flooding

    B. Broadcast routing

    C. Distance vector routing

    D. Multicast routing

21. Which of the following methods involves sending packets to a select group of computers?

   A. Flooding

   B. Broadcast routing

   C. Distance vector routing

   D. Multicast routing

22. Which of the following layers provides services to the Session layer?

   A. Network layer

   B. Presentation layer

   C. Data Link layer

   D. Transport layer

23. Which of the following services is not provided by the Session layer?

   A. Data exchange

   B. Dialog management

   C. Synchronization

   D. Congestion control

24. Which of the following layers is concerned with the syntax and semantics of the message being transmitted?

   A. Network layer

   B. Presentation layer

   C. Data Link layer

   D. Transport layer

25. Which of the following layers sends the data to the receiving computer in the form of bits — 0s and 1s?

   A. Network layer

   B. Physical layer

   C. Application layer

   D. Transport layer

26. Which of the following protocols does not operate at the Data Link layer?

   A. ARP

   B. SLIP

   C. PPP

   D. HDLC

27. Which of the following protocols is also known as connectionless transport protocol?

    A. ARP

    B. UDP

    C. PPP

    D. TCP

Answers to Chapter 18 Questions

1. A. Of the seven OSI layers, the Application layer interacts with the user.

2. D. Of the seven OSI layers, the Physical layer interacts with the hardware.

3. C. The Data Link layer performs the following functions:

    • Providing a service-interface to the Network layer

    • Framing

    • Switching

    • Error detection and recovery

    • Flow control

4. D. Token Ring implements acknowledged connectionless service. The acknowledged connectionless service consists of the source computer sending the data without establishing a connection. But in this case, the receiver sends back an acknowledgment for every frame that it receives. If the sender does not receive an acknowledgment within a stipulated time, the packet is retransmitted.

5. B. ATM and Frame Relay use unacknowledged connection-oriented service for data transmission.

6. C. TCP/IP networks implement acknowledged connection-oriented service. A typical example for such a communication is the dial-up connection for the Web browsing. In this, the user first connects to the server of the ISP to establish a path and then communicates with the server over this path during the period of connection.

7. C. The Data Link layer organizes the data into frames to make it more manageable and adds control information for error detection and correction. It computes a checksum for each frame, attaches the checksum to the trailer of the frame, and transmits it. When data is received by the receiver, it again computes the checksum and compares it with the checksum in the frame. If they differ, then an error is reported and the frames are retransmitted.

8. D. Different methods by which data is broken into frames include

- Character count

- Character stuffing

- Bit stuffing

9. A. The character count method includes the size of the frame in the header of the frame.

10. B. Character stuffing inserts an ASCII character sequence at the beginning and at the end of the frame.

11. C. In bit-stuffing a bit pattern called the *flag byte* is added at the beginning and end of the frame.

12. D. Switching can be defined as the process of sending data from a source to a destination through a set of intermediate devices. These intermediate devices are also referred to as switches. Data is transmitted from one station to the other by being routed through a network of nodes.

13. B. Circuit switching involves establishment of a dedicated communication path between two stations. The path is composed of a sequence of links between the source and the destination. A typical example of circuit switching is the telephone network.

14. C. Message switching is not suited for interactive applications or for real-time traffic because of the delay. It is also unsuitable for voice connections.

15. D. Packet switching is a technique that attempts to combine the best features of circuit switching and message switching. It gives the best advantages when used in a network where the volume of traffic is relatively high.

16. D. The Data Link layer creates the frames and passes them to the Physical layer for transmission. At the other end, the Physical layer on the receiver's computer accepts the frame and passes it to the Data Link layer.

17. C. Network layer is the third layer of the OSI model. It provides its services to the Transport layer and also the Data Link layer.

18. A. In flooding, every packet received by the router is sent on every outgoing line except the incoming line.

19. C. The distance vector routing algorithm method consists of maintaining a table giving the best path to reach the different destinations. These tables are exchanged between routers. The measurement may be in terms of distance, delay, and traffic.

20. B. Broadcasting refers to sending packets to all hosts attached to the network.

21. D. Multicasting is the process of sending packets to a select group of computers. The algorithm used to achieve multicasting is called multicasting algorithm.

22. D. The Transport layer provides its services to the Session layer.

23. D. Congestion control is provided by the Transport layer. The Session layer provides services to the layer above it, the Presentation layer. The services provided include

- Data exchange

- Dialog management

- Synchronization

- Activity management

- Exception reporting

24. B. The Presentation layer is concerned with the syntax and semantics of the message being transmitted.

25. B. The Physical layer does not add any header information to the packet. It sends data to the receiving computer in the form of bits — zeros and ones. The Physical layer is the only layer that interacts directly with its counterpart on the receiving computer.

26. A. ARP is a Network-layer protocol.

27. B. User Data Protocol (UDP) is a connectionless transport protocol. It does not guarantee delivery, nor does it guarantee duplicate protection.

✦   ✦   ✦

Lab Exercises

This appendix of exercises based on Chapters 5, 6, 8, and 9 tests your practical knowledge of configuring access lists, CBAC, routers, and PIX Firewall.

Chapter 5 Labs

The first two labs from Chapter 5 demonstrate how to create access lists that perform specific tasks: One denies access to hosts on a specified router and the other prevents ping traffic. The next two labs demonstrate how to create IPX and extended IPX access lists.

Lab 5-1: Denying access to hosts on a specific router

Create an access list that denies access to any host on the router with IP address 223.8.151.5.

1. Open Cisco HyperTerminal and enter privileged mode in global configuration mode.

2. In the notepad, enter the following commands:

   ```
   no access-list 1
   access-list 1 deny 223.8.151.5
   access-list 1 permit any
   ```

3. Save this file.

4. In the Cisco HyperTerminal window, right-click the Router prompt and choose Paste to Host.

5. To enter the Interface mode, type

   ```
   int e0
   ```

6. To apply the access list, type

   ```
   ip access-group 1 out
   ```

Lab 5-2: Preventing ping traffic

Create an access list that prevents `ping` traffic originating from node 205.7.5.7 on Router A from reaching host 223.8.151.3 on Router C.

1. Enter privileged mode in the global configuration mode of Router C.

2. In the notepad, enter the following commands:

```
no access list 101
access-list 101 deny tcp host 205.7.5.7
  host 223.8.151.3 eq icmp
access-list 101 permit icmp any any
```

3. Save this file.

4. In the Cisco HyperTerminal window, right-click the Router prompt and choose Paste to Host.

5. To enter the Interface mode, type

```
int e0
```

6. To apply the access list, type

```
ip access-group 101 out
```

Lab 5-3: Creating an IPX access list

Create an IPX Extended list that denies access to your network to all traffic from D0.

1. Enter the privileged mode in configuration mode.

2. In the notepad, enter the following commands:

```
no access list 801
access-list 801 deny D0 A0
access-list 801 permit -1 -1
```

3. Save this file.

4. In the Cisco HyperTerminal window, right-click the Router prompt and choose Paste to Host.

5. To enter the Interface mode, type

```
int e0
```

6. To apply the access list, type

```
ipx access-group 801 in
```

Lab 5-4: Creating an Extended IPX list

Create an Extended IPX list that blocks all IPX traffic from all sockets of a network with IPX address A0 from reaching your network on any socket.

1. Enter privileged mode in configuration mode.

2. In the notepad, enter the following commands:

```
no access list 901
access-list 901 deny    -1 A0 0 DE 0
access-list 901 permit -1 -1 0 -1 0
```

3. Save this file.

4. In the Cisco HyperTerminal window, right-click the Router prompt and choose Paste to Host.

5. To enter the Interface mode, type

```
int e0
```

6. To apply the access list, type

```
ipx access-group 901 in
```

Chapter 6 Lab

Configure E0 of your router as the inside interface and S0 as the outside interface. (Use `192.168.1.0/24` network for E0 and `10.1.1.0/24` for S0.) Also configure a dynamic pool of addresses, ranging from `172.16.1.1` to `172.16.1.254` so the pool is allocated to inside addresses. Use access-list mapping as you create the dynamic pool of IP addresses.

1. Go to the interface configuration mode of interface `Ethernet 0` and execute the following commands to specify it as the inside interface:

```
ip address 192.168.1.10 255.255.255.0
ip nat inside
```

2. Go to the interface configuration mode of interface S0 and execute the following commands to specify it as the outside interface:

```
ip address 10.1.1.10 255.255.255.0
ip nat outside
```

3. Go to the global configuration mode to create a standard access list that specifies the range of inside hosts:

```
access-list 1 permit 192.168.1.0 0.0.0.255
```

4. Go to the global configuration mode to create a dynamic pool of inside global addresses and create the mapping of access list 1 with this pool:

```
ip nat pool dynamic-lab 172.16.1.1 172.16.1.254
 netmask 255.255.255.0
ip nat inside source list 1 pool dynamic-lab
```

Chapter 8 Lab

Configure CBAC to provide security while permitting internal users to listen to songs from the Internet. (The application protocol is RealAudio.) Keep the timeout as 30 seconds. Apply this CBAC on interface E0, which is the internal interface.

1. Go to the router's global configuration mode and execute the following commands (in the given sequence) to create the CBAC inspection rule:

```
ip inspect name labtest realaudio timeout 30
```

2. Go to the interface-configuration mode of interface Ethernet 0 and execute the following command to apply the CBAC:

```
ip inspect labtest in
```

3. Go to privileged exec mode and execute the following commands to verify the access list:

```
show ip inspect config
show ip inspect interfaces
```

Chapter 9 Lab

Configure PIX Firewall to have a global pool of IP addresses from the range 192.168.1.100 to 192.168.1.200. Then configure the address translation of all internal IP addresses to this pool of addresses. (The internal IP addresses are in the range 172.17.0.100 to 172.17.0.200.)

1. Go to the configuration mode of PIX Firewall and execute the following command to configure the global pool of addresses:

```
global (outside) 1 192.168.1.100-192.168.1.200
```

2. Execute the following command to enable address translation of the internal IP address to the pool of addresses configured in Step 1:

```
nat (inside) 172.17.0.0 255.255.255.0
```

3. To view the translation when communication is occurring between the internal and external hosts, use the following command in privileged mode:

```
show xlate
```

✦   ✦   ✦

Glossary

Access control Measures taken to protect computer or network resources by restricting access.

Access list Common term for *access-control list (ACL)*, an electronic listing of users and groups — and their specific permissions to access network resources — used in packet filtering.

Accounting management The process of measuring the usage of network resources by users to determine costs, bill users, and set quotas.

ACSE Association Control Service Element, an Application-layer protocol that applications use to communicate with each other.

Acknowledged connection-oriented service A service in which the sender establishes a connection with a receiver and then sends frames; the receiver sends back an acknowledgment for every frame it receives.

Acknowledged connectionless service A service in which a source computer sends data without establishing a connection with a destination computer. The receiver sends back an acknowledgment for every frame it receives.

Active hub A network hub that regenerates a signal before retransmitting it, as does a repeater.

ActiveX A set of object-oriented program technologies and tools developed by Microsoft; its most familiar products are *ActiveX controls*, small programs that can be written once and deployed anywhere. Because ActiveX allows software components to interact with each other on a network, network administrators should regulate the use of ActiveX to avoid security problems.

Address Resolution Protocol (ARP) A protocol that maps an IP address to a computer's address on a local network.

Advanced Encryption Standard (AES) The replacement algorithm for the Data-Encryption Standard (DES). AES has key lengths of 128, 192, and 256 bits; DES has a 56-bit key.

Alert A message that describes a network event (for example, an attempted access) relevant to network function or security.

Algorithm Mathematical representation of a series of steps used to complete a task (for example, the encryption of data).

Alternate name The X.509v3 certificate extension that contains a user-friendly name of the entity, such as an e-mail address in addition to the subject name. The use of alternate names in X.509v3 certificates helps identify the entity without referring to the X.500 directory.

American National Standards Institute (ANSI) The organization that guides development of technology standards in the United States.

American Wire Gauge (AWG) A system of naming standard thickness values for wire. The AWG number decreases as the thickness of the wire increases.

Amplifier In networking, a device that amplifies an incoming signal — and its accompanying noise — by using analog technology.

Analog repeater Device that amplifies and re-sends analog signals to help them reach faraway destinations.

ANS.1 Abstract Syntax Notation 1, a standard set by ISO (International Standards Organization) for defining data structures.

Anti-replay service A service that blocks replay-type hacks by tagging a unique sequence number to every IP packet transmitted over a secure network. On the receiving end, the sequence number of the IP packet is checked to validate whether the sequence number falls within the allowed range. If not, the packet is blocked.

Application-coupled security Security measures imposed on an application itself or built into the Transport layer of the OSI model.

Application-layer attacks Attacks targeting the services that operate on the Application layer of the OSI model.

Application-layer firewall Server set up as a proxy server to inspect data at the Application layer; its functions include intercepting and checking packets sent by outside users, and forwarding such packets to the appropriate application at an internal location. As a result, the outside users don't have direct access to internal resources behind the firewall.

ARA AppleTalk Remote Access, an Apple Computer networking protocol (also known as *ARAP*).

Asymmetric encryption Encryption according to a concept of *key rings*—matched pairs of encryption/decryption codes set up as a public key and a private key. A public key is published widely and used to encrypt data packets before sending; only the designated owner knows the private key (which decrypts the data).

ATM Asynchronous transfer mode (also referred to as *cell relay*), a technology that transmits data as small, fixed-size packets (cells) of 53 bytes each. ATM is a network architecture often found on WANs.

Attachment A file sent to a user via an e-mail message.

Attack An attempt to avoid network-security measures and gain unauthorized access to a network.

Attribute certificates Certificates that contain the entity's attribute information.

Audit Assessment of activities to ensure compliance with security policy and procedures.

Authentication A process that serves to validate the integrity of the user who is attempting to access the network.

Authentication header A string of code attached to an IP datagram to ensure data integrity, provide a basis for authentication, and help ensure nonrepudiation.

Authority Revocation List (ARL) CRL that contains revocation information about CA (Certificate Authority) certificates. The ARL is issued by the same Certificate Authority that issues CA certificates.

Authorization The permission required to access resources on a network. Authorization has a close connection with authentication. When authenticated, a user is authorized to access the resources.

Autonomous system (AS) A stand-alone subnetwork considered as part of the Internet.

Bandwidth Data-carrying capacity, measured as data speed in bits per second.

Bastion host A host that intercepts incoming and outgoing data on a network. A bastion host also serves as a gatekeeper system that can accept access by outsiders without endangering the internal network.

Biometrics Using biological properties to identify individuals—for example, fingerprints, retina scans, and voice recognition.

Bit A digit (either 1 or 0) in binary code.

Bit stuffing A framing method in which a bit pattern called the *flag byte* is added at the beginning and end of the frame so the packet conforms to a uniform size.

Block A sequence of bits of fixed length.

Block cipher A symmetric cipher that encrypts and decrypts blocks of messages.

BNC connector A device used to connect coaxial cables to computers.

BNC T-connectors A device used for connecting two cables to a network interface card.

BNC terminator A device attached to the end of a bus cable to absorb stray signals.

Border Gateway Protocol (BGP) An exterior gateway routing protocol used for exchanging routing information between gateway hosts.

Bridge A device that connects two similar or dissimilar LANs.

Broadcast routing A routing method that sends a packet to all hosts attached to a network.

Broadcast storm A popular denial-of-service (DoS) attack method in which a large number of packets are introduced into the network, all showing a destination address that doesn't exist. The goal of such an attack is to tie up the server's processor and prevent legitimate traffic from getting through.

Brouter A combination of a bridge and a router. A bridge connects two LANs that use the same protocol. A router connects two or more LANs and uses protocols to govern the connection. A brouter, therefore, can handle communication processes both within a network and between networks.

Brute-force attacks Attacks performed using an application that runs across the network to log in to a shared resource.

Buffer-overflow attack Also known as *stack overflow*, a buffer-overflow attack identifies bugs in the applications running on the server and attacks them. As a result, the application overlays the system areas such as the system stack, and the hacker gains administrative rights on the system.

Bus topology Consists of a single cable that connects all the computers in the network.

CA certificate Certificate issued to a Certificate Authority to establish its legitimacy on the network, included as an electronic credential in the packets it sends.

CA Signature algorithm An algorithm used by the Certificate Authority to sign the CA certificate.

CCR (Commitment, Concurrency, and Recovery) A protocol in the Application layer, used by applications to communicate with each other.

Centralized network management architecture A network design that places the network management platform on a single computer with a centralized database.

Certificate Distribution Center (CDS) Name given to the online system that distributes certificates and users' private keys.

Certificate request A request made to a CA to issue a certificate.

Certificate Authority (CA) An authoritative agency responsible for managing security credentials and public keys. It is a part of the Public-Key Infrastructure. The user sends the request for a digital request to the Certificate Authority. The Certificate Authority then checks the information provided by the requestor with a Registration Authority. After the RA verifies the information, the CA issues the digital certificate to the requestor.

Certificate Revocation List (CRL) A digitally signed data structure that lists all certificates issued but revoked by a CA. Although these certificates have not expired, they are no longer valid.

Challenge-Handshake Authentication Protocol (CHAP) An authentication technique in which the server establishes a connection with a requestor and sends a challenge to him or her. The requestor then sends the value obtained by using a one-way hash function. The server compares this hash value with the expected hash value. If there is any kind of mismatch, the connection is terminated.

Challenge-response An authentication technique that prompts the user (challenge) to provide private information (response). Security systems that rely on smart cards implement challenge-response. In this case the user is provided with a unique code and can be asked to enter this code at any time. After the user enters this code, he or she is provided another code that the user should use when he or she logs in again.

Character count A framing method that includes the size of the frame in the header of the frame.

Character stuffing A framing method that inserts an ASCII character sequence at the beginning and end of the frame.

Character User Interface (CUI) A simple computer interface that a user controls by entering characters (that is, text).

Checksum The count of the number of bits in a transmission unit. This count is included with the unit to confirm that the transmission was complete and no data corruption occurred. The sender computes a checksum before sending the data. The receiver computes the checksum when the data is received. If the count matches, the transmission was complete.

Circuit switching Switching scheme that establishes a dedicated communication path between two stations.

Cisco Secure ACS for Unix (CSUNIX) Protects a network from unauthorized users by authenticating all users against a database of user and group profiles.

Cisco Secure ACS for Windows NT (CSNT) Uses a Windows NT service to manage authentication, authorization, and accounting of users on the network.

Cisco Secure Policy Manager (CSPM) A system that implements security according to the policies applied to the Cisco Firewall Virtual Private Network, IP security, and the sensors of the intrusion-detection system.

Cleartext Messages that have not been encrypted, also known as *plaintext*.

Client In the *client/server model*, the computer that sends requests to the server. For example, a user sending print jobs to the print server is actually requesting that the print server print the document.

Client/server model Network design that uses a *server* to share data and resources among several *client* computers. The clients send requests to the server and the server accepts or rejects these requests. After the request is accepted, the server processes the request.

Closed security policy A security policy that provides maximum security against all security threats, with emphasis on security monitoring and auditing. Often such a policy also entails minimum user convenience and makes business harder to transact.

CMIP A network management protocol designed to build on SNMP. The basic design of CMIP is similar to SNMP, whereby PDUs are employed as variables to monitor a network. CMIP contains 11 types of PDUs (compared to SNMP's five).

Coaxial cable Also abbreviated as *coax,* this cable consists of two (often concentric) conductors that share the same longitudinal axis.

Collaborative computing A system that provides platforms for group discussions and conferencing for the employees, irrespective of the geographical location of the users.

Common Gateway Interface (CGI) An interface used by a Web server to a transfer user's request to an application program and to send data back to the user. CGI has a number of security flaws, such as insecure file permissions that must be fixed before using it on a secure network.

Compression The process of reducing the size of a plaintext file by using a compression algorithm. This process takes place after fragmentation but before encryption.

Compression algorithm An algorithm used to compress plaintext.

Compromise In relation to network security, a compromise refers to a situation wherein a system has been invaded or intruded.

Compulsory tunneling A tunneling method in which a computer between the client computer and the server or a network device creates a secure tunnel on behalf of the client computer.

Confidential data Data strictly meant for use within the organization.

Confidentiality Keeping information private and secret so unauthorized parties cannot access or use it.

Configuration management The process of obtaining data from the network to manage the current network configuration, store the data to maintain an up-to-date inventory of all network devices, and produce reports according to the configuration information collected.

Content scanning or screening Reviewing the information that would be displayed on an end-user's screen while he or she is using a specific Internet application (for example, screening the content in e-mail messages).

Context-Based Access Control (CBAC) A stateful packet-inspection system, CBAC is an important component of Cisco IOS Firewall. CBAC filters and inspects network traffic, issuing alerts and establishing audit trails to keep tabs on network transactions and their contexts.

Conventional leased lines Analog lines that work on a single pair of telephone lines and offer a reliable medium for information transfer. Transfer speed ranges from 2.4Kbps to 19.2Kbps.

Cracker A person who indulges in criminal activities using other people's computers — in particular, cracking security codes.

Crypto engine Software used for encryption.

Cryptography A mechanism that involves converting data into unreadable form (encryption) for security purposes and then deciphering it (decryption). The data is encrypted using the public key, and only the person who possesses the secret key for the public key used for encryption can decrypt the message.

Cryptosystem The infrastructure for cryptography, which comprises an encryption/ decryption algorithm, plaintexts, ciphertexts, and keys.

Data diddling A security attack that involves capturing, modifying, and corrupting data on a trusted host.

Data-Encryption Standard (DES) A cryptographic algorithm approved by the National Bureau of Standards and Technology (NIST), published in Federal Information Processing Standards (FIPS) 46, mainly for government and public use. See also *AES*.

Data Link layer Second layer in the OSI model, which gives network services a consistent interface to the Network layer.

Database server Server that maintains a database — reading, writing, and storing useful data to share with all clients that access the server.

Decipher To convert encrypted data to readable and usable data.

Decryption The process of retrieving the original message from its encrypted form.

Demilitarized zone (DMZ) Network placed between a protected internal network and an untrusted external network. The DMZ has its own front-end servers, back-end servers, and firewalls, serving as an additional layer of security.

Denial-of-service (DoS) attack Attempted attack that uses an application to overload a server's processor with false requests. After a while, system resources are too busy dealing with false requests to process genuine requests — in effect, denying service to legitimate users.

Diffie-Hellman algorithm Algorithm used most commonly for key exchange — a process that does not exchange keys themselves but rather the information needed to generate identical keys.

Digest The output obtained after applying a hash algorithm to data.

Digested data A field displaying content type, as defined by standards such as PKCS#7.

Digital certificate A certificate of identity (such as an ID card) that binds the identity information with the public key.

Digital repeaters Devices that reconstruct a digital signal to its original level of quality before resending it.

Digital Signature Standard (DSS) A standard algorithm developed by the U.S. National Security Agency (NSA) in 1994 for creating digital signatures.

Digital signatures The result of encrypting a message hash by using the private key of the sender. This is proof of the integrity and authentication of the message.

Digital Subscriber Line (DSL) A technology that uses sophisticated modulation schemes to pack data onto existing copper phone lines.

Digital timestamp The process of signing a document to specify the time of its creation.

Directory Service Agents (DSA) Databases that maintain and store information of an organization per the X.500 directory standard. They can also contain information about multiple organizations.

Directory service server An X.500-compliant server on which all certificates are published in a directory-style list.

Directory User Agent (DUA) An intermediary between the user and the directory database to retrieve information from the directory.

Distance-vector routing algorithm method A dynamic routing method that involves maintaining a table of best paths to various destinations. The measurement may be in terms of distance, delay, and traffic. These tables are exchanged between routers.

Distinguished name (DN) A unique name assigned to each entity in a directory.

Distributed key A key split up into many parts and shared (distributed) among different participants. See also *Secret sharing*.

Distributed network management architecture A network design that uses multiple peer platforms. Each peer platform has a complete database of its own for devices on the particular network segment. Any report can be sent to the central computer.

DNS spoofing DNS spoofing is the process by which one breaches the trust relationship by portraying a DNS name of another system. This is usually done by either corrupting the name service cache of a system or by compromising a domain name server for a valid domain.

Domain A collection of hosts belonging to an organization or otherwise logically related as a subnetwork.

Domain Name System (DNS) A service used on the Internet to resolve user-friendly names into their corresponding IP addresses.

Dynamic address translation The administrator defines a pool of global addresses to be shared among local users when there are more users than available global IP addresses — and configures the system to use these shared addresses in times of heavy network traffic.

Dynamic NAT A security measure that provides users with access to the Internet while conserving registered IP addresses and hiding the actual IP addresses of network resources.

Dynamic routing A routing method in which each router decides its own best path to another computer and updates that path periodically.

Eavesdropping When an unwanted party listens to a conversation of two communicating parties without their consent. In networking, this happens electronically.

E-business Business transactions conducted over the Internet; includes buying, selling, and providing services.

E-commerce Commercial transactions conducted over the Internet.

E-mail Messages sent electronically from one person to another via the Internet.

Encapsulated Security Payload (ESP) A method of providing unencrypted packets as vehicles for encrypted packets to maintain confidentiality for IP datagrams transmitted over the Internet.

Encryption The process of converting plaintext to ciphertext. See also *ciphertext*.

Enveloped data A content type field as defined by PKCS#7.

Ethernet A protocol developed by Xerox Corporation (with help from DEC and Intel) in 1976. It defines a cabling scheme for local-area networks and supports data-transfer rates of up to 100Mbps.

Executable A special file that acts like an application and can be run on the computer. An executable file can be (for example) a Java applet, application, or virus.

Expiry date The date on which a digital certificate will expire.

Extensions Additional attributes stored in a certificate or a CRL. These were introduced in X.509 v3 certificates and v2 CRL.

External revocation request A certificate-revocation request made to a CA by an entity other than the subject of the certificate.

Extranet An intranet partially accessible to authorized outsiders.

Extranet VPN Virtual private network that connects an organization with its business associates, suppliers, and customers.

Fault management A process of locating and correcting network problems or faults.

Federal Digital Signature bill A bill passed by the U.S. government to give digitally signed electronic transactions the same legal weight as transactions signed in ink.

Fiber-Distributed Data Interface (FDDI) A set of ANSI protocols that serves to transfer digital data through fiber-optic cable. FDDI uses the token passing method of data transfer and supports a data transfer speed of 100Mbps.

Fiber-optic cable A cable that consists of a core of ultra-thin fiber of glass or fused silica.

File server Server used to share data for the client computers.

File Transfer Protocol (FTP) An Application-level protocol that standardizes the transfer of electronic files from one computer to another.

Filter A program that checks incoming and outgoing data for content that matches certain criteria (such as port number and source address). The data is not processed or forwarded unless these conditions are satisfied.

Firewall A security mechanism that serves to protect the resources present on a network from external networks. It is also used to prevent users on the Internet from accessing unwanted sites.

Flooding algorithm A static routing algorithm in which every packet received by the router is sent on every outgoing line except the incoming line.

Fractional T1 link A type of digital leased-line arrangement (a variation of the T1 link) in which the customer uses only a portion of the 24 channels available in a T1 link.

Frame Relay A standards-based technology defined by both American National Standards Institute (ANSI) and International Telecommunication Union (ITU). Frame Relay provides higher speeds and throughput rates for signaling, data transfer, and switching to route data to a desired destination.

Gateway A machine or service through which data passes while it is being transferred from one network to another.

Go back *n* method A method for handling errors during pipelining, in which the receiver discards all frames received after an erroneous packet arrives, sending no acknowledgments for them. Starting with the erroneous packet, all packets must be retransmitted.

Graphical User Interface (GUI) A computer interface that uses on-screen graphics as ways to organize information and activate commands. The most familiar example is the Microsoft Windows operating system.

Hacker A person who breaks into a system on the network without the consent of the system's owner.

Handshake protocol A protocol that allows two entities to agree upon the session information during a session establishment.

Hash function A function that takes a variable-sized input and returns an output of fixed size.

Hash-based MAC The MAC that uses a hash function to reduce the size of the data it processes.

Header A CMP component that contains the sender and recipient name, time of message, and the cryptographic algorithm used to encrypt the message.

Header Message Authentication code A hash function-based code developed by IETF for message authentication.

Hierarchical network management architecture An architecture that uses multiple computers. One computer acts as the central server and the others function as clients.

High-level Data Link Control (HDLC) protocol A bit-oriented protocol that uses a bit-stuffing method for creating frames.

Hijacking When a hacker gains control of a connection that an authentic user has established.

Hop A communication channel between two different computers.

Hub A central component to which all computers in a Star network are connected.

Hybrid hub A hub to which more than one type of cable can connect.

HyperText Markup Language (HTML) A computer language used to structure Web pages for the Internet.

HyperText Transfer Protocol (HTTP) A protocol that governs the exchange of hypertext files on the Internet. The files can incorporate text, graphics, sound, or multimedia.

Identification certificate A certificate that contains the identification information of the entity to whom the certificate is issued.

Impersonation A security threat where an entity pretends to be something it is not.

Inside global IP address A legal or public IP address assigned by the service provider that might represent one or more inside local IP addresses to the outer world.

Inside local address translation Address translation where the source IP address in the IP header of the packet is replaced with the inside or outside IP address.

Inside local IP address An IP address assigned to an inside network host.

Insider attack An attack on the resources of a server from within a protected network.

Institute of Electrical and Electronics Engineers (IEEE) A body that specifies various national and international standards in the fields of electrical engineering and computing.

Intangible assets Assets that do not have a physical form. Intangible assets include time and goodwill.

Integrated Services Digital Network (ISDN) A public, circuit-switched telephone system. Originally designed for carrying analog voice signals, this system is generally unsuitable for digital communication.

Integrity A property that ensures that the message content is not altered during transit.

International Data Encryption Algorithm (IDEA) A secret key cryptographic scheme fast gaining popularity.

International Standards Organizations (ISO) An international organization whose main purpose is to create and publish standards for different products.

International Telecommunications Union — Telecommunications (ITU-T) An organization that recommends worldwide technology standards.

Internet A network of computers from all over the world forming a worldwide network.

Internet Corporation for Assigned Names and Numbers (ICANN) ICANN coordinates the assignment of Internet identifiers, such as IP addresses and domain names.

Internet Domain Name System Security Extensions (IDNSSE) Security extensions included in DNS to provide host and data authentication.

Internet Engineering Task Force (IETF) An organization whose main purpose is to manage protocols used on the Internet.

Internet Key Exchange (IKE) A protocol responsible for providing authenticated keying material for security associations.

Internet Message Access Protocol (IMAP) A protocol used to monitor the operations of the Internet. The latest version of IMAP is IMAP 4.

Internet Protocol (IP) Protocol that serves to transfer data on the Internet from one computer to the other. Each computer on a network possesses a unique address that distinguishes it from other computers on the network.

Internet Protocol, Secure (IPSec) A standard for secure transmission of TCP/IP traffic over the Internet. This is one of the primary protocols used in virtual private network (VPN).

Internet Security Association and Key Management Protocol (ISKMP) A protocol that defines procedures for establishing and tearing down security associations.

Internet Service Provider (ISP) An organization providing Internet connections as a specific service.

Intranet A TCP/IP-based network that uses standard Internet services and applications within the confines of a particular organization.

Intranet VPN A virtual private network used to connect branch offices and corporate departments.

Intrusion detection Discovering break-ins or break-in attempts by examining the system logs or other information available on the network.

IP hijacking When an unauthorized user intercepts an already active connection and takes over the connection. As a result, the unauthorized user can impersonate the connected user on the network and cause damage to network resources.

IP spoofing An attack in which an attacker masquerades his computer as a host on the target network.

Java A strong, open-source, multiplatform programming language widely used to develop applications for the Internet.

Kerberos A system used for DES-based authentication, developed at MIT from a paper written by Needham and Schoeder, and named after the nine-headed hound that guarded the underworld in Greek mythology.

Key In cryptography, a string of bits used in the encryption and decryption of data. Given a cipher, a key determines the mapping of the plaintext to the ciphertext.

Key compromise An unintentional disclosure of the keys to an entity other than the owner of the key. Key compromise causes a certificate to lose its validity.

Key exchange A process used by two or more parties to exchange public or private keys, depending on the type of cryptosystem in use.

Key Exchange Algorithm (KEA) A variant of the Diffie-Hellman algorithm used for exchanging encryption keys.

Key generation The process of creating keys from numerical values by means of algorithms.

Key length Length of a key in bits.

Key management Coordination of the processes involved in the creation, distribution, authentication, and storage of keys.

Key pair Combination of a private key and its corresponding public key used in public-key cryptography.

Key recovery A special feature of a key-management scheme that allows messages to be decrypted even if the original key is lost.

Key recovery request and response message A type of message required for transferring a private key for backup purposes.

Key RR The *resource records* (RR) that contain the public key of an entity, along with other identifying information.

Layer 2 Forwarding (L2F) A tunneling protocol that encapsulates data packets in PPP-compliant packets before transmitting them to an L2F server.

Layer 2 Tunneling Protocol (L2TP) A tunneling protocol that combines the best features of PPTP and L2F, incorporating them for use over PPP. L2TP supports a variety of routed protocols, including IP, IPX, and AppleTalk.

Leased lines Permanent telephone lines used to connect two distant locations.

Legacy systems Leftover hardware and software from previous implementations that do not confirm to the strategic standards of the organization.

Lightweight Directory Access Protocol (LDAP) A protocol used to query the information stored in an X.500-compliant database and access data from the directory.

Link Control Protocol (LCP) A protocol that performs all the functions related to link management, such as encapsulation format options. LCP also handles negotiating limits on sizes of packets, detecting a looped-back link, and common misconfiguration errors.

Load balancing Distributing the processing activities evenly in a network so that all devices in the network share the load.

Local cache A place in the local name server where all addresses known by the local DNS server during the name-resolution process are stored.

Local-area network (LAN) A network that connects nearby computers in a single building, business, or campus environment.

Mail-bomb attack An attack in which a hacker repeatedly sends identical copies of e-mail messages to a target address.

Malicious code A code introduced in a program or data packet with an aim to harm or disrupt the function of the system.

Managed nodes A device capable of communicating status information.

Management Information Base (MIB) A database that contains information available from a device.

Management stations General-purpose computers that contain network management protocol and one or more network management applications.

Man-in-the-middle attack An attack in which a hacker captures the network packets traversing over the network using transport protocols and packet sniffers.

Manipulation The act of data alteration.

MD5 (Message Digest Algorithm 5) A message digest algorithm released by RSA Laboratories. This algorithm is for digitally signed messages and outputs a 128-bit message digest.

Member traffic IP traffic that flows between two workstations, both of which are within the VPN.

Message Authentication Code (MAC) A function that takes a variable length input and a key to produce a fixed-length output. An integrity-check value is computed after the data has been compressed—and recomputed at the receiving end to verify data integrity.

Message digest The result of applying a hash function to a message.

Message switching A switching method that involves the exchange of discrete logical units of data (messages).

Modem A device that enables a computer to transmit data over telephone lines. Modems can be internal or external.

MS-CHAP Microsoft proprietary CHAP protocol, supported only by Microsoft client/server architecture.

Multicasting The process of sending packets simultaneously to a select group of computers.

Multicasting algorithm The algorithm used to achieve multicasting.

Multimode fiber Fiber-optic cabling that allows multiple paths of light. In this fiber, the light waves bounce inside the fiber until they reach the detector.

Multipurpose Internet Mail Extensions (MIME) An Internet standard that allows the transmission of text, images, audio, or video in e-mail messages.

Network Access Server (NAS) A server (usually dedicated) that manages access to all network devices and resources.

Network Address Port Translation (NAPT) Enables configuring multiple server daemons on one physical server to listen on different port numbers.

Network Address Translation (NAT) The use of one or more registered IP addresses for a group of computers.

Network Control Centers (NCCs) Central contact points that control enterprise-wide networks.

Network-coupled security Security measures built into the Network layer and optimized for a particular network.

Network Device Group (NDG) A feature of Cisco Secure ACS that allows a set of network devices to be viewed and maintained as a group. A network device can be assigned to only one NDG at a time.

Network File System (NFS) Allows a set of computers to access files transparently.

Network Interface Card (NIC) Hardware device present on the motherboard. Using NIC, a computer connects to the network and is able to communicate with other computers on the network.

Network layer Third layer of the OSI model, providing services to the Transport and Data Link layers.

Network-management application Network applications developed by vendors of network devices to help customers manage their devices effectively.

Network-management platform Software that provides the generic functionality for managing a variety of network devices.

Network-management protocol Protocols designed to help regulate the flow of information in a network, supporting legitimate queries on the device name, network interface address, and the number of interfaces in the device.

Network Management System (NMS) Software designed to help network engineers manage a network effectively and efficiently.

Network Operating System (NOS) Software program that enables computers on a network to exchange data and communicate with each other.

Network-security policy A policy that defines an organization's vision of utilizing computer and network infrastructure for providing better service and productivity. It also outlines the procedures to counter and respond to the security threats.

Networking hardware All hardware devices used for networking, but especially those designed for connecting computers and transferring data among them.

Networking software Specialized software applications designed for implementing and operating a network.

Non-repudiation A property of a cryptosystem, which ensures that the users cannot deny actions performed by them.

One-Time Password (OTP) A password assigned only once during the challenge-response authentication process.

One-way hash function A function that takes a variable-sized input and creates a fixed-size output. It converts a variable-length string into a fixed-length binary character sequence set. The original string cannot be retrieved from a fixed-length string.

Open security policy A security policy that assumes minimum security risks and outlines easy authentication methods.

Open Shortest Path First (OSPF) protocol An interior-gateway routing protocol.

OSI model A hierarchical, seven-layer conceptual framework that describes how interaction takes place between computers over a standard network.

Outermost perimeter network A network that demarcates an internal network from an external network.

Outside global IP address An IP address assigned to an outside network host. It is allocated from the globally routable address space.

Outside local IP address The IP address of an outside host as it appears to the inside network, allocated from the routable address space or private address allocation.

Packet filtering A security measure that uses *access lists* to check—and then either permit or deny access to—packets coming into the network from outside.

Packet sniffer Software that captures all packets that travel over the network, often used by hackers and crackers to study the packets for possible network-security flaws.

Packet-Switched Data Network (PSDN) A form of public data network in which messages are transmitted in one or more fixed-length data packets after finding the best route for each packet.

Packet switching A switching technique that attempts to combine the best features of circuit-switching and message-switching methods by using self-contained logical units of data called *packets*.

Party A set of protocol entities that communicate through a management protocol and a transport service, using authentication and privacy features.

Passive hubs Hubs that act only as connection points, unable to regenerate a received signal before retransmitting it.

Password cracker A program designed to decrypt passwords or disable password-protection.

Password-Authentication Protocol (PAP) Using a two-way handshake, a protocol that provides a simple method for a remote node to establish its identity.

Peer A computer that requests and provides services to other computers on the network. In effect, it can act as a server as well as a client.

Peer-to-peer model A networking concept that avoids concentrating either the server functions or the client functions in just one machine. Each computer is required to act both as a client and a server.

Performance management The process of monitoring network devices (and their associated links) to determine utilization and error rates. The process also involves determining and providing a consistent level of service to users.

Physical layer The first layer in the OSI model, which defines the mechanical, electrical, and procedural events that take place when data is physically transmitted as electronic signals.

Ping of death A type of DoS attack in which the network is flooded with oversize ICMP packets targeted at a specific host server as a means of overloading and crashing it.

PKCS#7 A standard that defines the syntax for cryptographically signed data.

PKCS#10 A standard that defines the syntax for certificate requests.

PKI client A client application (such as e-mail or a Web browser) that requests resources and services on behalf of the server. See also *Public-Key Infrastructure (PKI)*.

PKI management protocol Protocol that enables Certificate Authorities to collect the information required for issuing and revoking certificates. See also *CA*.

Plaintext A message in an unencrypted form (also known as *cleartext*) that is simple to transmit but unsecured.

Point-to-Point Protocol (PPP) A Data Link-layer communication protocol that allows a node connected to a server to function as a part of the Internet.

Policy mapping An extension that helps one CA recognize the policy of another; the policy of the first CA should be mapped with the policy of the second CA.

Port A connection that allows transfer of data from one computer to another on a network.

Port scanning One of the most widely used techniques to discover and map services listening on a specific port.

Port-Address Translation (PAT) Uses port addresses to map inside (local) and outside (global) IP addresses.

Presentation layer The sixth layer of the OSI model, providing services to the Application layer.

Pretty Good Privacy (PGP) A public-key encryption program that has become a *de facto* standard for encrypting e-mail on the Internet.

Print server A server that treats the printer to which it is connected as a shared network resource. Client computers can request print jobs from the server, which queues them so the printer can print them.

Privacy A relative degree of separation, isolation, and/or protection from others, often involving the control of how much they are allowed to know. An essential concept for network security.

Private Communication Technology (PCT) protocol Protocol designed to provide privacy between two communicating applications in client/server architecture.

Private data Restricted data (such as personal information about employees) meant for use only by specific departments within the organization.

Private key In public-key cryptography, the secret part of a key pair that serves to decrypt the encrypted data received from someone using the public key of the pair. The private key is always kept with the owner, should be kept strictly secret, and can also be used for encryption with a digital signature.

Promiscuous mode of a network adapter card A mode in which a network adapter card, instead of capturing only the packets meant for it, captures all the network packets sent across a network even if the destination address of the packets is not that of the network card.

Protocol A set of rules that implement algorithms to perform the required functions.

Protocol Data Units (PDUs) The message units used by the management station and the managed device to interact with each other.

Proxy server A server that controls a client's access to the Internet. Acts as a gateway between an internal network and the Internet.

Public key A part of a key pair that serves to encrypt the data. Typically a public key is made available to general users and stored in a public directory. In public-key cryptography, this key is primarily for encryption but can also be used to verify digital signatures.

Public-key cryptography An encryption/decryption technique according to a combination of two keys, also called *asymmetric* cryptography.

Public-Key Cryptography Standards (PKCS) A series of cryptographic standards dealing with public-key issues, published by RSA Laboratories.

Public-Key Infrastructure (PKI) A public-key management system that involves a Certificate Authority, a Registration Authority, and DSS.

Public-Packet Data Network (PPDN) A network of separate packet networks.

Public Switched Telephone Networks (PSTN) A worldwide system of separately owned and operated networks.

RC2 Rivest's Cipher, a 64-bit block-cipher algorithm that uses variable-size keys.

RC4 An advanced version of the RC2 cipher algorithm that provides keys of variable size.

Record protocol A protocol that works following the handshake protocol to ensure a secure handshake process. The record protocol uses the session key negotiated during the handshake process.

Redirect CRLs CRLs that point to multiple CRL distribution points where the CRLs are located — which can be changed without affecting the status of the certificate.

Registration Authority (RA) An authority that acts as an interface between a user and a CA, receiving certificate requests from users, authenticating the identity of those users, and submitting certificate requests to the CA.

Reliable Transfer Service Element (RTSE) A protocol in the Application layer that applications use to communicate with each other.

Remote access Accessing an organization's network from a remote computing device, usually through communications lines such as ordinary phone lines.

Remote-Access Server (RAS) A server that supports and processes remote connections. Client computers can dial in from a remote location and access the resources on the server. The connection is established using the public telephone system.

Remote-access VPN VPN that connects a remote location and the corporate network.

Remote Authentication Dial-In User Service (RADIUS) This client/server protocol enables remote-access servers to communicate with a central server for authenticating and authorizing dial-in users.

Remote Operations Service Element (ROSE) A protocol in the Application layer that applications use to communicate with each other.

Remote Procedure Call (RPC) Enables building distributed client/server-based applications.

Repeater A device used to regenerate or replicate a signal. Repeaters are used in transmission systems to regenerate signals affected by attenuation (loss of signal strength over long distances).

Replay protection The protection against one transaction being recorded and replayed multiple times by a hacker.

Resolver An entity that issues a query to the DNS server to obtain the IP address of the requested name.

Revocation delay The time difference between when a certificate is revoked and when the revocation information is posted in the CRL.

Ring topology A topology in which the cabling that connects all the computers on the network makes the data travel in the logical equivalent of a ring.

Risk analysis The process of assessing assets to find the impact of potential damage on the organization.

RMON Remote MONitoring. A standards-based method for monitoring networks with products from multiple vendors.

RMON2 An extension of RMON. It monitors not just the network traffic, but also the applications (and their related protocols) that constitute the traffic.

RMON probe A combination of hardware and software that helps an administrator monitor network traffic.

Router A device that connects two or more LANs.

Routing The process of determining the path a packet will take from its source to its destination.

Routing Information Protocol (RIP) A protocol which standardizes the process of providing routing information.

RSA A public-key algorithm developed by Rivest, Shamir, and Adleman, used for both authentication and encryption.

Scalability Design factor of a computing solution that allows it to expand and support the growing needs of an organization without degrading system performance.

Secret key A key used for both encryption and decryption.

Secure channel A communications medium safe from the threat of eavesdroppers.

Secure Hash Algorithm (SHA-1) A hash algorithm (published by the U.S. government) that can create a 160-bit hash value for strong encryption.

Secure HyperText Transfer Protocol (S-HTTP) A secure version of HTTP, used to transfer sensitive information over the World Wide Web.

Secure Multipurpose Internet Mail Extension (S/MIME) A standard proposed by Internet Engineering Task Force (IETF) for e-mail applications and the secure transfer of electronic messages.

Secure Shell (SSH) protocol A *de facto* standard for securing remote-access connections over IP networks.

Secure Sockets Layer (SSL) The most widely used standard for providing secure access to Web sites. The server that uses SSL authenticates itself to its clients by using a digital certificate.

Security breach A successful attempt to break into a network.

Security policy Policy that governs an organization's use of cryptography and defines how the organization manages public and private keys.

Selective repeat method A method for error handling during pipelining. The Data Link layer of the receiver ignores the bad frame and stores all the other frames. The sender does not get acknowledgment for the bad frame and therefore must retransmit it.

Sensitive data Data extremely important to the organization, whether for its possible usefulness, its damaging potentials, or both. Special precautions must be taken to protect this data from security attacks.

Serial Line IP (SLIP) A communications protocol that allows a node connected to a server to function as part of the Internet.

Server A system entity that provides a service in response to requests from clients.

Session key A key for symmetric-key cryptosystems, used for the one message or communication session.

Session layer The fifth layer in the OSI model, providing services to the layer above it (the Presentation layer).

Session replay A security attack in which the hacker replays a counterfeit and manipulated data stream to gain unauthorized access and advantages.

Shared key The secret key shared by two (or more) users in a symmetric-key cryptosystem.

Shielded Twisted-Pair (STP) Consists of a copper-braid jacket and a foil wrap between and around the wires.

Shortest-path routing An algorithm used to decide the shortest path to be taken between two computers. The shortest path could be expressed as a physical distance (kilometers), number of hops (computers between source and destination), or how long it takes a packet to reach the destination computer.

Signal-regenerating repeaters Devices that filter data transmissions, separate signal from noise, and retransmit only the amplified signal.

Signed data A content type field as defined by PKCS#7.

Simple Network Management Protocol (SNMP) A network management protocol used for managing diverse commercial, educational, and research internetworks.

Single address translation Address translation that allows all users on the private network to have one global source.

Single-key cryptography A cryptographic technique according to a secret key (also called *symmetric* cryptography).

Single-mode fiber A fiber-optic cable in which the diameter is reduced to one wavelength of light, which forces the light to travel in a straight line without any bouncing.

Sliding window protocol A protocol that enables a sender to maintain a sending window, which keeps track of the packets that have been sent but whose acknowledgments have not been received.

Smurf DoS attack A network-level attack in which a large number of IP echo requests are sent to the IP broadcast address of the network.

SNMP v2.0 SNMP version 2.0 is an evolution of Simple Network Management Protocol. See also *SNMP*.

Social engineering Act of impersonating users or network administrators to reveal their username and passwords to unauthorized users.

Spam mailing A method of sending junk e-mail in which messages are sent with fake reply addresses.

SSL handshake An exchange of messages that takes place between client and server during an SSL session.

SSL handshake protocol A protocol that uses the SSL record protocol to establish an SSL connection between the two SSL-enabled devices by exchanging a series of messages.

SSL record protocol An SSL protocol that defines the format used to transmit data.

Star Bus topology A combination of Star and Bus topologies, consisting of one Bus segment that connects multiple Star hubs.

Star Ring topology A combination of Star and Ring topologies that connects the nodes to a central hub, much like a Star network. The Ring is implemented within the hub.

Star topology Consists of various computers connected to one central component (the hub).

Static NAT Defines a fixed address translation from the inside (local) network to the outside (global) network

Static routing Routing method that takes effect when the network is started, computing the path between two computers in advance of transmitting a message, and passing the result to the router.

Strategic system A system built around hardware and software that conforms to an organization's computing standards.

Switch A combination of a hub and a bridge, consisting of several RJ45 connectors that provide a physical link point between network systems. A switch not only amplifies signals but also acts as if a bridge were attached to each of the ports.

Switched Multimegabit Data Services (SMDS) A high-speed, packet-switched, datagram-based service for data communication, offered by telephone companies to subscribers.

Switching The process of sending data from a source to a destination through a set of intermediate devices.

SYN SYnchronized sequence Number. In a TCP connection, the first data packet that the host sends to the receiver is SYN. This SYN contains host ID.

SYN flood A type of DoS attack that uses up all new network connections at a site, preventing legal users from connecting to the network.

Synchronization A service, provided by the Session layer, that returns the system to a previous state after an error.

System Administrators' Tool for Analyzing Networks (SATAN) Identifies common network-related security problems and reports them to the administrator.

System backdoors Accounts created for administrators in case the original accounts are corrupted.

T1 link A 1.544Mbps dedicated link that consists of 24 multiplexed channels. The analog signals from the 24 channels are fed into a *codec* (coder/decoder) one at a time. The T1 link uses time-division multiplexing.

T1-C link A variation of a T1 link, which operates at 3.152Mbps.

T2 Link Four T1 lines multiplexed together.

T3 Link Six T2 links combined. T3 streams operate at a speed of 44.736Mbps.

T4 Link Seven T3 links combined. A T4 stream operates at 274.176Mbps.

Tactical systems Includes hardware and software that no longer falls in the category of strategic software but is still functional in the organization's current computing environment.

Tangible assets Assets that have physical form — such as computers, printers, network hubs, cables, network devices, and computer peripherals.

TCP load distribution A feature that relieves server overload by distributing the task load, located on the internal network, at minimal cost.

TCP session hijacking An attack in which a hacker takes over a TCP session between two computers.

Terminal Access Controller Access Control System (TACACS+) A protocol that allows a server to provide AAA services as independent, separate modules.

Thicknet cable A .5–inch-thick coaxial cable. Also referred to as *Standard Ethernet.*

Thinnet A .25-inch-thick coaxial cable. Thinnet cables can carry a signal up to about 185 meters before the signal suffers attenuation.

Threat A condition likely to adversely affect the working of a system. Such a condition can completely destroy a system, disclose confidential information to unauthorized users, or modify essential data.

Time-to-live (TTL) The time for which the entries in the local cache are stored.

TLS handshake protocol A TLS protocol that allows the client and the server to authenticate each other.

TLS record protocol A protocol that is layered over a transport protocol. It ensures a secure, reliable, and private connection between the communicating applications.

Traceroute A TCP/IP utility that serves to trace the route between a computer and a remote host.

Traffic analysis The study of the traffic flowing in a network to detect any abnormalities or attacks.

Transmission Control Protocol (TCP) A protocol designed to provide reliable communication between pairs of processes using reliable and unreliable networks as well as the Internet.

Transparent bridges Bridges that forward frames one hop at a time toward the destination.

Transport layer The fourth layer in the OSI model. This layer provides data transport from the sender computer to the destination computer.

Transport Layer Security (TLS) protocol A protocol that serves to encrypt all Web communications, providing a secure channel of communication.

Triple-DES A cryptographic algorithm that encrypts data three times. Also called *3DES.*

Trojan Horse A program that causes exploitation or destruction of data.

Trust list A compilation of trusted certificates used to authenticate other certificates.

Trusted certificate A certificate trusted by the users. This certificate consists of public keys, which initiate certification paths.

Trusted network A network within the security perimeter of an organization.

Trusted Third Parties (TTP) PKI systems operated by commercial CA outside an organization.

Tunnel Dedicated channels used to transmit data packets over the public network, such as the Internet.

Tunneling A method of data transmission in which the data packets are enclosed into a packet of another protocol.

Twisted-pair cable A cable that consists of two strands of copper wire twisted around each other.

Unacknowledged connectionless service A service where the source computer sends data without establishing a connection with the destination computer. The sender does not receive an acknowledgment.

Unacknowledged connection-oriented service A service where a connection is established between the source and the destination computer prior to the transmission of data. The sender does not receive an acknowledgment.

Unknown networks Networks neither trusted nor untrusted.

Unshielded Twisted-Pair (UTP) A cable that consists of two insulated copper wires twisted around each other.

Unsupported systems Includes hardware and software that can be no longer supported by the organization.

Untrusted networks Networks outside the security perimeter of your organization.

User certificate Certificates issued to individual entities or organizations for authentication.

User Datagram Protocol (UDP) A connectionless, unreliable data transmission protocol. This protocol works at the Transport layer.

User name Also called *user ID.* A string of characters used to identify a user in the network.

Validity A field that contains two dates. These two dates indicate the beginning and end of the certificate validity period.

Verification The act of finding out the correct identity of an entity.

Virtual LAN A group of computers that behave as if they are physically connected to each other to form a network.

Virtual Point Of Presence (VPOP) In VPOPs, the dial access outsource receives calls at its POP, and then the POP sends the traffic to the ISP over the VPN.

Virtual Private Network (VPN) An extension of an organization's private network across a public network, such as the Internet, by creating a secure private connection.

Virus A program alters other programs and hence changes their functionality.

Voluntary tunneling A tunneling method in which the client computer issues a VPN request to create a voluntary tunnel

Vulnerability A weakness in the software and/or hardware design that poses security threats.

Web Database Server A repository of information that can be accessed either using a query language like SQL or by a set of programming APIs.

Web server Server used to provide content on the Internet. Client computers can then connect to the Internet and browse the sites.

Wide-area network (WAN) A network spread over wide areas (such as across cities, states, or countries).

WWW browser software A client software that gives the user flexible options to browse the Web.

WYSIWYG What You See Is What You Get.

X.25 A standard that was developed during the 1970s to provide an interface between public-packet-switched networks and their customers.

X.500 A standard proposed by International Standards Organization (ISO) and International Telecommunication Union (ITU) for distributed global directory service. This directory service is for the storage of certificates and CRLs.

X.509 A standard proposed by ISO and ITU for certificates and CRLs. X.509 defines the authentication framework for global directory services and is globally accepted by companies involved in producing PKI products.

XML Extensible Markup Language, which allows developers to create custom tags when designing Web pages.

Index

continued

management of, 66
masking, 91
network address, 148–149
outside global IP addresses, 196
outside local IP addresses, 196
overlapping, 201–202, 207–209
static routes for, specifying, 307
subnet masking, 151–154
translation from internal to public, 194–195
wildcard masks of, 154–156
IP authentication, IP spoofing vulnerability, 21
IP backbone, for VPN connectivity, 386
IP datagrams, 610
headers for, 431
PPP frame conversion into, 403
with PPP packets in, 406–407
ip directed-broadcast command, 193
IP networks, L2TP over, 422–423
IP next generation, 195
IP over IP, 71
IP packets, source-routed, 22
IP permit lists, 135
ip route command, 192
IP session filtering, 173–180
IP spoofing, 8, 21–22, 45, 91, 216
preventing, 21–22
protecting against, with NAT, 211
for username and password information
detection, 45
IP traffic, filtering, 148
IP tunnels, VPN implementation with, 382–383
ip verify unicast reverse-path command, 193
IPSec, 62–64, 401, 430. See also Cisco IPSec
AHs, 62, 431
AHs, creating, 431–432
authentication proxy compatibility with, 357
CBAC compatibility with, 272
Cisco Secure VPN Client implementation of,
441–447
configuring, 439–441
data transfer, 437
deployment of, 64
Encapsulated Security Payload protocol, 62, 431
endpoint authentication, 424
extended authentication on PIX Firewall, 468
Hash Message Authentication Code, 63
IKE configuration, 438–439, 452–453
IKE phase 1, 436–437
IKE phase 2, 437

implementation of, 437–441
implementation planning, 451–452
Internet Key Exchange protocol, 431
planning for, 438
preparing for, 463
process initiation, 436
remote-access VPN use of, 465–469
security associations, 433–434
security policy, 438
transform sets configuration, 455–459
Tunnel Endpoint Discovery, 469
tunnel termination, 437
for tunneling, 395
verifying configuration, 441, 460–462
IPSec Tunnel Mode, 71
IPX, authorization services for, 351
IPX access lists, creating, 708
ISDN connections, VPN implementation with, 382–383
ISL trunking protocol, 68–69
ISO TLSP, 54

J

Java applets, 10
for Application-layer attacks, 46
blocking, 105
Cisco IOS Firewall blocking capabilities, 249
downloading, prevention of, 73
filtering at firewall, 252
inspection rules for, 258–259
Java blocking, 194
Java code, security vulnerabilities of, 87
Java-blocking error messages, 270
JavaScript code, security vulnerabilities of, 87

K

Kerberos authentication, 102, 333, 348–350
Cisco Secure ACS product support for, 328
for login authentication, 350
for PPP authentication, 348–350
for security servers, 365
Ticket Granting Ticket, 349
Key Distribution Center (KDC), 333, 348
Key Exchange Algorithm (KEA), SSL support of, 56
key management, for VPNs, 384
keyapp.exe program, 340
keying material, 437
key-string command, 464
KINIT software, 333, 349–350

L

continued

continued